T0143027

Lecture Notes in Computer Science 13308

Founding Editors

Gerhard Goos
Karlsruhe Institute of Technology, Karlsruhe, Germany

Juris Hartmanis
Cornell University, Ithaca, NY, USA

Editorial Board Members

Elisa Bertino
Purdue University, West Lafayette, IN, USA

Wen Gao
Peking University, Beijing, China

Bernhard Steffen
TU Dortmund University, Dortmund, Germany

Moti Yung
Columbia University, New York, NY, USA

More information about this series at https://link.springer.com/bookseries/558

Margherita Antona ·
Constantine Stephanidis (Eds.)

Universal Access in Human-Computer Interaction

Novel Design Approaches and Technologies

16th International Conference, UAHCI 2022
Held as Part of the 24th HCI International Conference, HCII 2022
Virtual Event, June 26 – July 1, 2022
Proceedings, Part I

Springer

Editors
Margherita Antona
Foundation for Research and Technology -
Hellas (FORTH)
Heraklion, Crete, Greece

Constantine Stephanidis
University of Crete and Foundation for
Research and Technology - Hellas (FORTH)
Heraklion, Crete, Greece

ISSN 0302-9743   ISSN 1611-3349 (electronic)
Lecture Notes in Computer Science
ISBN 978-3-031-05027-5   ISBN 978-3-031-05028-2 (eBook)
https://doi.org/10.1007/978-3-031-05028-2

© The Editor(s) (if applicable) and The Author(s), under exclusive license
to Springer Nature Switzerland AG 2022, corrected publication 2022
This work is subject to copyright. All rights are reserved by the Publisher, whether the whole or part of the material is concerned, specifically the rights of translation, reprinting, reuse of illustrations, recitation, broadcasting, reproduction on microfilms or in any other physical way, and transmission or information storage and retrieval, electronic adaptation, computer software, or by similar or dissimilar methodology now known or hereafter developed.
The use of general descriptive names, registered names, trademarks, service marks, etc. in this publication does not imply, even in the absence of a specific statement, that such names are exempt from the relevant protective laws and regulations and therefore free for general use.
The publisher, the authors and the editors are safe to assume that the advice and information in this book are believed to be true and accurate at the date of publication. Neither the publisher nor the authors or the editors give a warranty, expressed or implied, with respect to the material contained herein or for any errors or omissions that may have been made. The publisher remains neutral with regard to jurisdictional claims in published maps and institutional affiliations.

This Springer imprint is published by the registered company Springer Nature Switzerland AG
The registered company address is: Gewerbestrasse 11, 6330 Cham, Switzerland

Foreword

Human-computer interaction (HCI) is acquiring an ever-increasing scientific and industrial importance, as well as having more impact on people's everyday life, as an ever-growing number of human activities are progressively moving from the physical to the digital world. This process, which has been ongoing for some time now, has been dramatically accelerated by the COVID-19 pandemic. The HCI International (HCII) conference series, held yearly, aims to respond to the compelling need to advance the exchange of knowledge and research and development efforts on the human aspects of design and use of computing systems.

The 24th International Conference on Human-Computer Interaction, HCI International 2022 (HCII 2022), was planned to be held at the Gothia Towers Hotel and Swedish Exhibition & Congress Centre, Göteborg, Sweden, during June 26 to July 1, 2022. Due to the COVID-19 pandemic and with everyone's health and safety in mind, HCII 2022 was organized and run as a virtual conference. It incorporated the 21 thematic areas and affiliated conferences listed on the following page.

A total of 5583 individuals from academia, research institutes, industry, and governmental agencies from 88 countries submitted contributions, and 1276 papers and 275 posters were included in the proceedings to appear just before the start of the conference. The contributions thoroughly cover the entire field of human-computer interaction, addressing major advances in knowledge and effective use of computers in a variety of application areas. These papers provide academics, researchers, engineers, scientists, practitioners, and students with state-of-the-art information on the most recent advances in HCI. The volumes constituting the set of proceedings to appear before the start of the conference are listed in the following pages.

The HCI International (HCII) conference also offers the option of 'Late Breaking Work' which applies both for papers and posters, and the corresponding volume(s) of the proceedings will appear after the conference. Full papers will be included in the 'HCII 2022 - Late Breaking Papers' volumes of the proceedings to be published in the Springer LNCS series, while 'Poster Extended Abstracts' will be included as short research papers in the 'HCII 2022 - Late Breaking Posters' volumes to be published in the Springer CCIS series.

I would like to thank the Program Board Chairs and the members of the Program Boards of all thematic areas and affiliated conferences for their contribution and support towards the highest scientific quality and overall success of the HCI International 2022 conference; they have helped in so many ways, including session organization, paper reviewing (single-blind review process, with a minimum of two reviews per submission) and, more generally, acting as goodwill ambassadors for the HCII conference.

This conference would not have been possible without the continuous and unwavering support and advice of Gavriel Salvendy, founder, General Chair Emeritus, and Scientific Advisor. For his outstanding efforts, I would like to express my appreciation to Abbas Moallem, Communications Chair and Editor of HCI International News.

June 2022   Constantine Stephanidis

HCI International 2022 Thematic Areas and Affiliated Conferences

Thematic Areas

- HCI: Human-Computer Interaction
- HIMI: Human Interface and the Management of Information

Affiliated Conferences

- EPCE: 19th International Conference on Engineering Psychology and Cognitive Ergonomics
- AC: 16th International Conference on Augmented Cognition
- UAHCI: 16th International Conference on Universal Access in Human-Computer Interaction
- CCD: 14th International Conference on Cross-Cultural Design
- SCSM: 14th International Conference on Social Computing and Social Media
- VAMR: 14th International Conference on Virtual, Augmented and Mixed Reality
- DHM: 13th International Conference on Digital Human Modeling and Applications in Health, Safety, Ergonomics and Risk Management
- DUXU: 11th International Conference on Design, User Experience and Usability
- C&C: 10th International Conference on Culture and Computing
- DAPI: 10th International Conference on Distributed, Ambient and Pervasive Interactions
- HCIBGO: 9th International Conference on HCI in Business, Government and Organizations
- LCT: 9th International Conference on Learning and Collaboration Technologies
- ITAP: 8th International Conference on Human Aspects of IT for the Aged Population
- AIS: 4th International Conference on Adaptive Instructional Systems
- HCI-CPT: 4th International Conference on HCI for Cybersecurity, Privacy and Trust
- HCI-Games: 4th International Conference on HCI in Games
- MobiTAS: 4th International Conference on HCI in Mobility, Transport and Automotive Systems
- AI-HCI: 3rd International Conference on Artificial Intelligence in HCI
- MOBILE: 3rd International Conference on Design, Operation and Evaluation of Mobile Communications

List of Conference Proceedings Volumes Appearing Before the Conference

1. LNCS 13302, Human-Computer Interaction: Theoretical Approaches and Design Methods (Part I), edited by Masaaki Kurosu
2. LNCS 13303, Human-Computer Interaction: Technological Innovation (Part II), edited by Masaaki Kurosu
3. LNCS 13304, Human-Computer Interaction: User Experience and Behavior (Part III), edited by Masaaki Kurosu
4. LNCS 13305, Human Interface and the Management of Information: Visual and Information Design (Part I), edited by Sakae Yamamoto and Hirohiko Mori
5. LNCS 13306, Human Interface and the Management of Information: Applications in Complex Technological Environments (Part II), edited by Sakae Yamamoto and Hirohiko Mori
6. LNAI 13307, Engineering Psychology and Cognitive Ergonomics, edited by Don Harris and Wen-Chin Li
7. LNCS 13308, Universal Access in Human-Computer Interaction: Novel Design Approaches and Technologies (Part I), edited by Margherita Antona and Constantine Stephanidis
8. LNCS 13309, Universal Access in Human-Computer Interaction: User and Context Diversity (Part II), edited by Margherita Antona and Constantine Stephanidis
9. LNAI 13310, Augmented Cognition, edited by Dylan D. Schmorrow and Cali M. Fidopiastis
10. LNCS 13311, Cross-Cultural Design: Interaction Design Across Cultures (Part I), edited by Pei-Luen Patrick Rau
11. LNCS 13312, Cross-Cultural Design: Applications in Learning, Arts, Cultural Heritage, Creative Industries, and Virtual Reality (Part II), edited by Pei-Luen Patrick Rau
12. LNCS 13313, Cross-Cultural Design: Applications in Business, Communication, Health, Well-being, and Inclusiveness (Part III), edited by Pei-Luen Patrick Rau
13. LNCS 13314, Cross-Cultural Design: Product and Service Design, Mobility and Automotive Design, Cities, Urban Areas, and Intelligent Environments Design (Part IV), edited by Pei-Luen Patrick Rau
14. LNCS 13315, Social Computing and Social Media: Design, User Experience and Impact (Part I), edited by Gabriele Meiselwitz
15. LNCS 13316, Social Computing and Social Media: Applications in Education and Commerce (Part II), edited by Gabriele Meiselwitz
16. LNCS 13317, Virtual, Augmented and Mixed Reality: Design and Development (Part I), edited by Jessie Y. C. Chen and Gino Fragomeni
17. LNCS 13318, Virtual, Augmented and Mixed Reality: Applications in Education, Aviation and Industry (Part II), edited by Jessie Y. C. Chen and Gino Fragomeni

39. CCIS 1582, HCI International 2022 Posters - Part III, edited by Constantine Stephanidis, Margherita Antona and Stavroula Ntoa
40. CCIS 1583, HCI International 2022 Posters - Part IV, edited by Constantine Stephanidis, Margherita Antona and Stavroula Ntoa

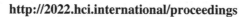

http://2022.hci.international/proceedings

Preface

The 16th International Conference on Universal Access in Human-Computer Interaction (UAHCI 2022), an affiliated conference of the HCI International (HCII) conference, provided an established international forum for the exchange and dissemination of scientific information on theoretical, methodological, and empirical research that addresses all issues related to the attainment of universal access in the development of interactive software. It comprehensively addressed accessibility and quality of interaction in the user interface development life-cycle from a multidisciplinary perspective, taking into account dimensions of diversity, such as functional limitations, age, culture, background knowledge, etc., in the target user population, as well various dimensions of diversity which affect the context of use and the technological platform and arise from the emergence of mobile, wearable, ubiquitous, and intelligent devices and technologies.

UAHCI 2022 aimed to help, promote, and encourage research by providing a forum for interaction and exchanges among researchers, academics, and practitioners in the field. The conference welcomed papers on the design, development, evaluation, use, and impact of user interfaces, as well as standardization, policy, and other non-technological issues that facilitate and promote universal access.

Universal access is not a new topic in the field of human-computer interaction and information technology. Yet, in the new interaction environment shaped by current technological advancements, it becomes of prominent importance to ensure that individuals have access to interactive products and services that span a wide variety of everyday life domains and are used in fundamental human activities. The papers accepted to this year's UAHCI conference present research, methods, and practices addressing universal access issues related to user experience and interaction, and approaches targeted to provide appropriate interaction means to individuals with specific disabilities, but also issues related to extended reality – a prominent technological medium presenting novel accessibility challenges, as well as advancements in learning and education, a domain which was considerably challenged in the context of the ongoing pandemic.

Two volumes of the HCII 2022 proceedings are dedicated to this year's edition of the UAHCI conference, entitled Universal Access in Human-Computer Interaction: Novel Design Approaches and Technologies (Part I) and Universal Access in Human-Computer Interaction: User and Context Diversity (Part II). The first focuses on topics related to novel approaches to accessibility, user experience, and technology acceptance in universal access, and multimodal and psychophysiological interaction, while the second focuses on topics related to universal access to learning and education, extended reality in universal access, design for cognitive and learning disabilities, and design for visual disabilities.

Papers of these volumes are included for publication after a minimum of two single-blind reviews from the members of the UAHCI Program Board or, in some cases, from members of the Program Boards of other affiliated conferences. We would like to thank all of them for their invaluable contribution, support and efforts.

June 2022   Margherita Antona
                                                    Constantine Stephanidis

16th International Conference on Universal Access in Human-Computer Interaction (UAHCI 2022)

Program Board Chairs: Margherita Antona, Foundation for Research and Technology – Hellas (FORTH), Greece, and Constantine Stephanidis, University of Crete and Foundation for Research and Technology – Hellas (FORTH), Greece

- João Barroso, INESC TEC and UTAD, Portugal
- Ingo Bosse, Interkantonale Hochschule für Heilpädagogik, Switzerland
- Laura Burzagli, IFAC-CNR, Italy
- Pedro J. S. Cardoso, University of Algarve, Portugal
- Silvia Ceccacci, Università Politecnica delle Marche, Italy
- Carlos Duarte, Universidade de Lisboa, Portugal
- Pier Luigi Emiliani, National Research Council of Italy, Italy
- Andrina Granic, University of Split, Croatia
- Gian Maria Greco, University of Warsaw, Poland, and POIESIS, Italy
- Simeon Keates, University of Chichester, UK
- Georgios Kouroupetroglou, National and Kapodistrian University of Athens, Greece
- Barbara Leporini, ISTI-CNR, Italy
- Jun-Li Lu, University of Tsukuba, Japan
- John Magee, Clark University, USA
- Daniela Marghitu, Auburn University, USA
- Jorge Martín-Gutiérrez, Universidad de La Laguna, Spain
- Troy McDaniel, Arizona State University, USA
- Maura Mengoni, Università Politecnica delle Marche, Italy
- Silvia Mirri, University of Bologna, Italy
- Federica Pallavicini, Università degli Studi di Milano-Bicocca, Italy
- Hugo Paredes, INESC TEC and UTAD, Portugal
- Enrico Pontelli, New Mexico State University, USA
- João M. F. Rodrigues, University of the Algarve, Portugal
- Frode Eika Sandnes, Oslo Metropolitan University, Norway
- J. Andrés Sandoval-Bringas, Universidad Autónoma de Baja California Sur, Mexico
- Volker Sorge, University of Birmingham, UK
- Hiroki Takada, University of Fukui, Japan
- Philippe Truillet, Université de Toulouse, France
- Kevin Tseng, National Taipei University of Technology, Taiwan
- Gerhard Weber, Technische Universität Dresden, Germany

The full list with the Program Board Chairs and the members of the Program Boards of all thematic areas and affiliated conferences is available online at

http://www.hci.international/board-members-2022.php

HCI International 2023

The 25th International Conference on Human-Computer Interaction, HCI International 2023, will be held jointly with the affiliated conferences at the AC Bella Sky Hotel and Bella Center, Copenhagen, Denmark, 23–28 July 2023. It will cover a broad spectrum of themes related to human-computer interaction, including theoretical issues, methods, tools, processes, and case studies in HCI design, as well as novel interaction techniques, interfaces, and applications. The proceedings will be published by Springer. More information will be available on the conference website: http://2023.hci.international/.

General Chair
Constantine Stephanidis
University of Crete and ICS-FORTH
Heraklion, Crete, Greece
Email: general_chair@hcii2023.org

http://2023.hci.international/

Contents – Part I

Contents – Part II

Extended Reality in Universal Access

Design for Cognitive and Learning Disabilities

Design for Visual Disabilities

Novel Approaches to Accessibility

Web User Interface Adaptation for Low Vision People: An Exploratory Study Based on a Grounded Theory Review Method

Maximiliano Jeanneret Medina[1,2(✉)] [ID], Cédric Baudet[1] [ID], and Denis Lalanne[2] [ID]

[1] HEG Arc, HES-SO//University of Applied Sciences Western Switzerland, Neuchâtel, Switzerland
maximiliano.jeanneret@he-arc.ch
[2] Human-IST Institute, University of Fribourg, Fribourg, Switzerland

Abstract. People with visual impairments (PVI) are characterized as a diverse population of users due to multiple vision impairments like visual acuity, light and glare sensitivity, contrast sensitivity, limited field of vision, color blindness. In that context, adaptation is a key element for coping with diversity in the field of Human-Computer Interaction (HCI). This study explores the adaptation to provide accessible web user interfaces for low vision people. To do so, we relied on Grounded Theory (GT) as a review method to cover academics and mainstream web perspectives. In the spirit of all is data, we collected a set of scientific publications, initiatives led by leading actors in Information and Communication Technology, and PVI organizations over the past ten years. Our findings show that academics followed particularist, user-centered, and proactive principles, but rarely included PVI in the early project stage. While most solutions are based on adaptivity, adaptation is still under investigation. Regarding the mainstream web perspective, recent initiatives followed universality, multi-stakeholder involvement, and proactivity principles. In opposition to the academic perspective, accessibility has been exclusively based on adaptability and tailored user interfaces. As the adaptability features become more and more advanced, the frontier between specialized assistive technology will be blurred. Hence, we recommend investigating environments of adaptation stacking with a better alignment between academics and industry.

Keywords: Accessibility · Universal access · Adaptation · People with visual impairments · Low vision · Web technology · Grounded theory

1 Introduction

According to the World Health Organization, 86% of people with visual impairments (PVI) have a low vision [1]. Low vision refers to visual impairments other than blindness including visual acuity, light and glare sensitivity, contrast sensitivity, limited field of vision, and color blindness [1, 2]. Moreover, most of PVI reported multiple types of visual impairment [2]. In that context, accommodating the diversity of users is challenging in

© The Author(s), under exclusive license to Springer Nature Switzerland AG 2022
M. Antona and C. Stephanidis (Eds.): HCII 2022, LNCS 13308, pp. 3–21, 2022.
https://doi.org/10.1007/978-3-031-05028-2_1

Human-Computer Interaction (HCI) [3]. Moreover, awareness of universal access must be increased [4].

To better address accessibility issues, the past few decades have been marked by multiple paradigm shifts: a shift from a *particularist* account to a *universalist* account of access, a shift from a *maker-centered* to a *user-centered* perspective, and a shift from a *reactive* to a *proactive* approach to accessibility [5]. Moving from an '*accessibility for users with disabilities*' approach to an '*inclusive-design*' approach benefits a wide range of users, those with disabilities but also those without [6].

In the context of web accessibility, the Web Content Accessibility Guidelines (WCAG) aims to make content accessible to a wider range of people with disabilities by providing a single shared standard that meets the needs of individuals, organizations, and governments internationally [7]. However, being compliant with web accessibility norms does not guarantee that a specific population can reach their goals with reasonable time and effort [8–11].

With the knowledge that *one size does not fit all* [12], adaptation is a key element for coping with diversity [13]. Recent efforts aim to cope with diversity towards adaptation. For example, the WCAG 2.1 makes a short mention of the term *visually customized* [14]. Moreover, the W3C Low Vision Task Force provides accessibility requirements dedicated to people with low vision [1]. Many requirement statements are oriented with a focus on adaptability (i.e., a user-invoked adaptation [13]). Hence, makers have to create an adaptable system to benefit low-vision people.

In this study, we review adaptation approaches applied to provide accessible but also usable web content to PVI. We were particularly focused on people with low vision because their diversity fit well with universal access. We endeavor to answer the following research question: *How web user interfaces are adapted for low vision people?* To answer this question, we conducted a literature review based on Grounded Theory (GT), including both academic and mainstream web perspectives.

This paper is organized as follows. The first section presents our methodological choices. The second section presents the results obtained. The third section highlights our research contributions, outlines the limitations, and suggests future avenues of research. Finally, the fourth section concludes the study.

2   Methodology

This research used GT as a review method [15]. The GT research process may be described as "*investigating an area of interest to the researcher in order to highlight the main concern that emerges from the field through collected data; the purpose of this process is to identify a core category that also emerges from the researcher's data as explaining this main concern*" [16]. The Grounded Theory Literature Review (GTLR) invokes GT as a method during the analysis stage, and uses the content from the papers as empirical material that is coded and constantly compared, thus grounding the insights of the review [15]. GTLR is composed of five stages, namely: 1) defining the scope of the review (inclusion and exclusion criteria, sources of information, search terms); 2) searching for the potential papers; 3) selection of the papers for the review (filtering, refine sample based on title and abstract); 4) in-depth analysis of the papers (through different coding levels); and 5) present the emerging categories from the papers. To include both academics and mainstream web perspectives, Fig. 1 illustrates the GT *zigzag* approach [17] (i.e., movement in the form of process) related to GLTR.

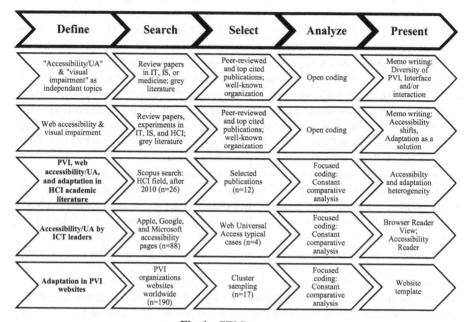

Fig. 1. GTLR process.

2.1 Review Scope

We first performed both iterations related to: a) accessibility and visual impairment as distinct topics, and b) web accessibility in the context of visual impairment. This led us to the topic of adaptation as a solution to support universal access. This orientation has been influenced by field observations of the research team (e.g. textbook adaptation for PVI), meta-review in HCI [12], W3C's low vision recommendations [1], and observations made on websites of organizations of and for PVI (e.g. World Blind Union, American Foundation for the Blind). Also, we clarified the PVI population singularity and their accessibility needs with experts (e.g. local PVI organizations) through informal interviews.

We delimited our research scope on web technology because most of the digital documents provided to PVI are in HTML [18], the importance of web accessibility to address a wide range of people with disabilities is recognized [19], and the web is the most popular technology in accessibility research related to Information and Communication Technology (ICT) [20]. At the end of both iterations, we obtained the core categories of our analytical framework (see Appendix 1).

PVI, Web Accessibility, and Adaptation in HCI Academic Literature. On the 7th of June 2021, we collected 26 scientific publications on Scopus based on the following query: *TITLE-ABS-KEY ((accessibility OR "universal access" OR "inclusive design" OR "accessible design" OR "design* all") AND (web OR www) AND (adaptation OR adaptab* OR adaptiv*) AND ("vis* disabilit*" OR "vis* impair*" OR "low vision" OR "partial vision" OR "residual vision" OR "vision loss" OR "color blind*" OR "color* defic*" OR sensitivity)) AND DOCTYPE (ar OR cp OR re) AND SUBJAREA (soci OR comp) AND (PUBYEAR > 2010) AND LANGUAGE (english).* This query includes different variations of accessibility and connected concepts [21], different formulations and types of vision impairment [22], and different kinds of adaptation [23]. We retained only publications published the last ten years because it characterized a period when accessibility paradigm shifts occured [5]. Regarding the choice of the metadatabase, Scopus is recognized as having a broader coverage of scientific publications [24]. Also, Scopus provides subject area filters that helped us to frame the research. The subject area Social Sciences (SOCI) contains Human Factors and Ergonomics while Computer Sciences (COMP) contains Human-Computer Interaction.

We analyzed the title, abstract, and keywords of each of the 26 scientific publications. Exclusion criteria covered extended abstract, publications on which the web technology, the adaptation, or PVI diversity were not the primary concern. For instance, we excluded studies concerned with hardware (e.g. TV device), or solely focused on blind users without aiming to widen the scope. When a research group published similar studies, we retained the most detailed one after a full document analysis. Finally, we obtained a set of 12 publications.

Web Accessibility to PVI through Adaptation by ICT Leaders. By embedding accessibility into mainstream solutions, we move towards Universal Design [25]. For that reason, we focused on mainstream user agents providing features to assist individuals with disabilities. The difference with assistive technologies is that mainstream user agents target broad and diverse audiences that usually include people with and without disabilities [14].

We searched for projects, products, or features within ICT leaders (GAFAM) websites and blogs related to accessibility or universal access. We narrowed the scope to Apple, Google, and Microsoft because they have a clear positioning in universal access, develop tools to consume information on the web (i.e. web browsers), and produce accessible information (i.e. authoring tools and guidelines). On the 23rd of August 2021, we extracted 88 titles and descriptions of projects, products, or features within accessibility and blog web pages published from 2010. We manually performed the filtering because websites do not provide advanced search options.

Adaptation is a primary concern of the three actors analyzed, but rarely linked with web technology. Apple and Microsoft are generally focused on assistive technology (AT) and accessibility features of their operating system. Related to web technology and adaptation, we noticed that: a) Apple briefly mentioned a dark mode that can be applied in several applications (i.e. Safari Browser), b) Microsoft provided adaptability features in the Immersive Reader, and c) Google explicitly mentioned adaptability in the Chrome browser, as well as developed an interactive experience of storytelling for PVI. We performed a typical case sampling (purposive sampling) based on these findings. We selected four cases covering adaptation and mainstream web user agents: Safari Reader Mode, Chrome Reader Mode, Auditorial (Google), and Microsoft Immersive Reader.

A Reader Mode or a Reader View reduces the colorfulness and visual complexity of web pages [26]. Reader Views are perceived as accessibility features by the PVI community [27]. Moreover, more advanced Reader Views (e.g. Immersive Reader) promote universal access because they benefit people with varying reading skills [26]. For example, simplifying the web page layout helps people with visual and those with cognitive impairments.

Adaptation in Website for PVI. To complete the mainstream web perspective, we retained a cluster 17 websites of PVI organizations (see Appendix 2). Each website is maintained by a PVI organization, member of the World Blind Union, and located in a top-ranked country by region according to the Digital Accessibility Rights Evaluation Index (DARE) Index 2020 [28].

2.2 Analysis

Analytical Framework. In line with a GT concept-centric review [16], our analytical framework is based on two core categories. The first one concerns the paradigm shifts on accessibility as reported by recent and valuable works related to universal access in HCI [5, 12, 25]. The second one places the adaptation as a solution to address accessibility issues in respect to these paradigm shifts [12, 13].

Paradigm Shifts on Accessibility. Greco [5] reported three paradigm shifts regarding accessibility in various fields including HCI: a shift from *particularist* accounts to a *universalist* account of access, a shift from a *maker-centered* to a *user-centered* perspective, and a shift from a *reactive* to a *proactive* approach.

The first shift considers the move from a *particularist* to a *universalist* approach to accessibility. Specialized adaptations and add-on assistive technologies are replaced by universal solutions catering to a diverse set of user needs [25]. It is also highlighted by a contemporary definition of accessibility: '*the extent to which products, systems, services, environments and facilities are able to be used by a population with the widest range of characteristics and capabilities (e.g. physical, cognitive, financial, social and cultural, etc.), to achieve a specified goal in a specified context.*' [21]. Moreover, moving from an '*accessibility for users with disabilities*' approach to an '*inclusive-design*' approach benefits a wide range of users, those with disabilities but also those without [6].

The second shift refers to the considered perspective when developing accessible solutions (hardware or software). The dominant attitude was based on the assumption that the maker's knowledge of users with disabilities is the only one that matters [5]. This approach caused a complex series of gaps between the different stakeholders involved, of which the *maker-user* and the *maker-expert-user* gaps were the most prominent. To bridge these gaps, inclusive design practices based on *user-centered* approaches emerged. Such practices take into account the knowledge of users, but also experts and other stakeholders, which are all as important as the maker's knowledge [5]. A suitable design process should be a co-construction where multiple agents must work together [5, 12, 25].

The third shift concerns the accessibility consideration within the design process. This process can be broken down into *ex-ante*, *in itinere*, and *ex-post* stages [5]. First efforts pursued accessibility via *a posteriori* adaptation, for instance, by employing assistive technology and add-ons to provide access to applications that were originally designed and developed for non-disabled [5, 12]. In that case, accessibility is reactive or an afterthought [29]. In rare cases, accessibility was addressed *in itinere* [5], which may produce a loss in functionality or provide limited and low-quality access [12]. Respecting the proactivity principle calls for a proactive attitude to comply with the access requirement, and building access features into a product as early as possible (e.g. design phase) [25, 29]. Best fixing complex accessibility issues require sometimes revisiting the overall approach [30].

In short, these paradigm shifts concern the target population, the population implied during the development process of accessible software, and the moment when accessibility efforts are performed.

Adaptation as a Promising Solution. On the one hand, users' needs vary widely across people with low vision, and one user's needs may conflict with another user's needs [1]. On the other hand, the industry is facing the necessity to target all people with disabilities, while developing multiple and completely different software is difficult [12]. Considering these constraints and the aforementioned paradigm shifts, taking the path of adaptation seems a promising solution [13].

Systems that can adapt according to various requirements and criteria, or even upon request is not new [23]. Coarsely, approaches to adaptation of interactive systems can be classified into two broad categories, namely user-invoked adaptation (*adaptability*) and automatic adaptation (*adaptivity*) [23]. Interactive systems may also mix both approaches [31]. An adaptable system (via adaptability mechanisms) offers its users the capability to alter the system's characteristics. Users select or set between different alternative presentation and interaction characteristics, among the ones built into the system. Adaptation is defined at the design time. A typical example includes customization of system presentation or behavior (i.e. navigation facilities) through preference dialogs. The second approach to adaptation, adaptivity, refers to the ability of the interface to dynamically derive knowledge about the user, the usage context, etc., and to use that knowledge to further modify itself to better suit the revised interaction requirements [13]. An adaptive system automatically alters its characteristics at runtime, based on assumptions about the user's current usage [31]. In addition to adaptability and adaptivity, a tailored adaptation refers to user interfaces (UI) adapted at design-time, by a maker or a system, and are instantiated at runtime [32].

To comprehend *what is adapted?*, we used the User Interface Markup Language (UIML) [33]. In UIML, a UI is a set of interface elements with which the end-user interacts. A UI is conceptualized as a stack of structure, style, content, and behaviors. The behavior needs to be considered as follows: *what behavior do parts have?*. We focused on graphical user interfaces because low vision people prefer to take advantage of their residual sight [4].

Coding Procedure. Following a constructivist GT approach [34], we combined various sampling techniques, constant comparison, and two coding cycles. In the first coding cycle, we coded paragraphs within each publication related to the two first iterations following a descriptive coding technique [35]. The goal was to obtain a categorized inventory of the data's contents. Once our analytical framework was developed, we performed deductive coding based on the list of codes [36]. This led us to a broader view of adaptation (adaptability, adaptivity, tailored UI) than that mentioned commonly in the literature (e.g. the adaptability-adaptivity distinction [23] or the tailored UI-adaptivity continuum [32]). In a second coding cycle, we developed the final list of codes. The categories did not change, but we performed continuous changes in codes as new papers were analyzed. Compared to an inductive approach, a top-down constructivist approach implied better questioning, theory integration, insight and a richer picture [37]. Also, a constructivist approach has been motivated by the fact that adaption in well defined in theory [13, 38–40]. One researcher performed the coding, while the analysis has been discussed through socialization between two researchers.

3   Results

3.1   Academics Perspective

Studies of our sample have been published between 2012 and 2021. Seven publications are conference proceedings, and five are journal articles. Publications have primarily been published in Universal Access in the Information Society (3), in Lecture Notes in Computer Science that includes UAHCI proceedings (3), and in Web for All (W4A) Conference (2). Almost all publications focused on web technology in a desktop context, and two focused on mobile web [41, 42]. Publications are varied in terms of goals. They addressed accessibility issues like non-accessible colors [43–46], unstructured table issues [47], unadapted multimedia on mobile devices [41], non-compliant websites [48]. Other authors address specific limitations of web content and assistive technologies [49], the limitations of voice-based systems [50], while others aim to improve user's navigation [51], skimming strategies [42], or the automated generation of UI [52].

Five studies provide a methodological outcome such as adaptation techniques for tailored UI or adaptive systems [47–49], as well as a theoretical outcome (e.g. ontology) [45, 51]. Regarding artifact outcome, studies mainly relied on the methodological or theoretical outcome they created [42, 47–49], rather than using a preexistent method or model [52] (Table 1).

Accessibility. Regarding the target population, most of the publications focused on a particular, sometimes diverse, type of PVI [48–50, 52], while two explicitly refer to a universal approach to accessibility. Such studies included sighted and blind users or target people with different disabilities [42, 43].

Regarding the design perspective, ten publications are user-centered. One concerns a trade-off between the user and the maker [44], and another adopts a holistic perspective by integrating multiple stakeholders [48].

Concerning the moment when accessibility features are taken into account during the development process, we coded all publications as proactive. We explain this choice because in accessibility studies, and authors think about accessibility from the start. Regarding the proactive principle's application, two studies asked for users' problems or requirements at the project design phase [48, 51]. Studies usually used a proxy such

Table 1. Accessibility Shifts and Adaptation as a Solution in the Academic Literature (n = 12)

Core category	Category	Codes	References
Accessibility/universal access	Target population	Particularist	[41, 44–52]
		Universalist	[42, 43]
	Design perspective	User-centered	[41–43, 45–47, 49–52]
		Maker/user-centered	[44]
		Multiple stakeholders	[48]
	Accessibility efforts	Proactive	All
		Design phase (direct)	[48, 51]
		Evaluation phase (direct)	[42, 45, 48, 49, 51]
Adaptation	Adaptation type	Adaptability	[50]
		Adaptivity	[41–43, 47, 51]
		Tailored	[46, 48, 49, 52]
		Adaptability-Adaptivity	[44]
		Adaptivity-tailored	[45]
	Adaptation on UI	Content, or structure, or style, or behavior	[41, 43–47, 50]
		Content-structure	[51]
		Content-behavior	[42, 48]
		Structure-style	[49]
		Content-structure-style	[52]
	Adaptation sources	User	[43, 46–48, 50–52]
		User-technology	[41, 42, 45, 49]

as a common accessibility issue, a PVI needs, or accessibility guidelines (e.g. WCAG). Regarding the evaluation phase, five studies directly involved PVI, one performed a technical evaluation related to accessibility [52], and six did not perform a user-centered evaluation.

Adaptation. Publications investigated adaptation in different ways. Five publications focused on adaptivity, four on tailored UI, one on adaptability, and two combined two types of adaptation.

Seven publications adopted a unidimensional approach to UI adaptation. It is important to highlight that advanced computations such as page recoloration [43], table restructuration [47], or multimedia adaptation [41] often implied one UI dimension. One study implemented a system that adapts the four dimensions of a UI [48].

Content adaptation is preferred over modality adaptation. Three UI dimensions are often considered, respectively the style (6), the content (5), and the structure (4), while the behavioral dimension is less studied (2). Regarding the style, the color [43–46], the font [49, 52], and the visual effects (i.e. contrast, blur) [49, 52] are investigated. Publications solely focused on the style exclusively focused on people with color deficiencies [43–46]. Regarding the content, transformation and filtering [41, 48], hiding [50, 52], and enrichment [42, 50] are investigated. Concerning the structure, layout adaptation [49, 52], table reorganization [47], and semantic-based restructuration [51] are developed. When the behavioral dimension is investigated, is it through links (that impacts user's navigation [42]), or the auditory modality (human to computer [50], or computer to human [48]).

Authors sometimes completed or compared adaptivity with makers (i.e. tailored UI) or users (i.e. adaptivity). Regarding colorblind people, manually colored interfaces obtained in the majority the best results [46]. Also, combining design-time generation with runtime adaptation through responsive design technology is a way to address the limitations of manual or automatic generated UI [52].

Regarding the source of the adaptation, researchers generally relied on user features, through their preferences [42, 44–46, 48], and/or disability [45, 46, 52], but rarely on user's knowledge (i.e. browsing activity) [42]. Pathology types, needs, and individual user preferences are simultaneously taken into account in the context of automatic color selection [45]. Four studies combined user features with the technology used (e.g. device, assistive technology). Regarding low vision people, some adaptation techniques depended on the type of assistive technology used to access the web [49]. In the context of color deficiencies, there are significant differences among the adaptation techniques according to different contexts [46].

3.2 Mainstream Web Perspective

The four accessible retained cases of ICT leaders, as well as 17 PVI organizations' websites analyzed were grouped into three implementations of adaptation (see Table 2). The *Website Template* approach is based on a responsive HTML/CSS template[1] that is often compliant with accessibility standards. Such an approach allows fitting a web interface to a user profile or user preferences and guarantees that the page layout will not be broken after a user-invoked adaptation. Our analysis shows that 53% (9 out of 17) of websites analyzed support adaptability (see Appendix 2). Also, ICT leaders support web accessibility by developing basic and advanced readers. A *Reader Views* and *Accessibility Readers* are both web user agents [53]. They aim to enhance the visual presentation of web content through a format for easy reading, without ads, navigation, or other distracting items. The origin of *Website Templates* for PVI dates back to before 2010,[2] *Reader Views* emerged around 2010 [54], while *Accessibility Readers* appeared at the end of the last decade.[3]

Accessibility Approach. The three types adopt a universalist approach because they target diverse users. Regarding the *Website Template*, websites target PVI and sighted people, and some go beyond these profiles. For example, the QSCCB website includes

---

[1] https://www.a11yproject.com/.

[2] The AFB website provided text size adaptation on the 1st of January 2010. See: https://web.arc hive.org/web/20100101192728/https://afb.org/.

[3] https://github.com/microsoft/immersive-reader-sdk/releases.

Table 2. Accessibility shifts and adaptation as a solution in mainstream web

Core category	Category	Website template	Reader view	Accessibility reader
Accessibility/universal access	Target population	Universalist	Universalist	Universalist
	Design perspective	Not mentioned	Not mentioned	Multiple
	Accessibility efforts	At itinere	At itinere	Proactive
Adaptation	Adaptation type	Tailored UI; adaptability	Tailored UI; adaptability	Tailored UI; adaptability
	Adaptation on UI	Content; structure; style; behavior	Content; structure; style; behavior	Content; structure; style; behavior
	Adaptation source	User	User	User
	Examples	PVI organization websites sample	Safari Reader [54]; Chrome Reader Mode [55]	Microsoft Immersive Reader [56]; Google Auditorial [57]

sighted, visually impaired, and blind people profiles. The RSB website provides a font suitable to dyslexic users, while the ONCB website provides sign language videos. *Browser Reader Views*, which initially did not mention accessibility [54], are now part of accessibility settings [55]. Such solutions benefit people with varying reading skills [26]. The Microsoft Immersive Reader primarily targets people with learning disabilities (e.g. dyslexia), but also PVI [56, 58]. Dedicated explicitly to blind and low vision people, RNIB, Guardian, and Google jointly developed Auditorial [57], an experiment in storytelling that can be adapted to suit the user's needs and preferences.

Regarding the stakeholders involved during the development process, *Accessibility Reader* implementations involved users and educators (Immersive Reader), as well as users, accessibility specialists, and journalists (Auditorial) [57].

Because PVI organization websites and *Browser Reader Views* included accessibility features during the evolutive maintenance,[4] adaptation has been integrated *in itinere*. Both *Accessibility Reader* cases emphasize the importance of including the user at an early project stage. The Immersive Reader is based on Universal Design, and is built on top of empirical research related to text appearance, readability, and reading comprehension [59]. In addition, Auditorial redesigned the overall storytelling experience with accessibility in mind.

---

[4] Safari integrated the Reader Mode in version 5 [54]. The original version of the AFB website did not integrate adaptability. See: https://web.archive.org/web/20000302105032/https://afb.org/.

Adaptation Approach. All kinds of mainstream web adaptations can mix tailored UI and adaptability approaches. Web designers are responsible for preparing the content that the user could further adapt.

In the majority of cases that use adaptation by a template, the user obtains the original/sighted version of the website first. If the user has a vision impairment, the interface can be adapted through customization. In the QSCCB website, the user needs to select a profile (sighted, visually impaired, blind) that will affect the web interface and then adapt the font size. Such interfaces are tailored because they consider the specific disabilities of the users at design time [32]. They are also adaptable due to the presence of user-invoked adaptation. Also, not all web pages are compatible with the *Reader Mode*.[5] Regarding the Immersive Reader, the designer has to markup the page elements that can be viewed within the reader.

Although the three implementations provide quite similar capabilities in terms of UI adaptation, they differ in terms of advances. This is particularly illustrated in the *Website Template* category. The AFB website provides one option to change the font size. Four websites provide additional color schemes options (ONCB, UNCU, ACB, AICB). The five remaining websites provide more advanced accessibility features that affect at least two dimensions of a UI, but rarely more. For instance, the VOS website presents page content on a narrow page with a menu moved to the left side, support a simplified style, and filter informational noise (e.g. logo). The CNIB website provides options to place the table of content at the top of the page and emphasize interactable inputs (i.e. links, buttons). *Reader Views* provide structure linearization, narrow page presentation, information filtering[6], and basic adaptability features (e.g. font, font size, and background color selection). When the read-aloud functionality is present, the user can rely on the auditive modality. *Accessibility Readers* such as Microsoft Immersive Reader and Auditorial are more advanced [27]. Microsoft Immersive Reader contains artificial intelligence-powered features like reading aloud, translating languages, focusing attention through highlighting, and extracting text from images.[7] Auditorial is highly customizable (zoom, color, image, motion) and provides two modalities (visual, auditive) to experiment with the story. Each content is thoroughly tailored to support an interactive and immersive experience.

4 Discussion

Regarding the accessibility approach, academics followed mostly particularist, user-centered, and proactive principles. They often used a proxy to access PVI needs (i.e. PVI report, common accessibility issues). In the mainstream web, recent initiatives led

---

[5] From a randomly selected sample of 100 website URLs, only 2% of homepages and 41% of child pages were available in Firefox Reader View [26].

[6] The logic behind *Browser Reader View* is provided by Mozilla Firefox in open-source. See: https://github.com/mozilla/readability.

[7] Microsoft Immersive Reader is built into Microsoft applications (e.g. Word, OneNote, Outlook, Edge web browser) or can be used as a cloud service (Azure Cognitive Services). At this moment, Azure is the only major cloud provider offering this type of reading technology [63].

by leading ICT actors followed a universalist, holistic and proactive approach to accessibility. We explain the misalignment of the academic literature in regards to accessibility shifts by the difficulty to find and involve people with disabilities in a study [22], and the incremental nature of research (i.e. prior knowledge about PVI is known). However, HCI academics should involve PVI in all project phases [4]. While ICT leaders market their solutions to the PVI community, we only found studies that evaluated such solutions with people with cognitive impairments or without disabilities [59]. Similar to *Reader Views* [26], the utility of accessibility reading tools must be empirically validated with PVI.

Regarding adaptation, the academic literature is characterized by a wide diversity of adaptation types, even in our limited research scope. On the mainstream web side, adaptation is pervasive. Basic to advanced adaptability and/or tailored UI enhance the visual presentation of web interfaces. Mainstream web agents are in line with W3C's low vision recommendations [1]. However, academics are still investigating the advantages and drawbacks of adaptation types in different contexts of use [46, 48, 49].

Unlike the academic literature, the mainstream web has not embraced adaptivity, yet well defined in theory [38]. Advanced computation, often through the form of deep learning for computer vision, has been reserved to assist PVI in their daily lives. For now, one *Accessibility Reader* uses artificial intelligence to support adaptability for an educational purpose (e.g. text styled and enhanced with metadata for dyslexic users). This can be explained by the fact that designing for diversity is difficult [38]. Moreover, even if academics investigated adaptivity, it was performed in a limited technical scope, or completed by other kinds of adaptation. We believe that mainstream web user interfaces will soon explore adaptivity by taking the latest advances in machine learning.

One solution rarely works in all situations, and no unique solution would meet the needs of all low-vision users [29]. However, the more mainstream products will provide advanced accessibility features, the more the frontier between mainstream user agents and assistive technologies will be blurred. Mainstream web user agents provide overlapping adaptation features with assistive technology. For instance, ZoomText contains a special reading environment in which text is reformatted for easier reading, as well as fonts, contrasts, and magnification levels can be customized.[8] In an overlay of adaptation layers, the user could customize the display options at the operating system level, at the browser level, at the reader level, and at the level of the assistive technology used (i.e. screen magnifier). In that sense, we suggest investigating the superposition [49], the complementarity or the replacement of assistive technologies and mainstream user agents, as well as exploring adaptive strategies used by PVI to reach their goals in these environments stacking adaptations. To facilitate the customization needed by numerous adaptation layers, we suggest deeper investigating solutions in which all users can create flexible and portable personal profiles that customize interfaces to their needs [29]. For instance, a disability profile approach has been investigated in the context of Open Educational Resources [60]. However, the task will be difficult because few people are aware of current accessibility features [61].

This research provides a rich description of the adaptation applied to address a wide variety of users, and illustrates this phenomenon through multiple perspectives. Rich

---

[8] ZoomText User Guide, January 2021.

descriptions obtained by GT are valuable because they serve as sources of new domain knowledge, and new phenomena must be documented and understood before explaining their causes and effects [62]. We call for further investigations about the reason for the misalignments exposed and analyze in-depth adaptation methods and techniques of both perspectives.

4.1 Limitations

The main limitations of this study are the following. Firstly, we covered a limited scope that caused a small sample of scientific publications. However, we believe that the varied adaptation coverage reflects well the subfield of research. Secondly, to prevent the use of Scopus as a unique data source, we recommend including another one such as Web of Science. Thirdly, we retained three ICT leaders, of which adaptation occurs the most often at the operating system level. Somewhat, we believe that typical cases we selected faithfully represent the landscape of mainstream accessibility on the web. Fourth, taking multiple perspectives does not allow to compare data in all aspects (i.e. industry gives only a few details about the development process). We minimized this limitation by creating a complete picture by analyzing blog articles, projects, and features related to accessibility.

5 Conclusion

This research is born from the observation that PVI are a heterogeneous population with different needs in terms of access to ICT, applying generic web accessibility guidelines does not guarantee a usable experience to the full range of PVI, and accessibility moved to a universal, proactive, and holistic approach. Considering all these elements, taking the path of adaptation seems a promising solution.

In this study, we investigated the adaptation of web content in a context of universal access by focusing on the wide range of people with low vision. We reviewed scientific publications and mainstream web user agents over the last decade. Our findings show that both perspectives covered adaptation differently. Academics mostly focused on adaptivity, indirectly involved users, and are still investigating the benefits and drawbacks of adaptability and tailored UI under different contexts of use. In the mainstream web, adaptability is widespread, solutions become universal with ever more advanced accessibility features, but must be proved empirically. Finally, there is no single approach to address accessibility issues through adaptation. Especially in environments that are stacking adaptation layers, both perspectives need to be better aligned to provide accessible and usable interactive systems to people with visual disabilities.

Appendix 1: Codebook

Category	Codes	References
Community of focus[*]	People with visual impairments (PVI); blind (B); people with low vision (PLV); people with color vision deficiency (PCVD); maker (M, e.g. web designers, developers); sighted or people without vision disabilities (S)	[1]
Study method[a]	Controlled experiment; interview; survey; usability testing; accessibility testing; case study; focus group; field study; workshop or design session(s); observation; other	[20]
Participant groups*	PVI; people with disabilities (PD); specialists (e.g., therapists, teachers); people without disabilities; researchers; no user study; other	[1, 20]
Use of proxies*	Yes; No	[20]
Contribution type[a]*	Empirical; artifact; methodological (accessibility guidelines/standards; adaptation technique; model); theoretical (e.g. model, ontology); survey	[20]
Target population (who is targeted)	Particularist (one disability, e.g. vision); Universalist (e.g. multiple disabilities, people with and without disabilities such as sighted and blind)	[5, 12, 25]
Design Perspective (who is involved)	Maker-centered; user-centered; maker/user-centered; multiple stakeholders	[5, 12, 25]
Accessibility Efforts (when and how accessibility is included)	Reactive (a posteriori adaptation) or proactive (accessibility thought by default). If proactive, can be direct (involve at early project stage; the design respect WCAG), undirect (start from a common accessibility issue), or N/A for design and evaluation phases	[5, 12, 25]
Adaptation Type*	Adaptability (user-invoked adaptation); adaptivity (system runtime adaptation); tailored (adaptation at design time, authored by the maker or generated by a system)	[13, 32]
Adaptation On* (what is adapted?)	Structure; style; content, behavior (of UI parts)	[33]

(continued)

(*continued*)

Category	Codes	References
Adaptation Source* (adapt from what)	User features (knowledge, preferences, task, disability, and position), technology used (device, connectivity, browser)	[32, 39, 40]

Note: An (*a*) indicates a category only for the academic perspective. A star (*) indicates if multiple codes are possible for the category.

Appendix 2: Sample of PVI Organization Websites

PVI Organization	Acronym	URL	Adaptation
African Union of the Blind	AFUB	http://www.afub-uafa.org/	Adaptability
Kenya Union of the Blind	KUB	http://kub.or.ke/	
The Royal Society for the Blind	RSB	https://www.rsb.org.au/	Adaptability
All Russia Association of the Blind	VOS	https://www.vos.org.ru/	Adaptability
Confédération Française pour la Promotion Sociale des Aveugles et Amblyopes	CFPSAA	http://www.cfpsaa.fr/	
Unione Italiana dei Ciechi e degli Ipovedenti	ONLUS-APS	http://www.uiciechi.it/	
Organização Nacional de Cegos do Brasil	ONCB	http://fundacaodorina.org.br/	Adaptability
Unión Nacional De Ciegos Del Uruguay	UNCU	https://www.uncu.org.uy/	
Qatar Social and Cultural Centre for the Blind	QSCCB	http://www.blind.gov.qa/en	Adaptability; Tailored UI
Canadian National Institute for the Blind	CNIB	https://www.cnib.ca/	Adaptability
American Foundation for the Blind	AFB	https://www.afb.org/	Adaptability
National Federation of the Blind	NFB	https://nfb.org/	
American Council of the Blind	ACB	https://www.acb.org/	Adaptability

(*continued*)

(*continued*)

PVI Organization	Acronym	URL	Adaptation
All India Confederation Of The Blind	AICB	https://www.aicb.org.in/	Adaptability
National Federation of the Blind	NFB	http://www.nfbindia.org/	
National Association for the Blind	NAB	http://www.nabindia.org/	
Pakistan Association of the Blind	PAB	https://pabnpk.org/	

Note: PVI Organizations (n = 17) are part of the World Blind Union, and in the top two countries in their respective region according to the DARE Index 2020.

References

1. W3C: Accessibility Requirements for People with Low Vision: W3C Editor's Draft 04 November 2021. https://w3c.github.io/low-vision-a11y-tf/requirements.html
2. WebAIM: Survey of Users with Low Vision #2 Results. https://webaim.org/projects/lowvisionsurvey2/
3. Shneiderman, B.: Universal usability (2000)
4. Power, C., Jürgensen, H.: Accessible presentation of information for people with visual disabilities. Univers. Access Inf. Soc. **9**, 97–119 (2010). https://doi.org/10.1007/s10209-009-0164-1
5. Greco, G.M.: Accessibility studies: abuses, misuses and the method of poietic design. In: Stephanidis, C. (ed.) HCII 2019. LNCS, vol. 11786, pp. 15–27. Springer, Cham (2019). https://doi.org/10.1007/978-3-030-30033-3_2
6. Schmutz, S., Sonderegger, A., Sauer, J.: Implementing recommendations from web accessibility guidelines: a comparative study of nondisabled users and users with visual impairments. Hum. Factors. **59**, 956–972 (2017). https://doi.org/10.1177/0018720817708397
7. W3C: Web Content Accessibility Guidelines (WCAG) 2.0. https://www.w3.org/TR/WCAG20/
8. Theofanos, M.F., Redish, J.G.: Bridging the gap: between accessibility and usability. Interactions **10**, 36–51 (2003). https://doi.org/10.1145/947226.947227
9. Sullivan, T., Matson, R.: Barriers to use: usability and content accessibility on the web's most popular sites. In: Proceedings of the Conference on Universal Usability, pp. 139–144 (2000)
10. Giraud, S., Thérouanne, P., Steiner, D.D.: Web accessibility: filtering redundant and irrelevant information improves website usability for blind users. Int. J. Hum. Comput. Stud. **111**, 23–35 (2018). https://doi.org/10.1016/j.ijhcs.2017.10.011
11. Power, C., Freire, A.P., Petrie, H., Swallow, D.: Guidelines are only half of the story: accessibility problems encountered by blind users on the Web. In: Proceedings of the SIGCHI Conference on Human Factors in Computing Systems (CHI 2012), pp. 433–442. Association for Computing Machinery, New York (2012). https://doi.org/10.1145/2207676.2207736
12. Stephanidis, C., et al.: Seven HCI grand challenges. Int. J. Hum. Comput. Interact. **35**, 1229–1269 (2019). https://doi.org/10.1080/10447318.2019.1619259
13. Stephanidis, C., Savidis, A.: Universal access in the information society: methods, tools, and interaction technologies. Univers. Access Inf. Soc. **1**, 40–55 (2001). https://doi.org/10.1007/s102090100008

14. W3C: Web Content Accessibility Guidelines (WCAG) 2.1. https://www.w3.org/TR/WCAG21/

15. Wolfswinkel, J.F., Furtmueller, E., Wilderom, C.P.M.: Using grounded theory as a method for rigorously reviewing literature. Eur. J. Inf. Syst. **22**, 45–55 (2013). https://doi.org/10.1057/ejis.2011.51

16. Walsh, I., Holton, J.A., Bailyn, L., Fernandez, W., Levina, N., Glaser, B.: What grounded theory is…a critically reflective conversation among scholars. Organ. Res. Meth. **18**, 581–599 (2015). https://doi.org/10.1177/1094428114565028

17. Bruce, C.: Questions arising about emergence, data collection, and its interaction with analysis in a grounded theory study. Int. J. Qual. Meth. **6**, 51–68 (2007). https://doi.org/10.1177/160940690700600105

18. Dorigo, M., Harriehausen-Mühlbauer, B., Stengel, I., Dowland, P.S.: Survey: improving document accessibility from the blind and visually impaired user's point of view. In: Stephanidis, C. (ed.) UAHCI 2011. LNCS, vol. 6768, pp. 129–135. Springer, Heidelberg (2011). https://doi.org/10.1007/978-3-642-21657-2_14

19. Petrie, H., Savva, A., Power, C.: Towards a unified definition of web accessibility. In: W4A 2015 - 12th Web All Conferences (2015). https://doi.org/10.1145/2745555.2746653

20. Mack, K., McDonnell, E., Jain, D., Lu Wang, L., E. Froehlich, J., Findlater, L.: What do we mean by "accessibility research"?: a literature survey of accessibility papers in CHI and ASSETS from 1994 to 2019. In: Proceedings of the 2021 CHI Conference on Human Factors in Computing Systems, pp. 1–18. Association for Computing Machinery, New York (2021). https://doi.org/10.1145/3411764.3445412

21. Persson, H., Åhman, H., Yngling, A.A., Gulliksen, J.: Universal design, inclusive design, accessible design, design for all: different concepts—one goal? On the concept of accessibility—historical, methodological and philosophical aspects. Univers. Access Inf. Soc. **14**(4), 505–526 (2014). https://doi.org/10.1007/s10209-014-0358-z

22. Brulé, E., Tomlinson, B.J., Metatla, O., Jouffrais, C., Serrano, M.: Review of quantitative empirical evaluations of technology for people with visual impairments. In: Conference on Human Factors in Computing Systems - Proceedings, pp. 1–14 (2020). https://doi.org/10.1145/3313831.3376749

23. Stephanidis, C.: Adaptive techniques for universal access. User Model. User-Adapt. Interact. **11**, 159–179 (2001). https://doi.org/10.1023/A:1011144232235

24. Harzing, A.-W., Alakangas, S.: Google Scholar, Scopus and the Web of Science: a longitudinal and cross-disciplinary comparison. Scientometrics **106**(2), 787–804 (2015). https://doi.org/10.1007/s11192-015-1798-9

25. Begnum, M.E.N.: Universal design of ICT: a historical journey from specialized adaptations towards designing for diversity. In: Antona, M., Stephanidis, C. (eds.) HCII 2020. LNCS, vol. 12188, pp. 3–18. Springer, Cham (2020). https://doi.org/10.1007/978-3-030-49282-3_1

26. Li, Q., Morris, M.R., Fourney, A., Larson, K., Reinecke, K.: The impact of web browser reader views on reading speed and user experience. In: Conference on Human Factors in Computing Systems - Proceedings (2019). https://doi.org/10.1145/3290605.3300754

27. Kelley, S.: Accessibility Features in Windows Web Browsers for Low Vision Users (2020). https://www.afb.org/aw/21/4/16975

28. Leblois, A.: The DARE index - monitoring the progress of digital accessibility around the world - a research conducted by advocates for advocates. In: The 23rd International ACM SIGACCESS Conference on Computers and Accessibility. Association for Computing Machinery, New York (2021). https://doi.org/10.1145/3441852.3487959

29. Theofanos, M.F., Redish, J.G.: Helping low-vision and other users with web sites that meet their needs: is one site for all feasible? Tech. Commun. **52**, 9–20 (2005)

30. Paiva, D.M.B., Freire, A.P., de Mattos Fortes, R.P.: Accessibility and software engineering processes: a systematic literature review. J. Syst. Softw. **171**, 110819 (2021). https://doi.org/10.1016/j.jss.2020.110819
31. Miraz, M.H., Ali, M., Excell, P.S.: Adaptive user interfaces and universal usability through plasticity of user interface design. Comput. Sci. Rev. **40**, 100363 (2021). https://doi.org/10.1016/j.cosrev.2021.100363
32. Miñón, R., Paternò, F., Arrue, M., Abascal, J.: Integrating adaptation rules for people with special needs in model-based UI development process. Univers. Access Inf. Soc. **15**(1), 153–168 (2015). https://doi.org/10.1007/s10209-015-0406-3
33. OASIS: User Interface Markup Language (UIML) Version 4.0: Committee Draft (2008)
34. Charmaz, K.: Constructing Grounded Theory. SAGE Publications Inc., Thousand Oaks (2014)
35. Saldaña, J.: The Coding Manual for Qualitative Researchers (2013). https://doi.org/10.1017/CBO9781107415324.004
36. Miles, M.B., Huberman, M.A., Saldaña, J.: Qualititative Data Analysis: A Methods Sourcebook. SAGE, Thousand Oaks (2014)
37. Furniss, D., Blandford, A., Curzon, P.: Confessions from a Grounded Theory Ph.D.: Experiences and lessons learnt. Conference on Human Factors in Computing Systems - Proceedings, pp. 113–122 (2011). https://doi.org/10.1145/1978942.1978960
38. Stephanidis, C.: Design for individual differences. In: Salvendy, G., Karwowski, W. (eds.) Handbook of Human Factors and Ergonomics, pp. 1189–1215. Wiley, Hoboken (2021)
39. Brusilovsky, P.: Adaptive hypermedia. User Model. User-Adapt. Interact. **11**, 87–110 (2001). https://doi.org/10.1023/A:1011143116306
40. Brusilovsky, P.: Methods and techniques of adaptive hypermedia. User Model. User-Adapt. Interact. **6**, 87–129 (1996). https://doi.org/10.1007/BF00143964
41. Zhang, D., Jangam, A., Zhou, L., Yakut, I.: Context-aware multimedia content adaptation for mobile web. Int. J. Netw. Distrib. Comput. **3**, 1 (2015). https://doi.org/10.2991/ijndc.2015.3.1.1
42. Zhang, D., Zhou, L., Uchidiuno, J.O., Kilic, I.Y.: Personalized assistive web for improving mobile web browsing and accessibility for visually impaired users. ACM Trans. Access. Comput. **10**, 1–22 (2017). https://doi.org/10.1145/3053733
43. Aupetit, S., Mereuță, A., Slimane, M.: Automatic color improvement of web pages with time limited operators. In: Miesenberger, K., Karshmer, A., Penaz, P., Zagler, W. (eds.) ICCHP 2012. LNCS, vol. 7382, pp. 355–362. Springer, Heidelberg (2012). https://doi.org/10.1007/978-3-642-31522-0_54
44. Bonavero, Y., Huchard, M., Meynard, M.: Reconciling user and designer preferences in adapting web pages for people with low vision. In: W4A 2015 - 12th Web All Conferences (2015). https://doi.org/10.1145/2745555.2746647
45. Bonacin, R., Reis, J.C.D, de Araujo, R.J.: An ontology-based framework for improving color vision deficiency accessibility. Univers. Access Inf. Soc. (2021). https://doi.org/10.1007/s10209-021-00791-6
46. de Araújo, R.J., Dos Reis, J.C., Bonacin, R.: Understanding interface recoloring aspects by colorblind people: a user study. Univers. Access Inf. Soc. **19**(1), 81–98 (2018). https://doi.org/10.1007/s10209-018-0631-7
47. Lai, P.P.Y.: Adapting data table to improve web accessibility. In: W4A 2013 - International Cross-Disciplinary Conference on Web Accessibility, pp. 5–8 (2013). https://doi.org/10.1145/2461121.2461143
48. Ferati, M., Vogel, B., Kurti, A., Raufi, B., Astals, D.S.: Web accessibility for visually impaired people: requirements and design issues. In: Ebert, A., Humayoun, S.R., Seyff, N., Perini, A., Barbosa, S.D.J. (eds.) UsARE 2012/2014. LNCS, vol. 9312, pp. 79–96. Springer, Cham (2016). https://doi.org/10.1007/978-3-319-45916-5_6

49. Moreno, L., Valencia, X., Pérez, J.E., Arrue, M.: An exploratory study of web adaptation techniques for people with low vision. Univers. Access Inf. Soc. **20**(2), 223–237 (2020). https://doi.org/10.1007/s10209-020-00727-6
50. González-Mora, C., Garrigós, I., Castelyn, S.: A web augmentation framework for accessibility based on voice interaction. In: Bielikova, M., Mikkonen, T., Pautasso, C. (eds.) ICWE 2020. LNCS, vol. 12128. Springer, Cham (2020). https://doi.org/10.1007/3-540-28218-1
51. Sorrentino, T., MacEdo, J., Santos, A., Ribeiro, C.: An adaptative semantic model for internet accessibility visually impaired users. In: 17th International Conference on Information Integration and Web-Based Applications & Services, iiWAS 2015 - Proceedings (2015). https://doi.org/10.1145/2837185.2837255
52. Rathfux, T., Kaindl, H., Thöner, J., Popp, R.: Combining design-time generation of webpages with responsive design for improving low-vision accessibility. In: Proceedings of ACM SIGCHI Symposium on Engineering Interactive Computing Systems, EICS 2018 (2018). https://doi.org/10.1145/3220134.3220141
53. W3C: User Agent Accessibility Guidelines (UAAG) 2.0. https://www.w3.org/TR/UAAG20/
54. Apple Inc.: Apple Releases Safari 5. https://www.apple.com/newsroom/2010/06/07Apple-Releases-Safari-5/
55. Google Inc.: Get help reading text on a screen. https://support.google.com/accounts/answer/7177379?hl=en&ref_topic=7189720
56. Microsoft: All about the Immersive Reader. https://education.microsoft.com/en-us/resource/9b010288. Accessed 4 Aug 2021
57. RNIB, Guardian, Google: Auditorial: Accessibility Notebook. https://auditorial.withgoogle.com/project-background
58. Microsoft: Special education: Vision. https://education.microsoft.com/en-us/resource/98d2a996
59. Microsoft: Research related to Immersive Reader. https://education.microsoft.com/en-us/resource/9786fb2a. Accessed 4 Aug 2021
60. Navarrete, R., Luján-Mora, S.: Bridging the accessibility gap in open educational resources. Univers. Access Inf. Soc. **17**(4), 755–774 (2017). https://doi.org/10.1007/s10209-017-0529-9
61. Wu, J., Reyes, G., White, S.C., Zhang, X., Bigham, J.P.: When can accessibility help? An exploration of accessibility feature recommendation on mobile devices. In: Proceedings of the 18th International Web for All Conference, W4A 2021 (2021). https://doi.org/10.1145/3430263.3452434
62. Wiesche, M., Jurisch, M.C., Yetton, P.W., Krcmar, H.: Grounded theory methodology in information systems research. MIS Q. **41**, 685–701 (2017). https://doi.org/10.1079/9781845938918.0127
63. Microsoft: Immersive Reader: An AI service that helps users read and comprehend text. https://azure.microsoft.com/en-us/services/cognitive-services/immersive-reader/. Accessed 4 Aug 2021

Evaluating the Potential Implementation of New Metrics in Automated Web Accessibility Testing Software for Managers

Jonathan Lazar[1]([⊠]), Mark Turner[2], Luis Velarde[2], and Jeremy Westerwiller[2]

[1] College of Information Studies (iSchool), Trace Research
and Development Center, and Human-Computer Interaction Lab (HCIL), University
of Maryland, College Park, MD 20742, USA
jlazar@umd.edu

[2] Optimal Solutions Group, College Park, MD 20742, USA

Abstract. Automated software tools for testing web accessibility are the only evaluation method that scales well to thousands or even millions of web pages. However, the automated testing tools can report incorrect and misleading results, as many aspects of web accessibility cannot be tested using automated means. Previous research identified a potentially useful metric, the "presence of accessibility features" metric for measuring web accessibility using automated testing tools in a way that is both more accurate and more useful for managers. This paper presents exploratory research and development on the use of this new metric for the development of web accessibility testing tools for managers, focusing specifically on 1) technical infrastructure, 2) dashboards and notifications for managers, and 3) the potential integration of historical archived data.

Keywords: Web accessibility testing · Web Content Accessibility Guidelines · Archives · Wayback Machine

1 Introduction

People with disabilities need to have equal access to the information, transactions, social networking, commerce, and education that exists in the form of web pages. People with disabilities often use assistive technologies, alternate input and output devices and techniques such as screen readers, captioning, voice recognition, and alternate keyboards, and web sites need to be built to be flexible enough to work with these various input and output techniques. To make a website accessible, developers should follow the Web Content Accessibility Guidelines (WCAG), which describes methods and techniques for making a website accessible. Recent research also found that designing a web site to conform with WCAG also makes it much more usable for people without disabilities [1]. But in addition to using the WCAG proactively in design, it is important to evaluate a website after being built, on a regular basis, to ensure that it remains accessible and usable by people with disabilities, using one of the three major evaluation techniques:

© The Author(s), under exclusive license to Springer Nature Switzerland AG 2022
M. Antona and C. Stephanidis (Eds.): HCII 2022, LNCS 13308, pp. 22–39, 2022.
https://doi.org/10.1007/978-3-031-05028-2_2

usability testing involving people with disabilities, manual inspections (a form of expert review), or automated accessibility testing.

The Web Content Accessibility Guidelines, version 1.0, were first issued by the Web Accessibility Initiative in 1999, based on the 1998 Trace Center Unified Web Content Accessibility Guidelines [2]. The current version of the WCAG is version 2.1, with a new 2.2 version potentially being issued in the year 2022 [3]. The WCAG are not new, yet they have recently received increased attention in the legal arena. As early as 1996, the U.S. Department of Justice publicly stated for public accommodations covered under Title III of the Americans with Disabilities Act (ADA), their websites must be accessible for people with disabilities [4], a position that the DOJ reconfirmed as recently as 2018 [5]. The DOJ explained much of the legal reasoning for how web site accessibility is a requirement under the ADA, even if the ADA doesn't mention web sites, in a statement of interest in the New v. Lucky Brand Dungarees Store, Inc. case [6]. According to the DOJ, even when an accessibility standard has not been defined yet for a particular technology (such as websites or point of sale terminals), the effective communication requirements of the Americans with Disabilities Act under Title III (Public Accommodations) still apply, as the ADA cannot predict, in advance, all technologies that potentially could be utilized in a public accommodation. However, even if websites are legally required to be accessible, the use of WCAG as the guideline is currently only a suggestion, not a legal requirement [7], even though the use of WCAG is a component of nearly every legal settlement related to web accessibility [8].

One of the first lawsuits related to web accessibility was the National Federation of the Blind v. Target (452 F. Supp. 2d 946, N.D. Cal, 2006). Yet with a 25-year history of web accessibility since the original DOJ announcement in 1996 and at least a 15-year history of lawsuits related to the topic of web accessibility, it has really gained increased attention in the past five years due to the increased numbers of lawsuits. The early lawsuits were generally done by disability rights lawyers. The tidal wave of lawsuits within the past five years were primarily done by lawyers not involved in disability rights, who would file lawsuits against hundreds of plaintiffs in a day, figuring that many of the plaintiffs would not be aware of the status of their web site accessibility, and would instead make a quick settlement [9]. The current legal situation for public accommodations covered under Title III of the ADA, where the WCAG can be used but is not required, and where some Federal circuit courts have said websites of public accommodations only need to be accessible if the public accommodations have a physical component, has made the situation more confusing for organizations [10]. Businesses, non-profit organizations, and government need reliable tools that they can use to determine and manage their web site accessibility, yet existing tools give misleading and confusing results. While there may be unclear legal guidance, the solutions to web accessibility come from the human-computer interaction and accessibility research communities. This paper presents the results of one research and development project to move the discussion forward, researching and developing new and more effective approaches for use in automated web accessibility testing tools.

2 Background Literature

2.1 Evaluating Web Pages for Accessibility

There are three core methods for evaluating web pages for accessibility: usability testing involving people with disabilities, expert inspections (also known as manual inspections), and automated accessibility testing [8]. Other methods, such as barrier walkthrough and subjective assessments, have been proposed in the literature but have not been used in practice [11]. A combination of usability testing involving people with disabilities and expert inspections is considered to be the ideal method, yet since both involve humans, the scalability is limited. Furthermore, a weakness of usability testing is that the user typically only identifies barriers that relate to their own disability and sometimes users with disabilities cannot provide useful feedback since portions of a web site are completely inaccessible [8]. Expert reviews typically identify different types of barriers for different disability populations and are more effective at determining compliance with standards, but often provide no useful information on usability, so accessibility barriers may technically be removed, but the website may still be impossible to use [12]. Furthermore, the amount of expertise present in the "expert" human in an expert review, has a major impact on the quality of the review, leading to inconsistent quality of reviews [13].

Regardless of which method (or combination of methods) is most effective, while human users or experts can examine all of the web pages on a 10 page, 50 page, or 100 page website, it becomes unreasonable and logistically impossible in terms of cost and time to have humans evaluate thousands or tens of thousands of web pages. With larger sites, when human users or experts evaluate web pages, they must use some form of sampling technique: either evaluating the most frequently visited pages, a random sampling of pages, or sampling pages that use different page templates. Because of scalability issues, automated tools for accessibility testing are often presented as an alternative, the only accessibility evaluation approach that can actually check all of the web pages on a site. Yet there are many drawbacks to using automated accessibility testing tools.

2.2 Automated Accessibility Testing Tools

Automated accessibility tools, while necessary due to the scalability issue, suffer from a large problem: they often give many misleading results, false positives, and require "manual checks" (human intervention to determine if an accessibility feature is implemented properly). The Web Accessibility Initiative (the accessibility component of the World Wide Web Consortium, also known as W3C) clearly states this on their website: "There are evaluation tools that help with evaluation. However, no tool alone can determine if a site meets accessibility standards. Knowledgeable human evaluation is required to determine if a site is accessible." [14]. Many aspects of web accessibility cannot be accurately evaluated using automated testing means. Only some of the WCAG 2.1 guidelines are currently machine-testable, and while AI may help make other guidelines machine-testable in the future, those AI approaches do not yet exist.

The automated web accessibility tools have a somewhat-negative reputation, for a number of reasons: 1) Many portions of the WCAG are not machine-testable, and require a human understanding of appropriateness and context, 2) When a tool determines the presence of a feature, it is often unable to determine if the feature is implemented properly (e.g. ALT text exists but the ALT text is identical for all 50 images, or says something useless like "imagename" to describe an image), and 3) the tools give developers feedback that is not useful (e.g. when a tool says that there are 58 violations and 653 potential violations on a single page) [8]. For novices to automated accessibility testing, they are often unaware of the strengths and weaknesses of different tools, and assume that the results of one tool give accurate results, leading to situations of being incorrectly led to believe that their web site is beyond repair, leading to "negative effects and undesirable consequences" [15]. In summary, existing automated testing tools generally do not provide data to users on what the tools can accurately do—determine the presence of an accessibility feature. Instead, the existing tools provide data on and claim to do what the tools can't accurately do—determine the correct implementation of an accessibility feature.

2.3   What Managers Need in Automated Tools

Automated web accessibility testing tools typically give feedback at a page level, listing the number of accessibility barriers, but they give limited information on a site or an organizational level. This means that the results of automated accessibility testing tools are geared towards developers or webmasters (at a micro level), but give very limited feedback at a macro level to policymakers and managers who are charged with implementing web accessibility. These existing tools often miss the distinction between web accessibility evaluation (which is focused at a page level), and compliance monitoring (which is at a web site or organizational level) which evaluates overall effectiveness of policies related to web accessibility [8]. Managing web accessibility for an organization is a compliance, higher-level activity. Furthermore, while WCAG is considered an international standard for guidelines, many different approaches for creating "scoring" for web accessibility have appeared in the literature, but none have been widely adopted or used [16].

Managers and leaders of organizations need to know whether they are making overall improvements in web accessibility, whether certain technical accessibility barriers are widespread, or if certain divisions of an organization are not effectively implementing accessibility. Existing tools do not provide that macro level of information, and furthermore, managers need ongoing information about web accessibility, not just information that is one-point-in-time. A recent (2020) study from Vollenwyder et. al. found that web accessibility is more frequently considered in the design and implementation phases of a web site, much more than during ongoing web site management and maintenance [17]. The challenges of managing web accessibility as a website frequently changes, was discussed more than 15 years ago by Lazar et al. (2004), and yet this management challenge is frequently forgotten about [18]. Since the content of web sites changes continuously, managers need tools that allow them to monitor the accessibility levels of websites on an ongoing basis, allowing for longitudinal analysis.

2.4 The "Presence of Accessibility Features" Approach to Metrics

Managers are interested in gaining a high-level understanding about the presence of accessibility features over hundreds or thousands of web pages in an organization, because it helps them understand whether organizational accessibility efforts are successful. For instance, if 90% of expected web accessibility features are present in one department, and only 20% of expected web accessibility features are present in another department, this data helps identify departments that may need further review. If one division of a large company has a high level of accessibility features implemented, but another division of a company has a low level of accessibility features implemented, this is useful feedback for management, given that the accessibility features are not implemented by accident, and they do not occur without some level of planning. This organizational-level data could potentially be useful in determining the level and success of accessibility policy implementation within a large organization, providing useful data to managers responsible for monitoring and implementing web accessibility.

Preliminary work published in 2017 examined the concept of the "presence of accessibility features" metric, where an automated tool could potentially identify all of the locations where accessibility features (such as ALT text) would be expected, and then compare the presence of accessibility features to the expected presence of accessibility features, throughout the websites of an organization or specific departments in an organization [19]. The previously published work presented the theoretical underpinnings, and did a one-point in time evaluation, of accessibility features on 629 web sites within the U.S. Federal Government, over a total of 28,429 webpages [19]. As an example, with ALT text, more than 500 of the 629 Federal web sites had ALT text present in over 80% of the circumstances where you would expect it. Yet both with labels for form controls, as well as <h1> headings, the distribution was bimodal. With form controls, 282 websites had labels on at least 80% of their form controls but 171 websites had less than 20% of their form controls with labels. This served to both identify patterns throughout the Federal government, and also to drill down to the Federal agency level, to determine where policy implementation on web accessibility was effective, and where it was not [19].

3 Research Questions and Methods

The current project has the following three exploratory research questions related to the design and development of improved automated web accessibility testing tools:

1. What type of technical infrastructure would be needed to collect data using the "presence of accessibility features" metric for measuring existing web sites on a longitudinal basis?
2. Based on the type of data collected (site-level presence of accessibility features) using this metric, what types of interface notifications and reporting could potentially be useful for managers?
3. How could historical archives of web pages be integrated into an automated tool to support longer-term analysis for managers?

Related to **RQ1**, to learn more about the potential use of this metric approach on a longitudinal basis in automated web accessibility testing tools, an existing web accessibility tool (iAccessible) which uses standard page-level approaches for evaluation and reporting, was modified to incorporate the new "presence of accessibility features" metric approaches. iAccessible is a part of the larger Revelo software package for web site and data management.

iAccessible is an accessibility tool that seeks to facilitate the extraction of web data and display relevant accessibility information. The results from the automated web accessibility testing tools are displayed in dashboards. The data is displayed in tables, bar charts, line graphs and pie charts, all comprised in different dashboards.

Related to **RQ2**, to understand the types of notifications and reports that might be useful for managers using the new metrics on a longitudinal basis, web accessibility data was collected using the modified iAccessible tool for a year-long period from four existing websites. One website was from a U.S. state agency/department. The other three websites were from three universities: a small private university (approx. 5,000 students), a medium-sized private university (approx. 20,000 students), and a large state university (approx. 40,000 students). These four websites were chosen because they were the same organizations involved in a year-long series of interviews of those who direct web accessibility policy (the results of the interviews are reported in [20]). The goal of the evaluation is to test the tool in real-world usage, and to examine how longitudinal data from the tool might potentially be used by managers. It is important to note that this stage of the research and development project does not have a goal of analyzing the accessibility data itself from the four websites, but rather, to learn more about the potential design space of a new approach to automated accessibility testing tools.

Each of the four organizations participating in the study also had subdomains associated with each parent domain. For example, a university's business school also needed scanning, resulting in the organization needing www.University.edu and www. Business.University.edu domains scanned for accessibility. All this resulted in 39 different domains needing to be scanned by iAccessible within one of the universities. Once these domains were identified, iAccessible used a crawling tool to identify all the webpages rooted to the original domain by identifying links on all scanned webpages. This method identified over 400,000 total webpages throughout the 39 domains. However, the total URLs identified far exceed what the website owners had expected, and so a sampling method needed to be used for this exploratory study.

A web design strategy often used to minimize the level of effort while providing consistent user experience is to use an HTML template across multiple pages with the design of all of the pages being the same and only the content of the page being different. A familiar example of this would be comparable to a company having multiple products with different URLs for each product, while the page layout remained the same. Understanding this was essential in lowering the total webpages scanned to a more reasonable level. An example of this approach is shown below between would be URLs identified and URL tested:

URLs Identified:

- www.University.edu/updates/01Jan2020
- www.University.edu/updates/02Jan2020

- www.University.edu/updates/03Jan2020
- www.University.edu/updates/04Jan2020
- www.University.edu/majors/business
- www.University.edu/majors/economics
- www.University.edu/majors/engineering

Using this type of sampling approach narrows down the URLs to only two:

- www.University.com/updates/01Jan2020
- www.Univeristy.com/majors/business

Implementing this approach lowered the total monthly URLs to be tested from 400,000 + webpages to 30,000 pages evaluated monthly. Using this sampling approach, during the 12 month period, a total of 523,000 webpages (across all 4 web sites) were scanned and evaluated for accessibility.

Related to **RQ3**, to learn more about the potential use of historical archives of web pages, the research team investigated the potential integration of data from the Wayback Machine into iAccessible. The Wayback Machine (https://archive.org/web/), an existing web tool that stores historical web pages, has been used to collect data for previously published historical studies of web accessibility [21, 22], but it does not appear to ever have been directly integrated into a web accessibility tool. A proof-of-concept to extract web pages from the Wayback Machine and place them directly into iAccessible for analysis was created by the co-authors.

Each of the next sections details the findings related to research questions 1, 2, and 3, respectively.

4   Technical Infrastructure to Implement the "Presence of Accessibility Features" (RQ1)

The Web Content Accessibility Guidelines are considered to be the gold standard for digital accessibility guidelines, used by countries around the world in their disability rights laws. Previous research about the use of metrics [19] identified three potential metrics from the WCAG where automated tools could accurately measure the "presence of accessibility features": the presence of ALT text (WCAG Success Criteria 1.1.1), the presence of labels for form controls (WCAG Success Criteria 2.4.6), and the presence of H1 Headings (WCAG Success Criteria 1.3.1). In this paper, we add three additional metrics that we identified could be used with the "presence of accessibility features" approach: Heading Elements (h1–h6) are properly nested (WCAG Success Criteria 1.3.1), tabular data tables have row/column headers (WCAG Success Criteria 1.3.1), and that a web page has at least one main landmark (WCAG Success Criteria 1.3.1).

WAVE is an evaluation tool that helps businesses and organizations to make web content more accessible. There are two versions of WAVE available: WAVE has a free browser extension that is available for Firefox and Google Chrome. The free extension identifies the most common accessibility errors and a possible solution to every error. Even though this tool is advantageous, the information WAVE extension provides is very limited, to only the most common errors. For an enterprise level, WAVE offers an API service that can be installed locally or in a cloud server. WAVE Enterprise version apply scripts to interact with page content before page analysis, capture full-page screenshots and produce a table with 107 variables of data for its analysis.

Much of this data for potential use in the iAccessible tool is already collected by the existing WAVE tool, but is not presented to WAVE users in the way that we had proposed. We modified iAccessible to integrate the information from WAVE by retrieving the WAVE tables into a database, applying formulas for the metrics and populating that information into the dashboards.

As one example, related to alternative text, the WAVE tool creates 13 different data variables related to alternative text: *alt_missing, alt_link_missing, alt_spacer_missing, alt_input_missing, alt_area_missing, alt_map_missing* (all of which are used when alt text is missing), as well as *alt, alt_null, alt_spacer, alt_link, alt_input, alt_map, and alt_area* (all of which are used when alt text is present). They need to be amalgamated by iAccessible into one overall score of the presence of expected accessibility features on that specific page. In this example, the formula used is displayed in Fig. 1. The variables used from WAVE data are also expressed as V1 – V13 in Table 1.

$$\frac{Number\ of\ instances\ alternative\ text\ is\ present}{Number\ of\ instances\ alternative\ text\ is\ expected\ to\ be\ present}$$

Fig. 1. Plain language formula representation for Alternative Text Present Metric

Table 1. WAVE variables used in the page-level and website-level formulas for Alternative Text Present

WAVE Variables used for when alternative text is missing: V1: alt_missing, V2: alt_link_missing, V3: alt_spacer_missing, V4: alt_input_missing, V5: alt_area_missing, V6: alt_map_missing	WAVE Variables used for when alternative text is present: V7: alt, V8: alt_null, V9: alt_spacer, V10: alt_link, V11: alt_input, V12: alt_map, V13: alt_area

The page-level score is calculated for every URL. The formula used for this is represented in Fig. 2:

$$\frac{V7 + V8 + V9 + V10 + V11 + V12 + V13}{V1 + V2 + V3 + V4 + V5 + V6 + V7 + V8 + V9 + V10 + V11 + V12 + V13} \times 100$$

Fig. 2. Formula and variables used to calculate a page-level Alternative Text Present metric score

The other metrics were created with a similar approach, specifically, all of the accessibility features present on a web page in the numerator, divided by all of the places that WAVE expected that there should be accessibility features (using all of the existing metrics built into WAVE), and multiplied by 100. Creating these formulas may seem straight-forward, but there are a number of complexities in the way that WAVE collects data about table headers. WAVE collects a data point called, table_data, which documents the number of tables in a webpage (by counting the number of < Table > tags). WAVE also collects two other variables, *th_col*, and *th_row*, which counts the number of table headers to mark rows or columns, respectfully. In this example, the formula used is displayed in Fig. 3. The variables used from WAVE data are also expressed as V1 – V3 in Table 2.

Data Tables with Row and or Column Headers
_____
All Data Tables

Fig. 3. Plain language formula representation for Rows/Columns Present metric

Table 2. WAVE variables used in the page-level and website-level formulas for Rows/Columns Present Metric

WAVE variables for Data Tables with Row and or Column Headers: V1: th_row V2: th_col	WAVE Variable for Data Tables: V3: table_data

The computation for the Rows/Columns metric is expressed in Fig. 4.

$$\frac{V1 + V2}{V3} \times 100$$

Fig. 4. Formula and variables used to calculate the page-level Rows/Columns Present metric score

This page-level score is then used as part of the average score for a website-level score. See formula used in Fig. 5

$$\bar{x}\left\{\Sigma(\frac{V1 + V2}{V3} \times 100)\right\}$$

Fig. 5. Formula and variables used to calculate the website-level Rows/Columns present metric score

If a webpage has two tables, to conform with WCAG it would need to have row headers and column headers present in both tables. Yet imagine a webpage where WAVE reports 3 tables, 9 row headers and 9 column headers. WAVE is not yet able to track if the 9 row headers and 9 column headers are spread out among the 3 tables, or if all 9 row headers and 9 column headers are in 1 table, and the other two tables are completely missing headers for rows and columns. Given the limited information coming out from WAVE, the following approach was used for creating the metric in iAccessible (Table 3):

Table 3. Criteria to calculate the website-level Rows/Columns present metric score

If table_data is NULL (no tables exist on the page) then metric = Not applicable (NA) If table_data is not NULL, see if th_row or th_col is not NULL If th_col => table_data and th_row => table_data then metric = 100% (meaning that there are at least as many th_row and th_col, as there are tables, so in a best-case scenario, each table has at least one row header and one column header) If th_col < table_data and th_row < table_data then metric= 0% (meaning that there are fewer th_row and th_col than tables, so all of the tables do not have row headers or column headers) If th_col < table_data and th_row => table_data then metric = 50% If th_col => table_data and th_row < table_data then metric = 50%

5 Types of Potential Interface Notifications and Reporting for Managers (RQ2)

From March 2020, using the modified iAccessible tool with the new metrics, web accessibility data was collected monthly from the four websites described in Sect. 3. An average of between 43,000 and 44,000 webpages were scanned on a monthly basis (it changed as webpages were added and removed from sites), for a total of approximately 523,000 pages being scanned for accessibility during the 12 month period. The goal of this exploratory research is to understand the design space, for how to present this data. Therefore, the data collected in iAccessible was used to help understand what types of notifications and reports are needed by managers.

To start with, one summary dashboard was created, showing the overall level of accessibility features present, for each of the six metrics discussed earlier in the paper, by month, at the organizational level. Data was examined to determine potential notifications that might be useful. For one of the college units within one of the universities, there was a large increase in the amount of alt text present, between June 2020-Aug 2020 (see Fig. 6). For all of the places where ALT text was expected to be present, amount of ALT text actually present increased from 47.7% in June 2020, to 54.2% in July 2020, to 95.6% in August 2020. Clearly something was going on. Was a new content management system put in place? Was a new policy implemented, requiring ALT text? Was there increased training over the summer? Were old legacy web pages removed from the site? This is the type of massive change in a short amount of time, that should trigger a notification to managers. It is good news, and perhaps there is a strategy that can successfully be used in other parts of the organization.

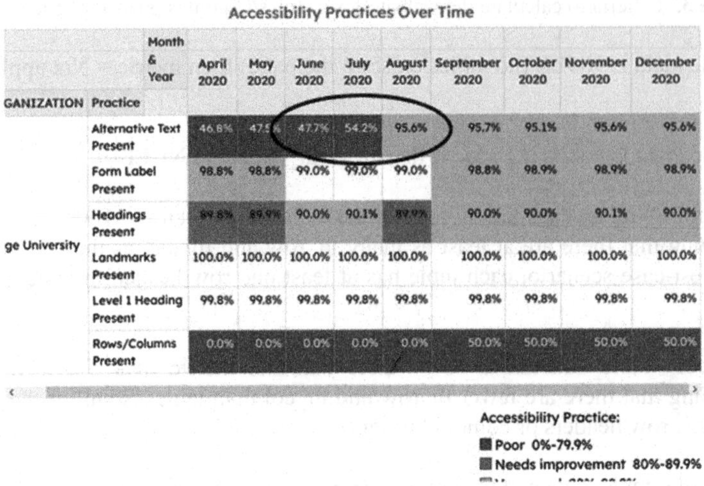

Accessibility Practices Over Time

GANIZATION	Practice	Month & Year	April 2020	May 2020	June 2020	July 2020	August 2020	September 2020	October 2020	November 2020	December 2020
ge University	Alternative Text Present		46.8%	47.5%	47.7%	54.2%	95.6%	95.7%	95.1%	95.6%	95.6%
	Form Label Present		98.8%	98.8%	99.0%	99.0%	99.0%	98.8%	98.9%	98.9%	98.9%
	Headings Present		89.8%	89.9%	90.0%	90.1%	89.9%	90.0%	90.0%	90.1%	90.0%
	Landmarks Present		100.0%	100.0%	100.0%	100.0%	100.0%	100.0%	100.0%	100.0%	100.0%
	Level 1 Heading Present		99.8%	99.8%	99.8%	99.8%	99.8%	99.8%	99.8%	99.8%	99.8%
	Rows/Columns Present		0.0%	0.0%	0.0%	0.0%	0.0%	50.0%	50.0%	50.0%	50.0%

Accessibility Practice:
■ Poor 0%-79.9%
■ Needs improvement 80%-89.9%

Fig. 6. Dashboard presenting data with a dramatic increase in ALT text between June-Aug 2020

Similarly, a drop or a massive shift in data over time, should cause a notification to be given to managers in the interface, with prompting for further analysis. Figure 7 shows that, for one web site, for the expected number of form labels present, 96.2% were present in September 2020, 69.2% were present in October 2020, and 87.4% were present in November 2020. This clearly should prompt drill-down analysis.

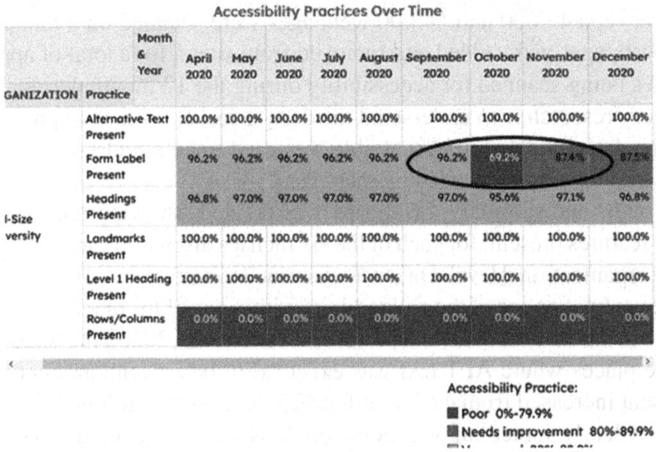

Accessibility Practices Over Time

GANIZATION	Practice	Month & Year	April 2020	May 2020	June 2020	July 2020	August 2020	September 2020	October 2020	November 2020	December 2020
l-Size versity	Alternative Text Present		100.0%	100.0%	100.0%	100.0%	100.0%	100.0%	100.0%	100.0%	100.0%
	Form Label Present		96.2%	96.2%	96.2%	96.2%	96.2%	96.2%	69.2%	87.4%	87.5%
	Headings Present		96.8%	97.0%	97.0%	97.0%	97.0%	97.0%	95.6%	97.1%	96.8%
	Landmarks Present		100.0%	100.0%	100.0%	100.0%	100.0%	100.0%	100.0%	100.0%	100.0%
	Level 1 Heading Present		100.0%	100.0%	100.0%	100.0%	100.0%	100.0%	100.0%	100.0%	100.0%
	Rows/Columns Present		0.0%	0.0%	0.0%	0.0%	0.0%	0.0%	0.0%	0.0%	0.0%

Accessibility Practice:
■ Poor 0%-79.9%
■ Needs improvement 80%-89.9%

Fig. 7. Dashboard presenting data with a dramatic decrease in form labels present between Sept-Nov 2020

One could also imagine where an organization is generally effective at some aspects of web accessibility (such as ALT text) or headings but is consistently ineffective at other aspects of web accessibility. For instance, Fig. 8 shows how an organization consistently has low levels of form labels present and row and column headers present. This would also trigger the need for interface notifications for managers.

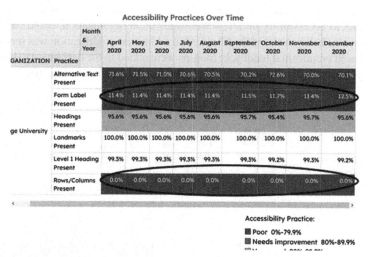

Fig. 8. Dashboard presenting consistently low accessibility data in terms of form labels present and row/column labels present

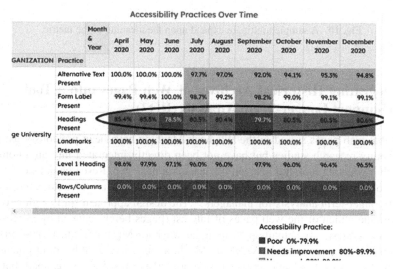

Fig. 9. Dashboard showing the problem of minor changes in data being reflected in heatmap shading.

One additional discovery from our prototype interface: if a scale is used, which shades data based on the perceived severity of the situation (basically, a heatmap), the shading will need to be adjusted so that small changes in data (e.g. back and forth across an 80% threshold) are not reflected in notifications to the manager. For instance, in Fig. 9, the shading keeps changing, as the level of headings present slightly changes above and below the 80% threshold, making it appear as if there are major changes, which there are not. While this is not unique to accessibility dashboards, it is certainly possible that a few tweaks to accessibility on a few webpages in an organization, could easily push a score above or below a stated threshold. One additional modification was made to the interface based on informal feedback: tooltips were added to the dashboard to help users potentially understand about what the different metrics meant (see Fig. 10).

Accessibility Practices Over Time

Organization & Department	Practice*	Month & Year					
		April 2020	May 2020	June 2020	August 2020	September 2020	October 2020
Small University, Covid-19	Alternative Text Present	99.6%	100.0%	100.0%	100.0%	100.0%	99.8%
	Form Label Present	100.0%	100.0%	100.0%	100.0%	98.9%	100.0%
	Headings Present	97.6%	97.5%	97.5%	97.5%	97.8%	97.9%
	Landmarks	At least one main Landmark present / All pages		0.0%	0.0%	0.0%	0.0%
	Level 1 Head Present			100.0%	100.0%	100.0%	100.0%
	Rows/Columns Present	0.0%	0.0%	0.0%	0.0%	0.0%	0.0%

*Hover over practices' names to see the formulas used to calculate the scores.

Fig. 10. A sample tooltip, to expand upon the meaning of the metric.

6 Integrating Historical Archives of Web Pages into a Tool to Support Longer-Term Analysis (RQ3)

Given that web pages stored in the Wayback Machine have been previously used for accessibility research studies but have not been directly integrated into an automated accessibility testing tool, this seemed like a natural next step. Research question 3 asks "How could historical archives of web pages be integrated into an automated tool to support longer-term analysis for managers?" The design approach starts with crawling to determine which of the web pages of interest (pages being scanned by iAccessible as per user request), are actually present in the Wayback Machine. If historical versions of webpages are present in the Wayback Machine, then iAccessible could potentially increase the longitudinal analysis to include not only pages directly scanned, but also pages available in previous years, extending analysis to 5, 10, 15, or even in rare circumstances, 20 years (as the earliest web archives in the Wayback Machine are from 1996, although they are by no means complete). Figure 11 shows the schematics developed for use in iAccessible for crawling the Wayback Machine archives. Table 4 describes the process for scanning the Wayback Machine and Table 5 describes the fields returned to iAccessible by the Wayback Machine.

WaybackMachine Scenario: Website scan

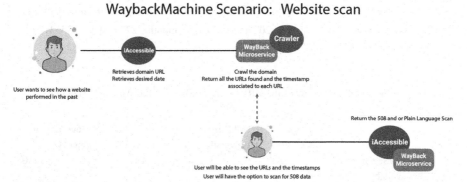

Fig. 11. Schematic drawing showing how iAccessible can crawl the web pages on the Wayback archive

Table 4. Table describing how iAccessible can crawl the web pages on the Wayback archive

Wayback Machine Scenario: Website Scan	
Reference	*Explanation/Description/Result*
User	User that wants to see how a website performed in the past
iAccessible	Web-based application
Crawler	Microservice that allows to crawl a website in the present to get all their URLs, Parent URLs, timestamp, URL status and internal vs external URL data
Wayback Machine Microservice	Microservice that calls the Wayback API for past data/information

To help explain how this proof-of-concept works, we choose one identified URL and extracted the most recent historical web-page URL (within the 12-months period for this study):

The identified URL:

- www.University.com/majors/business

The extracted URL from the WayBack Machine API:

- www.web.archive.org/web/20200227225541/University.com/majors/business

Table 5. Fields necessary to build an archived URL

From the Wayback Machine archive snapshot it extracts:	
Reference	*Explanation/Description/Result*
Availability	True if it is available, false if not
URL	www.web.archive.org/web/20200227225541/University.com/majors/business
Tmestamp	"20200227225541"; "2020" = year, "02" = month, "27" = day, "225541" = hours, minutes, and seconds

Table 6. Data on how many of the URLs were available in the Wayback Machine.

	Large University	Mid-size University	Small University	State Government Agency
Total URLs Scanned	5054	13157	10430	9630
# of URLs available in the Wayback	4263	11218	7255	6960
# of URLs not available in the Wayback	791	1939	3175	2670
# of URLs available between 2020/2021	2474	8716	6447	4813
% of URLs available in the Wayback Machine	84.35%	85.26%	69.56%	72.27%
% of URLs available in the Wayback Machine between 2020/2021	48.95%	66.25%	61.81%	49.98%

Using this crawling technique, we were able to determine that a majority of the ~ 43,000 webpages used in our previous evaluations using iAccessible were also available in the Wayback Machine (See Table 6), with their unique timestamp. While 84%, 85%, 69%, and 72% of webpages were available overall, when searching the Wayback Machine specifically to the 2020–2021 timeframe, those availability rates dropped to 48%, 66%, 61%, and 49%, respectively.

Based on the crawling approach described in previous sections, mockups were created to address how historical data from the Wayback Machine might be implemented into iAccessible. It was determined that there were three stages at which a user might enter the process of analyzing historical web page data: 1) the user wanted to find out which pages were available on the Wayback Machine for analysis and wanted to request a crawl, 2) crawling was done, and historical web pages available for analysis were identified but were not yet downloaded or analyzed for accessibility, and 3) pages had already been downloaded and scanned for accessibility. Understanding this distinction would help both in terms of limiting unneeded processing (e.g. webpages that existed on the Wayback Machine but were not of interest due to the timeframe and therefore did not need to be downloaded), and also in terms of setting realistic expectations in terms of response time (since presenting already-scanned webpages would be quick, but downloading and scanning thousands of webpages would not be quick). A mockup appears in Fig. 12, showing how users might potentially select webpages to be analyzed based on timestamp, for those that had already been crawled and were found to be available on the Wayback Machine.

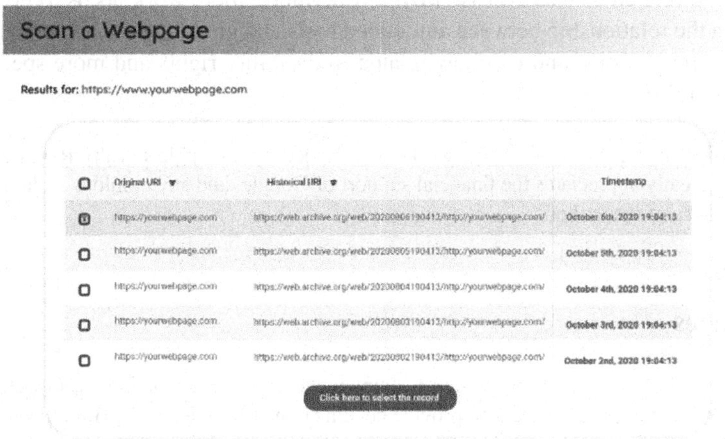

Fig. 12. Mockup for selecting the date ranges based on web pages that were already crawled and were available for scanning for accessibility.

7 Discussion and Summary

This research and development project explored three questions, relating to: 1) the technical infrastructure needed to collect longitudinal data using the "presence of accessibility features" metric, 2) interface notifications and reporting for managers related to the use of this metric, and 3) using historical archives of web pages (the Wayback Machine) to support longer-term analysis for managers. The proof-of-concept described in this paper laid out one type of technical infrastructure that could be used to create tools that provide a managerial-level analysis of web accessibility for managers. Using sample data of over half a million web pages scanned for accessibility during a 12-month period, it was possible to identify different types of notifications and reporting that would be helpful for managers. However, this paper presents only exploratory steps in understanding what is potentially possible for the next generation of automated web accessibility testing tools. Specifically, the formulas developed in this project, serve as an example of the limitation of existing approaches for collecting and analyzing data (such as the example of how WAVE parses table accessibility).

There are a few potential next directions for this research, both technical and organizational. From a technical research point of view, the next steps could be to investigate which other success criteria from WCAG could be added into this tool. Currently, only

6 WCAG success criteria are included in the tool (3 of which were first created as a part of this paper), and so it would be useful to evaluate which additional success criteria from WCAG could reliably be integrated using the "presence of accessibility features" metric. From an organizational research point of view, it would be useful to have web accessibility managers in an organization actually using the tool, using data from their organizations, giving feedback both on 1) the usability of the tool and interface, 2) the types of notifications and reporting, and 3) how the tool impacts their organizational decision making related to web accessibility. Furthermore, more work needs to be done to evaluating the relationship between automated tools and guidelines, and how they relate to statutes, regulations, and case law related to disability rights and more specifically, web accessibility.

Acknowledgements. Portions of this work were funded by a Google Faculty Research Grant. The author greatly appreciates the financial support of Google, and any opinions included herein are solely those of the author.

References

1. Schmutz, S., Sonderegger, A., Sauer, J.: Implementing recommendations from web accessibility guidelines: would they also provide benefits to nondisabled users. Hum. Factors **58**(4), 611–629 (2016)
2. Web accessibility initiative: Web content accessibility guidelines working group end-of-charter report (1999). https://www.w3.org/WAI/GL/end-charter2-report.html
3. Web accessibility initiative: Web content accessibility guidelines 2.2 working draft (2020a). https://www.w3.org/TR/WCAG22/
4. U.S. Department of Justice: Letter from assistant Attorney General Deval Patrick to Senator Tom Harkin (1996). http://www.justice.gov/crt/foia/readingroom/frequent_requests/ada_tal/tal712.txt
5. U.S. Department of Justice: Letter from assistant attorney general Stephen Boyd to Representative Ted Budd (2018). https://www.adatitleiii.com/wp-content/uploads/sites/121/2018/10/DOJ-letter-to-congress.pdf
6. US Department of Justice: Statement of Interest of the USA, New v. Lucky Brand Dungarees Store, Inc.: Point of Sale Machines (S.D. Fl. 14-cv-20574) . (2014). http://www.ada.gov/briefs/lucky_brand_soi.pdf
7. Lazar, J.: Due process and primary jurisdiction doctrine: a threat to accessibility research and practice? In: Proceedings of the ACM 2018 Conference on Accessible Technology (ASSETS), pp. 404–406 (2018)
8. Lazar, J., Goldstein, D.F., Taylor, A.: Ensuring digital accessibility through process and policy. Elsevier/Morgan Kaufmann, Waltham (2015)
9. Harris, E.: Galleries from A to Z sued over websites the blind can't use. The New York Times, 18 February 2019. https://www.nytimes.com/2019/02/18/arts/design/blind-lawsuits-art-galleries.html
10. Lazar, J.: The potential role of US consumer protection laws in improving digital accessibility for people with disabilities. Univ. Pennsylvania J. Law Soc. Change **22**(3), 185–204 (2019)
11. Brajnik, G.: A comparative test of web accessibility evaluation methods. In: Proceedings of the 10th International ACM SIGACCESS Conference on Computers and Accessibility, pp. 113–120 (2008)

12. Power, C., Freire, A., Petrie, H., Swallow, D.: Guidelines are only half of the story: accessibility problems encountered by blind users on the web. In: Proceedings of the SIGCHI conference on human factors in computing systems, pp. 433–442 (2012)
13. Brajnik, G., Yesilada, Y., Harper, S.: The expertise effect on web accessibility evaluation methods. Hum. Comput. Interact. **26**(3), 246–283 (2011)
14. Web Accessibility Initiative: Evaluating web accessibility overview (2020b). https://www.w3.org/WAI/test-evaluate/
15. Vigo, M., Brown, J., Conway, V.: Benchmarking web accessibility evaluation tools: measuring the harm of sole reliance on automated tests. In: Proceedings of the 10th International Cross-Disciplinary Conference on Web Accessibility, vol. 1 (2013)
16. Vigo, M., Brajnik, G.: Automatic web accessibility metrics: Where we are and where we can go. Interact. Comput. **23**(2), 137–155 (2011)
17. Vollenwyder, B., Opwis, K., Brühlmann, F.: How web professionals perceive web accessibility in practice: active roles, process phases and key disabilities. In: Miesenberger K., Manduchi R., Covarrubias Rodriguez M., Peňáz P. (eds.) Proceedings of the 2020 International Conference on Computers Helping People with Special Needs, pp. 294–302. Springer, Cham (2020). https://doi.org/10.1007/978-3-030-58796-3_35
18. Lazar, J., Dudley-Sponaugle, A., Greenidge, K.D.: Improving web accessibility: a study of webmaster perceptions. Comput. Hum. Behav. **20**(2), 269–288 (2004)
19. Lazar, J., Williams, V., Gunderson, J., Foltz, T.: Investigating the potential of a dashboard for monitoring US federal website accessibility. In: Proceedings of the 50th Hawaii International Conference on System Sciences, pp. 2428–2437 (2017)
20. Lazar, J.: Managing digital accessibility at universities during the COVID-19 pandemic. Universal Access in the Information Society (2021). https://doi.org/10.1007/s10209-021-00792-5
21. Hackett, S., Parmanto, B., Zeng, X.: Accessibility of Internet websites through time. In: Proceedings of the 6th International ACM SIGACCESS Conference on Computers and Accessibility, pp. 32–39 (2003)
22. Hanson, V.L., Richards, J.T.: Progress on website accessibility? ACM Trans. Web (TWEB) **7**(1), 1–30 (2013)

Expert Validation of the ICT Accessibility Requirements Tool Prototype

Márcio Martins[1]([⊠]) , Francisco Godinho[2] , Pedro Gonçalves[2] ,
and Ramiro Gonçalves[1]

[1] INESC TEC and University of Trás-os-Montes and Alto Douro, Vila Real, Portugal
{marciom,ramiro}@utad.pt
[2] University of Trás-os-Montes and Alto Douro, Vila Real, Portugal
{godinho,pgoncalves}@utad.pt

Abstract. The Accessibility Requirements Tool for Information and Communication Technologies (FRIATIC) was developed within the work of a doctoral
project, at the University of Trás-os-Montes and Alto Douro, and may be used at
various stages of public procurement processes as well as projects and developments that include ICT products and services. This tool helps to consult, determine and assess the accessibility requirements for ICT products and services in
European Standard EN 301 549 supporting the legislation in the field of public
procurement for the countries of the European Union – Directive 2014/24/EU.
This study focuses on the validation of the FRATIC prototype with 25 experts
in the areas of accessibility, assistive technologies and public procurement, by
conducting semi-structured interviews on this research subject and the FRATIC
tool in particular, which were conducted after performing usability tests with the
tool. A thematic analysis method was used to assess the qualitative data from the
interviews.

Keywords: Accessibility Requirements Tool for ICT · European Standard EN
301 549 · Public procurement · Accessibility · Usability

1 Introduction

The belief that equal capabilities ensure full cooperation and thus equal participation in
a given system for all is erroneous, or at least limited, as it neglects the peculiarities of
each individual and the notion of human diversity [1]. Human diversity in our society
can only be managed if we are able to overcome limitations, and if we all contribute
to increasing the full integration of everyone, regardless of each individual's difficulties
[1].

According to the World Health Organization (WHO) and the World Bank, a significant percentage (about 15%) of the world's entire adult population suffers from some
kind of disability. This percentage is likely to be higher in developing countries as
poverty, conflict, and poorer welfare states are all factors that exponentially increase the
risk of a fragile physical condition becoming a disability [2]. Overall, the percentage

© The Author(s), under exclusive license to Springer Nature Switzerland AG 2022
M. Antona and C. Stephanidis (Eds.): HCII 2022, LNCS 13308, pp. 40–58, 2022.
https://doi.org/10.1007/978-3-031-05028-2_3

of people with disabilities (PWD) is 15.9% for people aged between 50 and 59 years old and 29.5% for people aged 60 and over, according to figures from the WHO [3]. In the European Union (EU) an estimated 80 million European citizens have some type of disability or impairment [4] that inhibits them from participating in the many different dimensions of life and citizenship on an equal basis with others. In Portugal, this figure is close to 1 million people [5].

Disability is perceived as the result of a complex nexus between personal and contextual factors that triggers health consequences and adjacent economic effects [6]. Throughout history, not enough practices and policies have been observed to overcome inequalities, social injustices, and the exclusion of PWD and the elderly in various social areas. One of the areas where this problem has always been visible are the information and communication technologies (ICT), firstly in regards to their access and then in the conditions of use and interaction.

Improving the accessibility of ICT products and services for people with disabilities is an important step towards complying with the United Nations (UN) Convention on the Rights of Persons with Disabilities, signed and ratified by several countries, including Portugal [7], as it aims to promote, protect, and ensure the full and equal enjoyment of all human rights and fundamental freedoms by all PWD, and to promote the respect for their inherent dignity [8].

Within the work of a doctoral project, at the University of Trás-os-Montes and Alto Douro, where this study is also inserted, the ICT Accessibility Requirements Tool (FRATIC), based on Microsoft Excel, was developed. This tool may be used at various stages of public procurement processes as well as projects and developments that include ICT products and services [9], as it helps to consult, determine and assess the accessibility requirements for ICT products and services in EN 301 549 [10–14] that support the legislation in the field of public procurement for the countries of the European Union – Directive 2014/24/EU [15] – and is capable of providing comprehensive and detailed reports. This study focuses on the validation of the FRATIC prototype with 25 experts in the fields of accessibility, assistive technologies, and public procurement. To this end, a semi-structured interview was conducted [16] with the experts after they have completed the usability tests with the tool. The interview was designed so as to elicit objective answers to specific questions about the theme of this research and the FRATIC tool in particular, and comprised 19 open and closed questions.

2 State of the Art

Whenever an activity excludes someone merely because it is impossible to access a place, product or service, there is, by definition, a form of exclusion and, consequently, discrimination [17]. Accessibility is based on the basic and fundamental element of everyone's right to equal participation, regardless of each person's characteristics [18], and is increasingly relevant for full integration in a society where information technology is essential for sharing information and building knowledge [19], and where ICTs are used more frequently [20]. PWD have already shown through several technological resources that, when assistive products that enable them to access the systems are developed – products that turn out to be tools of great importance by enhancing equality in the access to products and services, and fighting exclusion [21]–, they are the first to adopt the new resources [22, 23].

So, in a society where more and more ICTs are being used, ensuring full accessibility for all is a priority and indispensable, since accessibility in this area is fundamental for achieving social and digital inclusion of people with special needs (PSN) – i.e. PWD and the elderly –, or even people in general [24–27]. Likewise, technological potential and political will must be leveraged, and no efforts should be spared to achieve the universal access goal for ICT products and services.

It was with this same focus that, in 1973, the United States of America (USA) implemented the Americans with Disabilities Act (ADA), in order to legislate the accessibility agenda [28]. Later, in 1998 and 2000, the US Access Board also published the Guidelines for Section 255 of the Telecommunications Act [29] and the Section 508 Standards of the Rehabilitation Act [30] – both of which have undergone several updates between their respective years of publication and until 2018. This process has allowed the US to acquire the necessary experience to understand the relevance of public procurement in providing accessible ICTs in the marketplace. It should be noted that the potential efficiency of public procurement as a mechanism to promote accessibility has been proven on several instances, and it was instrumental in creating the European Union's Directive 2014/24/EU [15], where the subject of accessible and usable ICTs for all is becoming increasingly visible.

In an effort to harmonize accessibility guidelines, and following in the US footsteps, the European Commission (EC) has asked three European bodies[1] (CEN, CENELEC and ETSI) to formally set out the European accessibility requirements in public procurement procedures for products and services in the ICT domain in order to harmonize the requirements among the Member States. To that end, the first version of EN 301 549 [10] was published in 2014 – and four updates were published afterwards, which also supported the European Accessibility Act [31, 32], Directive 2014/24/EU on public procurement procedures of Member States [15], and Directive 2016/2102/EU which provides the first European Union (EU) wide rules on the accessibility of websites and mobile applications for public sector bodies [33]. Furthermore, this standard also aims at a) promoting the free circulation of accessible goods and services and b) increasing the effectiveness of accessibility legislation [34, 35]. Therefore, it is easy to understand that Portugal should also review its policies and the relevant legal framework so that it can comply with the applicable legislation in other EU Member States regarding the acquisition and development of a wide range of ICT products and services [32].

The US has developed a web-based tool, the Accessibility Requirements Tool,[2] capable of assisting in determining relevant Section 508 accessibility requirements, and incorporating them into procurement and contract documentation that includes ICT products and services, as well as in internal ICT development. Similarly, the EU has

---

[1] Designations of the three European standardization organizations: European Committee for Standardization (CEN), European Committee for Electrotechnical Standardization (CENELEC) and European Telecommunications Standards Institute (ETSI).

[2] Accessibility Requirements Tool, available at https://www.section508.gov/art.

created under M 376 the Accessible ICT Procurement Toolkit[3] to assist public procurement officers in using and implementing EN 301 549, and to provide information on how accessibility applies to the different stages of the public procurement process [36]. However, this toolkit is no longer available.

3 Methodology

Qualitative research methodologies are the most suitable methods, although not exclusive, when it comes to thoroughly analyzing the meanings, statements, and interpretations of the subjects, particularly when it comes to studying less explored aspects of a given phenomenon [37, 38], as it is the case here.

This study focuses on the validation of the FRATIC prototype with 25 experts in the fields of accessibility, assistive technologies, and public procurement. To this end, semi-structured interviews were conducted [16], which were applied after performing the usability tests with the tool, about this investigation's subject and the FRATIC tool in particular. The interviews were designed so as to elicit objective answers to specific questions, and they comprised 19 open and closed questions. For the qualitative analysis of the interviews a thematic analysis was used, which is a widely used qualitative data analysis method aimed at identifying, analyzing, and reporting patterns (themes) in data, enhancing the understanding of explicit and implicit meanings associated with textual data [39, 40].

These interviews aimed at obtaining the participants' thoughts regarding the topics "European Standard EN 301 549", "other tools", "FRATIC usability", "FRATIC features" and "FRATIC target audience". Within each topic, it was intended to elicit answers to the following questions (indicators):

- European Standard EN 301 549: a) How can EN 301 549 be deemed sufficient to determine accessibility requirements and their means of verifying compliance for a specific ICT?
- Other tools: b) How can the technical accessibility criteria specified in EN 301 549 be evaluated globally?
- FRATIC usability: c) To what extent are there usability capabilities and/or limitations in FRATIC?
- FRATIC features: d) How can FRATIC contribute or benefit the creation and purchase of technologies accessible to all?
- FRATIC target audience: e) Who are the potential FRATIC users, stakeholders, beneficiaries or target audience (or to whom may it be useful)?

4 Study Elements

4.1 Participants

Participants in the interviews were required to meet certain inclusion criteria: 1) being an expert and/or a person interested in the areas of accessibility, assistive technologies,

---

[3] Accessible ICT Procurement Toolkit, available from December 2014 to February 2021 at http://mandate376.standards.eu/.

and public procurement; 2) having at least three years of experience in one of these areas; 3) having a computer with ZOOM® software, a sound system with speakers and microphone, a webcam, and strong Internet access.

4.2 Study Background

The restrictions imposed by the COVID-19 pandemic dictated that the interviews were carried out remotely, that is, through video calls via ZOOM® between the researcher and the participants, using several features of this platform, namely: video and audio of host and participant, video and audio recording of the session, screen sharing of the host, and remote control provided by the host.

4.3 Data Collection Techniques and Instruments

Based on the objectives defined for this study, supported by the defining characteristics of the paradigms and the research methods applied, several data collection techniques and instruments were used. Notably, we employed the observation technique and document collection, and the instruments for structured and semi-structured interviews, which are presented below.

It is important to mention that this study, including the instruments and the supporting materials used in the interviews and in the usability tests previously carried out, were previously examined and received a unanimous Ethical Favorable Opinion, with process reference Doc14-CE-UTAD-2021, by the Ethics Committee of the University of Trás-os-Montes and Alto Douro in Vila Real, Portugal.

Interviews

Cohen, Manion, and Morrison [16] state that semi-structured interviews are the most commonly used interview technique in qualitative research. This type of interview is based on a script, elaborated in advance by the researcher. It is open enough, giving the interviewer some leeway to rearrange the content, deviate from the script, or explore new additional questions that might emerge during the conversation. The post-test semi-structured interview was used in the study presented here. In general, the researcher's script (shown below) was followed. However, there were additional and complementary questions that were deemed important to explore and include in the study. This was an expected outcome – hence the decision to use semi-structured interviews – and we wanted to consider the added value of the interviewees' profiles, whose knowledge and experience in the research area were quite relevant.

However, it is important to mention that the structured interview technique was also used – in the pre-test interview – as a way to collect data related to the participants' characterization. This type of interview strictly follows the interview script outlined in advance, not allowing the researcher to deviate from it [16].

- Pre-test interview
    The pre-test interview aimed at analyzing the participants' characteristics in the usability tests and interviews, and a variety of information was collected. Participants

were asked their full name, age, occupation, education and qualification, type of disability (if any), experience with assistive technologies/accessibility, experience using Microsoft® Excel® software, and the computer screen/monitor size they were using.

- Post-test interview

The feedback from the participants who performed the usability testing on the use of FRATIC is important for this research. In order to collect it, semi-structured interviews were then conducted on the subject of this research and on the FRATIC tool, divided into 5 main themes: European standard EN 301 549, other tools, FRATIC usability, FRATIC features, FRATIC target audience. The post-test interview is composed by the 19 questions present in Appendix 1.

4.4 Documental Collection

- Audio and video recording

All data collection procedures were performed using the ZOOM® tool, and were logged in the form of audio and video recording. Screen recordings of the interviews were made in order to speed up the process for the participants.

- Data processing

The data resulting from the pre-test interviews were quantitatively processed and analyzed using Microsoft® Excel®.

First, the data from the post-test interviews were treated on an individual basis. The interviews were transcripted into Microsoft® Word® and relevant quantitative data were analyzed in Excel®. Word® documents with the interview transcripts were imported into MaxQDA software for qualitative data analysis. They were then divided into different categories, defined by the researcher, based on the methodology mentioned above.

5 Results

For the analysis and qualitative treatment of the data from the interviews, a content analysis of the participants' answers was performed, determining post-established categories of analysis, based on the expressions and judgments they formulated in each dimension. For further analysis, the MAXQDA Analytics Pro R20.2.1 software was used (Fig. 1).

The Similarity Matrix between codes that was determined allowed us to visualize the similarity between interviews in terms of the categories found, thus providing a means of gauging the agreement between the opinions of the different interviewees. Being the value 1 equivalent to total agreement, the higher the value, the greater the agreement between each interviewee. So, for example, we can see that Participant 1 and Participant 16 have closer opinions (0.94) than Participant 7 and Participant 21 (0.76), for example (Fig. 2).

Other tools
EN 301 549
FRATIC
Target audience
Usability
Features

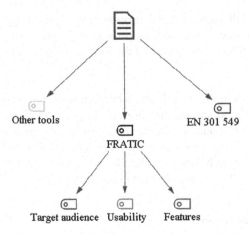

Fig. 1. Interview topics

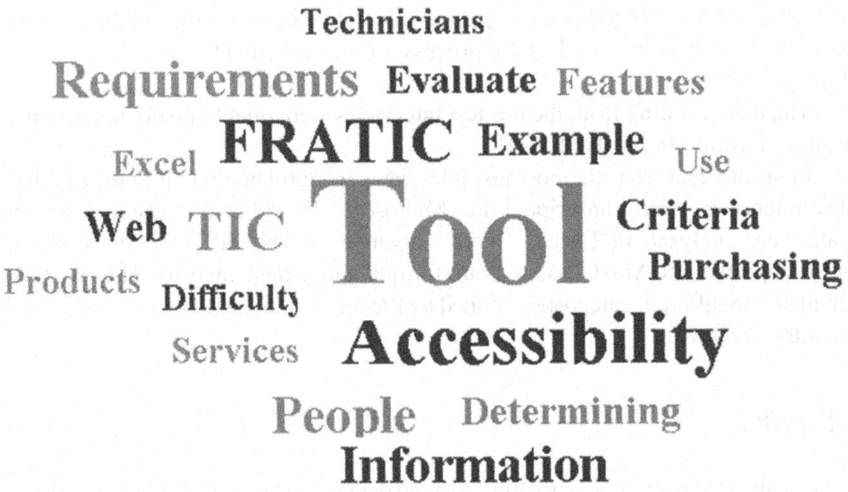

Technicians
Requirements
Evaluate
Features
Excel
FRATIC
Example
Use
Web
TIC
Tool
Criteria
Purchasing
Products
Difficulty
Services
Accessibility
People
Determining
Information

Fig. 2. Global word cloud from the interviews

The word cloud, shown in the above figure, refers to the expressions used most often by the participants in the overall tally of the interviews. Setting a minimum of 50 occurrences, we have chosen to gather the 20 most mentioned words. Words such as "yes" and "no", articles, adverbs, pronouns and verb tenses that are not relevant to the topic under discussion were excluded from the list – the verbs "to determine" and "to evaluate" were kept, the verb "to do", for example, was excluded. The larger a word is in the cloud, the more frequently that word was referenced by the participants.

It should be noted that the qualitative analysis of the interview data, conducted after the usability tests, also allowed us to obtain some quantitative details from the participants/experts' answers.

5.1 European Standard EN 301 549

From the 25 interview participants, 60% said they had already participated in some way in public procurement procedures for ICT products, and the remaining 40% admitted they never did. It should be noted that the vast majority of those who mentioned having already participated as professionals in public procurement/contracting entities has at least 10 years of professional experience in the area of Assistive Technologies and Accessibility.

Regarding EN 301 549, the aim was to understand if the official document itself is enough to determine the accessibility requirements and the respective means of verifying their compliance for a specific ICT. More specifically, if its content can be considered intuitive, easy to understand, and quick to use to be considered sufficient for potential stakeholders to perform such tasks. It should be noted that no expert considers the EN 301 549 document alone to be sufficient for the tasks: 88% believe the opposite to be true, with the most experienced experts in the field of assistive technologies/accessibility stating this with greater vigor and regularity, and 12% not knowing it well enough to answer with certainty.

Although three of the experts find EN 301 549 intuitive for those who "are in the accessibility area" (Participant 18) or are "more knowledgeable about it" (Participant 17), that is, for those who are well acquainted with the scope in the European standard, they also consider it "a complex document, with many requirements" (Participant 18), and that "it seems endless" (Participant 17), although this is understandable "because of the amount of information it has" (Participant 17). This complexity and extent entail possible difficulties in finding, determining, and evaluating accessibility requirements applicable to specific ICTs, as mentioned by other experts. In fact, participants consider that, overall, ENs "are many times very technical, dense, very confusing, difficult to interpret, and complex for the average citizen to decipher" (Participant 2). Regarding EN 310 549 in particular, they state that "it is not intuitive, nor is it quick to use" (Participant 22), and they believe that "it will be a barrier precisely to the preparation of adequate specifications" (Participant 22), stressing the need for "documentation of the interpretation of the standards themselves" (Participant 13). They also mention that "without the FRATIC tool" this interpretation is tiresome "and knowledge would be needed to identify the requirements" (Participant 12).

Fig. 3. Word cloud on the European standard EN 301 549

From the word cloud in Fig. 3, concerning the answers about the standard, it is clear that none of the experts considers it adequate to be used independently for several reasons, mainly because it is quite extensive, complex, difficult and time-consuming to use, and non-intuitive. However, although less frequently, experts also find it difficult to cross-reference information, dense, very technical, hard to understand, cumbersome, dull, repetitive, overwhelming, confusing, and having it available only in English is not helpful. Moreover, according to one of the experts (Participant 11), all these features can make it very difficult, and take a lot of time to perform certain tasks, and may lead some people to withdraw from applying the standard.

5.2 Other Tools

When asked if they were familiar with any tool capable of helping to globally evaluate the technical accessibility criteria specified in EN 301 549, the experts (100%) were not able to mention any such capable tool. About 28% of the experts reported that they were familiar with tools, namely TAW, Access Monitor, Accessibility Checklists from the AMA Digital Experience Team, and the Accessible ICT Procurement Toolkit (which is no longer available), but none of these were dedicated to the overall assessment of the standard's criteria, and some were used only for the assessment of some of the WCAG success criteria. One of the experts (Participant 17) mentions and precisely emphasizes FRATIC's pioneering role in the global evaluation of the criteria, as it provides "very good support in the global evaluation that did not exist until now".

5.3 FRATIC Usability

The knowledge in the area of assistive technologies and accessibility, and the completion of the thirteen tasks included in the usability tests with FRATIC helped the participants to perceive the existing capabilities and/or limitations in the tool's usability. Concerning the organization or amount of information, 24% of the experts reported having felt at least some adaptation difficulties when starting to use FRATIC: at the beginning because it was the first contact, and because they did not know the standard well and it was very extensive and complex, sometimes requiring the tool to present a considerable amount of information. The remaining (76%) experts said that they did not experience any difficulty in adapting to the tool. Experts mentioned that "it's a lot of information for the first impact, but the way it is presented helps" (Participant 15) and that "there is a lot of information in the same geographical space, but it's organized logically" (Participant 9), suggesting the inclusion of "colors for the sake of information availability, organization and sequence, using the same colors for identical tasks" (Participant 22).

Almost everyone (96%) considered that, as they used the tool, the features became intuitive, "especially for those who are familiar with the standard at least" (Participant 15), that "the consistent layout helps to understand" (Participant 3) and "to use the tool fluidly" (Participant 4), that "the messages provided are very pertinent and in the right time give feedback" (Participant 18), and that overall FRATIC "is simple, has a nice range of easily identifiable options and functions, and there are no adaptation problems" (Participant 12), being "easy to learn and use" (Participant 13) and "understand and work" with it. The screen/monitor size showed not to be a determining factor in terms of perceived usability or difficulties experienced by the experts, although experts with smaller screens/monitors needed to do some horizontal sweeping.

However, despite this, that the tool makes it possible to "easily create intuitive and very useful reports" (Participant 3) and that 72% of the experts reported having no difficulty using or creating content with FRATIC in the usability test tasks, others, also based on their expertise in the area, suggested improving some aspects of the tool in order to overcome some of the difficulties they felt. To this end, they mentioned that it would be beneficial to "improve the location of some buttons" (Participant 10), namely those that allow "creating and saving documents in Word®, Excel® and PDF" (Participant 20) and "evaluating accessibility" (Participant 14), as well as "increase and standardize the size of some buttons and text readability" (Participants 13 and 15), "change the color of the main buttons" (Participant 13) and "increase explanations and instructions" (Participant 7) and "notes with help associated to several fields" (Participant 14), "almost as if it were an assistant" (Participant 7). Several experts mentioned that a) they had some difficulties in scroll navigation, but that this was mainly due to the network signal strength and the performance of the tests on the ZOOM® platform, b) it would be interesting to improve the "linkage between tasks, by including steps" (Participant 4) "with colors" (Participant 22), that is, "guide the user through steps, have a sequence of steps because the tasks are all more or less sequential, so there is also some separation of information" (Participant 7), and c) that a search box in the Information section would be useful (Participants 12 and 17), as well as making the tool more graphic and interactive (Participants 13, 20 and 21).

FRATIC's accessibility requirements filtering mechanisms are fundamental for the use of some functionalities and in performing several tasks, namely in determining, accessing and cross-referencing information present in the standard. However, the abundance of information displayed on the screen can lead to usability problems. The experts were asked objectively whether they considered it relevant that the tool, when filtering the information on accessibility requirements, should load the notes for each requirement along with its description, or whether it was enough to filter the description of each requirement because, if necessary, more information could be consulted in the Consultation section. Most of the experts (52%) thought it was important that the filters had as much information as possible for a better understanding, i.e. the descriptions and notes of the requirements without having to use another section.

However, for example, some experts, among those who prefer to see the notes on the requirements, because they are not very experienced with the standard, mentioned that with the use and familiarization with the accessibility requirements they might not need to read so much of the notes afterwards. Similarly, 24% of the experts stated that it would suffice to display only the descriptions, without the notes, as they could consult such information in the Consultation section and thus avoid having too much information on the screen.

Additionally, there are even experts (24%) who think the notes are quite important, but that it would be pertinent to hide them, as well as the descriptions of the accessibility requirements, if such information could be directly accessed through a link, bookmark or expansion.

One of the relevant factors for some of these opinions is navigation: the more information the requirements are presented with, the more the participants will need to scroll through the tool. However, as previously discussed, some difficulties experienced in navigation were not due to this factor alone, but mainly to network delay and lag, as a result of performing the tests via ZOOM® platform.

During the usability test, some experts pointed out potential advantages of replicating FRATIC's functionalities for Web technology, mainly in terms of graphical interface, mass access and dissemination, and interaction by users with screen readers. When asked in the post-test interview about the relevance of FRATIC features being available on the Web, or simultaneously on both the Web and Microsoft® Excel®, 36% of the experts agreed that it was essential that they would be made available on the Web in the future.

Despite preferring the Web, some experts recognize the importance of working in Microsoft® Excel®, and refer that the choice depends on the preferences of each user. Likewise, being available simultaneously in both technologies, both on the Web and in Microsoft® Excel®, would be "pertinent and an added value" (Participant 3) according to the opinion of the majority of the experts (60%).

Enabling access and use of FRATIC without an Internet connection and the universality of the tool among the field professionals are the main advantages of Microsoft® Excel®, compared to the Web, as mentioned by the experts, according to their professional experiences, which advocates the maintenance of the tool in this format. There are even experts who, besides stating that the availability of the tool in both technologies is pertinent, consider that the integration and interconnection between both technologies is important and should be considered.

5.4 FRATIC Features

FRATIC version 1.1, which was used for the usability tests, had several features. In order to have a better perception of how these, as well as others suggested by the experts, can contribute to the increase of creation and procurement of accessible ICTs, questions were asked, namely about the determination and evaluation of technical criteria, covered by EN 301 549, for specific ICT, the introduction and fulfillment of technical accessibility criteria in public procurement for ICT products and services, to comply with legislation and to increase the creation and procurement of technology accessible to all.

Determining and Evaluating Technical Criteria

All (100%) experts feel that using FRATIC can provide advantages for those who need to determine and evaluate the technical criteria, covered by EN 301 549, for a specific ICT. The experts mention that yes, clearly, "it can bring many advantages" (Participants 1, 5 and 9), because the "standard document is so complex, unintuitive and difficult to use" (Participant 10) that "by itself it pushes people away from applying it, while this tool helps" (Participant 4) and "it can be a good solution to optimize the time to perform these tasks and even to get the very information one needs" (Participant 10). As mentioned by Participant 22, "any tool that provides access to information in a faster and more intuitive way is fundamental" and, in this particular case, FRATIC "is a more effective means, a means that allows more quickly obtaining data, a means that allows consulting" (Participant 25), "integrating information in an essential way" (Participant 8), and providing "the whole information very well organized" (Participant 9).

In short, the experts agree that FRATIC "allows one to determine the technical criteria for specific ICTs in a short time and directly, for several ICTs, even without any deep knowledge about the standards or even the field" (Participant 12), and it "offers benefits for the evaluation of the technical criteria" (Participant 14) as it allows doing it "in an easier and more intuitive way" (Participant 12).

One of the experts (Participant 15) stated that FRATIC's functionality to determine the technical criteria for specific ICTs can not only play an important role, but also cover more ICTs by sharing information from professionals and entities.

The consultation of the desired information from EN 301 549 can be performed dynamically and quickly using the filtering and search mechanism for accessibility requirements, and this can be done using several types of filters simultaneously. For this specific functionality, among all the others, FRATIC's availability of all the information in Portuguese is quite relevant, according to several experts.

FRATIC's Scope

FRATIC's ability to determine and evaluate the requirements for many different ICTs, as a result of the tool's functionality and the comprehensiveness of EN 301 549, may be a determining factor for its usefulness and success, as clearly stated by almost all experts (92%), since the tool standardizes the procedure for the entire spectrum of ICT uses and the standard is European.

The use of the scores and classifications, FRATIC Index, in the evaluation of ICT accessibility for each functional performance statement/PSN group and in the global evaluation was one of the highlighted aspects, for being a quick reference and allowing access to an accessibility indicator to all users, regardless of their knowledge on the matter.

Compliance with Legislation

Compliance with the rules in Directive 2016/2102/EU, on accessibility of the websites and mobile applications of public bodies, and with Decree Law No. 83/2018, of October 19, which transposes the aforementioned Directive into the national legal framework, is not always observed, despite the fact that, as mentioned by one expert (Participant 19), these instruments have been in place long enough for them to be applied. However, according to 92% of the experts, the FRATIC tool can contribute to achieving this goal, as the legislation's rules are not complied with deliberately or out of disregard.

According to the experts, the fact that Directive 2016/2102/EU, Decree-Law No. 83/2018 and EN 301 549 documents, to which the former refer, are extensive, complex and difficult to interpret makes it difficult to comply with the legislation's rules. However, on the other hand, the tool makes all this information operational. In addition to saving time, and simplifying and clarifying information, the tool simplifies its use and exempts users from the need for more in-depth, specialized knowledge about the directive and/or the standard, and acts as an encouragement for their implementation.

Overall, and as mentioned by Participant 12, the experts are aware that "as there is legislation in Portugal that adopts the Directive on accessibility of websites and mobile applications, therefore, this application will be able to support compliance with both, making it easier to demand, incorporate, and implement accessibility in ICTs". However, two of the experts, given its innovative character, think that FRATIC's contribution will be clearly greater "for the accessibility of mobile applications than for websites" (Participant 21) as the requirements for "apps are more recent and there is not so much experience with their implementation" (Participant 18). Others point out that compliance with legislation depends on other factors, namely the will of decision-makers and the replication of FRATIC's functionalities for Web technology.

Public Procurement

FRATIC offers several features, and almost all of them, directly or indirectly, can be used in the different phases of public procurement and commissioning for ICT products and services. Only 4% of the experts who participated in the usability tests and interviews state that they are not sure that the tool could contribute to the implementation and adherence to technical accessibility criteria in public procurement of ICT products and services. The remaining 96% consider that for anyone who knows the tool, it can be useful.

According to the experts, the comprehensive and detailed information that FRATIC provides, through the creation of the different reports, simplifies the work and makes communication between the multiple stakeholders in public procurement more effective, efficient, clear, and detailed, minimizing the occurrence of different interpretations, without requiring in-depth reading and interpretation. Therefore, in addition to contributing to the introduction of technical accessibility criteria, the tool can be a means of ensuring that these are met, should only the competing bids of vendors that meet them be admitted to the procurement process. It should be noted that the reference of technical accessibility criteria in public procurement, at the moment, is usually contemplated in the specifications, however, only in a very general manner. The tool allows this information to be detailed.

FRATIC provides detailed information that can be used at different times and for different purposes, namely by the procuring entity for drafting procurement advertisements, specifications, and contracts, as well as for evaluating the competence of potential vendors in terms of accessibility, and the proposals submitted by bidders and final solutions. This way it is easier for the different stakeholders and interested parties to understand the technical specifications and/or the award criteria they need to meet, as well as the accepted means of proof to ascertain that the proposed solution takes accessibility requirements into consideration. It even allows those responsible for introducing technical accessibility criteria in public procurement for ICT products and services, despite not having much knowledge on the subject of ICT or accessibility, to perform some tasks independently.

Depending on what an entity intends to contract and its purpose, being it possible and essential, weights can be considered in FRATIC for the evaluation of the technical criteria of a proposal for an ICT product or service, since the tool performs both the global evaluation, and also the individual evaluation of the functional performance statements list and/or PSN group statements.

Opposite to all the others, one of the participants considers that the tool as it is, in Microsoft® Excel®, will hardly be used by people who work with purchases. However, it could have an important role at the training level, especially in Academia.

Other features, which were not implemented in version 1.1 of the FRATIC prototype, were identified by the experts when conducting the usability tests and interviews, and were subsequently implemented. Among them, for tasks related to public procurement of ICT products and services, the interconnection of the CPV (Common Procurement Vocabulary) – itself extensive – with FRATIC, with the addition of a field with CPV code information, stands out.

Boosting the Creation and Purchase of Accessible ICTs

In general, the experts (96%) believe that FRATIC's features can also be used in the different phases, and contribute to the promotion of projects, developments and purchases in general, of technology accessible to all. This contribution, at the very least, can happen by raising awareness, building consciousness, and by facilitating understanding and access to information.

Increasing clarity of information about accessibility requirements and the importance of accessibility for ICT, according to experts, can even increase the trust of those financing assistive technologies and other ICTs.

The EN 301 549 standard covers a wide range of ICT products and services, it is recent and has been regularly updated, and therefore it may facilitate and contribute to vendors having up-to-date information on accessibility requirements that are appropriate to the evolution of ICTs and existing solutions, and overcome certain difficulties experienced by them. Several experts also mention that the tool has a great potential to contribute to the creation of projects and the procurement of ICT products and services accessible to all, but that legislation will be a determining factor for this to happen.

Another feature also identified by the experts during the usability tests and interviews, which was subsequently implemented, includes the possibility of creating VPAT® (Voluntary Product Accessibility Templates) reports, which could play a key role in compliance with legislation by distributors and importers, as well as in the various stages of public procurement, project development, and accessible ICT procurement.

5.5 Target Audience

The FRATIC tool functionalities potentialities, as previously shown, can contribute to the completion of many different tasks and, therefore, it will be useful for a wide group of users with distinct profiles – according to the experts: virtually everyone who works with and is interested in the assistive technologies area, namely companies, manufacturers and prescribing entities.

With the ultimate goal of achieving a more inclusive society, all (100%) experts consider that the tool could be useful for themselves or for other people they know.

The amount and scope of information available in the standard is overwhelming, and it is not always easy to convey, or verify all the requirements for what one needs. The simplifying and organizing nature of FRATIC, in its main purpose – promoting accessible ICT procurement in the public sector – stands out in terms of clarity and rigor in providing information for the different phases of public procurement procedures and ICT production, and therefore, according to the experts, those responsible for or involved in any way in ICT design, development, and procurement are the tool's main target audience.

Because of their professional experience in an academic environment, the experts regularly mention the usefulness of the tool for the people and services responsible for procurement in public entities. Some of the experts mention that FRATIC can have an important role in training, both in Academia and in professional training courses, about the content of the standard and the features in the tool that help in certain tasks.

The use of the tool is directly mentioned by the experts as being able to contribute to the promotion of a more inclusive society for all. The determination and evaluation of accessibility requirements for an ICT, by functional performance statements/PSN groups, will be useful, for example, for the ICT prescribing entities, as well as for the people with disabilities themselves, and the entities and professionals working in the areas of defense of their rights and promotion of their quality of life and access to information and communication.

Therefore, for a number of reasons, the experts found FRATIC to be useful for themselves and for purchasing entities, vendors, accessibility experts, political agents, designers, manufacturers, accessibility advocates, professionals who work or deal with people with disabilities, auditors and evaluators, and they also stressed the fact that it could be useful for public officials, Academia, consultants, public officials, prescribing entities and society in general.

6 Final Considerations

FRATIC's prototype intends to simplify the lives of a growing number of users, by creating and purchasing more accessible and usable products, at a competitive price and without additional costs. In conclusion, the international market will grow and society will be able to benefit from ICT products and services designed with appropriate responses for people of all ages and with any kind of disability or impairment. We hope that FRATIC can simplify the implementation of EN 301 549 accessibility requirements in public procurement procedures for ICT products and services, as well as the work of designers and developers to make ICT products and services more accessible and usable by all.

The semi-structured interviews with experts, as well as their analysis and data processing, allowed us to get participants' feedback and draw some conclusions on the different dimensions covered:

- Most experts stated they had already worked in public procurement procedures for ICT products and services, and most of them had at least 10 years of professional experience in the field. The official EN 301 549 document is considered unintuitive due to its length, density, complexity, difficult and time-consuming use, and technicality. This makes it difficult to cross-reference information, and determine and evaluate accessibility requirements and their means of verifying compliance for a specific ICT, to the point that it can be a barrier to the application of the standard.
- Experts know no other tool capable of assisting in the global evaluation of the technical accessibility criteria specified in EN 301 549, mentioning precisely FRATIC's pioneering character. Regarding FRATIC usability, the feedback was positive: although the tool offers a good range of options and functions, most of the experts had no

difficulties in adapting to it, mentioning the features' intuitiveness, the learning level, the possibility to filter, organize and present pertinent information. The experience in the field of accessibility/assistive technologies was crucial in suggesting improvements in some aspects, in order to overcome some difficulties felt, mainly related to the location and size of some content, navigation, amount of information presented, division and instructions in the different tasks, and graphical aspects of the interface. It is noteworthy that some of the experts mentioned potential advantages with the replication of the FRATIC functionalities for the Web and invoked the maintenance of the tool in Microsoft Excel, finding pertinent and an added value the concurrent availability in both technologies and the possible integration between them.

- The interviews gave further insight and evidence of FRATIC's features' relevance in increasing the creation and procurement of accessible ICTs, through the determination and evaluation of technical criteria, covered by EN 301 549, for specific ICTs, the introduction and compliance with technical accessibility criteria in public procurement for ICT products and services, compliance with legislation, and increasing the creation and procurement of technology accessible to all.
- The main FRATIC beneficiaries will be the professionals responsible for and involved in some way in the different phases of ICT procurement procedures and the design and development of accessible ICT products and services. However, the tool's utility is much more comprehensive and, according to the experts, it can be useful and an asset to many other entities and people – to society in general.

Suggestions and contributions from the participants, as well as some improvements to be made detected in the usability tests and the interviews have already been implemented, thus resulting in FRATIC version 1.2.

From this study's results, it is expected that the FRATIC development may simplify the management and use of the information in EN 301 549 in public procurement procedures for ICT products and services, as well as the work of ICT designers and developers.

Acknowledgements. This work is financed by FCT, Fundação para a Ciência e a Tecnologia (Portuguese Foundation for Science and Technology), supported by funding from POPH/FSE.

This article reflects the views only of the author, and FCT cannot be held responsible for any use which may be made of the information contained therein.

Appendix 1 – Semi-structured Interview (Post-test) Script

1. Have you ever participated, or are you participating in any way in public procurement procedures for ICT products and services?
2. In order to determine accessibility requirements and their means of verifying compliance for a specific ICT, do you think that the official EN 301 549 document (PDF) alone is intuitive, easy to understand, and quick to use, to be considered as sufficient for possible interested parties to perform such tasks? Why?
3. Do you know of any tools that can help to globally evaluate the technical accessibility criteria specified in EN 301 549?

4. If so, how often have you used them or how often do you use them?
5. Did you have any difficulties adapting when you started using FRATIC? Regarding organization or amount of information, for example.
6. As you were using the tool, did the features seem intuitive to you?
7. Did you experience any difficulties when using or creating content on FRATIC? In any of the tasks in this usability test or others.
8. If so, what do you think could be done to overcome these difficulties?
9. When filtering the accessibility requirements, do you find it pertinent to preview the notes for each requirement along with its description? Or do you think that the description of each requirement would suffice, since in case of need you would consult more information in the Consultation section?
10. Do you think that using FRATIC can bring some benefits to those who need to determine and evaluate the technical criteria, covered by EN 301 549, for a specific ICT?
11. Among the people you know, to whom would the FRATIC tool be useful? Describe this person professionally.
12. Considering the scope of EN 301 549, do you think the fact that the tool brings together the ability to determine and evaluate the requirements of many different ICTs could be a determining factor in its utility and success?
13. Do you think the FRATIC tool could contribute to the compliance with the Directive 2016/2102/EU rules, on accessibility of websites and mobile applications of public bodies, and the Decree Law No. 83/2018, of October 19, which transposes the aforementioned Directive into the national legal framework? Justify.
14. Do you think this tool could contribute to the introduction and compliance with technical accessibility criteria in public procurement of ICT products and services?
15. Do you think FRATIC can contribute to the creation and purchase of technology accessible to all?
16. Aiming at achieving a more inclusive society, do you think that the potential of this tool could be useful for you or for other people?
17. Do you think it is relevant to have FRATIC functionalities available on the Web, or simultaneously available both on the Web and in Microsoft Excel?
18. Given your knowledge in the area of assistive technologies/accessibility and the experience with FRATIC, do you have any remarks or suggestions to improve the features of the tool?
19. Finally, do you have any further comments, or thoughts?

References

1. Reicher, S.C.: Diversidade humana e assimetrias: uma releitura do contrato social sob a ótica das capacidades. SUR-Revista Int. Direitos Humanos **8**(14), 173–185 (2011)
2. WHO and WB: World report on disability (2011). https://www.who.int/. Accessed 10 June 2021
3. Silva, J.S.: Metodologia para engenharia de software inclusiva out-of-the-box. Universidade de Trás-os-Montes e Alto Douro, Vila Real (2019)

4. Comissão Europeia: People with disabilities have equal rights - TheEuropean Disability Strategy 2010–2020. Comissão Europeia. Comissão Europeia, Bruxelas (2010)
5. INE: Health and disabilities in Portugal: 2011. Instituto Nacional de Estatística, IP, Lisboa (2012)
6. Mitra, S., Palmer, M., Kim, H., Mont, D., Groce, N.: Extra costs of living with a disability: a review and agenda for research. Disabil. Health J. **10**(4), 475–484 (2017)
7. Amado-Salvatierra, H.R., Hernández, R., Hilera, J.R.: Implementation of accessibility standards in the process of course design in virtual learning environments. Procedia Comput. Sci. **14**, 363–370 (2012)
8. United Nations: Convention on the Rights of Persons with Disabilities. United Nations, New York (2006)
9. Martins, M., Gonçalves, R., Godinho, F., Novais, J.: Benefits of EN 301 549 for each group of people with special needs. In: Proceedings of the 8th International Conference on Software Development and Technologies for Enhancing Accessibility and Fighting Info-exclusion, pp. 123–128 (2018)
10. ETSI, CEN, and CENELEC: EN 301 549 V1.1.1 - Accessibility requirements suitable for public procurement of ICT products and services in Europe. European Telecommunications Standards Institute, França (2014)
11. ETSI, CEN, and CENELEC: EN 301 549 V1.1.2 - Accessibility requirements suitable for public procurement of ICT products and services in Europe. European Telecommunications Standards Institute, França (2015)
12. ETSI, CEN, and CENELEC: EN 301 549 V2.1.2 - Accessibility requirements for ICT products and services. European Telecommunications Standards Institute (2018)
13. ETSI, CEN, and CENELEC: EN 301 549 V3.2.1 - Accessibility requirements for ICT products and services. European Telecommunications Standards Institute (2021)
14. ETSI, CEN, and CENELEC: EN 301 549 V3.1.1 - Accessibility requirements for ICT products and services. European Telecommunications Standards Institute (2019)
15. Parlamento Europeu: Diretiva (UE) 2014/24 do Parlamento Europeu e do Conselho de 26 de fevereiro de 2014 relativa aos contratos públicos e que revoga a Diretiva 2004/18/CE. Jornal Oficial da União Europeia. Estrasburgo, 65–242 (2014)
16. Cohen, L., Manion, L., Morrison, K.: Research Methods in Education, 8th edn. Routledge, London (2017)
17. Klironomos, I., Antona, M., Basdekis, I., Stephanidis, C.: White paper: promoting design for all and e-accessibility in Europe. Univers. Access Inf. Soc. **5**(1), 105–119 (2006)
18. Iwarsson, S., Ståhl, A.: Accessibility, usability and universal design—positioning and definition of concepts describing person-environment relationships. Disabil. Rehabil. **25**(2), 57–66 (2003)
19. Castells, M.: A galáxia internet: reflexões sobre Internet. Negócios e Soc. Fundação Calouste Gulbenkian, Lisboa (2004)
20. Gouveia, L., Gaio, S.: Sociedade da Informação: balanço e implicações. Porto Edições Univ, Fernando Pessoa (2004)
21. Gonçalves, R., Martins, J., Pereira, J., Oliveira, M.A.-Y., Ferreira, J.J.P.: Enterprise web accessibility levels amongst the Forbes 250: where art thou o virtuous leader? J. Bus. Ethics **113**(2), 363–375 (2013)
22. Bares, R., Vickers, S., Istance, H.O.: Gaze interaction with virtual on-line communities: levelling the playing field for disabled users. Univers. Access Inf. Soc. **9**(3), 261–272 (2010)
23. Martins, M., Cunha, A., Oliveira, I., Morgado, L.: Usability test of 3Dconnexion 3D mice versus keyboard + mouse in Second Life undertaken by people with motor disabilities due to medullary lesions. Univers. Access Inf. Soc. **14**(1), 5–16 (2015)
24. Emiliani, P.L., Stephanidis, C.: Universal access to ambient intelligence environments: opportunities and challenges for people with disabilities. IBM Syst. J. **44**(3), 605–619 (2005)

25. McKinney, S., Horspool, A., Willers, R., Safie, O., Richlin, L.: Using second life with learning-disabled students in higher education. Innov. J. Online Educ. **5**(2) (2008)
26. Magnusson, L., Hanson, E., Borg, M.: A literature review study of information and communication technology as a support for frail older people living at home and their family carers. Technol. Disabil. **16**(4), 223–235 (2004)
27. Foley, A., Ferri, B.A.: Technology for people, not disabilities: ensuring access and inclusion. J. Res. Spec. Educ. Needs **12**(4), 192–200 (2012)
28. Benfer, E.A.: The ADA amendments act: an overview of recent changes to the Americans with disabilities act. Advance **4**, 53 (2010)
29. US Access Board: Information and Communication Technology (ICT) - Revised 508 Standards and 255 Guidelines. US Federal Register, Washington (2017)
30. US Access Board: Electronic and information technology accessibility standards. Fed. Regist. **15**, 2005 (2000)
31. Lecerf, M.: Briefing - EU Legislation in Progress, European Accessibility Act. Parlamento Europeu, Bruxelas (2017)
32. Parlamento Europeu: Diretiva (UE) 2019/882, relativa aos requisitos de acessibilidade dos produtos e serviços. Jornal Oficial da União Europeia (2019). https://eur-lex.europa.eu/legal-content/PT/TXT/HTML/?uri=CELEX:32019L0882&from=EN. Accessed 30 May 2021
33. Comissão Europeia: European Commission - Press release - Comissão saúda acordo para tornar mais acessíveis sítios Web e aplicações móveis do setor público. Comissão Europeia (2016)
34. Astbrink, G., Tibben, W.: ICT accessibility criteria in public procurement in OECD countries – the current situation. In: Stephanidis, C., Antona, M. (eds.) UAHCI 2013. LNCS, vol. 8009, pp. 155–164. Springer, Heidelberg (2013). https://doi.org/10.1007/978-3-642-39188-0_17
35. Ahtonen, A., Pardo, R.: The accessibility act-using the single market to promote fundamental rights. European Policy Centre, vol. 12 (2013)
36. ITU: Accessible Europe 2019 Background Paper, Standards in the Procurement of Accessible ICT Products and Services. International Telecommunication Union, Geneva, Switzerland (2019)
37. Esteves, A.J.: Metodologias qualitativas, perspectivas gerais. Metodol. Qual. para as Ciências Sociais, Inst. Sociol. da Fac. Let. da Univ. do Porto, Porto (1998)
38. Miles, M.B., Huberman, A.M.: Qualitative Data Analysis: An Expanded Sourcebook. SAGE, Thousand Oaks (1994)
39. Braun, V., Clarke, V.: Using thematic analysis in psychology. Qual. Res. Psychol. **3**(2), 77–101 (2006)
40. Braun, V., Clarke, V.: Successful Qualitative Research: A Practical Guide for Beginners. SAGE, Thousand Oaks (2013)

Usability and Accessibility Evaluation of the ICT Accessibility Requirements Tool Prototype

Márcio Martins[1]([envelope]) [ID], Francisco Godinho[2] [ID], Pedro Gonçalves[2] [ID], and Ramiro Gonçalves[1] [ID]

[1] INESC TEC and University of Trás-os-Montes and Alto Douro, Vila Real, Portugal
{marciom,ramiro}@utad.pt
[2] University of Trás-os-Montes and Alto Douro, Vila Real, Portugal
{godinho,pgoncalves}@utad.pt

Abstract. The Accessibility Requirements Tool for Information and Communication Technologies (FRATIC) was developed within the work of a doctoral project, at the University of Trás-os-Montes and Alto Douro, and may be used at various stages of public procurement processes as well as projects and developments that include ICT products and services. This tool helps to consult, determine and assess the accessibility requirements for ICT products and services in European Standard EN 301 549 that supports the legislation in the field of public procurement for the countries of the European Union – Directive 2014/24/EU. This study focuses on the standardized usability and accessibility features evaluation of the FRATIC prototype, based on ISO 9241-11 metrics, other usability and accessibility evaluation criteria, as well as various standardized measurement tools and methods – such as Single Ease Question (SEQ) and System Usability Scale (SUS) – after conducting usability tests and interviews with 25 experts in the fields of accessibility, assistive technologies, and public procurement.

Keywords: Accessibility Requirements Tool for ICT · European Standard EN 301 549 · Public procurement · Accessibility · Usability

1 Introduction

A high percentage of the European population has some kind of disability or impairment [1, 2], and not only is the distribution of opportunities between these people and the population in general unequal, but also the practices and policies to overcome inequalities, social injustice and exclusion of the former in various areas of society are insufficient. This problem can be observed in the area of Information and Communication Technologies (ICT), namely at the level of access and conditions of use and interaction. Because ICTs are available to and used by many people and because it is of paramount significance in today's society, the implementation of accessible ICTs is an effective way to promote the general principles of the Convention on the Rights of Persons with Disabilities [3]. Portugal has endorsed these principles, the United Nations Standard Rules on the Equalization of Opportunities for Persons with Disabilities [4], the Salamanca Declaration [5], and the accessibility rules for the design of e-government websites. These

© The Author(s), under exclusive license to Springer Nature Switzerland AG 2022
M. Antona and C. Stephanidis (Eds.): HCII 2022, LNCS 13308, pp. 59–78, 2022.
https://doi.org/10.1007/978-3-031-05028-2_4

instruments bind the Government to guarantee the dignity of life of persons with disabilities (PWD) – including granting equal rights and opportunities in access to ICTs – and its responsibility in this matter.

Within the work of a doctoral project, at the University of Trás-os-Montes and Alto Douro, where this study is also inserted, the ICT Accessibility Requirements Tool (FRATIC, *Ferramenta de Requisitos de Acessibilidade para TIC*), based on Microsoft® Excel®, was developed. This tool may be used at various stages of public procurement processes as well as projects and developments that include ICT products and services [6], as it helps to consult, determine and assess the accessibility requirements for ICT products and services in European Standard EN 301 549 [7], which supports the legislation in the field of public procurement for the countries of the European Union – Directive 2014/24/EU [8]–, and is capable of providing comprehensive and detailed reports. This study is based on a standardized evaluation of the usability and accessibility features of the FRATIC prototype, based on ISO 9241-11 metrics, other usability and accessibility evaluation criteria, and various measurement tools and methods, by conducting usability tests with 25 experts in the fields of accessibility, assistive technologies, and public procurement.

2   State of the Art

In a society where more and more ICTs are being used, ensuring full accessibility for all is a priority and indispensable, since accessibility in this area is fundamental for achieving social and digital inclusion of people with special needs (PSN) – i.e. PWD and the elderly –, or even people in general [9, 10].

In the United States of America (USA), regulatory legislation on accessibility has been in place since 1973, with the origin of the Americans with Disabilities Act (ADA) [11]. The Guidelines for Section 255 of the Communications Act and the original Section 508 Standards of the Rehabilitation Act were published by the US Access Board in 1998 and 2000, respectively [13, 14]. These two regulations have been revised and updated several times, most recently in 2018, with the corrections to the Final Rule on Information and Communication Technology Standards and Guidelines. The U.S. experience over the past decades has clearly illustrated the importance of public procurement in increasing the availability of affordable ICTs in the market. Public procurement has been used as a very effective tool to increase accessibility and it is this approach that lies at the very heart of Directive 2014/24/EU [8] and the European Union's Accessibility Act [16], where there is a growing awareness towards the need for accessible and usable ICTs for all.

The European Commission (EC), acknowledging the benefits of this approach from the US, issued a standardization request in 2005 to three European bodies[1], CEN, CEN-ELEC and ETSI, to establish the European requirements for accessibility in public procurement procedures for products and services in the ICT domain. This resulted in 2014 in the approval of version 1.1.1 of EN 301 549 [17] (and, in 2015, 2018, 2019

---

[1] Designations of the three European standardization organizations: European Committee for Standardization (CEN), European Committee for Electrotechnical Standardization (CEN-ELEC) and European Telecommunications Standards Institute (ETSI).

and 2021, in improved versions 1.1.2, 2.1.2, 3.1.1 and 3.2.1), containing the accessibility requirements mentioned above and which supported and originated the European Accessibility Act [18, 19], Directive 2014/24/EU on public procurement procedures for Member States [8] and Directive 2016/2102/EU containing the first rules at European Union (EU) level on the accessibility of the websites and mobile applications of public sector bodies [20]. The standard also aims to harmonize accessibility requirements among Member States and with the US, as well as to promote the free circulation of accessible goods and services, and to increase the effectiveness of accessibility legislation [21, 22]. This and the adopted legislation cover a wide range of ICT products and services and, therefore it pushes Portugal to reformulate its policies as well as the legal framework to be applied, in order to conform with the other EU Member States [19].

3 Methodology

The sociodemographic characterization of the participating experts was performed through a structured interview [23]. For the purpose of evaluating the usability of the tool with systematic methods, we have used usability tests, ISO 9241-11 [24] metrics, standardized instruments, namely post-task Single Ease Question (SEQ) [25, 26] and post-test System Usability Scale (SUS) [26, 27] questionnaires, as well as a subjective evaluation of seven accessibility features, considering the basic principles of Universal Design [28], and the existing content type and the platform where FRATIC was implemented, namely: Ease of use; Readability; Button size; Memorability; User friendliness; Language adequacy; Overall level of satisfaction.

4 Study Elements

4.1 Participants

Participants were selected based on the following inclusion criteria: 1) being an expert and/or a person interested in the areas of accessibility, assistive technologies, and public procurement; 2) having at least three years of experience in one of these areas; 3) having a computer with ZOOM® software, a sound system with speakers and microphone, a webcam, and reliable Internet access.

4.2 Study Background

The restrictions imposed by the COVID-19 pandemic dictated that data collection was carried out remotely, that is, through video calls using the ZOOM® tool, between the researcher and the participants, using several features of this platform, namely: video and audio of host and participant, audio and video recording of the session, screen sharing of the host, and remote control provided by the host.

4.3 Data Collection Techniques and Instruments

Based on the objectives defined for this study, supported by the defining characteristics of the paradigms and the research methods applied, several data collection techniques and instruments were used. Notably, we employed the observation technique and document collection, and the instruments usability tests, interviews, and questionnaires, which are presented below.

4.4 Usability Test Tasks

In the usability tests, in all four FRATIC sections, participants were given six specific tasks/13 subtasks to complete (see Table 1). These tasks were selected so as to encompass a variety of relevant activities of different lengths and difficulty levels that covered as much FRATIC content and functionality as possible, in order to achieve a representative and accurate performance in their use. The tasks were carried out individually in order to understand the complexity level and the main difficulties experienced when using the tool.

Table 1. Tasks and subtasks for the usability tests.

Task	Objective	Subtask	Section
1	Determining the accessibility requirements for a common ICT	1.1 Naming the ICT	EN 301 549
		1.2 Determining the requirements for the common ICT and functional performance declarations	
		1.3 Excluding accessibility requirements	
2	Generating the report "Request Text" with information about technical criteria for a cell phone	2.1 Creating the "Request Text" report	EN 301 549
		2.2 Saving filtered data and requirements	
3	Determining the accessibility requirements for a mobile application, with given conditions	3.1 Naming the ICT	Directive (Web and Mobile Applications)
		3.2 Determining the requirements for a mobile application by selecting the respective applicable conditions	
4	Creating the "Accessibility Evaluation" report with information about technical criteria for a mobile application, with its respective evaluation	4.1 Assessing accessibility	Directive (Web and Mobile Applications)
		4.2 Creating the "Accessibility Evaluation" report	
5	Querying to the accessibility requirements and the corresponding types of compliance check	5.1 Querying by type of technologies - European standard requirements	Querying

(continued)

Table 1. (*continued*)

Task	Objective	Subtask	Section
		5.2 Querying by common ICT type + text	
6	Finding a particular content in the Information section	6.1 a) Finding the link to Directive (EU) 2019/882 on accessibility requirements for products and services	Information
		6.1 b) Finding the link to download the Color Contrast Analyzer tool	

4.5 Remark

A questionnaire is a data collection tool characterized by objectivity, meaning it can be applied to a large universe of participants without the researcher's intervention [23]. However, because questionnaires were answered during or immediately after the usability tests, they were applied on a question-answer basis between researcher and participant. A structured interview was applied, as well as the following questionnaires:

- Pre-test interview: to collect personal data, namely: full name, age, occupation, educational and qualification area, type of disability (if any), experience with assistive technologies/accessibility, experience using Microsoft® Excel® software, and screen/monitor size used by the participant.
- Post-task questionnaire: using the single-item instrument SEQ, which helped in assessing the participant's degree of ease/difficulty or satisfaction in completing each subtask of the usability tests. This assessment was performed on a scale with seven rating levels, where level 1 meant that it was very difficult to perform the task and level 7 meant that it was very easy to perform the task.
- Post-test questionnaire: using the SUS instrument, consisting of 10 items, which assisted in assessing subjective usability, overall satisfaction, and the qualitative components of usability, as indicated by Nielsen, in the FRATIC usability tests. This assessment was performed on a scale with 5 rating levels, where level 1 meant that they strongly disagreed with the item and level 5 meant that they strongly agreed with the item.
- FRATIC content evaluation questionnaire: using the heuristic method, seven features were evaluated, selected based on the basic principles of Universal Design [28], as well as on the genre of content existing in FRATIC and in the platform where it was implemented: Ease of use, Readability, Button size, Memorability, User friendliness, Language adequacy and Overall level of satisfaction. This assessment was performed on a scale with 5 rating levels that meant: 1 – Very bad; 2 – Bad; 3 – Satisfactory; 4 – Good; 5 – Very good.

4.6 Documental Collection

- Audio and video recording: all data was collected using the ZOOM® tool and was logged in the form of audio and video recording. Screen recordings of the usability tests, interview and questionnaires were made in order to speed up the process for the participants.
- Observation guide: used to help record various information in the explanations and in each of the subtasks of the FRATIC tool usability tests, performed by the participants. The guide contains information such as the durations and types of questions or comments heard in the explanations and clarifications of doubts about the tests and the tool, as well as the following information for each subtask: the execution time, the comparison of task/participant execution times, the number of mistakes or how many attempts they had to start, the type of mistakes, the most frequent mistakes, whether they completed the task, the number of wrong clicks, whether they asked for help or guidance, whether they were comfortable, the type of questions or comments heard while performing the task, the evaluation of the participant's behavior while using the tool, and other observations.
- Data processing: the data resulting from the pre-test interview, the questionnaires and the assessment of accessibility characteristics were quantitatively processed and analyzed using Microsoft® Excel®.

5 Results

5.1 Participants' Characterization

Twenty-five experts in the fields of accessibility, assistive technologies, or public procurement participated in the usability tests. A large percentage (72%) of the participants was found to be in an age group above 40 years old, 40% of the participants were between 40 and 49 years old, and 32% of the participants were between 50 and 65 years old. More male participants were included (60%) than female (40%), and several participants reported having visual limitations. However, only one had very low vision, tunnel vision, which usually compromises interaction with interfaces and the execution speed of several tasks despite using a computer with 6x magnification and almost always a high-contrast theme. All participants (100%) held at least level 6 (Bachelor's Degree) of the National Qualifications Framework[2] (NQF), most of these (52%) held level 8 (Doctorate) of the NQF, and 72% held at least level 7 (Master's Degree) of the NQF. It was found that the main educational background of the participants was in Science and Technology (68%), followed by Humanities and Social Sciences (24%) and Health (8%), that the vast majority of the participants were Higher Education Professors/Researchers (64%) and had fifteen or more years (52%) of professional experience in the area of assistive technologies/accessibility. It should be noted that 72% had ten or more years of professional experience in assistive/accessibility technologies, and that only 20% had between three and five years of experience.

---

[2] National Qualifications Framework - created in 2007 and regulated in June 2009, became effective in October 2010 (Decree No. 782/2009, July 23), with reference to the principles of the European Qualifications Framework (EQF).

Regarding experience in using Microsoft® Excel® software, most of the participants reported having moderate experience (52%) or a lot of experience (40%), and only 8% reported having little experience.

5.2 Usability Test Data

The usability tests were conducted between September 1, 2020 and January 11, 2021. The total duration of these tests ranged from 01:16:10 to 03:20:11, and their average duration was 01:38:51.

We first sought to understand which computer screen/monitor size the participants used to perform the usability test tasks, in order to understand if this variable had any impact on task performance and the assessment of the FRATIC features. It was found that the screens of about half (48%) of the participants had between 13.5″ and 16″, that the ones from 32% had more than 16″, and that only 20% had less than 13.5″.

5.3 Objective Evaluation of FRATIC Usability

A variety of observation and data collection instruments and techniques were used to measure FRATIC's effectiveness and efficiency. Effectiveness is usually measured by the task completion rate and by counting the number of errors made during the interaction, while efficiency includes the level of effort and the user's use of resources to achieve the usability goals, and is usually measured by the execution time of each task and the average time between users and/or tasks [29].

Overall, participants needed little time to complete the subtasks: a few seconds for the simplest and quickest subtasks and a few minutes for the most complex and extensive subtasks. For most subtasks the average completion length was less than one minute and in none of the subtasks did it take more than three and a half minutes to complete. The subtasks that on average took less than a minute to complete include those for naming the ICT (subtasks 1.1 and 3.1), creating reports (subtasks 2.1 and 4.2), saving filtered data and requirements (subtask 2.2), and finding information (subtasks 6.1 a) and 6.1 b)). The subtasks for which, on average, more than one minute was required include those for determining accessibility requirements (subtasks 1.2 and 3.2), excluding accessibility requirements (subtask 1.3), performing accessibility assessment (subtask 4.1), and querying accessibility requirements (subtasks 5.1 and 5.2).

Some of the subtasks of the usability tests have somewhat similar purposes and difficulty levels for completion, namely: subtasks 1.1 and 3.1; subtasks 1.2 and 3.2; subtasks 2.1 and 4.2; subtasks 5.1 and 5.2; subtasks 6.1 a) and 6.1 b). By analyzing and comparing the average completion time for each of the above pairs of subtasks we found that the participants always took less time to complete the "second subtask", which shows an ease of learning and consistency in the different sections and features of FRATIC.

The ISO usability measure "efficiency" was determined through task execution time, that is, the time each participant needed to successfully complete each task. So, the following equation was used to calculate the time-based efficiency:

$$Time-based\ efficiency = \frac{\sum_{j=1}^{R} \sum_{i=1}^{N} \frac{n_{ij}}{t_{ij}}}{NR}$$

Where:

N = Total number of tasks;

R = Number of users;

n_{ij} = Result of task i by user j; if the user successfully completes the task, then $n_{ij} = 1$; if not, then $n_{ij} = 0$;

t_{ij} = Time used by user j to complete task i. If the task was not completed successfully, then the time was clocked up to the moment the user stopped performing the task.

In the results of the time-based average efficiency calculations for each subtask it was found that participants for subtasks 1.1, 2.2, 3.1, and 6.2.b) achieved an efficiency above three goals per minute; for subtasks 4.2 and 6.1 a) they achieved an efficiency above two goals per minute; for subtask 2.1 they achieved an efficiency above one goal per minute; for subtasks 1.2, 1.3, 3.2, 5.1 and 5.2 they achieved an efficiency above half a goal per minute; and only for subtask 4.1 they achieved an efficiency below half a goal per minute. Using the average time-based efficiency of all subtasks we found that participants achieved an efficiency of 1.77 goals per minute.

In terms of information about wrong clicks and mistakes while performing each of the subtasks, namely the total number of wrong clicks, and the total number and types of mistakes, as well as the most frequent mistake, it was found that overall participants did not make many wrong clicks nor made many mistakes while performing the subtasks.

For eleven of the thirteen subtasks the twenty-five participants combined had five or fewer mistakes, and for three of these subtasks, 1.1, 6.1 a) and 6.1 b), there were no mistakes. The two subtasks where there were more than five mistakes were 4.1 and 5.1, with seventeen and twelve mistakes respectively. Still regarding the verified mistakes, there are two interesting facts that are worth pointing out: (i) in all subtasks there was an average of less than one mistake per participant; (ii) in all subtasks there were only two or less mistakes, that is, even in the subtasks where there were more mistakes, they did not differ much.

For ten of the thirteen subtasks the twenty-five participants together made three or fewer wrong clicks. The three subtasks where there were more than three wrong clicks were 3.2, 4.1 and 5.1, with eight, six and twenty-one wrong clicks respectively. Yet, concerning the wrong clicks observed, there are three notable facts that are worth pointing out: (i) an average number of wrong clicks is individually verified in all subtasks below one wrong click per participant, existing concretely an average of 0.17 wrong clicks per participant in the subtasks in general; (ii) 61% of the wrong clicks were detected in the three subtasks where more than three wrong clicks occur, the subtasks 3.2, 4.1 and 5.1, and it was in subtask 5.1 that a great part (39%) occurred; (iii) the typology and reasons for the wrong clicks, especially in the three subtasks where more wrong clicks occurred, do not differ much.

The ISO usability measure "effectiveness" was determined through the task completion rate and the number of errors (mistakes and wrong clicks) that occurred per subtask. The completion rate is an easy-to-understand, simple metric, and can be represented as a percentage. While a 100% completion rate is always desired, according to a study by Sauro [30], the average task completion rate was about 78%, based on an analysis of 1189 tasks from 115 usability tests where 3472 users participated.

For the effectiveness calculation based on the task completion rate, given that the participants were able to complete all tasks, the following two scenarios were considered: (1) task completion without help: the participant successfully completes the task without any help – attributing the binary value "1"; (2) task completion with help: the participant successfully completes the task, but requested a little help/hint from the test leader – attributing the binary value "0". Using the simple equation below:

$$Effectiveness = \frac{Number\ of\ successfully\ completed\ tasks}{Total\ number\ of\ completed\ tasks} \times 100\%$$

From the results of the effectiveness calculations based on the completion rate of each subtask it can be seen that participants in subtasks 4.1 and 5.1 achieved 88% completion effectiveness rate, and in subtasks 1.3 and 3.2 they achieved 96% completion effectiveness rate. In the remaining nine subtasks there is an optimal completion efficiency rate (100%). The average effectiveness rate based on the completion of the thirteen subtasks was 97.54%.

Another measure that can be used for the ISO "effectiveness" calculation involves the amount and category of errors that each participant made while completing each of the tasks. Errors can be unintentional actions, slips, mistakes, or omissions that a user makes while trying to perform a task. It is best to assign a short description, a severity rating, and identify each error for its respective category. Although it is somewhat time-consuming, counting the number of errors provides very useful diagnostic information. Sauro [31], based on the analysis of a sizeable sample of tasks performed, concluded that the average number of errors per task is 0.7, with 2 out of 3 users making an error, and that in only 10% of the analyzed tasks were performed without any errors, thus leading to the conclusion that it is perfectly normal for users to make errors when performing tasks.

To calculate the effectiveness based on the number of errors (mistakes and wrong clicks), considering the level of relevance and severity of the errors that occurred while performing the tasks in FRATIC, we used the equations below with the following two categories and their respective classifications: (1) mistake: the participant made a mistake in a way that could compromise the performance of the task – one mistake is worth 1 error; (2) wrong click: the participant made a wrong click, not compromising, but unnecessary for the performance of the task – one wrong click is worth 0.5 errors.

$$Avarage\ number\ of\ errors = \frac{\sum_{j=1}^{R} \sum_{i=1}^{N} e_{ij}}{R}$$

$$Average\ number\ of\ wrong\ clicks = \frac{\sum_{j=1}^{R} \sum_{i=1}^{N} c_{ij}}{R}$$

$$Effectiveness\ based\ on\ the\ number\ of\ errors = \frac{\sum_{j=1}^{R} \sum_{i=1}^{N} e_{ij}}{R} + \frac{\frac{\sum_{j=1}^{R} \sum_{i=1}^{N} c_{ij}}{R}}{2}$$

Where:

N = Number of tasks;

R = Number of users;

e_{ij} = Number of mistakes in task i, by user j;

c_{ij} = Number of wrong clicks on task i, by user j.

The results of the effectiveness calculations based on the number of errors (mistakes and wrong clicks) show that in ten of the subtasks, the average number of errors was less than 0.2, i.e. with less than one in five participants making an error. In task 3.2 the average number of errors was 0.36, that is, with about one in three participants making an error, while in the two subtasks where the average number of errors was higher, 4.1 and 5.1, it was 0.8 and 0.9 respectively. It should be noted that the average number of errors per participant in the entire test across the thirteen subtasks was 3.16, i.e. just over three errors, and that the average number of participant errors per subtask was 0.24, i.e. that less than one in four participants made an error per subtask.

The number of wrong clicks and, mainly, the average duration of the subtasks and the number of mistakes in these subtasks, according to the analysis of the observation guide data and the comments from the participants themselves, is related to the required scrolling time for each subtask and the combination of several factors, including the type of navigation in Microsoft® Excel®, the usability tests carried out via ZOOM® and the existence of delay and/or lag in the internet connection. Furthermore, other factors contributed to the existence of wrong clicks and mistakes, such as the size of some interaction content, the lack of information in some fields, such as the complementary help, the mandatory and the dependency between them, the misplacement of some information, such as several buttons and tables, the lack of the locate feature, and the lack of textual and visual identification of different steps in the FRATIC sections.

Despite the wrong clicks and mistakes that occurred when performing the usability test subtasks in FRATIC, it should be noted that only on three occasions did any of the participants have to start a subtask again: one participant in subtasks 1.3 and 5.2, and another in subtask 3.2. To this end, the inclusion of guidelines and alert messages at various stages of the tool's use proved to be fundamental, thus providing tolerance and prevention of possible errors, as well as the possibility of correcting them without having to start the intended process or task.

The information collected through the observation guide and the recording of the usability tests also allowed us to understand that, as a whole, the participants resorted to some help or guidance in eight situations and, in general, were very comfortable in performing the defined tasks, concentrated, attentive and confident when using the FRATIC tool, always managing to complete each subtask.

5.4 Subjective Evaluation of FRATIC Usability

During the usability testing, in order to measure the participants' satisfaction, they were asked to provide a subjective evaluation of their experience when using FRATIC. In fact, satisfaction was objectively measured using available, widely known and used observation and data collection instruments and techniques, namely the SEQ and the

SUS, which were applied after the end of each task and at the end of the test (after all tasks were completed), respectively.

Task-Level Assessment

The post-task questionnaire, based on the SEQ instrument, was applied after the completion of each subtask. The question "Overall, this task was..." was asked, and the participants were free to answer a rating from a Likert scale with seven rating levels, where level 1 means that it was very difficult to perform the subtask and level 7 means that it was very easy to perform the subtask. This way, it was possible to analyze concretely and quantitatively, through feedback from the participants, how easy it was to perform the subtasks, that is, what was the participants' perception of usability based on the last subtask performed. The average level of ease of accomplishment of the thirteen subtasks felt by each participant ranged from a value of 5.3 for participant 21 to a value of 7 for participants 19 and 20. It should also be noted that for twenty-three of the twenty-five participants the average level of ease for completing the thirteen subtasks was above 6, and it was equal to or greater than 6.5 for twenty of those participants. Participants 15 and 21, besides the lowest values of the mean, scored the highest standard deviation values for the ease of completion level of the thirteen subtasks, 1.45 and 1.97 respectively.

The average level of ease felt in completing each of the thirteen subtasks, by the twenty-five participants, ranged from a value of 5.8 in subtask 4.1 to a value of 7 in subtasks 1.1 and 3.1. It should be noted that the average level for ease of completion of the thirteen subtasks felt by the twenty-five participants was 6.6, that in twelve of the thirteen subtasks it was above 6, and was equal to or above 6.5 in ten of the subtasks. Subtasks 1.3, 4.1 and 6.1. a) got the highest standard deviation values for their ease of completion level, 1.24, 1 and 1.29 respectively.

Test-Level Assessment

Subsequently, a questionnaire was applied so that we could indicate "the dimension" of the usability problems on a numerical scale. In this post-test questionnaire we used the SUS numerical scale, developed by John Brooke [32], which is a widely used tool and one of the best known methods for measuring subjective usability [33].

This modified instrument [34] has ten items, and for any of them, participants have answered on a scale with five levels of agreement, where level 1 means strongly disagree and level 5 means strongly agree. The ten items asked about FRATIC in the usability tests were as follows:

1. I would use the FRATIC tool regularly.
2. The FRATIC tool is unnecessarily complex.
3. The FRATIC tool is easy to use.
4. I would need help from a knowledgeable person to use the FRATIC tool.
5. The different functions of the FRATIC tool are well connected.
6. The FRATIC tool has many inconsistencies.
7. I think people will learn how to use the FRATIC tool very quickly.
8. I found the use of the FRATIC tool confusing (in terms of usability).
9. I felt confident using the FRATIC tool.
10. I had to learn several new things before I could use the FRATIC tool.

The answers from the twenty-five participants allowed us to check their level of agreement on each of the ten items above. In five of the items, in the positive "tone" items 1, 3, 5, 7, and 9, the participants responded to have a high level of agreement (they show a higher number of "agree" and "strongly agree" responses), between 4.4 and 4.7, while in the other five items, in the negative "tone" items 2, 4, 6, 8, and 10, the participants responded to have a low level of agreement (they show a higher number of "disagree" and "strongly disagree" responses), between 1.1 and 1.5. This suggests that participants are able, through the items, to assess the FRATIC features. It was in items 4 and 7 that we found the highest values of the standard deviation of the level of agreement with 0.91, and in items 5, 6 and 10 that we found the lowest values 0.48, 0.40 and 0.37, respectively.

The agreement levels for each item, gathered from the post-test questionnaire, allow us to indicate the overall satisfaction level of the participants using the formula for calculating the SUS raw scores [32]: $((I1-1) + (I3-1) + (I5-1) + (I7-1) + (I9-1) + (5-I2) + (5-I4) + (5-I6) + (5-I8) + (5-I10)) \times 2,5$. This way we can easily get the participants' SUS scores by item. All items scored highly on the SUS, between a score of 84 and a score of 98. The item that got the lowest SUS score was item 7, while the item that got the highest SUS score was item 6. In four of the items (3, 7, 8, and 9) it was found that the SUS score was equal to or higher than 84 and lower than 90, while in the other six items (1, 2, 4, 5, 6, and 10) it was found that the SUS score was equal to or higher than 90. In terms of standard deviation, items 4 and 7 had the highest value (22.68), while items 5, 6, and 10 had the lowest values, 11.9, 10, and 9.35, respectively (Fig. 1).

Using the formula mentioned above, we were able to determine the SUS raw score per participant. In 24 of the 25 participants a raw SUS score of 80 or higher was obtained, in five of these the maximum SUS score (100) was obtained, and only with participant 25 a modest score (60) was obtained. The mean and standard deviation values of the SUS raw scores obtained were 90.8 (8.89).

Among the 25 participants in the usability tests, 24 scored a raw score higher than the SUS average (68). According to the SUS curve rating scale and the adjective-based approach to interpreting SUS raw scores, FRATIC is rated by twenty-one participants as best imaginable (A+ rating), by one participant as excellent (A rating), by two participants as good (A− rating), and by one participant as OK (D rating). Similarly, according to the acceptance-based approaches and the NPS categories for interpreting the SUS raw scores, FRATIC is rated by 24 participants as acceptable and promising and by only one participant as marginal and detractor. The weighted mean value (90.8) of the SUS raw scores obtained indicates that, overall, participants rated FRATIC with A+ (84%), best imaginable (84%), acceptable (96%), and promising (96%) (Table 2).

The two-dimensional structure of the SUS discovered and advocated by several authors [35–37] and the scoring calculation method of this system allowed us to determine the participants' scores for the Usability and Learning subscales. The participants' scores on the learning subscale ranged from 50 to 100; 23 of the 25 participants scored higher than 80, and 16 of these scored the maximum (100). On the other hand, the participants' scores on the usability subscale ranged from 53 to 100; 23 out of 25 participants scored higher than 80, and five of these scored the maximum (100). The average and

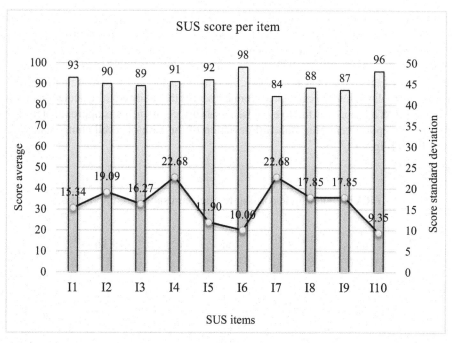

Fig. 1. Participants' SUS score by item.

Table 2. Frequency distribution according to the classification obtained in SUS (n = 25).

Classification	n (%)	Cumulative %
Worst imaginable	0	0
Poor	0	0
OK	1 (4.0)	4.0
Good	2 (8.0)	12.0
Excellent	1 (4.0)	16.0
Best imaginable	21 (84.0)	100.0
Total	25 (100.0)	

standard deviation values for the learning and usability subscales were 93.5 (11.5) and 90.1 (10.3) respectively.

The relationship mapping between the SUS items and the qualitative components indicated by Nielsen [38, 39] allowed us to determine the average score of the participants by the five usability components identified by Nielsen: Ease of learning (items 3, 4, 7 and 10), Efficiency (items 5, 6 and 8), Ease of recall (item 2), Minimization of errors (item 6), Satisfaction (items 1, 4 and 9).

We were able to get an overview of the score of each of the participants in the five usability components identified by Nielsen. All five qualitative components of usability scored highly, between 90 and 98 points. The error minimization component had the highest average score (98), the efficiency component scored 92.67, and the remaining three components, ease of learning, ease of remembering, and satisfaction scored 90. The standard deviation (σ) calculated from the scores that allowed the calculation of the average FRATIC score for the five Nielsen usability components is approximately 10, the only exception being the standard deviation of the ease of recall component with $\sigma = 19.09$ (Fig. 2).

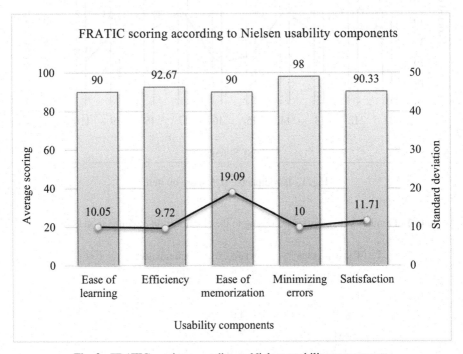

Fig. 2. FRATIC scoring according to Nielsen usability components.

Participants' Profiles, Experience, and Resources

The results of the descriptive statistics, concerning the two objective components and the subjective component of the ISO [24], were compared with the sociodemographic data to discriminate differences and similarities between the participants and their performance and satisfaction data, in order to verify whether the sociodemographic data can influence the results of the interaction with the FRATIC. For these comparisons, among the characteristics of the participants and the performance and satisfaction measures, we compared the participants' age group, gender, level of qualification, area of training, occupation, professional experience in the area of assistive technologies/accessibility and public procurement, experience using Microsoft® Excel® software, and screen/monitor size with effectiveness, efficiency, and satisfaction, obtaining the respective mean scores and standard deviations ($\overline{X}[s]$).

Participants in younger age groups, 20 to 29 years and 30 to 39 years, scored better, namely on effectiveness based on completion rate with 100, on effectiveness based on error rate with 0.13 (0.3) and 0.12 (0.3) errors per subtask, on efficiency based on task time with 1.89 (0.26) and 2.05 (0.12) goals completed per minute, and on satisfaction based on raw score obtained on the SUS with 92.5 (7.91) and 95 (5). It should be noted that, in addition to a better average in the various components measured, these participants always had a lower standard deviation relative to participants in older age groups (from 40 to 49 years and from 50 to 65 years). Female participants (F), compared to male participants (M), had better results in terms of mean and standard deviation of effectiveness based on completion rate (F: 98.46 [3.76]; M: 96.92 [5.18]), efficiency based on error rate (F: 0.18 [0.31]; M: 0,28 [0,29]), efficiency based on task time (F: 1.82 [0.33]; M: 1.76 [0.4]), and satisfaction based on SUS raw score (F: 92.5 [4.56]; M: 89.67 [10.89]).

In terms of the participants' qualifications, it was found that those with a Master's degree (MD) obtained better results in terms of mean and standard deviation in the various components measured, and that those with a Bachelor's degree (BD) or a PhD (PD) obtained identical results in terms of effectiveness based on the completion rate (BD: 97.8 [5.36]; MD: 100 [0]; PD: 96,45 [7,44]), efficiency based on error rate (BD: 0.23 [0.32]; 0.17 [0.27]; 0.28 [0.34]), efficiency based on task time (BD: 1.53 [0.36]; MD: 2.02 [0.13]; PD: 1,83 [0,37]), and satisfaction based on SUS raw score (BD: 89.64 [6.03]; MD: 98 [3.26]; PD: 88.65 [10.44]). Participants with backgrounds in Science and Technology (STS) and Humanities and Social Sciences (HSS) scored similarly to each other on completion rate-based effectiveness (STS: 97.29 [4.57]; HSS: 97,44 [6, 26]), efficiency based on error rate (STS: 0.22 [0.28]; HSS: 0,23 [0,36]), efficiency based on task time (STS: 1.87 [0.28]; HSS: 1,48 [0,45]), and satisfaction based on SUS raw score (STS: 93.09 [6.03]; HSS: 91,25 [5,65]), while Health participants (HS) scored better on effectiveness based on completion rate (HS: 100 [0]), and efficiency based on task time (1,92 [0,45]),but worse in terms of effectiveness based on the error rate (HS: 0,48 [0,83]), and satisfaction based on SUS raw score (HS: 70 [14.14]). Comparing the results obtained by the Higher Education Teachers/Researchers (S) and the other participants (N), there were no significant differences in the level of effectiveness based on the completion rate (S: 97.12 [6.05]; N: 98.29 [4.17]), efficiency based on error rate (S: 0.27 [0.33]; N: 0.2 [0.27]), efficiency based on task time (S: 1.82 [0.34]; N: 1,71 [0,42]), and satisfaction based on SUS raw score (HS: 89.22 [9.95]; N: 93.61 [6.14]).

The results showed that the participants' professional experience in the area of assistive technologies/accessibility and public procurement is not decisive nor significant. However, participants with less than ten years' experience (<5 and $5 < 10$) scored slightly better than participants with more experience ($10 < 15$ and $15 \leq$) at the level of effectiveness based on completion rate (<5: 100 [0]; $5 < 10$: 100 [0]; $10 < 15$: 95.38 [8.77]; $15 \leq$: 97.04 [5.91]), efficiency based on error rate (<5: 0.2 [0.41]; $5 < 10$: 0.15 [0.3]; $10 < 15$: 0.25 [0.33]; $15 \leq$: 0.27 [0.28]), efficiency based on task time (<5: 1.77 [0.32]; $5 < 10$: 1.92 [0.17]; $10 < 15$: 1.76 [0.29]; $15 \leq$: 1,77 [0,45]), and satisfaction based on SUS raw score (<5: 91 [7.42]; $5 < 10$: 95 [7.07]; $10 < 15$: 92 [7.58]; $15 \leq$: 89.62

[10.55]). Regarding the experience of using Microsoft® Excel® software, surprisingly, participants with little experience (LE) scored better than participants with moderate experience (ME) and a high level of experience (HE) on the level of effectiveness based on the completion rate (LE: 100 [0]; ME: 98.22 [4.61]; ME: 96.15 [5, 6]), efficiency based on error rates (LE: 0.08 [0.28]; ME: 0.27 [0.37]; ME: 0.25 [0.24]), efficiency based on task time (LE: 2.11 [0.07]; ME: 1.76 [0.3]; ME: 1.75 [0.46]), and satisfaction based on SUS raw score (LE: 98.75 [1.77]; ME: 87.88 [10.1]; ME: 93 [6.54]). Finally, as expected, participants with a screen/monitor size greater than 13.5″ scored better on effectiveness based on completion rate ($12″ \leq 13.5″$: 93.85 [12.61]; $13.5″ \leq 16″$ 99.36 [2.31]; $16″ \leq$: 97.12 [5.48]), and efficiency based on task time ($12″ \leq 13.5″$: 1.54 [0.57]; $13.5″ \leq 16″$: 1.82 [0.26]; $16″ \leq$: 1.87 [0.34]). However, against expectations, they scored worse on satisfaction based on the raw SUS score ($12″ \leq 13.5″$): 94 [4.87]; $13.5″ \leq 16″$: 90.83 [6.51]; $16″ \leq$: 88.75 [13.36]) and there was no significant difference in effectiveness based on error rate ($12″ \leq 13.5″$: 0.23 [0.36]; $13.5″ \leq 16″$: 0.24 [0.35]; $16″ \leq$: 0.25 [0.23]).

Despite the differences felt in some of the features, it should be noted that none were high or truly significant (correlation coefficient $p < 0.5$). However, the fact that this coefficient is close to the 0.5 value verified in the training area and the low representativeness of the participants in the Health area forces us to be somewhat cautious in our conclusions. In order to better understand and more accurately assess how the sociodemographic data of potential users of the FRATIC can influence the interaction results, namely the performance and satisfaction measures, more usability tests should be conducted, especially with participants with training in the Health area, with professional experience in the area of assistive technologies/accessibility and public procurement between five and ten years, and with little experience in the use of Microsoft® Excel® software, given the low representativeness of participants with these traits.

5.5   Evaluation of FRATIC Section Features

In the FRATIC usability tests the participants performed a subjective evaluation of some accessibility features. In the subjective evaluation of FRATIC's accessibility features, seven in total, participants were given a scale with five rating levels: 1 – Very bad; 2 – Bad; 3 – Satisfactory; 4 – Good; 5 – Very good. In this assessment, considering the basic principles of Universal Design [28], as well as the genre of existing content and the platform where FRATIC was implemented, for the four sections the features were contemplated: Ease of use; Readability; Button size; Memorability; User friendliness; Language adequacy; Overall level of satisfaction.

The methodology used in this evaluation, despite being a subjective evaluation because it considers the heuristic interpretation of each evaluator, allowed a quick and competitive analysis [40]. The accessibility feature in FRATIC that got the highest value in the subjective evaluation was adequate language (4.8 - Very Good), while the accessibility features button size and ease of navigation got the lowest evaluation value (4.4 - Good). In five of the accessibility features it was found that the evaluation value was equal to or higher than 4.5 (Very good). The standard deviations (σ) from the subjective evaluation values for each of the FRATIC accessibility features were never higher than

0.90, and it was in the ease of memorization, appropriate language, and general level of satisfaction features that they were lowest, 0.47, 0.36, and 0.5 respectively.

In all accessibility features evaluated, in all four FRATIC sections, the Information section was the one with the highest evaluation, followed by the Consultation section - both with very good in all seven features. The EN 301 549 section and the Directive section (Web and Mobile Applications) scored less highly in the evaluation of accessibility features, being identical to each other in most of the assessed features - very good in three features and good in the remaining four.

6 Final Considerations

Getting objective data from a product is important because the researcher's perceptions of the tasks and user performance may not be congruent with the performance data and subjective satisfaction felt by the user.

The participants' performance and satisfaction evaluations when using FRATIC, as well as the qualitative components of the tool's usability and accessibility features, have gotten very positive results, showing a great acceptance and satisfaction by the experts and potential users. These, and the performance and satisfaction results, evidence:

- the speed of completing each subtask, with an average efficiency based on the time of all subtasks of 1.77 goals per minute;
- a high subtask completion rate (97.54%), well above the average task completion rate found by Sauro [30];
- a low error occurrence rate (mistakes and wrong clicks) per subtask (0.24), far lower than the average error occurrence rate found by Sauro [31];
- a high average satisfaction (6.6, on a 7-point scale) in terms of the ease felt by the participants in completing each of the thirteen subtasks;
- that the overall satisfaction of 96% of the participants is higher than the SUS average (68) indicated by Sauro and Lewis [26]. The weighted mean value (90.8) of the raw SUS scores obtained indicates that overall the participants rated the FRATIC with A+, best imaginable, acceptable, and promising;
- that participant satisfaction on the usability and learning subscales and the qualitative usability components are equally high (always ≥ 90), higher than the SUS average (68);
- that trends in sociodemographic data, as well as the participants' IT knowledge and requirements, can have little influence on the interaction results.
- a high average subjective rating of the seven FRATIC content accessibility features.

Despite the performance and satisfaction results achieved, some objective data showed and pointed to the need for corrections, especially for certain information sections and subtasks. Suggestions and contributions from the participants, as well as some improvements to be made detected in these usability tests have already been implemented, thus resulting in FRATIC version 1.2.

It is our expectation that through the development of FRATIC and by the results of this study, the tool can simplify the enforcement of EN 301 549 accessibility requirements in public procurement procedures for ICT products and services, as well as the work of designers and developers to make ICT products and services more accessible and usable by an increasing number of users, at a competitive price and without additional costs.

Acknowledgements. This work is financed by FCT Fundação para a Ciência e a Tecnologia (Portuguese Foundation for Science and Technology), supported by funding from POPH/FSE.

This article reflects the views only of the author, and FCT cannot be held responsible for any use which may be made of the information contained therein.

References

1. Comissão Europeia: People with disabilities have equal rights - TheEuropean Disability Strategy 2010–2020. Comissão Europeia. Comissão Europeia, Bruxelas (2010)
2. INE: Health and disabilities in Portugal: 2011. Instituto Nacional de Estatística, IP, Lisboa (2012)
3. Nações Unidas: Convenção sobre os Direitos das Pessoas com Deficiência. Nações Unidas, Nova York (2006)
4. Nações Unidas: Standard Rules on the Equalization of Opportunities forPersons with Disabilities. Nações Unidas, Nova York (1993)
5. Nações Unidas: Declaração de Salamanca sobre princípios, políticas e práticas na área das necessidades educativas especiais, Conferência Mund. Educ. Espec. (1994)
6. Martins, M., Gonçalves, R., Godinho, F., Novais, J.: Benefits of EN 301 549 for each group of People with Special Needs. In: Proceedings of the 8th International Conference on Software Development and Technologies for Enhancing Accessibility and Fighting Info-exclusion, pp. 123–128 (2018)
7. ETSI, CEN, and CENELEC: EN 301 549 V3.1.1 - Accessibility requirements for ICT products and services. European Telecommunications Standards Institute (2019)
8. Parlamento Europeu: Diretiva (UE) 2014/24 do Parlamento Europeu e do Conselho de 26 de fevereiro de 2014 relativa aos contratos públicos e que revoga a Diretiva 2004/18/CE. Jornal Oficial da União Europeia. Estrasburgo, pp. 65–242 (2014)
9. McKinney, S., Horspool, A., Willers, R., Safie, O., Richlin, L.: Using Second Life with learning-disabled students in higher education. Innov. J. Online Educ. **5**(2) (2008)
10. Foley, A., Ferri, B.A.: Technology for people, not disabilities: ensuring access and inclusion. J. Res. Spec. Educ. Needs **12**(4), 192–200 (2012)
11. Benfer, E.A.: The ADA Amendments Act: an overview of recent changes to the Americans with Disabilities Act. Advance **4**, 53 (2010)
12. Architectural and Transportation Barriers Compliance Board: Telecommunications act accessibility guidelines (36 CFR Part 1193, RIN 3014-AA19). Federal Register, vol. 63, no. 22, pp. 5607–5641 (1998)
13. US Access Board: Electronic and information technology accessibility standards. Fed. Regist. **15**, 2005 (2000)
14. US Access Board: Information and Communication Technology (ICT) - Revised 508 Standards and 255 Guidelines. US Federal Register, Washington (2017)

15. US Access Board: Information and Communication Technology (ICT) Standards and Guidelines, pp. 2912–2916 (2018)
16. Easton, C.: Website accessibility and the European Union: citizenship, procurement and the proposed Accessibility Act. Int. Rev. Law Comput. Technol. **27**(1–2), 187–199 (2013)
17. ETSI, CEN, and CENELEC: EN 301 549 V1.1.1 - Accessibility requirements suitable for public procurement of ICT products and services in Europe. European Telecommunications Standards Institute. França (2014)
18. Lecerf, M.: Briefing - EU Legislation in Progress, European Accessibility Act. Parlamento Europeu, Bruxelas (2017)
19. Parlamento Europeu: Diretiva (UE) 2019/882, relativa aos requisitos de acessibilidade dos produtos e serviços. Jornal Oficial da União Europeia (2019). https://eur-lex.europa.eu/legal-content/PT/TXT/HTML/?uri=CELEX:32019L0882&from=EN. Accessed 30 May 2021
20. Comissão Europeia: European Commission - Press release - Comissão saúda acordo para tornar mais acessíveis sítios Web e aplicações móveis do setor público. Comissão Europeia (2016)
21. Astbrink, G., Tibben, W.: ICT accessibility criteria in public procurement in OECD countries - the current situation. In: International Conference on Universal Access in Human-Computer Interaction, pp. 155–164 (2013)
22. Ahtonen, A., Pardo, R.: The Accessibility Act-Using the single market to promote fundamental rights. Eur. Policy Cent. **12** (2013)
23. Cohen, L., Manion, L., Morrison, K.: Research Methods in Education, 8th edn. Routledge, London (2017)
24. ISO 9241-11: ISO 9241-11:2018 - Ergonomics of human-system interaction—Part 11: Usability: Definitions and concepts, Geneva, Switz. Int. Organ. Stand. (2018)
25. Sauro, J.: If you could only ask one question, use this one. MeasuringU (2010). https://measuringu.com/single-question/. Accessed 22 Apr 2020
26. Sauro, J., Lewis, J.R.: Quantifying the User Experience: Practical Statistics for User Research. Morgan Kaufmann, Burlington (2016)
27. Padrini-Andrade, L., et al.: Evaluation of usability of a neonatal health information system according to the user's perception. Rev. Paul. Pediatr. **37**(1), 90–96 (2019)
28. Story, M., Mueller, J.L., Mace, R.L.: The universal design file: designing for people of all ages and abilities, Revised edn. (1998)
29. ISO 9241-11: ISO 9241-11 - Ergonomic requirements for office work with visual display terminals (VDTs), Geneva, Switz. Int. Organ. Stand., vol. 45, no. 9 (1998)
30. Sauro, J.: What is a good task-completion rate? MeasuringU (2011). https://measuringu.com/task-completion/. Accessed 09 Apr 2021
31. Sauro, J.: 10 Benchmarks for user experience metrics. MeasuringU (2012)
32. Brooke, J.: SUS: a "quick and dirty'usability" usability scale. In: Usability Evaluation in Industry, p. 189 (1996)
33. Lewis, J.R.: Measuring perceived usability: the CSUQ, SUS, and UMUX. Int. J. Hum. Comput. Interact. **34**(12), 1148–1156 (2018)
34. Bangor, A., Kortum, P.T., Miller, J.T.: An empirical evaluation of the system usability scale. Int. J. Hum. Comput. Interact. **24**(6), 574–594 (2008)
35. Borsci, S., Federici, S., Lauriola, M.: On the dimensionality of the System Usability Scale: a test of alternative measurement models, no. July (2009)
36. Borsci, S., Federici, S., Bacci, S., Gnaldi, M., Bartolucci, F.: Assessing user satisfaction in the era of user experience: comparison of the SUS, UMUX and UMUX - LITE as a function of product experience, no. November (2015)
37. Lewis, J.R., Sauro, J.: The factor structure of the system usability scale. In: Kurosu, M. (ed.) HCD 2009. LNCS, vol. 5619, pp. 94–103. Springer, Heidelberg (2009). https://doi.org/10.1007/978-3-642-02806-9_12

38. Tenório, J.M., Cohrs, F.M., Sdepanian, V.L., Pisa, I.T., Marin, H.deF.: Desenvolvimento e avaliação de um protocolo eletrônico para atendimento e monitoramento do paciente com doença celíaca. Rev. Informática teórica e Apl. **17**(2), 210–220 (2010)
39. Boucinha, R.M., Tarouco, L.M.R.: Avaliaçao de ambiente virtual de aprendizagem com o uso do sus-system usability scale. RENOTE-Revista Novas Tecnol. na Educ., vol. 11, no. 3 (2013)
40. Lynch, K.R., Schwerha, D.J., Johanson, G.A.: Development of a weighted heuristic for website evaluation for older adults. Int. J. Hum. Comput. Interact. **29**(6), 404–418 (2013)

Cognitive Personalization in Microtask Design

Dennis Paulino[1,2(✉)], António Correia[1,2], Arsénio Reis[1,2], Diogo Guimarães[1,2], Roman Rudenko[1,2], Carlos Nunes[2], Tarcila Silva[2,3], João Barroso[1,2], and Hugo Paredes[1,2]

[1] INESC TEC, Porto, Portugal
dpaulino@utad.pt
[2] University of Trás-os-Montes e Alto Douro, Vila Real, Portugal
[3] Cefet/RJ, Rio de Janeiro, Brazil

Abstract. Today digital labor increasingly advocates for the inclusion of people who are excluded from society in some way. The proliferation of crowdsourcing as a new form of digital labor consisting mainly of microtasks that are characterized by a low level of complexity and short time periods in terms of accomplishment has allowed a wide spectrum of people to access the digital job market. However, there is a long-recognized mismatch between the expectations of employers and the capabilities of workers in microwork crowdsourcing marketplaces. Cognitive personalization has the potential to tailor microtasks to crowd workers, thus ensuring increased accessibility by providing the necessary coverage for individuals with disabilities and special needs. In this paper an architecture for a crowdsourcing system intended to support cognitive personalization in the design of microtasks is introduced. The architecture includes an ontology built for the representation of knowledge on the basis of the concepts of microtasks, cognitive abilities, and types of adaptation in order to personalize the interface to the crowd worker. The envisioned system contains a backend and a frontend that serve as an intermediary layer between the crowdsourcing platform and the workers. Finally, some results obtained to evaluate the proposed system are presented.

Keywords: Cognition · Crowdsourcing · Personalization · Microtasks

1 Introduction

Social exclusion designates individuals that cannot achieve equal access to several human rights, opportunities or resources that are usually available to other groups of individuals [1]. Disabled people usually face challenges such as the lack of employment opportunities, lower salaries, and a set of social and environmental barriers related but not limited to the lack of access to education and transportation [2]. Moreover, disabled individuals also face prejudice in work settings derived from the existence of stereotypes, being classified as having less capabilities compared to people without disabilities [3]. Employability can help people with disabilities to improve their economic status, to have greater social inclusion and to develop their civic capacities [4–6]. In line with this, employers' lack of knowledge about the characteristics of the different types of disability negatively influences the employability rate of people with disabilities [7]. A significant part

© The Author(s), under exclusive license to Springer Nature Switzerland AG 2022
M. Antona and C. Stephanidis (Eds.): HCII 2022, LNCS 13308, pp. 79–96, 2022.
https://doi.org/10.1007/978-3-031-05028-2_5

of people with disabilities have some kind of cognitive impairment or deficit which is considered as an obstacle in the cognitive process. In general terms, cognition can be explained as a group of capacities and mental processes that are used for the fulfillment of a goal [8, 9]. Furthermore, cognition represents all mental structures involving perception, attention, thinking and reasoning, learning, memory, and communication [10]. With this framing, cognitive impairment is the decline of the cognition as expected in an individual regarding the context such as age and education. In extreme cases it can affect the daily functions as well [11]. In this account, the worldwide cost of care for people suffering with cognitive impairment is increasing and could become untenable [12]. Based on the findings of Lopresti and colleagues [13], technology can increase the cost efficiency of care for people with cognitive impairment.

The International Classification of Functioning, Disability and Health (ICF) is a framework for the classification of health and disability [14]. In practice, it is regarded as an important reference in the classification of the human functioning and disabilities [15], and also a worldwide standard for health-related concepts [16, 17]. The systematic literature review conducted by Gillespie and co-authors [18] examined the role of assistive technology interventions from a cognitive lens and identified several concepts of ICF applied to cognitive functions, including but not limited to attention, memory, thought, and calculation. Problems found on assistive technology as applied to cognitive functions are mainly related with the mismatch between users and technology [13, 19, 20]. Thus, the main purpose of assistive technology is to help a person to mitigate a technology mismatch. In this regard, design-for-all has the objective of creating technology accessible and usable to a wide spectrum of users, including elderly and disabled people [21, 22]. However, this broad view may not focus on what an individual user can do. In consequence, design-for-one emerges as a paradigm where technology adapt itself to each individual through a modular, context-aware user interface [23]. In line with the premise of this paper, ability-based design [24] refers to a paradigmatic approach for technology development where the focus must be placed on user skills, not on disabilities. Thus, this approach can solve the mismatch between technology and users with cognitive impairments.

Technology can help people with disabilities in their daily activities and thus exert an important role in supporting remunerated work by providing more labor market opportunities [25–27]. One advantage of digital labor platforms is that they reduce the regulatory impact between recruiters and workers [28]. Digital workers are often self-employed and national labor laws rarely apply to them [29]. One benefit of the lack of regulation is that an effective allocation of capacities can be made. As there are no geographical limits, it helps workers to overcome the barriers of the local labor market and thus increase the price of labor [30]. Currently, the harmful effects of the COVID-19 pandemic have left a substantial amount of workers unable to work in person. The solution found for almost all workers was to work remotely. This has been applied in many countries as a matter of high priority [31]. The policies applied had to preserve the practicality of this solution for both employers and workers, and the accelerated implementation of this solution provides a unique perspective to evaluate the effectiveness of remote work, thus serving as a basis for future political laws that can significantly restructure the current work structure with the possibility of achieving even more flexibility. In this concern, the economic risk of COVID-19 was evaluated in detail at the geographic level [32]. The assessment includes a model that allows analyzing the vulnerability and resilience measures of the local economy to the pandemic impact, where several Asian and African regions present high economic risk. This highlights the need to use flexible teleworking strategies without geographical barriers.

Crowdsourcing is a new form of digital labor consisting mainly of microtasks, which can be performed in a short time due to their low level of complexity [33]. Thus, microtasks allow a wide spectrum of people to access the digital job market. However, Zyskowski and co-authors [34] detected a certain mismatch between the expectations of employers and the capabilities of workers in microtask crowdsourcing arrangements. The correct mapping will thus allow an increase in the quality of the work performed as well as an increase in workers' motivation. Cognitive personalization has the potential to tailor microtasks to workers, thus ensuring increased accessibility for people with disabilities. In crowdsourcing, there is already a strand of research on cognitive personalization taking into account the effective mapping of microtasks at the level of their distribution [35]. Nonetheless, it remains to explore the cognitive personalization of microtasks in its design. We believe that this will allow making that microtasks well suited to the abilities of each individual regardless of the type of tasks being published as well as who is going to execute them. To this end, we contribute towards this goal by introducing an architecture and ontological model for cognitive personalization applied to the design of microtasks in crowdsourcing.

This paper is organized as follows. Section 2 describes some preliminary research on cognitive adaptive assistive technology and task design in work settings. Section 3 presents a proposal for a cognitive personalization framework for crowd work along with a set of architectural, ontological and implementation details. Section 4 shows some preliminary results obtained through cognitive style tests, and the paper finishes in Sect. 5 with some concluding remarks and pointers to future work.

2 Background

2.1 Cognitive Adaptive Assistive Technologies for Supporting Daily Activities

Assistive technology has a valuable role in the activities of daily life for people with cognitive impairment by helping to rehabilitate cognitive functions. Rehabilitation or improvement of cognitive capacities mostly targets people with dementia, but also include other conditions like Alzheimer, brain injury, stroke, and alcoholic dependency. The interventions can be made in the form of serious games [36–43], support for executing daily activities [44–48], or others methods (e.g., [49, 50]) intended to rehabilitate cognition. The reason why many studies have used serious games is to upkeep motivation, revealing good results on the cognitive stimulation. Overall, technology was made commonly for computer programs, webpages, and mobile apps. There were other works using robot prototypes, testbed setups for smart homes, immersive virtual reality, and emotional intelligent assistants. Independently of the technology used, several works have described user evaluation on a functional prototype [36–38, 40–45, 48, 49]. Furthermore, from that works only one did not mentioned technology adaptation but addressed the remote evaluation of assistive technology [36]. In general, technology adaptation has been presented in two perspectives: adaptation from the user side or making the system adapt to the user needs. One recurring option for helping the user adapt to the system was by having one or multiple training sessions before the experiment [42, 44, 48]. The sessions explained how the participants should use the technology. On other hand, some experiments were done with a caregiver or a therapist present in the evaluation session [37, 38, 41, 45, 49]. During the intervention, the supporting person could guide the participant to have an optimal experience when interacting with the technology. One study even mentioned that this kind of face-to-face interaction could have a positive influence on the results in terms of motivation [37]. From the point of view of the system adapting to the user, only two studies were identified through our exploratory literature review [40, 43]. In one study, the adaptation was done taking into account the motor capabilities of the user when performing a simple virtual task. On another study, the difficulty presented to the user when competing with others was adapted from previous results, being adjusted to upkeep motivation. In both cases, the satisfaction assessment was positive. From the results presented, it seems that many studies still include a person to help before or during session. While this has better results on the cognition functions, it consequently raises two problems when considering how to handle the costs of having a dedicated person to help with the usage of technology and how the user can bring the learning technology at home and keep the cognition rehabilitation. Although the reported studies did not focus on the individual cognitive capabilities, we believe that having the system adapting to the user capabilities can solve both problems. The lack of adaption from the system side can deteriorate the motivation of the user with respect to the use of a certain technology [51]. Thus, a tailoring strategy towards the user abilities is needed to overcome the current barriers.

Implementing ability-based design principles becomes necessary to extend the spectrum of users while keeping the systems accessible and usable. This will shift the focus from the user disabilities towards the user abilities, with a more optimistic and empowerment of what users can do. System-driven adaptation in digital labor platforms can enable more people to be included in the digital labor market by having in consideration their abilities instead of their disabilities such as cognitive impairments.

2.2 Cognitive Adaptive Task Design in Digital Labor

In the literature, there is already a research focus on the cognitive adaptive task design in the context of digital labor, as it can be seen in Table 1. For instance, Sakurai et al. [52] created a content personalization method that takes into account the cognitive profile evaluated with the Web-OSPAN test [56]. In practice, the Operation Span (OSPAN) Task has remained broadly utilized for evaluating the working memory ability. The tasks include answering arithmetic questions while remembering disparate words [57]. An online edition of the OSPAN Task (Web-OSPAN) was created which records response latency, efficiency on calculations, and amount of correct words [56]. The research study of Sakurai and co-authors [52] investigated how to improve collaboration in online settings by applying the Web-OSPAN to measure the working memory ability of users. The privileged collaborative environment can diminish disagreements between users in the context of remote collaboration. Results indicated that the information presented could be dynamically adjusted by considering the working memory ability. In an analogous pattern, intelligence tests are commonly applied to foresee a personal performance in a job environment [58, 59]. Furthermore, these tests can be performed to evaluate intelligence aspects in crowdsourcing platforms. In [52] the cognitive assessment was conducted in the laboratory, so there is no evidence of remote collaboration in a real environment. Erskine and colleagues [53] conducted a study on spatial decision support to determine whether the attributes of tasks and users can be improved to achieve improved quality of work in decision making. Along with the attributes analyzed, the authors explored the Geospatial Reasoning Ability [60] and the consequences of problem difficulty and perceived task-technology fit on decision performance. It was underlined that the proper visualization and reduced difficulty of the problem can improve the performance of workers in geospatial tasks. Likewise, Engin and Vetschera [61] conducted a research to assess the impact of information representation regarding the relation of cognitive styles and decision-making performance. The results emphasized the adverse consequences that a disparity among information representation, task aspects and cognitive styles will have on problem solving. Other relevant research work on personalized cognition focused on the impact of cognitive bias on crowdsourcing, particularly in document relevance ranking tasks [54]. The goal of this study was to identify the incidence of cognitive bias in crowd workers. Some of the studied cognitive biases are:

- **Ambiguity Effect** – Lack of information makes the decision-making process seem more difficult [62];
- **Anchoring** – Intense focus on a specific piece of information (often the first one they observe) disregarding additional contradictory evidence [63];
- **Bandwagon Effect** – Presentation of an existing group of results can influence one individual to follow the group behaviour [64].
- **Decoy Effect** –When an individual has to choose between options A and B, individuals will choose B when a third option C is presented and is obviously inferior to option B [65].

The study concluded that a task design that does not consider the cognitive biases of crowd workers can lead to significant decrease in the work quality. In other study focused on cognitive load, Sampath et al. [55] investigated the progress of crowdsourcing task design from a cognitive perspective with a prominence on text-transcription tasks. During this research, a set of experiments were conducted to analyze cognitive parameters from crowd workers in terms of working memory characteristics and visual saliency. The findings outlined that usage of cognitive principles applied to task design can improve the crowd workers' performance. Others have examined the characteristics that can lead to a successful task design for online workers [66]. The characteristics were extracted from a set of transcripts from video meetings in order to model the processes of collaborative problem solving considering the skills required. This model could be used by the collaboration system to detect important processes of collaborative problem skills (CPS). The transcripts were analysed for identifying the CPS processes and an automatic identification mechanism was created using Random Forest Classifiers. The method used for identifying the CPS can be generalizable to new teams and then applied to construct intelligent collaborative interfaces while conducting collaborative task activities.

Kosinski and co-authors [67] introduced a distinct method for determining the intelligence of crowd workers across a general standpoint as an alternative of personal evaluations. The method applied consisted of breaking an IQ questionnaire based on the Raven's Standard Progressive Matrices [68], converting each question into a crowdsourcing task. Consequently, the intelligence of the crowd was applied to examine numerous aspects such as the impact of crowd worker status, compensation, and accumulation of outcomes. One of the main findings is that punishing the worker reputation for wrong and/or random answers can significantly improve performance. If the task requester offers a high reward, a psychological pressure can be exerted on the crowd worker and thus diminish their cognitive skills at the time of completing the task. Another main finding is that similar crowdsourcing campaigns can have significant different results just based on minor changes in task design. Other studies identified that the personality aspects of the extraversion and agreeableness have a positive effect in the task's performance [75, 76].

Table 1. Overview of the results on cognitive adaptive task design in digital labor. [*] Imp. – Implicit; Exp. – Explicit; Ab. – Abilities; Bi. – Bias; Eng. – Engagement.

Reference	Nature of collaboration		Cognitive features			Platforms
	Imp.[*]	Exp.	Ab.	Bi.	Eng.	
Sakurai et al. [52]		✗	✗			Project Wonderland
Engin and Vetschera [61]	✗		✗			–
Eickhoff [54]	✗			✗		Amazon Mechanical Turk
Stewart et al. [66]		✗	✗			Zoom
Sampath et al. [55]	✗		✗			Amazon Mechanical Turk
	✗		✗			
Mourelatos and Tzagarakis [75]	✗		✗			microWorkers
Mourelatos et al. [76]	✗		✗			microWorkers
Kosinski et al. [67]	✗		✗		✗	Amazon Mechanical Turk
Erskine et al. [53]	✗		✗			GISCloud
Saab et al. [77]	✗			✗		–
Ponciano and Brasileiro [78]	✗				✗	–

Some studies have used cognitive tests in the form of microtasks for evaluating the cognitive abilities of crowd workers [35, 69]. The main purpose of these works was to improve task assignment in crowdsourcing by assessing three different cognitive abilities (i.e., inhibition control, cognitive flexibility, and working memory) through the use of five cognitive tests: Stroop [70], Flanker [71], Task Switching [72], N-Back [73], and Self-ordered Pointing [74]. Before each test, a set of instructions were accompanied by an example to ensure that the workers understood the experiment. The experimental results indicated a significant increase in terms of performance when applying these short online tests to support task assignment in crowdsourcing settings. The most promising research works for cognitive adaptation in digital labor are those of cognitive tests transformed into microtasks [35, 69]. Decomposing traditional extensive cognitive tests into microtasks gives the possibility to obtain the cognitive profile of crowd workers in a few minutes [79]. However, the works mentioned focused only on the task assignment, and not on the task design which allows any task to be executed without being dependent on the current pool of tasks.

3 Architecture, Ontology and Implementation

The proposed architecture for cognitive personalization in microtask design requires following two fundamental aspects highlighted above: the ability-based design [24] principles, and the use of cognitive tests in the form of microtasks [79]. An introduction to this architecture is presented in [80]. Figure 1 presents a use-case diagram for cognitive personalization in a crowd work setting. It includes a framework that will serve as an intermediary between the crowd worker and the crowdsourcing platform. After registration and login, the crowd worker will perform a set of microtasks that contain cognitive tests with or without personalization. In this framework, it is envisioned that the crowd workers are not aware of the difference between the two and their view will be that when carrying out a microtask, thus allowing the seamless performance of the cognitive tests.

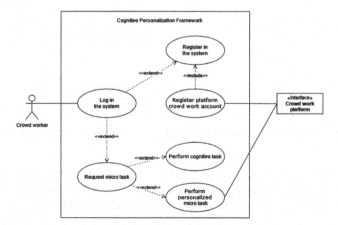

Fig. 1. UML use-case diagram for the cognitive personalization framework in a crowd work environment.

An E-R diagram is shown in Fig. 2 for the Crowd Work Cognitive Personalization Database (CWCPD). The diagram starts with the *User* table, where only an external ID is registered, which can come from a third-party provider for authentication purposes. Derived from increasingly demanding privacy policies such as the GPDR [81], it is crucial to keep the essential information. This allows an adequate privacy policy that takes the user's protection in high regard. Since the scope of this system is cognitive personalization, cognitive tests will be used to measure the cognitive profile of each worker. These tests do not imply the collection of sensitive user data. The *CognitiveTestRun* table identifies a test run by the crowd worker, containing the start and end date. The *CognitiveTestRun_Question* table maps a test to the question used. The question refers to an element of the cognitive test, but it is not mandatory to be associated with a *CognitiveTest*. An example is the question related to a demographic issue such as "What is the level of digital literacy?". Another example is the issue of containing information for a tutorial that helps the user in each test. Associated with the *Question* table is the *Question_Resource* table that identifies a resource such as an image or a video that is part of a cognitive test question. An example of this is the Navon test [82] which provides an image that forms the respective characters required in a question. Finally, the *HistoricalData* table contains historical data related to the adjustments made in the user interface (UI) taking into account the user's cognitive preferences. The fields are optional as records can be inserted only in cognitive tests, task results, or both situations simultaneously.

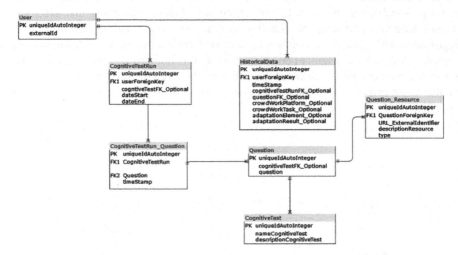

Fig. 2. E-R diagram for the crowd work cognitive personalization database (CWCPD).

An activity diagram is presented in Fig. 3 to explain the flow of the cognitive personalization of microtasks. The diagram starts at the step where the crowd worker requests a microtask. Therefore, the crowd worker's cognitive profile and historical data are then loaded. Afterwards, a crowdsourcing platform is asked to return microtasks. If no microtasks are available, the crowd worker is notified and the activity is finished. If there are microtasks available, their implementation details are loaded. Subsequently, the appropriate adaptation to the UI elements of the microtasks is carried out. If the user rejects at least one adaptation, then this preference is stored in the historical data and the adaptation step is performed again. In any step of the adaptation, the user preferences have always priority. This is in line with the discussion of personalization and customization, where preference should be given to user choices rather than automatic personalization [83]. If the crowd worker accepts all the adaptations, the microtask is then completed and the results are stored in the historical data and sent to the crowdsourcing platform.

The cognitive personalization framework also includes an ontology (see Fig. 4). In its general form, an ontology is a formal representation of knowledge that incorporates the concepts of an area and the relationships between concepts [84, 85]. Moreover, ontologies are an explicit specification of a shared conceptualization and provide an often agreed-upon understanding of a given area that can be reused and shared across multiple applications [86]. For instance, the Web Ontology Language (OWL) is a knowledge representation language standardized by the World Wide Web Consortium (W3C) [87] and considered the official language to define ontologies in the Web. An ontology must be able to answer questions in human language within an area of expertise. The resources explained by ontologies are instances (or individuals), concepts (or classes), attributes, and relations [88]. Those resources can be anything from real word entities to abstract concepts [89].

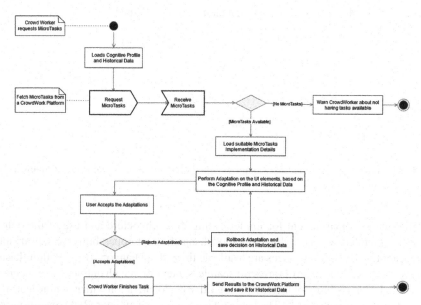

Fig. 3. UML activity diagram for the cognitive personalization framework in a crowd work environment.

For the cognitive personalization framework, an ontology[1] was created with the aim of representing the concepts of microtasks, cognitive abilities, and types of adaptation in order to personalize the interface to the crowd worker. To this end, we incorporated an existing ontology called ACCESIBILITIC [90] which represents knowledge about accessibility and activity-centered design and includes a taxonomy with the classification of cognition-related concepts from the ICF scheme [14]. For the representation of microtasks in crowd work settings, it was chosen a taxonomy that defined sixteeen types of microtasks [91].

The ontology created has five main classes: *User*, *Capability*, *Body_Functions*, *Tasks*, and *UserInterfaceElements*. In the User class, a crowd worker is defined, including only the identifier as an attribute to safeguard the GPDR. In the Capability Class, the user capabilities such as Cognitive Load or Cognitive Style are defined. In the case of Cognitive Load, it is defined as the limit of Working Memory when processing information, being essential in typical crowdsourcing microtasks [69]. The Cognitive Style relates to how information is processed taking into consideration its representation, such as Verbal-Visual or Wholist-Analytic dimensions [92]. For capabilities, Body Functions are needed as defined by the ACCESSIBILITIC ontology and the ICF taxonomy. Some defined Body Functions are executive functions (e.g., Cognitive Flexibility) or Memory Functions (e.g., Working Memory). The Task class represents the capabilities required to accomplish a microtask based on the associations made [69]. To define what is needed in the User Interface to carry out the microtasks, a class with several typical Web elements such as Buttons, Input Text or Dropdown elements was defined.

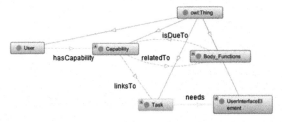

Fig. 4. Inferred ontology top-classes diagram for the cognitive personalization framework in Microtask design.

The runtime environment for implementing the architecture and use of the ontology follows a microservice architecture model, ensuring interoperability, scalability and manageability. The microservices are available through a Django[2] API, a Python-based framework chosen due to its libraries for seamless integration with ontologies (e.g., Owlready[3]) and the possibility of improving cognitive personalization with machine learning techniques (e.g. Scikit-learn[4]). The backend's main service allows CRUD operations on

---

[1] https://webprotege.stanford.edu/#projects/9ba01df2-48f9-4ab4-aede-4fd850b7f3ef.

[2] https://www.djangoproject.com/.

[3] https://pypi.org/project/Owlready2/.

[4] https://scikit-learn.org/stable/.

the database and the use of the ontology as a basis for customizing microtasks. Furthermore, it includes a REST API to increase the interoperability and scalability of the services provided. The end user layer is ensured by a frontend that consumes the microservices for the creation of a user-friendly Web interface for end users' interaction. The frontend was developed with React[5] for enhanced interoperability with the provided APIs. In Fig. 5 it is shown an example of the cognitive personalization framework shown in the user perspective when a crowd worker is executing a transcription microtask.

| I have been affected by the good disposition of my colleagues, | I have been much afflicted by Sickness | There is no such thing as being sick since last Fall, |

Do you like this Task Personalization?

● Yes ○ No

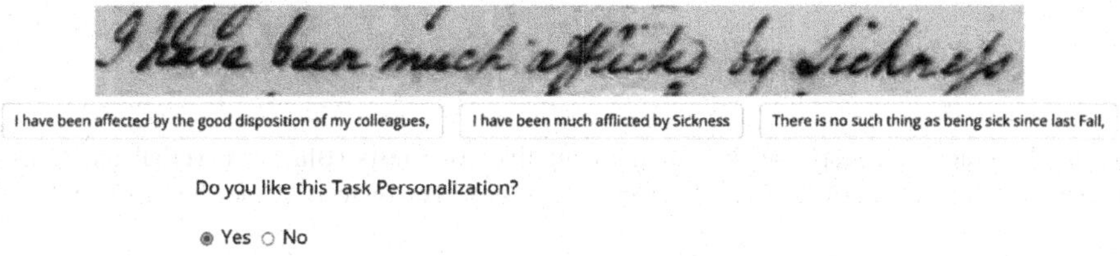

Fig. 5. Example of a transcription Microtask with cognitive personalization.

4   Case Study

A case study was conducted to validate some of the steps proposed in the cognitive personalization framework for microtasks design, following the same experimental setup defined in [80] to investigate a homogeneous group. The experimental setup included microtasks created to assess the cognitive style proposed by the CSA test (Verbal-Imagery and Wholist-Analyst) [93]. To measure the Verbal-Imagery dimension, the textual tasks of the CSA test were used with the inclusion of the image-based Shepard tests [94]. To measure the Wholist-Analytic dimension, the Navon test [82] was applied since it can be used to evaluate the different forms of visual representation with the cognitive style of wholist-analyst [95]. The microtasks chosen and implemented were based on the research of Hettiachchi and colleagues [35, 69] which obtained good outcomes in assigning microtasks to the cognitive profile of crowd workers. However, only four types of microtasks were chosen in this experimental setup: classification, counting, sentiment analysis, and transcription. Contrary to our previous work [80] where a significant heterogeneous group of crowd workers was recruited worldwide, this time the objective was to obtain a homogenous group to check for some predictive indicators in the data collected. To this end, a total of sixteen Informatics Engineering students (age: mean = 22.1; SD = 4.178) were recruited from a local university.

The results obtained from the cognitive tests and the crowdsourcing microtasks are compared with the previous related study [80]. In the cognitive tests (see Fig. 6), there is a substantial improvement in terms of effectiveness in the cognitive tests of the visual dimension (Text-Imager questions) and the Wholist-Analyst dimension (Navon test). The response times of the cognitive tests remain similar without outliers above 5 s.

---

[5] https://reactjs.org/.

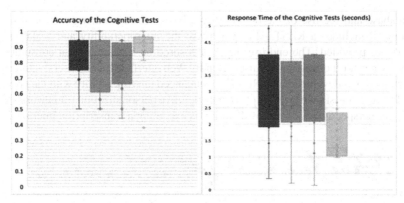

Fig. 6. Accuracy and response time of the cognitive style tests (Blue: text-verbal questions; Orange: text-image questions; Grey: Shepard test; Yellow: Navon test). (Color figure online)

In crowdsourcing microtasks (see Fig. 7), there is a strong improvement in the classification, counting and transcription tasks, while the response time remain similar. From the results obtained, it is possible to observe a positive tendency to correlate the verbal-visual test with tasks that require text transcription and the classification of images. Concerning the Wholist-Analyst dimension, it was observed a high score in the cognitive tests related to classification and counting, but not in the sentiment analysis. These results show the same tendency of the previous study, which supports the evidence that it is feasible to apply the cognitive style tests but having in consideration a homogeneous group which can be achieved by grouping crowd workers by their cognitive abilities.

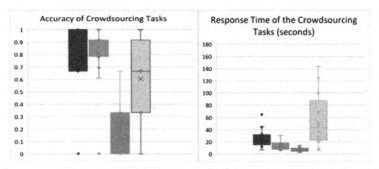

Fig. 7. Accuracy and response time of the crowdsourcing tasks (Blue: Classification; Orange: Counting; Grey: Sentiment Analysis; Yellow: Transcription) (Color figure online)

5   Final Remarks

Microtasks allow a wide spectrum of people to access the digital job market. However, there is a recurrent mismatch between the expectations of employers and the capabilities of workers in such forms of microwork crowdsourcing settings. A correct mapping will thus allow an increase in the quality of the work performed as well as an increase in crowd workers' motivation. Cognitive personalization has the potential of tailoring microtasks to workers and thus ensure increased accessibility for people with disabilities. In crowdsourcing, there is already research on cognitive personalization through the effective mapping of microtasks at the level of task assignment. Instead, this paper addresses the cognitive personalization of microtasks in terms of task design. This will allow that, regardless of the type of microtasks being published, as well as who is going to execute them, a microtask can be designed in accordance to the individual abilities of each worker. The results obtained from an experiment with a homogeneous group of students allowed to evaluate the proposed approach and provided more evidence on the feasibility of applying a cognitive personalization framework in microtask design.

For future work it is necessary to test this framework with active personalization based on cognitive abilities. This will allow testing the personalization on executive functions such as cognitive flexibility or working memory. Moreover, it is also worth mentioning that the task design should be tested using the personalized system presented in this paper in runtime.

Acknowledgements. This work is financed by the FCT – Fundação para a Ciência e a Tecnologia (Portuguese Foundation for Science and Technology) with research grant SFRH/BD/148991/2019. The authors also acknowledge support from the European Social Fund under the scope of North Portugal Regional Operational Programme.

References

1. Burchardt, T., Le Grand, J., Piachaud, D.: Social exclusion in Britain 1991–1995. Soc. Policy Adm. **33**(3), 227–244 (1999)
2. Barnes, C., Mercer, G.: Disability, work, and welfare: challenging the social exclusion of disabled people. Work Employ Soc. **19**(3), 527–545 (2005)
3. Rohmer, O., Louvet, E.: Implicit stereotyping against people with disability. Group Process. Intergroup Relat. **21**(1), 127–140 (2018)
4. Schur, L.: The difference a job makes: the effects of employment among people with disabilities. J. Econ. Issues **36**(2), 339–347 (2002)
5. Abberley, P.: Work, Disability, Disabled People and European Social Theory. Polity Press, Oxford, Disability Studies Today (2002)
6. Simplican, S.C., Leader, G., Kosciulek, J., Leahy, M.: Defining social inclusion of people with intellectual and developmental disabilities: an ecological model of social networks and community participation. Res. Dev. Disabil. **38**, 18–29 (2015)
7. Nota, L., Santilli, S., Ginevra, M.C., Soresi, S.: Employer attitudes towards the work inclusion of people with disability. J. Appl. Res. Intellect. Disabil. **27**(6), 511–520 (2014)
8. Ramsey, W.: Must cognition be representational? Synthese **194**(11), 4197–4214 (2017)
9. Miller, E.K., Wallis, J.D.: Executive function and higher-order cognition: definition and neural substrates. Encycl. Neurosci. **4**, 99–104 (2009)
10. Montello, D.R.: Cognitive research in GIScience: recent achievements and future prospects. Geogr. Compass **3**(5), 1824–1840 (2009)
11. Gauthier, S., Reisberg, B., Zaudig, M., Petersen, R.C., Ritchie, K., Broich, K., et al.: Mild cognitive impairment. Lancet **367**(9518), 1262–1270 (2006)

12. Wimo, A., Guerchet, M., Ali, G.C., Wu, Y.T., Prina, A.M., Winblad, B., et al.: The worldwide costs of dementia 2015 and comparisons with 2010. Alzheimer's Dementia **13**(1), 1–7 (2017)
13. Lopresti, E.F., Mihailidis, A., Kirsch, N.: Assistive technology for cognitive rehabilitation: state of the art. Neuropsychol. Rehabil. **14**(1–2), 5–39 (2004)
14. World Health Organization: International Classification of Functioning, Disability and Health: ICF, Geneva, Switzerland (2001)
15. Larkins, B.: The application of the ICF in cognitive-communication disorders following traumatic brain injury. Semin. Speech Lang. **28**(4), 334–342 (2007)
16. Üstün, T.B., Chatterji, S., Bickenbach, J., Kostanjsek, N., Schneider, M.: The international classification of functioning, disability and health: a new tool for understanding disability and health. Disabil. Rehabil. **25**(11–12), 565–571 (2003)
17. Cieza, A., Fayed, N., Bickenbach, J., Prodinger, B.: Refinements of the ICF linking rules to strengthen their potential for establishing comparability of health information. Disabil. Rehabil. **41**(5), 574–583 (2019)
18. Gillespie, A., Best, C., O'Neill, B.: Cognitive function and assistive technology for cognition: a systematic review. J. Int. Neuropsychol. Soc. **18**(1), 1–19 (2012)
19. Adolfsson, P., Lindstedt, H., Pettersson, I., Hermansson, L.N., Janeslätt, G.: Perception of the influence of environmental factors in the use of electronic planning devices in adults with cognitive disabilities. Disabil. Rehabil. Assist. Technol. **11**(6), 493–500 (2016)
20. de Joode, E., van Heugten, C., Verhey, F., van Boxtel, M.: Efficacy and usability of assistive technology for patients with cognitive deficits: a systematic review. Clin. Rehabil. **24**(8), 701–714 (2010)
21. Stephanidis, C., Salvendy, G.: Toward an information society for all: an international research and development agenda. Int. J. Hum. Comput. Interact. **10**(2), 107–134 (1998)
22. Harper, S.: Is there design-for-all? Univ. Access Inf. Soc. **6**(1), 111–113 (2007)
23. Ringbauer, B., Peissner, M., Gemou, M.: From "design for all" towards "design for one" - a modular user interface approach. In: Proceedings of the International Conference on Universal Access in Human-Computer Interaction, pp. 517–526 (2007)
24. Wobbrock, J.O., Kane, S.K., Gajos, K.Z., Harada, S., Froehlich, J.: Ability-based design: concept, principles and examples. ACM Trans. Accessible Comput. **3**(3), 1–27 (2011)
25. Morash-Macneil, V., Johnson, F., Ryan, J.B.: A systematic review of assistive technology for individuals with intellectual disability in the workplace. J. Spec. Educ. Technol. **33**(1), 15–26 (2018)
26. Miller, P., Parker, S., Gillinson, S.: Disablism: how to tackle the last prejudice. Demos (2004)
27. Tomczak, M.T.: Employees with autism spectrum disorders in the digitized work environment: perspectives for the future. J. Disability Policy Stud. **31**(4), 195–205 (2021)
28. Lodovici, M.S.: The impact of teleworking and digital work on workers and society. Eur. Parliament (2021)
29. Assemi, B., Jafarzadeh, H., Abedin, E., Rabhi, F., Mathies, C.: Who gets the job? Synthesis of literature findings on provider success in crowdsourcing marketplaces. Pacific Asia J. Assoc. Inf. Syst. **14**(1), 4 (2022)
30. Graham, M., Hjorth, I., Lehdonvirta, V.: Digital labour and development: impacts of global digital labour platforms and the gig economy on worker livelihoods. Transfer Eur. Rev. Labour Res. **23**(2), 135–162 (2017)
31. Vyas, L., Butakhieo, N.: The impact of working from home during COVID-19 on work and life domains: an exploratory study on Hong Kong. Policy Des. Pract. **4**(1), 59–76 (2021)
32. Noy, I., Doan, N., Ferrarini, B., Park, D.: Measuring the economic risk of COVID-19. Global Pol. **11**(4), 413–423 (2020)
33. Bhatti, S.S., Gao, X., Chen, G.: General framework, opportunities and challenges for crowdsourcing techniques: a comprehensive survey. J. Syst. Softw. **167**, 110611 (2020)

34. Zyskowski, K., Morris, M.R., Bigham, J.P., Gray, M.L., Kane, S.K.: Accessible crowdwork? Understanding the value in and challenge of microtask employment for people with disabilities. In: Proceedings of the ACM Conference on Computer Supported Cooperative Work & Social Computing, pp. 1682–1693 (2015)
35. Hettiachchi, D., Van Berkel, N., Kostakos, V., Goncalves, J.: CrowdCog: a cognitive skill based system for heterogeneous task assignment and recommendation in crowdsourcing. Proc. ACM Hum. Comput. Interact. 4(CSCW2), 1–22 (2020)
36. Westerberg, H., et al.: Computerized working memory training after stroke - a pilot study. Brain Inj. 21(1), 21–29 (2007)
37. De Luca, R., Bramanti, A., De Cola, M.C., Leonardi, S., Torrisi, M., Aragona, B., et al.: Cognitive training for patients with dementia living in a Sicilian nursing home: a novel web-based approach. Neurol. Sci. 37(10), 1685–1691 (2016)
38. Mansbach, W.E., Mace, R.A., Clark, K.M.: The efficacy of a computer-assisted cognitive rehabilitation program for patients with mild cognitive deficits: a pilot study. Exp. Aging Res. 43(1), 94–104 (2017)
39. Dethlefs, N., Milders, M., Cuayáhuitl, H., Al-Salkini, T., Douglas, L.: A natural language-based presentation of cognitive stimulation to people with dementia in assistive technology: a pilot study. Inform. Health Soc. Care 42(4), 349–360 (2017)
40. Rego, P.A., Rocha, R., Faria, B.M., Reis, L.P., Moreira, P.M.: A serious games platform for cognitive rehabilitation with preliminary evaluation. J. Med. Syst. 41(1), 1–15 (2017)
41. De Luca, R., Portaro, S., Le Cause, M., De Domenico, C., Maggio, M.G., Cristina Ferrera, M., et al.: Cognitive rehabilitation using immersive virtual reality at young age: a case report on traumatic brain injury. Appl. Neuropsychol. Child 9(3), 282–287 (2020)
42. Gamito, P., Oliveira, J., Lopes, P., Brito, R., Morais, D., Silva, D., et al.: Executive functioning in alcoholics following an mHealth cognitive stimulation program: randomized controlled trial. J. Med. Internet Res. 16(4), e2923 (2014)
43. Burdea, G., Polistico, K., Krishnamoorthy, A., House, G., Rethage, D., Hundal, J., et al.: Feasibility study of the BrightBrainer™ integrative cognitive rehabilitation system for elderly with dementia. Disabil. Rehabil. Assist. Technol. 10(5), 421–432 (2015)
44. Imbeault, H., Langlois, F., Bocti, C., Gagnon, L., Bier, N.: Can people with Alzheimer's disease improve their day-to-day functioning with a tablet computer? Neuropsychol. Rehabil. 28(5), 779–796 (2018)
45. Evald, L.: Prospective memory rehabilitation using smartphones in patients with TBI: what do participants report? Neuropsychol. Rehabil. 25(2), 283–297 (2015)
46. Seelye, A.M., Schmitter-Edgecombe, M., Cook, D.J., Crandall, A.: Naturalistic assessment of everyday activities and prompting technologies in mild cognitive impairment. J. Int. Neuropsychol. Soc. 19(4), 442–452 (2013)
47. Mihailidis, A., Boger, J.N., Craig, T., Hoey, J.: The COACH prompting system to assist older adults with dementia through handwashing: an efficacy study. BMC Geriatr. 8(1), 1–18 (2008)
48. Kwan, R.Y.C., Cheung, D.S.K., Kor, P.P.K.: The use of smartphones for wayfinding by people with mild dementia. Dementia 19(3), 721–735 (2020)
49. Alm, N., Astell, A., Ellis, M., Dye, R., Gowans, G., Campbell, J.: A cognitive prosthesis and communication support for people with dementia. Neuropsychol. Rehabil. 14(1–2), 117–134 (2004)
50. Abiri, R., McBride, J., Zhao, X., Jiang, Y.: A real-time brainwave based neuro-feedback system for cognitive enhancement. In: Proceedings of the Dynamic Systems and Control Conference (2015)
51. Braley, R., Fritz, R., Van Son, C.R., Schmitter-Edgecombe, M.: Prompting technology and persons with dementia: the significance of context and communication. Gerontologist 59(1), 101–111 (2019)

52. Sakurai, Y., Takada, K., Kawabe, T., Knauf, R., Tsuruta, S.: Evaluation of enriched cyberspace for adaptive support of remote collaboration. In: Proceedings of the IEEE International Conference on Signal-Image Technology and Internet Based Systems, pp. 225–232 (2010)
53. Erskine, M.A., Gregg, D.G., Karimi, J., Scott, J.E.: Individual decision-performance using spatial decision support systems: a geospatial reasoning ability and perceived task-technology fit perspective. Inf. Syst. Front. **21**(6), 1369–1384 (2019)
54. Eickhoff, C.: Cognitive biases in crowdsourcing. In: Proceedings of the ACM International Conference on Web Search and Data Mining, pp. 162–170 (2018)
55. Sampath, A.H., Rajeshuni, R., Indurkhya, B.: Cognitively inspired task design to improve user performance on crowdsourcing platforms. In: Proceedings of the SIGCHI Conference on Human Factors in Computing Systems, pp. 3665–3674 (2014)
56. Graf, S., Lin, T., Jeffrey, L.: An exploratory study of the relationship between learning styles and cognitive traits. In: Proceedings of the European Conference on Technology Enhanced Learning, pp. 470–475 (2006)
57. Turner, M.L., Engle, R.W.: Is working memory capacity task dependent? J. Mem. Lang. **28**(2), 127–154 (1989)
58. Nguyen, N.N., Nham, P.T., Takahashi, Y.: Relationship between ability-based emotional intelligence, cognitive intelligence, and job performance. Sustainability **11**(8), 2299 (2019)
59. Murtza, M.H., Gill, S.A., Aslam, H.D., Noor, A.: Intelligence quotient, job satisfaction, and job performance: the moderating role of personality type. J. Public Aff. **21**(3), e2318 (2021)
60. Erskine, M.A., Gregg, D.G., Karimi, J., Scott, J.E.: Geospatial reasoning ability: definition, measurement and validation. Int. J. Hum. Comput. Interact. **31**(6), 402–412 (2015)
61. Engin, A., Vetschera, R.: Information representation in decision making: the impact of cognitive style and depletion effects. Decis. Support Syst. **103**, 94–103 (2017)
62. Ellsberg, D.: Risk, ambiguity, and the Savage axioms. Q. J. Econ., 643–669 (1961)
63. Tversky, A., Kahneman, D.: Judgment under uncertainty: heuristics and biases. Science **185**(4157), 1124–1131 (1974)
64. Bikhchandani, S., Hirshleifer, D., Welch, I.: A theory of fads, fashion, custom, and cultural change as informational cascades. J. Polit. Econ. **100**(5), 992–1026 (1992)
65. Huber, J., Payne, J.W., Puto, C.: Adding asymmetrically dominated alternatives: violations of regularity and the similarity hypothesis. J. Consum. Res. **9**(1), 90–98 (1982)
66. Stewart, A.E., et al.: I say, you say, we say: using spoken language to model socio-cognitive processes during computer-supported collaborative problem solving. Proc. ACM Hum. Comput. Interact. **3**(CSCW), 1–19 (2019)
67. Kosinski, M., Bachrach, Y., Kasneci, G., Van-Gael, J., Graepel, T.: Crowd IQ: measuring the intelligence of crowdsourcing platforms. In: Proceedings of the Annual ACM Web Science Conference, pp. 151–160 (2012)
68. Raven, J.: The Raven's progressive matrices: change and stability over culture and time. Cogn. Psychol. **41**(1), 1–48 (2000)
69. Hettiachchi, D., van Berkel, N., Hosio, S., Kostakos, V., Goncalves, J.: Effect of cognitive abilities on crowdsourcing task performance. In: Lamas, David, Loizides, Fernando, Nacke, Lennart, Petrie, Helen, Winckler, Marco, Zaphiris, Panayiotis (eds.) INTERACT 2019. LNCS, vol. 11746, pp. 442–464. Springer, Cham (2019). https://doi.org/10.1007/978-3-030-29381-9_28
70. MacLeod, C.M.: Half a century of research on the Stroop effect: an integrative review. Psychol. Bull. **109**(2), 163 (1991)
71. Eriksen, B.A., Eriksen, C.W.: Effects of noise letters upon the identification of a target letter in a nonsearch task. Percept. Psychophys. **16**(1), 143–149 (1974)
72. Monsell, S.: Task switching. Trends Cogn. Sci. **7**(3), 134–140 (2003)

73. Owen, A.M., McMillan, K.M., Laird, A.R., Bullmore, E.: N-back working memory paradigm: a meta-analysis of normative functional neuroimaging studies. Hum. Brain Mapp. **25**(1), 46–59 (2005)
74. Petrides, M., Alivisatos, B., Meyer, E., Evans, A.C.: Functional activation of the human frontal cortex during the performance of verbal working memory tasks. Proc. Natl. Acad. Sci. **90**(3), 878–882 (1993)
75. Mourelatos, E., Tzagarakis, M.: Worker's cognitive abilities and personality traits as predictors of effective task performance in crowdsourcing tasks. In: Proceedings of the ISCA/DEGA Workshop on Perceptual Quality of Systems (2016)
76. Mourelatos, E., Giannakopoulos, N., Tzagarakis, M.: Personality traits and performance in online labour markets. Behav. Inf. Technol., 1–17 (2020)
77. Saab, F., Elhajj, I.H., Kayssi, A., Chehab, A.: Modelling cognitive bias in crowdsourcing systems. Cogn. Syst. Res. **58**, 1–18 (2019)
78. Ponciano, L., Brasileiro, F.: Finding volunteers' engagement profiles in human computation for citizen science projects. arXiv preprint arXiv:1501.02134 (2015)
79. Goncalves, J., Feldman, M., Hu, S., Kostakos, V., Bernstein, A.: Task routing and assignment in crowdsourcing based on cognitive abilities. In: Proceedings of the International Conference on World Wide Web Companion, pp. 1023–1031 (2017)
80. Paulino, D., Correia, A., Guimarães, D., Barroso, J., Paredes, H.: Towards a cognitive personalization framework for UI adaptation in crowd work. In: Proceedings of the IEEE International Conference on Computer Supported Cooperative Work in Design (2022)
81. Chaudhuri, A.: Internet of things data protection and privacy in the era of the general data protection regulation. J. Data Prot. Priv. **1**(1), 64–75 (2016)
82. Navon, D.: Forest before trees: the precedence of global features in visual perception. Cogn. Psychol. **9**(3), 353–383 (1977)
83. Paulino, D., et al.: Assessment of wizards for eliciting users' accessibility preferences. In: Proceedings of the International Conference on Software Development and Technologies for Enhancing Accessibility and Fighting Info-Exclusion, pp. 135–140 (2020)
84. George, G., Lal, A.M.: Review of ontology-based recommender systems in e-learning. Comput. Educ. **142**, 103642 (2019)
85. Gruber, T.R.: A translation approach to portable ontology specifications. Knowl. Acquis. **5**(2), 199–220 (1993)
86. Chandrasekaran, B., Josephson, J.R., Benjamins, V.R.: What are ontologies, and why do we need them? IEEE Intell. Syst. Their Appl. **14**(1), 20–26 (1999)
87. Group, O.W.: OWL 2 web ontology language document overview: W3C recommendation 27 October 2009 (2009)
88. Allemang, D., Hendler, J.: RDF - The basis of the semantic web. In: Semantic Web for the Working Ontologist, 2nd edn. (2011)
89. World-Wide Web Consortium: RDF 1.1 Primer (2014)
90. Mariño, B.D.R., RodríGuez-FóRtiz, M.J., Torres, M.V.H., Haddad, H.M.: Accessibility and activity-centered design for ICT users: accesibilitic ontology. IEEE Access **6**, 60655–60665 (2018)
91. Gadiraju, U., Kawase, R., Dietze, S.: A taxonomy of microtasks on the web. In: Proceedings of the ACM Conference on Hypertext and Social Media, pp. 218–223 (2014)
92. Riding, R.J.: On the nature of cognitive style. Educ. Psychol. **17**(1–2), 29–49 (1997)
93. Riding, R., Cheema, I.: Cognitive styles - an overview and integration. Educ. Psychol. **11**(3–4), 193–215 (1991)

94. Shepard, R.N., Metzler, J.: Mental rotation of three-dimensional objects. Science **171**(3972), 701–703 (1971)
95. Šašinka, Č, Stachoň, Z., Kubíček, P., Tamm, S., Matas, A., Kukaňová, M.: The impact of global/local bias on task-solving in map-related tasks employing extrinsic and intrinsic visualization of risk uncertainty maps. Cartogr. J. **56**(2), 175–191 (2019)

Tools for an Innovative Approach to Web Accessibility

Vincenzo Rubano, Fabio Vitali, and Chantal Lengua(✉)

Alma Mater Studiorum, Università di Bologna, Bologna, Italy
chantal.lengua2@unibo.it
https://www.unibo.it/en

Abstract. Standards, guidelines and many support resources to help developers create accessible websites and applications are widely available. Yet, the majority of web content available on the Internet still exhibits critical accessibility issues.

While some factors leading to this situation (such as a general lack of interest by stakeholders) cannot be controlled, we argue that there is room for improvements to the current situation from a technical point of view. In fact, we argue that:

- Creating truly accessible content still requires highly specialized knowledge often unavailable among web developers and content authors.
- Existing tools do little or nothing to let non-disabled people *perceive* accessibility issues in their code and their impact on people with disabilities.
- Accessibility is not *enforced* at the implementation level by existing web technologies and user agents.

Therefore, we propose a threefold approach to rethink web accessibility from the ground up, creating:

- *Saharian*, an innovative manual testing tool that can map accessibility issues to concepts that developers are already familiar with.
- *AX*, a declarative framework of web components capable of enforcing the generation of accessible markup as much as possible.
- *A11A*, a categorized, structured repository of accessibility-related resources currently available on the Internet.

Keywords: Web accessibility · Declarative markup · Accessibility testing

1 Introduction

Web Accessibility is the inclusive practice of ensuring the absence of barriers that prevent interaction with, or access to, websites and applications by people with physical disabilities, situational disabilities, and socio-economic restrictions on bandwidth and connection speeds. People with physical disabilities are individuals whose physical conditions can affect, either permanently or temporarily,

© The Author(s), under exclusive license to Springer Nature Switzerland AG 2022
M. Antona and C. Stephanidis (Eds.): HCII 2022, LNCS 13308, pp. 97–115, 2022.
https://doi.org/10.1007/978-3-031-05028-2_6

their capacity, mobility, stamina and/or dexterity. On the other hand, situational disabilities are difficulties accessing and/or interacting with a system due to the context or situation in which one finds oneself; scenarios like poor lighting, distractions, or the need to perform another task that requires the use of hands or eyes (such as pushing a baby stroller while walking) are situations in which one may experience "conditions" that are very similar to the ones experienced by people with physical impairments. Also, generally speaking people take their broadband and high-speed Internet connection for granted, but this is still not true for people living in many countries around the world or even large areas (such as suburbs and smaller villages) in more developed countries.

According to *World Health Organization*, more than one billion people worldwide (more than 15% of the world's population) experience some form of disability. Yet, if we consider the definition of web accessibility and all kind of disabilities, this number can only increase. Inaccessible content means preventing all of them from accessing information, and perpetuating an act of discrimination. Yet, the majority of web content available on the Internet still exhibits critical accessibility issues that prevent people from effectively perceiving, operating and understanding it and all interfaces that are needed to reach such information. How is this possible?

The factors leading to this scenario are various and heterogeneous, but can be broken down into two main groups: human factors and technical reasons. First, there is a general, very well-known lack of awareness and interest in the problem among the stakeholders who may have the most effective impact towards changing the current situation at any level: web developers, who can choose among different implementations to accomplish the same result, managers, who are responsible for allocating budgets and making project-level decisions, marketers, who are responsible for the spread of social media content and product advertising, legislators, who can dramatically influence market and business decisions with laws and regulations, etc. While not too much can be done to change people's mindsets, certainly advocating for web accessibility can help them realize the impact of their decisions on people with disabilities, that every decision can influence web accessibility, and perhaps make them more responsible so that they can make more informed decisions. Second, we argue that there are some technical issues that make it too difficult to create truly accessible user experiences.

Creating truly accessible content still requires highly specialized knowledge often unavailable among web developers and content authors. Currently, you need to be aware of (abstract) principles and guidelines that content should comply to, and how to test for its accessibility leveraging success criteria: this requires detailed knowledge about interaction models (such as keyboard navigation and screen reader usage) that developers are not familiar with, therefore adding the cognitive effort of learning how to perform accessibility testing to the required effort of learning how to make your product accessible. In addition to this, we argue that existing tools do little or nothing to let non-disabled people *perceive* accessibility issues in their code and their impact on people with disabilities. Understanding why a certain implementation choice results in accessibility issues while another does not is hard and requires developers either to rely on indirect witnesses or *blindly* trust the available documentation.

Finally, and perhaps most importantly, accessibility is not *enforced* at the implementation level. Web technologies allow developers to create both accessible and inaccessible versions of the same content that can result in the exact same visual rendering. HTML is neither sufficiently descriptive to provide the necessary tags to represent all user interface elements commonly required in web applications, nor sufficiently prescriptive to prevent web developers from abusing elements semantics and omitting required information necessary to ensure they are accessible.

In this paper, we aim to present our vision to improve the current situation, the tools we developed in order to *make it happen*, the challenges we faced during the process and how we think this may impact web accessibility. Undoubtedly, fully realizing our vision would require us to *rethink* the way in which we approach web accessibility from the ground up; however, given the current problematic situation, we argue that a paradigm shift could be necessary.

The remaining of this paper is organized as follows. In Sect. 2, we illustrate various standards and guidelines to help developers produce accessible content, existing laws and regulations that enforce the creation of accessible web content and interfaces, and briefly summarize the wide variety of accessible testing tools that are available. In Subsect. 2.4, we prove that, unfortunately, web accessibility is still far from being a reality in many different contexts. In Sect. 3 we illustrate our innovative approach to rethink web accessibility from the ground up, describing the tools we propose to *realize* our vision and the reasons why we believe they are necessary. In Sect. 4 we discuss how we implemented them, illustrating some of the challenges we faced during the process. Finally, in Sect. 5 we outline some final conclusions, illustrating various opportunities for future work to improve the tools we propose.

2 Related Works

2.1 Standards and Guidelines

Web Content Accessibility Guidelines (WCAG) 2.1 [5] provide the foundation to define how content should be made in order to be accessible. More specifically, the specification states that people with disabilities should experience content that is perceivable, operable, understandable and robust (synthesized under the acronym *POUR*). These guidelines also provide practically testable statements for evaluating whether or not web content satisfies a certain guideline: these statements are called *success criteria*. Moreover, the support document Understanding Web Content Accessibility Guidelines [23] expands on the topic by stating that depending on how many and which guidelines are met, web accessibility can be rated on 3 levels: A, AA and AAA.

Even more importantly, these documents make it clear that Web Content Accessibility Guidelines are meant to be *abstract enough* so that they can be applied to the widest possible variety of web technologies. In fact, examples illustrating how to comply with accessibility guidelines while using specific technologies are provided in a separate non-normative document, Implementing ATAG 2.0 [6].

But the current scenario is even more complex. The advent of AJAX techniques proved that an additional specification was necessary in order to guarantee people with disabilities access to web applications that extensively leveraged partial updates and complex controls not available in standard HTML. Thus, W3C published the WAI-ARIA specification [9] and provided an ontology of roles, states and properties for the information required by assistive technologies to create a representation of interfaces suitable for consumption by users with disabilities. Once again the specification is *technology agnostic*, and practical code examples demonstrating how to leverage it are provided in a separate document (sometimes not up to date) [32].

Accessibility guidelines go even beyond that. Indeed, Authoring Tools Accessibility Guidelines (ATAG) 2.0 [28] provide fundamental information on how the creation of accessible content should be made with authoring tools, i.e. any tool that allows people to produce, edit or manipulate in any way content, including automatic conversion processes. Guidance on how to meet such guidelines, perform conformance testing, and benefit from in-depth practical examples are outlined in a dedicated document [36].

In addition, further standards have been published in an attempt to regulate the ways in which the various parties involved (i.e. the browser, operating system, and assistive technologies) cooperate to achieve proper web accessibility. These are User Agent Accessibility Guidelines (UAAG) 2.0 [1] and Core accessibility API mappings 1.1 [31], the latter currently being extended with a newer standard specifically crafted for HTML. Finally, the Accessible name and description computation [12] W3C recommendation provides supplementary information on how assistive technologies should compute the accessible representation of the elements of a web page.

Given their nature, making sense of all the information contained in these incredibly valuable resources, as well as how each one fits into the big picture, necessitates a thorough understanding of "how things work under the hood" as well as hyper specialized knowledge of complex concepts that is difficult to obtain. As a result, a plethora of instructional materials have sprung up to assist developers in creating accessible content, understanding all of these standards, and providing more hands-on, practical material. Examples are the ones made available by WebAIM [26], Deque Systems [10], A11A [29] and many blogs curated by members of the accessibility community.

2.2 Laws and Regulations

Just as disability rights laws ensure that people with disabilities are included in society at large, laws have been enacted that also assure that people with disabilities are not being cut off from society through inaccessible websites.

A wide range of legal and policy approaches include web accessibility as a requirement of public sector body websites: treaties, human right documents and multinational alliances (e.g. the European Union), but also national, regional, and provincial statutes, regulations and enforcement actions. Moreover, in some cases both national and regional laws co-occur.

For example, in the United States, the Americans with Disabilities Act (ADA) [40] regulates accessibility at the federal level, but 18 States actually hold statutes related to technology accessibility [33]. Enacted in 1990, ADA ensures equal opportunities for people with disabilities in the areas of employment, public services and commercial facilities. Because it was enacted before the Internet became a center of social interaction and information, ADA does not explicitly include web accessibility; however, it is endorsing that direction [42], and there are other laws affecting Internet accessibility.

The Rehabilitation Act of 1973 [39] was the first major federal legislation aimed at ensuring equality for people with disabilities; amended three times (1993, 1998, 2015), today two of its sections directly pertain to web accessibility [24]. The first is Sect. 504, a civil rights law that, like ADA, protects qualified individuals from discrimination based on their disability. It applies to employers and organizations that receive financial assistance from federal departments and agencies, thus including hospitals, nursing homes, mental health centers, etc. [38]. Section 508, then, mandates access for people with disabilities to ICT developed, purchased, maintained, or used by federal agencies, including websites. At the operational level, the law directs the federal agency responsible for disability design guidelines development (U.S. Access Board) to set mandatory standards clearly identifying what constitutes "accessible" electronic and information technology services.

The European Union is also deeply aware of this issue and has built up a considerable corpus of disability laws and policies over the past three decades [15]. In 2009, the ratification of the Convention on the Rights of Persons with Disabilities (UNCRPD) [37] marked a turning point in establishing minimum standards for the rights of people with disabilities, along with the establishment of the Committee on the Rights of Persons with Disabilities (UNCRPD Committee). Specifically, the UNCRPD contextualizes web accessibility as a central element of the right to independent living. In addition, in line with the Charter of Fundamental Rights of the European Union, the European Commission also unveiled the European Disability Strategy 2010–2020 [7], later renewed in the Strategy 2021–2030 [8], which aims to ensure the full participation of persons with disabilities in society on an equal basis. To achieve this goal, it proposes a multi-year policy framework for the practical implementation of UNCRD. Two of these most relevant legislative initiatives are the Web Accessibility Directive and the European Accessibility Act (EAA).

The first one, also known as Directive (EU) 2016/2102 [14], intends to improve the functioning of the internal market, allowing websites and mobile applications of public bodies to be more accessible. It establishes minimum accessibility criteria that must be satisfied by public entities (such as administrative courts, police departments, public hospitals, universities, schools, etc.), while also encouraging Member States to make more far-reaching regulations and extend the application to private entities. It is guided by the Web Content Accessibility Guidelines (WCAG) 2.1, Level AA.

The European Accessibility Act (EAA) [13], on the other hand, remains under discussion and it is unclear when it will be enacted. It will require Member States to ensure that certain products and services on the market are available to people with disabilities. Its legislative breakthrough and legislative power stem from its coverage of certain private sector websites, as it seeks to ensure that online sales of products and services are accessible to people with disabilities, whether they are sold publicly or privately. Another key strength of this proposal, which aligns it with UNCRPD, is that it only delivers functional accessibility requirements, without specifying technical implementations and, thus, allowing for further innovation and flexibility.

As for other countries, some focus strongly on web accessibility, while others fall slightly behind [42]. Japan, for example, lacks web accessibility legislation, but does provide the Japanese Industrial Standard X 8341 (JIS X8341), an accessibility policy and set of guidelines for electronic technologies applicable to government entities, which also takes into account people with disabilities. With its Disability Discrimination Act of 1992 [2], Australia already required its government agencies and their websites to provide information and services without discrimination. Today they are also required to meet the Web Content Accessibility Guidelines (WCAG) 2.0 Level AA. A similar level of compliance is required by the Canadian government, with its Canadian Standard on Web Accessibility (2011) [19] which, however, outside of government facilities, does not apply to any business. In this, the United Kingdom has stricter laws: the Equality Act of 2010 [27], which "protects people from discrimination in the workplace and in wider society", requires that private website owners do not discriminate against or disadvantage people with disabilities.

In Italy, Law n.4, January 9, 2004, also known as Stanca Act [4], states that the government must protect the right of every individual to access information sources and services regardless of disability, in line with the principles of equality established by the Italian Constitution. In general, the Stanca Act applies to public sector organizations and agencies but not to those in the private domain. In 2018, an update through Legislative Decree No.106 incorporated Directive (EU) 2016/2102 into Italian legislation, de facto making public sector websites and mobile apps also subject to compliance with WCAG 2.1, Level AA.

2.3   Testing Tools

Many different tools have been developed throughout the years to assist developers in testing and evaluating the accessibility of their content. These tools are divided into two categories: automated accessibility testing tools, which do not require human participation in order to *do their business*, and manual accessibility testing tools, which are meant to assist humans when completing manual accessibility testing. All sorts of hybrid solutions in between them are being developed as well, constituting a new open research branch.

Automated accessibility testing tools have been released in many flavors to meet the widest variety of requirements from various development workflows: web services (both free to use [16] and commercial [22]), browser extensions

[18,35], and frameworks and command line tools to support test driven development and continuous integration [11]. Often, the same tool is offered in different versions, allowing developers to choose the one that best matches their needs and their workflow.

Generally speaking, automated testing tools let developers test the accessibility of a web page, either by taking as input its url or source code, or by testing the accessibility of an entire website; in the latter case, they also crawl web pages for links and visit all pages they find from the given starting point.

So far, all tools proposed in the literature have been focused on approaches to maximize the number of identified accessibility issues while reducing the number of *false positives*. In general, however, they rely either on *augmenting* the information displayed on the web page with visual cues to suggest issue to fix, or simply by pointing out the mistake in the source code. In certain cases, identified accessibility issues are accompanied with links to external resources that may assist in their resolution. However, it has not been explored whether this is the most effective representation to allow developers to *perceive* accessibility issues and their impact on users with disabilities.

2.4   The Current Situation

Given the plethora of standards, guidelines, tools and more specialized support resources available to help developers while producing, testing and evaluating accessible content, it is reasonable to question their effectiveness by attempting to evaluate their impact on web accessibility.

With regards to accessibility testing, there is no automated tool that can compete with a human in terms of quality and depth of the analysis. Evidence shows that only up to 50% of accessibility issues can be discovered by automated testing tools [41]. Unfortunately, manual accessibility testing is a time and money-consuming process that requires specific and non-trivial expertise.

However, even relying solely on automated testing yields discouraging results for web accessibility. According to WebAIM's annual Million Report [25], the top 1 million homepages exhibit an average of 51.4 severe errors per page, implying that people with disabilities should expect to encounter accessibility issues on 1 out of every 17 page elements they interact with. A study on special education cooperatives websites [3] shows that only 25% of them satisfy minimum WCAG 2.0 requirements, even if compliance is enforced by laws and regulations. Most European healthcare websites feature significant accessibility issues as well [34].

There is evidence that developers struggle to grasp accessibility standards and guidelines, which are perceived as excessively technical and lacking in problem-solving assistance [21]. Given the current scenario and the fact that most of website accessibility advances through the years have resulted from the adoption of more accessible technologies rather than an increased interest in digital accessibility [20], we argue that an innovative approach to accessibility testing is required [30]. We should rethink web accessibility from the ground up to minimize the effort demanded by developers to produce accessible content. This is the fundamental principle behind the innovative approach and the tools we propose.

3   A New Approach to Web Accessibility

After an in depth analysis of the existing literature, several discussions with web developers with different backgrounds who had varying degrees of expertise with regarding web accessibility, and the collection of all the experiences available in our team, we identified three main recurring problems that developers and content authors face.

First off, creating truly accessible content still requires highly specialized knowledge often unavailable among web developers and content authors. Currently, you need to be aware of (abstract) principles and guidelines that your content should comply with, and how to test its accessibility by leveraging the success criteria. This requires an in depth knowledge of interaction models (such as keyboard navigation and screen reader usage) that developers are not familiar with, therefore adding the cognitive effort of learning how to perform accessibility testing to the required effort of learning how to make your product accessible.

Second, producing accessible web pages and interfaces still requires highly specialized knowledge that is not always available within web development teams, and significant additional efforts to accomplish acceptable results: you need to be aware of different standards and guidelines, then figure out how to translate their (abstract) content into more actionable information (by using different support documents), and finally figure out how to solve the specific issues you are facing in your project. The fact that accessibility is not *enforced* at the implementation level naturally contributes to this problem: existing web technologies allow developers to create both accessible and inaccessible versions of the same content that can result in the exact same visual rendering. HTML, for instance, is neither sufficiently descriptive to provide the necessary tags to represent all user interface elements commonly required in web applications, nor sufficiently prescriptive to prevent web developers from abusing elements semantics and omitting required information necessary to ensure they are accessible.

Finally, existing tools do little or nothing to let non-disabled people *perceive* accessibility issues in their code, their severity and their impact on people with disabilities. Understanding why a certain implementation choice results in accessibility issues while another does not is hard and requires developers either to rely on indirect witnesses or *blindly* trust the available documentation and the feedback provided by existing testing tools. Speaking of which, accessibility test results reported by all currently available on the market do not use the most intuitive representation. In fact, existing tools either try to identify accessibility issues and simply report the line number in the source code of the page that originates the issue, or *augment* the page visualization in order to report accessibility issues by showing appropriate visual cues as close as possible to the element that is causing it: when you click on such cues, you are often presented with additional (technical) information to help you solve the problem, but still based on the exact same generic solutions available in even more generic support documents.

The abundance and wide variety of standards, guidelines, laws, regulations, support resources and testing tools suggests that perhaps the current scenario is caused by the more common approach they take, rather than the tools themselves. In fact, they all share the common idea that web developers need to understand accessibility-specific concepts and should acquire additional knowledge in order to create accessible content, designs and implementations. Therefore, we intend to *rethink* the way we approach web accessibility from the ground up by presenting several tools that can be seen as part of a threefold approach that involves:

1. The creation of *Saharian*, an innovative manual testing tool that can map accessibility issues to concepts that developers are already familiar with. This can be done by leveraging the fact that, stylistic opinions aside, there is a common sense of what common user interface elements are, how they should appear, and how they should behave. Therefore, we argue that accessibility testing tools should *replace* the visual rendering of a web page with a representation built by exploiting only the information exposed to assistive technologies so that:
   - the visual rendering of a page is replaced with a representation that reflects the information as it is exposed by the page to assistive technologies, by exploiting the *common sense* of what widgets are, how they should look like, and how they should behave.
   - keyboard operability is mapped to mouse operability. This means that a developer can operate a user interface control *if and only if* the equivalent action can be performed by people with disabilities using assistive technologies; these aids, in fact, require a page to support keyboard navigation and operability properly.

   The most obvious consequence that naturally arises from this approach is that whenever a non-disabled developer tests a widget for its accessibility, he or she is using his or her very well established knowledge; most notably, when he or she finds out that something is not working as expected, it becomes obvious what to look for. This is accomplished by means of the *Saharian* browser extension.

2. The creation of *AX*, a declarative framework of web components [17] capable of enforcing the generation of accessible markup as much as possible. Such components should be low-level enough to be used with any popular JavaScript library currently available on the market while remaining as unopinionated as possible, yet be high level enough to accomplish the desired result of shifting away from web developers the burden of determining whether or not a certain implementation of any page element is accessible, and determining which attributes and values *must* be specified for it to be truly accessible.

3. The creation of *A11A*, a categorized, structured repository of accessibility-related resources currently available on the Internet. Evidence shows that developers have a hard time understanding how accessible their work is, and eventually how to translate standards and guidelines into actionable items. In addition to this, it is currently necessary to know what to look for, where to look it for and evaluate whether the solution found is suitable for your project:

unfortunately, not all sources of accessibility-related information are equally authoritative. We believe that A11A can help with these aspects, as well as provide the opportunity to learn often unknown (and very useful) resources that can be leveraged during all phases of the development process. It can also contribute to spread the word about accessibility in general, increasing people awareness by leveraging the same terminology they use everyday rather than the language commonly used in official standards and guidelines.

4   Implementation

4.1   AX, Web Components for Accessible Markup

The first tool we propose to improve the current situation with regards to web accessibility is *Ax*, a declarative framework of web components capable of enforcing the generation of accessible markup as much as possible. These components are designed to be low-level enough to be used in conjunction with any other JavaScript library (Vue, React, Angular, etc.), and not to replace them. In addition to this, such components are designed to be as unopinionated as possible in order to facilitate their adoption: this is the reason why, for example, they do not ship with any default styling; instead, AX focuses *only* on the generation of accessible markup. Stylistic choices are made *if and only if* not making them would prevent the framework from achieving its ultimate goal.

The enforcement of accessible markup generation is done in two steps: first, static analysis enforces that the required properties are specified wherever possible; in this phase, the declarative nature of the framework is exploited as well in order to enforce aspects such as correct semantic relationships and hierarchical nesting of components. Secondly, an accessible testing engine is integrated to deal with issues that cannot be dealt statically (e.g. color contrast) as they are affected by factors that can only be determined dynamically (such as the final page rendering performed by the user agent) or are strongly influenced by *context* items that can be determined only at run time. All these aspects are taken care of by the framework itself: this implies that, other than using the framework itself, no additional efforts is required by the web developer in order to get such features working.

In both cases, results are tightly integrated into the development tools traditionally involved in web development workflows, and provide immediately actionable feedback that developers can handle even if they are not familiar with web accessibility-related concepts: being responsible for the markup generation phase, in fact, Ax can point exactly where problems arise, and the most suitable solution for them. This is something that cannot be achieved with the sole reliance on automated accessibility testing tools, as there are situations that may or may not represent accessibility problems depending on how they are used. Eventual accessibility issues are represented by rendering actual error messages wherever the component would be expected to render, even logging them in the browser console.

The end result is that Ax becomes a solution to *enforce* web accessibility within current web technologies: unlike HTML, where you can have multiple representations for the same exact element that result in the same exact visual rendering but with varying degrees of accessibility, Ax does not allow this to happen. This has two main benefits: first of, accessibility issues cannot go unnoticed during any phase of the web development process, as they are shown prominently in all places developers naturally use to test and debug their code; secondly, accessibility becomes tightly integrated within the projects since the earliest development phases without requiring any additional efforts from the developer.

Finally, Ax shifts away from web developers the burden of choosing among different implementations for the same element the one that is most accessible, thus preventing them from *studying and fully understanding* many accessibility standards, guidelines and supporting documents before they can actually produce accessible code.

The Ax framework has been developed by leveraging *Web Components*, small reusable, self-contained stand-alone code block suitable for performing a specific task in the context of a web page. Made popular by JavaScript frameworks such as Angular, React and Vue.JS, they are also the subject of a set of World Wide Web Consortium (W3C) specifications that standardize how they can be created and how user agents should support them. This mechanism de facto allows to *extend* the HTML markup language by introducing additional tags that can be mapped on the provided web components. This characteristic gives Ax the opportunity of being leveraged even in existing project, where parts of web pages and interfaces could already be developed with native HTML elements or by exploiting different frameworks: Ax can thus be adopted gradually.

However, there is another trend that is clearly emerging in web development, especially in the *Jamstack* world: it is the case of *statically rendered* websites. In contrast to more traditional rendering strategies, in this case the final HTML output is compiled once for all pages in a so-called *build phase*, and then served to all users as static HTML pages. In order to support this scenario, and given the fact that Web Components do require a full browser to work properly, we decided to introduce an additional API in Ax: being strongly inspired by Drupal's rendering system and Swift UI, it allows developers to represent web pages (or fragments of them) with function calls that can generate the proper output and perform the expected *enforcement* of the generation of accessible markup even if a full browser is not available (i.e. with a build step run in Node.JS).

4.2   The Saharian Browser Extension

Despite our efforts towards accessible markup generation and tightly integrating automated testing engines, we argue that manual accessibility testing is not going away anytime soon. However, there is room for improvement in the way in which we represent the accessibility of a web page. In order to implement this philosophy we developed *Saharian* (acronym for Sighted Architects Helper for Aria Notation), a browser extension currently available for Google Chrome.

Saharian can be activated on any web page rendered by the browser, and its business logic is executed entirely client-side: no server or cloud service is involved, making it suitable for accessibility testing in projects where confidential data might be involved, or the project might not be publicly available. Whenever it is activated, Saharian performs three operations:

1. it replaces the visual rendering of the page with a representation generated to reflect the information transmitted from its DOM to assistive technologies. The visual representation of each page element has been carefully crafted to reflect the developers' expectations on how a certain widget should look, make it obvious if each element exhibits accessibility issues (and if so what they are and how to fix them), and let them *perceive* the impact of such issues on people with disabilities.
2. it intercepts all mouse events, handling them with a more complex logic to mimic equivalent keyboard events. Such mappings have been carefully crafted so as to meet the expectations of non-disabled developers when widgets support proper keyboard navigation, and make it obvious what to look for whenever there is an issue: in the latter case, in fact, developers will not be able to operate the widget with a mouse in the way they would expect to.
3. it starts listening for DOM changes, in order to update the generated page representation to reflect the latest changes in the DOM. Nowadays, web pages can change dynamically at any time, potentially leading to a DOM that is completely different from the one created by analyzing the HTML code received after the initial request for the page. Therefore, it is important that Saharian reflects any DOM changes in a timely manner, so that its representation of the page is always accurate.

Figure 1 shows the visual rendering of the New York City Police Department's official web site from a traditional browser. As a comparison, Fig. 2 depicts its representation generated by Saharian: the page is despoiled of style and images in favor of a structure visualization functional to the accessibility analysis.

4.3   A11A - All About Accessibility

While there are objective technical difficulties to make a website, application or any content accessible, as discussed in Sect. 2 a very large number of standards, guidelines, laws, regulations, educational resources and support tools are available to help developers and content creators achieve the desired outcome. Unfortunately, there is evidence that developers have difficulties finding these resources: it is clear that you need to know what to look for, where to look it for, and then *select* the most suitable resources across a larger set of them, which may have different authority levels and may or may not be relevant to your project. Undoubtedly, this becomes part of the complexity of creating accessible content, increasing the additional effort (in terms of time, money, and cognitive efforts) required to achieve the desired result.

Unlock the key to NYC
Get the latest on the COVID-19 Vaccine
Agency service suspensions/reductions
NYPD
About
Bureaus
Services
Stats
Media
Careers
Policies
Search
NOV
12
BREAK
IN THE
CASE
Break in the Case Podcast
CITY OF NEW YORK
DETECTIVE

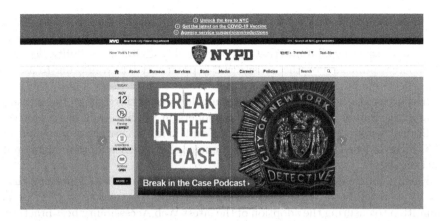

Fig. 1. The New York Police Department's official website

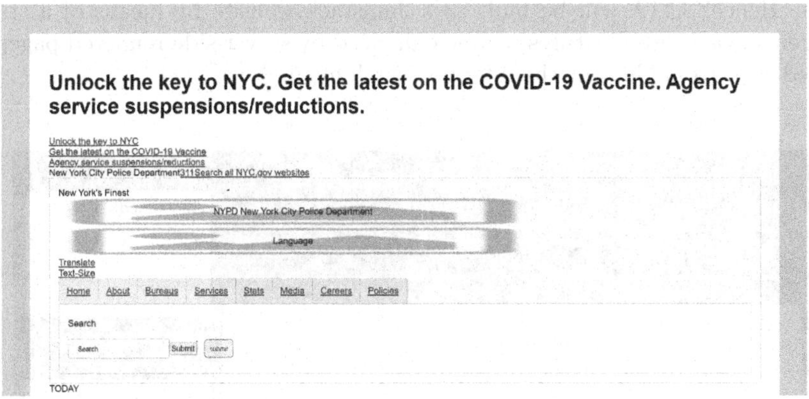

Unlock the key to NYC. Get the latest on the COVID-19 Vaccine. Agency service suspensions/reductions.
Unlock the key to NYC
Get the latest on the COVID-19 Vaccine
Agency service suspensions/reductions
New York City Police Department311Search all NYC.gov websites
New York's Finest
NYPD New York City Police Department
Language
Translate
Text-Size
Home
About
Bureaus
Services
Stats
Media
Careers
Policies
Search
Search
Submit
TODAY

Fig. 2. The Saharian rendering of the New York Police Department's website

This is the reason why we propose the creation of *A11A* [29], a sort of *accessibility wiki* to collect all the useful accessibility resources available on the Internet. In order to facilitate their retrieval, resources on the website will be classified according to different criteria:

- their nature, distinguishing between guides, tutorials, frameworks and libraries, other utilities, command line tools, plug-ins for existing tools, videos, etc.; clear indications on the intended audience for each resource will be provided as well;
- tags designed to group resources according to the matters they refer to; one can find tags for iOS or Android accessibility, common frameworks used in web development projects (Vue.JS, React, Angular, etc.), and specific subjects they relate to (Math, LaTeX, etc.); such tags will group only resources that are related to them, creating useful *entry points* to discover the most suitable accessibility resources for your needs.

While some repositories of accessibility resources do already exist, A11A features three main differences when compared to them. First, it will be a 360-degree wiki, covering all topics that can be related to digital accessibility. Second, all resources published on the website will be manually tested in order to assess their effectiveness, and validate that they work as advertised. Third, the way the resources are organized and the terminology used throughout the website is carefully crafted to facilitate web developers in finding available resources. Additional resources are also provided that explain how to use the more technical ones. Figure 3 provides a glimpse of the homepage of A11A and its minimal and functional style.

Finally, we think that from an educational standpoint there is nothing that can be more effective than good examples. This is the reason why A11A is committed to ensuring the adoption of the latest Web Accessibility best practices throughout the website: while this may seem counter-intuitive, unfortunately it is not uncommon for accessibility-related websites to exhibit minor accessibility issues. Hence, A11A will be built as a Jamstack website by means of a static site generator, whose features will be enhanced by server-side rendered pages as needed (e.g. to implement the internal search engine).

Fig. 3. The homepage of A11A - All About Accessibility

5   Conclusions and Future Developments

After describing the wide variety of standards, guidelines and educational resources available on the Internet to help web developers, designers and content authors produce accessible websites and applications, we outlined the main laws and regulations that require major entities (such as large companies providing services of public interest, public administrations, schools, universities, healthcare providers, etc.) to create accessible websites and applications. We also described the great diversity of accessibility testing and evaluation tools that have been developed over the years, illustrating their strengths and weaknesses. But we also proved that this is not enough to ensure truly accessible user experiences for people with disabilities: we can say that most of websites and applications available on the Internet still exhibit critical accessibility issues.

Given the large number of people who could benefit from enhancements in the accessibility of websites and applications, it definitely makes sense to question the reason why we are faced with the current situation. We argue that, in addition to human factors (such as a general lack of awareness and interest among stakeholders) there are several technical ones that have a significant impact. Therefore we presented our innovative approach to rethink web accessibility from the ground up, illustrating the tools we developed, how we implemented them, the technical challenges we faced and the impact we expect from each one. While these tools are independent, we see their combination as essential to improving the current situation with web accessibility. We argue that the fact that web accessibility is not enforced at the implementation level by actual web technologies, the complexity of web accessibility testing and evaluation, and the absence of a central repository to find any accessibility-related resource in a practical and developer-friendly way has a very significant impact in determining the current situation. As a consequence, we argue that, in order to get a more accessible web, we should make web accessibility more accessible: in this sense, a *paradigm shift* may be extremely beneficial. Evidence has shown that accessibility improves when technology makes it easier for developers to create accessible products, and not because of increased interest among stakeholders: we find this another compelling reason to pursue our approach.

Web technologies should mandate the generation of accessible markup as much as possible, shifting from developers the burden of determining whether or not a certain implementation is accessible, what information is needed for it to be accessible, and so on. On the other hand, accessibility testing and evaluation tools can be improved so as to map the complex concepts that are critical in the context of web accessibility on top of the concepts that non-disabled developers are already familiar with: in this way, accessibility testing would become much more developer friendly, requiring less additional cognitive efforts (as well as time and budget) in order to be performed effectively. In addition, this would allow non-disabled developers to *perceive* the impact of accessibility issues on people with disabilities in ways they can understand without reading any technical documentation.

We strongly believe that the approach we propose has great potential in facilitating more widespread production of accessible web content, as it offers tools to alleviate some of the most significant difficulties that developers, designers and content authors face in doing so with the resources that are available today.

A11A, the Ax framework and Saharian are being developed in an iterative process, so as to refine and improve them over time, gathering community feedback and taking it into account to maximize their impact; this means that a long term development process will be necessary for them to succeed. A good first step in this direction would be a comprehensive, large-scale user evaluation of these tools. In fact, at the moment they have been evaluated only internally (within our development team), and only with a very restricted group of people. However, the preliminary feedback we are gathering does show exciting results, as the tools are proving to be extremely effective in filling the gaps they were designed to fill.

Of course, this ongoing process opens up many opportunities for further research challenges and raises some interesting research questions. The main purpose of the Ax framework, for example, is to provide components commonly used when developing websites and applications that are accessible by default. But which components should be included in such a set to consider it complete? What are the most commonly used components in web pages? Finding an answer to this question can maximize the impact of the framework, as development can be prioritized by the popularity of (i.e. how necessary are) certain components over the others. For the time being, a prototype has been developed that includes only basic HTML components to represent links, tables, forms and form fields in order to prove the feasibility of the project.

With regards to Saharian, then, it would be important to validate our design assumptions. While, as we mentioned, there is a general idea of what each widget is, how it should look and how it should behave, there is obviously room for tweaks that could maximize the effectiveness of the extension based to the feedback received. The fact that it is only available for Google Chrome, for instance, is perceived as a limitation by developers who use different browsers to test and debug their projects. The effectiveness of A11A could be evaluated as well; at the moment, data collected through website statistics show very encouraging preliminary results.

Finally, as our approach leverages the usage of a declarative framework on top of existing web technologies, intriguing opportunities arise from this choice; for instance, the framework could be exploited in ways that would allow for the easy creation of accessible multi-modal applications for which the web is only one of the means of access. With the population aging phenomenon currently underway, the known difficulties of the elderly when it comes to dealing with modern technologies, the fact that the Web is becoming more and more fundamental in our lives, and the fact that many countries still lack access to fast and reliable Internet connections, this might become a critical aspect to address in the future. We believe that by definition our approach can help with these topics as well, thus there's another win for it!

References

1. Allan, J., Patch, K., Lowney, G., Spellman, J.F.: User Agent Accessibility Guidelines (UAAG) 2.0. W3C note, W3C, December 2015. https://www.w3.org/TR/2015/NOTE-UAAG20-20151215/. Accessed 8 Feb 2022
2. Australian Government Federal Register of Legislation: Disability Discrimination Act (1992). https://www.legislation.gov.au/Details/C2018C00125. Accessed 8 Feb 2022

3. Baule, S.M.: Evaluating the accessibility of special education cooperative websites for individuals with disabilities. TechTrends **64**(1), 50–56 (2020)
4. Camera dei deputati e Senato della Repubblica Italiana: Disposizioni per favorire l'accesso dei soggetti disabili agli strumenti informatici, January 2004. https://www.gazzettaufficiale.it/eli/id/2004/01/17/004G0015/sg. Accessed 8 Feb 2022
5. Campbell, A., Cooper, M., Kirkpatrick, A., Connor, J.O.: Web content accessibility guidelines (WCAG) 2.1. W3C recommendation, W3C, June 2018. https://www.w3.org/TR/2018/REC-WCAG21-20180605/. Accessed 8 Feb 2022
6. Champbell, A., Cooper, M., Kirkpatrick, A.: Techniques for WCAG 2.1. W3C note, W3C, July 2020. https://www.w3.org/WAI/WCAG21/Techniques/. Accessed 8 Feb 2022
7. Communication from the Commission to the European Parliament, the Council, the European Economic and Social Committee and the Committee of the Regions: European Disability Strategy 2010–2020: A Renewed Commitment to a Barrier-Free Europe, November 2010. http://eur-lex.europa.eu/LexUriServ/LexUriServ.do?uri=COM:2010:0636:FIN:en:PDF. Accessed 8 Feb 2022
8. Communication from the Commission to the European Parliament, the Council, the European Economic and Social Committee and the Committee of the Regions: Union of Equality: Strategy for the Rights of Persons with Disabilities 2021–2030, March 2021. https://eur-lex.europa.eu/legal-content/EN/TXT/?uri=COM%3A2021%3A101%3AFIN. Accessed 8 Feb 2022
9. Craig, J., Cooper, M., McCarron, S., Schwerdtfeger, R., Diggs, J.: Accessible Rich Internet Applications (WAI-ARIA) 1.1. W3C recommendation, W3C, December 2017. https://www.w3.org/TR/2017/REC-wai-aria-1.1-20171214/. Accessed 8 Feb 2022
10. Deque Systems, I.: Deque Systems: Web Accessibility Software, Services & Training, November 2021. https://www.deque.com. Accessed 8 Feb 2022
11. Deque Systems, INC.: Axe: accessibility testing for development teams, October 2020. https://www.deque.com/axe/. Accessed 8 Feb 2022
12. Diggs, J., Cooper, M., Garaventa, B.: Accessible Name and Description Computation 1.1. W3C recommendation, W3C, December 2018. https://www.w3.org/TR/2018/REC-accname-1.1-20181218/. Accessed 8 Feb 2022
13. European Commission: Proposal for a Directive of the European Parliament and of the Council on the Approximation of the Laws, Regulations and Administrative Provisions of the Member States as Regards the Accessibility Requirements for Products and Services, December 2015. https://eur-lex.europa.eu/legal-content/EN/TXT/?uri=celex:52015PC0615. Accessed 8 Feb 2022
14. European Parliament and Council of the European Union: Directive (EU) 2016/2102 of the European Parliament and of the Council of 26 October 2016 on the accessibility of the websites and mobile applications of public sector bodies, October 2016. https://eur-lex.europa.eu/legal-content/EN/TXT/?uri=CELEX%3A32016L2102&qid=1644420047022. Accessed 8 Feb 2022
15. Ferri, D., Favalli, S.: Web accessibility for people with disabilities in the European union: paving the road to social inclusion. Societies **8**(2), 40 (2018)
16. Gay, G., Li, C.Q.: AChecker: open, interactive, customizable, web accessibility checking. In: Proceedings of the 2010 International Cross Disciplinary Conference on Web Accessibility (W4A), pp. 1–2 (2010)
17. Glazkov, D., Ito, H.: Introduction to web components. W3C note, W3C, July 2014. https://www.w3.org/TR/2014/NOTE-components-intro-20140724/. Accessed 8 Feb 2022

18. Google, INC.: Lighthouse - Tools for Web Developers, October 2020. https://developers.google.com/web/tools/lighthouse. Accessed 8 Feb 2022
19. Government of Canada: Standard on Web Accessibility, August 2011. https://www.tbs-sct.gc.ca/pol/doc-eng.aspx?id=23601. Accessed 8 Feb 2022
20. Hanson, V.L., Richards, J.T.: Progress on website accessibility? ACM Trans. Web (TWEB) **7**(1), 1–30 (2013)
21. Henka, A., Zimmermann, G.: Persona based accessibility testing. In: Stephanidis, C. (ed.) HCI 2014. CCIS, vol. 435, pp. 226–231. Springer, Cham (2014). https://doi.org/10.1007/978-3-319-07854-0_40
22. LLC., T.: tenon.io (2017). https://tenon.io. Accessed 8 Feb 2022
23. Michael Cooper, J.O.C., Kirkpatrick, A.: Understanding WCAG 2.1. W3C note, World Wide Web Consortium (W3C), October 2016. https://www.w3.org/TR/2016/NOTE-UNDERSTANDING-WCAG20-20161007/. Accessed 8 Feb 2022
24. Web Accessibility in Mind: United States Law: Overview of the Rehabilitation Act of 1973 (2013). http://webaim.org/articles/laws/usa/rehab. Accessed 8 Feb 2022
25. Web Accessibility in Mind: The WebAIM Million - an annual accessibility analysis of the top 1,000,000 home pages (2021). https://webaim.org/projects/million/. Accessed 8 Feb 2022
26. Web Accessibility in Mind: WebAIM —Homepage, November 2021. https://webaim.org. Accessed 8 Feb 2022
27. Parliament of the United Kingdom: Equality Act 2010 (2010). https://www.legislation.gov.uk/ukpga/2010/15/contents. Accessed 8 Feb 2022
28. Richards, J., Spellman, J.F., Treviranus, J.: Authoring Tool Accessibility Guidelines (ATAG) 2.0. W3C recommendation, W3C, September 2015. https://www.w3.org/TR/2015/REC-ATAG20-20150924/. Accessed 8 Feb 2022
29. Rubano, V.: A11A - All About Accessibility, November 2021. https://a11a.disi.unibo.it. Accessed 8 Feb 2022
30. Rubano, V., Vitali, F.: Making accessibility accessible: strategy and tools. In: 2021 IEEE 18th Annual Consumer Communications & Networking Conference (CCNC), pp. 1–6. IEEE (2021)
31. Scheuhammer, J., Snow-Weaver, A., Diggs, J., Cooper, M., Leventhal, A., Schwerdtfeger, R.: Core Accessibility API Mappings 1.1. W3C recommendation, W3C, December 2017. https://www.w3.org/TR/2017/REC-core-aam-1.1-20171214/. Accessed 8 Feb 2022
32. Schwerdtfeger, R., et al.: WAI-ARIA Authoring Practices 1.1. W3C note, W3C, August 2019. https://www.w3.org/TR/2019/NOTE-wai-aria-practices-1.1-20190814/. Accessed 8 Feb 2022
33. Shaheen, N.L., Lazar, J.: K-12 technology accessibility: the message from state governments. J. Spec. Educ. Technol. **33**(2), 83–97 (2018)
34. Sik-Lanyi, C., Orbán-Mihálykó, É.: Accessibility testing of European health-related websites. Arab. J. Sci. Eng. **44**(11), 9171–9190 (2019). https://doi.org/10.1007/s13369-019-04017-z
35. Smith, J., Whiting, J.: WAVE - Web Accessibility Evaluation tool (2016). https://wave.webaim.org/. Accessed 8 Feb 2022
36. Spellman, J.F., Richards, J., Treviranus, J.: Implementing ATAG 2.0. W3C note, W3C, September 2015. https://www.w3.org/TR/2015/NOTE-IMPLEMENTING-ATAG20-20150924/. Accessed 8 Feb 2022
37. United Nations: Convention on the Rights of Persons with Disabilities, December 2006. https://www.un.org/development/desa/disabilities/convention-on-the-rights-of-persons-with-disabilities.html. Accessed 8 Feb 2022

38. United Nations Committee on the Rights of Persons with Disabilities - Office for Civil Rights: Your rights under Section 504 of the Rehabilitation Act (2006). https://www.hhs.gov/sites/default/files/ocr/civilrights/resources/factsheets/504.pdf. Accessed 8 Feb 2022
39. United States Congress: Rehabilitation Act of 1973, September 1973. https://www.eeoc.gov/rehabilitation-act-1973-original-text. Accessed 8 Feb 2022
40. US Congress: Americans With Disabilities Act of 1990. Public Law 101–336, 26 July 1990. https://beta.ada.gov/law-and-regs/ada/. Accessed 8 Feb 2022
41. Vigo, M., Brown, J., Conway, V.: Benchmarking web accessibility evaluation tools: measuring the harm of sole reliance on automated tests. In: Proceedings of the 10th International Cross-Disciplinary Conference on Web Accessibility, pp. 1–10 (2013)
42. Yang, Y.T., Chen, B.: Web accessibility for older adults: a comparative analysis of disability laws. Gerontologist **55**(5), 854–864 (2015)

The Simulated User Impairment Testing (SUIT) Protocol and Toolbox for Digital Artifacts

Joschua Thomas Simon-Liedtke[(✉)] [iD] and Till Halbach [iD]

Norwegian Computing Center, Gaustadalléen 23A, 0373 Oslo, Norway
{joschua,halbach}@nr.no
https://www.clothes4all.net/?

Abstract. User testing involving people with varying abilities and impairments are two of the key ingredients of universal design that can help to increase the accessibility and usability of an ICT artifact. However, recruiting adequate participants during the design and development process can be difficult, time-consuming and resource intensive. We suggest mitigating these challenges by employing user simulation as additional quality assessment measure throughout the design and development process of a digital ICT artifact.

In the present paper, we present a protocol and a toolbox for Simulated User Impairment Testing (SUIT) that enables non-impaired designers and developers to simulate the perception of people with some of the most common impairments related to cognitive, visual, auditory, vocal, mobility-related and motor-related functioning. We compile a list of possible tools and methods that are readily available or easily obtainable in a production and design setting. Moreover, we complement this list with relevant user examples for each category, as well as examples of the most common barriers. Finally, we point out how the Simulated User Impairment Testing (SUIT) toolbox can be used to add an additional layer of quality assessment during the design and development process of a digital artifact and argue that it cannot replace the user testing part.

Keywords: Universal design · Accessibility · Simulation · Impairments · Simulations

1 Introduction

Around 15% of the population in the world is living with some sort of impairment [37]. The number of people with impairments in Western societies is expected to increase due to increased life expectancy and ageing [35]. Thus, universal design, defined as the process of designing and implementing systems that are accessible and usable for the widest range of users possible, including people with impairments, has increased its importance in communities and societies around the globe [21,32]. Additionally, it has been shown that increased accessibility and usability of a product or service will benefit non-disabled users [29,30].

© The Author(s), under exclusive license to Springer Nature Switzerland AG 2022
M. Antona and C. Stephanidis (Eds.): HCII 2022, LNCS 13308, pp. 116–136, 2022.
https://doi.org/10.1007/978-3-031-05028-2_7

Moreover, universal design has become a legal requirement in many countries around the world. The United Nations' Convention on the Rights of Persons with Disabilities has been ratified by many of their member states, and national lawmakers have passed laws for the inclusion of people with impairment1 [16, 38]. The Norwegian anti-discrimination law states, for example, that ICT solutions like websites are universally designed [15, 16]. The Norwegian lawmakers, and likewise the legislative in other countries like the USA or UK have implemented legal obligations in practice by using a system of audit and certification to a set of guidelines or standards like the Web Accessibility Guidelines (WCAG) [11, 42].

User evaluations including people with impairments and varying abilities into the design and development process is one of the key elements of universal design to achieve increased accessibility and usability [4, 5]. Even though guidelines are a good starting point to eliminate common technical barriers, user-based evaluations involving real users interacting with an artifact are still necessary to detect and mitigate barriers while making the artifact as a whole more usable [28]. In the ideal case, such user evaluations are conducted with people of different abilities including people with impairments. However, such evaluations involving a wide set of users are often considered to be too time or resource intensive [28]. Thus, supplement methods that can be conducted by singular experts or developers have been proposed including the use of personas, and models or simulations, especially during the early stages of a development process [2, 26, 28].

We argue that the use of simulation methods can be an effective tool to increase accessibility and usability of an artifact, at the same time as simulations can easily be integrated by designers and developers in the early stages of design process without the need to rely on direct input from external users. On the one hand, the founders of Universal Design published guidelines spanning the spectrum of human abilities in architecture, and individual simulation methods for ICT are mentioned sporadically throughout the literature [1, 32, 33]. On the other hand, there is no comprehensive framework including practical examples for simulations for the whole spectrum of human abilities applicable in ICT.

In the present paper, we want to close the aforementioned gap by introducing a protocol and a toolbox for Simulated User Impairment Testing (SUIT) spanning the whole spectrum of human abilities relevant for the consumption of, usage of, and interaction with ICT, e.g., cognitive, sensory, voice and movement-related abilities. The SUIT toolbox includes concrete simulation methods that are practically applicable by designers and developers.

In the following sections, we will (I.) review relevant literature about universal design strategies and evaluation methods including guidelines, expert evaluations, personas, and simulations, (II.) introduce the protocol for Simulated User Impairment Testing (SUIT), (III.) list tools and examples for the practical implementation of the SUIT toolbox, (IV.) present a trial study of the SUIT protocol and toolbox evaluating an online artifact used as reference project for the visualization of WCAG 2.0 and 2.1 called Clothes4All, and (V.) discuss some general observations and recommendations collected during our trial study.

2   Background

One strategy to increase accessibility and usability for implementing universal design of a digital artifact is interactive, user-centered design processes with the following iterative phases [24]: (I.) the understanding of users, tasks, and contexts, (II.) the design of the artifact, (III.) the prototyping the artifact, (IV.) the evaluation of the artifact, and (V.) the integration and final implementation of the artifact. A prerequisite of such a design process is inclusive design, which means the inclusion of people with impairments and other marginalized groups as evaluators [24]. Most common evaluation methods include [24,28]: (I.) user testing through for example observations or thinking-aloud techniques; (II.) guidelines, checklists, and automated checking tools; (III.) expert evaluation, (IV.) cognitive walkthroughs, (V.) personas; and (VI.) simulations. These methods are not mutually exclusive. An expert can conduct an evaluation with or without simulation, cognitive walkthroughs can follow checklists, and so on. In an ideal world, user testing would always be the prioritized choice, as it allows detailed insight and first-hand experience by users of the relevant groups. However, user testing can sometimes be impractical, time consuming, resource intensive, and expensive, as well as qualified evaluators with impairments can be difficult to recruit [19,24,28]. Thus, we want to shortly present some of the alternatives that can supplement some user evaluation in some iterations of the design process.

2.1   Guidelines

Accessibility guidelines are tools that help developers to implement websites more easily in the most technically accessible and usable way possible. Guidelines provide best-practice solutions for common challenges and help to avoid common pitfalls. Examples for such guidelines are the Web Accessibility Guidelines (WCAG) that have been proposed in multiple versions [42,43]. WCAG 2.0 have been enshrined in law my the national lawmaker in Norway, while WCAG 2.1 is the standard in the Web Accessibility Directive (WAD) passed by the European Union (EU) [9,15].

2.2   Expert Evaluations and Personas

Other alternatives for user testing include experts in the field that follow either none, general or detailed guidelines or the usage of Personas [24,26]. Personas are defined as fictional characters representing individual users or user groups [7,26]. Personas were originally rough sketches used in marketing. However, these original Personas had the downsides of not being believable enough, having the characters being communicated poorly, not having provided a clear instruction on how to use the characters, and lacking high-level support within a company [26]. Eventually, Personas evolved to more detailed characters by including statistical data and anecdotes and observations from interviews with target users, having the Personas embedded within the design process and providing clear instructions on why, when, and how to use them [26]. Personas provide a variety of advantages and disadvantages: On the pro side, Personas can create a strong focus on users and work contexts through a fictionalized setting that can create engagement in designers and developers [26]. Moreover, creating Personas can help to make assumptions about the target audience more explicit [26]. Overall, Personas can help to focus the attention on a specific target group by creating a powerful medium for communicating results and improving the understanding of the target group [26]. On the contra side, it can be challenging to compile the right Persona or set of Personas for a specific target group [26]. What is more, designers and developers can be tempted to reuse existing Personas when it would be more appropriate to create new ones [26]. Likewise, overusing personas may replace other valid methods like user-testing, or product evaluation (leading to a so-called "Persona mania") [26]. Moreover, different groups or roles in the design process might have different needs requiring diverging Persona attributes or target audiences [26]. A marketing department, for example, might have different wishes to Personas than for example product development.

2.3   Comparison of User Testing, Expert Evaluation, and Personas

Expert evaluations and Persona testing are often considered to be insufficient, as they are not considering users and their needs well enough [28]. Especially persona testing is not considered to be an empirical method and requires decision-making that is likely subject to personal bias by the person interpreting any given persona [26]. For personas with impairments, a tester might base decisions on subjective assumptions that are not based in reality. In contrast, user testing involving users with impairments is often considered to be time or resource intensive, at the same time as it might be difficult to get access to relevant users [25,28]. Furthermore, it can be difficult to set up the testing environment in a way that is accessible for users with impairments [28].

To safe resources and minimize the problem of subjective bias, the testing can be supported by methods that simulate a given impairment. In other words, expert testing that includes simulations can be a feasible alternative to support expert testing or Persona testing. In this paper, we define simulation methods as models that can emulate the perception or experience of people with impairment as accurate as possible to a person without the impairment. Thus, simulations are most relevant where models are possible and economical [24]. Simulation-based testing is helpful in earlier stages of the design process before deploying user testing [3].

2.4   Impairments to Consider

The World Health Organization (WHO) published a document defining the whole spectrum of human functions and abilities [41]. Based on this document, we defined categories of human impairments that are relevant for ICT: (I.) Cognition [(i.) Vision, (ii.) Hearing, (iii.) Touch], (II.) Senses, (III.) Voice, (IV.) Movement [(i.) Mobility, (ii.) Motor] [12].

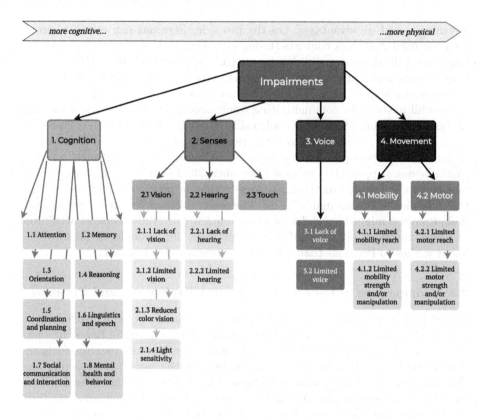

Fig. 1. The impairment categories considered for SUIT.

3   The Simulated User Impairment Testing (SUIT) Protocol

The main goal of Simulated User Impairment Testing (SUIT) is to discover possible barriers that people with impairments can encounter when interacting with a digital ICT artifact. In this paper, we are targeting digital artifacts in ICT, a term that encompasses all interactive digital products, systems and applications in the realm of ICT. Typical representations of digital artifacts are, for example, web sites, mobile apps, museum exhibitions, or automats. In other words, we intent to evaluate how accessible and usable the artifact is for people with impairments. A minor goal is to let a non-disabled developer experience an artifact through the eyes and body of a person with impairment. Thus, it is important to emulate the experience of users with impairment as accurate as possible. Another minor goal is to raise awareness around the needs and experiences of people with impairments.

Our Simulation User Impairment Testing (SUIT) Protocol and Toolbox is informed by strategies from the literature, as well as practical experiences from accessibility and usability testing that we have conducted throughout the years. The SUIT protocol is one key element that consists of five major steps:

(1.) The tester defines one or multiple tasks connected to the artifact. Tasks can be related to retrieving information, completing a routine, communication and more.
(2.) The tester defines a metric according to which they intent to evaluate the outcome of the tasks. Such metrics can, for example, measure the completion rate, completion time, accuracy, record the number of observed errors or issues, or simply record qualitative data from observational input.
(3.) The tester defines one or multiple impairments, and chooses an adequate simulation tool to emulate the experience of people with the chosen impairment.
(4.) The tester completes the task(s) with the chosen impairment(s) while recording qualitative observations and relevant data according to the chosen metric.
(5.) The tester evaluates the results from the metric.

We suggest including the SUIT protocol throughout the design and development phase as an additional accessibility and usability evaluation, as well as an additional quality assessment step. Moreover, a tester should apply multiple iterations of the SUIT Protocol throughout the design and development process of a digital artifact. It has been shown that a combination of automated checking tools, checklists, expert evaluation, and simulation methods can uncover a high percentage of accessibility and usability issues with respect to their cost [2]. Furthermore, the SUIT protocol is easily compatible with an agile workflow [2]. It can be beneficial to for example have multiple evaluation cycles in which the tester uses automated tools, followed by simulations, checklists, and finally expert evaluations [2]. It is not necessary to apply the complete set of tools represented in the SUIT toolbox at each step of the evaluation. It is possible to rather focus on one or two major impairments during each iteration of the SUIT protocol.

4   The SUIT Toolbox

In the following paragraphs, we will describe the various user impairment categories in more detail, including relevant user groups from each subcategory and typical barriers users from those user groups might encounter. Moreover, we list tools, equipment and environments that can be used to carry out simulated user testing. This list includes various assistive devices that users with impairments might employ when interacting with websites online. A system developer or designer should ensure that information on their artifact can be accessed and retrieved both with and without simulating one of the impairments mentioned above (cf. Fig. 1).

4.1 Cognitive and Mental Functions

Cognitive and mental functions are functions of the brain, including both global and specific mental functions, as well as various emotional functions [41]. They can be subcategorized into attention, memory, orientation, reasoning, coordination and planning, linguistics and speech, social communication and interaction, and mental health and behavior.

Attention is defined as all "specific mental functions of focusing on an external stimulus or internal experience for the required period of time" [41] encompassing all functions related to concentration, focus, and motivation. *Examples* of individuals with attention difficulties are people with attention deficit hyperactivity disorder (ADHD) and plain attention deficit disorder (ADD). We are not aware of any typical *assistive technology (AT)* used by this group, but it is worth mentioning that distractions can be reduced by removing distracting devices like mobile phones and services such as social media. Examples of potential *barriers* include situations with complex and over-complicated graphical screen layouts, lengthy text, moving, blinking or flickering content, or background audio [40]. We propose the following *simulation strategies*:

(1.) Use the artifact with an audio source in the background playing at a sufficiently high level.
(2.) Use the artifact with an additional screen on the side, playing for instance a movie or showing a TV program.
(3.) Use the artifact browser extension like Web Disability Simulator (concentration) [20].

Memory is defined as all "specific mental functions of registering and storing information and retrieving it as needed" [41] encompassing both short-term and long-term memory. *Examples* of individuals with memory difficulties are those with short-term or long-term memory loss, dementia, Alzheimer's, and similar [40]. In many cases, ADHD and its variant ADD can have an impact on memory functions as well. We are not aware of any typical *AT* used by this group, but it is worth mentioning that for instance reminder and note taking applications may in general support an individual's memory functions. Examples of potential *barriers* include situations with lengthy text, multiple-step task and problem solving, complex and over-complicated graphical screen layouts, and similar [40]. We propose the following simulation strategies:

(1.) For every instance of use, solve a new task that involves new, unfamiliar parts of the artifact without help and instructions [32].
(2.) Perform multiple-step tasks on the artifact out of order [32].
(3.) In the middle of the solving of a multiple-step task, start over again [32].

Orientation is defined as all "general mental functions of knowing and ascertaining one's relation to self, to others, to time and to one's surroundings" [41]. For digital artifacts, orientation is the ability to orientate to particular targets and to navigate within a given artifact. *Examples* of individuals with orientation difficulties are people with seizure disorders, as well as dementia patients [40]. We are not aware of any typical *AT* used by individuals in this impairment category. Examples of potential *barriers* include situations with complex and over-complicated graphical screen layouts, as well as multiple-step tasks and problem solving. We propose the following simulation strategies:

(1.) For every instance of use, solve a new task that involves new, unfamiliar parts of the given artifact without help and instructions [32].
(2.) Perform multiple-step tasks on the artifact out of order [32].
(3.) Make deliberate mistakes, and try to correct them afterwards [32].
(4.) In the middle of the solving of a multiple-step task, start over again [32].

Reasoning encompasses consciousness function "of the state of awareness and alertness, including the clarity and continuity of the wakeful state" [41], thought functions "related to the ideational component of the mind" [41], and intellectual functions "required to understand and constructively integrate the various mental functions, including all cognitive functions and their development over the lifespan" [41]. For digital artifacts, reasoning is the ability to understand, fathom and explain concepts, ideas, and other abstract aspects of a given artifact, such as an ICT application or system. *Examples* of individuals with reasoning difficulties are people with learning impairments, individuals with Down's syndrome, and others [18,40]. We are not aware of any typical *AT* used by this group. Examples of potential *barriers* include situations with complex and over-complicated screen layouts, lengthy sentences and unusual terms [40] We propose the following simulation strategies:

(1.) For every instance of use, solve a new task that involves new, unfamiliar parts of the given artifact without help and instructions [32].
(2.) Perform multiple-step tasks on the artifact out of order [32].
(3.) Make deliberate mistakes, and try to correct them afterwards [32].
(4.) In the middle of the solving of a multiple-step task, start over again [32].

Coordination and planning encompasses higher-level cognitive functions "including complex goal-directed behaviors such as decision-making, abstract thinking, planning and carrying out plans, mental flexibility, and deciding which behaviors are appropriate under what circumstances; often called executive functions" [41]. For digital artifacts, coordination and planning describes the ability to plan strategies, make decisions, execute tasks and evaluate outcomes of one's behavior. *Examples* of individuals with coordination and planning difficulties are individuals with Down's syndrome [18]. We are not aware of any typical *AT* used by this group. Examples of potential *barriers* include situations with multiple-step problem solving and change of problem-solving strategies [18]. We propose the following simulation strategies:

(1.) For every instance of use, solve a new task that involves new, unfamiliar parts of the given artifact without help and instructions [32].
(2.) Perform multiple-step tasks on the artifact out of order [32].

(3.) Make deliberate mistakes, and try to correct them afterwards [32].
(4.) In the middle of the solving of a multiple-step task, start over again [32].

Linguistics and speech encompasses "specific mental functions of recognizing and using signs, symbols and other components of a language" [41]. This category has some intersections with Sect. 4.3. *Examples* of individuals with speech or linguistics difficulties are people with dyslexia, non-native speakers, speakers with strong accents or dialects, shy/quiet speakers, and individuals with Down's syndrome [18,40] Typical *AT* used by this group are text-to-speech converters, speech synthesizer, digital grammar assistants, translation and lookup services, and similar. Examples of potential *barriers* include situations with complex and over-complicated graphical screen layouts, complex sentences and unfamiliar vocabulary, long text without illustrations, moving, blinking or flickering content, or background audio [40] We propose the following simulation strategies:

(1.) Use the website as if you cannot read [32].
(2.) Use uncommon accents or dialects.
(3.) Use browser extensions like Web Disability Simulator (dyslexia, small vocabulary, etc.) [20].

Social communication and interaction functions are defined as "general mental functions [...] required to understand and constructively integrate the mental functions that lead to the formation of the interpersonal skills needed to establish reciprocal social interactions, in terms of both meaning and purpose" [41]. For digital artifacts, this social communication and interaction encompasses the ability to ask for support or help from, interact with, or take contact with others. *Examples* of individuals with social communication and interaction difficulties are Autism spectrum disorder (ASD) [40]. We are not aware of any typical *AT* used by this group. Examples of potential *barriers* include situations with complex and over-complicated graphical screen layouts, complex sentences and unfamiliar vocabulary, long text without illustrations, moving, blinking or flickering content, or background audio [40] We are not aware of any simulation strategies at the moment.

Mental health and behavior encompasses emotional functions "related to the feeling and affective components of the processes of the mind" [41]. temperament and personality functions "of constitutional disposition of the individual to react in a particular way to situations, including the set of mental characteristics that makes the individual distinct from others" [41]. *Examples* of individuals with mental health and behavior difficulties are anxiety, stress, delirium, depression, paranoia, schizophrenia [40]. We are unaware of any typical *AT* used by this group. Examples of potential *barriers* include situations with complex and over-complicated graphical screen layouts, complex sentences and unfamiliar vocabulary, long text without illustrations, moving, blinking or flickering content, or background audio [40] We propose the following simulation strategies:

(1.) For every instance of use, solve a new task that involves new, unfamiliar parts of the given artifact without help and instructions [32].

(2.) Perform multiple-step tasks on the artifact out of order [32].

(3.) Make deliberate mistakes, and try to correct them afterwards [32].

(4.) In the middle of the solving of a multiple-step task, start over again [32].

(5.) Let yourself get distracted by a radio, or TV, or let yourself be interrupted by a colleague. [32].

(6.) Use a browser extension like the Funkify disability simulator [10].

4.2 Senses

In this section, we discuss the human senses relevant for digital artifacts including seeing, hearing, and touching [41].

Vision addresses all functions related "to sensing the presence of light and sensing the form, size, shape and color of the visual stimuli" [41]. We can subcategorize vision impairments into lack of vision, low vision, reduced color vision, and light sensitivity

Examples of individuals with a lack of vision are those who are blind or deaf-blind [40]. Typical *AT* used by this group are screen readers, refreshable braille displays, magnifiers, and similar. Examples of potential *barriers* include situations where no text alternative is given for visual elements, missing text or audio alternative for videos, or browsing without full keyboard support [40]. We propose the following simulation strategies:

(1.) Use the artifact with screen reader (and turned-off monitor): Jaws, NVDA, VoiceOver, TalkBack, Voice Assistant and others [23, 31].

(2.) Use the artifact with a keyboard only.

(3.) Use the artifact with a non-graphical browser.

Examples of individuals with limited or low vision are those with reduced focus or acuity (i.e., increased blurriness), tunnel vision, central field loss, clouded vision, as well as those affected by cataract, glaucoma, age-related macular degeneration, retinitis pigmentosa, stroke, diabetes retinopathy, and others [40]. Typical *AT* used by this group are magnifiers (both optical and digital), screen readers, and separate color schemes. Examples of potential *barriers* include situations where it is impossible to resize text or images sufficiently, change contrast, or use custom color schemes [40]. We propose the following simulation strategies:

(1.) Increase the distance between eye and monitor, or reduce the browser zoom.

(2.) View the artifact through a tube.

(3.) View the artifact with one eye closed or with peripheral vision only [32].

(4.) View the artifact with a single or multiple layers of Cambridge Simulation Glasses [39].

(5.) Use a browser extension: NoCoffee, Web Disability Simulator, SEE, A11Y, and others [17, 20, 27, 34].

Examples of individuals with reduced color vision are those affected by color vision deficiencies, including deuteranomaly, and protanomaly [40]. Typical *AT* used by this group are special color schemes and frequency band switching glasses. Examples of potential *barriers* include situations where differentiation between two elements is only possible by color alone, or layout ordered by color alone [40]. We propose the following simulation strategies:

(1.) Use low-brightness glasses.
(2.) Use a browser extension: NoCoffee, Web Disability Simulator, SEE, A11Y, and others [17,20,27,34].
(3.) Use of special user style sheets.

Examples of individuals with light sensitivity are people with seizure disorders, including epilepsy and migraines, and people with conditions like retina detachment and meningitis [40]. Typical *AT* used by this group are light-filtering glasses and shields, as well as special color schemes like dark mode. Examples of potential *barriers* include constellations with high-brightness screens, viewing screens in combination with stray light or strong reflections, and visual flickering at certain frequencies and with particular patterns [40]. We propose the following simulation strategies:

(1.) View the artifact with maximum screen brightness.
(2.) View the artifact with a direct strong light source from above, below or from the sides.

Hearing encompasses all functions related "to sensing the presence of sounds and discriminating the location, pitch, loudness and quality of sounds" [41]. We can subcategorize hearing impairments into lack of hearing, and limited hearing.

Lack of hearing is synonymous with deafness [40]. Typical *AT* used by this group are cochlear implants, and transcript and caption services, as well as speech-to-text converters and services [6]. Examples of potential *barriers* include situations where applications rely on the voice alone, such as calling services, and a lack of sign language support [40]. We propose the following simulation strategies:

(1.) Use a muted speaker or headset output.
(2.) Use high-fidelity noise cancellation headsets.

Examples of individuals with a limited hearing function are people with hearing aids, implant-operated, people affected by Tinnitus, as well as many elder individuals and people with Down's syndrome [14,40]. Typical *AT* used by this group are various hearing aids including conversation amplifiers and teleloop systems, various assistive listening and alerting devices, speech-to-text and transcription services, and media playing and volume controls [22,40]. Examples of potential *barriers* include situations where audio content is presented without captions or transcripts, situations with a high level of background noise, and services which lack media playing and volume controls. We propose the following simulation strategies:

(1.) Use reduced speaker or headset volume for media and sound playback.
(2.) Listen to the audio source with background noise.
(3.) Use high-fidelity noise cancellation headsets (with or without additional background noise), or ear plugs.

Touch is defined as all functions related to "sensing surfaces and their texture or quality" [41]. *Examples* of individuals with decreased touch sensation are those affected by numbness (hypoesthesia) caused by illnesses and injuries. We are not aware of any typical *AT* used by this group. Examples of potential *barriers* include situations where alerts are only signaled through vibration, and where temperature is only communicated through heat radiation. We propose the following simulation strategies:

(1.) Use gloves or mittens to decrease sensitivity [32].
(2.) Use the artifact with wet or oily fingers [32].

4.3 Voice

encompasses all functions related to producing sounds and speech [41]. Vocal functions can be sub-categorized into lack of voice, and limited voice.

Examples of individuals with limited voice and lack of voice include people with muteness, stuttering, cluttering, dysarthria, speech sound disorder, individuals affected by stroke, foreign language speakers, and those speaking language dialects [32,40]. Typical *AT* used by this group are augmentative and alternative communication/AAC devices, picture boards, and text-to-speech converters [22]. Examples of potential *barriers* include situations where device control relies on interaction by voice alone, systems that rely on phone lines as only means of communication, home assistants, as well as noisy environments [40]. We propose the following simulation strategies:

(1.) Use without voice, or muted/lowered microphone on headset.
(2.) Use speech distortion.
(3.) High background noise (for interference with voice input).

Examples of limited voice include stuttering, cluttering, dysarthria, speech sound disorder, and similar, stroke-affected, people using a electrolarynx, non-native language speakers, people with a low speaking voice, and those speaking with strong dialects [32,40]. Typical *AT* used by this group are augmentative and alternative communication or AAC devices, picture boards, and text-to-speech converters [22]. Examples of potential *barriers* include situations where device control relies on interaction by voice alone, systems that rely on phone lines as only means of communication, home assistants, as well as noisy environments [40]. We propose the following simulation strategies:

(1.) Use a voice distorter.
(2.) Use the artifact while lowering the microphone input.
(3.) Use uncommon accents or dialects.
(4.) Use the website with loud background noises.

4.4 Movement

This section addresses all human functions related to movement and mobility including functions of joints, bones, reflexes and muscles [41].

Mobility or lower body functions encompasses all functions and impairments related to the lower body structures (legs, feet, pelvis, etc.) and their related actions (standing, walking, getting up, or sitting down) [35,36]. Mobility functions can sub-categorized into limited mobility reach, and limited mobility strength and/or manipulation.

Examples of individuals with limited mobility reach are wheelchair users, amputees, and people suffering from arthritis [32]. Typical *AT* used by this group are wheelchair, crutches, and protheses of various fidelity [32]. Examples of potential *barriers* are stairs, stepping thresholds, narrow aisles, and so on. We propose the following simulation strategies:

(1.) Use the artifact in a wheelchair (manual and/or electrical).
(2.) Use the artifact while using a stroller or walker.
(3.) Use the artifact while using crutches.
(4.) Use the artifact while resting on one leg.

Examples of individuals with limited mobility strength and/or manipulation are people of extreme size or weight, those suffering from Parkinson's disease or multiple sclerosis, stroke or similar, as well as some affected by cerebral palsy [32]. Typical *AT* used by this group are crutches [32]. Examples of potential *barriers* include situations where one has to rise from a seated position or stand upright, games with a stepping mat, and exhibits that need to be controlled by a foot or feet [32]. We propose the following simulation strategies:

(1.) Use the artifact with crutches.
(2.) Use the artifact while resting on one leg.
(3.) Use the artifact with balancing shoes or B-shoes.

Motor or upper body functions are defined as all functions and impairments related to the upper body structures (arms, hands, neck, back, etc.) and their related actions (lifting, grasping, or pushing/pulling) [35,36]. Motor functions can be sub-categorized into limited motor reach, and limited motor strength and/or manipulation.

Examples of individuals with limited motor reach are people with amputations, those suffering from arthritis, carpal tunnel syndrome, and others, as well as conditions related to cerebral palsy [32]. Typical *AT* used by this group are head-operated pointing devices, mouth stick, on-screen keyboard with trackball, joystick, or switch-operated by foot, shoulder, or head [40]. Examples of potential *barriers* include situations that require two arms or two hands for interaction, and situations with the need to push a button or lever or to turn a wheel [32]. We propose the following simulation strategies:

(1.) Use the artifact with the hand tied to body through rubber band, or elbow fixated against the body [32].
(2.) Use the artifact with a rope with weight around wrist [32].
(3.) Use the artifact with a single hand or single arm [32].
(4.) Use a Browser Extension: Web Disability Simulator [20].

Examples of individuals with limited motor strength and/or manipulation are those suffering from Parkinson's disease, multiple sclerosis, stroke, people with muscular dystrophy, tremor and spasms, as well as repetitive stress injury/RSI, and many affected by cerebral palsy [32,40]. Typical *AT* used by this group are ergonomic keyboard or mouse, voice recognition, eye tracking, and exoskeleton [40]. Examples of potential *barriers* for these users include situations that require precise input on screen or keyboard, repeated input over time, no full or limited keyboard support, insufficient time limits, faulty navigation mechanisms and page functions, and the simple need to push a button or turn a wheel [32,40]. We propose the following simulation strategies:

(1.) Use the artifact with plastic or simulation gloves (such as Cambridge Simulation Glasses, with various material thicknesses, increased push resistance, larger area of touch, and similar [39]).
(2.) Use the artifact with mittens or fists.
(3.) Use the artifact with single (unfamiliar) finger of the dominant and non-dominant hand [32].

5   Pilot Study of SUIT on Clothes4All

We tested the protocol on an artifact we developed, called Clothes4All, which is website that can be used to study different aspects of web accessibility. The artifact is a fictive online shop that sells clothes for all, and can be accessed under www.clothes4all.net (cf. Fig. 2a). The website shows how the WCAG 2.1 can be implemented in practice, at the same time as it gives the user the option to toggle on/off conformance to various WCAG success criteria (cf. Fig. 2b). By toggling WCAG success criteria on/off, the user can investigate how a website with high conformance to WCAG can compare to a website with low conformance to WCAG, at the same time as experienced developers and designers can inspect the source code of the website for best-practice examples.

When designing the pilot study of SUIT on Clothes4All, we defined a set of tasks relevant to the content of the website:

" (1.) Scenario 1: Obtaining information about the products. You want to know more about the various offers and deals.
  (a.) What is the product for women with the lowest price currently on sale? How much do you save compared to previously?

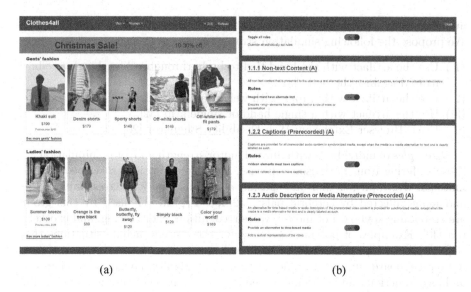

(a)   (b)

Fig. 2. (a) The homepage of Clothes4All, a fictive online shop selling clothes that fit all. (b) Examples for some of the WCAG 2.1 rules that users can toggle on/off.

> (b.) Is the leather coat for men on sale?
> (c.) Are the slim-fit denim jeans for women on sale?
> (d.) ...
> (2.) Scenario 2: Buying men's clothing. You want to buy some men's clothing. Complete the following tasks. Please start with an empty shopping basket.
> (a.) How many categories of men's fashion do you find?
> (b.) How many fashion items for men are in the following categories:
>   i. Suits.
>   ii. Blazers.
>   iii. Shirts.
> (c.) ...
> (3.) ...

Examples of possible tasks for Clothes4All   "

Then, we defined a metric according to which the tasks should be evaluated:

> (1.) Could you solve the task? Yes/No (If you cannot solve the task within XX minutes, you should mark the case as unsolvable.)
> (a.) If No: What prevented you from completing the task? What barriers did you encounter?
> (2.) How much time did you use for solving the task? Measure the so-called time-on-task, e.g. from the beginning of solving the task until either it is completed or abandoned.

(3.) Please write down some descriptions, explanations, or comments around the process.

(4.) How satisfied are you with the process? Pick a number on a scale from 1 to 10, where 1 is least satisfied, and 10 is most satisfied. Set a number on how you experienced the process. Think of the variety of feelings that may have been involved, e.g. joy, frustration, like, dislike, curiosity, surprise, or confusion.

The SUIT metric for Clothes4All   ''

Finally, we customized the SUIT protocol (cf. Sect. 3) for the Clothes4All website:

''
(1.) Choose a single or multiple user impairments that you want to simulate. Please consult Sect. 2.4 for a list of impairments.

(2.) Pick the appropriate tools, e.g. assistive technologies (ATs) or equipment, from the SUIT toolbox. A collection of tools for any particular impairment is included in Sect. 4.

(3.) Turn off one or several of the associated success criterion switches in the settings/rule set of Clothes4All.

(4.) Now pick one task of your choice from the provided list. Try to solve the task once with the relevant success criterion switches turned off as described in the previous step (this equals the first trial), and then with all switches turned on (equals the second trial). Write down your observations according to the metric defined before.

The SUIT protocol for Clothes4All   ''

During the test trial, we went through all categories and picked one simulation tool for each category. We then recorded the data according to the results. The goal of this trial run was to investigate the feasibility and practicability of the SUIT protocol and toolbox, rather than uncovering barriers on the website. After all, the website was designed in a way that it offered one version that was more accessible and usable than the others. Thus, we knew where we could expect to find barriers and challenges. In other words, the purpose of the trial was not to discover barriers themselves, but to investigate whether or not the protocol and the tools where appropriate to discover barriers and challenges on the artifact.

6 Discussion

To begin with, we could conduct the trial successfully simulating each of the categories mentioned in the toolbox above (cf. Sect. 4). However, performance and relevance differed for some of the categories. Simulations of sensory impairments performed quite well, and sensory tools could easily be obtained. There is, for example, a variety of models and tools that predict various visual impairments like color vision deficiencies and others. Thus, we could choose among multiple tools, plug-ins and products to simulate the experience of people with sensory impairments. The same can be said about auditory impairment simulation tools. Likewise, movement-related impairments simulation tools were easily available and applicable in a regular office setting. At the same time, the motor-related simulation tools were more relevant for our digital artifact than the mobility-related tools. The reason for this is the fact that the user interacts mostly with their upper body extremities, e.g., the arms and hands, rather than their lower body extremities. In contrast, tools representing cognitive impairments had limited availability, and questionable accuracy. Cognitive process can be very subjective, and models are not readily available. Some of the tools or methods for simulation described in this paper can be very vague or inaccurate. Thus, the results should be interpreted carefully.

Moreover, the relevance for some of the tools depend strongly on the type of digital ICT artifact that is investigated. We were testing on a website artifact that mainly stimulates visual and auditory senses while relaying on input from upper body extremities. At the same time, the tasks required significant cognitive interaction. Lower body and touch-related functions were not as relevant for the investigated artifact. This could be different for other digital ICT artifacts like museum exhibitions, where users are encouraged to watch, touch, interact with, walk into, lift, or manipulate the artifact [13]. Testing for wheelchair accessibility is for example more relevant for a museum exhibition that a user can walk into than it is for a website. We want to evaluate the relevance of the SUIT protocol and toolbox for other areas by testing them on other digital ICT artifacts like museum exhibits in future research.

One of the strengths of the SUIT toolbox is that it can help to raise awareness and increase visibility for people with impairments and their needs. While using a screen reader, a tool that is very common among people with low-vision or blindness, we became aware of how missing labels and alt-texts can significantly decrease the user experience of a given digital ICT artifact. Likewise, retrieving auditory information from a video without subtitles while the sound was turned off was obviously impossible. We argue that designers and developers using the simulation tools will more easily understand the importance of accessibility and usability guidelines for their products. Likewise, the tools can increase the acceptance and dissemination of accessibility and usability guidelines, checklists, and best-practice examples.

One challenge of the SUIT toolbox was the accuracy of the categorization. The list of simulation methods in Sect. 4 does not represent a complete set of simulation methods for the experiences that people with impairments may encounter. In the same way, the (sub)categories do not represent all possible impairments. The (sub)categories can be organized differently depending on a given project or user needs. For online artifacts, for example, mobility barriers are less relevant than for museum exhibits [13]. It is very common that the categorization of human impairments differ throughout the literature [8,13,28,44].

Moreover, we intended to integrate the SUIT simulation toolbox into a meaningful testing routine for accessibility and usability following clearly defined procedures. As described in Sect. 3, designers and developers should define concrete tasks and their desired outcome beforehand. The outcome should be measurable according to observable metrics like pass/fail, success rate, or completion time. By defining observable metrics, testing results will become comparable over time, as well as allowing developers and designers to compare and weigh various options and solutions against each other. These comparisons will not only help development within any ongoing project but have the potential of being transferable to other future or previous projects as well.

Finally, the SUIT simulation toolbox is not intended to replace thorough user testing including people with impairments. It is intended as additional quality assessment during the production and development process that has the potential of mitigating some of the most basic barriers that can arise during the development of a project. Thus, it is still necessary to conduct multiple iterative cycles with user testing involving people with impairments to increase accessibility and usability of the digital ICT artifact. One reason for this is that simulation methods will never be able to capture the complete experience of people with impairments. People that use simulation tools for a limited time span, will experience digital ICT artifacts differently than people who must live with the limitations of an impairment on a daily basis. People with impairments have, for example, strategies and mechanisms to cope with and mitigate some of the most common challenges and barriers of typical ICT artifacts. These strategies might be unknown to non-disabled people who can develop alternative coping strategies that might be irrelevant for people with impairments. In other words, user testing with people with impairment is still the most important necessity to increase accessibility and usability of a digital ICT artifact for all.

7   Conclusion

In this paper, we present a protocol and toolbox for Simulated User Impairment Testing (SUIT) that allows designers and developers to experience the perspectives of users with impairments during the development of a digital ICT artifact through simulation tools. By using simulation tools, designers and developers can assess their digital ICT artifact through the eyes and bodies of a person with impairments and varying abilities. With The tools of the Simulated User Impairment Testing (SUIT) toolbox, designers and developers can simulate the experience of people with cognitive, visual, auditory, vocal and movement-related impairments. We show how these tools can be used to evaluate the design process of a digital ICT artifact using the SUIT protocol. The observations from our prototype trial show that the tools and methods can be easily implemented and integrated into an agile design and development workflow. We show that the SUIT toolbox can meet the economical and practical demands and restrictions imposed by the industry. At the same time, we observed that sensory impairments, related to vision, hearing, and touch, as well as physical impairments could be easily simulated. However, there were only a few reliable simulations for cognitive impairments. Finally, we argue that this kind of simulation approach can raise awareness for and acceptance of the needs and experiences of people with impairments. In future research, we see the need to extend the simulation strategies specifically for cognitive impairments. In the present paper, we could only test the SUIT protocol and toolbox on websites, which was within the scope defined in our research project called Clothes4All. However, other digital ICT artifacts like museum exhibits can have more focus on other human functions like mobility or motor than websites. Thus, we want to test the SUIT protocol and toolbox on other digital ICT artifacts like museum exhibits in future research as well.

Acknowledgement. This work was partly supported by the UnIKT program of the Norwegian Directorate for Children, Youth and Family Affairs.

References

1. Bai, A., Fuglerud, K.S., Skjerve, R.A., Halbach, T.: Categorization and comparison of accessibility testing methods for software development. Stud. Health Technol. Inform. **256**, 821–831 (2018). https://europepmc.org/article/med/30371447
2. Bai, A., Mork, H.C., Stray, V.: A cost-benefit evaluation of accessibility testing in agile software development. ICSEA **2016**, 75 (2016)
3. Bai, A., Skjerve, R., Halbach, T., Fuglerud, K.: Evaluating accessibility testing in automated software build processes. In: Norsk IKT-konferanse for forskning og utdanning, November 2019. https://ojs.bibsys.no/index.php/NIK/article/view/646
4. Begnum, M.E.N.: Universal design of ICT: a historical journey from specialized adaptations towards designing for diversity. In: Antona, M., Stephanidis, C. (eds.) HCII 2020. LNCS, vol. 12188, pp. 3–18. Springer, Cham (2020). https://doi.org/10.1007/978-3-030-49282-3_1
5. Bonacin, R., Dos Reis, J.C., Baranauskas, M.C.C.: Universal participatory design: achievements and challenges. SBC J. Interact. Syst. **10**(1), 2–16 (2019)
6. Clerk Center, Gallaudet University: Assistive Technology (2017). https://clerc center.gallaudet.edu/national-resources/info/info-to-go/assistive-technology.html. Accessed 24 Feb 2022
7. Cooper, A.: The inmates are running the asylum. In: Software-Ergonomie 1999. Springer, Cham (1999). https://doi.org/10.1007/978-3-322-99786-9_1
8. European Telecommunications Standards Institute (ETSI): EN 301 549 v3.1.1 (2019–06): Accessibility requirements for ICT products and services, June 2019
9. European Union (EU): Web Accessibility Directive (WAD) - Directive (EU) 2016/2102, October 2016. https://eur-lex.europa.eu/eli/dir/2016/2102/oj. Accessed 23 Feb 2021
10. Funkfiy: Funkify (2022). https://www.funkify.org/. Accessed 24 Feb 2022
11. Giannoumis, G.A.: Implementing web accessibility policy. Case studies of the United Kingdom, Norway, and the United States. Ph.D. thesis, The University of Bergen, June 2019. http://hdl.handle.net/1956/21054
12. Halbach, T., Simon-Liedtke, J.T.: Categories of user impairment. In: IADIS International Conference on Interfaces and Human Computer Interaction 2021 (part of MCCSIS 2021) (2021). https://nr.brage.unit.no/nr-xmlui/handle/11250/2766973

13. Halbach, T., Tjøstheim, I.: Towards reliable accessibility assessments of science center exhibits. In: Lamas, D., Loizides, F., Nacke, L., Petrie, H., Winckler, M., Zaphiris, P. (eds.) INTERACT 2019. LNCS, vol. 11746, pp. 33–41. Springer, Cham (2019). https://doi.org/10.1007/978-3-030-29381-9_3

14. Hørselshemmedes Landsforbund (HLF): Om HLF (2022). https://www.hlf.no/kontakt-oss/om-hlf/. Accessed 24 Feb 2022

15. Kommunal-og moderniseringsdepartementet: Forskrift om universell utforming av informasjons-og kommunikasjonsteknologiske (ikt)-løsninger (for-2013-06-21-732), June 2013. https://lovdata.no/dokument/SF/forskrift/2013-06-21-732. Accessed 17 Sept 2020

16. Kulturdepartementet: Lov om likestilling og forbud mot diskriminering (likestillings-og diskrimineringsloven, lov-2017-06-16-51), June 2017. https://lovdata.no/dokument/NL/lov/2017-06-16-51. Accessed 17 Sept 2020

17. Leventhal, A.: NoCoffee - Vision simulator for chrome, February 2013. https://accessgarage.wordpress.com/2013/02/09/458/. Accessed 24 Feb 2022

18. Malt, E.A., et al.: Health and disease in adults with Down syndrome. Tidsskrift for Den norske legeforening, February 2013. https://doi.org/10.4045/tidsskr.12.0390, https://tidsskriftet.no/en/2013/02/health-and-disease-adults-down-syndrome

19. McFadden, E., Hager, D.R., Elie, C.J., Blackwell, J.M.: Remote usability evaluation: overview and case studies. Int. J. Hum.-Comput. Interact. 14(3–4), 489–502 (2002). https://doi.org/10.1080/10447318.2002.9669131

20. Metamatrix: Web Disability Simulator - Chrome Nettmarked (2019). https://chrome.google.com/webstore/detail/web-disability-simulator/olioanlbgbpmdlgjnnampnnlohigkjla. Accessed 24 Feb 2022

21. Miljøverndepartementet: T-1468 B/E Universell utforming, November 2007. https://www.regjeringen.no/no/dokumenter/t-1468-universell-utforming/id493083/

22. National Institute on Deafness and Other Communication Disorders (NIDCD): Assistive Devices for People with Hearing, Voice, Speech, or Language Disorders, November 2019. https://www.nidcd.nih.gov/health/assistive-devices-people-hearing-voice-speech-or-language-disorders. Accessed 9 Nov 2020

23. Norges Blindeforbund: Skjermleser, March 2021. https://www.blindeforbundet.no/hjelpemidler-og-produkter/skjermleser. Accessed 24 Feb 2022

24. Petrie, H., Bevan, N.: The evaluation of accessibility, usability, and user experience. In: The Universal Access Handbook, vol. 1, pp. 1–16 (2009)

25. Power, C., Petrie, H.: Working with participants. In: Yesilada, Y., Harper, S. (eds.) Web Accessibility. HIS, pp. 153–168. Springer, London (2019). https://doi.org/10.1007/978-1-4471-7440-0_9

26. Pruitt, J., Grudin, J.: Personas: practice and theory. In: Proceedings of the 2003 Conference on Designing for User Experiences, DUX 2003, San Francisco, California, pp. 1–15. Association for Computing Machinery, June 2003. https://doi.org/10.1145/997078.997089

27. Q42: SEE, June 2014. https://github.com/Q42/SEE. Accessed 24 Feb 2022

28. Sauer, J., Sonderegger, A., Schmutz, S.: Usability, user experience and accessibility: towards an integrative model. Ergonomics 63(10), 1207–1220 (2020). https://doi.org/10.1080/00140139.2020.1774080

29. Schmutz, S., Sonderegger, A., Sauer, J.: Implementing recommendations from web accessibility guidelines: would they also provide benefits to nondisabled users. Hum. Factors 58(4), 611–629 (2016). https://doi.org/10.1177/0018720816640962

30. Schmutz, S., Sonderegger, A., Sauer, J.: Effects of accessible website design on nondisabled users: age and device as moderating factors. Ergonomics **61**(5), 697–709 (2018). https://doi.org/10.1080/00140139.2017.1405080

31. Statlig spesialpedagogisk tjeneste (Statped): Skjermleserne TalkBack og Voice Assistant for Android (2019). https://www.statped.no/laringsressurser/syn/opplaring-i-mobil-og-nettbrett/android-for-synshemmede/skjermleserne-talkback-og-voice-assistent-for-android/. Accessed 24 Feb 2022

32. Story, M.F., Mueller, J.L., Mace, R.L.: The Universal Design File: Designing for People of All Ages and Abilities, Revised Edition. Center for Universal Design, NC State University, Raleigh (1998). https://eric.ed.gov/?id=ED460554

33. Stray, V., Bai, A., Sverdrup, N., Mork, H.: Empowering Agile project members with accessibility testing tools: a case study. In: Kruchten, P., Fraser, S., Coallier, F. (eds.) XP 2019. LNBIP, vol. 355, pp. 86–101. Springer, Cham (2019). https://doi.org/10.1007/978-3-030-19034-7_6

34. The A11Y Project (2021). https://a11yproject.com/. Accesed 24 Feb 2022

35. The US Census Bureau: Americans with Disabilities: 2010, July 2012. https://www.census.gov/library/publications/2012/demo/p70-131.html

36. The US Census Bureau: Americans with Disabilities: 2014, November 2018. https://www.census.gov/library/publications/2018/demo/p70-152.html

37. United Nations High Commissioner for Refugees (UNHCR): Disability: Prevalence and Impact - Syrian Arab Republic. Humanitarian Needs Assessment Programme (HNAP), September 2019. A Nationwide Household Survey Using Washington Group Methodology

38. United Nations (UN): Convention on the rights of persons with disabilities (CRPD) (2006). https://www.un.org/development/desa/disabilities/convention-on-the-rights-of-persons-with-disabilities.html

39. University of Cambridge: Cambridge Simulation Glasses (2017). http://www.inclusivedesigntoolkit.com/csg/csg.html. Accessed 24 Feb 2022

40. W3C Web Accessibility Initiative (WAI): Diverse Abilities and Barriers, October 2020. https://www.w3.org/WAI/people-use-web/abilities-barriers/. Accessed 15 Oct 2020

41. World Health Organization (WHO): International Classification of Functioning, Disability and Health (ICF), May 2001. https://www.who.int/classifications/icf/en/. Accessed 10 Nov 2020

42. World Wide Web Consortium (W3C): Web content accessibility guidelines (WCAG) 2.0, December 2008. https://www.w3.org/TR/WCAG20/. Accessed 17 Sept 2020

43. World Wide Web Consortium (W3C): Web content accessibility guidelines (WCAG) 2.1, June 2018. https://www.w3.org/TR/WCAG21/. Accessed 17 Sept 2020

44. World Wide Web Consortium (W3C): Web content accessibility guidelines (WCAG) 2.2 [working draft], August 2020. https://www.w3.org/TR/WCAG22/. Accessed 17 Sept 2020

Ensembling and Score-Based Filtering in Sentence Alignment for Automatic Simplification of German Texts

Nicolas Spring[(✉)] [iD], Marek Kostrzewa [iD], Annette Rios [iD], and Sarah Ebling [iD]

Department of Computational Linguistics, University of Zurich, Zurich, Switzerland
{spring,mkostr,rios,ebling}@cl.uzh.ch

Abstract. Among the well-known accessibility services for audiovisual media are subtitling for the deaf and hard-of-hearing, audio description, and sign language interpreting. More recently, automatic text simplification has emerged as a topic in the context of media accessibility, with research often approaching the task as a case of (sentence-based) monolingual machine translation. This approach relies on large amounts of high-quality parallel data, which is why monolingual sentence alignment has gained momentum. Alignment for text simplification is a complex task, with alignments often taking the form of n:m (in contrast to the standard case of 1:1 in machine translation). In this contribution, we evaluate the performance of different alignment methods against a human-created gold standard of standard German/simplified German sentence alignments created from a number of parallel corpora. Two of the corpora contain multiple levels of simplification.

We employ a variety of alignment methods developed for monolingual tasks and bilingual sentence alignment. We explore strategies such as ensembling and score-based filtering to further improve the performance over these baselines. We show that combining multiple alignment methods with various hard voting strategies can outperform even the best individual methods and that we achieve similar results with score-based filtering of extracted alignments to find the most promising candidates. Our results motivate the notion that the overall task of sentence alignment for automatic simplification of German should be viewed as a two-step process that goes beyond the application of individual alignment methods.

Keywords: Media accessibility · Text simplification · Sentence alignment · Simplified language

Funded by the Austrian Research Promotion Agency (*Österreichische Forschungsförderungsgesellschaft*, FFG) General Programme under grant agreement number 881202.

ⓒ The Author(s), under exclusive license to Springer Nature Switzerland AG 2022
M. Antona and C. Stephanidis (Eds.): HCII 2022, LNCS 13308, pp. 137–149, 2022.
https://doi.org/10.1007/978-3-031-05028-2_8

1 Introduction

Simplified language[1] is a variety of standard language characterized by reduced lexical and syntactic complexity, the addition of explanations for difficult concepts, and clearly structured layout. Simplified German has received ever growing attention due to a number of legal and political developments in German-speaking countries, such as the introduction of a set of regulations for accessible information technology (*Barrierefreie-Informationstechnik-Verordnung, BITV 2.0*) in Germany, the approval of rules for accessible information and communication (*Barrierefreie Information und Kommunikation, BIK*) in Austria, and the ratification of the United Nations Convention on the Rights of Persons with Disabilities (CRPD) in Germany, Austria, and Switzerland.

In today's society, accessibility is a primary concern in the audiovisual media. Traditional accessibility services include subtitling for the deaf and hard-of-hearing, audio description, and sign language interpreting. More recently, text simplification, i.e., the process of generating simplified language, has become important. In its automated form, as automatic text simplification (ATS), in order to be approached with neural models, the task relies on large quantities of data. With research often approaching ATS as a case of sentence-based monolingual machine translation, the need for tools to produce high-quality sentence alignments emerges.

Automatically obtaining sentence alignments in the context of ATS is a challenging task due to a variety of factors. Crucially, sentence alignment in ATS is less parallel when compared to other fields such as (traditional) machine translation. Alignments of the form n:m are common, which means that multiple source segments can be aligned to multiple target segments. This is due to sentence splitting and sentence compression, which are frequently used in text simplification. In addition, there can be unaligned segments on the source (deletion of unnecessary content) and target (additional explanations) sides. The order of information is not fixed and often changes in the simplification process to create a more clear and concise text structure.

This paper reports on experiments applying various tools for automatic sentence alignment to pairs of standard German/simplified German documents and evaluating them against a human-created gold standard. We show that the tools have varying strengths and weaknesses and propose ways to improve the results *post-hoc*, i.e., after generating the alignments. In particular, the contributions of this paper are the following:

---

[1] The term "simplified language" is used to denote the sum of all "comprehensibility-enhanced varieties of natural languages" [6, p. 52], i.e., what is commonly termed "Easy Language" (German *leichte Sprache*) and "Plain Language" (German *einfache Sprache*). "Easy-to-understand language" has been mentioned as an umbrella term subsuming these varieties [6, p. 52]. However, in this contribution, we prefer the term "simplified language" to emphasize the notion of the result of a simplification process.

– We analyze the performance of various alignment methods on a human-created gold standard and show how design choices of the alignment methods influence the results.
– We show that a combination of alignment tools can outperform even the best of the selected alignment tools in isolation.
– We propose filtering the alignments by calculating various overlap-based metrics between the two sides of an alignment only to keep the most promising candidates.

Our results suggest that after applying tools to extract alignments, there is room for improvement by reducing the set of these candidates in a separate step.

The remainder of this paper is structured as follows: Sect. 2 describes previous work in alignment for ATS as well as metrics for evaluating ATS, which we use for filtering. Section 3 reports on our evaluation of the alignment tools and our approaches to ensembling and filtering. We discuss our results in Sect. 4 and conclude the paper in Sect. 5 with further thoughts on improving automatic sentence alignment in the context of ATS and current challenges to overcome.

2   Previous Work

2.1   Sentence Alignment in Automatic Text Simplification

The popularity of Newsela [16] and the Parallel Wikipedia [4,19] corpora have contributed towards the dominance of research on monolingual sentence alignment predominantly in the English language. Many tools and techniques [7,8,15] have been proposed to extract alignments between corresponding complex and simple sentences. In addition, tools initially developed for multilingual alignments such as SentenceBERT [12] and Vecalign [13] have been applied to text simplification [14].

Evaluating alignment methods requires a gold standard. As such gold alignments have to be created manually, they are comparatively rare in text simplification research. The most recent gold standards for English are NEWSELA-MANUAL and WIKI-MANUAL [5]. The authors used a neural alignment model to capture paraphrases and the context of surrounding sentences and manually annotated these results in addition. Non-English resources for sentence alignment in the context of ATS are scarce.

2.2   Automatic Evaluation of Text Simplification

Research on automatic evaluation of machine translation and ATS is concerned with finding metrics that correlate well with human judgement. To this end, a variety of metrics have been proposed: BLEU [9] is a commonly applied metric when evaluating ATS models and the *de-facto* standard for automatic evaluation of machine translation. It computes token n-gram overlap between a hypothesis and one or multiple references. While BLEU is widely used, it has been criticized for its reliance on exact token matches, which ignore different lexical choices (e.g. inflections or synonyms) that naturally occur in translation. The METEOR metric [1] has been proposed to address this by matching morphological variants. It is thus able to take into account differences due to inflection and synonyms. Another approach to this problem was proposed with BERTScore [18]. BERTScore foregoes the use of (near-)exact matches and instead uses token similarities with contextual embeddings to measure similarity.

For ATS, SARI [17] is often used, a metric developed specifically for this task. It is designed to punish excessive copying behaviour. SARI considers the input and rewards correct additions (tokens in the hypothesis that are not in the input but in one of the references) as well as deletions (tokens in the input that are neither in the hypothesis nor any of the references) and correctly retained tokens (tokens in the hypothesis that are in the input and one of the references). Because SARI requires a source text, which does not exist for pairs of aligned sentences, it is not included in our experiments on score-based filtering (cf. Sect. 3.4).

3   Improving Sentence Alignment for Simplified German

3.1   Gold Standard

For our experiments, we used a gold standard of sentence alignments manually created within our group [10,11,14]. It contains alignments for standard German/simplified German document pairs from four different corpora: The first is the Austria Presse Agentur (*Austrian Press Agency*; APA) corpus consisting of news articles simplified into two levels, A2 and B1, according to the Common European Framework of Reference for Languages (CEFR) [3]. The simplification levels are linguistically operationalized (concerning permitted constructions and content retention requirements) and follow the guidelines of capito[2], the largest provider of human simplification services for German. The news articles cover topics such as sports, culture, politics and economy. The second corpus consists of texts produced in-house by capito. These are mainly information and legal texts as well as websites. Here, simplifications exist on three levels: A1, A2, and B1. For the two remaining corpora, there are no distinct simplification levels: The first is the Web Corpus [2], a collection of web documents from Germany, Austria and Switzerland that cover politics, health and culture. The second corpus is a parallel corpus of articles from the German Wikipedia aligned with translations of the Simple English Wikipedia generated via DeepL[3].

For the gold standard, documents corresponding to a total length of 1,500 simplified German sentences per corpus were randomly selected and manually aligned by two human annotators. A third person acted as arbitrator and made the final decision in cases of disagreement. All persons involved were native speakers of German. The alignments in the gold standard are n:m, meaning that a complex segment can have multiple simple counterparts and *vice versa*.

---

[2] https://www.capito.eu/.
[3] https://www.deepl.com.

3.2   Alignment Methods

In our experiments, we evaluated three alignment methods developed for monolingual tasks, namely CATS [15], MASSAlign [8], and LHA [7], and two alignment methods developed in the context of bilingual sentence alignment, SentenceBERT [12] and Vecalign [13]. They offer different functionalities and utilize various strategies to localize alignment between sentences in comparable corpora, influencing the number and nature of obtained alignments. MASSAlign [8] uses an incremental vicinity search and TF-IDF cosine similarity applied on a paragraph and sentence level. CATS [15] aligns sentences based on Most Similar Text (MST) and the Longest Increase Sequences of Most Similar Text (MST-LIS) heuristics. It uses the word embeddings or surface-level character n-grams. LHA [7] applies hierarchical search over pre-trained embeddings of sentences.

For all tools, alignments were created using the Sentence Alignment Tools Evaluation Framework (SATEF)[4]. This framework provides a controlled environment for evaluating and testing different alignment tools. It unifies the processing pipeline, handles different input formats, and produces standardized output enriched with various evaluation metrics. The alignments were extracted using the default configuration settings of the tools.

The gold standard and the extracted alignments were converted into 1:1 alignments using the Vecalign[5] scoring script to enable a standardized comparison. This means that all alignments of a higher order than 1:1 were expanded to their individual edges (e.g., an alignment of the order 3:1 was split into three 1:1 alignments with different source IDs all pointing to the same target ID; cf. Fig. 1).

From the resulting set of 1:1 alignments, precision, recall and F1 scores were calculated against the human-created gold standard. These baseline results are displayed in Tables 1, 2, and 3. As can be seen, the results differ considerably between the alignment methods and the corpora making up the gold standard. LHA, SentenceBERT, and Vecalign were the best alignment methods in terms of F1. However, the F1 scores do not give the complete picture, as there are significant differences in precision and recall among these three best-performing methods: While SentenceBERT had the highest recall of all tools, the alignments of LHA (and MASSAlign) were much more precise. This shows that the methods have different strengths and weaknesses. Moreover, the gold standard is not homogeneous and the corpora of which it is composed differ in the degree of challenge that they pose for the alignment task. Generally, according to the scores, APA and Wiki data was more problematic to align than Web and capito.

3.3   Ensembling

As was shown in Sect. 3.2, LHA, SentenceBERT, and Vecalign performed best. Following the common practice of ensembling in machine learning, where a combination of systems often outperforms the best single system, we combined the

---

[4] https://github.com/kostrzmar/SATEF.

[5] https://github.com/thompsonb/vecalign.

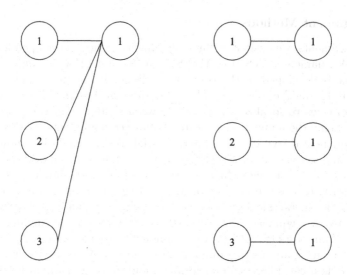

Fig. 1. An example for splitting complex alignments: The source segments 1, 2, and 3 are all aligned with target segment 1 (sentence compression), rendering it a single 3:1 alignment. This is converted to three individual 1:1 alignments.

Table 1. Precision of the evaluated alignment methods.

Method	APA A2	APA B1	Web	Wiki	Cap A1	Cap A2	Cap B1	Mean
CATS C3G	0.055	0.057	0.021	0.02	0.036	0.035	0.031	0.036
CATS WAVG	0.036	0.043	0.016	0.017	0.025	0.025	0.024	0.027
CATS CWASA	0.048	0.048	0.017	0.019	0.031	0.029	0.023	0.031
LHA	**0.153**	**0.186**	0.35	0.127	0.102	0.371	**0.714**	0.286
MASSAlign	0.115	0.156	**0.458**	**0.254**	**0.24**	**0.463**	0.373	0.294
SentenceBERT	0.072	0.07	0.157	0.058	0.134	0.27	0.237	0.143
Vecalign	0.076	0.06	0.185	0.071	0.217	0.448	0.168	0.175
Mean	0.148	0.164	0.304	0.142	0.219	0.388	0.357	

Table 2. Recall of the evaluated alignment methods.

Method	APA A2	APA B1	Web	Wiki	Cap A1	Cap A2	Cap B1	Mean
CATS C3G	0.194	0.193	0.046	0.212	0.06	0.039	0.033	0.111
CATS WAVG	0.131	0.151	0.036	0.177	0.046	0.032	0.028	0.086
CATS CWASA	0.173	0.166	0.039	0.2	0.055	0.034	0.026	0.099
LHA	0.147	0.251	0.329	0.257	0.096	0.283	0.4	0.252
MASSAlign	0.042	0.066	0.108	0.087	0.06	0.151	0.066	0.083
SentenceBERT	**0.274**	**0.253**	**0.355**	**0.461**	**0.44**	**0.489**	**0.498**	0.396
Vecalign	0.105	0.077	0.192	0.076	0.214	0.348	0.153	0.166
Mean	0.173	0.177	0.212	0.239	0.213	0.291	0.243	

Table 3. F1 scores of the evaluated alignment methods.

Method	APA A2	APA B1	Web	Wiki	Cap A1	Cap A2	Cap B1	Mean
CATS C3G	0.086	0.088	0.029	0.037	0.045	0.037	0.032	0.051
CATS WAVG	0.057	0.067	0.022	0.031	0.032	0.028	0.026	0.038
CATS CWASA	0.075	0.074	0.024	0.035	0.039	0.031	0.024	0.043
LHA	**0.150**	**0.213**	**0.339**	**0.170**	0.099	0.321	**0.513**	0.258
MASSAlign	0.062	0.092	0.175	0.13	0.096	0.228	0.112	0.128
SentenceBERT	0.114	0.11	0.218	0.104	0.205	0.348	0.321	0.203
Vecalign	0.088	0.067	0.188	0.073	**0.215**	**0.392**	0.16	0.169
Mean	0.112	0.119	0.195	0.111	0.165	0.277	0.231	

alignments extracted by these three methods. This was done via hard voting, which means that each alignment method had a single vote (classifying a segment pair as an alignment or not) and all votes were weighted equally, ignoring internal metrics of the alignment methods such as cosine similarity. The votes of the different classifiers were combined through three strategies:

- With the "any" strategy, all alignments found by any tool were included in the output. This strategy is expected to yield the highest recall.
- The "all" strategy is the opposite: Only alignments found by all three tools were included in the final set. This strategy likely results in the highest precision, assuming that good alignments tend to be found by multiple tools.
- Following the "majority" strategy, only alignments found by at least two of the three tools were included in the alignment output. This strategy results in a middle ground between precision and recall.

The results of our ensembling experiments are shown in Tables 4, 5, and 6. The "all" and "majority" voting strategies improve the mean F1 score of the best single alignment method (LHA with a mean of 0.258): With "all", we reach an F1 score of 0.275, while the "majority" strategy results in an F1 score of 0.336. We also observe that the "any" strategy maximized recall and the "all" strategy maximized precision, as expected. The "majority" method, which has no bias towards either of the two metrics precision and recall, achieved the best combined result. The higher F1 score of the "all" method compared to "any" can be explained by the composition of our gold standard corpora and the nature of the alignment task itself. The number of correct alignments is much smaller than the number of theoretically possible alignments, which means that a focus on recall is prone to returning a large number of bad alignments. This harms precision to a greater extent than a focus on precision would harm recall. Thus, these experiments motivate the notion that a focus on recall is less essential in terms of F1 than a focus on precision when creating sentence alignments on our corpora.

Table 4. Precision of the three hard voting strategies combining LHA, SentenceBERT, and Vecalign.

Method	APA A2	APA B1	Web	Wiki	Cap A1	Cap A2	Cap B1	Mean
All	**0.586**	**0.792**	**0.92**	**0.538**	**0.667**	1	1	0.786
Any	0.068	0.062	0.167	0.054	0.153	0.307	0.214	0.146
Majority	0.271	0.164	0.751	0.266	0.582	0.936	0.786	0.537

Table 5. Recall of the three hard voting strategies combining LHA, SentenceBERT, and Vecalign.

Method	APA A2	APA B1	Web	Wiki	Cap A1	Cap A2	Cap B1	Mean
All	0.094	0.137	0.195	0.1	0.182	0.185	0.28	0.168
Any	**0.389**	**0.355**	**0.569**	**0.571**	**0.692**	**0.886**	**0.716**	0.597
Majority	0.179	0.122	0.252	0.25	0.281	0.465	0.232	0.254

3.4   Score-Based Filtering

Our second set of experiments was focused on score-based filtering of extracted alignments. It was motivated by the high recall achieved by SentenceBERT in our baseline experiments (cf. Sect. 3.2). The baseline results suggest that increasing precision by other means could substantially improve specific alignment methods, with SentenceBERT being a good candidate because it tends to find a high number of alignments, most of which are not part of the gold standard. The metrics calculated by SATEF between the two sides of an alignment (BLEU, BERTScore, and METEOR) can be used to judge matches aside from the internal cosine similarity. We performed a grid search on the alignments extracted by SentenceBERT with these metrics: BLEU, BERTScore (precision, recall and F1) and METEOR (cf. Sect. 2.2). All metrics range between 0 and 1. We used threshold values with a step size of 0.05. Only the alignments with a score higher or equal to the value were evaluated at a given threshold. A threshold of 0 indicates the absence of filtering; thus, scores were identical to the baseline Sentence-BERT result with this value. For the grid search, results were calculated for the combined corpus, which corresponds to the "mean" column in the ensembling experiments (cf. Sect. 3.3).

Table 6. F1 scores of the three hard voting strategies combining LHA, SentenceBERT, and Vecalign.

Method	APA A2	APA B1	Web	Wiki	Cap A1	Cap A2	Cap B1	Mean
All	0.162	**0.233**	0.322	0.169	0.286	0.312	**0.438**	0.275
Any	0.115	0.106	0.258	0.099	0.25	0.456	0.329	0.23
Majority	**0.215**	0.14	**0.378**	**0.258**	**0.379**	**0.621**	0.359	0.336

The results of our grid search experiments are shown in Tables 7, 8, and 9. As expected, increasingly rigorous filtering improved precision but lowered recall. However, interestingly, this behaviour reverses at a certain point, with more strict filtering lowering precision. For all metrics except METEOR, the ideal threshold for precision was between 0.85 and 1.0 but not always 1.0. Regarding F1 scores, BERTScore_P and BERTScore_R both reached their highest F1 score of 0.36 at a threshold of 0.75. Consequently, filtering improved over the ensembling results presented in Sect. 3.3 by 0.024. In addition, there were differences between the various metrics: While the best results with BLEU were achieved at 0.30, BERTScore performed best with a threshold value of 0.75, and METEOR, with 0.05 and 0.10. Note that the performance of METEOR was substantially lower compared to the other metrics.

Table 7. Precision results from the grid search with five different metrics and threshold values between 0 and 1.

Metric	0.00	0.05	0.10	0.15	0.20	0.25	0.30	0.35	0.40	0.45	0.50
BLEU	0.14	0.18	0.19	0.22	0.27	0.34	0.42	0.51	0.61	0.67	0.71
BERTScore_F1	0.14	0.14	0.14	0.14	0.14	0.14	0.14	0.14	0.14	0.14	0.14
BERTScore_P	0.14	0.14	0.14	0.14	0.14	0.14	0.14	0.14	0.14	0.14	0.14
BERTScore_R	0.14	0.14	0.14	0.14	0.14	0.14	0.14	0.14	0.14	0.14	0.14
METEOR	0.14	0.17	0.17	0.17	0.17	0.18	0.20	0.22	0.28	0.21	0.00

Metric	0.55	0.60	0.65	0.70	0.75	0.80	0.85	0.90	0.95	1.00
BLEU	0.76	0.77	0.76	0.74	0.78	0.78	0.87	0.69	0.79	0.79
BERTScore_F1	0.14	0.15	0.19	0.32	0.54	0.69	0.79	0.76	0.74	0.80
BERTScore_P	0.15	0.15	0.19	0.30	0.49	0.65	0.74	0.80	**0.90**	0.80
BERTScore_R	0.15	0.15	0.19	0.29	0.50	0.66	0.75	0.78	0.75	0.80
METEOR	0.00	0.00	0.00	0.00	0.00	0.00	0.00	0.00	0.00	0.00

4 Discussion

When comparing the performance of the different alignment methods on the gold standard, the results varied considerably across tools. This is most likely due to the different algorithms used in the evaluated tools and our choice to apply them with their standard settings, which ensured a fair comparison. The tools that performed best in terms of F1 were LHA, SentenceBERT, and Vecalign, but they differed in the way in which these high F1 scores were reached: LHA (and MASSAlign, which did not perform as well overall) achieved a very high precision, while SentenceBERT showed a very high recall.

Looking at the ensembling results, we can see that combining these well-performing but different tools can be worthwhile. Incorporating multiple alignment methods with the "all" or "majority" strategies resulted in higher F1 scores than LHA, the best single alignment method. This can be explained by

Table 8. Recall results from the grid search with five different metrics and threshold values between 0 and 1.

Metric	0.00	0.05	0.10	0.15	0.20	0.25	0.30	0.35	0.40	0.45	0.50
BLEU	**0.40**	0.38	0.37	0.35	0.32	0.29	0.26	0.23	0.20	0.17	0.15
BERTScore_F1	**0.40**	**0.40**	**0.40**	**0.40**	**0.40**	**0.40**	**0.40**	**0.40**	**0.40**	**0.40**	**0.40**
BERTScore_P	**0.40**	**0.40**	**0.40**	**0.40**	**0.40**	**0.40**	**0.40**	**0.40**	**0.40**	**0.40**	**0.40**
BERTScore_R	**0.40**	**0.40**	**0.40**	**0.40**	**0.40**	**0.40**	**0.40**	**0.40**	**0.40**	**0.40**	**0.40**
METEOR	**0.40**	0.30	0.30	0.28	0.23	0.13	0.05	0.02	0.01	0.00	0.00

Metric	0.55	0.60	0.65	0.70	0.75	0.80	0.85	0.90	0.95	1.00
BLEU	0.13	0.12	0.10	0.09	0.08	0.06	0.06	0.05	0.04	0.04
BERTScore_F1	**0.40**	0.39	0.38	0.34	0.26	0.18	0.12	0.08	0.06	0.03
BERTScore_P	**0.40**	0.39	0.38	0.34	0.29	0.22	0.16	0.11	0.06	0.03
BERTScore_R	**0.40**	0.39	0.38	0.33	0.28	0.21	0.15	0.11	0.06	0.03
METEOR	0.00	0.00	0.00	0.00	0.00	0.00	0.00	0.00	0.00	0.00

Table 9. F1 scores from the grid search with five different metrics and threshold values between 0 and 1.

Metric	0.00	0.05	0.10	0.15	0.20	0.25	0.30	0.35	0.40	0.45	0.50
BLEU	0.20	0.23	0.24	0.26	0.29	0.31	0.32	0.31	0.30	0.27	0.24
BERTScore_F1	0.20	0.20	0.20	0.20	0.20	0.20	0.20	0.20	0.20	0.20	0.20
BERTScore_P	0.20	0.20	0.20	0.20	0.20	0.20	0.20	0.20	0.20	0.20	0.20
BERTScore_R	0.20	0.20	0.20	0.20	0.20	0.20	0.20	0.20	0.20	0.20	0.20
METEOR	0.20	0.21	0.21	0.20	0.18	0.14	0.08	0.04	0.01	0.00	0.00

Metric	0.55	0.60	0.65	0.70	0.75	0.80	0.85	0.90	0.95	1.00
BLEU	0.22	0.20	0.18	0.15	0.13	0.11	0.10	0.09	0.08	0.07
BERTScore_F1	0.20	0.21	0.25	0.32	0.35	0.28	0.21	0.14	0.10	0.05
BERTScore_P	0.21	0.21	0.25	0.32	**0.36**	0.32	0.25	0.18	0.12	0.05
BERTScore_R	0.21	0.21	0.24	0.31	**0.36**	0.32	0.24	0.18	0.12	0.05
METEOR	0.00	0.00	0.00	0.00	0.00	0.00	0.00	0.00	0.00	0.00

the behaviour of the two voting strategies, which exclude alignments found by a single tool only that are conceivably more likely not to be part of the gold standard. This is corroborated by our results for precision and recall, where the gap was considerably smaller between the "all" and "majority" strategies than between the "majority" and "any" strategies. Overall, the "majority" voting strategy worked best in terms of F1 and reached a mean score of 0.336, balancing precision and recall better than "all" and "any", which had a clearer bias towards one of the two metrics.

Our grid search for SentenceBERT for score-based filtering showed that improving on a single alignment method with high recall is also a viable option. With filtering, we reached a mean F1 score of 0.36 when only keeping alignments with a BERTScore_P or BERTScore_R of greater than or equal to 0.75 between source and target. Interestingly, the ideal threshold for BLEU and the BERTScore metrics to reach a high precision was not always 1.0 but ranged between 0.85 and 1.0. This is best explained with the fact that many gold alignments are not perfect matches, and when filtering very strictly, a disproportional number of correct matches are removed. A principal drawback of this method is increased cost, as calculating the metrics (specifically, BERTScore) can be expensive.

Evaluation of sentence alignments is also a difficult task in itself, even if a gold standard exists. While F1 score is a well-established metric for these tasks and combines precision and recall, it is, at the same time, sensitive to the configuration of hyperparameters. An overly restrictive configuration results in high precision and low recall, while an unrestricted configuration swaps the outcome. Additionally, comparing the F1 score between tools in isolation allowed us to distinguish between those tools that generate more valid alignments that exist in the gold standard (high recall and low precision) from those tools that deliver precisely the alignments from the gold standard only.

5 Conclusion and Outlook

Our experiments have shown that the quality of the automatic sentence alignments generated by various alignment methods for standard German/simplified German documents varies considerably. This leaves space for optimization as a second step after generating the raw alignments. A first possibility is to combine multiple alignment methods (ensembling) to leverage their individual strengths and to arrive at a single combined classification. We experimented with three voting strategies, using alignments that were found by either at least one, all, or a majority of the methods, respectively. We showed that the quality of the alignments when using the "all" or "majority" strategies improved over the quality of the best single alignment method. The majority vote was the best ensemble voting strategy in terms of F1 score.

We also performed experiments in score-based filtering of matches with a grid search to find optimal combinations of metrics and threshold values for scores. These experiments were performed on alignments extracted with SentenceBERT, which achieved a high recall but low precision in our initial experiments, rendering it an ideal candidate for additional filtering. We showed that BERTScore_P and BERTScore_R achieved the best results at a threshold value of 0.75. With this filtering method of SentenceBERT alignments, we outperformed the majority voting strategy for combining alignment methods.

The experiments reported in this paper motivate the notion that the complex task of sentence alignment in the context of ATS is best approached as a two-step process, with the automatic creation of alignments being the first and narrowing down these candidates the second step. We plan on conducting further experiments on this second step, using other, non-overlap-based filtering metrics such as edit distance. Also, conceptually, ensembling could be extended to soft voting, combining different embedding methods to represent inputs and calculate cosine similarity. We also plan to perform similar experiments on other pairs of standard/simplified languages with existing gold standards to judge the effectiveness of this approach for other language pairs. Moreover, we intend to perform a human evaluation of neural text simplification models trained on the aligned data together with the simplification experts at capito. As these models have been shown to be sensitive to noise, this will allow for a better understanding of the consequences of strict filtering and the tradeoff between data quality and quantity in a practical scenario.

Acknowledgements. The authors would like to thank the Austria Presse Agentur and CFS GmbH for providing the data for two of the parallel corpora of standard German documents with their simplified counterparts.

References

1. Banerjee, S., Lavie, A.: METEOR: an automatic metric for MT evaluation with improved correlation with human judgments. In: Proceedings of the ACL Workshop on Intrinsic and Extrinsic Evaluation Measures for Machine Translation and/or Summarization, pp. 65–72. Association for Computational Linguistics, Ann Arbor, Michigan, June 2005. https://aclanthology.org/W05-0909
2. Battisti, A., Pfütze, D., Säuberli, A., Kostrzewa, M., Ebling, S.: A corpus for automatic readability assessment and text simplification of German. In: Proceedings of The 12th Language Resources and Evaluation Conference, pp. 3295–3304. European Language Resources Association, Marseille, France, May 2020. https://www.aclweb.org/anthology/2020.lrec-1.403
3. Council of Europe: Common European Framework of Reference for Languages: Learning, Teaching, Assessment. Cambridge University Press, Cambridge (2009)
4. Hwang, W., Hajishirzi, H., Ostendorf, M., Wu, W.: Aligning sentences from standard Wikipedia to simple Wikipedia. In: Proceedings of the 2015 Conference of the North American Chapter of the Association for Computational Linguistics: Human Language Technologies, pp. 211–217. Association for Computational Linguistics, Denver, Colorado, May–June 2015. https://doi.org/10.3115/v1/N15-1022. https://aclanthology.org/N15-1022
5. Jiang, C., Maddela, M., Lan, W., Zhong, Y., Xu, W.: Neural CRF model for sentence alignment in text simplification (2021)
6. Maaß, C.: Easy Language–Plain Language–Easy Language Plus. Balancing Comprehensibility and Acceptability, Easy–Plain–Accessible, vol. 3. Frank & Timme (2020)
7. Nikolov, N., Hahnloser, R.: Large-scale hierarchical alignment for data-driven text rewriting. In: Proceedings of the International Conference Recent Advances in Natural Language Processing, RANLP 2019 (2019)

8. Paetzold, G., Alva-Manchego, F., Specia, L.: MassAlign: alignment and annotation of comparable documents. In: Park, S., Supnithi, T. (eds.) Proceedings of the IJCNLP 2017, Tapei, Taiwan, 27 November–1 December 2017, System Demonstrations, pp. 1–4. Association for Computational Linguistics (2017). https://aclanthology.info/papers/I17-3001/i17-3001

9. Papineni, K., Roukos, S., Ward, T., Zhu, W.J.: BLEU: a method for automatic evaluation of machine translation. In: Proceedings of the 40th Annual Meeting of the Association for Computational Linguistics (ACL), pp. 311–318, Philadelphia, PA (2002)

10. Pfütze, D.: Sentence alignment gold standards for neural text simplification, University of Zurich (2020)

11. Pfütze, D., Ebling, S.: Sentence alignment in the context of automatic text simplification. Poster Presented at KLAARA 2021–2nd Conference on Easy-to-Read Language Research, Switzerland (Online), August 2021

12. Reimers, N., Gurevych, I.: Making monolingual sentence embeddings multilingual using knowledge distillation. In: Proceedings of the 2020 Conference on Empirical Methods in Natural Language Processing. Association for Computational Linguistics, November 2020. https://arxiv.org/abs/2004.09813

13. Schwenk, H., Douze, M.: Learning joint multilingual sentence representations with neural machine translation. In: Proceedings of the 2nd Workshop on Representation Learning for NLP, pp. 157–167. Association for Computational Linguistics, Vancouver, Canada, August 2017. https://www.aclweb.org/anthology/W17-2619

14. Spring, N., Pfütze, D., Kostrzewa, M., Battisti, A., Rios, A., Ebling, S.: Comparing sentence alignment methods for automatic simplification of German texts. Presentation Given at the 1st International Easy Language Day Conference (IELD), Germersheim, Germany (2021)

15. Štajner, S., Franco-Salvador, M., Rosso, P., Ponzetto, S.: CATS: a tool for customized alignment of text simplification corpora. In: Proceedings of the Eleventh International Conference on Language Resources and Evaluation (LREC 2018), pp. 3895–3903, Miyazaki, Japan (2018)

16. Xu, W., Callison-Burch, C., Napoles, C.: Problems in current text simplification research: new data can help. Trans. Assoc. Comput. Linguist. 3, 283–297 (2015)

17. Xu, W., Napoles, C., Pavlick, E., Chen, Q., Callison-Burch, C.: Optimizing statistical machine translation for text simplification. Trans. Assoc. Comput. Linguist. 4, 401–415 (2016)

18. Zhang, T., Kishore, V., Wu, F., Weinberger, K.Q., Artzi, Y.: BERTScore: evaluating text generation with BERT. In: International Conference on Learning Representations (2020)

19. Zhu, Z., Bernhard, D., Gurevych, I.: A monolingual tree-based translation model for sentence simplification. In: Proceedings of the 23rd International Conference on Computational Linguistics (Coling 2010), pp. 1353–1361. Coling 2010 Organizing Committee, Beijing, China, August 2010. https://aclanthology.org/C10-1152

Access@tour: A Digital Platform to Promote Accessible Tourism

Pedro Teixeira[1] , Leonor Teixeira[2(✉)] , and Celeste Eusébio[3]

[1] Department of Economics, Management, Industrial Engineering and Tourism,
University of Aveiro, 3010-193 Aveiro, Portugal
pmiguel@ua.pt
[2] Department of Economics, Management, Industrial Engineering and Tourism, Institute of
Electronics and Informatics Engineering of Aveiro, University of Aveiro, 3010-193 Aveiro,
Portugal
lteixeira@ua.pt
[3] Department of Economics, Management, Industrial Engineering and Tourism, Governance,
Competitiveness and Public Policies, University of Aveiro, 3010-193 Aveiro, Portugal
celeste.eusebio@ua.pt

Abstract. The aim of this study is to present an innovative solution, a web-based
information system (WBIS) named *access@tour*, which can support knowledge
and information transfer in the context of accessible tourism. A first prototype of
this solution was developed in Adobe XD and includes a broad set of requirements
in terms of information and accessibility. These were identified in a rigorous process of requirement engineering involving three important stakeholders of this
market: demand (people with special needs, caregivers, and social organizations);
supply agents; and teaching institutions. To present the concept and demonstrate
the solution, some interfaces of *access@tour* will be explained and detailed, illustrating the layout, content, and main functionalities available in the system. Thus,
from a theoretical perspective, it was possible with this study to demonstrate a
concept of exchange and sharing of information suitable for promoting tourism
for all. From a practical perspective, this study creates a communication channel
between different stakeholders in the accessible tourism market.

Keywords: Accessible tourism · Information system · Tourism information
technologies

1 Introduction

Accessible tourism is a social response [1] for a more inclusive society, enhancing access
to tourism among people with special needs (PwSN), including people with disabilities
(PwD) [2]. Although digitalization enables access to tourism information, PwSN face
several constraints to accessing this information [3]. To overcome these constraints, and
to take all stakeholders of the accessible tourism market into perspective, information
systems can be potential solutions, as explained by Michopoulou and Buhalis [4]. Essentially, these systems are software tools, capable of helping PwD [5] reach the right type
of accessibility-related information in a relatively accessible format [6].

© The Author(s), under exclusive license to Springer Nature Switzerland AG 2022
M. Antona and C. Stephanidis (Eds.): HCII 2022, LNCS 13308, pp. 150–163, 2022.
https://doi.org/10.1007/978-3-031-05028-2_9

On the other hand, technology is changing the tourism sector, with new digital trends and applications emerging on a daily basis. Nevertheless, the implementation of technological solutions brings not only benefits but also challenges for the tourism industry [7]. A big challenge which has emerged recently is how new technologies can contribute to the social inclusion of PwSN [8], integrating both user-centred requirements and accessibility concepts. Accessible tourism is a crucial topic for the development of a more inclusive society, where PwD are not discriminated against due to their limitations. Since technology needs to be at the service of society, the integration of accessibility in various tourism activities using various technologies can be seen as a great example. Tourism is an activity that enriches people in many dimensions. However, without the necessary information, it is difficult for visitors with disabilities to travel without constraints [9]. Often PwSN are unable to travel due to various factors such as accessibility in transport and accommodation. In addition to this, tourism supply agents have difficulty promoting accessible offers and reaching the accessible tourism market. Furthermore, the role of higher education institutions is often disregarded, which has a negative impact on training of human resources with the necessary skills to help tourists with special needs [10]. In general, the lack of information related to accessibility and communication difficulties between offer and supply [11] create accessibility constraints in tourism, which can lead to the loss of a very important market share, composed of tourists with special needs.

With the growth of the accessible tourism market and all the economic potential associated with it [2], information and communication technologies (ICT), in which web applications are included, can be an excellent way to capitalize on it. In addition, the success rate of these systems depends on how well they fit the users' needs [12]. Therefore, it is imperative to understand how information exchange should be processed. This interaction is mainly defined by the mechanisms of the input (data) and output (information) that users have in the platform [13]. It is important to assure that the system in this area can work as a technological solution to overcome constraints on accessibility in tourism. Additionally, the literature points out that existing tourism information systems in the field of accessibility only tend to meet market needs from a demand perspective [14]. Therefore, a mixed perspective that includes the view of all stakeholders involved in the creation of accessible offers (e.g. demand, tourism supply, and higher education institutions with tourism programs) for the accessible tourism market should be taken into consideration.

To address these problems, the main objective of this work is to present a web-based information system (WBIS) prototype named *access@tour* to promote the exchange of information and stimulate communication among the main players involved in accessible tourism. To obtain this prototype, a user-centered methodology [15] was followed. The intention is now to show how the prototype meets the needs of the users involved in the accessible tourism market across different interfaces and thus validate the WBIS concept.

This work is structured in four sections. The present section contains the introduction, with a brief contextualization and objectives. The Sect. 2 presents a literature review on the importance of information systems in accessible tourism. The Sect. 3 clarifies the methodology used to develop *access@tour* and some results materialised in interfaces that illustrate some functionalities. The Sect. 4 contains the main conclusions and describes some limitations and future work.

2   Literature Review: Accessible Tourism and the Importance of Information Systems

Accessible tourism has been gaining some prominence in recent times; however, there are still numerous barriers that prevent PwSN, specifically PwD, from participating in tourism activities, [16]. If accessibility conditions are not ensured, it can give rise to barriers to the practice of tourism, which threatens the independence of PwSN [17]. Amongst various environmental barriers, it is worth highlighting the risk of the lack of information regarding accessibility, as well as the lack of accessible information [18]. Access to the right type of information is still the major factor in providing accessibility to tourism environments [19]. The information on accessibility allows us to understand whether the tourist's requirements will be taken into account during tourism experiences, as well as whether all the conditions for tourism are met, without any constraint [20].

With a new digital era transforming tourism, it is of utmost relevance to develop technological solutions that contribute to improving the flow of information in this area. Moreover, accessibility is one of the themes that have gained relevance, not only in academia but also in the tourism industry [2, 21–23]. The accessible tourism market is a growing market due to the ageing population. Thus, the investment in accessible tourism is an excellent business opportunity and also a social responsibility issue. In this scope, ICTs in the form of information systems can be potential solutions [24], improving accessibility through information sharing and connectivity [24].

Information systems can be perceived as platforms that not only serve information needs but can also be very useful within an accessibility extent. Essentially, some types of technological solutions are capable of helping PwSN by providing the right type of information at the right time and in an accessible format [6]. For example, technologies related to location systems are essential in building accessible geographic databases [25]. In addition, mobile applications can present proactive mechanisms and collaborative features [26]. In short, ICTs focus not only on the technological component of information dissemination but also on mechanisms to ensure connection to the digital world, namely assistive and/or adaptive technologies [27]. Some practical examples of the application of ICTs in accessible tourism are related to assistive technologies in museums, as shown in the studies performed by Mesquita and Carneiro [28].

In order to promote more accessible tourism offers, the specific needs [7], of different PwSN (PwD—e.g. mobility, vision, hearing, and cognitive/intellectual, and people with other special needs—e.g. seniors, pregnant women, people with respiratory allergies, people with food allergies) [29] should be taken into account by tourism supply agents and by entities responsible for providing accessible tourism competencies to future professionals in the sector, educational institutions. Bearing in mind the goal of achieving such a gateway, information technologies can be the path to success. This is linked with the importance of information within accessibility environments. In the specific case of tourism, the process of planning a trip is done in much more detail in the case of

PwSN, since the greater the accessibility requirements, the greater the requirements for detailed information [30]. Moreover, the interface and subsequently interaction of tourism platforms are directly related to human–computer interaction (HCI) in tourism and have been explored as a major challenge, since information must be available in an accessible way so that PwD can reach and understand its content [31, 32]. Despite the importance of these technological solutions, currently there are still few platforms available on the market [33–35] that aim specifically at promoting more accessible and inclusive tourism.

The application of information systems, within specific environments and users, presents a great challenge [36]. This was observed in previous studies from several research areas, such as tourism [37], healthcare [38], and education [39], where new methodological approaches needed to be developed to address particular user requirements. This is the case of the accessible tourism market, with PwSN and other stakeholders having different and particular requirements. Some authors [40] recommend for this purpose a user-centered design (UCD) approach, making systems more usable, by putting the focus on the users' needs and requirements [41]. There is, however, a gap in terms of available methodological approaches regarding the integration of accessibility-related requirements. The information developed within the scope of this work included the user's perspectives in different phases of its conceptualization, so that it can be acknowledged as an actual user-oriented solution.

3 Access@tour: An Accessible Tourism Platform

3.1 Objectives and Methodology

This study aims to present a WBIS prototype named *access@tour*, an innovative application to promote the exchange of information and stimulate communication among the main actors involved in accessible tourism, and consequently to enhance the co-creation of tourism experiences, helping in the dissemination of personalized tourism services and tourism experiences. This WBIS is designed to be dynamic, contributing to the elimination of some travel constraints caused by the absence of information related to accessibility and the lack of adequate communication channels to transmit it (from supply to demand). It also promotes the right conditions for training oriented to the needs of accessible tourism.

To achieve this goal, a specific methodology was followed, as shown in Fig. 1. More details on the methodology can be found in Teixeira et al. [15]. In a nutshell, this framework, defined according to previous methodological studies in different fields of information systems [37–39], and integrating a UCD and iterative development approach, also take accessibility factors into consideration [42]. To ensure that the requirements are correctly collected and converted into actual user functionalities, a total of six tasks, aggregated in three phases—exploratory, development and implementation—conducted in an iterative and incremental way, make up this methodology.

In the exploratory phase, the environment encompassing the accessible tourism market was studied, with special attention to the requirements of PwSN, supply agents, and institutions responsible for training in tourism. The results of this exploratory analysis

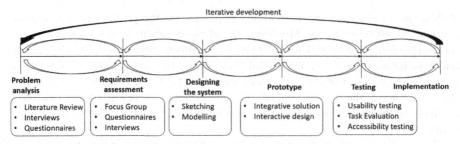

Fig. 1. UCD methodology used to develop *access@tour*.

allowed the collection of different users' requirements that served as inputs for the development phase. In the second phase, which aims to convert the gathered requirements into the actual system functionalities, the main conceptual models were defined. Therefore, a combination of techniques is applied to create the desired technological solution. In this phase, a set of acceptance tests to evaluate the concept with potential users was conducted. The objective was to identify improvement opportunities and improve the obtained solution. The last phase concerns the implementation of the solution and integration within a digital transformation context.

3.2   Results: Description of the Prototype from a Functional Perspective

As already briefly mentioned, *access@tour* aims to incorporate the contributions of different accessible tourism market stakeholders: (i) demand (PwSN, informal caregivers and formal caregivers—social organizations); (ii) supply agents (e.g. producers—accommodation units, food & beverage units, transport companies, tourism attractions, and tourism animation enterprises, intermediaries—travel agents and tour operators, and public organizations with responsibility in the sector); and (iii) teaching institutions responsible for training in tourism (e.g. universities and other higher education institutions).

Overall, from a functional perspective, the platform aims to promote the sharing and exchange of information between the mentioned relevant actors by allowing a user-platform interaction through different inputs (insert information into the platform) and outputs (search information within the platform) (Table 1).

Demand agents intend to use the platform to search for accessible tourism offers adequate to their particular needs, and also participate in making offers more accessible to other PwSN. On the other hand, supply agents want to make sure the platform is meant to divulge their accessible offers and reach a specific segment of the job market composed of people with experience in accessible tourism. Finally, teaching institutions can either use the application for academic research, or contact the other stakeholders directly and consequently get a better understanding of the accessible tourism market.

Table 1. Main functionalities of *access@tour*

	Functionalities	
Stakeholders	Outputs (Search for)	Inputs (Insert)
Demand	• Accessible tourism offers • Tourism support services • Legislation on accessible tourism	• Accessibility requirements • Evaluations of tourism offers
Supply agents	• Accessibility requirements • Evaluations of tourism offers • Human resources with training in accessible tourism	• Accessible tourism offers • Job offers
Teaching institutions — Students	• Training opportunities • Job opportunities • Academic research in accessible tourism • Training courses in accessible tourism	• Work experience in accessible tourism
Teaching institutions — Teachers	• Characteristics of accessible tourism • Market needs • Training courses in accessible tourism • Academic research in accessible tourism	• Academic research in accessible tourism • Training opportunities related to accessible tourism

As the platform intends to channel information in the field of accessible tourism, it is important to foster interactivity between all stakeholders, so they can also establish communication amongst themselves. The involvement of all these stakeholders through a requirement collection procedure was crucial for the creation of the intended application, as they can contribute in very particular ways to the creation of innovative and accessible tourism solutions. Therefore, all functionalities available were directly developed based on the requirements gathered from the different stakeholders.

It is important to note that *access@tour* integrates a set of innovative features which are not present in the platforms related to accessible tourism currently on the market. On this subject, it is worth mentioning that the available platforms [33–35] often just focus on a specific type of disability and fail especially at integrating the diversity of users present in the accessible tourism market. To fill this gap, *access@tour,* in addition to considering the needs of demand and supply-side agents, includes education institutions due to their involvement in training tourism programs, with many benefits to accessible tourism solutions, as explored in previous studies [10]. The *access@tour* platform is also intended to respect accessibility standards, namely Web Content Accessibility Guidelines (WCAG) [42]. These standards make sure the platform not only provides accessibility-related content but it is also accessible itself. On this detail, it is important that, in addition to the aforementioned system functionalities, *access@tour* also integrates accessibility standards such as: i) alternatives to content containing text/videos/images, ii) integration of a simple navigation system; iii) presentation of content in a simple and understandable format; iv) straightforward layout; and v) compatibility with assistive technologies.

With the goal of exhibiting some of the functionalities, a prototype for *access@tour* was produced in Adobe XD. The following section presents some screenshots of the interfaces available in the actual prototype, in an effort to give a general overview of the WBIS. For simplifying the process, interfaces will be shown to give a general idea of the functionalities which are part of the platform.

3.3   Results: Description of the Prototype from a Usage Perspective

In the first three interfaces of the *access@tour* platform, a clear description of the platform and its objectives are presented (Fig. 2).

Fig. 2. Interfaces of the initial screens of the *access@tour* (interfaces in Portuguese)

There are three paths offered according to the type of user: (i) demand agents that intend to search for accessible tourism experiences; (ii) supply agents that intend to offer accessible tourism experiences, and (iii) education institutions, aimed at tourism students and tourism teachers (Fig. 3). Once a navigation path is selected, it is possible to better specify the type of user and to navigate with a set of information oriented to that user profile. For example, the supply agent can indicate the system if they are a tourism supply agent (e.g. hotel manager, museum manager, restaurant owner), a tour operator, or a municipality entity. A user that belongs to a teaching institution should indicate if they are a tourism student or teacher. In addition, a demand agent can enter the system as a PwSN (including PwD), an informal caregiver (relatives or friends), or a formal caregiver (social organization). The interfaces representing the different navigation paths are illustrated in Fig. 3. At a later stage, the objective will be to implement an identification system (login) that will automatically guide the user to a specific starting page.

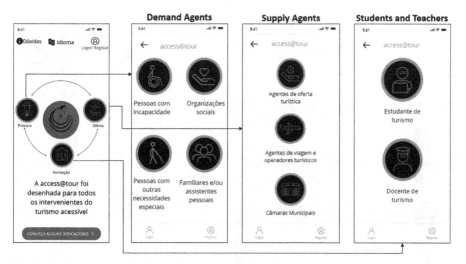

Fig. 3. Interfaces representing navigation paths within *access@tour* (interfaces in Portuguese)

Functionalities for the Demand Agents. For the case of demand agents (PwD, PwD, formal caregivers, and informal caregivers), there are different possible interactions with the platform (Fig. 4). The platform allows the user to search for accessible tourism offers; evaluate previously made tourism offers; search for investigations related to accessible tourism and search for legislation about accessible tourism. As well as this, there is a toolbar available to the users to connect them with other points of the platform. These connections include accessing a saved page of tourism offer favourites; a chat interface to interact with other users; a notification alert page; access to some basic definitions of the system; and a home button so users are easily able to return to their homepage. Finally, at the top of the interface, there is a research bar available for searching different aspects within the platform, using keywords.

Functionalities for the Supply Agent. An additional important piece for the system to work correctly is the presence of supply agents (tourism supply agents, travel agents and tour operators, and public organizations—municipalities) that wish to share their accessible experiences within the platform and obtain relevant information to improve the accessibility of their products. Bearing this in mind, the main interface aims to allow the users to have different interactions with the system (Fig. 5). Supply agents are able to insert and edit tourism offers; search for accessible tourism offers; search for support activities; search for qualified human resources; search for accessible tourism projects and financial support; and also register employment offers. Beyond these basic interactions, supply agents also have access to a toolbar where they can communicate with other users; set notifications and alerts; access the definitions of the system; and return to their homepage. As mentioned before for other users, supply agents can also search within the platform by inserting keywords in the top research bar.

Functionalities for Teachers of Tourism Education Programs. Tourism study programs are an significant tool in improving accessible tourism conditions. In this regard,

Fig. 4. Interfaces representing interactions that a demand agent can have with the platform (interfaces in Portuguese)

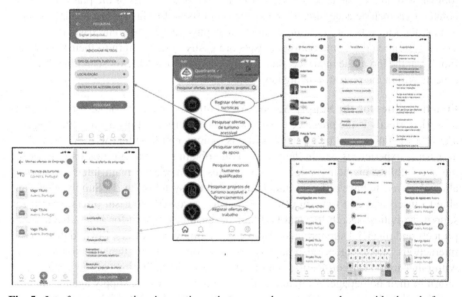

Fig. 5. Interface representing interactions that a supply agent can have with the platform (interfaces in Portuguese)

the platform intends to encourage academic knowledge in accessible tourism. On the home page for tourism teachers (Fig. 6) it is possible to search for accessible tourism offers (with the same standards as tourists) in order to increase their knowledge on accessible tourism; search for employment positions (e.g. university teaching positions) or insert employment opportunities; look up training in the area of accessible tourism; search for academic-level research, investigations, and projects regarding accessible tourism; and also find funding programs. This type of user also has the possibility of inserting their curriculum vitae (CV) into the platform. Similarly, for supply agents, the bottom toolbar and the top research bar intend to serve the same proposes as mentioned earlier. Overall, the insertion of this type of user hopes to foster academic interest in the topic of accessible tourism.

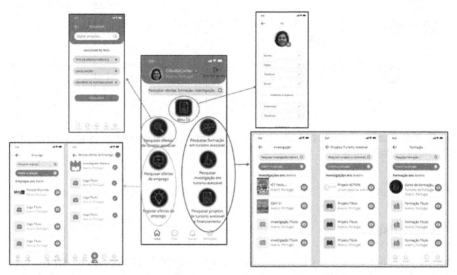

Fig. 6. Interfaces representing interactions that a tourism teacher can have with the platform (interfaces in Portuguese)

Functionalities for Tourism Students. Similarly to teachers, tourism students also play a crucial role in ensuring that tourism industry staff have the necessary knowledge and skills to work with the accessible tourism market. The *access@tour* platform (Fig. 7) allows students to search for accessible tourism offers (similarly to consumers) to increase their knowledge concerning the accessibility of the tourism industry; insert their CVs and explore job offers in accessible tourism; look up training and education aspects related to accessibility promotion in tourism; and also access academic research regarding accessible tourism. As with supply agents, the bottom toolbar and top research bar intend to serve the same basic functionalities. In a similar way to teachers, having students as an important component of the system will allow better divulgation of scientific knowledge regarding accessible tourism. The fact that students are part of this platform can help them to be more proactive towards the accessible market, as training options for students provide them with more skills to be better prepared to help tourists with special needs.

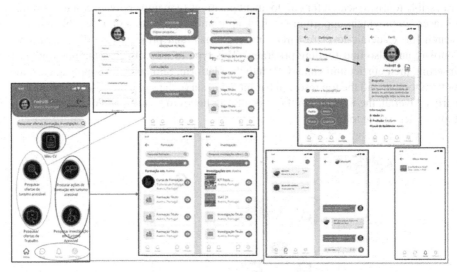

Fig. 7. Interfaces representing interactions that a tourism student can have with the platform (interfaces in Portuguese)

4   Conclusion

One of the main challenges in accessible tourism is to deliver accessible information to disabled tourists. WBIS are excellent platforms for information sharing between disabled tourists and tourism organizations. Despite this, this research shows that the existing number of platforms currently promoting accessible tourism is low and they are limited in terms of functionalities. To answer this need, this work presented a WBIS concept—*access@tour*. To achieve this goal, some functionalities of the platform were illustrated in interfaces obtained directly from the initial WBIS prototype, showing how technologies and a specific web application could contribute to making tourism more accessible by integrating the needs of different types of users.

With this study, the hope is to contribute with a proposal for a technological solution that promotes effective channels and forms of communication between the demand (i.e., tourists with special needs), the tourism supply, and teaching institutions. This guarantees conditions of accessibility for PwSN, as well as the dissemination of services and training/academic instances associated with the different stakeholders involved in accessible tourism.

Despite the relevant contribution of this study, as a result of complexity issues, some limitations should be pointed out. Due to fact that the prototype is being developed horizontally and built in Adobe XD, only some system functionalities could be presented.

Moreover, it was not possible to demonstrate all types of implemented accessibility standards, although the project has included them.

In terms of future work, it is hoped to continue assessing the viability and reliability of the system with actual stakeholders, namely visitors who suffer from some kind of disability, tourism supply agents that wish, on the on hand to improve the accessibility level of their products, or on the other to promote their accessible products, as well as students and teachers in education tourism programs. Following the explained iterative and incremental building approach, the project will proceed with the conduction of the set of usability tests, with the intention of validating the solution (understanding the relevance of features and information present in the system), as well as identifying new features. It will be necessary to compare the views of the different evaluator entities to perform all necessary modifications to the obtained WBIS. Furthermore, after obtaining a fully functional version of *access@tour*, the project hopes to integrate concepts of digital transformation and Tourism 4.0 [43], so that *access@tour* is capable of transforming itself and consolidating digital innovation. This can be achieved by studying the emerging technological drivers and understanding their application within the accessible tourism environment.

Acknowledgments. This work was financially supported by the project ACTION – Accessible Tourism: Co-Creation of Tourism Experiences Through Web-Based Intelligent Systems, funded by FEDER, through COMPETE2020 – Programa Operacional Competitividade e Internacional-ização (POCI-01–0145-FEDER-030376), and by national funds (OE), through FCT/MCTES (PTDC/EGE-OGE/30376/2017).

References

1. McCabe, S., Diekmann, A.: The rights to tourism: Reflections on social tourism and human rights. Tour. Recreat. Res. **40**(2), 194–204 (2015)
2. Kastenholz, E., Eusébio, C., Figueiredo, E.: Contributions of tourism to social inclusion of persons with disability. Disability Soc. **30**(8), 1259–1281 (2015)
3. Carneiro, M.J., Teixeira, L., Eusébio, C., Kastenholz, E., Moura, A.A.: Use of the internet to plan tourism trips by people with special needs. In: Eusébio, C., Teixeira, L., Carneiro, M.J. (eds.) ICT Tools and Applications for Accessible Tourism, pp. 74–95 (2021)
4. Michopoulou, E., Buhalis, D.: Information provision for challenging markets: the case of the accessibility requiring market in the context of tourism. Inf. Manag. **50**(5), 229–239 (2013)
5. Teixeira, P., Teixeira, L., Eusébio, C., Silva, S., Teixeira, A.: The impact of ICTs on accessible tourism. In: Eusébio, C., Teixeira, L., Carneiro, M.J. (eds). ICT Tools and Applications for Accessible Tourism, pp 1–25. (2021)
6. Kołodziejczak, A.: Information as a factor of the development of accessible tourism for people with disabilities. Quaestiones Geographicae **38**(2), 67–73 (2019)
7. Buhalis, D., Michopoulou, E.: Information-enabled tourism destination marketing: addressing the accessibility market. Curr. Issues Tour. **14**(2), 145–168 (2011)
8. Manzoor, M., Vimarlund, V.: Digital technologies for social inclusion of individuals with disabilities. Heal. Technol. **8**(5), 377–390 (2018). https://doi.org/10.1007/s12553-018-0239-1
9. Lee, B.K., Agarwal, S., Kim, H.J.: Influences of travel constraints on the people with disabilities' intention to travel: an application of Seligman's helplessness theory. Tour. Manag. **33**(3), 569–579 (2012)

10. Teixeira, P., Alves, J., Eusébio, C., Teixeira, L.: The role of higher education institutions in the accessible tourism ecosystem: requirements for the conceptualization of an information system. In: Rocha, Á., Adeli, H., Dzemyda, G., Moreira, F., Ramalho Correia, A.M. (eds.) WorldCIST 2021. AISC, vol. 1367, pp. 151–162. Springer, Cham (2021). https://doi.org/10.1007/978-3-030-72660-7_15

11. Michopoulou, E., Darcy, S., Ambrose, I., Buhalis, D.: Accessible tourism futures: the world we dream to live in and the opportunities we hope to have. J. Tour. Futures 1, 179–188 (2015)

12. Irestig, M., Timpka, T.: Politics and technology in health information systems development: A discourse analysis of conflicts addressed in a systems design group. J. Biomed. Inform. 41, 82–94 (2008)

13. Levy, Y., Ellis, T.J.: A systems approach to conduct an effective literature review in support of information systems research. Informing Sci. 9, 181–212 (2006)

14. Yim, K.: Equal access to integrated resort amenities for people with disabilities. Int. J. Hosp. Tour. Adm. 16(3), 251–274 (2015)

15. Teixeira, P., Alves, J., Teixeira, L., Eusébio, M.: Methodological approach for the conceptualization of an information system for accessible tourism. In: Proceedings of the 20th European Conference on Research Methodology for Business and Management Studies, pp. 181–191. ACPIL, Aveiro (2021)

16. Pühretmair, F.: It's time to make eTourism accessible. In: Miesenberger, K., Klaus, J., Zagler, W.L., Burger, D. (eds.) ICCHP 2004. LNCS, vol. 3118, pp. 272–279. Springer, Heidelberg (2004). https://doi.org/10.1007/978-3-540-27817-7_41

17. Popiel, M.: Barriers in undertaking tourist activity by disabled people. Bibl. Główna Akad. Im. Jana Długosza w Częstochowie. 15(3), 103–110 (2016)

18. Stumbo, N.J., Pegg, S.: Travelers and tourists with disabilities: a matter of priorities and loyalties. Tour. Rev. Int. 8(3), 195–209 (2005)

19. Magnelli, A., Pantile, D., Falcone, R., Pizziol, V.: The video guides at the Musei Civici in Rome: an example of technological innovation in touristic cultural heritage experiences. In: Rocha, Á., Abreu, A., de Carvalho, J., Liberato, D., González, E., Liberato, P. (eds.) Advances in Tourism, Technology and Smart Systems. Smart Innovation, Systems and Technologies, vol. 171, pp. 199–209. Springer, Singapore (2019)

20. McKercher, B., Darcy, S.: Re-conceptualizing barriers to travel by people with disabilities. Tour. Manag. Perspect. 26, 59–66 (2018)

21. Ozturk, Y., Yayli, A., Yesiltas, M.: Is the Turkish tourism industry ready for a disabled customer's market? Tour. Manag. 29(2), 382–389 (2008)

22. Figueiredo, E., Kastenholz, E., Eusébio, C.: How diverse are tourists with disabilities? A pilot study on accessible leisure tourism experiences in Portugal. Int. J. Tour. Res. 14(6), 531–550 (2012)

23. Dickson, T., Darcy, S., Johns, R., Pentifallo, C.: Inclusive by design: transformative services and sport-event accessibility. Serv. Ind. J. 36(11), 532–555 (2016)

24. Ribeiro, F.R., Silva, A., Barbosa, F., Silva, A.P., Metrôlho, J.C.: Mobile applications for accessible tourism: overview, challenges and a proposed platform. Inf. Technol. Tour. 19(1–4), 29–59 (2018). https://doi.org/10.1007/s40558-018-0110-2

25. Barbeau, S., Georggi, N., Winters, P.: Global positioning system integrated with personalized real-time transit information from automatic vehicle location. Transp. Res. Rec. J. Transp. Res. Board. 2143(1), 168–176 (2010)

26. Emrouzeh, M.P., Dewar, K., Fleet, G., Bourgeois, Y.: Implementing ICT for tourists with disabilities. In: Proceedings of 2017 International Conference on E-Education, E-bus, E-Technology, pp. 50–53 (2017)

27. Fall, C.L., et al.: A multimodal adaptive wireless control interface for people with upper-body disabilities. IEEE Trans. Biomed. Circuits Syst. 12(3), 564–575 (2018)

28. Mesquita, S., Carneiro, M.: Accessibility of european museums to visitors with visual impairments. Disabil. Soc. **31**(3), 373–388 (2016)
29. Buhalis, D., Darcy, S.: Accessible Tourism Concepts and Issues. Channel View Publications, Bristol (2011)
30. Buhalis, D., Eichhorn, V., Michopoulou, E., Miller, G.: Accessibility Market and Stakeholder Analysis. One-Stop-Shop for Accessible Tourism in Europe (OSSATE). University of Surrey, London (2005)
31. Daniels, M.J., Drogin Rodgers, E.B., Wiggins, B.P.: "Travel Tales": an interpretive analysis of constraints and negotiations to pleasure travel as experienced by persons with physical disabilities. Tour. Manag. **26**(6), 919–930 (2005)
32. Devile, E., Kastenholz, E.: Accessible tourism experiences: the voice of people with visual disabilities. J. Policy Res. Tour. Leis. Events. **10**(3), 265–285 (2018)
33. IBCCES: Autism Travel. https://autismtravel.com/. Accessed 21 Jan 2022
34. Jaccede: Jaccede. https://www.jaccede.com/en/. Accessed 21 Jan 2022
35. Tourism for All. www.tourism-for-all.com. Accessed 21 Jan 2022
36. Kotusev, S.: The hard side of business and IT alignment. IT Prof. **22**(1), 47–55 (2020)
37. Sandfreni, S., Adikara, F.: The implementation of soft system methodology (SSM) for systems development in organizations (Study case: the development of tourism information system in Palembang City). In: Proceedings of the First International Conference of Science, Engineering and Technology, ICSET 2019, p. EAI, Jakarta, Indonesia (2020)
38. Teixeira, L., Saavedra, V., Santos, B.S., Ferreira, C.: Integrating human factors in information systems development: user centred and agile development approaches. In: Duffy, V.G.G. (ed.) DHM 2016. LNCS, vol. 9745, pp. 345–356. Springer, Cham (2016). https://doi.org/10.1007/978-3-319-40247-5_35
39. Reis, A., Martins, P., Borges, J., Sousa, A., Rocha, T., Barroso, J.: Supporting accessibility in higher education information systems: a 2016 update. In: Antona, M., Stephanidis, C. (eds.) UAHCI 2017. LNCS, vol. 10277, pp. 227–237. Springer, Cham (2017). https://doi.org/10.1007/978-3-319-58706-6_19
40. Rinkus, S., et al.: Human-centered design of a distributed knowledge management system. J. Biomed. Inform. **38**(1), 4–17 (2005)
41. ISO 9241–210:2019. International Organization for Standardization: Ergonomics of human-system interaction—Part 210: Human-centred design for interactive systems (2019)
42. W3C: How to Meet WCAG 2.1. https://www.w3.org/WAI/WCAG21/quickref/. Accessed 21 Jan 2022
43. Peceny, U.S., Urbančič, J., Mokorel, S., Kuralt, V., Ilijaš, T.: Tourism 4.0: challenges in marketing a paradigm shift. In: Reyes, M. (ed.) Consumer Behavior and Marketing. Intech open (2019)

Animated Backgrounds on the Web Reduce Reading Speed: Some Empirical Evidence from a Remote Experiment

Ana Flávia Vital, Mark van der Baan, Øyvind Ødegård Stenberg,
and Frode Eika Sandnes[(✉)] [ID]

Oslo Metropolitan University, 0130 Oslo, Norway
frodes@oslomet.no

Abstract. It is generally considered a bad practice to place animations as backgrounds to text. There are many convincing arguments against using animated backgrounds, yet there are few empirical studies that have assessed effects of animated backgrounds in the context of the web. This study therefore set out to collect empirical evidence to support the recommendation of avoiding animated backgrounds. A remote web-based controlled reading experiment was conducted. The results showed that an animated background led to a significant slower reading speed and lower preference scores. Hence, the empirical evidence supports the established practices.

Keywords: Readability · Luminance contrast · Animation · Web · Accessibility · Augmented reality

1 Introduction

In the early days of the web, it was not uncommon to find websites with animated background behind body text. As the web has matured over the last decades such cases have become increasingly rare. It is generally considered bad practice to place animations behind text. Advice on the use of animations on the web has been proposed, for example Weir and Heeps [1] who argued that animations should not distract and not cause cluttering.

There are several obvious arguments for not using animated backgrounds. First, animated backgrounds may temporarily result in too little contrast between the text and the background. For instance, if the text is white on a black background, while the animation for some seconds is white in the neighborhood of a specific text the text will obviously be unreadable (white on white). This is because visual perception is based on detecting differences also known as luminance contrast [2–4]. This is why closed captions in videos often are presented on a solid or semi-transparent background, or with a clear contrasting outline [5]. Similar issues hold for transparent menus [6].

Second, animations usually involve motions, and motions within the visual field of view are known to attract the attention of the visual system, thereby heightening the risk

© The Author(s), under exclusive license to Springer Nature Switzerland AG 2022
M. Antona and C. Stephanidis (Eds.): HCII 2022, LNCS 13308, pp. 164–174, 2022.
https://doi.org/10.1007/978-3-031-05028-2_10

of drawing the attention away from the text reading process. For example, Hong et al. [7] demonstrated that flash animations on websites attract users' attention.

The problems associated with animated text backgrounds may seem obvious and trivial. This problem has gained renewed relevance in contexts of see-through augmented reality and heads-up displays [8] where text information is mixed with images of the world [9–11]. This is especially critical for low-vision users [12] that relies on visual cues as opposed to tactile or auditory cues [13, 14] or alternative strategies [15]. We therefore designed a simple controlled reading experiment to measure the impact of animations on the reading process, measured both objectively and subjectively.

The rest of this paper is organized as follows. The next section presents related work. Section 3 outlines the methodology used. The results are presented in Sect. 4 with a discussion in Sect. 5. The paper is closed with concluding remarks in Sect. 6.

2   Related Work

There is a vast body of literature on aspects that may improve usability and accessibility on the web (see for instance [16, 17]) and interactive elements that may affect web use (see for instance [18, 19]). Some of the literature has focused luminance contrast between text and background on the web [2–4]. There has recently also been interest in effects of so-called interface dark mode [20]. Several studies have focused on the process of selecting colors [21] and others have suggested tools that help designers select color pairs for text and background that has sufficient contrast [22].

To the best of our knowledge there are few studies of readability of text with animated background on the web. However, there are several related studies that have addressed readability of text superimposed on 3D visualizations [23] and the readability of text in see-through displays [9, 10, 24] where text is mixed with the image of the background.

Scharff et al. [9] measured readability using search times. They explored several factors, including type text contrast level, level of transparency (additive and multiplicative transparency) and background type (wave and plain). Their results indicated that all these factors affected readability. They claimed that an adjusted global masking index could be used to predict the readability of text.

In a similar study [10] Scharff et al. varied the text contrast and four spatial frequency filtered textures. They found that background texture only affected readability when the text contrast was low.

Rzayev et al. [24] explored the readability of text presented in smart see-through glasses where text is mixed with the background. Their results showed that text positioned in the top-right region of the field of view led to a higher perceived workload and lower comprehension. Moreover, they found that text presented sequentially in a serial manner was the most effective when participants were sitting, while scrolling text was more effective when participants were walking.

In a study of text overlays on three-dimensional (3D) visualizations and video [23] showed that that reading performance was unaffected by whether the type of background consisted of videos or 3D visualizations. They found that negative polarity resulted in a higher reading performance than positive polarity. They also found that participants preferred billboard drawing styles.

There has been some interest in the effects of webpage backgrounds in the context of advertising. For instance, Stevenson et al. [25] found that simple backgrounds were perceived as more positively, while Noiwan [26] found that users ignore animated ads. Benway [27] confirmed banner blindness in a controlled experiment, while Lee and Ahn [28] used eye-tracking to find that animations in banner ads had a negative effect on attention. Zhang [29] found that animation as a secondary cue reduces reading comprehension, while this disturbance diminishes with the complexity of the reading task. They also noticed that irrelevant animations and strong colors had negative effects on reading. Hong et al. [7] observed that flash animations helped information seeking, while Zhu and Grabowski [30] found no significant effects of animated versus still images.

Other studies have addressed the technical quality of different web animation techniques including animated gifs and flash [31]. More recent works have focused on CSS animations [32]. The effect of auditory distractions on reading [33] is another active area of research. Some claim that reading comprehension is negatively affected by fast and loud music [34]. Halin [35] explored an exciting connection between the visual and the auditory in that hard to read fonts requiring more concentration could help readers mask out disturbing speech from the environment.

One may suspect that animations used as carefully designed aesthetic elements on the web may be perceived positively by users. In fact, an interesting experiment conducted by Tractinsky, Katz, and Ikar [36] showed that users' perceptions of usability were more affected by the aesthetics of the interface than actual usability.

3   Method

3.1   Experimental Design

A within groups experimental design with background type as independent variable and reading time and preference as dependent variables. The background type independent variable had two levels, namely uniform (no disturbance) and animated (disturbance).

3.2   Participants

A total of 14 participants were recruited for the experiment from 20 to 35 years of age.

3.3   Materials

Two different texts comprising 260 words were selected from the text Little Women by Louisa May Alcott. The two texts were considered to be at the same level of difficulty since they were from the same work by the same author. The reading levels of the two texts were assessed using six well-known readability indices (using https://readab ilityformulas.com/free-readability-formula-tests.php). The shown in Table 1 shows that both texts were at an average to difficult reading level. The indices also suggest that the text used with the animated background was somewhat less readable (23%–43% difference) than the text used with plain background and may thus be a source of bias in the experiment. However, the literature on readability indices suggests that such indices should be interpreted with caution as they only present a simplistic view on readability [37–39].

Table 1. Readability of the two texts according to six common readability indices.

Index type	Plain		Animated		
	Score	Interpretation	Score	Interpretation	Diff.
Flesch Reading Ease sc.	62.7	Average	47.3	Difficult	24.5%
Gunning fog	14.3	Hard	18.4	Difficult	28.6%
Flesch-Kincaid Grade L.	11.8	12th grade	14.8	College	25.4%
The Coleman-Liau index	7.0	7th grade	10.0	10th grade	42.8%
The SMOG index	8.5	9th grade	12.1	12th grade	42.3%
Auto. readability index	13.1	College level	17.1	College graduate	30.5%
Linear write formula	16.8	College graduate	20.7	College graduate	23.2%

Both texts were presented in white foreground color on a black background (see Fig. 1 (f)). However, one of the texts had an additional cyclically repeating animated background with a multicolored wire-frame ball exploding in a fireworks-like manner covering the entire screen (see Fig. 1 (c-d)). The animation was achieved with an animated gif-file.

3.4 Procedure

The experiment was conducted online and remotely due to the COVID-19 pandemic. A simple custom-made website was designed where participants first were given a start screen where they would select path A or path B (see Fig. 1 (a)). Path a would lead to the text with the plain background first, followed by the animated background second. Similarly, path B would show the text with the animated background first, followed by the text with plain background. The web instrument is available at (https://anafvana.git hub.io/MMI_Background_Test/).

The experiment was balanced by randomizing the presentation order. About half of the participants recruited were instructed to choose either path A, the other half were instructed to choose path B.

The participants were asked to read each of the texts and press next. The time the participants were on the text page was automatically recorded.

At the end of the experiment a screen showing the recorded reading times for the two text were shown (see Fig. 1 (g)). The participants were asked to return these results to the experimenter via email.

Finally, the participants were redirected to a google form with questions about their perceptions on how much they learned from reading the two texts and how they found the reading experience using five-item Likert scales.

(a) Welcome screen, selecting path

(b) Getting ready

(c) Animated background

(d) Animated background (later)

(e) Getting ready for part 2

(f) Plain background

(g) Summary

Fig. 1. Reading experiment instrument.

The experiment was anonymous, and no linking data was necessary as it was conducted in a single session [40].

3.5 Analysis

The reading speeds in words per minute (wpm) [41, 42] were calculated based on the observed time to read the 260 words using

$$Reading\ speed = \frac{60 \times words}{reading\ time}$$

The reading speed was checked for normality using a Shapiro Wilks test and analyzed using parametric procedures, while the Likert responses were analyzed using non-parametric procedures as the data were ordinal. Statistical analyses were performed using JASP version 0.16.1.0 [43].

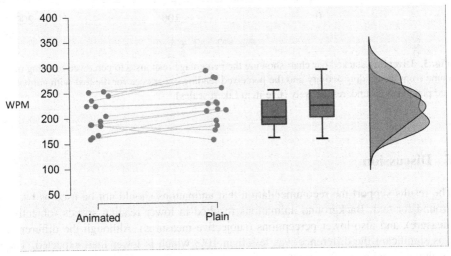

Fig. 2. Raincloud plot showing the distribution of reading speed observations with plain and animated backgrounds (words per minute).

4 Results

The observed mean reading speeds in words per minute (see Fig. 2) shows that the reading speed with the plain background ($M = 225.4$, $SD = 41.0$) was 9.2% higher than the reading speed with the animated background ($M = 206.1$, $SD = 33.1$) and this difference was statistically significant ($t(13) = 3.172$, $p = .007$, Cohen's $d = 0.848$).

The perception results from the five-item Likert questions (see Fig. 3) show that with plain background the reading experience ($M = 3.3$, $SD = 0.7$) and learning outcome ($M = 3.3$, $SD = 0.7$) where higher than the reading experience ($M = 2.0$, $SD = 1.0$)

and learning outcome ($M = 1.7$, $SD = 0.6$) with the animated background. No 5 Likert scoring was given for any of the questions. A two-way analysis of variance using Durbin tests shows that the effect of background was significant ($\chi^2(1) = 17.8$, $p < .001$). Furthermore, a Durbin test shows that there was no significant difference in reading experience and reading outcome for each of the two types of background ($\chi^2(1) = 0.140$, $p = .708$).

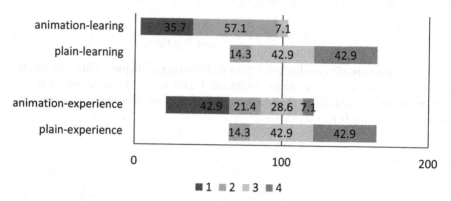

Fig. 3. Diverging stacked bar chart showing the percentage responses to perceived learning outcome from the reading activity and the perceived reading experience for the text with animated and plain background, respectively (five-item Likert scales).

5 Discussion

The results support the recommendation that animations should not be used as background for text. Background animations resulted in lower reading speeds (objective measure), and also lower perceptions (subjective measures). Although the difference was significant the difference was less than 10% which is lower than expected. The result agrees with previous work (see for instance [9, 10]).

Moreover, the perceived learning and reading experience scores were also comparably low overall. With the animated background these were at the negative side of the scale though not at the lowest point. The mean scores for the text with plain background was just slightly above neutral on the positive side. This may be a result of the text used. Perhaps this text was too hard or not sufficiently engaging?

5.1 Limitations

One weakness of the current experiment is the possibility of bias due to the differences in reading level detected by the readability indices. Although such indices are especially sensitive to variations for such short texts, they do provide a neutral perspective. Moreover, the fact that all six totally different readability scores placed the readability of the text with plain background over the animated background suggests that there indeed may be an actual difference. Clearly, the results for the text with plain background were also the most beneficial and we can therefore not be completely certain that it is the text itself or the animated background, or a combination that is the cause of the slower reading speed and lower preference scores. In hindsight, the experiment should have been further balanced into four conditions where both texts were presented in both background conditions. This would have eliminated any text readability bias.

However, one may also defend the legitimacy of the experiment. If it is in fact so that the text with animated background was harder to read, it may also be that the harder reading task has helped mask out the potential disturbance of the background animation, in a similar manner as was observed in the experiments by Zhang [29] and Halin [35].

The search for text passages focused on getting equal length texts. In hindsight the focus should be on finding text passages with similar readability scores as the exact equal lengths are probably not as important as equal reading levels. Such a choice can be justified as the reading speed is analyzed and presented as a normalized measure that is independent of the actual text length.

Also, the experiment was based on simply measuring the time it took to read the text. We therefore could not control the way the text was read. Some may have read the text carefully, while others may have skimmed the text, although the spread suggests relatively consistent reading patterns across the participants. In other readability studies often search tasks are introduced to better control the way the text is read (see for instance [9, 10]).

According to Scharff et al. [9, 10] the effect of the visual background noise is related to the contrast level of the text. In this study we did not control contrast level and we must therefore assume that the contrast level was sufficiently low. However, it must also be noted that the type of experiment deployed herein were quite different from that of Sharff et al.

Another weakness of this experiment is the small number of participants, comprising a relatively narrow cohort. Although this was a pragmatic choice during the COVID-19 pandemic, a larger scale study with cohorts at different reading ability levels could give relevant insight into the effect of the background.

6 Conclusions

This study attempted to provide concrete empirical evidence in support of the recommendation that animations should not be used as text background on the web. A simple reading experiment was conducted. The results support the recommendation as the text with animated background resulted in a slower reading speed and lower responses in terms of perceived learning and reading experience. These findings also give support to voices that argue for ensuring sufficient text contrast in see-through displays such as used for augmented reality. It must be noted that the results may be somewhat biased as readability indices indicate that the text used with the animated background was less readable than the text used with the plain background.

References

1. Weir, G.R., Heeps, S.: Getting the message across: ten principles for web animation. In: 7th IASTED International Conference on Internet and Multimedia and Applications, pp. 121–126. IASTED (2003)
2. Sandnes, F.E., Zhao, A.: An interactive color picker that ensures WCAG2. 0 compliant color contrast levels. Procedia Comput. Sci. **67**, 87–94 (2015). https://doi.org/10.1016/j.procs.2015. 09.252
3. Sandnes, F.E.: Understanding WCAG2.0 color contrast requirements through 3D color space visualization. Stud. Health Technol. Inform **229**, 366–375 (2016). https://doi.org/10.3233/ 978-1-61499-684-2-366
4. Sandnes, F.E.: An image-based visual strategy for working with color contrasts during design. In: Miesenberger, K., Kouroupetroglou, G. (eds.) ICCHP 2018. LNCS, vol. 10896, pp. 35–42. Springer, Cham (2018). https://doi.org/10.1007/978-3-319-94277-3_7
5. Huang, Y.P., Hsu, L.W., Sandnes, F.E.: An intelligent subtitle detection model for locating television commercials. IEEE Trans. Syst. Man Cybern. Part B (Cybern.) **37**(2), 485–492 (2007). https://doi.org/10.1109/TSMCB.2006.883428t
6. Harrison, B.L., Vicente, K.J.: An experimental evaluation of transparent menu usage. In: Proceedings of the SIGCHI Conference on Human Factors in Computing Systems, pp. 391–398. ACM (1996). https://doi.org/10.1145/238386.238583
7. Hong, W., Thong, J.Y., Tam, K.Y.: Does animation attract online users' attention? The effects of flash on information search performance and perceptions. Inf. Syst. Res. **15**(1), 60–86 (2004)
8. Sandnes, F.E., Eika, E.: Head-mounted augmented reality displays on the cheap: a DIY approach to sketching and prototyping low-vision assistive technologies. In: Antona, M., Stephanidis, C. (eds.) UAHCI 2017. LNCS, vol. 10278, pp. 167–186. Springer, Cham (2017). https://doi.org/10.1007/978-3-319-58703-5_13
9. Scharff, L.F., Ahumada, A.J.: Predicting the readability of transparent text. J. Vis. **2**(9), 7 (2002). https://doi.org/10.1167/2.9.7
10. Scharff, L.F., Hill, A.L., Ahumada, A.J.: Discriminability measures for predicting readability of text on textured backgrounds. Opt. Express **6**(4), 81–91 (2000). https://doi.org/10.1364/ OE.6.000081
11. Leykin, A., Tuceryan, M.: Automatic determination of text readability over textured backgrounds for augmented reality systems. In: Third IEEE and ACM International Symposium on Mixed and Augmented Reality, pp. 224–230. IEEE (2004). https://doi.org/10.1109/ISMAR. 2004.22
12. Sandnes, F.E.: What do low-vision users really want from smart glasses? Faces, text and perhaps no glasses at all. In: Miesenberger, K., Bühler, C., Penaz, P. (eds.) ICCHP 2016. LNCS, vol. 9758, pp. 187–194. Springer, Cham (2016). https://doi.org/10.1007/978-3-319-41264-1_25
13. Lin, M.W., Cheng, Y.M., Yu, W., Sandnes, F.E.: Investigation into the feasibility of using tactics to provide navigation cues in pedestrian situations. In: Proceedings of the 20th Australasian Conference on Computer-Human Interaction: Designing for Habitus and Habitat, pp. 299–302 (2008). https://doi.org/10.1145/1517744.1517794
14. dos Santos, A.D.P., Medola, F.O., Cinelli, M.J., Garcia Ramirez, A.R., Sandnes, F.E.: Are electronic white canes better than traditional canes? A comparative study with blind and blindfolded participants. Univ. Access Inf. Soc. **20**(1), 93–103 (2020). https://doi.org/10. 1007/s10209-020-00712-z
15. Huang, Y.P., Chang, Y.T., Sandnes, F.E.: Ubiquitous information transfer across different platforms by QR codes. J. Mobile Multimedia **6**(1), 003–014 (2010)

16. Hofseth, K.Å., Haga, L.K., Sørlie, V., Sandnes, F.E.: Form feedback on the web: a comparison of popup alerts and in-form error messages. In: Chen, Y.-W., Zimmermann, A., Howlett, R.J., Jain, L.C. (eds.) Innovation in Medicine and Healthcare Systems, and Multimedia. SIST, vol. 145, pp. 369–379. Springer, Singapore (2019). https://doi.org/10.1007/978-981-13-8566-7_35

17. Sandnes, F.E., Lundh, M.V.: Calendars for individuals with cognitive disabilities: a comparison of table view and list view. In: Proceedings of the 17th International ACM SIGACCESS Conference on Computers & Accessibility, pp. 329–330. ACM (2015). https://doi.org/10.1145/2700648.2811363

18. Aschim, T.B., Gjerstad, J.L., Lien, L.V., Tahsin, R., Sandnes, F.E.: Are split tablet keyboards better? A study of soft keyboard layout and hand posture. In: Lamas, D., Loizides, F., Nacke, L., Petrie, H., Winckler, M., Zaphiris, P. (eds.) INTERACT 2019. LNCS, vol. 11748, pp. 647–655. Springer, Cham (2019). https://doi.org/10.1007/978-3-030-29387-1_37

19. Skogstrøm, N.A.B., Igeltjørn, A., Knudsen, K.M., Diallo, A.D., Krivonos, D., Sandnes, F.E.: A comparison of two smartphone time-picking interfaces: convention versus efficiency. In: Proceedings of the 10th Nordic Conference on Human-Computer Interaction, pp. 874–879. ACM (2018). https://doi.org/10.1145/3240167.3240233

20. Pedersen, L.A., Einarsson, S.S., Rikheim, F.A., Sandnes, F.E.: User interfaces in dark mode during daytime – improved productivity or just cool-looking? In: Antona, M., Stephanidis, C. (eds.) HCII 2020. LNCS, vol. 12188, pp. 178–187. Springer, Cham (2020). https://doi.org/10.1007/978-3-030-49282-3_13

21. Brathovde, K., Farner, M.B., Brun, F.K., Sandnes, F.E.: Effectiveness of color-picking interfaces among non-designers. In: Luo, Y. (ed.) CDVE 2019. LNCS, vol. 11792, pp. 181–189. Springer, Cham (2019). https://doi.org/10.1007/978-3-030-30949-7_21

22. Hansen, F., Krivan, J.J., Sandnes, F.E.: Still not readable? An interactive tool for recommending color pairs with sufficient contrast based on existing visual designs. In: The 21st International ACM SIGACCESS Conference on Computers and Accessibility, pp. 636–638. ACM (2019). https://doi.org/10.1145/3308561.3354585

23. Jankowski, J., Samp, K., Irzynska, I., Jozwowicz, M., Decker, S.: Integrating text with video and 3d graphics: the effects of text drawing styles on text readability. In: Proceedings of the SIGCHI Conference on Human Factors in Computing Systems, pp. 1321–1330. ACM (2010). https://doi.org/10.1145/1753326.1753524

24. Rzayev, R., Woźniak, P.W., Dingler, T., Henze, N.: Reading on smart glasses: the effect of text position, presentation type and walking. In: Proceedings of the 2018 CHI Conference on Human Factors in Computing Systems. ACM (2018). https://doi.org/10.1145/3173574.3173619

25. Stevenson, J.S., Bruner, G.C., Kumar, A.: Webpage background and viewer attitudes. J. Advert. Res. 40(1–2), 29–34 (2000). https://doi.org/10.2501/JAR-40-1-2-29-34

26. Noiwan, J., Norcio, A.F.: Cultural differences on attention and perceived usability: Investigating color combinations of animated graphics. Int. J. Hum. Comput. Stud. 64(2), 103–122 (2006). https://doi.org/10.1016/j.ijhcs.2005.06.004

27. Benway, J.P.: Banner blindness: the irony of attention grabbing on the World Wide Web. In: Proceedings of the Human Factors and Ergonomics Society Annual Meeting, vol. 42(5), pp. 463–467. SAGE Publications, Los Angeles, CA (1998). https://doi.org/10.1177/154193129804200504

28. Lee, J., Ahn, J.H.: Attention to banner ads and their effectiveness: an eye-tracking approach. Int. J. Electron. Commer. 17(1), 119–137 (2012). https://doi.org/10.2753/JEC1086-4415170105

29. Zhang, P.: The effects of animation on information seeking performance on the World Wide Web: Securing attention or interfering with primary tasks? J. Assoc. Inf. Syst. 18, 648–686 (2000). https://doi.org/10.17705/1jais.00001

30. Zhu, L., Grabowski, B.: Web-based animation or static graphics: is the extra cost of animation worth it? J. Educ. Multimedia Hypermedia **15**(3), 329–347 (2006)
31. Schmidt, W.C.: Presentation accuracy of Web animation methods. Behav. Res. Methods Instrum. Comput. **33**(2), 187–200 (2001). https://doi.org/10.3758/BF03195365
32. Garaizar, P., Vadillo, M.A., López-de-Ipiña, D.: Presentation accuracy of the web revisited: animation methods in the HTML5 era. PLoS ONE **9**(10), e109812 (2014). https://doi.org/10.1371/journal.pone.0109812
33. Vasilev, M.R., Kirkby, J.A., Angele, B.: Auditory distraction during reading: a Bayesian meta-analysis of a continuing controversy. Perspect. Psychol. Sci. **13**(5), 567–597 (2018). https://doi.org/10.1177/1745691617747398
34. Thompson, W.F., Schellenberg, E.G., Letnic, A.K.: Fast and loud background music disrupts reading comprehension. Psychol. Music **40**(6), 700–708. (2012). https://doi.org/10.1177/0305735611400173
35. Halin, N.: Distracted while reading? Changing to a hard-to-read font shields against the effects of environmental noise and speech on text memory. Front. Psychol. **7**, 1196 (2016). https://doi.org/10.3389/fpsyg.2016.01196
36. Tractinsky, N., Katz, A.S., Ikar, D.: What is beautiful is usable. Interact. Comput. **13**(2), 127–145 (2000). https://doi.org/10.1016/S0953-5438(00)00031-X
37. Kaushik, H.M., Eika, E., Sandnes, F.E.: Towards universal accessibility on the web: do grammar checking tools improve text readability? In: Antona, M., Stephanidis, C. (eds.) HCII 2020. LNCS, vol. 12188, pp. 272–288. Springer, Cham (2020). https://doi.org/10.1007/978-3-030-49282-3_19
38. Eika, E., Sandnes, F.E.: Authoring WCAG2.0-compliant texts for the web through text readability visualization. In: Antona, M., Stephanidis, C. (eds.) UAHCI 2016. LNCS, vol. 9737, pp. 49–58. Springer, Cham (2016). https://doi.org/10.1007/978-3-319-40250-5_5
39. Eika, E., Sandnes, F.E.: Assessing the reading level of web texts for WCAG2.0 compliance—can it be done automatically? In: Di Bucchianico, G., Kercher, P. (eds.) Advances in Design for Inclusion, pp. 361–371. Springer, Cham (2016). https://doi.org/10.1007/978-3-319-41962-6_32
40. Sandnes, F.E.: HIDE: Short IDs for robust and anonymous linking of users across multiple sessions in small HCI experiments. In: CHI 2021, Conference on Human Factors in Computing Systems Extended Abstracts Proceedings. ACM (2021). https://doi.org/10.1145/3411763.3451794
41. Sandnes, F.E., Thorkildssen, H.W., Arvei, A., Buverad, J.O.: Techniques for fast and easy mobile text-entry with three-keys. In: Proceedings of the 37th Annual Hawaii International Conference on System Sciences 2004. IEEE (2004). https://doi.org/10.1109/HICSS.2004.1265675
42. Sandnes, F.E.: Evaluating mobile text entry strategies with finite state automata. In: Proceedings of the 7th International Conference on Human Computer Interaction with Mobile Devices & Services, pp. 115–121. ACM (2005). https://doi.org/10.1145/1085777.1085797
43. JASP Team. JASP (Version 0.14.1) [Computer software] (2020)

User Experience and Technology Acceptance in Universal Access

Design of Human-Centered Adaptive Support Tools to Improve Workability in Older Workers. A Field of Research of Human-Centered AI

Patricia Abril-Jimenez[1]([🖂]) [ID], María Fernanda Cabrera-Umpierrez[1] [ID],
Sergio Gonzalez[1] [ID], Rosa Carreton[2], Ginger Claassen[3],
and María Teresa Arredondo Waldmeyer[1] [ID]

[1] Universidad Politécnica de Madrid, ETSIT, Avda. Complutense 30, 28040 Madrid, Spain
pabril@lst.tfo.upm.es
[2] Asociación Nacional de Fabricantes de Áridos, Pl de las Cortes, 5,6, 28014 Madrid, Spain
[3] Accessibility Competence Center, Fürstenallee 11, 33102 Paderborn, Germany

Abstract. Advanced digitalization and other advanced technologies have proven their value to effectively address our social needs and have played a crucial role in the creation and transformation of society itself. Our daily life operates in an increasingly high-tech environment and revolutionize health provision, but also working conditions. Artificial intelligence (AI) related technologies can provide support at workplaces to compensate for the daily occupational dangers, reducing their impact on long-term worker health status. The purpose of this study is to identify relevant factors to improve long-term workability of aged workers that can be addressed through the use of new AI-based solutions, such as IoT, virtual reality, and interactive virtual coaches. In addition to a state-of-the-art research review, a set of workshop focus groups with the participation of middle-aged workers from different countries and an online European survey were conducted. An overview of the main factors that influence positive and negative on workability have emerged. This paper shows that factors in different working areas and how technology can provide skills and methods to cope with functional decline are relevant to improve workers' workability as they age. Further research is necessary to propose effective technological-based solutions to address the identified results and measure their impact on worker's long-term health.

Keywords: Ageing workforce · Advanced interaction · Digital support · Artificial Intelligence · Collaborative design · Workability

1 Introduction

Artificial intelligence (AI) is an umbrella term for multiple smart and adaptive products and services that aim to automatically support and solve problems that arise during

This work has received funding from the European's Union Horizon 2020 research and innovation programme under Grant Agreement No. 826299.

© The Author(s), under exclusive license to Springer Nature Switzerland AG 2022
M. Antona and C. Stephanidis (Eds.): HCII 2022, LNCS 13308, pp. 177–187, 2022.
https://doi.org/10.1007/978-3-031-05028-2_11

routine activities. AI models can learn from the increasing availability of data and information, discover patterns, and solve classification problems in a way that has never been done before. These smart technologies have become powerful tools that can bring benefits not only for key economic sectors, but also for individuals and society as a whole, especially in our rapidly changing society.

One of the sectors in which AI is penetrating much faster is industry [1]. In fact, over the past decades, the industry sector has emerged at the forefront of AI technology development and advanced use, with the combination of smart manufacturing technologies, cyberphysical infrastructure, and data control to improve productivity, predict, and adapt to sectors changing needs. This strong digitalization of the industry, known as Industry 4.0, has allowed the efficiency of optimized production systems in terms of time, cost, and resources needed [2].

However, this focus on processes and routines digitalization improvement usually neglects including human factors in the loop [3]. This lack is even more striking in modern western companies due to the continuous age of workers growth due to societal demographic change. The demographic development of the society obviously affects the workforce. More than 45% of the workers in the European Union are older than 45 years [4]. In addition, the pressure of the baby boomer generation on the public health and welfare systems is forcing governments to prolong the working lifetime.

This situation adds complexity to the effective deployment of adaptive manufacturing and management systems [5], with a focus on promoting occupational safety, increased long-term workability, and skills-based training that allow the adaptation of the workforce to the needs of production. From the point of view of human factors, ergonomics, and well-being at work policies, multiple challenges are open to face the influence of aging on work performance, and AI related technologies have the potential to include ageing workers' specific needs and abilities into their highly innovative process. However, the performance of the AI algorithms and their real usefulness depend on the quality of their design, the data used for their training, and the learning mechanisms. At the core of this process, human-centred design methodologies are crucial to manage the growing complexity of the involved systems while adapting to workers' needs for the aging process and making their control, management, and maintenance easier [6]. Furthermore, since there is a need to measure AI performance to clearly understand the requirements and expectations of workers, including the specific needs of minority groups or aspects related to context, benchmarking completes collaborative discovery of needs and requirements, and provides a target for discovering key objectives and improving performance and acceptance.

In this context, the present research explores the need to include a more focused human-centred approach in the digitalization processes of the industry sector, with an emphasis on maintaining the well-being and workability of older workers for longer. In particular, this research proposes a human-centered approach within the approach of the Ageing@Work project [7], to define the necessary requirements and functionalities of a smart system aimed at analysing the functional decline of aged workers and automatically propose techniques, strategies, and tools to enhance their natural capacity to cope with job demands, also considering their health status (i.e., physical, cognitive, and social) and skills.

2 Methods and Materials

This study addresses the analysis of industrial cases focused on human-related problems, including special ageing management at the company level, adaptive workstations (e.g., ergonomics, physical limitations, activity reassignments, etc.), workers' attitudes (i.e., intergenerational relationships and knowledge exchange, relationship management) and other human factors geared toward prolonging a healthy and productive work life, by improving workplace activities using AI-powered technology.

The methodology used consisted of a mixed method process oriented to improve the understanding of the current situation of aged workers in industry, with a focus on physically demanding jobs. Data collection and analysis were carried out using an iterative method of literature review, individual interviews, and focus groups. Two industrial sectors were involved in the process, the aggregated extraction and manufacturing industries, where aging workers are very common and age-related problems occur frequently [8].

2.1 Review of the Literature

The review of previous technology-related research and state-of-the-art research aimed to discover current trends in smart environment monitoring and interaction at work with a focus on maintaining well-being and healthy workplaces. Based on available research, the secondary objective was the definition of the most appropriate adaptive functionalities, according to work conditions, the tasks of the workers and their physical and cognitive abilities.

To perform the necessary initial search for technologies, applications, and best practices, we followed the recommendations offered by the PICO model [9]. The PICO process is a technique used in evidence-based practice to frame and answer a clinical question in terms of the specific patient's problem that helps to find evidence in the literature. To carry out this search, we have adapted the research questions of the PICO model to the work environment and workability, with a special emphasis on older workers, as can be seen in Table 1.

Using these research questions, the search terms of the research team were defined. The terms were combined using a Boolean OR operator.

This method was conducted by systematically searching for relevant journals and articles through two established databases, Scopus and Web of Science, but also analysing European Commission, OCDE and OSHA reports. The selected articles and reports were analysed to determine eligibility and the selected ones were incorporated into the analysis. The process was carried out in two phases with the aim of incorporating the results of the workshops into the research process and enhancing search and analysis. During the second phase, the impact of Covid-19 on working activities were also taken into account in the research.

Table 1. PICO design questions for literature research.

Question	Scope
In what population are we interested?	Active workers over 50 years of age. There is no restriction on the type of work
What kinds of interventions are we interested in?	Any kind of tools, technologies, adaptations or best practices that cover the main domains and areas of interest (Policy for older workers, increasing job retention (postponing early retirement), Improving productivity and workability, Healthy habits programs, Adaptation, and compensatory mechanisms
Would the study need a *comparison* group?	The comparison could be with those workers or companies that do not use any kind of compensatory mechanism, tool, technology, or best practice
What are the outcomes in which we are interested?	Improvement documented in the following areas Learning and cognitive functions, sensory ability, physical ability, psychology/mental abilities (including sleep problems) and workability (including promotion and workplace design; redeployment and transition to retirement)

2.2 Collaborative Focus Group Methodology

Parallel to this process, collaborative sessions were held with workers, using on-site and online workshops using a focus group approach, and individual surveys to support the iterative design of potential AI system. The goal of these sessions was to understand the daily tasks of older workers in their work routines, what were their needs and how they can receive technological support, with a focus on improving human interaction. The focus group workshops followed the same format, both online and offline. After an initial welcome to the participants and a short description of the main functionalities and dynamic of the workshop, the objectives were introduced. The informed consent was asked, and the sessions were recorded. A series of questions were used to guide the different discussions during the focus group sessions, and the discussion proceed organically. The session recordings were transcribed verbatim before analysing the results. Sample questions for the focus group data collection included:

- Tell me about your experience with smart devices at work.
- During the pandemic lockdown, have you started using any technological solution, application, or device that you have not used before at work?
- In your opinion, are smart devices at work beneficial?
- In your opinion, what are the most problematic?
- Have smart devices and applications such as the ones proposed by Ageing@Work met your expectations in your daily routines?

Three workshops were held between May 2020 and October 2021 with the participation of five to ten workers aged 45+ years in each of them.

2.3 Online Survey

Finally, the individual survey was conducted online. Industrial pilot setting workers were asked about their experiences related to the ageing process at their work and their strategies to cope with the functional decline due to aging, about performing daily work routines using new technologies, their skills training needs, and their intentions to use these solutions in the future, also for private life needs. Participants who had already used some type of technological system in their work setting were also asked about the barriers they had encountered before becoming familiar and skilled with the solution and their actual experiences. The survey had a total of 45 questions separated into four domains: 1) aspects related with the use of technology, aimed at discovering participants' use and know-how about technology; 2) well-being at work, aimed at finding main aspects to improve with the use of technology; 3) job satisfaction; and 4) technological acceptance, functionalities, privacy, and security.

3 Results

3.1 Summary of Results of the Literature Review

Different existing tools that support active and healthy lifestyles, from nutritional and physical activity apps to work schedule and daily life organizers, which may be used by workers in their daily life, were analysed. Furthermore, this analysis aimed to provide a thorough assessment of best practices and persuasive technologies that can be used to realize an effective motivating AI-supported system.

The benchmarked best practices, tools, and technologies cover the following domains closely related with the dimensions of age management initiatives in Europe: learning and cognitive functions, sensory ability, physical ability, psychology/mental abilities (including sleep problems) and workability (including promotion and workplace design; redeployment and transition to retirement).

- Domain 1. Policy for older workers: tools and technologies that aim to improve interpersonal communication between the later and other workers in the workplace.
- Domain 2. Increasing job retention (postponing early retirement): learning and training tools and technologies oriented to workability enhancement based on better psychological and stress management training, workplace adaptability, and management and enjoy new career challenges, in order to reduce the desire for early retirement and increase the workability index
- Domain 3. Improving productivity and workability: this domain includes health promotion programs based on physical, psychological and stress management training accompanied by diet counselling. Furthermore, this domain also reports interventions focused on productivity, absenteeism, sickness absence, and presentism, including alternative therapies such as yoga, mindfulness, or Tai chi.

- Domain 4. Healthy habits programs that promote physical activity, better nutrition, cessation of smoking, and health education seminars. This domain also includes educational leisure programs and early prevention programs, such as vaccines and medical check-ups.
- Domain 5. Adaptation and compensatory mechanisms to adapt the work environment to the functional decline of aging and to chronic diseases.

A total of 103 technologies, tools and best practices were analysed (62 during the first stage and 41 during the second stage). Each of the elements was analysed and classified according to the usefulness of tools, technology, sensors, devices, and best practices in each of the five domains (Fig. 1).

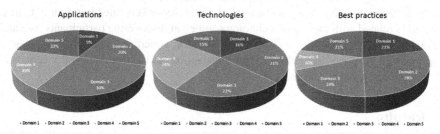

Fig. 1. Summary of the three categories of elements researched during the literature review, per domain.

Other important aspect commonly highlighted in consulted sources is the need of the worker to be already interested in having a healthy way of living, otherwise, the adherence to the application, advice, or activities purposes is very low. Usability and navigability of apps and tools with major acceptance should be carefully analysed together with the results of the focus groups in order to adapt the user experience.

During the second stage of this phase, after the Covid-19 outbreak, it was found the importance of technology on adapting working environments, and in some way, the pandemic boosted the uptake of new technologies in most of the working environments. We can highlight here the enormous number of new applications oriented to improve communication between peers that evidence of the importance of intergenerational relationships at work. These tools are key in the process and can break down the barriers of ageing stereotypes.

Other practices, tools and technologies, investigated aimed to provide long-term learning approaches, that mean, adaptation to changing environments.

3.2   Overview of the Results of the Focus Groups

A total of 35 workers participated in the focus groups. All participants reported their need to improve the daily conditions of work. They considered tailored recommendations and advice, as well as other more advanced solutions, such as persuasive virtual coaches, to have the potential to improve physical conditions and overcome work-related problems such as back pain, stress management, or overload. The general feeling was that such solutions could be useful for all workers independently of their age, but they recognized that aged workers were more aware of the physical and mental problems of daily working and more willing to adopt medium- and long-term solutions to solve or reduce the impact of working conditions in their health.

Several concerns emerged when they were asked about the practical implications of using this type of solutions to improve their health and well-being habits at work and to improve, in this way, their workability and work performance. They argued that it seems difficult to use a virtual coach while working, especially the recommendations about healthy habits, such as playing more sports or having relaxation time. When discussing about this specific topic and the reason for this general statement, the main reasons given were the resistance to change behaviours, for example, lack of willingness to introduce new routines into their daily habits. Besides this, the participants recognised the usefulness of a personal virtual coach to acquire healthy habits not only at work but also at home. However, when considering its use at home, new concerns emerged about data privacy and data flow between home and work. Some participants deemed such type of solutions as very useful, but annoying if they have to follow regular recommendations that may lead to change their habits. In this sense, adding rewards could be a way of maintaining medium- and long-term engagement with this kind of digital solutions (Fig. 2).

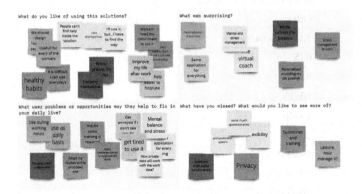

Fig. 2. Canvas with the results of one of the workshop sessions.

The results of the interviews provided preliminary information on the needs for a successful preservation of ageing and well-being at work and the role of digital tools in this. There were several positive experiences and expectations, but there were also concerns. In general, participants were confident with their functional capabilities, but recognize that the acquisition or improvement of their well-being habits could improve in the medium-term health outcomes, and the digital tools could facilitate, in the same way this acquisition. However, privacy and security concerns appeared, especially if the same tool or solution could be used for both work and private life support.

3.3 Overview of Interviews

A total of 574 responses were obtained from the survey. The profile description for the participants is summarized in Table 2.

Table 2. Sociodemographic characteristics of the survey participants

Category	Participants
Age	
>55 years	36,55%
Gender	
Male	50%
Job position	
Office worker	54.8%
Plant operator	1,6%
Maintenance	6,5%
Mobile machinery operator	8,1%
Remote technical assistant	3,2%
Other	35,5%
Years of experience	
0–5	1,6%
6–10	3.2%
10–15	1,6%
15–20	24,2%
20–25	27,4%
More than 25	41,9%
Highest level of education completed	
Primary school	0%
Secondary school	11,3%
University	75,8%
Vocational training	12,9
Other	3.2%

Most of the participants (over 75%) use digital tools and the Internet regularly for daily routines. Among them, more than 50% use digital tools in their daily work routines. The use of personal monitoring devices is extensive in younger men (50% of men between 45 to 55, however, only the 35% of women in the same age range). None of the participants use these types of monitoring devices for working purposes, but for personal monitoring and leisure. In addition, there is a relationship with the daily use of digital tools had the age of the participants (higher daily use, and more types of applications in younger users) and the professional profile (more in administrative and management profiles). Virtual Reality (VR) devices are used by 23% of the participants, but only 1% for work-related tasks. The main usage of VR tools is leisure.

Regarding well-being at work, the results are very positive. The worst result is the one related to the hours worked, with 20% of those surveyed declaring themselves dissatisfied or totally dissatisfied while the physical demand of the job is positively assessed. Both results are consistent with the interviewees profession with the vast majority working in offices.

Concerning the level of satisfaction and commitment at work, the results are very positive in terms of both vigour, dedication, and absorption. The highest percentage refers to absorption at work, so that 77.5% feels that time flies when they work intensively on a daily basis or regularly throughout the year. This is explained taking into consideration the profession and the tasks performed. Concentration and dedication are more likely to be intense in an office job than when doing a physical and repetitive task.

About the 65% of participants considers that digital solutions could support their tasks and even improve their work performance, however, a similar number of participants considers some of the new technologies introduced in their work are unnecessary and they reduce the engagement of the workers and the employment opportunities. Moreover, 75% of the participants expressed their willingness to use AI based technologies to improve their well-being at work and facilitate training and skills acquisitions, but they also expressed their concern about data privacy and how the continuous monitoring of the data could affect the internal management of the workplaces and the impact on their work relationships. At this point, ethical issues were found to be the main concerns among the participants.

4   Conclusions

The research proposes a human-centered approach to discover the requirements of adaptative systems to support ageing workers in the context of Industry 4.0. As aging workers (over 45 years) are increasing in Europe as well as worldwide, there is an urgent need to understand their needs and maintain their well-being and workability, improving the design of smart industrial systems. These systems have the potential to adapt their behaviours to support the interaction of workers, while compensating for the functional decline due to their age and also maximizing their skills and productivity capacity [10]. System adaption can be defined on the basis of technology state of the art, applying human-centered design technologies to reduce the resistance to change and enhance the adaptive behaviour of the user. Preliminary results demonstrate very positive attitudes towards these AI based systems, but a collaborative design strategy such as the proposed in this paper should be systematically adopted in industrial digitalization processes for promoting the regular inclusion of human factors, with special focus on ageing.

Current technologies have proven their usefulness in supporting ageing and increasing life expectancy and supporting independent living of the citizen when ageing. Additionally, some of the tools, technologies, and applications explored in this document have a wide acceptance in the population to support activities of fitness and wellness.

This can be appreciated by the large number of applications and tools in the areas of physical activity and wellbeing analysed.

Furthermore, these results also give an in-depth understanding of the dynamic multidimensional factors that influence the self-perceived well-being of aged miners. This can contribute to better awareness on how to adapt working environments to the ageing natural functional decline process, preserving workability and job satisfaction. Suitable working time models are one important measure for maintaining or even improving the working capacity of older workers. Furthermore, stress relieves employees who care for elderly relatives or children, and thus maintains their productivity and decreases the risk of accidents or negligence in general. Personalization of the models should take into account social and family context in other to better fix the possible solutions and achieve with the proposed objective. Close collaboration with managers is absolutely necessary for the success of the proposed solution.

The interviews and focus group results illustrate that workers are positive towards adopting digital technology applications that will allow them to better deal with their work-life balance, but specific reported needs and preferences should be considered in advance for developing such AI supported of services. These types of solution could be a good point to address, since we know from previous economic recession that people who are closer to retirement are usually not the preferred group to hire and train [11]. The use of new technologies such as eLearning or VR can make intergenerational training more attractive, open new opportunities for retraining older individuals, and address the need or wish to work for longer.

Next steps in research should be the design of customized interventions, the proposed services and applications, taking advantage of sensor technology, artificial intelligence, and other key enabling technologies adopted by the Ageing@Work project, which uses the results of our study as a starting point. These interventions will be positively influenced by a more productive and successful personal and social life of the workers. The identified factors should be considered in developing strategic plans to maintain health and promote ageing workers.

References

1. Furman, J., Seamans, R.: AI and the economy. Innov. Policy Econ. **19**(1), 161–191 (2019)
2. Lasi, H., Fettke, P., Kemper, H.-G., Feld, T., Hoffmann, M.: Industry 4.0. Bus. Inf. Syst. Eng. **6**(4), 239–242 (2014). https://doi.org/10.1007/s12599-014-0334-4
3. Manuti, A., Monachino, D.: Managing knowledge at the time of artificial intelligence: an explorative study with knowledge workers. East Eur. J. Psycholinguist. **7**(2) (2020). https://doi.org/10.29038/eejpl.2020.7.2.man
4. Buzzelli, G.: Class structure and technological replaceability of the European workforce (2021)
5. Guerin, R.J., Castillo, D., Hendricks, K.J., Howard, J., Piacentino, J., Okun, A.H.: Preparing the future workforce for safe and healthy employment (2020)
6. Zarte, M., Pechmann, A., Nunes, I.: Principles for human-centered system design in Industry 4.0 – a systematic literature review. In: Nunes, I.L. (ed.) AHFE 2020. AISC, vol. 1207, pp. 140–147. Springer, Cham (2020). https://doi.org/10.1007/978-3-030-51369-6_19

7. Giakoumis, D., Votis, K., Altsitsiadis, E., Segkouli, S., Paliokas, I., Tzovaras, D.: Smart, personalized and adaptive ICT solutions for active, healthy and productive ageing with enhanced workability. In: Proceedings of the 12th ACM International Conference on PErvasive Technologies Related to Assistive Environments, pp. 442–447, June 2019

8. Calzavara, M., Battini, D., Bogataj, D., Sgarbossa, F., Zennaro, I.: Ageing workforce management in manufacturing systems: state of the art and future research agenda. Int. J. Prod. Res. **58**(3), 729–747 (2020)

9. Frandsen, T.F., Nielsen, M.F.B., Lindhardt, C.L., Eriksen, M.B.: Using the full PICO model as a search tool for systematic reviews resulted in lower recall for some PICO elements. J. Clin. Epidemiol. **127**, 69–75 (2020)

10. Cabrita, M., op den Akker, H., Tabak, M., Hermens, H.J., Vollenbroek-Hutten, M.M.R.: Persuasive technology to support active and healthy ageing: an exploration of past, present, and future. J. Biomed. Inform. **84**, 17–30 (2018). https://doi.org/10.1016/j.jbi.2018.06.010

11. Berg-Beckhoff, G., Nielsen, G., Ladekjær Larsen, E.: Use of information communication technology and stress, burnout, and mental health in older, middle-aged, and younger workers – results from a systematic review. Int. J. Occup. Environ. Health **23**(2), 160–171 (2017). https://doi.org/10.1080/10773525.2018.1436015

Modified User Experience Evaluation Methods Applied to Blind Users in Latin America: Case Study TriviaBlind

Teresita Álvarez-Robles[1]([⊠]) ⓘ, Francisco Javier Álvarez-Rodriguez[2] ⓘ,
and J. Andrés Sandoval-Bringas[1] ⓘ

[1] Universidad Autómoma de Baja California Sur, Sur Km. 5.5, CP 23080 La Paz, B.C.S.,
México
alvarez88.t@gmail.com
[2] Universidad Autónoma de Aguascalientes, Av. Universidad 940, CP 20100 Aguascalientes,
Ags., México

Abstract. The main objective of this work is to evaluate through different user experience evaluation methods which have been modified to be implemented with blind users, the accessibility, utility, ease of use, among other factors of the UX with blind people from Mexico and Costa Rica. The approach used based on the methods used was qualitative and quantitative, the first to know the opinion of the target users and the second to evaluate some aspects such as time or the fulfillment of the task in a general way. The study sample consisted of 10 users, 5 Mexicans and 5 Costa Ricans, between 18 and 41 years old, of both genders with knowledge in the use of mobile devices and screen readers. As a result, we observed that regardless of being users from different countries, the methods are easy to follow and implement as they are designed for blind users. Therefore, the research allows us to conclude that it is relevant to make minor adjustments to existing methods to evaluate the prototypes of systems, products, or services from the early stages with the target users to guarantee a UX that meets the characteristics of blind participants.

Keywords: Human-computer interaction (HCI) · User eXperience (UX) · Evaluation methods · Blind users

1 Introduction

Several software systems focus on supporting people with visual disabilities, whether the user is entirely blind or has some type of low vision; currently, most of these systems focus on offering the best quality products, systems, or services being developed. With the quality, we mean that each product is easy to learn, easy to use, and accessible to the target user. The above mention some of the factors that we must meet within the user experience to provide a product, system, or service to the user with visual impairment that meets its characteristics.

© The Author(s), under exclusive license to Springer Nature Switzerland AG 2022
M. Antona and C. Stephanidis (Eds.): HCII 2022, LNCS 13308, pp. 188–199, 2022.
https://doi.org/10.1007/978-3-031-05028-2_12

Some works, such as [1–3], focus on specific characteristics that are important when considering a system for people with visual disabilities development. For example, some factors are considered so that the development system has compatibility with the device's screen reader. In addition, both haptic and auditory feedback meet the user's needs or focus on implementing touch aids.

In the case of [1], it focuses on the user locating physical objects in the environment both horizontally and vertically. Although the tests in [1] were carried out by two groups, (1) blind users and (2) normal vision people, the difference was that the blind group quickly detected sounds in the horizontal plane, and normal vision users performed best on ascending sounds, that is, vertical sounds. In [2], feedback strategies such as the touch part and the auditory part are combined to support both blind and low vision users; based on the tests carried out, it is possible to determine that the system developed is usable and users enjoy interacting with the interface. Finally, in [3], use is made of the navigation technique, which is useful to help people with visual impairment since it reduces the cognitive load of having to detect, locate and plan simultaneously. The system evaluated in [3], NavCog sends three types of messages: (1) remote announcements, (2) action instructions, and (3) point of interest (POI) descriptions.

In general, these works are presented to exemplify some cases in which certain types of feedback are used for the visually impaired user, such as these, there are various and newer methods to offer information to the target users. However, it is essential to highlight that, even with satisfactory results in their tests, in some cases, specific evaluation methods are not followed to carry out the evaluation tests.

In cases [2] and [3], it is specifically observed that the evaluation is carried out with satisfaction questionnaires, an open-ended questionnaire, and the direct observation of the researchers. On the other hand, in the second case, the researchers did not carry out a specific evaluation method because the tests were carried out in the same field of study. Therefore, in this case, the users followed simple instructions given by the facilitators, and subsequently, this test is evaluated with a video.

In this work, we want to highlight why it is crucial to consider the evaluation methods of the user experience in the early phases of software development where the target users are involved to guarantee the product, system, or service that is being made.

1.1 The User Experience (UX) Evaluation Importance

At the first point, the user experience (UX) allows us to know our users' needs, capabilities, and limitations. Once we get results, the goal is to produce simple, user-friendly, and accessible products to learn. In a few words and based on [4], "user experience" encompasses all aspects of the end-user interaction with the company, its services, its systems, and its products.

The importance of carrying out a UX evaluation with the target users is that if we involve them from the first stages of software development (Sw), such as analysis and design, we can avoid future large-scale errors that can lead to monetary losses or the cancellation of the product that we are making.

There are cases such as studies [1–3], among others found in the literature, where despite obtaining good results, they do not guarantee the user experience by not evaluating it with the established methods for it.

It is important to carry out the necessary tests because this guarantees, if not all, at least most of the factors that make up the UX (see Fig. 1).

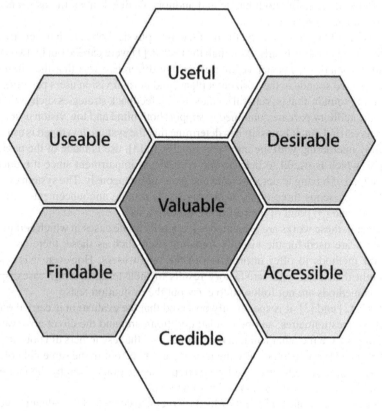

Fig. 1. The user experience honeycomb. [Public domain], via Semantic Studios [5]. (http://sem anticstudios.com/user_experience_design/).

Based on [5], at the core of UX is ensuring that users find value in what you are providing to them. For this reason, it is important to carry out the tests with the corresponding methods and do the tests with the end-users of the system.

1.2 User Experience Evaluation Method

Within the literature and based on [6], there are 86 methods for evaluating user experience. This collection of methods is distributed in different categories to help the evaluator detect their needs and identify which methods apply to the case we want to evaluate.

Some main categories that exist within UX evaluation methods are: (1) types of methods, (2) development phase, (3) studied period of experience, and (4) evaluator/information provider; and each of them has subsections, such as the methods applied in *the field of study, in laboratory studies, in early prototypes, in functional prototypes, before usage, snapshot during the interaction, one user at a time* and *group of users*, to mention some of those found in [6].

The UX evaluation methods that we used to evaluate our case study were: Hedonic and utility Scales (HED/UT Scale) and Positive and negative affect scale (PANAS).

It is important to note that the evaluation method Thinking aloud is modified for blind users [7]; however, we did not consider this case study due to the extent required by its results.

In the HED/UT Scale method, we followed the steps established in [8]. In general, the method consists of filling out some forms based on the realization of tasks by the blind user; in this way, we obtain results that allow us to know if the product, system, or service is useful and meets the needs of the end-user. Although the method evaluates two UX factors, (1) desirability and (2) utility, it should be mentioned that this method, like the previous one, can be carried out in the development stages based on the software engineering definition [9].

For the PANAS method, the process is very similar to that defined in the previous method [8], the only aspect that changes are that the elements to be evaluated focus on the percentage of positive and negative affect that it causes to users once they perform specific tasks within the system. This method can also be implemented in the development stages based on the Software engineering ISO [9] and evaluates the desirability, usability, and value of UX factors.

So, suppose the minimum percentages are met in each implemented method. In that case, it is guaranteed that the result will provide a satisfactory UX for the blind user by meeting at least four of the six user experience factors.

2   Study Case: TriviaBlind

TriviaBlind [10] is an entertainment Interactive Software System (ISS) developed for visually impaired/blind people. The purpose of TriviaBlind is to support users with visual disabilities in learning general culture in various areas of knowledge. Through this application, they can acquire knowledge to support their studies (if the blind person is studying) or just for sharing information with someone else.

It is important to point out that different systems have the same function and objective; before starting this project, the best-known ones were evaluated, i.e., Maraton [11] and Preguntados [12]. These systems were evaluated with blind users, and we could see that they are not accessible since it does not read to users what they are touching on the mobile device's screen, so they easily stop using the system.

Based on the previous, TriviaBlind focuses on providing all the necessary audios for the blind user; in the same way, it is expected to meet the expectations of our visually impaired users by offering an acceptable UX. For this reason, we involve our users in the testing phases to get feedback on contingencies that were overlooked at the time of development.

2.1   Participants

Our users must comply with a profile to participate in the ISS TriviaBlind evaluation.

The points that we are taking into account are:

- The user must be blind from birth or acquired.
- Their age ranges between 18+
- The user must understand using a mobile device with TalkBack (screen reader) enabled.

Tables 1 and 2 show the characteristics of the users who participated in the UX evaluation; the users in Table 1 are the participants from Costa Rica. The participants in Table 2 are the Mexican participants, respectively.

Table 1. Costa Rica users information.

User	Age	Gender	Blindness type
1	25	Female	Born-blind
2	23	Male	Born-blind
3	36	Female	Acquired blind
4	25	Male	Acquired blind
5	26	Male	Born-blind

Table 2. Mexican users information.

User	Age	Gender	Blindness type
1	18	Female	Born-blind
2	27	Female	Born-blind
3	40	Male	Born-blind
4	41	Female	Acquired blind
5	38	Male	Acquired blind

Once the participants were defined, the tasks that the user had to perform in the TriviaBlind system were established.

2.2 Tasks

We established three tasks, each with its identified objectives. The tasks' purpose is for each of the ten participants to carry out the activities and subsequently evaluate their interaction with the application with each of the modified UX methods for blind users.

The tasks are described below:

- Main Screen Navigation

  - Identify *Home* and *Help* buttons
  - Activate the *Help* button
  - Complete the tutorial

- Level identification and modality.

  - Identify the levels.
  - Select a level.
  - Identify the game modes.
  - Select a game mode.

- Question Round Practice.

  - Start round.
  - Identify the layout of the question screen.
  - Finish the round.
  - Identify the Back button and activate it.

When carrying out the evaluations, the user had to evaluate by task or in a general way; based on this, we decided to start with the HED/UT Scale method test and end with PANAS.

3 Test and Results

For each of the methods, tests were carried out with users from both countries to visualize whether a system developed for blind people and evaluated by blind people has the same impact or not in another country and, in the case of not meeting the expectations of the end-users, assess the changes that we can make not only to the system but also to the modified method.

3.1 HED/UT Scale Test and Results

The HED/UT Scale method measures whether it is useful and gives the user pleasure to use a system, product, or service. It is evaluated by rating 18 items of the ISS each time the user completes each of the established tasks.

We can do the evaluation in two ways with blind users, and they can choose to do it in Braille or verbal mode. The scale to evaluate this method ranges from 1 to 5, where one equals terrible and five equals excellent. It is important to note that there are cases where the item may not apply depending on the characteristic of the ISS; if that is the case, it must be specified in the format where each item is evaluated [8]. Some results in the original layout are shown in Figs. 2 and 3 (usernames are omitted for privacy reasons).

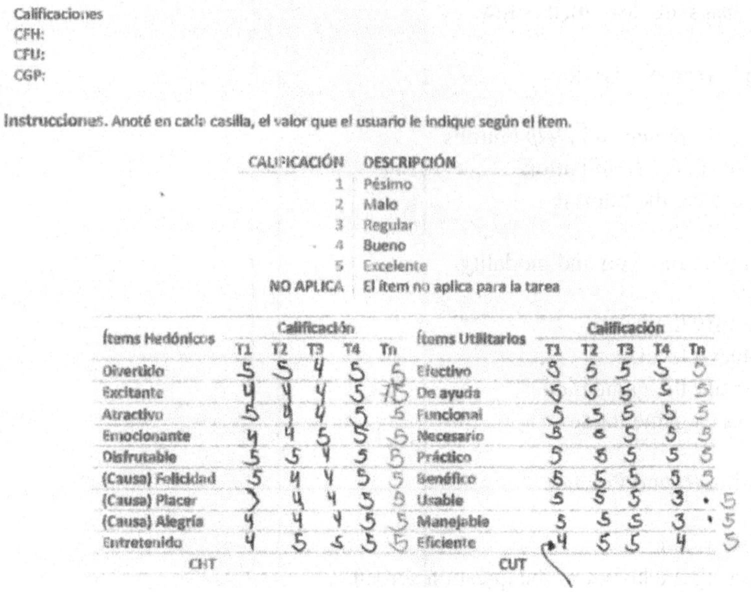

Calificaciones
CFH:
CFU:
CGP:

Instrucciones. Anoté en cada casilla, el valor que el usuario le indique según el ítem.

CALIFICACIÓN	DESCRIPCIÓN
1	Pésimo
2	Malo
3	Regular
4	Bueno
5	Excelente
NO APLICA	El ítem no aplica para la tarea

Ítems Hedónicos	Calificación					Ítems Utilitarios	Calificación				
	T1	T2	T3	T4	Tn		T1	T2	T3	T4	Tn
Divertido	5	5	4	5	5	Efectivo	5	5	5	5	5
Excitante	4	4	4	5	5	De ayuda	5	5	5	5	5
Atractivo	5	4	4	5	5	Funcional	5	5	5	5	5
Emocionante	4	4	5	5	5	Necesario	5	5	5	5	5
Disfrutable	5	5	4	5	5	Práctico	5	5	5	5	5
(Causa) Felicidad	5	4	4	5	5	Benéfico	5	5	5	5	5
(Causa) Placer	3	4	4	3	3	Usable	5	5	5	3	5
(Causa) Alegría	4	4	4	5	5	Manejable	5	5	5	3	5
Entretenido	4	5	5	5	5	Eficiente	4	5	5	4	5
CHT						CUT					

Fig. 2. A blind user results when taking the HED/UT Scale test. Source: own.

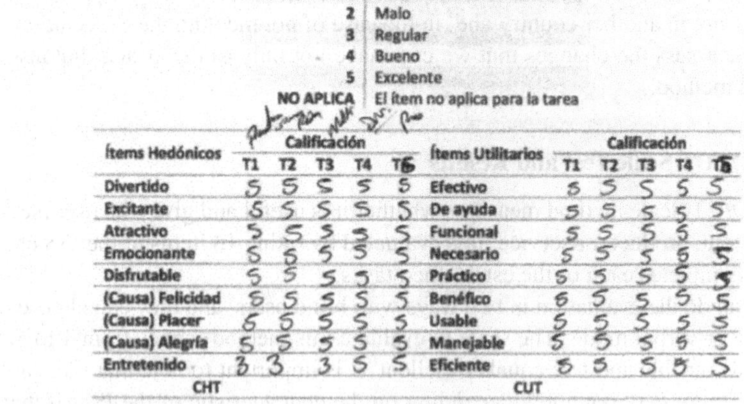

Calificaciones
CFH:
CFU:
CGP:

Instrucciones. Anoté en cada casilla, el valor que el usuario le indique según el ítem.

CALIFICACIÓN	DESCRIPCIÓN
1	Pésimo
2	Malo
3	Regular
4	Bueno
5	Excelente
NO APLICA	El ítem no aplica para la tarea

Ítems Hedónicos	Calificación					Ítems Utilitarios	Calificación				
	T1	T2	T3	T4	T5		T1	T2	T3	T4	T5
Divertido	5	5	5	5	5	Efectivo	5	5	5	5	5
Excitante	5	5	5	5	5	De ayuda	5	5	5	5	5
Atractivo	5	5	5	5	5	Funcional	5	5	5	5	5
Emocionante	5	5	5	5	5	Necesario	5	5	5	5	5
Disfrutable	5	5	5	5	5	Práctico	5	5	5	5	5
(Causa) Felicidad	5	5	5	5	5	Benéfico	5	5	5	5	5
(Causa) Placer	5	5	5	5	5	Usable	5	5	5	5	5
(Causa) Alegría	5	5	5	5	5	Manejable	5	5	5	5	5
Entretenido	3	3	3	5	5	Eficiente	5	5	5	5	5
CHT						CUT					

Fig. 3. Second blind user results when taking the HED/UT Scale test. Source: own.

A form filling was performed for each user, as shown in Figs. 2 and 3. Once the test with the users is done, the results shown in Table 3 are obtained. Once the test with the users has been carried out, the final results shown in Table 3 for Costa Ricans and in Table 4 for Mexicans are obtained.

Table 3. Costa Rican users information

	U1	U2	U3	U4	U5
CFH	4.2	4.7	5	3.9	5
CFU	4.9	5	5	4.3	5
CGP	4.5	4.8	5	4.1	5

Table 4. Mexican users Information

	U6	U7	U8	U9	U10
CFH	4.9	4.8	5	4.9	4.64
CFU	4.8	4.35	5	4.9	4.04
CGP	4.85	4.57	5	4.9	4.34

The terminology used in Tables 3 and 4 are described above:

- U# = the user number
- CFH (for its acronym in Spanish) = Final Hedonic Rating
- CFU (for its acronym in Spanish) = Final Utility Rating
- CGP (for its acronym in Spanish) = General Product Qualification

The scale used to evaluate the results of each user generally is shown in Table 5.

Table 5. HED/UT scale rating scale

Rating	Description
0–0.99	Terrible
1–1.99	Bad
2–2.99	Regular
3–3.99	Okay
4–5	Excellent

Based on the results and the general rating range of the HED/UT Scale method, it is observed that the two groups rated the application of Trivia Blind as excellent.

Therefore, it can be said that the modified method is understandable and easy to apply with any group of blind users and that the application is useful and gives the user pleasure.

3.2 PANAS Test and Results

This method consists of evaluating twenty items which allow knowing through the result if the ISS has a good acceptance on the part of the user with visual impairment; the scale to perform the evaluation is similar to that of the HED/UT Scale method, therefore can be seen in Table 5.

We obtain the positive and negative affections of the TriviaBlind system with this test. Despite being similar to the assessments of PANAS with the HED/UT Scale method, the items change; in Figs. 4 and 5, the results of some users are shown. The above occurs due to the affection scale where if the result is greater or equal to 29.7 (SD 7.9), the ISS has a positive affection on the user; otherwise, if it is less or equal to 14.8 (SD 5.4), the preference of the ISS will be negative. If the result will be in the middle, it means that we can improve it based on comments from the end-user; The general results obtained from doing this test with blind users are shown in Table 6, wherein terms of standard deviation (SD) the ISS TriviaBlind shows an optimal positive affect.

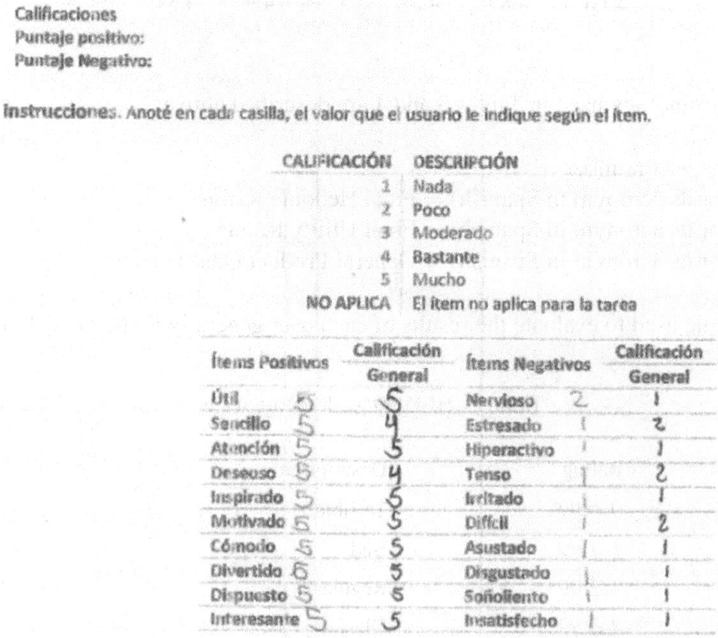

Calificaciones
Puntaje positivo:
Puntaje Negativo:

Instrucciones. Anoté en cada casilla, el valor que el usuario le indique según el ítem.

CALIFICACIÓN	DESCRIPCIÓN
1	Nada
2	Poco
3	Moderado
4	Bastante
5	Mucho
NO APLICA	El ítem no aplica para la tarea

Ítems Positivos	Calificación General	Ítems Negativos	Calificación General
Útil 5	5	Nervioso 2	1
Sencillo 5	4	Estresado 1	2
Atención 5	5	Hiperactivo 1	1
Deseoso 5	4	Tenso 1	2
Inspirado 5	5	Irritado 1	1
Motivado 5	5	Difícil 1	2
Cómodo 5	5	Asustado 1	1
Divertido 5	5	Disgustado 1	1
Dispuesto 5	5	Soñoliento 1	1
Interesante 5	5	Insatisfecho 1	1

Fig. 4. A blind user results when taking the PANAS test. Source: own.

Each group's scores are obtained by taking the item's mean of each group and once the result is obtained, the standard deviation is too. The general result of the TriviaBlind

Calificaciones
Puntaje positivo:
Puntaje Negativo:

Instrucciones. Anoté en cada casilla, el valor que el usuario le indique según el ítem.

CALIFICACIÓN	DESCRIPCIÓN
1	Nada
2	Poco
3	Moderado
4	Bastante
5	Mucho
NO APLICA	El ítem no aplica para la tarea

Ítems Positivos	Calificación General	Ítems Negativos	Calificación General
Útil	5	Nervioso	1
Sencillo	5	Estresado	1
Atención	5	Hiperactivo	1
Deseoso	5	Tenso	1
Inspirado	5	Irritado	1
Motivado	4	Difícil	1
Cómodo	5	Asustado	1
Divertido	4	Disgustado	1
Dispuesto	5	Soñoliento	1
Interesante	5	Insatisfecho	2

Fig. 5. Second blind user results when taking the PANAS Scale test. Source: own.

Table 6. General final results of the UX evaluation method application, PANAS. Source: own.

Average positive score	24.3
Average negative score	5.3

application with Costa Rican users is shown in Table 7 and the results of Mexicans in Table 8.

Table 7. The general final result of the Costa Ricans. Source: own.

Average positive score	23.8
Average negative score	1.1

Table 8. General final results of the UX evaluation method application, PANAS. Source: own.

Average positive score	24.1
Average negative score	1.3

As can be seen in both tables, the results are within the standards; therefore, we can say that the application of TriviaBlind positively affects blind users regardless of their nationality without saturating users with information that the negative affection is shallow, which is good.

4 Conclusions

Through the tests we carried out using the user experience evaluation methods, we observed that when we applied the methods, they were easy to follow by blind users. The above, regardless of nationality, due to an application made with the support of blind users from the early phases, is accessible, useful, and usable, among others.

When applying the modified UX methods, we observed that both methods are easy to implement with blind users. Furthermore, both methods have the option of being carried out verbally or with Braille, allowing the user to choose which way to go to evaluate a system, product, or service.

The previous is fundamental since having these options and including users guarantees the UX. Based on the general results obtained from the tests carried out with the HED/UT Scale and PANAS methods, we can conclude that not only 4 of the 6 UX factors are met, but based on quantitative and qualitative aspects, we guarantee UX in the development of the final product.

As future work, we hope to expand the modified UX evaluation tests for blind users and, at the same time, make relevant modifications to the TriviaBlind system based on feedback provided by blind users.

References

1. Wersényi, G.: Virtual localization by blind persons. J. Audio Eng. Soc. **60**(7/8), 568–579 (2012)
2. Ferati, M., Mannheimer, S., Bolchini, D.: Usability evaluation of acoustic interfaces for the blind. In: Proceedings of the 29th ACM International Conference on Design of Communication (2011)
3. Ahmetovic, D., Gleason, C., Ruan, C., Kitani, K., Takagi, H., Asakawa, C.: NavCog: a navigational cognitive assistant for the blind. In: Association for Computing Machinery. New York (2016)
4. Norman, D., Nielsen, J.: Nielsen Norman Group, NNg (2016). https://www.nngroup.com/art icles/definition-user-experience/. Accessed 13 Jan 2021
5. Morville, P.: Semantic Studios, SS, 21 June 2004 (2004). http://semanticstudios.com/user_e xperience_design/. Accessed 13 Jan 2021
6. Roto, V., et al.: All about UX (2013). https://www.allaboutux.org/
7. Álvarez Robles, T.d.J., Álvarez Rodríguez, F.J.B.-G.E.I.: Process of the usability evaluation method "thinking aloud" modified and applied to blind users in mobile devices. DYNA New Technol. **6**(1), 12 (2019)
8. López, E.E.R., Chery, J.S., Robles, T.d.J.Á., Rodríguez, F.J.Á.: Hedonic utility-scale (HED/UT) modified as a user experience evaluation method of performing talkback tutorial for blind people. In: User-Centered Software Development for the Blind and Visually Impaired: Emerging Research and Opportunities, pp. 62–77. IGI Global (2020)

9. ISO/IEC. International Organization for Standarization (2015). https://www.iso.org/standard/63711.html. Accessed 15 Jan 2021
10. Robles, T.d.J.Á., Orozco, L.A.M., Mariscal, J.L.P., Rodríguez, F.J.Á.B.-G.E.: TriviaBlind: sistema de software interactivo enfocado en la experiencia del usuario de personas ciegas como juego serio para el aprendizaje de cultura general. In: Avances Sobre Reflexiones, Aplicaciones y Tecnologías Inclusivas, La Paz, p. 10. IEEE (2019)
11. Maselu. Google Play, Creaciones Culturales Maselu, 15 May 2017 (2017). https://play.google.com/store/apps/details?id=com.juegomaraton.maratonclasico.Premium&hl=en&gl=US. Accessed 23 Jan 2021
12. Etermax. Google Play, Etermax, 18 January 2021 (2021). https://play.google.com/store/apps/details?id=com.etermax.preguntados.lite&hl=es_419&gl=US. Accessed 23 Jan 2021

Deaf and Hard of Hearing Viewers' Preference for Speaker Identifier Type in Live TV Programming

Akher Al Amin[1,2], Joseph Mendis[1,2], Raja Kushalnagar[1,2], Christian Vogler[1,2], Sooyeon Lee[1,2], and Matt Huenerfauth[1,2(✉)]

[1] Rochester Institute of Technology, Rochester, NY, USA
{aa7510,slics,matt.huenerfauth}@rit.edu
[2] Gallaudet University, Washington, DC, USA
{joseph.mendis,raja.kushalnagar,christian.vogler}@gallaudet.edu

Abstract. When there are multiple people shown onscreen at one time, people who are Deaf and Hard of Hearing (DHH) viewing captions may find it challenging to determine who the current speaker is, especially when speakers interrupt each other abruptly or when there is a lot of turn-taking. Prior research has proposed several methods of indicating speakers, including in-text methods and methods in which the caption is dynamically located onscreen. However, prior work has not examined the effectiveness of various speaker-identifier methods for conveying who is speaking when the number of speakers on the screen increases. To determine which speaker-identifier methods are effective for DHH viewers, as the number of speakers on screen varies, we have conducted an empirical study with 31 DHH participants. We observed DHH viewers preference for speaker-identifier types, for videos that vary in the number of speakers shown onscreen. Determining the relationship between DHH viewers' preference for speaker-identifier methods and the number of onscreen speakers can guide broadcasters to select appropriate speaker-identifier methods based on the number of speakers that appear on the screen.

Keywords: Caption · Speaker-identifier · Live-TV

1 Introduction

More than 15% of US adults who are Deaf and Hard of Hearing (DHH) rely on captioning while watching live television programming [1]. Captioning conveys auditory information, including non-speech information, such as indicating

The contents of this paper were developed under a grant from the National Institute on Disability, Independent Living, and Rehabilitation Research (NIDILRR grant number #90DPCP0002). NIDILRR is a Center within the Administration for Community Living (ACL), Department of Health and Human Services (HHS). The contents of this paper do not necessarily represent the policy of NIDILRR, ACL, HHS, and you should not assume endorsement by the Federal Government.

© The Author(s), under exclusive license to Springer Nature Switzerland AG 2022
M. Antona and C. Stephanidis (Eds.): HCII 2022, LNCS 13308, pp. 200–211, 2022.
https://doi.org/10.1007/978-3-031-05028-2_13

who is currently speaking – to provide information to DHH viewers about the spoken content. Simultaneously reading the captions and following which person onscreen is the current speaker can be challenging, especially when several people speak in an overlapping manner or with quick turn-taking.

To indicate change of speaker and to effectively convey who is speaking, current regulations recommend broadcasters to use a set of speaker-identifier methods, e.g., a double chevron ($>>$) in the text of the caption to indicate a change of speaker. Other options include providing the speaker's name in the caption text, changing the color of text for each person speaking, or "voice narration" (providing some text that conveys characteristics or role of the speaker, e.g., [Female Speaker] or [Host]) [2–4]. However, prior research has revealed that DHH viewers do not find speaker-identification methods as being satisfactory in a scenario where multiple speakers are engaging in rapid turn-taking [5].

In fact, prior work has revealed that DHH viewers have subjective preferences among various speaker-identifier methods, and these preferences vary depending upon the content and attributes of the captioned video [6, 7]. In addition, prior research has explored how the presence of multiple speakers at once on the screen may increase overall cognitive load, since DHH viewers have to perform both reading the captions and seeking the person who is speaking [5, 8]. This research has shown how important it is for DHH viewers to determine who the current speaker is, in order to comprehend the video content holistically. Motivated by the importance of identifying current onscreen speaker from several speakers, our current paper has made use of prior methodology [5, 9] to explore DHH viewers' subjective preferences among various speaker-identifier methods when watching live captioned TV programs that include several speakers.

Generally, broadcasters employ human captioners to generate captioning services for live television broadcasts [10]. Captioners tend to use speaker-identification methods that are recommended by broadcasters. Based on regulatory policy, broadcasters typically use two forms of speaker identification: (1) in-text representation and (2) placement of the captions. Among these, in-text speaker identification methods are [9, 11] more commonly used by broadcasters to indicate a change of speaker or to identify the current speaker. However, this in-text presentation of speakers might be confusing for DHH viewers because of the obvious time-delay during live captioning—ranging from 3 to 6 s—between the actual speech and the appearance of a caption on the screen [11–14]. Due, in part, to this delay, identifying who spoke which part of the captioned text can be challenging, especially when several speakers speak together or frequent turn-taking occurs. Considering this limitation of live settings, there is a need to understand DHH viewers' perspective in terms of their preference for in-text speaker identifier types when multiple speakers appear on the screen.

In a recent paper that presented a preliminary empirical study, we observed that DHH viewers preferred the current speaker to be indicated using a double chevron ($>>$) along with the speaker's name in the caption text, as compared to showing a double chevron alone [9]. This initial finding suggested that the double-chevron-only in-text speaker identifier method recommended by regulators and used by many broadcasters may not be satisfactory to DHH viewers.

Fig. 1. Sample images of captioned videos with speaker identifier based on (a) double chevron with speaker's name, (b) color, (c) voice narration, or (d) emoji

To the best of our knowledge, no prior research has investigated how the number of onscreen speakers may also influence DHH viewers' preferences for in-text speaker indicator types. To understand this effect, we conducted an empirical study to collect DHH users' subjective feedback on a set of video stimuli containing a wide range of speaker-identifier methods and with multiple speakers on the screen. The key contribution of this research is demonstrating how the number of speakers on screen may influence DHH viewers' reported preferences among speaker-identifier methods.

2   Related Work

2.1   Existing Speaker Identification Types

A wide-range of speaker-identifier methods have been employed by broadcasters. For instance, double chevron, speakers' name, or new color [2–4,15,15–18] are used to indicate change of speaker in a video. In addition, caption-placement approaches can also be used to indicate speakers, e.g., a caption may be located on screen in a manner that follows the position of the person speaking on the screen [19] or a comic-book-style speech bubble may be used [20] or Real-Time Text Display with Speaker-Identification (RTT-ID), which displays location of a speaker in a group [6]. Among these various speaker-identifier methods used in live television programming, prior research has found that DHH viewers have specific preferences among speaker-identification methods [5,6]. For instance, prior work has discussed how, in live television broadcast settings where captions are generated by human captioners, in-text speaker identification methods are preferred over placement-based approach, due to time and resource constraints that prevent careful placement of captions at specific locations onscreen [2,21].

2.2   Factors Influencing DHH Viewers' Preference for Speaker Identifier Types

Prior work has identified several video attributes that influence DHH viewers' preferences among certain speaker identification methods. For instance, users, while playing games or watching videos in augmented reality environment, prefer speakers' images to be included alongside caption text, as a speaker identifier [22]. Also users' preferences among speaker identification methods varies depending upon whether the speakers are known to the viewers or not. If someone who is known, then viewers reported that the speakers' name as an identifier could be useful; otherwise, the speaker's name may not be useful [23]. In a recent research, DHH viewers reported a preference for speaker identification methods that include additional information about the speaker [9]. However, including more textual information could lead to additional cognitive load on DHH viewers [8]. In addition, prior research has revealed frustration among DHH viewers in seeking the current speaker among multiple speakers visible on the screen while watching live captioned TV programming. To the best of our knowledge, no prior research has investigated which speaker identification methods will allow viewers to determine the current speaker effectively among multiple speakers on screen in live TV programs.

3 Research Question

As discussed above, prior work on speaker identification methods has not yet investigated how DHH viewers' subjective judgment for a video differs based on various speaker identifier methods in a real-time setting. Therefore, in this study, we experimentally evaluate how variations in the number of speakers on the screen affect viewers' judgments of video quality, in the following research question:

RQ: Do DHH viewers' preferred speaker identifier types vary based on the number of onscreen speakers?

4 Methods

4.1 Construction of Video Stimuli

As discussed above, several speaker-identification methods have been used in the television industry to indicate which onscreen person is speaking each segment of the caption text. This includes a wide-range of in-text speaker identification methods, e.g., double chevrons, the speakers' name, text color changes, in-line emoji, voice narration of the speaker's identity [2–4,15,15–18]. Among this set, in this study, we selected four speaker identification approaches that are highly used in live settings [2,4]. A list of speaker identification methods investigated in this study are as follows:

- Double Chevron with speakers' name
- Color of the text
- Voice Narration (Narration of the speaker identity)
- Emoji

After selecting these four speaker-identification methods to investigate, we then fixed the number of speakers that we planned to include in the video stimuli for the study. We examined a variety of live-broadcast videos from news, interviews, or talk shows, and we observed how many speakers appeared on the screen [24]. From our observation, we determined that, commonly, when multiple people were speaking in a video, it was 2, 3, or 4 people [5]. Therefore, we have selected these numbers of speakers when selecting video stimuli in our study, so that we could determine which speaker-identification methods would be preferred under each condition.

Based on the factors above, we needed to select potential video stimuli. We began by examining videos that had been broadcast live on various TV channels. A total of 150 video stimuli were examined from several broadcasters, including:

NBC, ABC, and CNN. From this video stimuli dataset, we selected a subset of videos for the final experiment. These selection of video stimuli were informed by the number of speakers (2, 3, or 4) that appear on the screen. We selected a total of 9 video stimuli, 3 for each different number of speakers.

As discussed in previous section, in this study, we will examine 4 types of in-text speaker identifier methods. Thus, for each of these 9 videos, we engineered four different versions of the caption files, each using one of the four speaker-identifier methods. Then, we burned these caption files into the video stimuli. In this way, a total of 36 video stimuli were prepared for evaluation during our study.

4.2   Recruitment and Participants

Participants were recruited by posting an advertisement on social media websites and a university-internal discord group. The advertisement included two key criteria: (1) identifying as Deaf or Hard of Hearing and (2) regularly using captioning when viewing videos or television. Participants received $25 cash compensation for this remotely conducted 30-min study, using video-conferencing software. A total of 31 people participated in the study, including 17 women, 13 men, and one person who identified as non-binary. Their ages ranged from 18 to 28 years (median = 25). All participants identified as Deaf, and they reported regularly using American Sign Language at home or work.

4.3   Study Design and Procedure

For this study, a website was developed to display to participants several videos with variations of speaker-identifier types, and participants responded to questions, to provide their subjective impression of the quality of the speaker-identifier types included in captions. The 30-min study was partitioned into three time-segments, with stimuli shown during each segment consisting of videos that had a specific number of speakers present on the screen. After participants watched each video stimulus, they responded to three subjective scalar questions, of which Question 1 was adapted from [25] and Question 3 from [9].

Q1: *How useful did you find the captions?* Participants were asked to respond to this question on a five-point scale from 'Not Useful' to 'Very Useful.' For the remainder of this paper, this question may be briefly referred to as the "Usefulness" question.

Q2: *Did you enjoy watching the video with the caption?* Participants responded to this question on a standard five-point Likert-scale from 'Strongly Disagree' to 'Strongly Agree.' For the remainder of this paper, this question may be referred to as the "Enjoyability" question.

Q3: *It was easy to follow the video.* Participants responded to this question on a standard five-point Likert-scale from 'Strongly Disagree' to 'Strongly Agree.' For the remainder of this paper, this question may be referred to as the "Easy-to-follow" question.

Table 1. Example schedule of stimuli shown to a participant in the study.

Segment	Video stimulus no.	Video stimuli attributes	
		Number of speakers appear on the screen	Speaker identifier type
1	1	2	Double chevron (>>) with speakers' name
	2	2	Color
	3	2	Voice narration
	4	2	Emoji
2	5	3	Double chevron (>>) with speakers' name
	6	3	Color
	7	3	Voice narration
	8	3	Emoji
3	9	4	Double chevron (>>) with speakers' name
	10	4	Color
	11	4	Voice narration
	12	4	Emoji

Table 1 illustrates that participants watched a total of 12 videos, 4 in each time-segment. Videos shown in each segment had a specific number of onscreen speakers (2, 3, or 4 speakers). Within each segment, four types of speaker identifier methods were included in each captioned video. Samples of these speaker identifiers have been illustrated in Fig. 1.

5　Results

For videos with **2 onscreen speakers**, we did not observe any difference in participants' preference across the four speaker-identifier types.

For videos with **3 onscreen speakers**, we observed significant differences between responses for some speaker-identification methods for the **usefulness question**, but not for other two questions. For the usefulness question, a Friedman test revealed a main effect, $\chi^2 = 8.81$, $p = .03$, with post-hoc pairwise comparison revealing significant pairwise differences between: color vs. double chevron with speakers' name ($p < 0.05$), as shown in Fig. 2.

In the segment with 4 onscreen speakers, for the **usefulness question**, a Friedman test revealed a main effect, $\chi^2 = 11.1$, $p = .01$, with post-hoc pairwise comparison revealing significant pairwise differences between: voice narration vs. color ($p < 0.05$), voice narration vs. emoji ($p < 0.05$). Also for the **easy-to-follow** question, a Friedman test revealed a main effect, $\chi^2 = 9.24$,

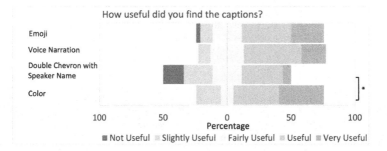

Fig. 2. Subjective user responses comparing four type of speaker identification method for videos that includes **3 speakers**: emoji, voice narration, double chevron with speakers name and color, for how "useful" the captions is the video were (Significant differences are marked with: * $p < 0.05$).

$p = .02$, with post-hoc pairwise comparison revealing significant pairwise differences between: voice narration vs. emoji ($p < 0.05$), voice narration vs. color ($p < 0.05$). Figure 3(a) and (b) displays participants' subjective preference for voice narration over emoji and color. For videos with 4 onscreen speakers, no significance was observed for the **enjoyability** question.

6   Discussion

The goal of this study was to determine which speaker-identifier methods are better at conveying to DHH viewers who the current speaker is when there are several speakers onscreen. Our findings broadly revealed how DHH viewers' TV or video-watching experience is influenced by various speaker-identifier methods.

Our findings demonstrate that a variety of speaker-identifier methods seem effective at conveying change of speaker, and they work well in the presence of only 2 speakers onscreen. However, when the number of speakers on the screen increases to 3 or 4, DHH viewers reported that some speaker-identifier methods were more satisfactory. For example, 'color of the text' was reported to be a significantly more useful speaker identification method than 'double chevron with speaker name' when 3 speakers appear in a video. Similarly, 'voice narration' was reported as being a significantly more useful and easy-to-follow method, as compared to color of the text or emoji, in videos with 4 onscreen speakers.

A key challenge for DHH viewers of videos with multiple speakers is to both follow the current speaker and read the captions, and conducting both activities at the same time can increase cognitive load [5,8]. As discussed in our results above, we did not observe any preference between speaker-identification methods when only 2 speakers appeared on the screen. However, when the number of speakers increased to 4, DHH viewers reported 'voice narration' as being more effective than other speaker-identifier methods. This finding suggests that when the number of speakers grows, DHH viewers may want to see captions that

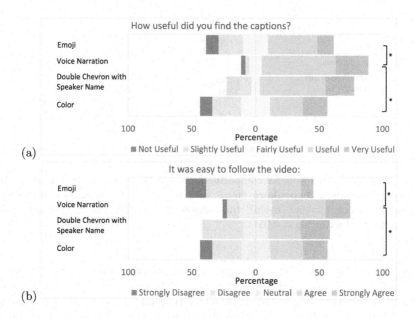

Fig. 3. Subjective user responses comparing four type of speaker identification method for videos that includes **4 speakers**: emoji, voice narration, double chevron with speakers name and color, for (a) how "useful" the captions is the video were and (b) whether the video was" easy-to-follow" (Significant differences are marked with: * $p < 0.05$).

include a straightforward method for indicating the current speaker, which may reduce overall cognitive load.

A main objective of this research was to determine how DHH viewers' preferences among speaker-identifier methods may vary, depending upon the number of speakers on screen. Apart from eliciting DHH viewers' preference, our findings may also inform how current speaker-identification guidelines and standards can be improved in this context. It may also be possible to implement an automatic in-text speaker identification recommendation system, to suggest to a human captioner which speaker-identifier method to use based upon automatically counting the number of onscreen speakers. For instance, existing computer vision algorithms, e.g., EAST [26], are capable of identifying speakers' faces in video.

The findings from this analysis have revealed that use of certain speaker-identifier methods can influence DHH viewers' video-watching experience. For instance, if captions include text color to indicate the current speaker when there are 4 speakers on the screen, DHH viewers' subjective judgment of that video stimuli might be poor. Thus, our findings may also inform researchers investigating how to best evaluate the overall quality of captioning for a television broadcast, i.e., a criterion may include whether the form of speaker-identification used was well-suited to the number of speakers in the video.

7   Limitations and Future Work

There were several limitations in our study, and some of these limitations suggest potential future avenues of research:

- We conducted this study with participants recruited from a university setting. Therefore, our findings reflect a particular subset of DHH community. More importantly, DHH viewers' preference for speaker-identifier methods may vary based on their demographic background. Future research would be needed to collect preferences from DHH viewers with a more diverse demographic background.
- Our motivation in this work was to investigate the relationship between DHH viewers' preferences among speaker-identifier methods, given various numbers of onscreen speakers. We therefore selected videos mostly from interviews and or news genres that were broadcast live and with the number of speakers appearing bring 4 or fewer. Future research would be needed to investigate stimuli from more diverse genres, e.g., panel discussions, sports, on-location interviews, or stimuli with more than 4 speakers on the screen. The presence of an even greater number of speakers may reveal different preferences among viewers.
- In this study, we have investigated only four types of speaker identification, which had been selected based on their usage currently in the live television broadcast industry. Beyond these four methods, other forms of speaker identification have been used at times by broadcasters, e.g., indicating speaker changes using hyphens or newlines, or simply including a speaker name. Thus, a future study could investigate other forms of speaker identification among DHH viewers.
- Our study investigated how DHH viewers' subjective judgment is affected by speaker identification, in terms of enjoyment, usefulness, and whether captions were easy-to-follow. Specifically, in this study, we did not explore how DHH viewers' comprehension of the video may have been affected by different speaker-identification methods. Future research could investigate how such methods may affect DHH viewers' understanding of the video, e.g., based on responses to objective comprehension questions.

8   Conclusion

This study was conducted as an initial step in determining whether DHH viewers' preferences for speaker identifier types vary depending on the number of speakers on the screen. This study contributes to addressing gaps in current practices in the television broadcast industry and guidelines. Our study provides an empirical understanding of DHH viewers' subjective preferences among speaker-identification methods, and it provides a foundation for designing future experimental studies to explore this aspect more broadly. The ultimate goal is that this line of work will provide guidance for television broadcasters to provide captions that better meet the needs and preferences of DHH viewers, and it may also shed light on how regulators should improve current guidelines to ensure the quality of captioning in live television broadcasts from DHH viewers' perspective.

References

1. Zhu, X., Guo, J., Li, S., Hao, T.: Facing cold-start: a live TV recommender system based on neural networks. IEEE Access **8**, 131286–131298 (2020)
2. Federal Communication Commission: Closed Captioning Quality Report and Order, Declaratory Ruling, FNPRM (2014)
3. BBC: BBC Subtitle Guidelines 2018 (2018)
4. The Described and Captioned Media Program: Captioning key for educational media, guidelines and preferred technique
5. Yoon, J.-O., Kim, M.: The effects of captions on deaf students' content comprehension, cognitive load, and motivation in online learning. Am. Ann. Deaf **156**(3), 283–289 (2011)
6. Kushalnagar, R.S., et al.: RTTD-ID: tracked captions with multiple speakers for deaf students. In: 2018 ASEE Annual Conference & Exposition (2018)
7. Hirvenkari, L., Ruusuvuori, J., Saarinen, V.-M., Kivioja, M., Peräkylä, A., Hari, R.: Influence of turn-taking in a two-person conversation on the gaze of a viewer. PLoS ONE **8**, 1–6 (2013)
8. Kruger, J.-L., Hefer, E., Matthew, G.: Measuring the impact of subtitles on cognitive load: eye tracking and dynamic audiovisual texts. In: Proceedings of the 2013 Conference on Eye Tracking South Africa, ETSA 2013, New York, NY, USA, pp. 62–66. Association for Computing Machinery (2013)
9. Amin, A.A., Glasser, A., Kushalnagar, R., Vogler, C., Huenerfauth, M.: Preferences of deaf or hard of hearing users for live-TV caption appearance. In: Antona, M., Stephanidis, C. (eds.) HCII 2021. LNCS, vol. 12769, pp. 189–201. Springer, Cham (2021). https://doi.org/10.1007/978-3-030-78095-1_15
10. Society of Cable Telecommunications Engineers. SCTE: Standard for carriage of VBI data in cable digital transport streams. Technical report (October 2012)
11. Amin, A.A., Hassan, S., Huenerfauth, M.: Effect of occlusion on deaf and hard of hearing users' perception of captioned video quality. In: Antona, M., Stephanidis, C. (eds.) HCII 2021. LNCS, vol. 12769, pp. 202–220. Springer, Cham (2021). https://doi.org/10.1007/978-3-030-78095-1_16
12. Nam, S., Fels, D.I., Chignell, M.H.: Modeling closed captioning subjective quality assessment by deaf and hard of hearing viewers. IEEE Trans. Comput. Soc. Syst. **7**, 621–631 (2020)
13. Gulliver, S.R., Ghinea, G.: How level and type of deafness affect user perception of multimedia video clips. Inf. Soc. J. **2**(4), 374–386 (2003)
14. Gulliver, S.R., Ghinea, G.: Impact of captions on hearing impaired and hearing perception of multimedia video clips. In: Proceedings of the IEEE International Conference on Multimedia and Expo (2003)
15. Pérez-González, L.: The Routledge Handbook of Audiovisual Translation, 1st edn. Routledge (2018)
16. Szarkowska, A.: Subtitling for the deaf and the hard of hearing. In: Bogucki, Ł, Deckert, M. (eds.) The Palgrave Handbook of Audiovisual Translation and Media Accessibility. PSTI, pp. 249–268. Springer, Cham (2020). https://doi.org/10.1007/978-3-030-42105-2_13

17. Lavner, Y., Rosenhouse, J., Gath, I.: The prototype model in speaker identification by human listeners. Int. J. Speech Technol. **4**, 63–74 (2001)
18. Ge, J., Herring, S.C.: Communicative functions of emoji sequences on Sina Weibo. First Monday **23** (November 2018)
19. Brown, A., et al.: Dynamic subtitles: the user experience. In: Proceedings of the ACM International Conference on Interactive Experiences for TV and Online Video, pp. 103–112 (2015)
20. Peng, Y.-H., et al.: SpeechBubbles: enhancing captioning experiences for deaf and hard-of-hearing people in group conversations. In: Proceedings of the 2018 CHI Conference on Human Factors in Computing Systems, CHI 2018, New York, NY, USA, pp. 1–10. Association for Computing Machinery (2018)
21. Ofcom: Measuring live subtitling quality, UK
22. Gallagher, A., McCartney, T., Xi, Z., Chaudhuri, S.: Captions based on speaker identification (2017)
23. Vy, Q.V., Fels, D.I.: Using avatars for improving speaker identification in captioning. In: Gross, T., et al. (eds.) INTERACT 2009. LNCS, vol. 5727, pp. 916–919. Springer, Heidelberg (2009). https://doi.org/10.1007/978-3-642-03658-3_110
24. Amin, A.A., Hassan, S., Huenerfauth, M.: Caption-occlusion severity judgments across live-television genres from deaf and hard-of-hearing viewers. In: Proceedings of the 18th International Web for All Conference, W4A 2021, New York, NY, USA. Association for Computing Machinery (2021)
25. Kafle, S., Huenerfauth, M.: Predicting the understandability of imperfect English captions for people who are deaf or hard of hearing. ACM Trans. Access. Comput. **12**, 1–32 (2019)
26. Zhou, X., et al.: EAST: an efficient and accurate scene text detector. In: The Proceedings of 2017 IEEE Conference on Computer Vision and Pattern Recognition (CVPR) (2017)

Perceptions of Digital Nudging for Cervical Testing: A Comparison Four Nudge Types

Thea Bratteberg Ytterland[2], Siri Fagernes[1,2], and Frode Eika Sandnes[1,2(✉)]

[1] Oslo Metropolitan University, 0130 Oslo, Norway
{sirifa,frodes}@oslomet.no
[2] Kristiania University College, 0153 Oslo, Norway

Abstract. Cervical cancer consumes many lives around the world. Many of these lives could be saved if more women were screened for cervical cancer. This study explored the potential of digital nudging through short electronic messages as a means of increasing women's participation in cervical screening programs. A questionnaire-based study was designed to explore Norwegian women's perceptions towards five different types of nudges, with a total of 280 respondents. The results show that women were generally positive towards text message nudging. The type of nudge had a significant effect on the respondents' perceptions. Messages that invited to an explicit appointment was perceived most positively, and incentives nudges were perceived least positively. About 87% of the participants expressed that it was desirable to receive such invitations via text messages although younger participants were more positive towards digital text messages than older participants. The results may be useful in designing more effective campaigns for increased participation in cervical cancer screening programmes.

Keywords: Digital nudging · Persuasion · Motivation · Perception · Cervical cancer screening · Short messages

1 Introduction

Cervical cancer typically affects women between the ages of 25–69 and is one of the cancer types that can be prevented if diagnosed early through screening. In 2018 The World Health Organization (WHO) issued a goal to eliminate cervical cancer worldwide [1]. It is therefore commonly recommended that all women between the ages of 25–69 regularly attend screening, which involves taking a pap smear. Still, many women are not regularly tested. In Norway, statistics indicate that approximately 250,000 women of screening age have not participated in screening during the last ten years [2]. In 2018, there were 12.8 diagnosed cancer cases per 100,000 women. Moreover, 50% of those who were diagnosed with cervical cancer had not followed the national recommendations regarding screening frequency [3]. It has been shown that there are varying reasons why women do not participate in cervical screening, e.g., forgetting to schedule an appointment [4–6], having to actively book an appointment [7], and insufficiently motivating invitations [7].

© The Author(s), under exclusive license to Springer Nature Switzerland AG 2022
M. Antona and C. Stephanidis (Eds.): HCII 2022, LNCS 13308, pp. 212–228, 2022.
https://doi.org/10.1007/978-3-031-05028-2_14

In Norway, all women in screening age receive invitations to participate in cervical screening. In 2020, approximately 40% of these invitations were sent through physical mail, and 60% electronically. According to a study on non-attendees to the Norwegian cervical screening program, the current invitation strategy was ineffective in motivating women to participate in screening [7]. Moreover, it was suggested that changing the invitation strategy may help increase attendance.

Persuasive technology (PT) has been widely used to ethically change, shape, or influence behavior [8, 9] in several areas, including public health [10]. PT often involves the use of digital nudges [11] to influence changes in behaviors. Thaler and Sunstein defined a nudge as a choice architecture that alters people's behavior in a predictable way without constraining the options or significantly altering the economic incentives [10]. Several studies have demonstrated that nudges have been effective in influencing behavioral changes in health-related context [12–14]. Health-related nudges are often implemented using persuasive messages communicated through Short Message Service (SMS) text messages [15]. Digitalization is an important step in making the health services more efficient [16] and several studies have shown that digital text message invitations have been effective in many healthcare contexts including screening [15, 17, 18].

The goal of the current study is to explore whether and how digital nudging can contribute to getting more women to participate in screening programs to reduce the number of incidences of cervical cancer. According to Jung and Mellers [19] successful implementation of nudges depends on how the public perceives the nudges. If the public does not accept nudging it may provoke strong reactions and prevent the nudging from being effective [20]. Four common digital nudge types, that is, social norms (our desire to choose the same as others), default (the convenience of a default choice), affect (attach emptions to choices), incentives (being penalized or rewarded for a chioice) [21], and no nudge, were addressed and women's perceptions to these nudges were investigated using a quantitative approach involving a questionnaire. The study is structured around four research questions:

1. *Motivation*: Do women find each of the nudge types motivating?
2. *Ethics*: Do women find it ethically justifiable to receive a message with the different nudges?
3. *Acceptance*: Do women want to receive an invitation to cervical screening through a text message?
4. *Experience*: Do different age groups respond differently to the nudges?

The different nudges were contrasted. Motivation was chosen as a key dimension in the study as motivation is one of three elements that change behavior [9]. Perceived ethics were chosen as another key dimension as responsible nudging is a fundamental assumption [22–24]. Moreover, public acceptance is an important criterion for policy makers when adopting such technologies with the best intentions for the citizens in mind [20], and gaining the public's trust [25]. Acceptance to such digitalization measures were also addressed to corroborate reports of the positive report of text messages as substitutes for letters and telephone reminders within healthcare [18]. Finally, age was identified as a key factor as several studies have documented correlations between age to technology acceptance [26].

Related studies typically investigated the effectiveness of the nudges. The method deployed in this study differs from what is commonly used in related studies as it focused on how the recipients perceived the digital nudges.

The rest of this paper is organized as follows: Sect. 2 presents related works. Section 3 introduces the methodology and the questionnaire design. The results are presented in Sect. 4 and discussed in Sect. 5. Concluding remarks are provided in Sect. 6.

2   Related Work

Persuasive technology has been widely used to change, shape, or influence behavior in a variety of application domains [9]. Persuasive technology typically builds on three different elements, namely motivation, ability, and triggers [27] which must coincide to change behavior. A review of 85 studies showed that persuasive technologies have been used by governments and policy makers to improve the health and wellness of the population [10], and that it has been an effective approach for changing behaviors that affect public health. As much as 92% of these studies reported positive outcomes, and that persuasive technology was most frequently used in conjunction with mobile and handheld devices.

Nudging is one facet of persuasive technology, which has been used to guide, change, or influence human behavior within many areas such as nudging for better decisions within computer security [28–30], nudging in human-robot interaction [31], nudging people together [32], nudging visitors at cultural heritage sites [33], nudging learning decisions [34], nudging in the supermarket [35, 36] and for healthier food choices [37]. According to Thaler and Sunstein [11] small details can have a significant impact on people's behavior. A nudge should not exclude any alternatives, it is only supposed to influence people's behavior in a predictable way. It should be easy to avoid. Based on this principle researchers have designed online environments that guide users towards desired behaviors by making small changes in how information is presented. Such changes require little effort and are cost-efficient. According to Schneider [38] people are nudged every day as how something is presented affects our decisions. There are also situations where nudging can be ineffective, for example a study on physical activity trackers [39] showed that feedback based on social comparison was only motivating if the participants were performing close to the group they were compared to.

Research indicates that women do not attend screening because they either forget to schedule appointments [4–6], need to initiate the scheduling action themselves [7], do not perceive the screening important [7], or are not motivated by the invitations [7].

Digital nudging has increasingly been utilized to improve the health of the population [12–14]. Harrison et al. [40] argued that some nudges can be more effective than others in certain health interventions, especially if provided at the time decisions are made. Lehmann et al. [14] studied how a nudge containing information about a scheduled appointment affected health care workers' likelihood of taking a flu vaccine. A total of 122 health workers were divided into two groups; one group received the scheduled appointment and the other only received an encouragement to take the vaccine. The results showed that participants who received the scheduled appointment were more likely to take the vaccine. People may be more likely to choose the default option when faced with several choices because it does not require any active considerations or effort.

A large randomized controlled study of how eight different persuasive message variants influenced people's willingness to sign up as organ donors was carried out in the UK [13]. The nudges included social norms, loss/gain frames, reciprocity, and affect. The reciprocity nudge had the most positive effect on getting people to sign up as organ donors. People were told that if they would ever need an organ donor, they would probably want people to sign up.

Nudging has also been employed to increase participation in screening programs [22], including cervical screening [12]. Some of the most used interventions to increase screening attendance are persuasive messages, pre-screening reminders, personalized letters, and scheduled appointments [22, 24]. According to a review of 109 studies related to nudging in screening [22] the outcome of a nudge is dependent on the context. One target population may react completely differently than another. It is therefore important that the design and implementation of a nudge are adapted to fit the context. Several studies have addressed the question of nudging in screening, and whether this may be effective or not. However, there are fewer empirical studies on how nudging has performed in screening, especially cervical screening. A few exceptions include Huf et al. [12], who investigated how text message reminders impacted cervical screening rates in an area of London with declining screening rates. The recruited participants were grouped in different age cohorts. The youngest cohort either received no text message reminder or got a reminder directly from their medical general practitioner (GP). This was done to test the effect of a text message reminder. The older cohort was exposed to different nudges to see which one was the most efficient, including a social norms nudge and two gain-and loss frame nudges and a message directly from their GP. Results showed that SMS reminders improved overall attendance. The message from the GP proved most effective and the message with no nudge had the second-highest effect, while the effects of the social norms nudge and the two gain- and loss nudges only had marginal effects.

Gotlieb et al. [41] proposed the use of gamification to nudge more women to attend cervical screening using a smartphone app, however, no results have been published. Klasjna and Pratt [42] investigated whether the combination of a text message and an app could increase cervical screening rates. The study involved 1,464 women who were at least six months overdue for screening. The participants received a text message that they were overdue for screening with a link to an app they could download to schedule an appointment. The results showed that scheduling an appointment through an application was more acceptable among younger women. Only 10% ended up making an appointment, and only a quarter of these downloaded and used the app. The researchers concluded that the text messages had more impact than the app.

Several approaches, frameworks, and toolkits for designing digital nudges have been proposed [43]. Two common frameworks are the MINDSPACE framework [21] and Caraban et al.'s [44] framework for technology-mediated nudging in HCI. MINDSPACE consists of nine elements for behavior change. Caraban et al.'s [44] framework based on a systematic review of nudge types that have been identified in the field of HCI comprises

23 nudging mechanisms organized into 6 categories, namely facilitate, confront, deceive, social influence, fear, and reinforce.

However, some nudge types that can be found in both frameworks are more commonly used in health interventions. The default nudge is frequently mentioned as one of the most effective nudges [21, 40, 44]. Nudges based on social norms are described as effective nudges [45], and they have similarities with Fogg´s social cues for designing persuasive technology [9], that is what is considered an acceptable way of behaving within a group of people or a society. Emotional messages that depend on affect are considered powerful in decision-making [46] and have therefore been used in several studies [12, 13, 46]. Affect nudges can be implemented by presenting something in a manner that makes the recipient afraid of missing out or afraid of losing something. Economic (monetary) incentives nudges are believed to influence behaviours, as individuals dislike losing more than then they like winning the same amount. Volpp et al. [15] investigated whether incentives could motivate weight loss. The participants deposited an amount of money and were told that they would get it back if they lost weight. Results showed that the incentives worked, as the participants lost a significant amount of weight. It has also been reported that incentives have helped individuals stop smoking [17].

Some screening programs have been criticized for resulting in over-diagnosis [22] and provoked a discussion about whether nudging in screening is ethical. One view is that nudging is ethical if participants are free to choose. Hofmann and Stanek [22] argue that nudging in screening is ethical if the benefits of screening outweigh the disadvantages. They contend that it is not a question of whether to nudge or not, but rather how to nudge ethically.

3   Method

3.1   Experimental Design

A questionnaire-based study was designed where the respondents' responses to four common digital nudge types and one control were observed. Women at different age groups between 25–69 years old were targeted as age has been shown to be a factor that can affect attitudes to and perceptions of technology. There were thus two main independent variables, namely nudge type and age. The within-groups independent variable nudge type had five levels, namely fear, default, social norm, incentives, and control. The between-groups independent variable age had three levels. Three main dependent variables were observed, namely perceived motivation, perceived likelihood of action and perceived ethical justifiability.

The data was gathered through an anonymous online questionnaire. The motivation for this procedure was that cervical screening is a sensitive and private topic, and it was deemed more likely to solicit responses from a larger sample of women because of the anonymity and non-confrontative nature of the questionnaire. Also, the study was carried out during the COVID-19 pandemic and social distancing regulations complicated the administration of physical interviews. Finally, an interview-based study dealing with sensitive medical information would require comprehensive ethical approval permits and data-storage permits which was not feasible for the available time frame of the project.

3.2 Participants

A total of 280 women successfully completed the questionnaire. Of these, 154 respondents (55.6%) were between 25–39 years old (younger cohort), 87 respondents (31.4%) were between 40–54 years old (middle aged cohort), while 36 respondents (13%) were 55 years old or older (senior cohort). We decided to use the same age cohorts as deployed in the national cervical screening program in Norway. The respondents were recruited using convenience sampling using the first author's network.

Table 1. Message (nudge) examples.

Type	Message
Fear (affect)	About 300 women are diagnosed with cervical cancer in Norway annually, of which approximately 70 dies. It is now time to take a new pap smear. Schedule an appointment with your GP
Unbiased/neutral information (default)	It is now time to take a new pap smear. You have received a scheduled appointment with your GP on 20.04.2021 at: 09.30. Click here to change the appointment
Exploiting social norms (social norms)	Approximately 400,000 women take a pap smear each year, so should you. It is now time to take a new pap smear. Schedule an appointment with your GP
Reward/penalty (incentives)	You have received a scheduled appointment with your GP on 20.04.2021 at: 09.30 to take a pap smear. You will be charged a fee of €50 for not attending the scheduled appointment. Click here to change the appointment
Neutral reminder (control)	It is now time to take a new pap smear. Schedule an appointment with your GP

3.3 Materials

A questionnaire was designed for the purpose of this study. Four digital nudge types were incorporated into the questionnaire (see Table 1).

Note that the main difference between the neutral reminder and the neutral information nudges were the presence of the proposed appointment.

Each nudge was associated with three 5-item Likert questions addressing motivation, change and ethics, namely: Did you become motivated to take a smear test? Is it more likely that you will take a smear test? and Do you think it is ethically acceptable for authorities to send this message?

The messages were presented as messages on a smartphone to make these appear more authentic (see Fig. 1), placing the respondents in the specific mindset of text message context, as it has been pointed out that the presentation of nudges can be as influential as the nudge itself [38].

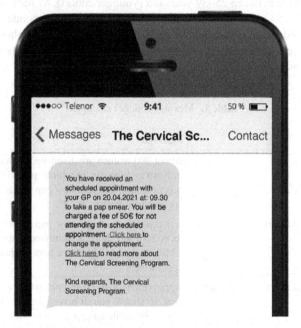

Fig. 1. Visual presentation of the messages.

In addition, the questionnaire asked respondents about their age range, whether they had taken a smear test previously, or had any negative experiences with smear tests. The questionnaire also asked about the respondents' opinions regarding whether it is important to get regularly tested, whether they are motivated to be tested, whether it is desirable to receive such notification using short messages, and whether they found the topic of cervical testing too personal (5-item Likert scales). Respondents were also invited to provide additional comments as free text.

The questions were written in Norwegian (free translations of individual questions are provided herein). The questionnaire was implemented using Google Forms. The questionnaire was subjected to several rounds of pilot testing with subsequent minor adjustments before it was deployed.

3.4 Procedure

Respondents were invited via personal contacts and through social media. The total number of invitees were not recorded, which makes it challenging to calculate the response rate.

The participants spent between 5–7 min to complete the questionnaire. The questionnaire was deployed for approximately one month during March 2021. Participation was voluntary and anonymous as there was no need to link any data across multiple sessions [47].

3.5 Analysis

The Likert responses were analyzed using two-way repeated measures ANOVAs with the different nudges as a within-group factor and age as a between-group factor. The Likert responses were ordinal which called for non-parametric testing procedures. However, it has been argued that it can be acceptable to analyze Likert responses using parametric tests [48] and this allowed us to explore possible interactions. This study therefore reports parametric results. Non-parametric tests were also conducted to validate the parametric tests. In cases where the assumption of sphericity was not satisfied, Greenhouse-Geisser corrections were applied. The responses to the questionnaire were analyzed using the JASP statistical software package version 0.13.1.0. The textual comments were manually processed using thematic analysis [49] which involves identifying reoccurring themes.

4 Results

Figure 2 shows how the five messages affected the respondents' motivation to take a pap test. Clearly the default nudge was perceived as most motivating (a skew towards positive responses) followed by the affect nudge, social norm nudge, and no nudge. The incentives nudge was the least effective in motivating the participants (a balanced set of responses). The differences between the nudges effect on motivation was statistically significant ($F(3.583, 985.279) = 42.132, p < .001$). Post Hoc tests showed that there was a significant difference between all nudges ($p < .05$), except the social norm nudge and no nudge ($p = .434$).

Neutral responses may indicate uncertainty associated with a message. The no nudge message yielded the highest portion of neutral answers (31%), while the incentives nudge (16%) and the default nudge (18%) exhibited the lowest portion of neutral answers.

Although some differences can be observed for how motivated the different age groups are by the messages, these differences were not statistically significant ($F(2, 272) = 0.392, p = .676$).

A majority (90.1%) of the respondents reported that they had taken a pap test at some point, while 8.9% reported that they had not. We did not find any significant difference in the motivational effect of the different nudges for those who had previously taken a pap test versus those who had not ($F(1, 268) = 2.46, p = .118$).

Of the respondents who reported that they had previously taken a pap test at some point 86.7% reported that they had no negative experiences, 12.6% reported that they had negative experiences and 1.1% did not respond to the question. No significant effect of negative previous experience with pap tests on motivations was observed ($F(3, 272) = 0.21, p = .888$).

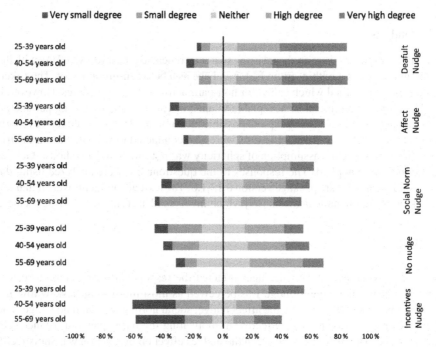

Fig. 2. A diverging stacked bar chart showing to what degree participants were motivated by the messages.

Figure 3 shows how the five nudge message types were likely to make the respondents take a pap test. The default nudge stands out as the most positively perceived, followed by the affect nudge, social norm nudge, no nudge, and the incentives nudge (balanced distribution of responses). The effect of the different nudge types was statistically significant ($F(3.373, 917.508) = 40.929, p < .001$). Post Hoc tests confirmed that there was a significant difference between all the nudges ($p < .05$), except for the social norm nudge and the incentives nudge ($p = .247$), social norm nudge and no nudge ($p = .799$), and incentives nudge and no nudge ($p = .276$). There was no significant effect of age ($F(2, 269) = 0.865, p = .422$).

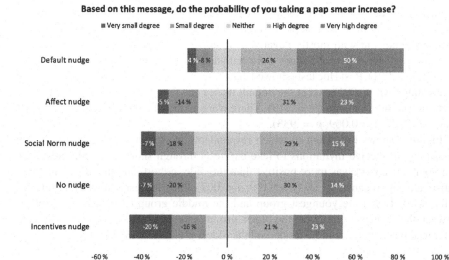

Fig. 3. A diverging stacked bar chart showing the respondents' perceived probability of taking a smear test after receiving the messages.

Figure 4 plots the degree to which the respondents find it ethically justifiable to receive the nudge messages. Again, the default nudge is associated with most positive

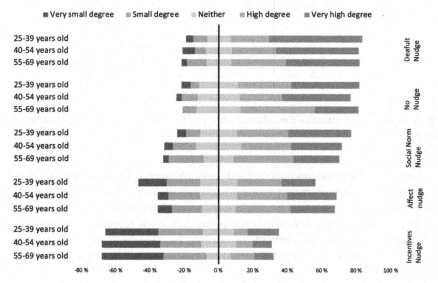

Fig. 4. A diverging stacked bar chart showing to what degree participants found it ethically justifiable to receive the messages.

responses, closely followed by the no nudge. Next follows the social norm nudge and affect nudge – both with a skew towards positive responses. The incentives nudge, however, stands out with mostly negative responses. Participants' views on the ethical justifiability of the different nudges were statistically significant $(F(3.621, 988.465) = 100.995, p < .001)$. Post Hoc tests showed that there were significant differences between all the nudges $(p < .001)$ except the default nudge and no nudge $(p = .119)$, and social norm nudge and no nudge $(p = .119)$. There were no significant differences attributed to age $(F(2, 270) = 0.069, p = .933)$.

Figure 5 shows the extent to which respondents within the three age groups find it desirable to receive invitations to take pap tests through short electronic messages. The youngest cohort was more positive than the older cohort, and this difference was statistically significant $(F(2, 274) = 5.109, p < .007)$. Post Hoc tests showed a significant difference between the youngest group and the middle group $(p = .027)$, as well as between the youngest group and the oldest group $(p = .036)$. There was no significant difference between the middle group and the oldest group $(p = .834)$.

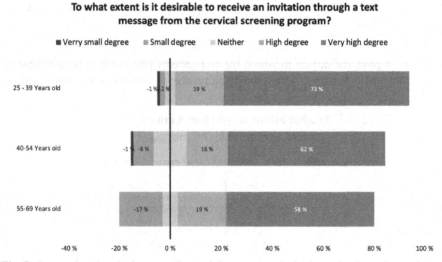

Fig. 5. Respondents' attitudes towards receiving pap test invitations via short electronic text messages.

A total of 42 respondents provided additional comments. Thematic analysis of these data resulted in three emerging themes; fixed appointments, form of delivery of the invite, and where to take the test. Eight respondents believes that fixed appointments may increase attendance. The argument was that even if one receives a notification with an invitation to schedule an appointment, one may forget to do so. On the other hand, it was also stated that a notification of a fixed appointment could be perceived as invasive by the receivers.

Six respondents commented that that they believed electronic text messages were more likely to make the recipient take a pap test compared to a letter sent via postal mail.

A total of nine respondents commented on reservations taking the pap test at one's regular general practitioner (GP). It was commented that the waiting time could be long at the regular GP, that the information and follow-up procedure was unsatisfactory, and that one would prefer to have the test done with a specialist instead.

5   Discussion

The results show that persuasive messages in the form of digital nudges have the possibility to increase participation in cervical screening and thus agree with several previous studies [12, 24, 50]. The nudge type with the highest potential to increase participation in cervical screening was the one including a scheduled appointment (default nudge), followed by the nudge with an emotionally informed message (affect nudge). When faced with several choices people tend to choose the default option because it involves the least effort. Moreover, it may be a type of nudge that respondents were familiar with, as it is the type of message that is currently used in the country of the study. Familiar choices may be perceived as safe.

One explanation for why the emotional message (affect nudge) received the second-highest positive responses may be that the message was perceived as intimidating and unpleasant, as it contained the negative words death and cancer. This may have alerted the respondents to realize the importance of screening, but the possible consequences of not participating. Previous studies have also shown that messages relying on fear can change behaviour [12, 13, 46].

The social norm nudge and no nudge resulted in similar results which were less favourable than that for the default nudge and affect nudge. Both messages had the highest portion of neutral responses suggesting that participants were indifferent to, or uncertain of, these messages.

A possible explanation as to why the message without a nudge was perceived as motivating by some may be because it was less complex compared to the other nudges. This was the shortest message and therefore probably required less cognitive effort from the recipient. Similar positive effect of no nudge was also found in [12].

A possible explanation as to why some respondents did not perceive the social norm nudge as motivating could be that the statistical facts presented did not match their expectations. In a previous study [39] it was found that social comparison only motivated the participants if the comparison were close to the participant's performance. According to Dolan et al. [21] descriptive norms should match the expectations people have, to be the most efficient. It is therefore possible that some respondents expected that the number of women attending screening should be higher than the numbers presented.

One possible explanation why the incentives nudge (penalty for missing the appointment) received the least positive responses may be that they do not want to pay the fee. Most people would probably have chosen to avoid a fee if possible. One respondent commented that it may be problematic with a fee for not showing up to a scheduled appointment. Negative perceptions of such penalties are aligned with the view that indicated that people are sensitive to costs and monetary losses.

The observation that there were no significant differences in which women from the different age groups are influenced by the nudges is consistent with a previous study that reported no difference in how women from different age groups reacted to a message with a scheduled appointment [50]. This indicates that it is not necessary to adapt the messages to different age groups, but that a one fits all approach should suffice.

Since the respondent reacted differently to the different nudges it seems that the most positively perceived nudges show more potential as pap testing motivators than the others. Similar results have also been observed in the context of organ donation where eight messages were tested, and the most successful message resulted in the recruitment of more organ donors [13]. Small changes in the text may result in considerable differences. For example, two messages were nearly identical, except that the message with the Incentives nudge contained an additional sentence with a fee for not showing up to the scheduled appointment.

A possible explanation why the message with the scheduled appointment (default nudge) was found as the most ethically justifiable may be that participants were familiar with this invitation approach and perceived it as normal. According to Hofmann et al. [22] a scheduled appointment is one of the most common ways of nudging in screening programs. Most women also found the message without a nudge and the one with the social norm nudge ethical. None of these messages contained any uncomfortable or confrontative text.

Most respondents indicated that the penalty message (incentives nudge) was not ethically justifiable. According to Thaler and Sunstein [11] a nudge must be easily avoidable. However, the penalty message requires the participants the three choices of attending the scheduled appointment, changing the appointment, or paying the penalty and there are no options for opting out. This nudge may therefore be considered unethical as participation is not voluntary. Previous studies have also shown that participants have not been positive with regards to monetary incentive nudges [51].

Approximately 40% of the invitations to cervical screening in the country of the study are sent via physical mail, and this may explain respondents' positive responses to receiving such notifications electronically. Previous studies have shown that text messages have been effective in health-interventions [18, 52]. The youngest age group was slightly more positive about receiving electronic invitations than the older groups. One possible explanation may be that this group is more accustomed to using new technologies while the older group was generally more accustomed to traditional paper-based regimes.

5.1   Limitations

One potential weakness of the questionnaire was that the nudge presentation orders were not randomized. There is therefore a chance of bias due to presentation order (learning effect). For example, one may have expected that respondents were more positive towards the first nudge and be fatigued when reaching the last nudge. However, the resulting preference order did not match the presentation order which does not give support to any suspicion of presentation order bias.

The incentive nudge was a negative incentive incurring a monetary penalty. It would have been interesting to also see if similar results would be obtained with a positive incentive through the promise of a monetary reward.

An attempt was made to spread the survey in various channels by people in different age groups, to get a representative sample of the population. Also, the questionnaire was only disseminated to women. Still, we cannot be completely certain that the sample is representative of the female population. There is thus a risk that the responses could be biased. Clearly, the younger cohort was much larger than the older cohort, and this imbalance is not representative of the population. Still, the number of responses in the older cohort was considered sufficiently large to provide statistical power.

There was also a mistake in the form where the intended age range of 40–54 years were noted as 40–55 years. Participants that were 55 years old could therefore have assigned themselves to either the middle tier or the senior tier. One may assume that respondents typically would identify with the youngest group of the two when given the option to choose. If we assume that the age distribution is uniform, then 5.8 participants of the 87 participants in the middle age group of 15 participants would be 55 years old. According to this calculation about 2% of the participants could potentially have been incorrectly assigned to the wrong group.

The nudge types selected for this study represent just a small subset of nudge types that have been discussed in the literature. It is therefore possible that other nudge types not addressed herein would have affected the results differently. Moreover, it is also possible that if designed differently the studied nudges would give different results.

5.2 Implications

The method deployed herein differs from other studies as it investigated how participants perceived the messages, while other studies have investigated the effectiveness of messages. Furthermore, the results of this study make a relevant contribution to the ongoing discussion about the ethics of nudging. Several frameworks for ethical nudging exist, but few empirical studies have investigated what is perceived as ethical by the users.

6 Conclusions

This study measured women's perceptions regarding five nudge types for cervical screening testing. A total of 280 women in three age groups responded to a questionnaire presenting the five nudges in the form of simulated text messages. The respondents' perceptions of the nudges in terms of motivation, likelihood of stimulating participation, and ethics were measured using the questionnaire. The results showed that the most positively perceived message was one with a specific invitation to an appointment, while the least positive message was one with a specific invitation to an appointment with a monetary penalty for not turning up (incentives nudge). There were no significant differences across the age groups regarding perceptions to the various nudges implying that the different age groups could be targeted with the same messages. Although most of the participants (87%) were positive regarding receiving invitations to cervical testing via electronic text messages, the younger generation (25–39 years) was more positive towards receiving electronic messages related to cervical testing than the older groups. The empirical results from this study may be helpful for organizations to design effective digital nudges with the goal of implementing effective cervical testing programmes.

Future work includes investigating the effect of nudges in context, that is, how effective such nudges are in promoting participation in practice. Another key issue is to investigate the timing of sending such messages as timing may be a determining factor for whether a recipient participates or not.

References

1. World Health Organization. Launch of the global strategy to accelerate the elimination of cervical cancer. WHO (2020). https://www.who.int/news-room/events/detail/2020/11/17/default-calendar/launch-of-the-global-strategy-to-accelerate-the-elimination-of-cervical-cancer. Accessed 30 Dec 2021
2. Cancer Registry of Norway. Life could have been saved. https://www.kreftregisteret.no/Generelt/Nyheter/-liv-kunne-vart-reddet/. Accessed 19 Aug 2020
3. Cancer Registry of Norway. Annual Report Cervical Cancer Program 2017–2018. Cancer Registry, 2017–2018 edition. Cancer Registry of Norway (2018)
4. Marlow, L.A., Chorley, A.J., Haddrell, J., Ferrer, R., Waller, J.: Understanding the heterogeneity of cervical cancer screening non-participants: data from a national sample of British women. Eur. J. Cancer **80**, 30–38 (2017)
5. Bosgraaf, R.P., et al.: Reasons for non-attendance to cervical screening and preferences for HPV self-sampling in Dutch women. Prev. Med. **64**, 108–113 (2014)
6. Ekechi, C., Olaitan, A., Ellis, R., Koris, J., Amajuoyi, A., Marlow, L.A.: Knowledge of cervical cancer and attendance at cervical cancer screening: a survey of Black women in London. BMC Publ. Health **14**(1), 1–9 (2014)
7. Aasbø, G., Solbrække, K.N., Waller, J., Tropé, A., Nygård, M., Hansen, B.T.: Perspectives of non-attenders for cervical cancer screening in Norway: a qualitative focus group study. BMJ Open **9**(8), e029505 (2019)
8. Waller, J., Jackowska, M., Marlow, L., Wardle, J.: Exploring age differences in reasons for nonattendance for cervical screening: a qualitative study. BJOG: Int. J. Obstet. Gynaecol. **119**(1), 26–32 (2012)
9. Fogg, B.J.: Persuasive technology: using computers to change what we think and do. Ubiquity (2002)
10. Orji, R., Moffatt, K.: Persuasive technology for health and wellness: state-of-the-art and emerging trends. Health Inf. J. **24**(1), 66–91 (2018)
11. Thaler, R.H., Sunstein, C.R.: Nudge: improving decisions about health, wealth, and happiness. Penguin (2009)
12. Huf, S., et al.: Behavioral economics informed message content in text message reminders to improve cervical screening participation: Two pragmatic randomized controlled trials. Prevent. Med. **139**, 106170 (2020)
13. Sallis, A., Harper, H., Sanders, M.: Effect of persuasive messages on National Health Service Organ Donor Registrations: a pragmatic quasi-randomised controlled trial with one million UK road taxpayers. Trials **19**(1) (2018)
14. Lehmann, B.A., Chapman, G.B., Franssen, F.M., Kok, G., Ruiter, R.A.: Changing the default to promote influenza vaccination among health care workers. Vaccine **34**(11), 1389–1392 (2016)
15. Volpp, K.G., John, L.K., Troxel, A.B., Norton, L., Fassbender, J., Loewenstein, G.: Financial incentive–based approaches for weight loss: a randomized trial. JAMA **300**(22), 2631–2637 (2008)
16. Blandford, A.: HCI for health and wellbeing: challenges and opportunities. Int. J. Hum Comput Stud. **131**, 41–51 (2019)

17. Volpp, K.G., et al.: A randomized, controlled trial of financial incentives for smoking cessation. N. Engl. J. Med. **360**, 699–709 (2009)
18. Uy, C., Lopez, J., Trinh-Shevrin, C., Kwon, S.C., Sherman, S.E., Liang, P.S.: Text messaging interventions on cancer screening rates: a systematic review. J. Med. Internet Res. **19**(8), e296 (2017)
19. Jung, J.Y., Mellers, B.A.: American attitudes toward nudges. Judgm. Decis. Mak. **11**(1) (2016)
20. Diepeveen, S., Ling, T., Suhrcke, M., Roland, M., Marteau, T.M.: Public acceptability of government intervention to change health-related behaviours: a systematic review and narrative synthesis. BMC Publ. Health **13**(1), 1–11 (2013)
21. Dolan, P., Hallsworth, M., Halpern, D., King, D., Metcalfe, R., Vlaev, I.: Influencing behaviour: the mindspace way. J. Econ. Psychol. **33**(1), 264–277 (2012)
22. Hofmann, B., Stanak, M.: Nudging in screening: literature review and ethical guidance. Patient Educ. Couns. **101**(9), 1561–1569 (2018)
23. Hansen, P.G., Jespersen, A.M.: Nudge and the manipulation of choice: a framework for the responsible use of the nudge approach to behaviour change in public policy. Eur. J. Risk Regulat. **4**(1), 3–28 (2013)
24. Duffy, S.W., Myles, J.P., Maroni, R., Mohammad, A.: Rapid review of evaluation of interventions to improve participation in cancer screening services. J. Med. Screen. **24**(3), 127–145 (2017)
25. Katner, K., Jianu, R.: The effectiveness of nudging in commercial settings and impact on user trust. In: Extended Abstracts of the 2019 CHI Conference on Human Factors in Computing Systems. ACM (2019)
26. Arning, K., Ziefle, M.: Different perspectives on technology acceptance: the role of technology type and age. In: Holzinger, A., Miesenberger, K. (eds.) USAB 2009. LNCS, vol. 5889, pp. 20–41. Springer, Heidelberg (2009). https://doi.org/10.1007/978-3-642-10308-7_2
27. Fogg, B.J.: A behavior model for persuasive design. In: Proceedings of the 4th International Conference on Persuasive Technology. ACM (2009)
28. Turland, J., Coventry, L., Jeske, D., Briggs, P., van Moorsel, A.: Nudging towards security: developing an application for wireless network selection for android phones. In: Proceedings of the 2015 British HCI Conference, pp. 193–201. ACM (2015)
29. Zimmermann, V., Renaud, K.: The nudge puzzle: matching nudge interventions to cybersecurity decisions. ACM Trans. Comput. Hum. Interact. **28**(1), 1–45 (2021)
30. Kankane, S., DiRusso, C., Buckley, C.: Can we nudge users toward better password management? an initial study. In: Extended Abstracts of the 2018 CHI Conference on Human Factors in Computing Systems. ACM (2018)
31. Ali Mehenni, H., Kobylyanskaya, S., Vasilescu, I., Devillers, L.: Children as candidates to verbal nudging in a human-robot experiment. In: Companion Publication of the 2020 International Conference on Multimodal Interaction, pp. 482–486. ACM (2020)
32. Mitchell, R.: Levelling, nudging, and easing: inspirational design patterns for supporting new encounters. In: Proceedings of the 5th International ACM In-Cooperation HCI and UX Conference, pp. 116–127. ACM (2019)
33. Wecker, A., Kuflik, T., Stock, O.: Reflections on persuasive and digital nudging methods for cultural heritage. In: Adjunct Publication of the 28th ACM Conference on User Modeling, Adaptation and Personalization, pp. 370–372. ACM (2020)
34. Zamprogno, L., Holmes, R., Baniassad, E.: Nudging student learning strategies using formative feedback in automatically graded assessments. In: Proceedings of the 2020 ACM SIGPLAN Symposium on SPLASH-E. ACM (2020)
35. Fechner, W., Herder, E.: Digital nudging for more ecological supermarket purchases. In: Adjunct Proceedings of the 29th ACM Conference on User Modeling, Adaptation and Personalization, pp. 284–292. ACM (2021). https://doi.org/10.1145/3450614.3464620

36. Kalnikaite, V., et al.: How to nudge in Situ: designing lambent devices to deliver salient information in supermarkets. In: Proceedings of the 13th International Conference on Ubiquitous Computing, pp. 11–20. ACM (2011)
37. Starke, A.D., Kløverød, E., Hauge, S., Løkeland, L.S.: Nudging healthy choices in food search through list re-ranking. In: Adjunct Proceedings of the 29th ACM Conference on User Modeling, Adaptation and Personalization, pp. 293–298. ACM (2021). https://doi.org/10.1145/3450614.3464621
38. Schneider, C., Weinmann, M., Vom Brocke, J.: Digital nudging: guiding online user choices through interface design. Commun. ACM **61**(7), 67–73 (2018)
39. Gouveia, R., Pereira, F., Karapanos, E., Munson, S.A., Hassenzahl, M.: Exploring the design space of glanceable feedback for physical activity trackers. In: Proceedings of the 2016 ACM International Joint Conference on Pervasive and Ubiquitous Computing, pp. 144–155. ACM (2016)
40. Harrison, J.D., Patel, M.S.: Designing nudges for success in health care. AMA J. Ethics **22**(9), 796–801 (2020)
41. Gotlieb, A., Louarn, M., Nygard, M., Ruiz-Lopez, T., Sen, S., Gori, R.: Constraint-based verification of a mobile app game designed for nudging people to attend cancer screening. In: Twenty-Ninth IAAI Conference (2017)
42. Klasnja, P., Pratt, W.: Healthcare in the pocket: mapping the space of mobile-phone health interventions. J. Biomed. Inf. **45**(1), 184–198 (2012)
43. Caraban, A., Konstantinou, L., Karapanos, E.: The nudge deck: a design support tool for technology-mediated nudging. In: Proceedings of the 2020 ACM Designing Interactive Systems Conference, pp. 395–406. ACM (2020)
44. Caraban, A., Karapanos, E., Gonçalves, D., Campos, P.: 23 ways to nudge: a review of technology-mediated nudging in human-computer interaction. In: Proceedings of the 2019 CHI Conference on Human Factors in Computing Systems. ACM (2019)
45. von Wagner, C., et al.: The impact of descriptive norms on motivation to participate in cancer screening–evidence from online experiments. Patient Educ. Couns. **102**(9), 1621–1628 (2019)
46. Tannenbaum, M.B., et al.: Appealing to fear: a meta-analysis of fear appeal effectiveness and theories. Psychol. Bull. **141**(6), 1178 (2015)
47. Sandnes, F.E.: HIDE: short IDs for robust and anonymous linking of users across multiple sessions in small HCI experiments. In: Extended Abstracts of the 2021 CHI Conference on Human Factors in Computing Systems. ACM (2021)
48. Norman, G.: Likert scales, levels of measurement and the "laws" of statistics. Adv. Health Sci. Educ. **15**(5), 625–632 (2010)
49. Guest, G., MacQueen, K.M., Namey, E.E.: Applied Thematic Analysis. Sage (2011)
50. Lönnberg, S., et al.: Impact of scheduled appointments on cervical screening participation in Norway: a randomised intervention. BMJ Open **6**(11), e013728 (2016)
51. Reisch, L.A., Sunstein, C.R.: Do Europeans like nudges? Judgm. Decis. Mak. **11**(4), 310–325 (2016)
52. Kerrison, R.S., Shukla, H., Cunningham, D., Oyebode, O., Friedman, E.: Text-message reminders increase uptake of routine breast screening appointments: a randomised controlled trial in a hard-to-reach population. Br. J. Cancer **112**(6), 1005–1010 (2015)

Shift Scheduling for the Effective Management of the Ageing Workforce

Ioannis Chatzikonstantinou[1]([✉]) [iD], Aris Papaprodromou[1], Maria Loeck[2],
Rosa Carreton[2], Sofia Segkouli[1] [iD], Andreas Triantafyllidis[1] [iD],
Dimitrios Giakoumis[1] [iD], Konstantinos Votis[1] [iD], and Dimitrios Tzovaras[1] [iD]

[1] Information Technologies Institute, Center for Research and Technology Hellas,
6th km Harilaou-Thermis Road, Thessaloniki, Greece
`ihatz@iti.gr`
[2] Asociación Nacional de Empresarios Fabricantes de Áridos, Plaza de las Cortes,
5 -7o, Madrid, Spain
`http://www.certh.gr`

Abstract. Aiming to address the needs of the ageing workforce in the context of shift work, we introduce a Participatory Work Orchestration Support Tool, with the aim of supporting decision making in deriving the periodic shift schedule of an organization. The proposed tool comprises two main components, an extensive and intuitive web-based platform that enables managers to gain an overview of their workforce and schedule, and an optimizing shift scheduler that works in the background to propose suggestions to the managers to improve scheduling, based on considerations of worker welfare and specifically targeting the ageing workforce. Preliminary testing of the tool in simulation yields encouraging results.

Keywords: Shift scheduling · Ageing workforce · Decision support tools · Participatory scheduling

1 Introduction

Shift scheduling is an integral part of any business or organization that operates on shift work as it is a very complex issue, especially when many shifts and large number of workers of various skills are involved. The aim of shift planning is to establish schedules for all activities and to assign each activity to a specific employee as effective planning helps in reducing labor costs while improving efficiency and employee satisfaction [1]. In addition, shift scheduling also needs to comply with certain labor regulations and each organization's rules and policies. Despite its advantages, unrestricted application of shift work is detrimental to various aspects of human health and well-being, among which

This work is part of the project entitled "Smart, Personalized and Adaptive ICT Solutions for Active, Healthy and Productive Ageing with enhanced Workability (AgeingAtWork)", which has received funding from the European Union's Horizon 2020 Research and Innovation Programme under grant agreement no 826299.

© The Author(s), under exclusive license to Springer Nature Switzerland AG 2022
M. Antona and C. Stephanidis (Eds.): HCII 2022, LNCS 13308, pp. 229–241, 2022.
https://doi.org/10.1007/978-3-031-05028-2_15

the biological rhythm, sleep and social life of workers in general [2]. In addition, shift work leads to a number of clinical and non-clinical problems while at the same time being responsible for delaying human performance and increasing the likelihood of accidents at work. In order to meet organization production needs, without sacrificing health and well-being of an increasingly ageing workforce, it is mandatory to consider an approach to shift management that is respectful to both health- and regulation-mandated constraints, as well as individual preferences of the workers.

Aiming to address the needs of the ageing workforce in the context of shift work, a Participatory Work Orchestration Support Tool has been developed, which is addressed to organization managers, and with the aim of providing sufficient decision support tools to improve management of the ageing workforce. The developed tool comprises two major components: The first is an intuitive web-based manager platform, which facilitates workforce and shift management, with a focus on the needs of the ageing workforce, and also aiming to facilitate transfer of knowledge within the organization. The platform enables organization managers to visualize at a glance organization schedule and cumulative figures regarding their workforce occupation, as well as interact and respond to worker requests.

The second is an optimizing shift scheduling decision support tool, which works in the background, providing schedule suggestions to managers, in order to further facilitate decisions in complex scenarios. With respect to shift schedule optimization, we formulate the shift scheduling problem as a Mixed-Integer Linear Problem, which incorporates a single objective and multiple constraints, derived in accordance to established shift scheduling literature, but adapted to the specifics of managing the ageing workforce.

With respect to the shift schedule optimizer we validate the results of our proposed approach in synthetic scheduling data, and with respect to the web platform, we present the results of an Acceptance Study. Future validation plans involve a pilot trial, in the context of the AgeingAtWork project [3], to be carried out in one of end user premises, involving managers and workforce.

2   Related Work

This section presents a brief review of the state of art in the field of workforce orchestration and scheduling, addressing the need for orchestration solutions to enhance ageing workers' well-being, health and workability.

The mathematical problem associated with orchestrating a workforce within an organization is known as the shift scheduling problem. In it's basic form, the shift scheduling problem involves determining the number of employees to be assigned to various shifts and the timing of their breaks within the limits allowed by legal, union, and company requirements [4]. This problem definition has been variably extended and altered to address specifics in different applications and industries, considering a constantly changing repertoire of constraints, objectives and problem parameters, that align with trends in legal and organizational requirements and considerations [5].

In [6] authors report on a novel Binary Integer Goal Programming (BGP) model for the Shift Scheduling Problem with days-off preferences, applied to scheduling of shifts for power station workers. The problem formulation presented in the study considers a detailed, real-world set of rules and common practices used in the power industry. In addition, several soft constraints are introduced, stemming from organization practices. This study is of high relevance, as it includes worker preferences as an integral part of the model, and may form the base for further extending and incorporating age-related objectives and constraints.

In [7], authors report on a Genetic Algorithm-based approach to the homecare staff scheduling problem which involve identifying the optimal assignment of caregivers to outpatients with the aim of minimizing travel times on different means of transportation.

In [8] authors consider the problem of staff scheduling in a security department where workers work in shifts to cover a 24h per day operation. The problem formulation presented in the study considers physical workload balancing (e.g. avoiding consecutive workdays and "heavy" shifts), as well as satisfaction of worker preferences, which is introduced as the sole objective in the problem linear model formulation. Authors present scheduling results that balance worker's physical workload and good satisfaction of worker preferences.

In [9] authors report on the problem of staff scheduling in a pharmacology research company, considering workload sharing equity as the primary criterion. Workload equity, as a criterion, also accounts for soft skill levels and preferences of personnel. As an example, the paper outlined the workload of two nurses, one of which is more confident in writing medical reports than the other. Equity in this case is achieved by assigning additional clinical tasks to the employee with less administrative capabilities, while at the same time relieving the other of such tasks to better focus on medical report writing. Authors use constraint programming and a series of problem-specific search strategies in order to achieve objective value improvement.

In [10] authors address the aspect of operational variability in organizations, which is inevitably introduced as unforeseen external factors contribute to changes in the organization requirements or resource availability over time, thus mandating changes in staff scheduling. In particular, three types of variability are considered: Uncertainty of capacity, uncertainty of demand and uncertainty of arrival. Authors propose a problem formulation, the Integrated Personnel Shift and Task re-Scheduling Problem (IPSTrSP), which aims to address static and dynamic scheduling needs in an integrated manner. They propose a metaheuristic algorithm that relies on solution perturbation and local search, to provide with reactive optimization in the face of unexpected scheduling changes. Authors present an extensive section with experimental results and parametric analyses on different parameters of the proposed algorithm.

In [11] authors present a Mixed Integer Programming (MIP) formulation for the problem of preference-based staff scheduling. The problem at hand comprises hard constraints (e.g. restrictions on working hours, vacations, training sessions etc.) and soft constraints (e.g. minimum allowable staff levels, maximum on-duty hours for each employee, employee requests etc.). The aim thus is to minimize soft constraint violation while satisfying hard constraints. Authors demonstrate that allowing near-optimal solutions using the proposed MIP model in fact results in well-performing solutions that are on par with manually generated schedules.

In [12] authors propose an optimization approach for train crew scheduling considering the fair distribution of unpopular tasks within the organization. In particular, a triplet of objectives is considered, namely minimization of schedule costs, minimization of schedule unfairness and minimization of schedule unpopularity. Authors present an extensive review of the notion of fairness in the context of scheduling, and go on to propose a constructive algorithm based on column generation to solve the scheduling problem, on instances that are taken from real-world scenarios.

Despite the wealth of related works, there is a need to cater to requirements concerning the ageing workforce, which is not fully covered in the existing state of art. The present work strives to contribute to this through the proposed Participatory Work Orchestration Support Tool, by introducing the elements of participatory management, through enabling requests of workers to be answered by managers, and introducing an intelligent optimizing decision support system, which makes suggestions based on a comprehensive range of decision criteria, including schedule fairness and ageing workforce-specific objectives and constraints.

3   Architecture

The architecture of the proposed Participatory Work Orchestration Support Tool follows the Model-View-Controller paradigm. An overview with key components is displayed in Fig. 1. Four main components are distinguished: The first is the Manager Platform Front-end, which undertakes the Human-Machine interfacing task and organizes and displays information to the user, in this case the organization managers. The second is the Platform Controller, which is responsible for data aggregation and communication with the shift scheduling optimization module. The Shift Scheduling Optimization Module is responsible for generating optimal schedules based on constraints imposed by the managers and organization. Finally, the Model store includes all relevant information regarding the workforce and organization operations. In the following sections, the two key components of the Participatory Work Orchestration Support Tool, namely the Manager Platform and the Shift Scheduling Optimization module are presented in greater detail.

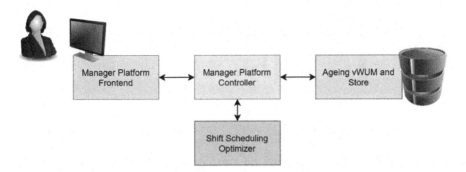

Fig. 1. The architecture of the proposed Participatory Work Orchestration Support Tool.

4   Manager Platform

The Work Orchestration platform is the first component of the Participatory Work Orchestration Tool that allows managers to receive an overview of the current situation regarding their organization shift and task assignments, and act on it to better adapt it to the needs of the organization and individual workers. The work orchestration platform is a web application that includes a number of separate views, all integrated into a main dashboard, each of which highlight a different aspect of the work organization schedule.

The main dashboard includes a series of overview panes on top, which highlight the main characteristics of the organization schedule: Workers, tasks, stations, remote sessions and worker requests. The manager can click on each pane to view a detailed view of each section.

In addition to the top panes, in the main section a series of views exist that give further insight into organization schedule. These can be selected via tabs on top. The first view is the Task-Shift table (Fig. 2), which provides a Gantt chart-style depiction of the weekly tasks assigned to each shift as well as individual worker assignments. Each row corresponds to an instance of a task to be performed, and each column to a specific shift in a day. The cells in the table show where each task is scheduled to be performed, and to which worker the task is principally assigned. By hovering over the task assignment, it is possible to see details about the task, the skills required and the assigned worker.

Another view is the Weekly Shift view (Fig. 3), which provides a more detailed breakdown of worker status for each shift. Columns in this display reflect shifts organized by day, while rows represent individual workers. Different situations can be visualized using distinct visual markers, allowing for a quick overview of the organization task assignments. In addition to the worker/task assignment overview, by hovering over the table cells the manager is able to obtain additional information regarding the particular assignment, such as the task being assigned, the state of the task etc.

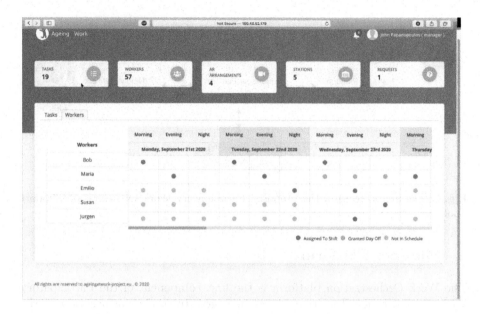

Fig. 2. The task-shift table view of the proposed Participatory Work Orchestration Tool.

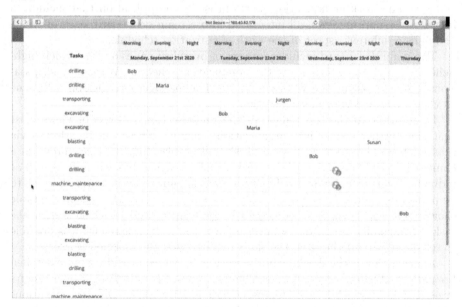

Fig. 3. The weekly shift view of the proposed Participatory Work Orchestration Tool.

5   Shift Scheduling Optimization

Shift scheduling is an integral part of any business or organization that operates on shift work as it is a very complex issue, especially when many shifts and large number of workers of various skills are involved. The aim of shift planning is to establish schedules for all activities and to assign each activity to a specific employee as effective planning helps in reducing labor costs while improving efficiency and employee satisfaction [13]. In addition, shift scheduling also needs to comply with certain labor regulations and each organization's rules and policies.

5.1   Problem Formulation

We formulate the shift scheduling problem as a Mixed-Integer Linear Problem, which incorporates a single objective and multiple constraints, derived in accordance to established shift scheduling literature, but adapted to the specifics originating from the goals defined in the AgeingAtWork project.

The main objective is to minimize worker assignments to shifts, subject to constraints related to production, safety and legal aspects. To model production-related constraints, we assume that in each shift a number of tasks need to be completed. Each task requires one or more skills. Each worker is associated to one or more skills in many-to-many relationships. As such, the main production-related constraint in scheduling is to ensure that workers with the required skills are present in each shift to successfully complete the corresponding tasks. Safety constraints stipulate minimum number of workers present during each shift, as well as presence of workers with safety-related skills. Finally, legal constraints limit the individual worker assignments on a daily, weekly and monthly basis, and prevent overnight continuous shifts. In addition to the essential problem definition outlined above, we consider a number of additional aspects that are outlined hereby.

Shift Difficulty and Fairness. Fairness of shift schedule is a term that has been proposed to highlight the need of including the inevitable differences in difficulty that characterize each shift throughout the day and week. Factors determining shift difficulty may depend on the specifics of the organization or not. For instance, night shifts carry an intrinsic difficulty due to the time they occupy, which may lead employees to develop issues with sleep, or to socialization problems. On the other hand, specific shifts in an organization may include tasks of varying complexity, which is a factor affecting the perceived difficulty of the shift.

Remote Work. The AgeingAtWork project introduces a suite of tools aimed at remote collaboration, which allow flexible assignment of senior, experienced workers, who can be assigned to work from home or standby roles, while younger workers undertake tasks in the facility, under the remote guidance of seniors. These tools obviously introduce novel opportunities for shift scheduling, which are exploited in our approach. To the extent that shift scheduling is involved, this enables senior workers to be assigned to remote shifts, which are considered lighter load, while on-site workers can undertake multiple tasks that they are not experts in.

Shift Preferences. Workers can indicate their preferences regarding shift assignments, which are then considered in the generated schedule. This is performed by adjusting the difficulty factor of preferred shifts, thus guiding the scheduling algorithm to select them.

5.2   Mathematical Definition

Considering the following sets:

W, the set of workers
T, the set of tasks
H, the set of shifts
D, the set of days
S, the set of skills

the following problem parameters:

K_{st}, parameter indicating task t needing skill s
P_{sw}, parameter indicating worker w having skill s
Q_{thd}, parameter indicating presence of task t in day d and shift h
U_{wd}, parameter indicating worker w unavailable in day d

and the following decision variables:

W_{whd}, worker w assigned to shift h in day d
R_{whd}, worker w assigned to remote work in shift h in day d
F_{wd}, worker w assigned day off in day d
$G_{df,max}$, aux variable representing the max assignment shifts of any worker

minimize:
$$G_{df,max} \tag{1}$$

s.t.:

$$K_{st} \times Q_{thd} \leq \sum_{w \in W, h \in H, d \in D, s \in S} (W_{whd} + R_{whd}) \times P_{sw}, \forall s \in S, t \in T \tag{2}$$

$$W_{\text{whd}} + R_{\text{whd}} + F_{\text{whd}} = 1, \forall w \in W, h \in H, d \in D \tag{3}$$

$$\sum_{h \in H} W_{whd} + \sum_{h \in H} R_{whd} \leq 1, \forall w \in W, d \in D \tag{4}$$

$$W_{wnd} + W_{wm(d+1)} \leq 1, \forall w \in W, d \in D, n = H_{-1}, m = H_0 \tag{5}$$

$$U_{wd} + W_{whd} + R_{whd} \leq 1, \forall w \in W, h \in H, d \in D \tag{6}$$

$$\sum_{w\in W} W_{\text{whd}} \geq \sum_{t\in T} Q_{\text{thd}} \,, \forall h \in H, d \in D \tag{7}$$

$$\sum_{w\in W} W_{whd} \geq c_{W,\text{min}}, \forall h \in H, d \in D \tag{8}$$

$$\sum_{w\in W} W_{whd} \leq c_{W,\text{max}}, \forall h \in H, d \in D \tag{9}$$

$$G_{DF\,\text{max}} \geq \sum_{h\in H, d\in D} (W_{\text{whd}} + R_{\text{whd}} \times Z_{\text{remote}}) \times Z_h \times Z_d, \forall w \in W \tag{10}$$

Equation 1 is the objective function that seeks to minimize the assigned tasks to workers. Inequality 2 ensures each task in a shift can be performed by at least one worker. Inequality 3 ensures no worker is assigned to multiple states at the same time. Inequality 4 ensures each worker only gets a maximum of one shift assigned per day. Inequality 5 ensures no worker gets consecutive shifts i.e. assigned to morning shift after a night shift. Inequality 6 ensures no worker is assigned to a shift on an unavailable day. Inequality 7 ensures for each shift there are at least as many workers as tasks. Inequality 8 ensures there are at least workers in each shift. Inequality 9 ensures there are at most workers in each shift. Inequality 10 is an auxiliary constrain that ensures the objective function variable corresponds to the max worker assignment. The above problem is solved using an open-source branch-and-cut mixed integer programming solver, CBC [14].

6 Experimental Results

6.1 Simulated Scheduling Data

This application example focuses on highlighting the potential of the AI-enabled shift scheduler in identifying favorable shift schedules, which ensure organization functional requirements, and at the same time satisfy worker preferences, to the extent possible given the scheduling problem definition. In order to illustrate this application, we assume the following scenario: A rapid-prototyping unit within an organization has 7 workers that tend two machines: A 3D printer and a Computer Numerical Control (CNC) router. Each of the two machines requires a different set of skills to operate; some skills are common (such as e.g. some safety-related skills), but others are unique. Workers also have different skill sets, depending on their specialization.

Here we consider a team of two 3D print technicians, three CNC technicians, and two safety technicians. In order to highlight the flexibility of the approach, we have designated one CNC technician and one 3D print technician to also have safety qualifications. In accordance to the tasks, a 3D print technician is required to operate the 3D printer, a CNC technician similarly is required to operate the CNC machine, and at least one safety technician needs to be present at all times. Each working day has three shifts: Morning, evening and night. Night

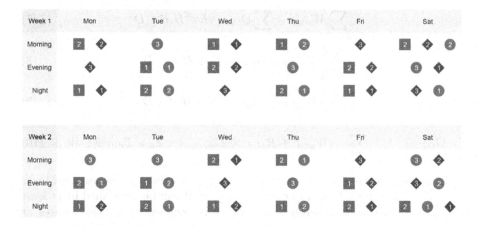

Fig. 4. Bi-weekly schedule generated by the Participatory Work Orchestration Tool for a team of seven workers.

shifts are considered the most challenging ones, with high difficulty rating, and morning shifts the easiest ones, with low difficulty rating. A two-week schedule is considered, with six working days, except Sunday. Saturdays are considered undesirable days, so they have greater difficulty rating. Assuming the above scenario, a MILP problem has been formulated, for determining the two-week shift schedule. The objectives, as outlined in Subsect. 5.2, are to maximize schedule fairness, subject to constraints as outlined in the same subsection. The schedule was successfully generated and the resulting task distribution is shown in Fig. 4. We observe that all constraints (e.g. no consecutive shifts, no more than a single shift per day) are observed, and in addition, it was possible to distribute "difficult" shifts (e.g. night shifts or weekend shifts) efficiently, maximizing schedule fairness.

6.2 Acceptance Study

An acceptance study regarding the Participatory Work Orchestration Support Tool was held from May 2021 to June 2021. The surveys were conducted entirely online after presenting the tool via video demonstrations and screenshots. As such there was no need to make personal contact with the respondents, reducing the dangers associated with the ongoing COVID-19 outbreak. Google forms were used to make the surveys accessible. The profiles of participants ranged among several groups, including directors, company owners, healthcare and safety specialists, and persons committed to teaching or research in mining fact, which enhanced the validity of acceptance findings.

A total of 36 persons were contacted for the acceptability studies, with a median age of 52 and a male/female ratio of 21/15. Perceived Ease of Use (PEU), Perceived Usefulness (PU), Behavioural Intention to Use (BI), and Self-efficacy questions were used to assess technology adoption, according to the dimensions of the Technology Acceptance Model [15].

An overview of the survey results is available in Table 1. Results indicate a strongly favorable disposition of the respondents towards the engagement with work orchestration tools. With respect to PEU, more than 85% or respondents expressed agreement or partial agreement to questions of ease of learning to operate the tool, ease of learning to command the tool and ease of becoming skilled with the tool. In addition, with respect to PU, more than half of the respondents completely agreed on the tool's usefulness in assigning task per worker, supporting daily tasks, putting worker skills to work and overall improvement of time and quality of work. For the same questions a total of 80% of the respondents expressed either complete or partial agreement. With respect to the sole BI question, more than 70% of the respondents expressed complete or partial agreement, while for the sole SE question, the percentage was more than 90%.

Table 1. Survey results

Question	Completely agree	Somewhat agree	Neutral	Somewhat disagree	Completely disagree
Perceived Ease of Use (PEU)					
Learning to operate this tool would be easy for you	41,6%	50%	5,6%	2,8%	–
You would find it easy to get this tool to do what you want it to do	30,6%	55,6%	11%	2,8%	–
It would be easy for you to become skilful in the use of this tool	36,1%	47,2%	13,9%	2,8%	–
Perceived Usefulness (PU)					
Using the information of vacations and absences provided in the tool would help you effectively assign tasks per worker, saving time and cost	52,8%	36,1%	11,1%	–	–
Using the Work-Scheduling tool daily notifications would be a good practice to support workers' daily tasks	58,3%	30,6%	11,1%	–	–
Using this tool, the overall time and quality of your work would be improved	55,6%	27,8%	13,8%	2,8%	–
Using this tool better exploitation of workers skills would be possible	55,6%	25%	13,8%	5,6%	–
Behavioral Intent (BI)					
If you could use this tool it to support you at your work, you would appreciate working with it	41,7%	33,3%	25%	–	–
Self-Efficacy (SE)					
You can use this tool if someone shows you how to do it	52,8%	38,9%	8,3%	–	–

7 Discussion and Conclusion

This work aims primarily to address the needs of the ageing workforce in the context of shift work, a form of work that is commonly employed in industrialized society. Towards this aim, a Participatory Work Orchestration Support Tool has been developed, which is addressed to organization managers, and with the aim of providing sufficient decision support tools to improve management of the ageing workforce. The platform enables organization managers to visualize at a glance organization schedule and the status of their workforce, respond to worker requests, and get intelligent suggestions for schedule improvement through an optimizing shift scheduler module.

The proposed tool has undergone preliminary validation, in the form of an Acceptance Study, as well as simulated benchmarks of the scheduler-generated shift schedules. Both forms of validation concluded into encouraging results, demonstrating on one hand an overall positive acceptance and on the other hand capability of generating promising and sound shift schedules.

From a development standpoint, the next steps of the research involve on further elaboration and enrichment of the visual overview provided to organization managers through the manager platform, as well as development of the shift scheduler with the aim of generating even more relevant results, taking into account a more detailed picture of worker preferences and shift difficulty. In addition, from a validation standpoint, we aim to extend the validation of the proposed solution to studies performed in end-user premises, with the aim of further consolidating the contribution of the proposed tool based on real data.

References

1. Yeung, A.K., Berman, B.: Adding value through human resources: reorienting human resource measurement to drive business performance. Hum. Res. Manag. **36**(3), 321–335 (1997)
2. Kang, M.-Y., et al.: The relationship between shift work and mental health among electronics workers in South Korea: a cross-sectional study. PloS One **12**(11), e0188019 (2017)
3. Giakoumis, D., et al.: Smart, personalized and adaptive ICT solutions for active, healthy and productive ageing with enhanced workability. In: Proceedings of the 12th ACM International Conference on PErvasive Technologies Related to Assistive Environments, pp. 442–447 (2019)
4. Aykin, T.: A comparative evaluation of modeling approaches to the labor shift scheduling problem. Eur. J. Oper. Res. **125**(2), 381–397 (2000)
5. Petrovic, S.: "You have to get wet to learn how to swim" applied to bridging the gap between research into personnel scheduling and its implementation in practice. Ann. Oper. Res. **275**(1), 161–179 (2019)
6. Shuib, A., Kamarudin, F.I.: Solving shift scheduling problem with days-off preference for power station workers using binary integer goal programming model. Ann. Oper. Res. **272**(1), 355–372 (2019)

7. Sinthamrongruk, T., et al.: Homecare staff scheduling problem using a GA based approach with local search techniques. In: 2019 9th International Conference on Cloud Computing, Data Science & Engineering (Confluence), pp. 250–257. IEEE (2019)
8. Herawati, A., et al.: Shift scheduling model considering workload and worker's preference for security department. IOP Conf. Ser. Mater. Sci. Eng. **337**(1), 012011 (2018)
9. Lapègue, T., Bellenguez-Morineau, O., Prot, D.: A constraint based approach for the shift design personnel task scheduling problem with equity. Comput. Oper. Res. **40**(10), 2450–2465 (2013)
10. Maenhout, B., Vanhoucke, M.: A perturbation matheuristic for the integrated personnel shift and task re-scheduling problem. Eur. J. Oper. Res. **269**(3), 806–823 (2018)
11. Ásgeirsson, E.I., Sigurardóttir, G.L.: Near-optimal MIP solutions for preference based self-scheduling. Ann. Oper. Res. **239**(1), 273–293 (2016)
12. Jütte, S., Müller, D., Thonemann, U.W.: Optimizing railway crew schedules with fairness preferences. J. Sched. **20**(1), 43–55 (2016). https://doi.org/10.1007/s10951-016-0499-4
13. Van den Bergh, J., et al.: Personnel scheduling: a literature review. Eur. J. Oper. Res. **226**(3), 367–385 (2013)
14. Forrest, J., et al.: coin-or/Cbc: version 2.9.9. version releases/2.9.9, July 2018. https://doi.org/10.5281/zenodo.1317566
15. Lee, Y., Kozar, K.A., Larsen, K.R.T.: The technology acceptance model: past, present, and future. Commun. Assoc. Inf. Syst. **12**(1), 50 (2003)

Stakeholder Perceptions on Requirements for Accessible Technical Condition Information in Residential Real Estate Transactions

Jo E. Hannay[2]([✉]) [iD], Kristin S. Fuglerud[1] [iD], and Bjarte M. Østvold[1] [iD]

[1] Norwegian Computing Center, Pb. 114 Blindern, 0314 Oslo, Norway
{kristins,bjarte}@nr.no
[2] Simula Metropolitan Center for Digital Engineering, Center for Effective
Digitalization of the Public Sector, OsloMet, Pb. 4 St. Olavs plass, 0130 Oslo, Norway
johannay@simula.no

Abstract. Buyers of residential real estate frequently experience dissatisfaction with the property they have purchased. Recent findings suggest that insufficient knowledge about the property is a key trigger to ensuing disappointment and claims for compensation. Further, a good technical condition report reduces the probability of dissatisfaction and insurance claims. For the purpose of designing services for improving technical condition information and its flow, we elicited stakeholder perceptions on the suitability of residential real estate technical condition reports. Specifically, we conducted multiple surveys which we content analyzed and used as the basis for a conceptual model of information products and dependencies needed to deliver better information to stakeholders in a real estate transaction process. The conceptual model, in turn, forms the basis for specific service design in future work.

Keywords: Residential real estate transactions · Technical condition information · Information services · Conflict reduction

1 Introduction

Buying and selling a home is a stressful ordeal. Few other transactions affect the family economy as much, while being based on a limited understanding of what is being transacted, in a relatively short transaction process.

Information asymmetry [9], where one party has more salient information about a transacted product than the other, can lead to market distortions [8,14], where residential real estate stakeholders do not end up transacting the property in question at a sustainable price, thus resulting in dissatisfaction and conflict. More specifically, lacking knowledge on the part of the buyer about the property in question and a good technical condition report have been found to be key determinants of (dis)satisfaction [11].

© The Author(s), under exclusive license to Springer Nature Switzerland AG 2022
M. Antona and C. Stephanidis (Eds.): HCII 2022, LNCS 13308, pp. 242–259, 2022.
https://doi.org/10.1007/978-3-031-05028-2_16

In this study, we investigate various stakeholders' perceptions on what information is salient in a property transaction process. We also specifically investigate the stakeholders' perceptions on a particular document used in the Norwegian residential real estate market; namely, a technical condition report written by an authorized property assessor. Then, on the basis of those perceptions, we develop a conceptual model of information requirements that should guide the design of information services that are intended to facilitate stakeholders' information processing during a residential real estate transaction process.

2 Background

Earlier, we conducted a stakeholder journey analysis [6], where we elicited possible technology touch points in a residential real estate transaction process (Fig. 1). The technology in question was "smart" property transaction (SPT) services to support stakeholders in a property transaction process. The services are briefly outlined in Fig. 2, and we will return to a few of them below.

The stakeholder journeys were developed through three workshops with stakeholders, and then refined by the researchers. The analysis was conducted for five groups of stakeholder. Figure 1 depicts five swimlanes, one for each stakeholder, from bottom to top: the residential real estate buyer, the estate agent, the seller, the technical condition assessor and the insurance company providing latent defects cover, an insurance policy that protects the seller against claims from the buyer after the real estate transaction has taken place.

In Fig. 1, the technical condition report appears as a technology touchpoint in the Assessor swim lane. Although real estate assessors use digital editing tools to generate technical condition reports, in the analysis, the technical condition report is simply an information source used as input to the touchpoint in the Estate Agent swim lane ("Explain set asking price"). That touchpoint involves the property scoring service (Fig. 2), which summarizes the technical condition of a property in a numerical score between zero and 100 and other metrics that are intended to be easy to grasp. Important goals of providing these metrics are to make it easier for non-experts to grasp the technical condition of a residential property, and also to make it easier to compare the technical condition of different properties. Moreover, several comments in the workshops were related to managing expectations about price. Real estate agents experience that sellers often expect a higher price for their home than agents think realistic according to the technical condition. They also experience that buyers often do not accept that any devaluation for technical condition has already been taken into account in the asking price. Thus, when the assessor has reviewed the property and written the technical condition report, the estate agent can use the property scoring service to document how the asking price is calculated. The user story "Explain set asking price" indicated in Fig. 1 reads as follows:

> Explain set asking price: As an estate agent, I can get a seller to understand the rationale for my suggestion for asking price by using the SPT property scoring service to show the technical condition of the property.

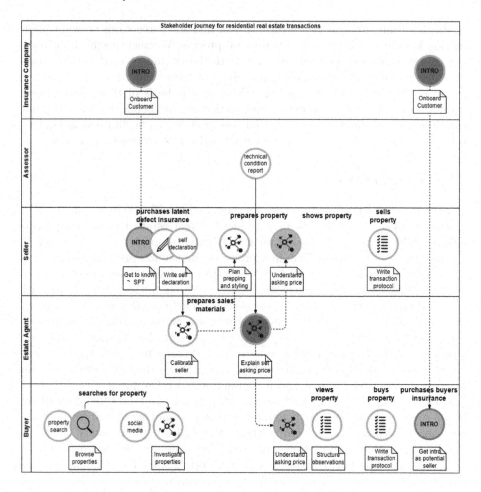

Fig. 1. Planned stakeholder journeys [6].

Incidentally, the first version of the stakeholder journey analysis also included the following user story at the same touchpoint:

> Generate sales prospect: As an estate agent, I can generate a sales prospect automatically by using the SPT property scoring service to retrieve key technical information on the property.

However, this user story was later dropped, since estate agents came to the conclusion that automated prospectus generation would probably give little added value to their work.

Starting with the current study, we set out to elaborate on the technical condition report touchpoint. The goal is to suggest service requirements for producing "better" technical condition reports. The intent being that the improved reports should benefit stakeholders directly, and also that they should benefit

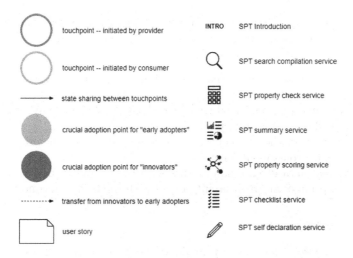

Fig. 2. Symbols for Stakeholder Journey Framework.

the functioning of the property scoring service touchpoint in Fig. 1. Indirectly, we also address the "Explain set asking price" and the two "Understand asking price" touchpoints, in the sense that better reports should facilitate the functioning and effects of these touchpoints as well, and also because it may be necessary to help explain and understand technical condition reports even when the reports may be better than before.

The technical condition report is a document prepared by an assessor before a dwelling is sold. The assessor visits the apartment or house and writes down an assessment of the technical condition in a semi-structured form, based on a standard [12]. For each part of the building, the report contains the following: a technical condition grade (TG) being an ordinal scale ranging from TG0 (best) to TG3 (worst) or, exceptionally, TGNE (not examined). A TG0 signifies pristine conditions for a building part not more than 5 years old, while a TG1 signifies an intact building part older than 5 years. A TG2 should be given when there is an observable flaw, or likely grounds (e.g., age or unfortunate circumstances) for expecting a flaw if not observable, that needs attention in due course, while a TG3 signifies an acute need for attention to a flaw. In the case of TG2 and TG3, a textual explanation of probable cause and necessary measures to attend to the flaw is expected. In practice, reports may contain technical terms that buyers, who are mostly laypersons, have problems understanding. Also, the actual building parts that appear in reports and the organization of reports vary and are to some degree at the discretion of the assessor.

3   Survey

To understand what "better" technical condition reports means, we conducted surveys on the five stakeholder groups, querying respondents on quality issues and on idiosyncrasies (that may not necessarily be unfortunate) that are known to occur in technical condition reports. The survey focused on the following perceptions of the stakeholder group:

- what information they perceived as most important for prospective real estate buyers prior to bidding
- what problems they perceived that prospective real estate buyers have with the technical condition report
- what information they perceived as most important for themselves in performing their professional function
- their perception of given quality issues with the technical condition report
- their perception of given variability issues with the technical condition report

3.1 Survey Method

We followed survey methodology in [5,10,13]. Specifically, we used semantic differential scales, rather than Likert scales, we used 7-point scales, rather than 5-point scales and we used non-extreme labels (e.g., "not important"–"important", rather than "extremely non-important"–"extremely important").

The survey questionnaires were similar across groups, varying in wording to match the particular group's terminology and understanding. Variants are indicated with square brackets below. For the professional stakeholders, the questionnaire opened with the following questions:

p1 What single source of information do you see as the most important for potential buyers prior to their placing a bid?   *free-text response*

p2 Indicate how important you see the following [information sources] are for potential buyers prior to their placing a bid:
                    sem. diff. "not important"–"important"

p3 To what degree do you think potential buyers think it is easy to read technical condition reports?   *sem. diff. "to a minor degree"–"to a major degree"*

p4 To what degree do you think potential buyers understand the technical condition report prior to placing a bid?
                    sem. diff. "to a minor degree"–"to a major degree"

p5 To what degree do you think potential buyers read the technical condition report prior to placing a bid?
                    sem. diff. "to a minor degree"–"to a major degree"

p6 What issues do you think potential buyers experience with technical condition reports?   *free-text response*

p7 What single source of information is most important for you in [your role] to [perform your tasks]?   *free-text response*

The two first questions were also given in a mirrored form to buyers:

b1 What single source of information do you see as the most important for you prior to placing a bid?   *free-text response*

b2 Indicate how important you see the following [information sources] are for you prior to placing a bid: *sem. diff. "not important"–"important"* and to sellers:

s1 What single source of information do you see as the most important for you to provide when selling a dwelling?   *free-text response*

s2 Indicate how important you see the following [information sources] are for you when selling a dwelling: *sem. diff. "not important"–"important"*

For technical condition assessors, p7 was formulated as

c7 What single source of information is most important for the parties in a property transaction   *free-text response*

Then the following questions were posed to all stakeholders:

a8 To what degree do you find it easy to read technical condition reports?
                    sem. diff. "to a minor degree"–"to a major degree"

a9 To what degree do you understand technical condition reports [prior to performing your task]?   *sem. diff. "to a minor degree"–"to a major degree"*

a10 How much time do you usually spend reading a technical condition report?
                    numeric response in minutes

a11 In [your role], what issues do you experience with technical condition reports?
                    free-text response

a12 Overall, how satisfied are you with the technical condition reports [you process in your role]   *sem. diff. "dissatisfied"–"satisfied"*

a13 Indicate to what degree the following quality deficiencies in technical condition reports affect [what you do in your role]:
                    sem. diff. "to a minor degree"–"to a major degree"

a14 Indicate to what degree you think the following variations in technical condition reports are advantageous or disadvantageous for [what you do in your role]:   *sem. diff. "disadvantage"–"advantage"*

a15 What is the most important improvement you can see for technical condition reports?   *free-text response*

a16 Are there other things you think can reduce discontent and conflict in residential real estate transactions?   *free-text response*

The survey was primarily designed for conceptualization, and we did not focus on statistical analyses of the ordinal responses. For this paper, we therefore present qualitative analyses for these questions. For each question with free-text responses, we content analyzed the responses as follows [7]: First, the three authors individually formed categories to characterize the semantic content of the responses. This was done by reading responses systematically and categorizing (coding)[1] phrases in the responses. New codes where declared when needed;

---

[1] All coding was performed in NVivo (various versions) and Microsoft Power BI.

otherwise, previously declared codes where used as categories. In this manner, categories were formed *inductively* from the material. Then, the three authors discussed the resulting categories in plenum. Joint categories were synthesized from the discussion. A third *abductive* step was performed on some of the material, in which the researchers formed themes (concepts) from the categories using their knowledge of the domain explicitly [7].

3.2   Survey Results

The questionnaire in its various forms was deployed as an online survey through channels provided by partners in an ongoing research project. Thus, we used convenience samples consisting of 11 responses from technical condition assessors supplied through an organization that trains and certifies assessors, 14 responses from sellers and 25 responses from buyers supplied through the social media channel of a company developing services for real estate transactions, 30 responses from a real estate agency and 32 responses from a company that processes latent defect insurance claims.

Below, we present figures[2] and analyses for the survey questions. Each heading indicates the survey questions that are addressed.

The Most Important Information for Buyers (p1–p2, b1–b2, s1–s2) (p7, c7). The first topic of the survey was what information the participants perceived to be most important for prospective buyers prior to bidding. Question p1 (b1, s1) prompted for unsolicited responses, while question p2 (b2, s2) asked for the relative importance of seven specifically given information sources.

Fig. 3. Stakeholders' classification of information.

---

[2] To distinguish between data that is based on content analysis and quantitative survey data, we use different colour schemes in Fig. 3 and in other figures. We use colour schemes that are accessible also for those with colour vision deficiency https://colorbrewer2.org/#type=sequential&scheme=BuGn&n=3 and https://personal.sron.nl/~pault/#sec:qualitative.

The free-text answers in questions p1, b1, s1, p7, and c7 were content ana-lyzed. The professional stakeholders were asked both which source of information was most important to themselves (p7) and which source of information they thought was most important for the buyers (p1), or, in the case of the assessors, for other stakeholders (c7). The buyers and sellers were only asked about what information was most important for themselves.

Most participants cited only one source of information, but some mentioned several sources, such as both the digital sales description and the technical con-

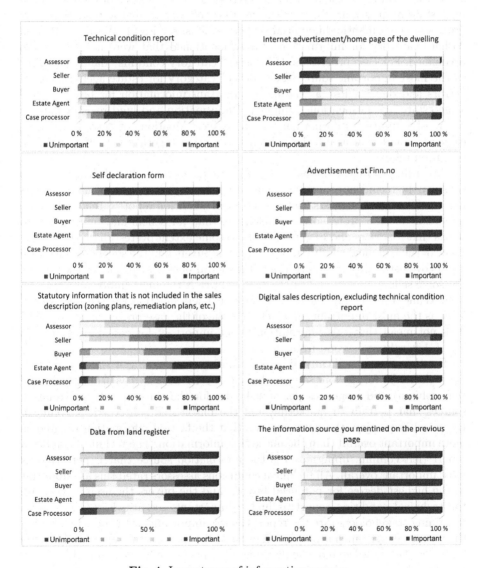

Fig. 4. Importance of information sources.

dition report. In these cases, the answer was divided and coded for each source mentioned, so that the total number of information sources counted is greater than the number of participants. Note that the respondents used alternative names and notions for these information sources, thus necessitating the content analysis for these responses.

Figure 3 presents the resulting information sources from that content analysis, that were mentioned most frequently as the most important information source. These are the technical condition report, the digital sales description, the self-declaration form, the internet advertisement and the price of the residential real estate in question. These categories were all covered by the predefined categories in the semantic differential scale questions, see Fig. 4. We also coded an "other" category for information sources mentioned that were not among the predefined. For case processors, the "other" category contains "damage report" as the most important source. The "other" category for estate agents includes "errors and deficiencies" as the most important information for buyers, while some estate agents mentioned municipal information and land register data as the most important information for themselves. Mentions of "errors and deficiencies" could conceivably have been categorized together with the technical condition report.

According to Fig. 3, the majority of participants from all stakeholder groups consider the technical condition report to be the most important source of information. The figure suggests that the technical condition report is relatively more important for the professional stakeholders than for sellers and buyers. It also seems that assessors and case processors to some extent overestimate the importance of the technical condition report for the buyers and the sellers, while estate agents overestimate the importance of the digital sales description for the buyers. For some sellers, buyers and estate agents, price is the most important information. While a few estate agents, buyers and sellers mention the self-declaration form as the most important information, none of the case processors do so. This does not mean that this information is not important for case processors; see Fig. 4, left column, second from the top.

For the seven specifically given information sources, Fig. 4 shows responses per stakeholder for the four sources that can be characterized as primarily factual (left column) and responses per stakeholder for the three specific information sources that pertain to marketing and the unsolicited source (right column). By visual inspection, the data suggests that the factual information is rated as more important overall than the marketing information. The technical condition report (left column, uppermost) is the information source that is perceived as most important overall. All technical conditions assessors rated this as important to the highest degree for potential buyers, and the buyers themselves also rate the technical condition report as highly important; see also Fig. 3. The three remaining stakeholders rate the reports as less important, with the sellers giving the lowest rating, which is notable since the seller pays for the report and has the most detailed knowledge of the dwelling. Conversely, sellers give a higher rating to both advertisement information sources than do the other stakeholders.

Our rationale for posing an open question on information sources and then asking respondents to rate a set of given information sources was to see if there might be any social-desirability bias toward the technical condition report being the "correct" choice as the most important information source. Overall, responses to the open question were in harmony with the responses to given information sources, even if a few information sources were not covered by the latter.

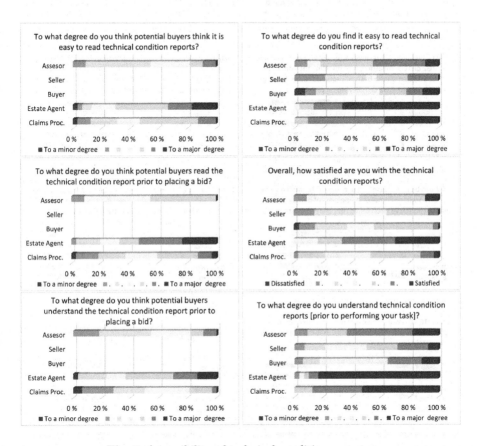

Fig. 5. Accessibility of technical condition reports.

Accessibility of Technical Condition Reports (p3–p5, a8–a9, a12). The next survey topic was the accessibility of technical condition reports. These questions can be divided into two groups: First, there are questions to professional stakeholders—technical conditions assessors, estate agents and insurance claims processors—about their thoughts on buyers' and/or sellers' relationship to reports. The responses to these questions are in the left column of Fig. 5. Overall, among the professional stakeholders, the estate agent has the highest confidence in the buyers' and sellers' ability and willingness to process the reports. The

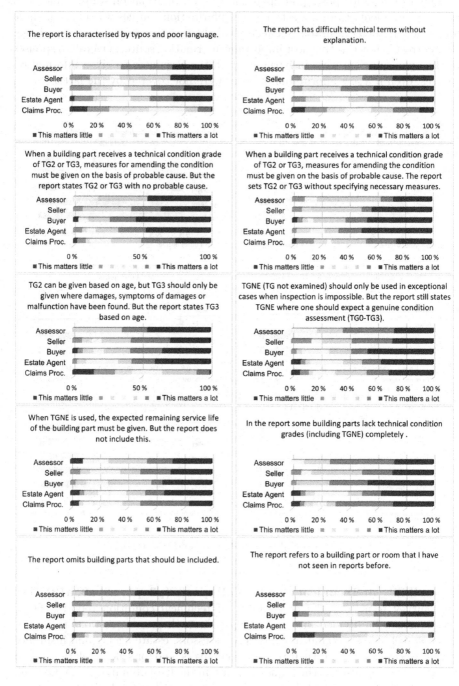

Fig. 6. Perceptions on technical condition report quality issues.

second group of questions, in the right column, were posed to all five stake-holders, and here the stakeholder rates his or her own relationship to technical condition reports. The professional stakeholders claim a higher ability to process reports than the non-professional ones, with the technical conditions assessors claiming a somewhat lower level than the estate agents and the insurance claims processors. The estate agents both claim the highest processing ability and has the highest confidence in the buyers' and sellers' ability and willingness. The assessors and claims processors have low confidence in the buyers and sellers. In the question on how satisfied stakeholders are with reports in general (middle of right column), the estate agent is markedly more satisfied than the rest, and furthermore, the non-professionals are the least satisfied.

Perceptions of Quality Issues (a13). The questionnaire listed a selection of known quality issues with technical condition reports and asked stakeholders to rate their seriousness, see Fig. 6. On most questions, the technical conditions assessors are more critical than the other stakeholders, whereas the insurance claims processors are generally the least concerned about the quality issues. The latter may be explained by the fact that for insurance claims, more recent information is typically processed – for example, a damage report – that is more important to the claim than the technical condition report.

Perceptions of Variability Issues (a14). The questionnaire listed a selection of known variability issues with technical condition reports (Fig. 7), and stakeholders were asked to indicate the degree to which they are advantageous

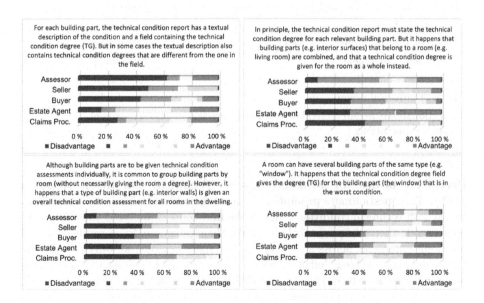

Fig. 7. Perceptions on technical condition report variability issues.

or not. These variabilities may be interpreted as the result of decisions by technical conditions assessors in order to capture the observed technical conditions in a report format that does not quite fit. The assessors stand out as rating at the extremes. This may be because they are experts on the topic and have more refined criticisms. At the same time, they may want the flexibility that variability gives, since this could make their job simpler.

Table 1. Perceived issues with technical condition reports. All stakeholders, joint categories and themes.

Joint category	Theme
Inadequate information	Content
Incorrect information	Content
Too much information	Content
Unspecific and ambiguous information	Content
Uninformative	Content
Poor language	Form
Difficult, unclear or messy, illogical layout, repetitions	Form, Standardization
Difficult to find information	Form, Standardization
Difficult to compare information	Standardization
Lack of standardization	Standardization
Poor description	Content
Challenge to explain condition to buyers	Content
Hard to understand or lacking info on consequences	Content
Technical terms	Content
Different understanding and use of grades and age	Assessment
Insufficient assessments	Assessment
Reservations and disclaimers	Assessment
Lack of universal design	Standardization
Questionable neutrality/credibility, due to sales language, seller's expectations	Assessment

Perceived Issues for Stakeholders in Technical Condition Reports (a11). The questionnaire prompted all the stakeholders to list issues they experience with technical condition reports. We first content analyzed these free-text responses inductively per stakeholder. We then categorized the resulting codes into joint categories across stakeholders. For space reasons, we only present the joint categories (Table 1, leftmost column). We only include joint categories representing responses from at least two different types of stakeholder.

In addition, and for the interest of concept building, we constructed themes abductively (Table 1, rightmost column). The theme *Content* concerns the nature of information and its role in communicating with other stakeholders. Examples of challenges include information that is inadequate or incorrect. Too much information can make it difficult to spot the essential information, as can poor descriptions. Other content problems include reports with unspecific and ambiguous information, that are uninformative, hard to understand, with difficult technical terms, or lacking information about consequences of serious flaws.

The theme *Form* concerns inconveniences and difficulties arising from unfortunate, or lacking, informational structure. *Form* is related to the theme *Standardization*, which includes issues on variations of layout and structure and how information is presented. Several of the joint categories in Table 1 are placed in both *Form* and *Standardization*.

Moreover, we have mapped issues related to difficulties with comparing technical conditions reports and lack of universal design into *Standardization*. Lack of universal design pertains to issues that could have been resolved by adhering to widely accepted standards for digital accessibility and accessible web content [3,4]. These standards are in line with the European Accessibility Act which covers websites and mobile applications provided by public bodies [2]. According to the Norwegian regulations universal design of ICT, private sector bodies must also adhere to the WCAG 2.1 standard [1].

The theme *Assessment* includes inconsistent applications of technical condition grades, inferior inspections and assessments, disclaimers on the part of the assessor and trust issues triggered by sales language and the fact that the assessor's commission is covered by the seller.

Most Important Improvement to Technical Condition Reports (a15). We content analyzed the free-text responses for each stakeholder on what they see as the most important improvements for technical condition reports. As for the previous question, we compiled the codes for each stakeholder into joint categories across stakeholders (Table 2). We then constructed themes abductively from the joint categories. Since this, and the previous question, are thematically similar, themes for this question and for the previous question were compiled together. Question a16 is also thematically similar, but we omit the analysis of this question for brevity, since the contribution beyond what we are already presenting is marginal.

The themes in Table 2 cover improvements on several issues covered by the categories in Table 1. However, there also emerged categories which gave rise to a new theme *Coordination*. Both the coordination of responsibilities and the coordination of specific types of information are mentioned in the responses. Other categories in this theme include illegalities, which are significant in insurance claims, the self-declaration form from the seller and information about technical value. Under *Standardization*, a new category emerged that concerns better support for communication between stakeholders. Under *Content*, a category emerged that is about providing a summary of the technical conditions report. When there is a poor technical condition grade there is a need for better descriptions of the condition itself, but also descriptions of potential consequences if not fixed, and necessary measures to repair the flaw. Further issues concerning assessors' expertise and the quality of the assessors' work and practices were placed in *Assessment*.

4 Conceptual Model

From the themes devised from the content analyses and shown in Tables 1 and 2, we constructed the conceptual model in Fig. 8. The model shows the two themes of *Form* and *Content* for the technical condition report as what needs to be addressed concretely for producing better reports. Alongside to the right is the *Assessment* theme that calls for increasing the competence of those who produce the reports. Overarching the technical conditions report and the assessment profession is the theme of *Coordination* which calls for explicating and delineating the roles of various documents that are involved in a real estate transaction process and seeing to it that information is coordinated across those documents. Cross-cutting all of this is the theme of *Standardization*, which calls for the systemic oversight on the part of relevant regulatory and advisory bodies to provide ample support in the form of mandatory standards to ensure improvement in all the other themes.

There is, perhaps, nothing surprising in this conceptual model. On the one hand, one might say that what is called for in the model is so obvious that

Table 2. Improvement to technical condition reports: Joint categories and themes.

Joint category	Theme
Explicated legal issues	Coordination
Clarified responsibilities	Coordination
Self-declaration from seller used	Coordination
Technical value included	Coordination
Technical conditions in sales documentation	Coordination
Crosscutting expertise	Coordination
Better support for communication	Standardization
Standardized reports	Standardization
Understandable language and readability	Form
Summary	Content
Consequences and secondary damages	Content
Necessary measures	Content
Better descriptions (condition)	Content
Less general and irrelevant information	Content
Broad expertise	Assessment
TG for each building part	Assessment
Thorough investigations during inspection	Assessment

one might expect that all this should already be in place. What is noteworthy, though, is that this is what five groups of stakeholder have expressed more or less uniformly as necessary to improve on (albeit compiled as our conception of it) so that, clearly, this is *not* in place, as perceived by those stakeholders. It is also interesting that a category on universal design emerged, since there is legislation and standards in place to address these issues. It is not unlikely that this category signifies a lack of awareness and knowledge of universal design among those responsible for the artefacts relevant to real estate transactions. It may also reflect that there are barriers to implementing such standards.

When looking closer at the model, it becomes clear that there is, in fact, a lot to undertake in order to reach the state of affairs declared in the model. Initiatives have to be started to improve the form and content of technical conditions reports on many aspects, and this relies on educating assessors, on standardization and on adequate support in the situation of producing the report. Standardizing form and content and ensuring universal design for reports and other relevant documents would seem to be year-long endeavours, if anything like other standardization initiatives. One must develop procedural support so that stakeholders can ensure that information is coordinated across documents and placed appropriately and can maintain this consistent information picture over time.

Fortunately, in the case we are studying, standardization is under way, and new requirements have been developed with the intention that more readable technical condition reports will be produced, where consequences and necessary measures are mandatory. This means that in our case, *regulations* for several of the asked-for improvements will be in place in the near future. As is often the

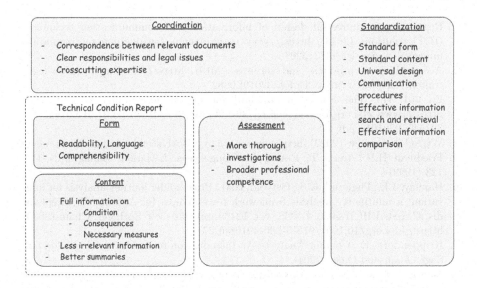

Fig. 8. Conceptual model of information products and relationships.

case, though, when new regulations are introduced, the corresponding operationalization of those regulations are not supplied. This means that stakeholders must find out ways to meet these new regulations.

All this only makes the conceptual model more relevant and the situation ripe for developing tool support for stakeholders accordingly.

5   Conclusion

The conceptual model in Fig. 8 is currently the basis for designing services for stakeholders in residential real estate transaction processes. Two focus groups have been held in which representatives for the five stakeholder groups suggested service functionality in line with the conceptual model developed in this paper. This raw service functionality material will be refined by service design and presented in a more detailed stakeholder journey map showing how stakeholders envision how, for whom and in which situations IT tool support can facilitate the production of better technical condition reports, the *in situ* education of assessors, the utilization of standardization for improving information retrieval and processing and the coordination of information across sources and responsibilities.

Acknowledgements. This research is funded by the Norwegian Research Council under project number 296256 *Smart Real Estate Transactions*. The authors are grateful to Vendu AS for organizing the respondents for the surveys.

References

1. Regulation for universal design of information and communication technology (ICT) solutions (2013). https://www.regjeringen.no/en/dokumenter/regulation-universal-design-ict/id731520/
2. Accessibility of products and services (2019). https://eur-lex.europa.eu/legal-content/EN/LSU/?uri=CELEX:32019L0882
3. En 301 549: The European standard for digital accessibility v3.1.1 (2019). https://www.etsi.org/deliver/etsi_en/301500_301599/301549/03.01.01_60/en_301549v030101p.pdf
4. WCAG 2 overview (2022). https://www.w3.org/WAI/standards-guidelines/wcag/
5. Friedman, H.H., Amoo, T.: Rating the rating scales. J. Market. Manag. **9**(3), 114–123 (1999)
6. Hannay, J.E., Fuglerud, K.S., Østvold, B.M.: Stakeholder journey analysis for innovation: a multiparty analysis framework for startups. In: Antona, M., Stephanidis, C. (eds.) HCII 2020. LNCS, vol. 12189, pp. 370–389. Springer, Cham (2020). https://doi.org/10.1007/978-3-030-49108-6_27
7. Krippendorff, K.: Content Analysis: An Introduction to Its Methodology, 2nd edn. Sage, Thousand Oaks (2004)
8. Levitt, S.D., Syverson, C.: Market distortions when agents are better informed: the value of information in real estate transactions. Rev. Econ. Stat. **90**(4), 599–611 (2008)

9. Lofgren, K., Persson, T., Weibull, J.W.: Markets with asymmetric information: the contributions of George Akerlof, Michael Spence and Joseph Stiglitz. Scand. J. Econ. **104**(2), 195–211 (2002)

10. Roster, C.A., Lucianetti, L., Albaum, G.: Exploring slider vs. categorical response formats in web-based surveys. J. Res. Pract. **11**(1), 108–143 (2015)

11. Schjøll, A., Holth Thorjussen, C.B.: A housing for trouble? Conflict in buying used homes in Norway. Technical Report SIFO RAPPORT 16–2019, Oslo Metropolitan University, Forbruksforskningsinstituttet SIFO (2019)

12. Standard Norge: Teknisk tilstandsanalyse ved omsetning av bolig. Technical report (2018). NS3600:2018 (no)

13. Verhagen, T., van den Hooff, B., Meents, S.: Toward a better use of the semantic differential in IS research: an integrative framework of suggested action. J. Assoc. Inf. Syst. **16**(2), 108–143 (2015)

14. Wong, S.K., Yiu, C.Y., Chau, K.W.: Liquidity and information asymmetry in the real estate market. J. Real Estate Finance Econ. **45**(1), 49–62 (2012)

Bridging the Gap Between Usability and Security: Cultural Adaptation of a Graphical User Authentication

Yvonne Kamegne[✉], Eric Owusu, and Joyram Chakraborty

Department of Computer, and Information Sciences, Towson University, 7800 York Road, Towson, MD 21252, USA

{ykamegne,jchakraborty}@towson.edu, eowusu@brockport.edu

Abstract. Authentication tasks are becoming more important, since these tasks are performed daily by millions of users across diverse cultures that share distinct characteristics and behaviors. Alphanumerical password authentication is often criticized because of its memorability issues. Thus, graphical passwords, which require users to select images as their password, have been proposed to increase memorability and ease the user authentication process. However, graphical passwords are globalized without considering that people from distinct cultures understand and interact with technologies differently. Culturally familiar graphical passwords allow the user to select pictures that relate to his cultural background. Such passwords exhibit a higher level of memorability, and leverage humans' cognitive strengths.

This paper reports the finding of an investigation of the effect of cultural elements on graphical password usability. A pilot study was conducted with thirty-four participants to examine the usability impact of culture on a customized graphical user authentication application. Two groups of participants were part of the study, namely Cameroonian and American users. Participants were asked to create a graphical password with the option of selecting cultural related images as opposed to non-related cultural images. Data gathered was used to measure the correlation between cultural related images and memorability and user preferences. The results showed that cultural elements are well considered as factors that influence password choices and the memorability of users during the registration and the authentication process. Findings underpin the necessity to consider cultural differences in the design of graphical password authentications, to enhance usability features and strengthened security.

Keywords: Usability · Security · Graphical password · Cross-cultural design

1 Introduction

User Authentication is one of the essential components in security. Several authentication mechanisms such as alphanumeric password-based authentication, multi-factor authentication, certificate-based authentication, biometric authentication, and token-based authentication are being implemented nowadays to protect user accounts from

© The Author(s), under exclusive license to Springer Nature Switzerland AG 2022
M. Antona and C. Stephanidis (Eds.): HCII 2022, LNCS 13308, pp. 260–269, 2022.
https://doi.org/10.1007/978-3-031-05028-2_17

unauthorized access [1]. Alphanumeric passwords are said to be the most ordinary form of authentication. Ironically, they are often criticized for their usability challenges. Graphical password authentication has been proposed to bypass these challenges. Research into graphical passwords revealed that it is easier for the human memory to remember pictures as compared to words, a picture is worth a thousand words. Moreover, graphical user authentication schemes encompass two major aspects namely security and usability. For these reasons, they are evolving and offer a promising alternative to traditional alphanumeric passwords, as they increase memorability and facilitate the user authentication process.

The problem with memorability is that users do not want to put a lot of mental effort into remembering passwords; they prioritize convenience over increased security. Graphical passwords provide a better memorability than alphanumeric passwords. One reason is that image processing delivers a better representation of semantic features than word processing [2]. Images are recognized with 98% of accuracy after a two-hour delay, which is higher than the accuracy for words. Additionally, error rates in image recognition are only 17% after viewing 10,000 images [3].

In order to develop secure authentication systems, several additional factors must be taken into consideration. In this study, human aspects, notably cultural elements are investigated to assess their impacts on graphical password usability [4]. Research studies revealed that users whose graphical passwords are comprised of images belonging to their cultural background have the highest memorability rate because these images are familiar to them, as cultural familiarity with images aid at better processing visual information. There is a positive correlation between cultural elements and the ability to retrieve memories, which is triggered by visual stimuli. Thus, a user's visual behavior can also affect the strength and security of a graphical password.

In this paper, the impact of cultural elements on graphical password usability is investigated. In doing so, the results can provide informative insights that could address distinct cultural preferences in user authentication design and positively affect security and usability of graphical passwords.

2 Background of the Study

Cultural differences highly impact the user experience (UX), User interface design (UI), eCommerce, trust, advertising, technology adoption, and communication of a product. If the product does not fit a users' cultural background, it will not meet needs and expectations. The results of products design requirements in one culture does not automatically apply to other cultures, because the traditions, behaviors, values, and beliefs of users in one culture are different from those in other cultures.

Authentication tasks are performed daily by millions of users from diverse cultural background, and cultural differences directly influence the way authentication systems are used and should be considered during the design process [5]. In the case of graphical passwords, users often relate to familiar images during the registration or authentication process. For instance, a user who is formulating a new graphical password will initially think about something he is familiar with. For a French-speaking user, it could be an image of the Eiffel tour. For a Cameroonian user, it could be a Cameroonian meal such as peanut sauce, or a picture of traditional dancers. A US user could think of traffic light signs, fries chicken wings, or burgers. The relationship that a user has with these familiar images impact the user experience. Moreover, from a memorability perspective, the human memory is more efficient in pictures recall when compared to words. One reason is that image processing delivers a better representation of semantic features than word processing [6]. From a security perspective, literature reviews outlined that the design of security systems should take into consideration the social and cultural contexts of the end-users (e.g., marital status, native populations) in order to facilitate their needs (e.g., trust in a relationship, limited banking services) [2].

An advantage of graphical passwords is that images are presented in a way that users can recall the perceptual features being observed, whereas textual passwords are represented with symbols that convey cognitive meaning. Thus, the additional steps required for verbal memory creates a more difficult cognitive task [7]. It is effortless for humans to remember images, pictures, familiar places, and things they have seen several times.

2.1 User Interface Design and Culture

Cross-cultural design research aims at enhancing the development of graphical user interfaces that can be usable to users of distinct cultural backgrounds. Designing products for people with different cognitive styles cross-culturally needs to accommodate the differences in the tendency of information organization and present the information accordingly [8]. A user may adapt to an interface that fails to respect his cultural background, while another user may choose to reject the interface. English-speaking countries represent about 8% of the world's population, and 75% of internet users are non-English speakers. Yet, this cultural factor is still overlooked. Translation should happen not just in terms of language, but also in terms of cultural content. The design of the UI must fit certain cultural aspects, which in turn influence the user's acceptance or rejection of a product [9].

Applying a single cultural model for UIs design could indeed be a poor choice because distinct levels of customization and cultural adaptations may be needed in different situations for different group of users. By carefully examining distinct cultures, it should be possible to find design approaches that can be transferred and adapted from one culture to another.

2.2 Research Motivation

Literature reviews provide evidence that cultural related images affect memorability and security of selected graphical password authentication schemes. Mohamed's previous research examined the effect of culture on the usage of Recognition Based Graphical Passwords (RBG-P) for the Chinese and Saudi Arabian cultures. She highlighted that culturally oriented images affect the ability to memorize the password and shapes the user's satisfaction of graphical passwords [10].

Although a considerable amount of research has been conducted in the area of graphical passwords usability, there has not been an adequate amount of research for understanding the impact of one's cultural background on graphical passwords for Western

African users notably Cameroonian users. However, to enhance the potential of security mechanisms, it is essential to investigate how users perceive and behave towards graphical passwords that encompass cultural elements.

This research specifically applies to Cameroonian users who are often an overlooked target group. Investigating these impacts will enable designers to better reflect such elements in the design of personalized authentication mechanisms. Cameroon and USA are two countries with distinct cultural characteristics and with immense cultural dimensions [11], that influence their adoption and usage of technology, and their attitudes toward usability and information security.

3   Methodology

The objective of this research study is to investigate the impact of a user cultural background on graphical password usability. For doing so, a culturally centered design web-based Graphical User Authentication (GUA) that was comprised of Cameroonian

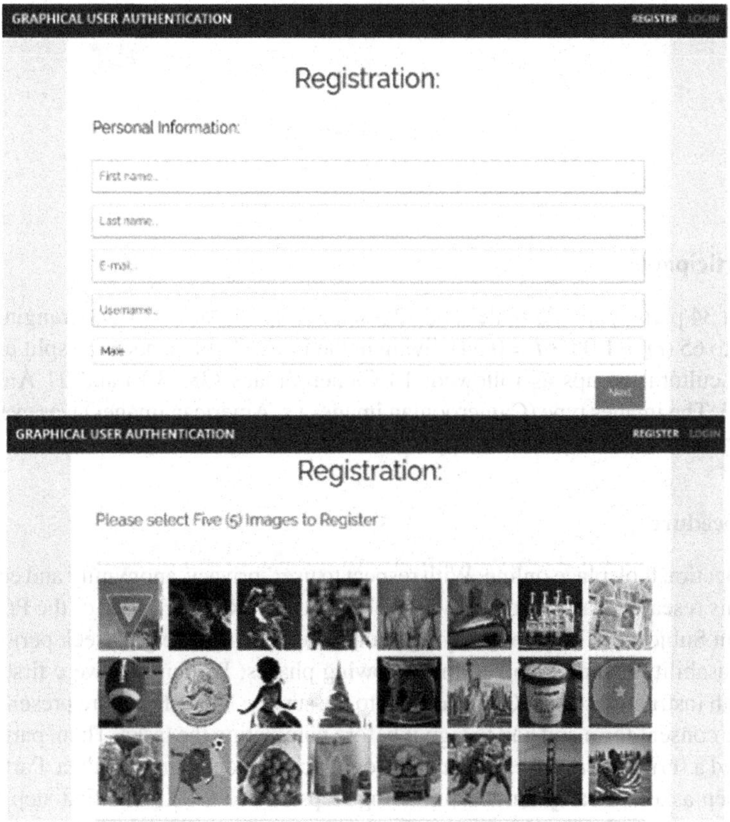

Fig. 1. Registration screens

and American related images was developed and tested to assess the impact of cultural elements on graphical passwords usability factors, namely memorability and user preference.

The GUA application was developed using PHP (Hypertext Preprocessor), CSS (Cascading Style Sheets), and HTML (Hypertext Markup Language). The screenshots of the GUA application are displayed in Figs. 1 and 2. Additionally, a database server with the purpose of storing user's login information such as, number of failed login attempts, number of successful login attempts, and images chosen during the registration and the authentication was designed using MySQL.

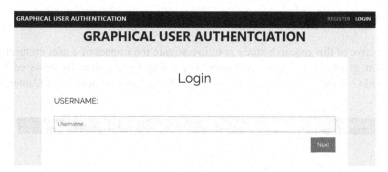

Fig. 2. Login screen

3.1 Participants

A total of 34 participants 22 males and 12 females ($m = 1.35$, $sd = 0.48$), ranging in age from 18 to 65 ($m = 1.06$, $sd = 0.34$), living in the USA. Participants were split unevenly into two cultural groups as followed: 13 Cameroonians (38.23%) and 21 Americans (61.76%). The images type (Cameroonian images vs. American images) was evenly and randomly distributed in the GUA application.

3.2 Procedure

Data collection took place online. With respect to user' privacy, anonymity and confidentiality, this research was approved by IRB (Institutional Review Board of the Protection of Human Subjects). The pilot study was conducted during an eight-week period.

The usability testing involved the following phases: Participants were first sent an email with instructions and a Qualtrics link to the survey. Next, they were presented with an online consent form and had to sign it before completing the tasks. Then, participants completed a series of pre-assessment questions to collect demographic data. Participants where then asked to carry out the following steps on the GUA: The first step was the registration phase. During this phase, participants were required to create a username and select 5 images from a set of 24 images, the set of images include 12 images form the Cameroonian culture and 12 images from the American culture. Each image could be used only once. The next phase was the authentication phase. During this phase, participants were asked to authenticate using the same username and the identical five images in the same sequence used during the authentication phase. Right after, participants were instructed to fill out a series of post-assessment questions comprised of quantitative (Likert scale) and qualitative (Open-ended) questions about their experience towards GUA. Participants were then thanked for their time and feedback.

Data was collected, cleaned, coded, and analyzed with IBM SPSS. The factors that were considered when measuring the impacts of cultural elements on graphical password usability were, memorability and user preference. Memorability was measured using Likert scale questions, successful and failed login attempts. User preference was measured using images selection and post-assessment questionnaire.

4 Results

4.1 The Impact of Culture on Memorability

Findings from the data collection indicated that memorability is very well influenced by background type images. participants selected cultural-related images for their graphical password because of their familiarity with these images, and because they increase memorability. The main Likert scale question used to access memorability with its result is as follows (Fig. 3):

Familiarity with the images improves my memorability of the graphical password (Table 1).

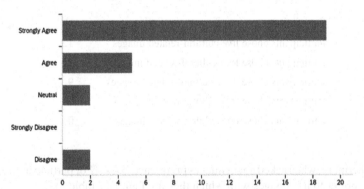

Fig. 3. Relationship between cultural images and memorability

Additionally, the database server that allowed the compiling of information such as number of successful log in attempts revealed findings that most of the participants who used images from their own cultural backgrounds made more successful login than failed login attempts.

Table 1. Descriptive summary

#	Field	Minimum	Maximum	Mean	Std Deviation	Variance	Count
1	Familiarity with images improves my memorability of the graphical password	1.00	5.00	1.61	1.11	1.24	28

#	Answer	%	Count
1	Strongly Agree	67.86%	19
2	Agree	17.86%	5
3	Neutral	7.14%	2
4	Strongly Disagree	0.00%	0
5	Disagree	7.14%	2
	Total	100%	28

4.2 The Impact of Culture on User Preference

To assess the impact of culture on user preference, factors such as user's choice of images was investigated. The database server that stored each user image selection provided the evidence that participants prefer cultural-related images. Table 2 below described the images selection of the participants.

Table 2. Image selection categories

Category	Description	No. of participants
A	Participants chose five cultural-related images	12
B	Participants chose four cultural-related images	11
C	Participants chose three cultural-related images	9
D	Participants chose two cultural-related images	0
E	Participants chose one cultural-related image	0

Furthermore, when asked about images preference, 57.14% of participants responded that they prefer to use images with which they are familiar (Table 3).

Table 3. Descriptive summary

#	Field	Minimum	Maximum	Mean	Std Deviation	Variance	Count
1	I prefer using images I am familiar with	1.00	5.00	1.68	1.07	1.15	28

#	Answer	%	Count
1	Strongly Agree	57.14%	16
2	Agree	32.14%	9
3	Neutral	3.57%	1
4	Strongly Disagree	0.00%	0
5	Disagree	7.14%	2
	Total	100%	28

5   Discussion

The purpose of this research study was to investigate the effect of cultural elements on the usability of graphical passwords. The main usability factors examined in this study were memorability and user preference.

The results of the study showed that there is a positive correlation between cultural-related images and memorability, as well as cultural-related images and user preference. The memorability of graphical passwords is enhanced by a user's cultural background. One of the reasons is that graphical passwords are based on cue recall (the retrieval of memory is facilitated by the feeding of cues) and recognition (the user views stimuli such as collecting pictures, whereas alphameric passwords are based on pure recall (retrieves information from the memory by generating the right answer without retrieval cues) [3]. Images related to one's cultural background influences the interaction behavior during password creation, and thus, password memorability. Users from diverse cultures display differences in visual processing, comprehension, and exploration of the picture content prior to making their password selections and can be encouraged to create more memorable passwords by providing them with cultural-related images during the graphical password authentication process, to better process visual information, and trigger deeper information processing and recall.

Users' preferences vary. Thus, product designers might want to design personalized products to target users in a way that fit the user preferences and provide user satisfaction. The findings of this study clearly revealed that users prefer to use images that fit into their cultural background. User preference is linked to user satisfaction and usability. A lack of user satisfaction leads to a lack of usability, which in turn could result in the rejection of a product or technology.

Overall, cultural familiarity with images provides better usability and security features. From a usability perspective, integrating familiar images in the GUA provides better memorability performance [12]. From a security perspective, pictures that fit into a user's culture increase the possibility of the image being selected as a user's password and minimizes the possibility of a brute force/guessability attack. Thus, designers should encourage users to create memorable and enjoyable passwords by providing them with the option to select personalized cultural related images to improve the GUA process.

According to the result of the post-assessment questionnaires, one significant finding was that the study revealed a high number of participants (75%) preferred alphanumeric passwords when asked about their preference between graphical and alphanumeric passwords.

One participants said:

"I prefer alphanumerical passwords because I am used to that authentication routine."

Another participants said:

"I prefer alphanumerical password because sometimes, it can be a little bit challenging to remember the exact order of the images, but I think graphical passwords are easier to remember, as memorability increase over time."

This goes to highlight that users want the effortless way of authentication; they prioritize usability over security. However, this may compromise the security of this authentications. This fact will be further investigated in our next study.

6 Conclusion

This research study provides evidence that cultural elements influence the user's visual behavior which in turn influence usability aspects of graphical passwords. This implies that design choices should not only focus on functionality and usability, but also on cultural relevance. Security and usability are both important in authentications. However, the requirements for security while preserving usability are often incompatible, and finding a suitable balance remains a challenge. Cultural-centered design graphical passwords could potentially contribute to bridging the gap between usability and security in authentication.

Understanding how the culture of a country affects authentication mechanisms is a high area of cross-cultural interest which need further investigation.

References

1. Maayan, G.: 5 Authentication Methods that Can Prevent the Next Breach (2019). https://www.idrnd.ai/5-authentication-methods-that-can-prevent-the-next-breach/
2. Weldon, M.S., Roediger, H.L., Challis, B.H.: The properties of retrieval cues constrain the picture superiority effect. Mem. Cognit. 17(1), 95–105 (1989). https://doi.org/10.3758/BF03199561
3. Wiedenbeck, S., Waters, J., Birget, J.C., Brodskiy, A., Memon, N.: Authentication using graphical passwords: effects of tolerance and image choice. In: Proceedings of the 2005 symposium on Usable privacy and security, pp. 1–12, July 2005

4. Aljahdali, H.M., Poet, R.: Users' perceptions of recognition-based graphical passwords: a qualitative study on culturally familiar graphical passwords. In: Proceedings of the 7th International Conference on Security of Information and Networks, pp. 279–283, September 2014
5. Czaja, S.J., Boot, W.R., Charness, N., Rogers, W.A.: Designing for Older Adults: Principles and Creative Human Factors Approaches, 3rd edn. CRC Press, Boca Raton, FL (2019)
6. Riley, C., Buckner, K., Johnson, G., Benyon, D.: Culture and biometrics: regional differences in the perception of biometric authentication technologies. AI society **24**(3), 295-306. Symposium on Usable Privacy and Security ({SOUPS} 2015), pp. 123–140 (2009)
7. Gao, H., Jia, W., Ye, F., Ma, L.: A survey on the use of graphical passwords in security. JSW **8**(7), 1678–1698 (2013)
8. Woods, N., Siponen, M.: Improving password memorability, while not inconveniencing the user. Int. J. Hum Comput Stud. **128**, 61–71 (2019)
9. Singh, S., Cabraal, A., Demosthenous, C., Astbrink, G., Furlong, M.: Security design based on social and cultural practice: sharing of passwords. In: Aykin, N. (ed.) UI-HCII 2007. LNCS, vol. 4560, pp. 476–485. Springer, Heidelberg (2007). https://doi.org/10.1007/978-3-540-73289-1_55
10. Mohamed, M., Chakraborty, J., Pillutla, S.: Effects of culture on graphical password image selection and design. J. Syst. Inf. Technol. (2020)
11. Hofstede Insights Organizational Culture Consulting (hofstede-insights.com)
12. Constantinides, A., Fidas, C., Belk, M., Pitsillides, A.: On the personalization of image content in graphical passwords based on users' sociocultural experiences: new challenges and opportunities. In: Adjunct Publication of the 27th Conference on User Modeling, Adaptation and Personalization, pp. 199–202, June 2019

Transformation of Plants into Polka Dot Arts: Kusama Yayoi as an Inspiration for Deep Learning

Jingjing Li[1][(✉)] [ID], Xiaoyang Zheng[2], Jun-Li Lu[1], Vargas Meza Xanat[1], and Yoichi Ochiai[1]

[1] Library and Information Media, University of Tsukuba, Tsukuba, Japan
li@digitalnature.slis.tsukuba.ac.jp
[2] Graduate School of Pure and Applied Sciences, University of Tsukuba, Tsukuba, Japan

Abstract. Museums and galleries are places that stimulate the imagination and creativity of people. However, against the backdrop of the COVID-19 pandemic, many museums have been forced to close. As a result, more visitors have had to start visiting online exhibitions. Under this trend, the quality of the online exhibition experience is facing unprecedented challenges, and visitors need to be provided with a high-quality online experience. With the rapid development of emerging technologies, museums and galleries have started to use technology to create "digitalization" experiences, such as 3D virtual exhibitions and VR interactive experiences. The current online exhibition format focuses more on improving the visitor's experience of viewing and browsing works and related information and less on how visitors create their artworks. In order to remedy the experience of visitors actively creating artworks, this study uses Yayoi Kusama's works as a case study to help form an utterly interactive process between visitors and artworks. We propose a Polka Dot Arts Transfer Network (PDAT-net), mixing realistic-looking and Polka Dot Art-style reference images. The output image looks like an actual natural image "drawn" in the polka dot art style. The PDAT-net is trained to compose an image in the style of Polka Dot Arts, based on neural style transfer. Convolutional networks implemented the training. Plant images performed the final test. The results showed that the generated polka dot images have similar styles to the style images, proving that our PDAT-network has good transfer performance of Polka Dot Arts.

Keywords: COVID-19 · Museums · Galleries · Online exhibition · Kusama Yayoi · Polka dot arts · Plants · PDAT-net · Deep learning

1 Introduction

1.1 Online Exhibition Under the COVID-19 Pandemic

People could not visit museums and art exhibitions in the physical world during the COVID-19 pandemic [1], so online art exhibitions could help people understand the artists and their works. ICOM reported that online activities will continue to increase,

© The Author(s), under exclusive license to Springer Nature Switzerland AG 2022
M. Antona and C. Stephanidis (Eds.): HCII 2022, LNCS 13308, pp. 270–280, 2022.
https://doi.org/10.1007/978-3-031-05028-2_18

in particular through the creation of new digital communication channels in the wake of lockdown [2]. Within the growing trend of online activities, exhibitions also show an increasing trend. Also, online exhibitions are more inclusive, allowing access to groups that would not normally have access to these spaces (physical museums and galleries). In fact, museum and art exhibitions belong to the experiential realm characterized by sensations, engagement, and esthetics, among other things [3–5]. Based on this background the authors want to explore a new online interaction method that allows visitors to better understand contemporary artworks. In this paper, we take the works of contemporary artist Yayoi Kusama as an example, who is known as the queen of polka dots because her artwork style has many elements of polka dots. In order to make visitors feel the polka dot style more deeply, we use deep learning to transform real photos into polka dot style images.

1.2 Yayoi Kusama and Polka Dot Arts

Yayoi Kusama is a famous contemporary artist born in Japan. Over the course of her seventy-year career, Yayoi Kusama has created a vast body of work across a wide range of media. Her art is characterized by its expression of single-minded repetition, proliferation, and accumulation, manifesting in the recurrent motifs of polka dots, net patterns, or protrusions, said to be the result of the visual and auditory hallucinations she has frequently experienced since childhood [6]. Since the 1990s, she has exhibited a large number of public artworks and largescale installations, winning enormous popular acclaim for her pop colors and works featuring familiar motifs like pumpkins and flowers. Since Kusama's artworks are most representative of plant elements, we chose photos of plants for the style conversion. First visitors upload an image of a plant on the PC, and then they can get a polka dot style picture. In this way, visitors can see things in their daily lives anew through the artist's perspective.

Polka dots have always held a special meaning for Yayoi Kusama. As she said, maybe polka dots are not feminine but symbols of energy and change. "A polka-dot has the form of the sun, which is a symbol of the energy of the whole world and our living life, and also the form of the moon, which is calm. Round, soft, colorful, senseless, and unknowing…Polka dots become a movement," she wrote in her 2005 book Manhattan Suicide Addict [7]. "Polka dots are a way to infinity." Alternatively, at the very least, polka dots provide another way to begin understanding the infinitely diverse expressions of human gender, identity, and selfhood.

1.3 About Our Research

Our research work focuses on the exploration of creating polka-dot artworks in everyday life. Polka Dot Art has long development history and is mainly used in painting, clothing design, and sculpture. Since the characteristics of its style require high painting skills, it is difficult for people without the foundation of art creation to try this style in daily life. We use a deep learning approach to accomplish real-time style transformation to solve this problem. Our study transforms the photos taken by participants into polka-dot style artworks in real-time. "Real-time style transfer" will help participants understand Yayoi Kusama and polka dots from their perspective and significantly reduce creating them.

The current online exhibition focuses on unidirectional input, feeding visitors' artwork and related information. The input and output of information is a complete participatory process, and this study is essentially exploring a way for visitors to export information. The "information output" is the process of understanding and thinking about the artwork (see Fig. 1). In this process, the visitor's active creativity is promoted, helping to understand the artwork deeper.

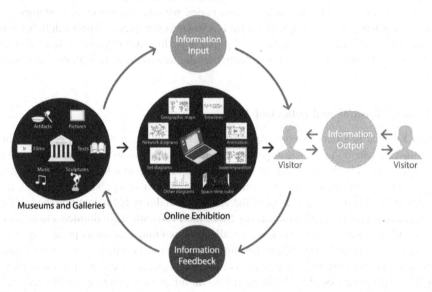

Fig. 1. The relationship map between museums and galleries, online exhibitions, visitors (including visitors to each other)

2   Related Work

2.1   Previous Methods Used to Draw Polka Dot Style Images

Polka dots have a richer history than we might think. Since first appearing in men's fashion in England in the mid-19th century, polka dots have occupied a surprisingly important place in modern history art. As shown in Table 1, this study summarizes five famous polka dot artworks currently created in style and represented by, among others.

Table 1. A summary of the current polka dot arts creation

Methods of creating polka dot arts	Descriptions	Representative persons & works	Ref.
Pointillism	Coming on the heels of Impressionism in the late 19th century, pointillism took the radical practice of leaving visible brush strokes a step further: composing images from many tiny dots (quite similar to how modern printers operate, actually)	Georges Seurat, "La Parade de Cirque" (1889); "A Sunday Afternoon on the Island of La Grande Jatte" (1884)	[8, 9]
Ben-Day Dots	In the 1950s, comic books adopted a cheap way to achieve a spectrum of color, using just the four printing process colors – cyan, magenta, yellow and black. Named after illustrator Benjamin Henry Day, Jr., the "Ben-Day" method overlaps (or spaces out) dots at different intervals to create the perception of new tones	Roy Lichtenstein, "Forms In Space" (1985); "M-Maybe" (1964)	[10, 11]
Infinity Dots	Infinity Dots displays Kusama's favorite art medium: dots! Infinity means a number that is larger than any known countable numbers. Abstract artist Yayoi Kusama uses what appears to be hundreds of tiny dots or adds color to her artwork to capture this effect. In this painting, the dots overwhelm the viewer and invites them to see the world through her eyes	Yayoi Kusama, "Infinity Dots Mirrored Room" (1996); "Passing Winter" (2009)	[12, 13]
Damien Hirst	The "dots" are all about representation. They may not actually depict anything, but as a field of messy marks on a surface each one stands for the most basic component in a traditional art of depiction—the simple act of applying a dollop of paint	Damien Hirst, "For the Love of God"	[14, 15]

(*continued*)

Table 1. (*continued*)

Methods of creating polka dot arts	Descriptions	Representative persons & works	Ref.
Pixel Dot	The computer screens consist of rows and rows of pixels, each of which consists of a red, green and blue sub-pixel that, illuminated in different combinations, produce a spectrum of perceived color as a result of additive color processing. Printers meanwhile, spray out ink as tiny dots at a density of somewhere between 300 and 600 per inch	Square Enix, The Art of Final Fantasy (2018)	[16, 17]

In the above summary, the "Infinity Dots" art style of Yayoi Kusama, a famous contemporary artist, was chosen as a case study for this research.

2.2 Image Style Transfer – Deep Learning

Neural style transfer (NST) is the most widely used deep learning application in image style transformation. NST refers to a class of software algorithms that manipulate a digital image or video to adopt another image's appearance or visual style. NST algorithms are characterized by using deep neural networks to perform image transformations. Typical use of NST is to create artificial artwork from photographs, such as transferring the appearance of a famous painting to a user-supplied photograph. Several well-known mobile applications use NST technology for this purpose, including DeepArt and Prisma. Artists and designers worldwide use this method to develop new artwork based on existing styles [18]. NST is an example of image styling, a problem that has been studied in the field of non-realistic rendering for more than two decades. The first two example-based style transfer algorithms are image analogies [19] and quilting [20], and both methods are based on patch-based texture synthesis algorithms. NST is a fascinating deep learning application with considerable research and application potential in the coming years [21]. This study, also based on deep learning, develops a new network for images style transformation.

3   Method

3.1   General Intro

In this work, we harness deep learning to transform natural plants images into polka dot arts images. We proposed a polka dot arts transfer network (PDAT-net, as shown in Fig. 2) that takes a realistic appearance and a polka Dot arts style reference image and blends them. The output image looks like the actual natural image "painted" in the Polka dot art style. The PDAT-net was trained to compose one image (content image) in the style of a polka dot art style image (style image) based on neural style transfer. The training was implemented using a convolutional network.

3.2 Dataset

To begin with, the Pl@ntView dataset (see Fig. 2), containing 26077 pictures of 250 herb and tree species, was used as authentic natural images. Five different polka dot art style images were used as style reference images. The training dataset trained the network based on supervised learning using Tensorflow.

Fig. 2. Images of plants from the Pl@ntView dataset

3.3 Detailed Algorithm

Figure 3 shows the network architecture of PDAT-net on the basis of VGG-Network, a deep convolutional network for large-scale image classification. The network starts from extracting the content and style representations of the input images, and the final few layers represent higher-level features. The style of an image can be described by the means and correlations across the different feature maps. These feature correlations are given by the Gram matrix:

$$G_{cd}^l = \frac{\sum_{ij} F_{ijc}^l(x) F_{ijd}^l(x)}{IJ} \tag{1}$$

Where F_{ijc}^l is the activation of the ith filter at position j in layer l. We use the gradient to optimize the style representation of the original image. During the training process, a lot of high-frequency artefacts are produced, and the optimization aims to decrease the high-frequency components of the image using an explicit regularization. this high-frequency component is basically an edge-detector, and the regularization loss associated with this is the sum of the squares of the values. Adam optimizer was used with a learning rate of 0.02, beta1 of 0.99, and epsilon of 0.1.

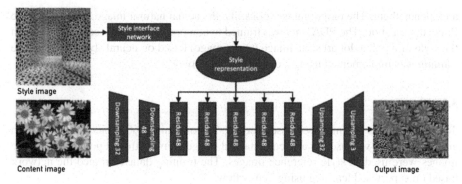

Fig. 3. The neural network of PDAT-net

4   Results and Discussion

4.1   Results of Feature Extraction

Figure 4 illustrates how to extract features from high-frequency components of a content image. As this high-frequency component is basically an edge-detector, the outline of flowers in the original figure can be easily detected. However, after style transfer, the outline becomes blurred and scatters emerge as a result of polka pots transferring.

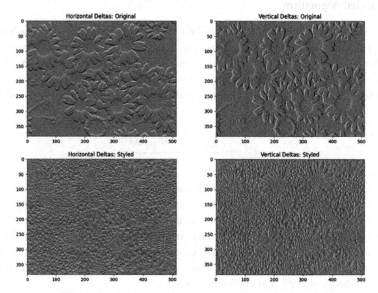

Fig. 4. High-frequency components of a content image

4.2   Results of the Loss Function and Mean Square Error

Figure 5 shows the change of loss during the training epoch. The results show that the loss gradually converges during training, demonstrating the stability of PDAT-net. During training, the content image is trained to gradually transfer into the style-like image.

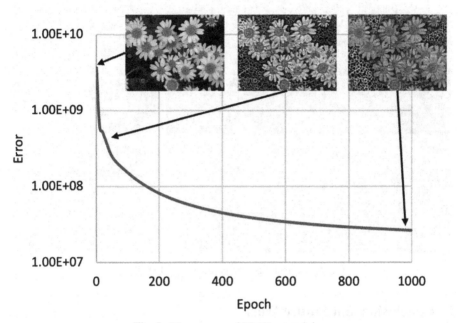

Fig. 5. The process of PDAT-net training

4.3   Generated Plant Images vs Original Images

Figure 6 shows some typically generated plant images using well-trained PDAT-net. Each generated image is compared with its content image and style image. The results demonstrate that the generated polka dot images have a similar style to the style images, proving that our PDAT -net has a good polka dot style of transformation performance.

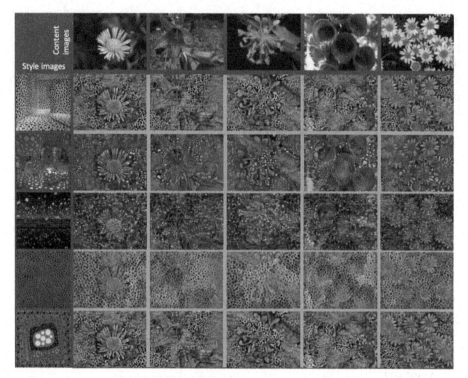

Fig. 6. Typically generated images by PDAT-net

5 Conclusion and Future Work

In conclusion, we propose a PDAT-net capable of transforming plants images into polka dot style images. Visitors to the tour scene of the online exhibition can take photos of the plants in real-time and transform them through PDAT-net's style to end up with a unique kind of polka dot artwork. The "visitor" role has changed to "creator" during the process, from a passive recipient of information to an active exporter of information. The whole network of style change promotes the creativity and motivation of the participants.

In the future, we will convert more artists' work styles, and users can upload photos to get new images in different art styles. We also hope to apply this interactive format to the actual museum and art exhibition experience to enhance visitors' understanding of the works' styles while adding fun to the process of visiting the exhibition. We will continue to explore combining this method with other art styles to help promote active creativity in visitors' online experiences (see Fig. 7). The online exhibition system can eventually use visitors' data to produce their digital artworks and share them with other visitors, and visitors will become creators.

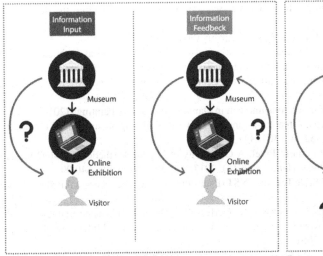

The current model of online museums   **Future work of this research**

Fig. 7. Positioning of this study in future work on online exhibitions

Acknowledgments. This work was supported by JST SPRING (grant number JPMJSP2124), and CREST (grant number JPMJCR19F2).

References

1. United Nations Educational, Scientific and Cultural Organisation: UNESCO Report: Museums around the world in the face of COVID-19. UNESCO (2021). https://unesdoc.unesco.org/ark:/48223/pf0000376729_eng/PDF/376729eng.pdf.multi
2. International Council of Museums: ICOM Report: Museums, museum profes-sionals and Covid-19: third survey. ICOM (2021). https://icom.museum/wp-content/uploads/2021/07/Museums-and-Covid-19_third-ICOM-report.pdf
3. Hassenzahl, M., Tractinsky, N.: User experience-a research agenda. Behav. Inform. Technol. 25(2), 91–97 (2006)
4. Holbrook, M.B.: The millennial consumer in the texts of our times: experience and entertainment. J. Macromark. 20(2), 178–192 (2000)
5. Pine, B.J., Pine, J., Gilmore, J.H.: The Experience Economy: Work is Theatre & Every Business a Stage. Harvard Business Press, Boston (1999)
6. Kusama, Y.: Infinity Net: The Autobiography of Yayoi Kusama. Tate Enterprises Ltd., New York (2021)
7. Clavez, B.: Yayoi Kusama. Manhattan Suicide Addict. Critique d'art. Actualité internationale de la littérature critique sur l'art contemporain (26) (2005)
8. Darragon, E.: Pégase à Fernando. A propos de «Cirque» et du réalisme de Seurat en 1891. Revue de l'Art 86(1), 44–57 (1989)
9. Seurat, G., Morris, J.: A Sunday afternoon on the island of La Grande Jatte. Delta Image (1991)
10. Markowitz, S.: A Taste for Pop: Pop Art, Gender, and Consumer Culture (1999)

11. Summers, S.: Adapting a Retro Comic Aesthetic with Spider-Man: Into the Spider-Verse (2019)
12. Dell'Aria, A.: Yayoi Kusama: Infinity Mirrors (2017)
13. de la Calleja, E., Zenit, R.: Fractal dimension and topological invariants as methods to quantify complexity in Yayoi Kusama's paintings. arXiv preprint arXiv:2012.06108 (2020)
14. Galenson, D.: Artists and the market: from Leonardo and Titian to Andy Warhol and Damien Hirst (2007)
15. Blanche, U.: Reflections of consumerism in Damien Hirst's Spot Paintings (2011)
16. Yu, L., Cao, J., Chen, Z.: A feature-aware method for dot painting on images. J. Comput.-Aid. Des. Comput. Graph. **32**(1), 130–139 (2011)
17. Mondloch, K.: From Point to Pixel: A Genealogy of Digital Aesthetics, by Meredith Hoy. Dartmouth College Press, Hanover (2018). 2017. 270 pp.; 26 b/w ills. $40.00
18. WIKIPEDIA: Neural Style Transfer (NST) Page. https://en.wikipedia.org/wiki/Neural_style_transfer
19. Hertzmann, A., Jacobs, C.E., Oliver, N., Curless, B., Salesin, D.H.: Image analogies. In: Proceedings of the 28th Annual Conference on Computer Graphics and Interactive Techniques, pp. 327–340, August 2001
20. Efros, A.A., Freeman, W.T.: Image quilting for texture synthesis and transfer. In: Proceedings of the 28th Annual Conference on Computer Graphics and Interactive Techniques, pp. 341–346, August 2001
21. Singh, A., Jaiswal, V., Joshi, G., Sanjeeve, A., Gite, S., Kotecha, K.: Neural Style Transfer: A Critical Review. IEEE Access (2021)

A Virtual Coach and a Worker Dashboard to Promote Well-Being and Workability: An Acceptance Study

Evdoxia-Eirini Lithoxoidou[1]([✉]), Rafail-Evangelos Mastoras[1], Aris Papaprodromou[1], Charalampos Georgiadis[1], Patricia Abril Jimenez[2], Sergio Gonzalez[2], Maria Fernanda Cabrera-Umpierrez[2], Maria Loeck[3], Rosa Carreton[3], Sofia Segkouli[1], Andreas Triantafyllidis[1], Dimitrios Giakoumis[1], Konstantinos Votis[1], and Dimitrios Tzovaras[1]

[1] Centre for Research and Technology Hellas, Information Technologies Institute, 6th Km Charilaou-Thermi, 57001 Thessaloniki, Greece
elithoxo@iti.gr
[2] Life Supporting Technologies Research Group, Universidad Politénica de Madrid, Avda Complutense 30, 28040 Madrid, Spain
[3] Asociación Nacional de Fabricantes de Áridos, Pl. de las Cortes, 5, 7, 28014 Madrid, Spain

Abstract. Behavioral monitoring tools can be proven to be especially helpful for aging workers for whom it is of paramount importance to avoid sedentary lifestyle, decreasing the possibility to exhibit musculoskeletal, cardiovascular and other health/mental related problems, which could impede their workability and job performance. Towards this direction, we have developed an unobtrusive pervasive health monitoring framework, enabling activity and location tracking, as well as self-reporting. The collected data is used to provide meaningful health-related suggestions through a life-like Virtual Coach aiming to encourage the engagement of workers with healthy lifestyle and behaviors. In this paper, we present the design and functionality of the solution, which was implemented as a mobile app accompanied with a dashboard for data overview, and demonstrate the results of its acceptance through a conducted survey. Survey participants were asked to answer questions related to their work experience, frequency of use of technology and type of applications used, well-being and satisfaction at work as well as their data privacy concerns. Finally, the participants also answered questions about the level of acceptance of the system and the perceived usefulness. Within the survey, video demonstrations and images were included, so that the participants have the chance to receive a better understanding of solution functionality. The acceptability study was conducted with the participation of 52 people, from which 90.4% reported that they found the Virtual Coach recommendations useful, while 84.6% reported intention of using the proposed solution in their daily life. The results indicate the virtue of such tools in promoting worker well-being.

Keywords: Design for aging · Pervasive health · Mobile · Digital phenotyping · Ageing · Human computer interaction · Acceptance study

© The Author(s), under exclusive license to Springer Nature Switzerland AG 2022
M. Antona and C. Stephanidis (Eds.): HCII 2022, LNCS 13308, pp. 281–295, 2022.
https://doi.org/10.1007/978-3-031-05028-2_19

1 Introduction

Pervasive behavioral monitoring technologies can enhance perception of both harmful and positive health behaviors of individuals and have the potential to improve their overall quality of life and workability [1]. Therefore, the use and adoption of such technologies by the aging workforce could promote their well-being, e.g. through engagement with healthy habits, such as regular physical activity and social interactions. Nonetheless, events of force majeure such as the COVID-19 pandemic, due to which strict isolation measures were imposed, the vast majority of world's population [2] have been restricted or hesitant to participate in physical/social activities and perform habits they previously enjoyed, thereby affecting their quality of life, mental and general health.

Meanwhile, due to demographic changes, the average employee age is changing dramatically, urging the development of suitable jobs [3]. There are studies suggesting an extended model of relation between work motivation and health through socio-demographic parameters and work-related stress parameters [4, 5]. German companies have developed strategies for adjusting work organization, health promotion and working-time designs to meet the ageing workers' life phases [6]. Another approach examines the effects of individual retention measures on early retirement behavior of workers in Norway [7, 8]. In this paper, the novelty lies in integrating different data modalities, including interventions specially targeted for the worker such as breaks at workplace, and providing a Virtual Coach (VC) to promote engagement by integrating persuasive techniques. This way, the system supports the elder workers' daily routine and encourages their retention in the workplace.

Towards providing tools which could bring improvements to elders' everyday lives and promoting healthier habits, we have developed an unobtrusive pervasive health monitoring framework [9], able to collect multimodal data related to activities, location categorization, keystroke typing, general phone usage statistics, questionnaire self-reports and data derived from wearable devices and popular third-party applications such as Google Fit and Samsung Health. Such data modalities have been reported in the past, each individually but also in combinations, to be suitable for monitoring and classification purposes among healthy controls and patients with health/mental related issues/disorders [10, 11]. Given the proposition value of multimodality, an application able to collect multimodal data in order to provide meaningful insights could be the groundwork towards analyzing and predicting digital biomarkers related to a variety of health/mental problems thus promoting early disease detection and prevention. As for a starting point, the data being collected can be used to infer behavioral aspects of user's everyday life and provide invaluable health related suggestions following international recommendations and guidelines. In this context, our implemented application has been designed to provide multiple health related interventions coupling both the context of user's location and activity tracking.

In order to increase user's adherence [12–14], a life-like VC with speech to text and lip sync capabilities was chosen to be the main means of delivering health recommendations based on captured data. Through its embodiment, the main target of the VC was to appear as a persuasive avatar, with adaptable appearance according to the personality of the user. In addition to the VC providing health recommendations, users are able to overview their data in a daily or aggregated manner through the virtual dashboard and receive insights related to their physical activity, stress and work-related wellbeing.

2   Application Design

2.1   Data Collection Modalities

In our previous work [9], we described a framework for data collection and virtual coaching in pervasive healthcare in depth. The framework supported the capturing of a very rich set of data sources, including activity information from wearable devices, smartphones, and third-party apps, keystroke-typing data, location information, and self-reports, towards building virtual coaching applications.

These framework capabilities have been extended to measure activities' intensity, so as to be able to distinguish physical activities from deliberate exercise. For example, while the user is at supermarket the walking activity will probably be of Sedentary/Light intensity, while if the user is walking to exercise the intensity would be Moderate to Vigorous. This was achieved by using the step rate to infer the activities Metabolic Equivalent of Tasks (METs) according to the Eq. (1) proposed by O'Brien et.al [15], which was solved for METs by the usage of a cubic equation solver. Then according to Bushman et al. [16] based on METs, we can calculate the calories, while Strath et al. [17] provides us also with the means to categorize each activity's intensity based on the estimated METs following the Table 1.

$$Step\,Rate = 73.490 - (0.513 \times height) + (59.867 \times METs) - (8.500 \times METs^2)$$
$$+ (0.436 \times METs^3) \tag{1}$$

Table 1. Activities' intensity based on METs range

METs range	Intensity
1.0–1.5	Sedentary
1.6–2.9	Light
3.0–5.9	Moderate
≥ 6.0	Vigorous

Moreover, the location categorization system was extended to also use manually user-recorded location categories, in order to be able to recognize additional socialization aspects like visiting a friends or family place or to improve the location categorization granularity.

Finally, the outcomes of our previous work [18] for the prediction of sedentary behavior solely from daily step counts, was integrated within the framework offering additional predictive and personalized capabilities. Machine learning algorithms are using as an input the daily steps of the last seven days in order to predict the possibility of sedentary behavior the upcoming day. Taking these predictions in consideration the system is able to emphasize the importance of following the system's suggestions so as to avoid sedentarism beforehand.

2.2 Virtual Coach Design

A life-like Virtual Coach (VC) was embedded within the application as the main mean of communicating with the user. The aim was to create an engaging interaction between the user and the VC, which could motivate workers to adopt a healthy lifestyle. The VC is adapting its appearance and behavior based on the Brunswick Lens Model [19], in order to appear more life-like and likeable whereas feelings of trust and engagement have been considered of high importance of design prerequisites. The final design includes verbal and non-verbal communication cues which adapt the VC's behavior and appearance in order to address the mirroring framework [20].

Adaptations concern gender, age and extroversion level perceived by users through verbal and non-verbal communication cues. Consequently, there are 12 profiles of the VC based on age*gender*extroversion level, which are listed as:

- male/young/extrovert, male/young/introvert, male/young/neutral
- male/elder/extrovert, male/elder/introvert, male/elder/neutral
- female/young/extrovert, female/young/introvert, female/young/neutral
- female/elder/extrovert, female/elder/introvert, female/elder/neutral

In Table 2 the verbal and non-verbal cues are shown, which are used to operationalize the contrasting personalities of the VC in terms of extroversion. Speech rate, volume, frequency and pitch are taken from Liew and Tan study in 2016 [21] where a virtual agent was designed in a way to appear either as extrovert persona or as introvert persona.

Table 2. Nonverbal cues adaptations for different personas of agents

Prosodic features	Intensity for extrovert persona	Intensity for introvert persona
Speech rate	216 WpM	Extrovert -10%
Volume	65 dB	Extrovert -10%
Frequency	140 Hz	Extrovert -10%
Pitch	40 Hz	Extrovert -10%

With the adaptation of prosodic features of speech of the VC, non-verbal communication cues give the perception of extrovert and introvert personas. Moreover, the VC's profiles are enhanced by adapting verbal and behavioral cues used from the VC to communicate with the user. In Table 3, the variations of motivators, feedback text, gaze and gesturing [21–24] are presented:

In order to adapt in a mirroring and empathic way, the VC is connected with user's information stored in the user model which includes data regarding gender, age and level

Table 3. Verbal and behavioral cues for introvert/neutral and extrovert personas of the VC

Communication dimension	Introvert	Neutral	Extrovert
Motivational text	Hey! I know, including a new stretching routine might be overwhelming. Maybe you think it is hard to find the time and motivation. No worries, I will work with you to create a stretching plan that works best for you. Keep calm and press the button to start."	"Welcome to the stretching section. Push the button to see the available exercises"	"Hello there! You probably know that motivation is what gets you started. However, habit is what keeps you going. Let's make stretching a habit and become better and better! Here is the button, push it and try to stretch with me!"
Facial expression/Gaze	Conservative smiley/ Gaze in front while talking, then look the button to proceed to the exercises	Neutral face	Wide smile/ Gaze in front while talking, keep gazing in front and use deictic gesture to the button to proceed to exercises
Welcome gesturing	Hands in front, holding one another during the whole talk. Small head movements to feel natural	Default hands	Hands lifted up during the "Hello there!". Hands open, vivid-"welcome" movements
Feedback/Done/Text	"Very nice, keep up the good work!"	"Well done!"	"Great! Next time let's go a bit outside the comfort zone. You can do it!
Feedback/Done/ Gesturing	Head nods once with a gentle bend of the body	Default hands/ Default face	Open hands, raised eyebrows and wide open smile for "Great! Next time let's go a bit outside the comfort zone!" and comes closer to the camera and blinks one eye for "You can do it!"

(continued)

Table 3. (*continued*)

Communication dimension	Introvert	Neutral	Extrovert
Feedback/Later/Text	"I know it may seem hard, ok, let's try later"	"See you in a while"	"Can't wait to get back to do some more stretching exercises together!"

of user's extroversion. The VC is formed with same gender, age and extroversion level as the user who uses it in order to evaluate acceptance of technology with these parameters.

2.3 Health and Wellbeing Suggestions

The data being collected, and their contextual combinations, can be proven to be a great behavioral information pool, which empowers our system to offer a wide variety of health-related recommendations.

First and foremost, our system aims to contribute towards increasing user's activity and promote a non-sedentary lifestyle. Avoiding sedentarism could have enormous benefits for anyone's physical or mental health, since among other benefits, it reduces the risk of heart attack and musculoskeletal issues and improves mental health.

Towards this goal, interventional features were developed. The system is able to recognize, using the location and information provided by the users, when they are at home, work or any other place. Additionally, due to the activity and step tracking modalities, the system can recognize sedentary behavior.

During the day, if the user is at home or work and stationery for longer than one hour, the Break@Work intervention is triggered (see Fig. 1a), reminding the user to stand up and walk for at least 5 min [25]. If this sedentary behavior is continuing for 2 consecutive times, then the system suggests performing some Stretching Exercises (see Fig. 1b). During this intervention the VC can show the user how to perform few predefined stretching exercises (see Fig. 1c).

Moreover, during the afternoon hours and when the user is not at the workplace, the VC suggests going for a leisure walk. This suggestion is triggered if the user has not reached his daily step goal, which should be at least 5000 steps and optimally 10000 steps [26]. When the user reaches the daily step goal the VC shall congratulate her/him.

The intensity categorization allowed our system to extend its capabilities and monitor user's moderate to vigorous activity time. According to the World Health Organization (WHO), adults should exercise every week for at least 150 min of moderate or 75 min of vigorous intensity or any equivalent combination [27] to avoid a sedentary lifestyle. These guidelines have been integrated within our system so as to offer a weekly goal to the users.

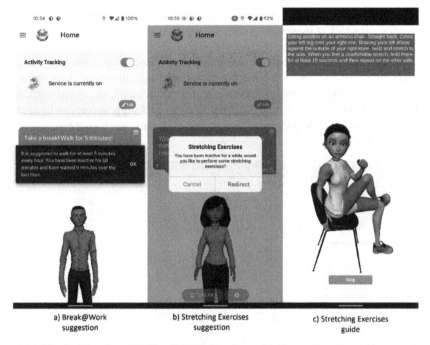

a) Break@Work suggestion	b) Stretching Exercises suggestion	c) Stretching Exercises guide

Fig. 1. Virtual coach's Break@Work and stretching exercises suggestions.

At last, the sedentary predictions pipeline tries to predict the possibility of the current day being sedentary based on previous daily steps observations. The pipeline is triggered during the first steps of the day and the system uses machine-learning algorithms to make the prediction. If the system detects the possibility of a sedentary behavior this day, then the user is informed accordingly.

Another challenge of the framework was to provide suggestions which aim to improve the mental health state and socialization. To this end additional suggestions have been integrated.

Depending on the location categorization, the system understands if the user spends time in social places. Our previous work [9], has described the location categorization pipeline, which was extended to also include manually categorized places. This was done to offer additional granularity, but most importantly for the users to be able to manually label locations visited as social interactions (e.g., friend's or family's place). The system suggests to the users to spend some additional time with their beloved ones or at their favorite social places. If a social interaction (e.g., exit event from a place categorized as "Social". "Friend" or "Family") is detected then the system congratulates the user and informs her that she gained socialization points.

Since the system can record questionnaire answers, some of which require to be answered daily while others weekly or one time, we are able to estimate the stress levels based on the self-reported questionnaire answers. Consequently, the estimated stress score is used to trigger suggestions aiming to reduce the stress level which can be a simple leisure walk, stretching exercise or to complete a Cognitive behavioral therapy (CBT) exercise which is integrated within the application.

Other than the VC's wellbeing suggestions, users are able to overview their data in an aggregated manner through the integrated Dashboard. Within this view, they can overview their daily habits in a longitudinal setting, including their daily steps (see Fig. 2a), sleep duration, visited location's categorization, mood, stress and workability self-reports (see Fig. 2b). Additional helpful insights and suggestions can be received through the dashboard while they can also review their daily goals (see Fig. 2c).

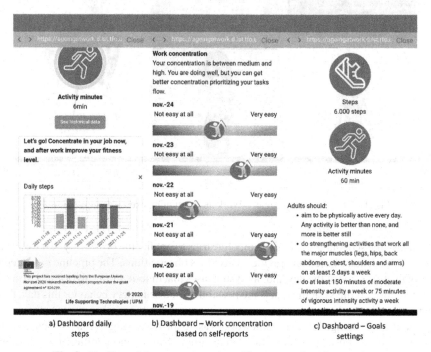

| a) Dashboard daily steps | b) Dashboard – Work concentration based on self-reports | c) Dashboard – Goals settings |

Fig. 2. Dashboard data, questionnaire self-reports and goals overview

3   Acceptance Study

The acceptance study has taken place from May to June 2021 through the usage of Google form surveys. The surveys were shared online to the targeted group of people, instantly without the need to come into direct contact with the respondents. This issue is essential since it had to be taken into consideration because of the restrictions imposed by the COVID-19 pandemic. Moreover, it saves considerable time and resources while the participants can respond more quickly. Participants' profiles varied amongst different groups such as directors, owners of companies, experts in healthcare and safety and people dedicated to training or research in mining, fact which enriched the validity of acceptance results.

The acceptability studies were contacted with a participation of 52 people, 30/22 males/females, with a median (std) age of 48 (8.861). Technology acceptance was examined via Perceived Ease of Use questions (PEU), Perceived Usefulness questions (PU), Behavioral Intention to Use (BI) and Self-efficacy which are based on the Technology Acceptance Model (TAM) [28].

The questions included were related to the intention of the users to use this technology for receiving advice for their health and well-being as well as daily feedback in respect to their performance in terms of healthy activities and prioritization of tasks. Moreover, the participants were asked the frequency they would like to receive notifications and messages from the VC.

3.1 Results

Regarding the perception of the ease of use of the tool, the results presented in Table 4, show positive impact, since the participants consider that the VC tool is clear and easy to understand, and that it will be easy for the user to use the tool (73% of respondents are extremely in favor). The results are less consistent with respect to the ease of interaction with the VC. A means of interaction with the VC is included if the user is not able to follow the recommendation including sending a message of encouragement to the worker and retrying sending recommendations at another time.

When participants have expressed their opinion on the usefulness of the VC as a way to improve their health, the results have been positive with 96% of the participants agreeing or quite agreeing that it will be useful for the coach to measure these parameters.

It is also considered very useful for the VC to include the security button in its services to be able to respond quickly in emergency situations. The greatest reluctance exists regarding the usefulness of receiving recommendations during work time. This reluctance is reasonable since the employee may be immersed in a task and not have enough time to check their device and see if the VC has made a recommendation. That is why the VC must be respectful with the performance of the worker and not conflict with the development of their tasks. Recommendations are made in such a way that the user can access them during their breaks at work or in their free time. Regarding the Behavioral Intention to Use (BI), 90% strongly agree or quite agree that, if possible, they would like to try the VC and the Dashboard.

Regarding self-efficacy, 90% strongly agree or agree that they could use the VC if someone taught them how. Again, we are facing a public of workers for whom this type of tools may seem strange, so it will be essential to focus our efforts on education and training. Finally, when asking users specific questions about how often they think they should receive recommendations, and the nature of them, a minority percentage of respondents would like to receive two messages a day (9.6%). The highest percentages of frequency are those referred to 1 message per day (28.8%), while the rest requested 1 to 4 messages per week. However, when asked if they would be interested in receiving feedback on their daily results or recommendations on how to organize work time, a vast majority would agree to receive these types of messages. The workers find the recommendations useful, and even make suggestions about the content they would like to receive, but do not want to feel "overwhelmed" by the VC. It is essential to design the tool in a way that is not invasive in working time.

Regarding the technology acceptance for the VC and the Worker Dashboard, we can conclude that the results are very positive regarding the perceived ease of use. It is a tool whose installation and usage are simple, since very few inputs are required from the users and once configured the application can run without any effort from them.

Regarding the perceived usefulness, the results are still very positive, with between 80–90% of the respondents being strongly in favour or in agreement on the questions regarding usefulness. The worst results are obtained with respect to the emergency button, which is explained by its limited usefulness in office environments.

As for the intention to use it in the future, 84.6% somewhat or completely agree that they would use it in the future. Although the result is positive, efforts will have to be made in communication and training to convey the usefulness of the tool and encourage its use.

Regarding the need for someone to use it previously so that the user knows how the tool works, only 10% is considered somewhat in agreement, which indicates that the tool, as it appears configured, is easy to use and may not need as many training efforts as others.

Results related to VC messages' content can been found at Table 5 whereas 88.46% of the respondents would like to receive advice on health and well-being from the tool, 84.62% would like to receive a summary of their daily results and 78.6% are in favour of receiving advice on how to organize their work time.

Table 4. Detailed question results

Question	Completely agree	Somewhat agree	Neutral	Somewhat disagree	Completely disagree
Perceived Ease of Use Questions (PEU)					
The virtual coaching tool was clear and easy to understand	73,3%	26,6%	-	-	-
It would be easy for you to interact with the virtual coaching tool	56,67%	40%	-	3,33%	-
It would be easy for you to learn to use the virtual coaching tool	60%	36,6%	3,33%	-	-
Perceived Usefulness Questions (PU)					
Receiving virtual coaching recommendations would provide you useful measurements for your health	48.08%	42.31%	3.85%	5.77%	-

(continued)

Table 4. (*continued*)

Question	Completely agree	Somewhat agree	Neutral	Somewhat disagree	Completely disagree
Using virtual coaching services such as emergency buttons would help you address effectively emergency situations at your work	55.77%	30.77%	9.62%	1.92%	1.92%
Virtual coaching advice/recommendations during the working day would be useful as a motivation to change your health habits whenever is necessary	42.31%	42.31%	5.77%	7.69%	1.92%
Behavioral intention to Use (BI)					
If possible, you will try to use such a virtual coaching solution	50.00%	34.62%	7.69%	5.77%	1.92%
Self-efficacy					
You can use the virtual coaching tool if someone shows you how to do it first	70%	20%	6,7%	3,3%	0%

Table 5. Assessment for additional VC feedback

Question	True	False
You would be interested in receiving advice for your health and well-being via your mobile phone/smartphone?	88.46%	11.54%
You would be interested to receive feedback about your daily score of achieving healthy activities also in respect to your performance the previous days/weeks	84.62%	15.38%
You would be interested to receive recommendations from a virtual coach about scheduling your job (e.g., when to take a day-off, when to change shift, etc.)	78.85%	21.15%

4 Discussion

The purpose of this paper was to present a VC accompanied with a worker dashboard, designed to promote the worker's well-being. This technology is responsible for the self-monitoring of the worker anytime-anywhere, and present recommendations through a user-friendly interface, the VC, which is embodied at the worker's smartphone. Functionality of the VC is implemented based on the multi-modal system for user's interaction which is orchestrated by the perceptible functions. In this paper, the discreet behavior of the VC is presented as a result of both visual and auditory modules that consist of the persuasive framework along with its acceptance study by the elder workers.

Regarding the monitoring functions, an extended description has been presented regarding how the VC is triggered at work in order to perform activity that can enhance productivity. Furthermore, we describe how it provides reminders and suggestions based on the worker's behavior analysis and detection of adverse signs which may need to be counteracted for. There are sections that present how we have achieved this target by explaining the system design and model which has taken place, and which follows OSH, behavioral and ergonomics factors. Besides, based on behavior analysis, sensor-based monitoring and self-reports, this paper showcases the VC's interaction with the worker. Involved cases are illustrated in detail and the reaction of the VC is presented based on the adaptations that take place for integrating persuasive techniques.

The results are encouraging and show that the VC is accepted as a technology solution of self-monitoring and supporting guide for maintaining good health and well-being. Most of the respondents found it easy to use the tool while they enjoyed receiving recommendations about their health once a day as a feedback message. However, results are a bit inconsistent with respect to the ease of interaction with the VC and no information is provided regarding whether the workers tried to start a conversation with the VC. On the other hand, they found the coaching services useful for either effectively facing the emergency situations at work or changing their health habits whenever it is necessary. The greatest reluctance in this case, is whether the workers should receive recommendations during worktime which is addressed by the VC's system developed to offer accessibility to them during the worker's breaks at work or their leisure time. Besides, when asked if they would be interested in receiving feedback on their daily results or recommendations on how to organize work time, a vast majority agree to receive these types of messages. Regarding self-efficacy, a high percentage of workers strongly agree that they could use the VC if someone taught them how, inferring the importance of focusing efforts on education and training when it comes to this type of tools and technology.

All in all, the workers find the recommendations useful, and even make suggestions about the content they would like to receive, but do not want to feel "overwhelmed" by the virtual coach. In order to evaluate this technology acceptance, data regarding perceived ease of use, usefulness of the VC, behavioral intention to use it and self-efficacy have been gathered for analysis and are interestingly encouraging. Results have shown an overall positive effect regarding users' opinion about the VC and accompanied dashboard, and their intention to use the solution for getting feedback about their physical and mental health. Additionally, they were font of receiving recommendations on how to improve their daily life regarding being more active and follow a healthier schedule during their daily routine but in a way that is not invasive in working time.

Based on previous acceptance studies [29–32], it is essential that our solution is accepted as well thus, we consider it as a first step for further studies regarding integration of virtual agents and user dashboards in health sector. Our future steps involve the evaluation of this technology in larger group of people and in different contexts to further assess its usefulness and value in promoting healthy behaviours.

Acknowledgment. This work has been supported by the EU Horizon 2020 funded project "Smart, Personalized and Adaptive ICT Solutions for Active, Healthy and Productive Ageing with enhanced Workability (Ageing@Work)", under grant agreement no: 826299.

References

1. Peruzzini, M., Pellicciari, M.: A framework to design a human-centred adaptive manufacturing system for aging workers. Adv. Eng. Inform. **33**, 330–349 (2017)
2. Tisdell, C.A.: Economic, social and political issues raised by the COVID-19 pandemic. Econ. Anal. Policy **68**, 17–28 (2020)
3. Wolf, M., Kleindienst, M., Ramsauer, C., Zierler, C., Winter, V.: Current and future industrial challenges: demographic change and measures for elderly workers in industry 4.0. Ann. Fac. Eng. Hunedoara-Int. J. Eng. **16**(1), 10 (2018)
4. Feißel, A., Peter, R., Swart, E., March, S.: Developing an extended model of the relation between work motivation and health as affected by the work ability as part of a corporate age management approach. Int. J. Environ. Res. Public Health **15**(4), 779 (2018)
5. Versluis, A., Verkuil, B., Spinhoven, P., Brosschot, F., J.: Effectiveness of a smartphone-based worry-reduction training for stress reduction: A randomized-controlled trial. Psychol. Health **33**(9), 1079–1099 (2018)
6. Knauth, P., Karl, D., Gimpel, K.: Development and evaluation of working-time models for the ageing workforce: lessons learned from the KRONOS research project. In: Age-Differentiated Work Systems, pp. 45–63. Springer, Heidelberg (2013)
7. Hermansen, Å.: Retaining older workers: The effect of phased retirement on delaying early retirement (2015)
8. Hermansen, Å.: Additional leave as the determinant of retirement timing—retaining older workers in Norway. Retaining Older Workers **4**(4) (2016)
9. Mastoras, R.E., Triantafyllidis, A., Giakoumis, D., Kordonias, R.K., Papaprodromou, A., Nalbadis, F., Tzovaras, D.: A mobile-based multimodal framework for pervasive health monitoring. In 2021 IEEE International Conference on Pervasive Computing and Communications Workshops and other Affiliated Events, PerCom Workshops, pp. 194–199. IEEE (2021)
10. Abdullah, S., Choudhury, T.: Sensing technologies for monitoring serious mental illnesses. IEEE Multimedia **25**(1), 61–75 (2018)
11. Zahid, A., Poulsen, J.K., Sharma, R., Wingreen, S.C.: A systematic review of emerging information technologies for sustainable data-centric health-care. Int. J. Med. Informatics **149**, 104420 (2021)
12. Trinh, H., Shamekhi, A., Kimani, E., Bickmore, T.W.: Predicting user engagement in longitudinal interventions with virtual agents. In: Proceedings of the 18th International Conference on Intelligent Virtual Agents, pp. 9–16 (2018).

13. Corrigan, L.J., Peters, C., Küster, D., Castellano, G.: Engagement perception and generation for social robots and virtual agents. In: Toward Robotic Socially Believable Behaving Systems, vol. 1, pp. 29–51. Springer, Cham (2016).
14. Yu, Z., He, X., Black, A.W., Rudnicky, A.I.: User engagement study with virtual agents under different cultural contexts. In: International Conference on Intelligent Virtual Agents, pp. 364–368. Springer, Cham (2016)
15. O'Brien, M.W., Kivell, M.J., Wojcik, W.R., d'Entremont, G., Kimmerly, D.S., Fowles, J.R.: Step rate thresholds associated with moderate and vigorous physical activity in adults. Int. J. Environ. Res. Public Health 15(11), 2454 (2018)
16. Bushman, B.A.: Wouldn't you like to know: how can I use METs to quantify the amount of aerobic exercise? ACSM's Health Fitness J. 16(2), 5–7 (2012)
17. Strath, S.J., et al.: Guide to the assessment of physical activity: clinical and research applications: a scientific statement from the American Heart Association. Circulation 128(20), 2259–2279 (2013)
18. Papathomas, E., Triantafyllidis, A., Mastoras, R.E., Giakoumis, D., Votis, K., Tzovaras, D.: A machine learning approach for prediction of sedentary behavior based on daily step counts. In: 2021 43rd Annual International Conference of the IEEE Engineering in Medicine & Biology Society, EMBC, pp. 390–394. IEEE (2021)
19. Brunswik, E.: Perception and the representative design of psychological experiments. University of California Press, Berkeley (1956)
20. Zhou, M.X., Mark, G., Li, J., Yang, H.: Trusting virtual agents: the effect of personality. ACM Trans. Interact. Intell. Syst. (TiiS) 9(2–3), 1–36 (2019)
21. Liew, T. W., Tan, S. M.: Virtual agents with personality: Adaptation of learner-agent personality in a virtual learning environment. In 2016 Eleventh International Conference on Digital Information Management, ICDIM, pp. 157–162. IEEE (2016)
22. Gratch, J., Wang, N., Gerten, J., Fast, E., Duffy, R.: Creating rapport with virtual agents. In: International workshop on Intelligent Virtual Agents, pp. 125–138. Springer, Heidelberg (2007)
23. Tapus, A., Ţăpuş, C., Matarić, M.J.: User—robot personality matching and assistive robot behavior adaptation for post-stroke rehabilitation therapy. Intel. Serv. Robot. 1(2), 169–183 (2008)
24. Ivaldi, S., Lefort, S., Peters, J., Chetouani, M., Provasi, J., Zibetti, E.: Towards engagement models that consider individual factors in HRI: On the relation of extroversion and negative attitude towards robots to gaze and speech during a human–robot assembly task. Int. J. Soc. Robot. 9(1), 63–86 (2017)
25. Hengel, K.M.O., Blatter, B.M., Joling, C.I., Van der Beek, A.J., Bongers, P.M.: Effectiveness of an intervention at construction worksites on work engagement, social support, physical workload, and need for recovery: results from a cluster randomized controlled trial. BMC Public Health 12(1), 1–10 (2012)
26. Tudor-Locke, C., Craig, C.L., Thyfault, J.P., Spence, J.C.: A step-defined sedentary lifestyle index:< 5000 steps/day. Appl. Physiol. Nutr. Metab. 38(2), 100–114 (2013)
27. https://www.who.int/news-room/fact-sheets/detail/physical-activity. Accessed 21 Jan 2022
28. Lee, Y., Kozar, K.A., Larsen, K.R.: The technology acceptance model: Past, present, and future. Commun. Assoc. Inf. Syst. 12(1), 50 (2003)
29. Dupuy, L., Micoulaud-Franchi, J.A., Philip, P.: Acceptance of virtual agents in a homecare context: Evaluation of excessive daytime sleepiness in apneic patients during interventions by continuous positive airway pressure (CPAP) providers. J. Sleep Res. 30(2), e13094 (2021)
30. Esposito, A., Amorese, T., Cuciniello, M., Esposito, A. M., Troncone, A., Torres, M. I., Cordasco, G.: Seniors' acceptance of virtual humanoid agents. In: Italian Forum of Ambient Assisted Living, pp. 429–443. Springer, Cham (2018).

31. Rietz, T., Benke, I., Maedche, A.: The impact of anthropomorphic and functional chatbot design features in enterprise collaboration systems on user acceptance (2019)
32. Esposito, A., et al.: Elder user's attitude toward assistive virtual agents: the role of voice and gender. J. Ambient. Intell. Humaniz. Comput. **12**(4), 4429–4436 (2019). https://doi.org/10.1007/s12652-019-01423-x

Blood Pressure Concerns: Findings from a Usability Study of Culturally Infused mHealth Design

Helina Oladapo$^{(\boxtimes)}$ and Joyram Chakraborty$^{(\boxtimes)}$

Department of Computer and Information Sciences, Towson University, 7800 York Road, Towson, MD 21252, USA
{holadapo,jchakraborty}@towson.edu

Abstract. High blood pressure BP (i.e., hypertension) is a chronic condition and risk factor for cardiovascular disease, stroke, and heart failure, occurring in populations across the globe. Currently, smart phones and applications are developing rapidly, and mobile health applications are being used to manage hypertension. The goal of this study was to understand the usability findings from an iterative cross-cultural mHealth application to identify the perceived usefulness among African migrant adopters in Maryland, United States. Qualitative and quantitative statistical method were used to collect participants' data. Usability findings reported that the behavioral intention of using the recommended features was influenced by the perceived usefulness of the AfriBP. The cultural dimensions were rated as the most preferred recommended features, followed by the health management feature. The perceived usefulness had a strong significant effect on attitude in adopting the AfriBP. Female participants adopted the AfriBP more than the male participants. The results regarding ethnicity found that the Nigerian participants considered the perceived usefulness of the AfriBP more than the Ghanaian participants. Few participants owned and or publicly used BP machines to monitor their BP. Few number of participants were less likely to use a smartphone health application to monitor their BP for health. The health status of the participants for BP readings and body mass index (BMI) was of great concern which supported prior research on Africans ancestry having the highest concern for BP.

Keywords: Africans · Blood pressure · Cross-cultural · mHealth application · mHealth design · Usability

1 Introduction

mHealth is the use of mobile devices, such as smartphones and tablets for diagnosis, treatment, or health management functions that are delivered through a software interface, known as an application or app [1]. The increase in the number of patients experiencing chronic diseases has led to the use of smartphone applications to manage and improve

The original version of this chapter was revised: See the "Chapter Note" section at the end of this chapter for details. The correction to this chapter is available at
https://doi.org/10.1007/978-3-031-05028-2_37

© The Author(s), under exclusive license to Springer Nature Switzerland AG 2022, corrected publication 2022
M. Antona and C. Stephanidis (Eds.): HCII 2022, LNCS 13308, pp. 296–305, 2022.
https://doi.org/10.1007/978-3-031-05028-2_20

health conditions [2]. mHealth is considered to be a new area of growth [3] which is made available by information and communication technology (ICT) to solve healthcare issues [4]. mHealth offers alternative solutions to the quality of care, cost reduction, time savings, accessibility, convenience, integration with internet, and monitoring of illness and access to data for faster recovery [5–7].

The integration of cultural components, values, and beliefs is significant to the user interface design for adoption of mHealth intervention tools across cultures. As a result, usability plays a major role in mHealth applications, as individuals have difficulties and limited experience with the use of mobile devices [8]. Blood pressure (BP) occurs when the force of blood pushes against the walls of arteries. BP is measured using systolic and diastolic blood pressure. Systolic BP is the upper number which measures the pressure during contraction of the heart while diastolic BP is the lower number which measures the pressure during the relaxation of the heart [9, 10]. Both systolic and diastolic pressure are measured in millimeters of mercury (mmHg). A normal BP level is less than 120/80 mmHg and has the potential to change throughout the day. Hypertension (HTN), diabetes, and coronary heart disease are the leading causes of chronic disease affecting most countries [11]. One third of adults in developed and developing regions have experienced HTN [12]. The population in sub-Saharan Africa is expected to experience an increase in high blood pressure, also called HTN, to 68% (125.5 million) by 2025 [14]. HTN is most common in individuals (25 years and older) with African ancestry [12, 15]. This high prevalence is driven by the increasing age of the population, obesity, and high dietary salt intake that affects the communities [12]. Most people experiencing HTN are unable to control their BP, but are aware that lowering BP can lessen the risk for renal and cardiovascular disease [13]. The blood pressure levels in black patients are much more severe than in white patients [12]. The fact that most Africans are unaware of their high blood pressure that suddenly occurs and poses risk to health is startling.

Adopting an mHealth application intervention that is designed to promote health behaviors and lifestyle changes such as physical activity, healthy diet, and self-management of BP will improve behavioral patterns and health management for the African community. This study developed an intervention for a culturally infused mHealth smartphone application for blood pressure called AfriBP. The aim is to understand the usability findings from the iterative cross-cultural mHealth application and identify the perceived usefulness in the adoption of AfriBP for African migrants located in Maryland, United States. Therefore, designing the user interface with the Africans' culture in mind becomes useful for adoption.

2 Literature Review

Culturally infused mHealth applications help foster behavioral lifestyle changes and health management leading to adoption and usage. Designing mHealth user interfaces and incorporating compatibility with cultural characteristics is essential for adoption and usage [16]. Culture aspects of interface design are cross-cultural elements that are essential for successful adoption, such as language, writing and reading direction, fonts, measures, calendar, and date and time formats [17]. There are limited studies which has investigated culturally infused mHealth applications design specifically for BP management, but this research data addresses such an approach. User interface design for specific cultures is an area that still needs to be addressed [18].

2.1 Culturally Infused mHealth Approach

Findings from previous study on culturally infused mHealth approaches reported that integrating cultural values such as language, colors, layout, and images significantly influenced participants' behavioral intention in using mobile user interface (UI) design based on Arabic culture [19].

2.2 Lack of Culturally Infused mHealth Approach

Previous study have discussed a lack of culturally tailored mHealth design. Although the authors argued that a culturally tailored approach was needed. It was reported that with the case of Breathing awareness medication (BAM) and individually culturally tailored designs and preferences for Pre-essential hypertension (preEH) for White or African American participants, due to limited sample size and that intervention might not be culturally tailored to these specific groups [20]. There is a need for development of culturally infused mHealth applications for the local community.

Perceived usefulness is a construct derived from Davis's Technology Acceptance model (TAM) as "the degree to which an individual believes that using a particular system would enhance his or her job performance" [21] which directly and indirectly affects attitudes and behavioral intentions [22]. When participants perceive that the AfriBP is useful, they will be more inclined to adopt the mHealth application.

Usability is defined as ease of use plus usefulness, including characteristics such as "learnability, speed and accuracy of user task performance, user error rate, and subjective user satisfaction" [23, 24] and plays a significant role in the development of usable products.

3   Methodology

A matured version of AfriBP that was tested by participants and modified/redesigned for usability testing was deployed on an Android platform using a tablet and a mobile emulator. The mHealth application was designed using Flutter framework, a Google cross-platform framework for iOS and Android. Flutter used the Dart programming language to create the AfriBP application. The data of the AfriBP application was securely stored in the Google Firebase system, Cloud Firestore.

The usability and design for the AfriBP application integrated cultural features, health features, and cultural elements. The cultural recommended features (cultural dimensions) are options provided to improve health and lifestyle management of the target populations. These include the Exercise Fitness and Eat Healthy Diet recommendations. These recommendations are based on the BP category, readings, and BMI for: normal, elevated, and high blood pressure (hypertension) in stage 1 and 2 for the users. Exercise Fitness options: pick-up soccer, basketball, volleyball, soccer, tennis leagues; African Dance Fitness; and Eat Healthy Diet, Nigerian and Ghanaian foods are recommended to enhance and improve health management of BP. The user clicks to check the nearest healthy shop within their zip code to provide recommendations based on where the user lives (geolocation). Other recommendations such as Spa (i.e., massage) were included to improve the stress management based on the zip code where the user lives (i.e., geolocation). The health features enabled users to register an account on the AfriBP: demographics, nutritional diet, and geolocation (i.e., zip code) recommendation based on where the user lives. Another aspect of the features includes the manual entry of BP measurements, calculation of body mass index (BMI), generation of health history and bar chart showing the patterns of the health history data, indication of cultural elements, exportation of health data and BMI in PDF and printable format, notification reminders, and the user profile display. The cultural elements features include navigation, data presentation, and icons on the home, add data, history, reminder, and profile screens. The date and time zones for the United States and West Africa are determined by the users' login. The BMI measurement unit uses US pounds and inches and kilograms and centimeters for West Africans. The food images specific to Nigerian and Ghanaian cultures were integrated into the design of the AfriBP.

A usability testing experiment was conducted to evaluate the usability of the culturally infused mHealth smartphone application for blood pressure (AfriBP) for Africans. The study used random sampling to recruit participants from local churches and by word of mouth. A qualitative and quantitative statistical method was used to collect participants' data by using the Zoom platform and Qualtrics software (survey). Institutional Review Board (IRB) approval was obtained for the study.

In total, 50 Nigerian and Ghanaian participants male (n = 21) and female (n = 29), were recruited for the usability testing experiment. The study was carried out for each participant by invitation via email to join an online Zoom platform and meet with the principal investigator (PI). Each participant used an Excel spreadsheet to sign-in with a pre-provisioned credentials identifier and a link provided to the Qualtrics software (survey). The purpose of the study was explained to the participants carefully before they agreed to the online consent form on the Qualtrics software (survey). Participants were eligible for the study if they were aged 18 to 69 years. Participants were informed of the study being voluntary and their right to withdraw at any time with the assurance of the confidentiality of data. The participants were also required to agree to have their BP recorded in the AfriBP application upon successful completion of the online consent form on the Qualtrics software (survey). In the first stage, the participants were informed to complete the pre-test questionnaire information about their demographics and use of smartphone health applications. In the second stage, a brief training was provided, and participants had to navigate on the user interface by completing a series of tasks to test the usability of the AfriBP application and log-out. At the end of the usability testing experiment, users were asked to complete the post-questionnaires. The matured version of the AfriBP was carried out for a 9-month period. The procedure was completed within 40 min by the participants after which the data were stored, cleaned, and coded using Excel and analyzed using SPSS software to understand the usability findings from the iterative cross-cultural mHealth application and identify the perceived usefulness in adopting AfriBP for Africans in Maryland, United States.

4 Results

The ages of the participants ranged from 18 to 69 years. Most (30.0%) participants were within the ages of 30–39 years. Female participants (58.0%) were the majority in the study, while the Male participants were (42.0%). Many (52.0%) participants were Nigerian. Almost all (92.0%) of the participants were on a regular diet.

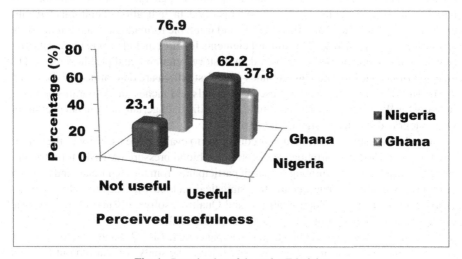

Fig. 1. Perceived usefulness by Ethnicity

Chi-square result: ($\chi 2 = {}^{F}$; p = 0.024).
* - Significant at 0.05; ^{F} – Fisher's Exact Test.

The participants' acceptance of usefulness of the AfriBP by ethnicity were more among Nigerian (62.2%) than Ghanaian (37.8%) (p=0.024) (Fig. 1).

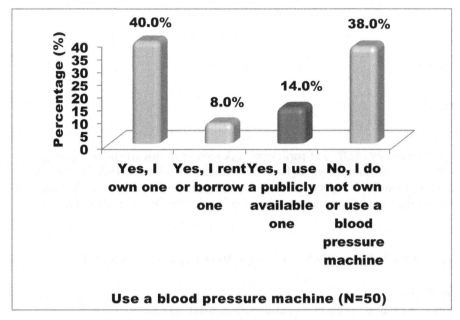

Fig. 2. Participants' usage of blood pressure machine

All (100.0%) participants reported that they used smartphones and 66.0% of them were using iPhone. Few (28.0%) participants reported using smartphones for measuring their blood pressure for health while 62.0% accepted that smartphone health apps are comfortable to use. The health status of the African community showed that many (56.0%) participants noted that their BP reading was normal and those who had normal BMI made up (48.0%) (Table 1).

Table 1. Health Status of the African community

Variable	N	%
Number of BP readings		
Low	2	4.0
Normal	28	56.0
Elevated	14	28.0
High blood pressure (stage 1)	3	6.0
High blood pressure (stage 2)	3	6.0
Number of BMI		

(*continued*)

Table 1. (*continued*)

Variable	N	%
Normal	24	48.0
Overweight	14	28.0
Obese	12	24.0

The majority (52.0%) of participants acknowledged that AfriBP was perceived as useful in cultural dimensions for Exercise Fitness and Eat Healthy Diet, and followed by those who felt that it is good for health management (36.0%). Many (46.0%) supposed that the app features were more useful in Eating Healthy Diet and (40.0%) for Exercise Fitness.

Table 2. Behavioral intention of using AfriBP (Perceived usefulness) (N = 50)

Question	N	%
Perceived usefulness to use in cultural dimensions, health management, and user interaction. Features found useful: Exercise Fitness (Pick-up soccer or African Dance fitness), and/or Eat Healthy Diet [Nigerian and Ghanaian food]		
Cultural dimensions	26	52.0
Health management	18	36.0
User interaction	6	12.0
Which of the following features did you find useful: Exercise Fitness (Pick-up soccer or African Dance fitness), and/or Eat Healthy Diet [Nigerian and Ghanaian food]		
Exercise Fitness	20	40.0
Eat Healthy Diet	23	46.0
Spa	1	2.0
Undecided	6	12.0

5 Discussion

The adoption of technology by gender significantly differs among countries [25]. The implication of the results for gender is that the female participants are adopting the AfriBP more than their male counterparts. In perceived usefulness, females had a higher intention to adopt mHealth than males, while in perceived ease of use, males adopted more than the females [26]. In Fig. 1, there is a relationship between ethnicity and the perceived usefulness to adopt the AfriBP. The hypothesis which stated that ethnicity will have no effect on perceived usefulness to adopt the AfriBP is therefore rejected ($p<0.05$). This implies that perceived usefulness by ethnicity shows that Nigerian participants perceived the acceptance of AfriBP as more useful than the Ghanaian participants to change and improve behavior, lifestyle, and health. Participant who owned and or publicly used the blood pressure machine to control and manage BP were limited in number (Fig. 2). The results indicated that 100% of the participants used smartphones considering the potential benefits derived. Moreover, participants who used smartphone applications specifically to monitor their BP were limited in this study. Participants usage of the Apple Health App for BP were 12%, Samsung Health App for BP were 16%, and 72% were not utilizing the health app for BP. As some participants did not understand the severity of BP. In the US, people with hypertension were less likely to use health-related apps on their smartphone or tablets than those without the health conditions [27]. Since people of African ancestry have the highest risk concern for BP [12], awareness of the usage of BP monitoring machines and mHealth applications for BP are essential. African participants' health statuses are disquieting. Some participants found the use of some smartphone health applications to be uncomfortable, so usability findings became a critical factor while designing the user interface for mHealth technology. A large portion of the participants' BMIs indicated they were overweight and obese, while some were prone to the risk and considered as having high BP (Table 1). This can be attributed to starchy food consumption leading to unhealthy eating and the lack of physical activity. Since the participants' statuses are troubling, they should recognize the usefulness of using the AfriBP. Designing the user interface of the AfriBP and integrating the cultural values, customs, and attitudes will lead to possible increase in adoption, usage, and healthy lifestyle. The participants' behavioral intentions around using the recommended features of the AfriBP were influenced by perceived usefulness of the AfriBP for cultural dimensions and health management, and user interaction.

The attitude of the participants rated a higher behavioral intention for cultural dimensions as the recommended feature: P11, "I feel it is culturally related"; P19, "It is convenient and gives alternatives to a healthier lifestyle"; P20, "Eat Healthy Diet was the element I found most useful because it gave clear images of what all the food I like. I was able to recognize some of the meals by image rather than name"; P7, "African Dance, helps to get fit, and encourages exercising within my comfort zone"; P15, "Soccer, it is more convenient for me to engage actively in sport". This implies that the participants will consider the AfriBP useful when their cultural values, customs, and attitudes of the participants are integrated into the design. This was followed by health management: P35, "BP and BMI will help me to take control of health, known when to see the doctor and change my lifestyle"; P38, "BP reading, BMI and geolocation has helped me to be on my toes about my health and also finding other locations for groceries is really nice for me". Then user interaction: P37, "The AfriBP is better because it is easy to navigate". The Eat Healthy Diet, participants find it more useful, followed by Exercise Fitness, and Spa which is offered as stress management.

The implication of the results is that perceived usefulness will have no effect on attitude to adopt the AfriBP. The hypothesis could only be illustrated by a descriptive analogy of the frequency and percentage of participants who have intention to use the features of the AfriBP (Table 2) since all participants reported having intention of using the features of the AfriBP. Thus, perceived usefulness has a strong significant effect on attitude in adopting the AfriBP (P = 0.000).

6 Conclusion

In conclusion, the usability findings indicate that designing for cross-cultures on mHealth applications as cultural components facilitate the perceived usefulness of adopting mHeath application. The interactive mHealth application tool is expected to enhance accessibility, increase adoption and use, and support user satisfaction as well as lifestyle changes in blood pressure health management. This can potentially add to the body of knowledge to help researchers and user interface designers enhance the usability and satisfy participants. Therefore, increasing the awareness of mHealth applications about health management and behavioral lifestyles of African migrants in the United States is critical.

References

1. Kumar, N., Khunger, M., Gupta, A., Garg, N.: A content analysis of smartphone–based applications for hypertension management. J. Am. Soc. Hypertens. **9**(2), 130–136 (2015)
2. Parati, G., Torlasco, C., Omboni, S., Pellegrini, D.: Smartphone applications for hypertension management: a potential game-changer that needs more control. Curr. Hypertens. Rep. **19**(6), 1–9 (2017)
3. Rai, A., Chen, L., Pye, J., Baird, A.: Understanding determinants of consumer mobile health usage intentions, assimilation, and channel preferences. J. Med. Internet Res. **15**(8), e2635 (2013)
4. Lee, E., Han, S. Determinants of adoption of mobile health services. In: Online Information Review, 2015, vol. 39(4), pp. 556–573. Emerald Group Publishing Limited. August 10 2015. https://www-emerald-com.proxy-tu.researchport.umd.edu/insight/content/doi/10.1108/OIR-01-2015-0007/full/html
5. Deng, Z., Mo, X., Liu, S.: Comparison of the middle-aged and older users' adoption of mobile health services in China. Int. J. Med. Inform. **83**(3), 210–224 (2014)
6. Yusof, A.F., Iahad, N.: Review on online and mobile weight loss management system for overcoming obesity. Paper presented at the 2012 international conference on computer & information science (ICCIS) (2012)
7. Kalem, G., Turhan, Ç.: Mobile technology applications in the healthcare industry for disease management and wellness. Procedia Soc. Behav. Sci. **195**, 2014–2018 (2015)
8. Zapata, B.C., Fernández-Alemán, J.L., Idri, A., Toval, A.: Empirical studies on usability of mHealth apps: a systematic literature review. J. Med. Syst. **39**(2), 1–19 (2015)
9. Centers for Disease Control and Prevention High Blood Pressure (2021). https://www.cdc.gov/bloodpressure/about.htm
10. Silva, P.M.P.D.: A pervasive system for real-time blood pressure monitoring (2013)
11. Hacibekiroglu, S., Kucukkose, A.F., Korucu, C., Kilic, A., Acemi, N.: Chronic disease management model in Acibadem Mobile Health. Int. J. Integr. Care (IJIC) **13**, 1–2 (Nov 2013)
12. Weber, M.A., et al.: Clinical practice guidelines for the management of hypertension in the community: a statement by the American Society of Hypertension and the International Society of Hypertension. J. Clin. Hypertens. **16**(1), 14–26 (2014)

13. Chow, C.K., et al.: Prevalence, awareness, treatment, and control of hypertension in rural and urban communities in high-, middle-, and low-income countries. JAMA **310**(9), 959–968 (2013)
14. Oladapo, H., Owusu, E., Chakraborty, J.: Effects of culturally tailored user interface design. In: Ahram, T.Z., Falcão, C.S. (eds.) AHFE 2021. LNNS, vol. 275, pp. 845–853. Springer, Cham (2021). https://doi.org/10.1007/978-3-030-80091-8_100
15. Ilhan, I.: Smart blood pressure holter. Comput. Meth. Prog. Biomed. **156**, 1–12 (2018)
16. Oladapo, H., Chakraborty, J.: Cross-cultural differences of designing mobile health applications for Africans. In: Stephanidis, C., et al. (eds.) HCII 2021. LNCS, vol. 13094, pp. 554–563. Springer, Cham (2021). https://doi.org/10.1007/978-3-030-90238-4_39
17. Evers, V., Day, D.: The role of culture in interface acceptance. In: Human-Computer Interaction INTERACT 1997, pp. 260–267. Springer, Boston (1997). https://doi.org/10.1007/978-0-387-35175-9_44
18. Khaddam, I., Vanderdonckt, J.: Towards a culture-adaptable user-interface architecture. Romanian J. Hum.-Comput. Interact. **7**(2), 161–194 (2014)
19. Alsswey, A., Umar, I., Al-Samarraie, H.: Towards mobile design guidelines-based cultural values for elderly Arabic users. J. Fundam. Appl. Sci. **10**(2S), 964–977 (2018)
20. Sieverdes, J.C., et al.: Formative evaluation on cultural tailoring breathing awareness meditation smartphone apps to reduce stress and blood pressure. mHealth **3**, 44 (2017). https://doi-org.proxy-tu.researchport.umd.edu/10.21037/mhealth.2017.09.04
21. Davis, F.D.: User acceptance of information technology: system characteristics, user perceptions and behavioral impacts. Int. J. Man Mach. Stud. **38**(3), 475–487 (1993)
22. Davis, F.D.: Perceived usefulness, perceived ease of use, and user acceptance of information technology. MIS Q. **13**(3), 319–340 (1989). https://doi.org/10.2307/249008
23. Hix, D., Hartson, H.R.: Developing User Interfaces: Ensuring Usability Through Product & Process. Wiley, Hoboken (1993)
24. Schneiderman, B.: Developing the User Interface. Addison-Wesley, Reading (1992)
25. Alam, M.Z., Hoque, M.R., Hu, W., Barua, Z.: Factors influencing the adoption of mHealth services in a developing country: a patient-centric study. Int. J. Inf. Manage. **50**, 128–143 (2020)
26. Hoque, M.R.: An empirical study of mHealth adoption in a developing country: the moderating effect of gender concern. BMC Med. Inform. Decis. Mak. **16**, 1–10 (2016)
27. Langford, A.T., et al.: Mobile phone ownership, health apps, and tablet use in US adults with a self-reported history of hypertension: cross-sectional study. JMIR mHealth uHealth **7**(1), e12228 (2019)

The Communicability of the Interaction of the Elderly User with the WhatsApp Application

Regina Oliveira(✉) [iD], Bruno Merlin [iD], and Heleno Fülber [iD]

Universidade Federal do Pará, Tucuruí, PA, Brazil
reginioliveira@gmail.com

Abstract. The advances in digital technologies and the widespread use of *smartphones* have greatly changed the way people communicate, mainly through social platforms. At the same time, the sharp growth of the elderly population raises the question of the relationship of the elderly and the new digital media, especially with the Covid-19 pandemic that has conditioned social isolation. This research aims to investigate the communicability of the interaction of elderly users with the WhatsApp application. Methodologically, a case of study was conducted with a group of 10 elderly. The Communicability Evaluation Method of Semiotic Engineering was applied. The results showed interaction problems related to the attribution of meaning, perception, recognition of icons; highlighted the most frequent communicability ruptures during the interaction; confirmed low vision as the most impacting change of aging; presented a global report of the usage experiences by elderly and also mitigated the satisfaction and classification of the service.

Keywords: Semiotic Engineering · Communicability · Elderly users · WhatsApp

1 Introduction

Due to the increase of life expectancy and the decrease in birth rate, the elderly population has grown rapidly in Brazil and worldwide in the last two decades [11]. Along with the evolution and spread of digital technologies, the elderly are gradually making more use of technologies, especially through the smartphone, which is one of the main technological devices currently used [3, 10]. Smartphones are becoming increasingly indispensable in people's lives. They are largely responsible for changing the way we live, work and communicate, by allowing a large number of daily activities and services that can be performed through it [3, 12]. During the Covid-19 pandemic, directly influenced by social isolation, their use rate increased especially for the communication services [12].

Elderly people tend to find smartphone services difficult to use, according to studies that point to problematic issues that range from the size of the device's screen to the user's interpretations of interface elements, such as icons, menus, buttons and others [17, 26]. These issues usually influence the quality of use for all types of users, however, for

© The Author(s), under exclusive license to Springer Nature Switzerland AG 2022
M. Antona and C. Stephanidis (Eds.): HCII 2022, LNCS 13308, pp. 306–324, 2022.
https://doi.org/10.1007/978-3-031-05028-2_21

the elderly, they become much more significant. In the use of computacional systems, graphical interfaces are the direct communication way between user and system, so they must be intuitive and well planned so that their interpretation provides quality in the interaction [5]. Thus, the good communicability of a system is important to guarantee that the message transmitted by the interface (metacommunication) is understood in the user-system interaction, preventing communication failures from hindering its use [21].

The relationship between seniors and digital technologies has not always been friendly. In the aging process, physical, cognitive and motor skills decline, limiting the performance of certain activities. This means that older people not only need to learn how to use the tools, but also that the tools should be adapted to feed their needs [22, 23]. Therefore, designers should know, understand and consider their characteristics and capabilities of use and interpretation when designing devices and computer applications [9, 14].

According to a survey by the IBGE (Brazilian Institute of Geography and Statistics) [10], the age group that grew the most in internet use, after young adults, were people over 60 years old by using smartphones. Elderly people show interest and willingness to digital inclusion, but still face barriers such as lack of training, lack of clarity in instructions, lack of help and support in use [25, 29].

Digital inclusion directly impacts the full exercise of citizenship of contemporary subjects, since cyberspace hypermedia languages permeate various social practices [15]. The increase in the elderly population brought new challenges to society, such as ensuring the social and digital inclusion of this public. Furthermore, they tend to naturally suffer from social isolation, which has been specifically aggravated during the current pandemic. Then, some initiatives use social platforms as facilitating means to contribute to the social inclusion of ederly [4, 27].

Social interaction modes are changing as technological advances provide new ways of communication. In Brazil, the number of elderly users of social platforms increased largely [10]. This generation became familiar with new ways of communicating and socializing, such as WhatsApp messaging application [13] among other platforms. In this context, the WhatsApp messaging application appears now as one of the main ways of communication, with a large number of active users (about 2 billion in 2020) and in continuous growth [12].

Given this scenario, this research aims to assess the communicability of the elderly user's interaction with the WhatsApp messaging application, using the theory of Semiotic Engineering. Methodologically, it is a qualitative research that, through a case of study, proposes to explain the interaction between the user and the system, knowing the particularities and individual experiences of each participant, even more influenced by the Covid-19 pandemic scenario. It seeks to identify the communicative problems of the interaction and the possible causes related to the characteristics of aging.

The rest of the article is organized as follows: Sect. 2 presents the theory of Semiotic Engineering and the method of evaluating communicability; Sect. 3 presents related works; Sect. 4 describes the methodology; Sect. 5 presents the application of the method; Sect. 6 addresses results and discussions; and, Sect. 7 brings the conclusions of this work.

2 Semiotic Engineering and MAC

Semiotic Engineering is a theory that focuses on the communication between the user and the designer's message, carried out through a system's interface. It understands the interface as a message being transmitted from the designer to the user (metamessage). It is an explanatory theory of HCI (Human-Computer Interaction), which allows us to understand the phenomena involved in the interaction. To assess the quality of the interaction, it defined the communicability property, which refers to the ability of a system to convey to the user the intentions and principles of interaction in an effective and efficient way [5, 18].

Semiotic Engineering defined methods to examine the communicability of systems. The MAC (Communicability Assessment Method) aims to assess the reception of the metamessage by the user. It investigates the user's experience with the system based on potential communication disruptions experienced during the interaction [5, 6, 18]. The evaluator is responsible for observing the interactive process, identifying communication breaks and performing the interpretation.

The MAC has five stages for its application (Fig. 1): test preparation, test application, labeling, data interpretation and preparation of the semiotic profile [1, 6].

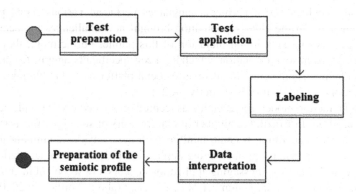

Fig. 1. MAC application steps.

The test preparation step aims to define all the general test parameters and prepare all the necessary material. The test application stage corresponds to the observation of the participants' interaction. Data collection is done by observing the participant performing the tasks in the system.

In the labeling, the evaluators use the collected data to make the tabulation, examining the communicative flaws/ruptures found [1]. Each identified break is assigned a label according to its characteristic and meaning. There are 13 (thirteen) labels defined in the MAC, which can be used in this step. They are categorized by type of communicative failure [1, 6], as shown in Table 1.

Table 1. Communicability labels and categories.

Label	Category
Where?	Temporary failures
Hey, what happened?	
And now?	
Where am I?	
Oops!	
That's not possible	
What is this?	
Help!	
Why does it not work?	
No, thank you!	Partial failures
Let's try another way	
It is good for me	Complete failures
I give up	

In the data interpretation stage, interaction problems are exposed and detailed. The evaluator analyzes and interprets the frequency and context of occurrence of each label [1, 6]. It provides indications of the causes of failures and possible solutions or suggestions to improve the interface.

The elaboration of the semiotic profile consists in producing a report that presents the reconstruction of the application's metamessage. It rewrites the metamessage from the results obtained in the labeling and interpretation, based on observations of the user's behavior and characteristics [1].

3   Related Works

This section presents works that discuss the elderly user's relationship with digital technologies, ederly needs and critical points of this relationship.

The works by Rocha and Padovani [19, 20] sought to identify the characteristics of aging and relate them to the implications for smartphone interface design and also raise suggestions from the elderly public to contribute to the teaching-learning process of smartphones.

The first work [19] related aspects arising from the aging process with smartphone interface design principles. The most evident aspects of aging impacting negatively the interaction of elderly users were related to vision, hearing, memory, tactile control, perception. They indicated a possible social exclusion that can occur with the elderly due to their unfamiliarity with digital technologies.

The second work [20] reports the experience of 9 seniors focusing on their learning desires and the difficulties they face with this technology. The results showed that they need training to master the device or they need support from an experienced person. They proposed a specific learning course for this audience. They highlighted that family members do not have the patience to teach. They pointed out the most common functions, doubts and where they make more mistakes and failures. They mentioned functions or applications most used by the elderly, such as: WhatsApp, calls and Facebook. They also highlighted a greater interest in communication with the family nucleus.

The work carried out in [21], dealt with the communicability of the social network Facebook, comparing different types of users. The research used the MAC to assess the social network Facebook with two types of profiles: younger users and older users. The objective was to assess whether the limitations of the aging process caused different results between profiles. As a result, aspects to be revised in the interface were observed, for example, improving the meaning system, defining more clearly the information organization criteria and correcting usability and accessibility problems that contributed to communicability breaks during the interaction of the elderly.

The survey was conducted with 10 participants, 5 elderly and 5 young adults. The rate of completion of tasks by the elderly was lower compared to younger participants. Task execution time was longer with the elderly. They had a higher number of communication breaks. They had difficulty understanding icons and non-textual information so as to find items in the interface. Another aspect common to the ederly interaction is the fact that they type slowly and looking at the keyboard, preventing immediate use of the system's auto-complete feature. The most frequent limiting aging consequence was low vision, which limited the recognition of interface elements.

The study [4] dealt with the experience of sociability of the elderly using the social network Facebook. It presents the use of information and communication technologies as a way to promote social inclusion and combat social isolation, which occurs with the elderly. These online social networks, when appropriate, can help seniors interact with their family, friends and other interest groups, in addition to keeping them updated on everyday matters. However, they find difficulties in the process of digital sociability. Aspects such as communicability, usability, accessibility and sociability influence the experience of using social platforms. They seem poorly suited to the needs of this group.

Among the potential problems identified, it is possible to exemplify the difficulty in perceiving and accessing the options for functions that are not very explicit. Options that are not statically explicit in the interface go unnoticed and are not intuitive to the elderly user. The results also showed that the reported interaction problems often impact the user's autonomy.

The works presented similar points in the relationship of the elderly with digital technologies, knowing aspects of how they interact and how aging changes interfere. They discuss and promote the demand for new research that characterizes the needs of the elderly on social platforms and the barriers they still face, despite the potential for inclusion they represent.

In this scenario, no studies were found in the literature that had assessed the communicability of WhatsApp for the elderly user, as aimed at in this study. Thus, this research contributes to and complements the area by investigating this relationship, in order to continue discussions that enhance more inclusive technologies for the elderly.

4   Methodology

This research aims to investigate the communicability of the elderly user's interaction with the WhatsApp messaging application. It is hypothesized that the interaction difficulties faced by the elderly are strongly related to changes resulting from aging.

The execution of the research followed the procedures defined in the Communicability Assessment Method (MAC) of Semiotic Engineering. Data collection used the techniques of interviews and observation of ederly users. Data analysis was performed in an interpretive way, explaining the phenomena and behaviors that occurred during the interaction.

4.1   System Definition

The WhatsApp application was the chosen system because it is part of the group of social platforms that has the largest number of active users in the world, with users of different age groups [12].

The original purpose of the system was to facilitate the exchange of messages on cell phones, but its use goes far beyond, becoming part of the daily routine of its users [12, 13]. In Brazil, WhatsApp is one of the most popular means of communication, where more than 90% of its Brazilians use the application daily [3].

4.2   Method Definition

There are several scientific methods to evaluate a system with a user. They have some characteristics in common, mainly in the part of test preparation and execution, varying in the type of data to be collected or in the analysis to be carried out [18]. The communicability tests seek to assess the implicit and explicit process of designer-user communication, which takes place through the interface, identifying the points in the system that were not well communicated by the designer to the user [18].

The choice of MAC considered its relevance in analyzing the quality of communication by observing the reception of the metamessage by the user [1, 6]. Therefore, among the methods of Semiotic Engineering, it was chosen because it allows the direct participation of users in the research. Thus, the method is used in the research to examine the elderly user's interpretation of the system interface message, how they understand and how they communicate with the intention to use the interface.

4.3   Selection of Participants

The participants selected for the research were elderly people, according to what is defined in the Elderly Statute [2], aged over 60 years. All elderly participants were users of the WhatsApp application and had their own smartphone. They had no history of exercising professional activities including the use of digital technologies.

Due to the Covid-19 pandemic, data collection was planned to be carried out in the participants' homes, following the prevention measures against the virus, in accordance with them. They set a date and time. Invitations to volunteers were made by phone call or message via WhatsApp.

When applying the MAC, it is recommended that there are 6 to 8 participants [18]. In this research, a total of 10 participants were evaluated, selected through the saturation sampling technique [8]. The main data on the profile of the participants are presented in Table 2. To maintain anonymity, they were referenced from P1 to P10.

Table 2. Participant data.

ID	Age	Profession	Sex	Schooling	Time of use
P1	60	From home	F	Elementary	2 years
P2	65	Bakery assistant	F	High	4 years
P3	61	General services	F	Elementary	3 years
P4	62	Watchman	M	Elementary	5 years
P5	64	Teacher	M	Higher	5 years
P6	76	Candymaker	F	High	2 years
P7	76	Sales representative	F	Higher	5 years
P8	65	From home	F	Elementary	5 years
P9	68	Seamstress	F	Elementary	1 year
P10	60	Construction worker	M	High	2 years

The age of the group ranged between 60 and 76 years. Among them, 70% declared themselves female and 30% male. As for education, 50% had completed elementary school, 30% high school and 20% higher education.

Due to the Covid-19 pandemic, the recruitment of participants was a cautious step, which took place after the first wave of contagion, when prevention measures were relaxed. Some elderly people refused to participate in the research or their children did not allow it, with the justification of remaining in social isolation until complete vaccination. Others refused to participate because they felt they did not have enough knowledge and because they were ashamed of making mistakes, even though the purpose of the research was explained. Also, it was difficult to find elderly people over 70 years old users of WhatsApp.

4.4 Definition of Functions Evaluated in the System

The most commonly used functions in WhatsApp were defined to be evaluated: sending messages (text, audio, image), image forwarding and changing the profile picture. Tasks are typical and realistic in system usage. All participants performed the test using the same smartphone device. The test scenario with task execution script is presented in Table 3.

It is noteworthy that the test interaction occurred with no simultaneous interaction between the participant and another person in the conversation.

Table 3. Test scenario and tasks.

Test scenario (script):
WhatsApp is a messaging and voice and video calling app for smartphones. In addition to text messages, users can send images, videos, audio and various documents, make calls and video calls, all through an internet connection. In this context, you want to communicate with a friend by sending text, audio and image messages. You also want to change your profile picture for a new one that is in your phone's gallery. For this, you will carry out the following activities: **1** - Start a conversation with the contact 'João' and send the text message "Good morning"/"Good afternoon"; **2** - Send an audio in the conversation asking "How are you?"; **3** - Send any image in the conversation (images in the cell phone gallery); **4** - Delete the image sent in the conversation; **5** - Forward an image of the conversation with 'Maria' to the friend 'João'; **6** - Delete the conversation with 'João'; **7** - Change the profile picture (images in the cell phone gallery);

4.5 Equipment and Application Configuration

The equipment used in the test to record the data were: 1 smartphone Samsung Galaxy A50 6.4″ screen and 1 Canon digital camera.

The WhatsApp application was properly installed and configured on the smartphone. In the system configuration, a specific user profile was created for the test, as well as two random conversations, in one of the conversations text messages and images were exchanged. Some contacts were saved in the list, with fictitious names, they were aware of the research and that they should not to interact with the participants during the tests. Folders with random images were created in the phone's gallery. The internet connection was made using mobile data from the cell phone. The text of the task execution script (test scenario) was formatted for printing in Arial font, size 20, in order to make it easier for the elderly to read.

The tests were recorded using the smartphone's native 'screen recorder' function and a digital camera. The audio recordings of the interviews pre- and post-test were made using the smartphone's native 'voice recorder' function.

5 Method Application

In this section the process of carrying out the steps of the method is presented.

5.1 Preparation

This first phase is where the elaboration and configuration of all the materials necessary for the test begins. The following activities were carried out: 1) definition of the profile of participants and recruitment; 2) definition of test objectives and tasks; 3) inspection of system design; 4) preparation of the scenario (script for the execution of tasks); 5) elaboration of the consent form; 6) pre- and post-test interview script elaboration; 7) elaboration of the observation script; 8) equipment and system configuration; 9) printing of all materials; 10) carrying out a pilot test.

5.2 Test Execution

The collections took place from December 2020 to the beginning of February 2021. The activities of this phase involved: 1) punctuality and organization of the test environment; 2) provide the necessary explanations and request the signature of the consent form; 3) conduct a pre-test interview, recording it in audio; 4) observe the participant interacting with the system (execution of test tasks), with video recording and cell phone screen recording; 5) carry out the post-test interview.

The tests were carried out in the participants' homes, in a space with a table, usually the kitchen or living room. The digital camera was positioned in front of the participant, about 80 cm away, while the audio recorder (native to the smartphone) was about 30 cm away. It is recommended that the test environment be controlled without interference. In approximately half of the tests, the elderly were alone at home.

The pre-test interview questions collected personal and health data, and experience about digital technologies. The post-test interview focused on answering the evaluators' doubts about the participant's test execution. The interviews took place in a conversation format to make the elderly more comfortable to report their perceptions and experiences.

Some seniors had difficulty reading the test script and performing tasks simultaneously. The tasks were listed in sequence, however, most participants had doubts and asked what was the next task to perform or if they had already completed the current one. For this reason, it was necessary to read the tasks slowly and repeatedly as they interacted.

During the execution of the tasks, most participants reported feeling strange when using a smartphone that was different from what they were used to. Almost all had a smartphone with an Android operating system (similar to the test device), only one participant used an Apple smartphone, which has an iOS system. The smartphone used in the test, Samsung Galaxy A50, was a device with very current characteristics, it had an infinite 6.4″ screen, 4G RAM memory, Android 10 operating system.

In the post-test interview, the elderly who reported feeling strange about the device, took the opportunity to demonstrate how they performed the tasks on their own cell phone, however, they committed the same test failures.

At the end of each test run, a written summary was made on paper of the relevant points of observation, noting what the elderly person did wrong or right and what the behavior or justification was for what happened.

5.3 Labeling

At this stage, the collected data were evaluated: the participants' interaction videos, audio and interview notes. Twenty videos were analyzed (approximately 148 min of recording), in addition to the interviews, which helped a lot in this stage, especially the post-test. From the videos, the communicability ruptures identified in the participant's interaction were tabulated. In this step, the notes made about each test were also considered.

The videos were watched repeatedly until evaluators identified and assigned the label related to the break. The labeling was registered in a spreadsheet where the time (time range) in which the rupture occurred and the corresponding label were informed.

The Table 4 records the occurrences of the test labels of all participants, specified for each task.

Table 4. Test labeling.

Labels	Tasks							Total
	T1	T2	T3	T4	T5	T6	T7	
Where?	7	2	4	3	2	0	0	**18**
Oops!	1	0	0	0	0	1	0	**2**
Hey, what happened?	1	0	0	0	0	1	0	**2**
And now?	0	0	1	2	0	2	3	**8**
Where am I?	0	0	0	0	0	0	1	**1**
Why does it not work?	0	0	1	0	0	0	0	**1**
No, thank you	0	0	0	0	0	0	0	0
It is good for me	0	0	0	0	1	8	2	**11**
Let's try another way	0	0	2	0	2	0	0	**4**
What is this?	0	0	0	0	0	0	0	0
Help!	3	1	2	2	1	2	1	**12**
That is not possible	0	0	0	0	0	0	0	0
I give up	0	0	0	0	0	0	6	**6**
Total	**12**	**3**	**10**	**7**	**6**	**14**	**13**	**65**

5.4 Data Interpretation

In general, regarding the rate of completion of tasks by the group, no elderly person was able to complete all the tasks without disruptions in communicability. The participants who performed better were P4 and P8, as they completed the tasks with fewer failures and quicker. The average duration of the tests was approximately 7 min. The slower participant was P1 and took about 14 min, and the fastest was P4 who took about 4 min. The longer task was task 3 (send an image) followed by task 5 (forward an image between conversations). Task 2 (send an audio) was the faster one.

Sixty-five breaks of communicability were recorded for all tests in the group. With predominance of the labels "Where?", "It is good for me" and "And now?". Since "Where?" and "And now?" constitute temporary failures, where the interpretation is temporarily inconsistent. In the "Where?" label, the user knows what to do but keeps looking in the interface for an element to perform the task, while in the "And now?" label, he doesn't know what to do, so he wanders through the interface looking for clues with indications how to perform the task. The label "It is good for me" constitutes a complete failure, as the user is not aware of the failure and believes that he has achieved the goal.

The interpretation of each task will be presented below:

Task 1: Start conversation by sending a text message

In carrying out the first task, the rupture most committed by the participants was looking for the contact or the list of contacts on the screen, corresponding to the label "Where?". An interaction problem related to navigation and meaning assignment. The icon referring to the list of contacts at the bottom right of the screen (Fig. 2) went unnoticed by 70% of the participants, which caused some explicit requests for help, registering the label "Help!". Generally, the focus of the users' view is at the top of the screen, where the options menu is usually located. So some have explored the menu bar (Conversations, Status and Calls) in order to find contacts.

Fig. 2. WhatsApp home screen.

Through the reports of the elderly, it was observed that in some cases the conversations are initiated by other people and are not deleted, continuing for future interactions. Thus, the elderly make little use of the contact list button and were slow to find it.

Task 2: Send an audio in the conversation

The task of sending an audio into the conversation was where the least disruptions in the interaction occurred. Only participants P1 and P7 demonstrated difficulty in locating the audio button, causing the label "Where?". One of the reasons suggested was the low vision and also the fact that the audio button is the same as the send message ('Enter' button), possibly generating a problem of attribution of meaning and confusion in the users' understanding.

The audio function stood out as very common for most participants because it is more practical and quicker in everyday conversations in the app, especially for those who have difficulty typing texts and low vision for reading.

Task 3: Send an image in the conversation
In this task 60% of the participants committed ruptures identified with the labels "Where?", "Let's try another way", "And now?" and "Why doesn't it work?". These are interaction problems related to the perception and attribution of meanings to the interface elements.

The "Where?" were caused by the difficulty in locating in the interface where to get an image from the gallery. There are two ways to access the gallery through the application interface, the 'Attachments' icon and the 'Camera' icon in the message type bar (Fig. 3).

Fig. 3. Access to the gallery by 'Attachments' and 'Camera'.

The label "Let's try another way" occurred when the participants left the app, went to the cell phone gallery and from there they sent an image. Participants reported knowing and using this path more often when sending an image in the conversation. They learned this path first and therefore find it easier to view and search by going to the gallery app, rather than accessing it from within WhatsApp.

The "And now?" happened to participant P7 who wandered into the interface and admitted not knowing how to send an image. The label "Why doesn't it work?" happened to participant P6 who mistakenly tapped the audio button but actually wanted to tap the 'Camera' icon to open the gallery. She justified the failure by saying that she was not distinguishing the symbol because of her low vision.

Task 4: Delete the image sent in the conversation
In general, participants knew how to quickly delete the image sent in the conversation. In this task, the labels "Where?", "And now?" and "Help!" happened. In the label "Where?",

two seniors selected the image holding it, but later did not find the trash, even though it was available on the top bar. They had difficulty identifying or distinguishing the icon, which, due to low vision, can become blurred. For the "And now?" label, two other seniors showed not knowing how to perform the task. They started by opening the image, where a menu appeared in the upper right corner. But they did not explore it, so they could not see the options. They were wandering the interface and following a less productive path. Thus, P6 and P10 asked for help to carry out the task (label "Help!").

Task 5: Forward an image between conversations
In carrying out this task, there were few occurrences of communicative breaks. Participant P1 registered the label "Where?" because he opened the image and kept looking for the icon "forward", did not find the icon at the top of the screen or could not make the attribution of the meaning.

Participant P2 started with the label "Where?", as she kept looking in the interface for the arrow icon next to the image to forward it, but she did not find it because it disappeared when she selected the image, leaving only the icon in the top bar. She gave up that way, exited the application and went to the cell phone gallery to look in the WhatsApp images folder and shared the image, indicating the label "Let's try another way". As mentioned earlier, some seniors prefer to browse the gallery app directly.

Participant P3 successfully completed the task, however, taking a slightly longer path inside the application, activating the label "Let's try another way". While participant P5 forwarded the image to the contact Maria, and did not notice the mistake, indicating a slight flaw and the label "It is good for me".

Overall, the group of participants showed recognition of the function of the application's image forwarding/sharing icons (Fig. 4), even though they followed different paths.

Fig. 4. Forward/share icons.

Task 6: Delete the conversation
The result of this labeling revealed that the task was misinterpreted by the participants. The entire group of elderly people showed similar disruptions and behaviors. The objective was to delete the conversation that normally is in the list of conversations on the system's home page.

The predominant label was "It's good for me", identified in 80% of the participants who deleted the messages from the conversation, leaving the conversation still open. One possibility for the misinterpretation is that as they had finished performing task 5, they stayed on the conversation screen and from that point on they tried to start task 6, causing a misunderstanding.

The most common action was to select all or some messages from the conversation and delete them in the trash can icon, and thus, mistakenly, they concluded that the task had been performed successfully. Participant P10 cleared the messages by going to the 'Clear conversation' function. P7 and P9 stated that they did not know how to delete the conversation. They tried to discover the function in the interface, within the conversation, but they were unsuccessful. At the end, they asked for help to carry out the task (label "Help!").

In the post-test interview, it was possible to verify that some of the participants initially labeled "It's good for me" knew how to erase the conversation correctly. They demonstrated the step-by-step instructions on their own cell phone.

Task 7: Change profile picture
The most recorded label was "I give up", by participants who explicitly admitted not knowing or not being able to perform the task. Interaction problem in the full execution of the task, as they could not even start a productive path. In this case, some preferred not to try. They reported that they rarely change their profile picture and that this task is done with the help of someone else.

Participants P1 and P2 inserted a photo in the Status, believing they were doing the task correctly (label "It is good for me"). Elderly P4 was the only one who succeeded in completing the task on the test, and showed good ability. However, other participants said they had performed the task before, but failed the test. They reported not having good memorization of the sequence of steps to be followed.

Overall, this task proved to be quite complex for most elderly people, due to lack of practice or because of the longer and less intuitive path. Some seniors said that there should be a more accessible button or label that indicates this function.

5.5 Semiotic Profile

The last step is the elaboration of the semiotic profile, which consists in reconstructing the system's metamessage. The semiotic profile helps to present an overview of meta-communication, answering about what the system does, who its users are, what they want or need to do, how they prefer to use the functions, issues and suggestions. It is presented in a paraphrased message.

The reconstructed meta message is: "In my interpretation, you are an elderly user, with average experience using WhatsApp and very interested in communicating with family and friends. I learned that you want to exchange messages in different formats that allow you to interact socially and feel closer to people, in a simple and intuitive way. You also want to be more digitally included and get information on a daily basis. You are a user who often has low vision and wears glasses, types slowly and prefers to speak and listen. Here, then, is the system for you: a system for exchanging text messages, audio, images, videos and documents, which allows you to make voice or video calls. Most functions are available in the interface through icons. I learned that you have difficul-ties interpreting some interface icons, such as the 'Search' magnifying glass and the 'Attachments' clip. You also have difficulty locating your contact list, a green button at the bottom right of your screen and to identify the interface dynamic and contextual changes performed during the interaction. I understand that you prefer textual indica-tions or icon labels to identify functions more easily. Some terms are difficult for you to interpret, such as 'Settings'. I learned that you know little about the menu functions in the upper right corner, symbolized by three small dots. Therefore, you have difficulties changing the application's settings. Changing your profile picture is complex for you. I realized that the visuals need to be sharp and larger for you to recognize and select them appropriately, like the trash icon".

6   Results and Discussions

For the limitations of the research, some points were identified that could somehow threaten its results. The first point is about how realistic the configuration of the app and the smartphone used in the tests. As well as, how realistic was the test scenario and if the tasks defined to be performed were all common to the elderly user. Another point is about the time when the participants were users of the application, which ranged from one to five years apart. Also, it is important to note the case of participant P7, for two different reasons: she was in the early stages of Alzheimer's and has always used an Apple branded smartphone, which has its own operating system. The WhatsApp application undergoes some interface changes in Apple's operating system. Regarding Alzheimer's disease, it was not possible to determine whether there was memory loss during the test, as there was no specialist for this analysis.

The participants who performed better were P4 and P8, aged 62 and 65 respectively. Both with elementary education and users of the application for about 5 years. Participant P4 was very interested in exchanging information about politics and current news, so he actively participated in various groups. He demonstrated that he knew how to perform all the tasks, even though he had a complete loss of vision in one eye. The label "Oops!", committed by him when interacting very quickly with the system, may be related to this characteristic.

The participant P8 communicates a lot with her children and grandchildren. She performed the first five tasks properly and the failures in the last two tasks do not correspond to her vision problem, which is pterygium, but to the misinterpretation of task 6 and low memorization in task 7. She highlighted that the frequency of communication with the family through the app has increased due to the Covid-19 pandemic. The functions she uses the most are: making a video call, sending photos and videos, and participating in family groups. Overall, the average time the group of participants used the system was about 3 years.

The main change that occurred in the aging process of the tested group is related to vision (cataract, myopia, astigmatism, glaucoma, pterygium) and memory (forgetfulness). Vision problems are commonly mentioned in the literature, confirming what has been presented in related works [15, 19, 26]. All seniors wore glasses. The main difficulties are in reading and distinguishing symbols/icons, so the larger size and good sharpness are recommended. As for forgetting, they reported not interfering in their daily lives, but they have difficulty learning and memorizing functions that have many steps, such as changing the profile picture for instance. Participant P7, as informed by her family, is in the early stages of Alzheimer's disease, but it was not possible to identify whether there was memory loss during the test. She assumed that she didn't know how to carry out the tasks of sending images, deleting conversations and changing profile pictures. She had higher education and was an iPhone user.

Low vision can also be related to mistaken taps, for example, when the participant wanted to tap the 'Back' icon on the smartphone, but repeatedly tapped the app's 'Enter' and didn't get the expected result. Slower typing is also related to low vision and the size of keys and fonts, even typing little text during the test, it was possible to notice the slowness and delay in finding the letters on the keyboard.

The frequency of labels and their categorization illustrates how the interaction takes place. With emphasis on the temporary failures "Where?", "And now?", "Help!" and the complete failures "It is good for me" and "I give up", as shown in Table 5.

Table 5. Categorization of frequent labels in the test.

Category	Label	Feature
Temporary failure	Where?	It mainly occurred when the elderly could not find the contact list. Also when he did not find the gallery and did not identify the trash icon (delete) or other contextual menus. The user knew what to do, but his interpretation was temporarily interrupted
	And now?	It occurred when the elderly did not know what to do and looked for clues on the interface on how to perform the task. With emphasis on the tasks of sending and forwarding images
	Help!	It happened every time the elderly person tried to restore productive interaction, explicitly asking the evaluator for help. Almost always after the "Where?" and "And now?"
Complete failure	It is good for me	It mainly occurred in the task of deleting the conversation, as they only deleted the messages, without being aware of the flaw. There could be 'Delete conversation' option in the internal menu, as there is 'Clear conversation'
	I give up	When, consciously, the elderly admitted not being able to perform the task. Occurred only in the task to change the profile picture. Either because I had never done it before or because of the difficulty in memorizing it

As seen in Table 5, the high frequency of the label "Where?", a temporary failure, was closely related to the low vision of the participants, as in the occurrences the item was in the interface, but not located. As pointed out in the work by Paula et al. [4], when the options are not very explicit in the interface, they become less intuitive and go unnoticed by the user. The label "Where?" was often succeeded by the label "Help". The occurrence of partial failures was minimal.

The semiotic profile brought clues and suggestions that serve for a possible redesign of the interface. Difficulty in interpreting texts and assigning meanings to symbols on the application's interface is something common in smartphone use, as reported by the group and already pointed out in studies [4, 21]. The suggestion is the larger size in fonts and icons. The font size can be set directly in the application or in the operating system. There was also the suggestion of labels on the icons, as some symbols have unknown meanings, and the text helps in interpreting the function. Moreover, the discrete dynamic and contextual changes performed during the interaction are rarely observed by ederly and static menu would be preferred.

Participants reported that they ask for help from younger family members when they need to solve a problem or learn something new. They are afraid of 'moving' and 'unconfiguring' the cell phone. They also reported not knowing how to use the device and application settings, showing a possible dependence experienced by them, when they need other people to help or perform these functions. However, they sometimes reported that they face people's impatience to teach, as indicated in [20].

Regarding the motivation to use the app, they stated that communication with the family is the most important reason and that they feel comfortable interacting through the app. They reinforced that the daily usage time increased in the Covid-19 pandemic, and started to use more video call function to see the family, which was previously more rare.

Finally, the participants evaluated that the tasks requested in the test were not difficult or complex and that they did not experience many difficulties in performing them alone, with the exception of task 7 (changing profile picture). However, they rated their level of knowledge of the application's functions as low or medium and that they find the service offered by WhatsApp very important and useful.

7 Conclusions

This research addressed the communicability of the WhatsApp application for elderly users, evaluating the interaction through the MAC of Semiotic Engineering. It aims at knowing how the interaction between user and system takes place, identifying communicative problems and verifying their relationship with the aging characteristics of the elderly.

The main errors and breaks found in the test were generally temporary failures, in common routine usage tasks, while complete failures happened in less usual tasks. The predominance of the label "Where?" was very related to the users' view. Vision problems were the most common feature within the researched group, which is commonly pointed out in related works [4, 19, 21]. However, they did not cause a total interruption in the interaction with the system, but suggest possible improvements that can be made in the interface to minimize some identified communicability problems.

It was also noticed that, even with the problems of communicability, WhatsApp is a system well accepted by the elderly, as they see it as an important means of current communication with their social nucleus, especially the family. Thus, the research brings important contributions to understand the perceptions of the elderly about the application and to emphasize the potential that digital technologies have to improve communication in the lives of the elderly.

In future works, it is expected to investigate other functions of the application or carry out a comparative study with different types of users, carry out tests in laboratories and use a support tool to optimize the steps of applying the method. It is also believed that new researches assessing the quality of interaction of the elderly on social platforms contributes to enhance this group inclusion.

References

1. Barbosa, S., Silva, B.: Interação Humano-Computador, 1st edn. Campus/Elsevier, São Paulo (2010). ISBN 978-85-352-3418-3
2. Brasil: Estatuto do Idoso: Lei Federal n° 10.741, de 01 de outubro de 2003. Secretaria Especial dos Direitos Humanos, Brasília, DF (2003)
3. Deloitte: Global Mobile Consumer Survey 2019. Disponível em. pesquisas.lp.deloittecomu nicacao.com.br/global-mobile-consumer-19. Acesso em 20 de jan de 2021 (2019)
4. de Paula, N., Barbosa, G., Silva, I., Silva, T.: Evaluation of user experience and sociability on social softwares in an elderly people perspective: a facebook case study. In: Proceedings of the 17th Brazilian Symposium on Human Factors in Computing Systems (IHC 2018), Belém, Brazil (2018)
5. de Souza, C.: The Semiotic Engineering of Human-Computer Interaction, vol. 1. The MIT Press, Cambridge (2005)
6. de Souza, C., Leitão, C.: Métodos de Engenharia Semiótica para Pesquisa Científica em IHC, 1st edn. Morgan & Claypool, San Francisco (2009)
7. Gil, A.: Como elaborar projetos de pesquisa, 6th edn. Atlas, São Paulo (2017)
8. Glaser, B., Strauss, A.: The Discovery of Grounded Theory: Strategies for Qualitative Research. Aldine de Gruyter, New York (1967)
9. Guner, H., Acarturk, C.: The use and acceptance of ICT by senior citizens: a comparison of technology acceptance model (TAM) for elderly and young adults. Univ. Access Inf. Soc. 19(2), 311–330 (2018). https://doi.org/10.1007/s10209-018-0642-4
10. IBGE Notícias: PNAD Contínua TIC 2018. Disponível em (2018). https://agenciadenot icias.ibge.gov.br/agencia-sala-de-imprensa/2013-agencia-de-noticias/releases/27515-pnad-continua-tic-2018-internet-chega-a-79-1-dos-domicilios-do-pais. Acesso em: 09 de dez. de 2020
11. IPEA – Instituto de Pesquisa Econômica Aplicada: População idosa brasileira deve aumentar até 2060. Disponível em (2018). www.ipea.gov.br/portal/index.php?option=com_content& view=article&id=33875. Acesso em: 09 de dez. de 2020
12. Kemp, S.: Digital 2021: the latest insights into the 'state of digital'. We Are Social. Disponível em (2021). https://wearesocial.com/blog/2021/01/digital-2021-the-latest-insights-into-the-state-of-digital. Acesso em: 28 de jan. de 2021
13. Matassi, M., Boczkowski, P., Mitchelstein, E.: Domesticating WhatsApp: Family, friends, work, and study in everyday communication. Novas mídias e sociedade 21(10), 2183–2200 (2019). https://doi.org/10.1177/1461444819841890
14. Muriana, L., Hornung, H.: Including older adults into the design process: challenges and lessons learned. In: Proceedings of the 16th Brazilian Symposium on Human Factors in Computing Systems (IHC 2017), Joinville, Brazil (2017)
15. Oliveira, W., Hessel, A., Pesce, L.: Envelhecimento e inclusão digital: autonomia e empoder-amento à luz da pedagogia crítica freireana. Revista Prâksis 3, 85–101 (2020). https://doi.org/ 10.25112/rpr.v3i0.2150
16. Oppl, S., Stary, C.: Game-playing as an effective learning resource for elderly people: encouraging experiential adoption of touchscreen technologies. Univ. Access Inf. Soc. 19(2), 295–310 (2018). https://doi.org/10.1007/s10209-018-0638-0
17. Petrovcic, A., Rogelj, A., Dolnicar, V.: Smart but not adapted enough: Heuristic evaluation of smartphone launchers with an adapted interface and assistive technologies for older adults. Comput. Hum. Behav. 79, 123–136 (2018). https://doi.org/10.1016/j.chb.2017.10.021

18. Prates, R., Barbosa, S.: Introdução à Teoria e Prática da Interação Humano Computador fundamentada na Engenharia Semiótica. In: Kowaltowski, T., Breitman, K. (Orgs.) Jornada de Atualização em Informática, 2007. Editora PUC, Rio de Janeiro (2007)

19. Rocha, E., Padovani, S.: Usabilidade e acessibilidade em smartphones: identificação de características do envelhecimento e suas implicações para o design de interface de smartphones. Ergodesign HCI **4**, 58–66 (2016). https://doi.org/10.22570/ergodesignhci.v4iEspecial.119

20. Rocha, E., Padovani, S.: Conduzindo Focus Group com idosos: Compreendendo como interagem e querem aprender a utilizar smartphones. In: 16° USIHC, Blucher Design Proceedings, vol. 3 (2017). ISSN 2318-6968. https://doi.org/10.5151/16ergodesign-0258

21. Sacramento, C., et al.: Comunicabilidade no Facebook: uma Avaliação da Interação de Jovens e Idosos com o MAC-g. In: Proceedings of the 14th Brazilian Symposium on Human Factors in Computing Systems (IHC 2015), Salvador, Brazil (2015)

22. Salman, H., Ahmad, W., Sulaiman, S.: Usability evaluation of the smartphone user interface in supporting elderly users from experts' perspective. IEEE Access **6** (2018). https://doi.org/10.1109/ACCESS.2018.2827358

23. Salman, H.M., Wan Ahmad, W.F., Sulaiman, S.: Heuristic evaluation of the smartphone applications in supporting elderly. In: Saeed, F., Gazem, N., Mohammed, F., Busalim, A. (eds.) IRICT 2018. AISC, vol. 843, pp. 781–790. Springer, Cham (2019). https://doi.org/10.1007/978-3-319-99007-1_72

24. Tsai, T.-H., Tseng, K., Chang, Y.-S.: Testing the usability of smartphone surface gestures on different sizes of smartphones by different age groups of users (2017). https://doi.org/10.1016/j.chb.2017.05.013

25. Vaportzis, E., Clausen, M., Gow, A.: Older adults perceptions of technology and barriers to interacting with tablet computers: a focus group study. Front. Psychol. (2017). https://doi.org/10.3389/fpsyg.2017.01687

26. Wildenbos, G., Peute, L., Jaspers, M.: Aging barriers influencing mobile health usability for older adults: a literature based framework (MOLD-US). Int. J. Med. Inform. **114**, 66–75 (2018). ISSN 1386-5056. https://doi.org/10.1016/j.ijmedinf.2018.03.012

27. .Yang, H.-L., Lin, S.-L.: The reasons why elderly mobile users adopt ubiquitous mobile so-cial service. Comput. Hum. Behav. **93**, 62–75 (2019). https://doi.org/10.1016/j.chb.2018.12.005

28. Zain, A.: Aging-friendly smartphones: an analysis of design and user-interface to understand smartphone 'usability' for elderly citizens. In: Conference: Senex: III. Congress of Aging Studies for Graduate Students. Akdeniz University, Antalya, Turkey (2019)

29. Zhao, X., et al.: Smartphone application training program improves smartphone usage competency and quality of life among the elderly in an elder university in China: a randomized (2020). https://doi.org/10.1016/j.ijmedinf.2019.104010

Users' Perceptions of a Digital Stress Self-monitoring Application: Research Insights to Design a Practical Innovation

Myriam Sillevis Smitt[1]([✉]), Mehdi Montakhabi[1,2], Jessica Morton[3], Cora van Leeuwen[1], Klaas Bombeke[3], and An Jacobs[1]

[1] imec-SMIT, Vrije Universiteit Brussel, Pleinlaan 9, 1050 Brussels, Belgium
myriam.sillevissmitt@imec.be

[2] Center of Energy Technologies (CET), Department of Business Development and Technology (BTECH), Aarhus University, Aarhus, Denmark

[3] imec-mict-UGent, De Krook, Miriam Makebaplein 1, 9000 Ghent, Belgium

Abstract. Self-monitoring is considered a promising tool for self-management in clinical mental health, such as for coping with excessive stress. Detecting debilitating stress before the onset of a psychopathology is becoming more of interest both for practitioners and the scientific community. However, the development of mental well-being technology focusing on stress is disrupted by the complexity of accurately measuring stress, as no clear idea exists on the construct and how it should be measured. There is also limited knowledge on the perception of perceived quality of the outcomes from a stress algorithm and the variety in its behavioural consequences. Therefore, the purpose of this study is to explore the impact of such digital self-monitoring technology for stress. It applies a qualitative method, by using semi-structured interviews. The most important resulting themes to users of this application were data-interpretation and a request for transparency. Results indicated that the majority of the predictions of the stress algorithm were not in line with the expectations of the users. The implications of these findings reveal how stress algorithms can make participants doubt their own self judgment on assessing their daily stress levels.

Keywords: Self-monitoring · Personal informatics · Mental health · Stress · Stress algorithm

1 Introduction

It is well documented that the experience of stress, and the many forms it can manifest itself, are considered an important precursor for mental, cognitive and physical health problems [1, 2]. Stress can be triggered by negative thoughts about the past, present and future, inducing a physiological response [3]. The inability to recover from repetitive stress related events, could lead to chronic stress responses and cause diseases. The use of personal informatics, referring to personal data derived from behaviour and physiological

© The Author(s), under exclusive license to Springer Nature Switzerland AG 2022
M. Antona and C. Stephanidis (Eds.): HCII 2022, LNCS 13308, pp. 325–341, 2022.
https://doi.org/10.1007/978-3-031-05028-2_22

parameters, has been considered to be a promising tool for self-management in clinical mental health, such as managing excessive stress by digital self-monitoring [4].

The detection of debilitating stress before the onset of a psychopathology has become more relevant to both practitioners and the scientific community [5, 6]. However, the development of technology to measure mental well-being is inhibited by the complexity of accurate measurement [7] as there is no clear construct of how stress, for instance, should be measured [8, 9].

Advances in wearable technology have allowed for continuous data collection. The abundance and combination of different physiological data can be used by algorithms to predict and determine behavioural patterns. The complexity of measuring stress could possibly be handled by machine learning algorithms [10]. The problem is that sensor measurements have a tendency to reduce complex phenomena to variables that can be measured, such as stress being simplified to particular heart rate patterns [8]. This is why algorithm development requires consistent and ongoing involvement with users and their data during the development of stress detection technologies.

Additionally, there is limited knowledge on how users interact with algorithmically detected stress, what the perceived quality is and what the behavioural consequences are of these stress detections [11]. Therefore, the purpose of this study is to explore the influence of digital self-monitoring for stress on participants. The core research question this study aims to answer is: 'What are users' perceptions when using a digital self-monitoring for stress tool?'.

The novel contributions of this paper are 1) describing the different perceptions towards using a digital self-monitoring tool for stress, 2) demonstrating the relevance and need of interpretable algorithms for measuring stress, and 3) showing the influence of a self-monitoring for stress application on participant's their confidence in self-judgment.

The remainder of this paper is structured as follows. First, we elaborate on the current state of self-monitoring technology. Next, we introduce the relationship between self-monitoring data and algorithms. This is followed by the methodology and results of the qualitative interviews. Finally, we present a discussion and the key findings that reflect on the design and ethical implications that arose from the study.

2 Background

2.1 Self-monitoring

Self-monitoring is the collection of a person's physiological, behavioural, and physical data at repetitive intervals, in order to reveal the consistency or variation of patterns in between data points, allowing for intra or inter comparison [12]. By collecting data on oneself, self-reflection can be facilitated, providing new insights and behavioural change as a consequence [13]. Several processes are required before the data can lead to behavioural change. These processes have been developed into frameworks over the last decade and delineate the user's relationship with personal informatics and how that impacts the user [14–17]. All frameworks delineate a similar process, starting with creating awareness, and then reflecting and processing the data, which eventually results in an action. This reflection phase is considered to be the quintessential aspect of self-monitoring. In a qualitative systematic review on self-management for chronic diseases, a recurring theme is the "in-the-moment-understanding" that participants develop through the insights provided by self-monitored data. Seemingly, it is the skill of "in-the-moment-understanding" that users apply to associate the personal informatics with their personal beliefs of their current health [18]. Only recently a few articles shed light on the different interactions users can have with self-monitored data. There is little known about the negative consequences of (self-monitoring) data presented to a user, also known as the dark side of tracking [19]. Eikey and colleagues [11] highlight the negative thought cycles that self-monitoring can provoke, positing that limited attention has been dedicated to understanding the relationship between self-reflection in personal informatics. These negative thought cycles can lead to rumination [3], and potentially undermine the purpose of self-monitoring for health [11]. By rumination we mean recurring negative thoughts that identify with feelings of anxiety, self-doubt, insecurity or low self-efficacy. Feng and colleagues [19] conducted a systematic review on self-tracking studies and state 1) the dearth of information on how participants process the information from self-tracking and 2) the relation between self-monitoring and compulsive thoughts/behaviours.

2.2   Use of Algorithms in Health

Personal informatics can be used by algorithms to predict and determine behavioural patterns. Researchers and experts have shown interest in exploratory data-mining techniques to develop algorithms that may uncover new knowledge hidden within the data that cannot be seen by data inspections through the human eye.

Stress measurements are associated with several challenges that could be handled by machine learning algorithms [9]. Stress experiences are very personal, and individual and subjective differences related to stress and health perception provide another layer of potentially misleading information that algorithms can't easily account for [20]. For example, the differences between stress measures can be related to genetic predispositions, or ethnicity-related differences [21]. Likewise, self-learning algorithms need to be trained with sensor data as well as users' feedback to improve the accuracy of detecting stress.

However, technologies such as machine learning algorithms have come with new challenges. In particular unsupervised machine learning algorithms can have no objective for what the outcome should be, similar to measuring stress. Due to the reliance of algorithmic interpretation of data for wellbeing applications, ethical questions have been raised, such as the misleading societal implications of a non-representative sample [22]. These questions are related to every socio-technological enquiry, but their importance needs to be emphasized when used for determining human health data collected through sensors and wearables [23]. Sensors have a tendency to reduce a complex phenomena such as stress to measurable variables [8], which predominantly exposes the interpretation of sensor data and the tweaking of the algorithm feature statistics to a researchers' bias. Although the source of data collection for a stress algorithm can be clearly stated (such as heart rate, skin conductance, temperature, accelerometer), the functionality of a stress algorithm can remain opaque to users [22]. More attention has been directed in improving the explainability and transparency of complex algorithms [24] to assess potential biases and reduce any barriers of technology adoption. The urge for more transparency and explainability has also been shown through the rise in publications on algorithms that try to win user trust.

3 Methodology

3.1 Participants

A qualitative method with semi-structured interviews was used to evaluate twelve participants' perceptions on their stress predictions. Through a purposive selection method, the interviewees were recruited from a cohort of one hundred and thirty participants taking part in the second epoch of data collection (February 2021) in a study called 'Nervocity', which investigated stress experiences in the city of Ghent. The selection of the interviewees was based on variety in education, stress levels, gender, living circumstances, and living location that represented the demographic characteristics of Ghent's citizens.

In this study, participants were excluded if they were younger than 18 years and had been diagnosed with: schizophrenia, bipolar disorder, borderline, psychotic episodes, personality disorder, or post traumatic stress disorder. In case of doubt, candidates could request a consultation with a clinical psychologist, who judged their readiness for participation. The research design was approved by the ethical commission of the research institute.

3.2 Experimental Design

For two weeks, all participants wore an arm wrist wearable and answered questions about their daily stress experiences, triggered by an Ecological Momentary Assessment (EMA) methodology, on a specifically developed smartphone application for the Nervocity study (see Appendix 1). The data from the wearable and the EMA's were processed through imec's predictive stress algorithm [10] and visually accessible in the UI.

The wearable and wireless bracelet, called Chill+, was developed by the research company imec (see Appendix 2 for the technical features of the wearable). It can monitor multiple parameters through the user's wrist, such as skin conductance (measured by Galvanic skin response), heart rate (with a Photoplethysmogram, PPG sensor), temperature and movement. On the basis of these parameters and by the use of imec's algorithm [10] the degree of stress experienced by participants was estimated. These measurements were stored on the wearable and could be sent via Bluetooth for analysis, or they were read out via USB.[1]

---

[1] The Nervocity application had some boundary conditions due to the technical restrictions. The stress outcomes had a 15 min delay in being shown in the smartphone application, which did not allow for a realtime association between the participant's experience and the algorithm predictions. Additionally, the participants were not able to associate stress outcomes from previous days through a timeseries. This was a conscious choice by the design team as stress classification happened per minute and timeline graphs would become too variable to be interpreted at all. The technology also encompassed EMA's that were triggered through wearable data. For the purpose of this study we only address the qualitative data related to interpretation of the stress algorithm and not the EMA interactions.

All participants were informed on the purpose of the study and what personal data the stress algorithm used to detect stress. All study related information was written in an informed consent form and recorded in video material. No detailed information was provided on the EMA trigger methodology for questions received in the Nervocity application. Participants were informed that those smartphone questions could be linked to the wearable data, but also could be sent arbitrarily.

Interviews took place in a digital environment, through Microsoft Teams software. All interviews were recorded and during the interview the researcher took notes. After every interview the researcher wrote a summary and categorised the data by the topics discussed in the interviews (i.e., motivation, self-awareness, personal stress experience, covid impact on life, stress reduction, self-monitoring, ecological momentary assessment, user interface experience, and use of wearable). After transcribing the topics of interest for this study, the data was coded in MAXQDA through a thematic analysis [25] and resulted in themes that reflected participants perceptions on the experiences of the stress predictions.

4   Results

4.1   Demographics

In total, 12 participants (8 female, 4 male) were interviewed, with an average age of 53 years old (SD = 12). Several relevant variables were inquired at the intake moment before the start of the study (see Table 1). Tech proficiency was very high in the current sample, measured with an average score of 4 on a 5-point Likert scale (ranging from 'totally disagree' to 'totally agree'), originating from the annual imec.digimeter report about the possession, use and attitude towards media and technology in Flanders [26]. Next, the overall happiness level reported by the current sample is moderate to high, as measured with the question "All things considered, how happy would you say you are?" on a slider scale ranging from 0 (very unhappy) to 10 (very happy). Individual stress levels were measured with the Perceived Stress Scale (PSS) inquiring experienced stress feelings and thoughts (i.e., the degree to which they feel their life has been unpredictable, out of control and overloaded) during the last month on a 5-point Likert scale (ranging from 'never' to 'always', scored 0–4) [27]. The total sum score of the 10 items answered by the current sample is considered as moderate individual stress (cut-off range between 14–26). Additionally, the average daily stress level, subjectively reported during the 2 week field study on a slider scale ranging from 1 (not stressed at all) to 10 (totally stressed), was rather low to moderate. The coping style for stress feelings during the past 2 weeks before study participation was also inquired with the Emotion Regulation Scale [28]. For each subtype of emotion regulation, three items were rated on a 5-point Likert scale (ranging from 'totally disagree' to 'totally agree', scored 1–5). Participants reported rather high integrative emotion regulation (e.g., " I mostly tried to understand why I was experiencing stress"), moderate to high suppression (e.g., "I almost always tried not to show my stress") and somewhat lower scores for dysregulation (e.g., "I sometimes did things that I really didn't want to do because of the stress"). Finally, user experience was inquired after study participation with the question "Did the study meet your expectations?" and a 5-point Likert scale, resulting in rather mixed answers and thus a neutral average. Also, the User Burden Scale was used to get an idea of the user burden when using the Nervocity technology (wearable + application) with 20 items on a 5-point Likert scale (ranging from 'never' to 'always', scored 0–4). These items touched upon the physical, time and social, mental and emotional and privacy burden, and general difficulty of use [29]. In general, experienced user burden was very low.

Table 1. Summary of demographic and context variables measured before, during and after study participation.

Variable	Mean (SD)/N (%)
Gender	8 females (67%)
Age	53 years (12)
Tech proficiency (1:5)	4.29 (0.69)
Happiness level (0:10)	6.92 (1.0)
Perceived stress (0:40)	17.33 (5.37)
Daily subjective stress level (1:10)	3.78 (1.67)
Integrative emotion regulation (1:5)	3.75 (0.62)
Suppressive emotion regulation (1:5)	2.92 (0.79)
Dysregulation (1:5)	2.47 (0.90)
Study expectations met (1:5)	3.33 (0.89)
User burden (0:80)	13.58 (7.57)

The thematic analysis yielded two main themes: "data interpretation" and "request for transparency". These themes were further divided in five subthemes (Fig. 1 shows a brief overview of the theme structure). The sub-theme "Discrepancy between self evaluation and algorithm" is the most substantial of the (sub)themes and further consists of two distinct categories "the ruminators" and "the rejectors", explained in more detail below. These are preliminary findings and are subject to change and recategorization when the other additional thirteen interviews from the Nervocity study have been analysed.

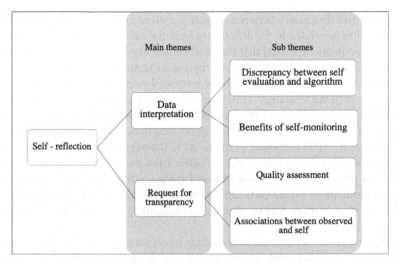

Fig. 1. Qualitative data theme overview

4.2 Data-Interpretation Theme

Discrepancy Between Self Evaluation of Stress and Algorithmic Stress.
The majority of the participants experienced a discrepancy between their perception of daily experienced stress and the stress predictions coming from the stress algorithm. The most frequent occurring comment was that the algorithm categorized stress high(er) and more frequent in contrast to the participant's perception: "It was indicated that I was stressed while I was actually feeling very good." (P01) and "I don't like it when the wearable says something different from what I experience." (P02). Due to this perceived disparity it was possible to discern two types of participants, being 1) ruminator and 2) rejector of the technology. These types were based on the behaviour and reported reactions towards the algorithmic detected stress.

As the name implies, the "ruminators" are the group of participants that experienced a lot of worry associated with the predicted stress. They tended to accept the indicated stress level and this resulted in them questioning their own perception and judgement. Furthermore, this resulted in feelings of insecurity, as they were mostly concerned about what they should do with this information: "If I showed the app to my friends, they would tell me that I should look for another job." (P03).

Indeed, these participants would overanalyse the results and tended to trust the findings of the algorithm more than their own perception of experienced stress levels: "The app indicated much more stress than I felt. Is it the app or is it my perception?" (P02). Another example is: "I started to think that maybe it was just me. I know that I am sensitive to tension and stress, but participation still makes me doubt, should I do something with this information now?" (P03). This confusion was experienced by ruminators in regard to their supposed actions towards the detected stress: "The wearable registers stress at times when I think I don't experience stress. I do not know to what extent it is correct." (P04) and "I have stress [referring to technology] when I don't expect it, and I have no solution for it." (P05).

The cognitive dissonance between the self perceived and the algorithmic stress outcome seemed to be related to the differences in initial motivation to join the study. For instance, participants expressed that they had certain expectations, such as confirming their self-perception of low or high stress by use of technology: "The theme interests me. I want to gain more insight into my own stress. I want to know if my feelings and experiences match the wearable." (P03) and "I know myself that I regularly experience stress. I've been thinking about the idea of buying a smartwatch for a while now. By joining the study I thought it would be a good idea to see if it works effectively and what I think of it." (P04). Another example is "In the beginning I did not trust the system, but because the second week did not differ from the first week and the type and frequency of the recorded stress was similar, I started to think that It was me after all." (P03). The participants expressed being sensitive to experiencing stress and partaking in this study resulted in more doubts: "But do I do something with this information [stress detection]?" (P03).

The second group of participants decided to reject the technology as the discrepancy between their own stress experience and the algorithmic findings resulted in a disbelief of distrust in the technology. This group was therefore called "the rejectors of technology". The rejection was a result of a fair bit of reflection, for instance if the participant started to worry at first due to high recorded stress, however instead of adopting the results from the algorithm she decided to take distance from the self-monitored data: "I thought it was very frustrating, and started to worry. I started to wonder if I am so stressed that I can't even detect it myself anymore." (P08). After a week she came to the conclusion that it was not her fault but the system. Then she was able to let it go emotionally.

For another participant the initial motivation was to prove herself how successful her stress reduction techniques were. However, when she experienced that the stress data was not in line with her perception she got annoyed: "I only see orange [high stress] while I think I do not experience any stress." (P07). Later in the conversation, she indicated that this made her a bit angry: "I feel a bit resented." (P07). Eventually, she dismissed the data completely: "I am not experiencing any stress at the moment and I think the study did not measure any stress either." (P07).

Rejecting the personal informatics can take place due to disagreement, but can also be a means to avoid thoughts of rumination and self-doubts. One participant mentioned she was avoiding looking at the data. She describes that when she is not experiencing stress but the stress algorithm is, she does not want to know: "If it doesn't bother me, it is better to leave it that way." (P11). Implying that she rather did not want to look at the user interface anymore. She even expressed that the difference between her own opinion and the algorithm outcome was quite funny: "Sometimes I was just busy with work, household work, then it indicated that as a stress peak, while I didn't think it was. I thought it was comedic." (P11).

In contrast to the discrepancy between self-perception and the algorithmic outcomes, one participant did not question the self-monitored data and identified completely with the stress outcomes: "It confirmed to me that I am quickly triggered by stress." (P09).

Benefits of Self-monitoring. The use of self-monitoring for stress made several participants reflect on their behaviour, emotions and cognition. Although several participants expressed doubts about the accuracy of the algorithmic predictions, partaking in the study did have advantages that were independent from the evaluation of the technology. Regularly, self-monitoring studies have delineated the influence of personal informatics. In this study we found that participants expressed more 1) self-awareness, such as "I have been listening more to my body" (P04), 2) better recognition of behavioural patterns when stressed, such as "I became more aware of the hours in the day and what I did at that time because of the study." (P04), referring to the smartphone questions about their stress experience, and 3) a better sense of time and activities due to the reflective questions. It made participants reflect on their day and on their emotions more than they would do without the use of the wearable, together with the triggered smartphone questions: "If I think about it, I act differently when I am stressed compared to when I am at ease, I am more on edge when I am stressed, otherwise I never have that." (P09).

4.3 Request for Transparency Theme

Associations Between Observed and Self. Regardless of the type of emotional response the participants had to their stress predictions, most of them expressed a curiosity to understand how stress can be determined. For instance, participants expressed an interest in wanting to know how their heart rate was associated with stress: "I want to be able to make associations between the data and my own experiences." (P06). Or participants looked for explanations themselves: "I think that when my wrist is on my chest when I am resting, it raises the temperature and measures high stress. I think that's not right. Similarly, there were times when the sun was shining on the watch, causing the temperature to rise and incorrectly measuring stress and making me sweat a lot. So every time I am active, stress is measured." (P12). Another participant interpreted the stress predictions as positive stress: "I came to the conclusion that I did not understand that stress was detected while I did not experience it and so I thought it was interpreted as positive stress, but I do not think that was correct." (P01).

Quality Assessment of Algorithm. Participants who expressed a discrepancy between the self perceived stress and the algorithm outcome, wondered about the quality of the stress algorithm. The stress predictions were considered to be of interest, but due to the distrust in the stress algorithm, participants felt the need to identify the reliability of the algorithm. There was a need for accountability and explainability of the algorithmic predictions. As one participant stated he finds it difficult to deal with the high stress values. If he understands better what the cause of it is or how it is detected he would feel more at ease: "I want to know more about how stress is determined, what is the cause? If I can understand it better, then I know how to deal with it better." (P05).

Another participant stated that she thought the frequency of her high stress prediction was very excessive: "I am in the orange zone [high stress] a lot, I wonder if this is correct. I thought to myself more to be in the yellow zone [light stress]. I started to question what has actually been measured?" (P04). She questioned the possibility of measuring stress: "Only two parameters are measured, temperature and heart rate, how can that measure stress? Is that possible?" (P04).

Also the question for comparing own predictions with that of other participants was raised: "I would like to be able to compare my data with that of others, do they also register that much stress? I also would like to know more about how they detect stress, so I can better assess if it actually is stress or not. Now I have no clue and it makes me doubt. Although I know I am sensitive to stress...but is it really the case? I can't interpret it very well." (P03).

A few participants did not articulate strong thoughts on the algorithmic stress outcomes. It seemed that the lack of interpretability of the data resulted in assuming that the technology is still in development: "I assumed that it is a study and that it [stress algorithm] is still under development." (P12). One participant expressed that human interpretation is not always correct and sometimes technology is flawed: "It is an interplay, it depends from situation to situation. Sometimes the wearable is wrong, sometimes I'm wrong. I assume that technology is not always correct and that we are not robots." (P06).

5   Discussion

This study has shown that the algorithm categorised higher stress than participants perceived to be correct, leading to differing attitudes. The primary attitudes that were observed were participants who kept ruminating, those who rejected algorithmic stress detection and a few who remained indifferent. It is this variety of the different attitudes towards the use of the stress algorithm that provided new insights and further discussion for its future development.

It is only recently that studies demonstrated the dark side of self monitoring [11, 19]. They have shown that too much emphasis on individuals' thoughts can impede their mental health. Eikey and colleagues [11] pointed out that the difference between negative thought cycles (such as rumination) and constructive self-reflection could relate to parameters such as motivation, goals that identify with the user's self-worth and culturally valued morals. Stress continues to have a negative connotation and the purpose in western societies remains to reduce stress or to improve oneself to better deal with stress [30]. Participants focusing on determining how high their stress levels are can potentially demonstrate the emotional battle they have with the concept of stress and their work life balance.

In the current data, we found that several participants wanted to confirm their own stress observations, which could indicate that they initially doubted or questioned their own judgment of stress perception. Participants showed a high interest in their own stress levels, reflected by high integrative emotion regulation scores (see Table 1). Commencing the study with high levels of self-doubts or low self-efficacy on their stress judgment could be of influence in how participants interpreted the stress detections from the algorithm. Although for some participants the algorithmic stress detection confirmed their initial ideas, the frequency of high stress that was recorded for them could have felt like a moral judgment and made them question themselves or the technology.

Lupton [31] and Feng and colleagues [19] mention the neoliberal shift to feeling responsible for one's individual health and well-being. Commercial digital health innovations are built on the premise of improving well-being, and tracking technologies imply the individual as deficient in being knowledgeable enough to make health and well-being related decisions [23]. This implicit tendency could possibly influence the relationship users nowadays have with technology and makes them susceptible to depend on algorithmic data to confirm the beliefs one has about oneself. Interestingly enough, a few participants pointed out the experiences of self-doubt when being confronted with the stress predictions, yet decided to be in disagreement with this algorithmic stress output at some point.

The secondary theme in this study originated from the discrepancy participants experienced with their stress predictions. All participants were informed of the type of data collection to determine the stress outcome and were aware that the answers to the smartphone questions, not further discussed in this article, helped them to further personalise their stress predictions. In order to detect biases or to determine the trustworthiness in the algorithmic stress predictions, participants followed their own explanations or expressed their need for explainability of the algorithm. Verifying and understanding an algorithm for personal use is an important aspect for adopting the technology [32].

Independent from how participants interpreted their detected stress, many expressed that reflecting on their stress benefited their own self-awareness. This is in line with many other studies that use self-monitoring for well-being [13, 33–35].

5.1 The Insights to Design a Self-monitoring Practical Innovation

Technology developers should be aware of the behavioural implications of applications that show personal informatics and algorithmic predictions. Although the characteristics of the group of participants that experienced rumination is unclear, it is suggested to take the potential negative consequences of personal informatics into account in the design of mental well-being technologies. Additional emphasis must be placed on the differences in data interpretation and if technology meets the initial purpose of its design. A few aspects need to be considered when designing user interfaces that show well-being related algorithmic predictions:

- A need for greater explainability when using algorithmic predictions related to health. This will help to increase the users confidence in deciding to trust or distrust the algorithm.
- Increase interpretability through developing a comparative framework, such as linking the algorithmic predictions of users to their notes and their calendar activities.
- Increase interpretability and trustworthiness by developing normality curves, enabling anonymous data comparison between other users.
- Defining 1) the user's motivation to use the technology, 2) their self-efficacy in self-evaluation, and 3) their perceived stress levels in order to shape the type of information and communication style that is provided in the design of the UI.

5.2 Limitations and Opportunities for Future Research

The current study has limitations and therefore opportunities for further research. The study had a small sample size and was performed during Covid restrictions. This could be remedied in the future by a larger sample size which represents society more broadly and in more representative living circumstances.

Measuring stress is subject to individual interpretation. For this study we provided a broad description of stress as the debilitating effect of stress, which is very subjective. The qualitative data, not discussed in the findings of this study, demonstrated a homogeneous interpretation that stress is predominantly a negative term [20]. However, when participants felt unable to associate the predicted algorithmic stress data with their own perception, they classified the predicted stress as a form of positive stress or as physiological stress through exercising. Therefore, studying the ontology of stress and its associations with psychological traits is required for future research.

Many interviewed participants who participated in the Nervocity study expressed an interest in technology or expressed a curiosity in understanding their stress levels. Due to this selection bias, it could be that participants were more prone to be influenced by the outcomes of the stress algorithm. Future research should be aware of the impact of stress predicting algorithms and account for potential adverse effects. A shift in focus is also needed to determine what kind of psychosocial parameters are related to having a debilitating interaction instead of a constructive relationship with self-monitoring for stress.

The UI design of the smartphone application undoubtedly had an influence on how participants perceived and interacted with the stress detections. The technical limitations did not allow for more granularity and variation in design choices. Aspects that were of influence were: colour choice, wording, timeline format, etc. Future research should perform A/B testing on different types of UI designs while involving end users.

Participant involvement required two weeks of usage of the technology and interacting with stress predictions. This short time window can not establish stable behavioural patterns when it comes to the usage and interpretation of predicted stress outcomes. The novelty and motivation overruled the honest judgement of the technology. Longitudinal data would demonstrate differences more thoroughly when it comes to evaluation of the stress data and how it could have impacted their lives.

Finally, although the technology for the stress algorithm is a self-learning algorithm, the initial dataset for this algorithm was developed on a white-collar dominated data set and therefore biases could be present. For instance, one of the most recurring observations by the participants was high stress during office hours or during long periods of sitting. Participants consequently associated their predicted high stress with work activities and assumed that their work caused more stress than they were able to realise themselves. This could be true, but could be a default feature of the previous trained dataset of this algorithm, with false assumptions as a consequence. Qualitative user input is required to highlight contextual situations that could improve and correct the efficacy of the predictive model.

6   Key Insights

- Participants had a tendency to consider the predicted stress outcomes being more objective than their own self-evaluation of stress. This resulted in self-doubt or rejection of the technology. The important take-away message here is the influence technology can have, regardless of its reliability.
- Using a stress prediction algorithm can help to reflect on daily behaviour patterns and create more self-awareness. This is independent from the perceived reliability of the algorithm.
- The type of intention or motivation for using a stress algorithm could possibly be associated with negative thought cycles and lead to rumination and aggravating mental well-being.
- Participants that expressed a low interpretability of the predicted stress measures, resulted in a distrust in the algorithm or development of their own theories to explain the data. More explainability of the algorithm is required to support the user's decision making if and when an algorithmic stress prediction can be trusted and therefore utilised.

7   Concluding Remarks

The study explored users' interaction with digital self-monitoring for stress. Based on the results of twelve semi-structured interviews, two main themes were derived: 'data interpretation' and 'request for transparency'. A majority of the predictions of the stress algorithm were not in line with the expectations of the participants. This resulted in a high level of self-reflection that instead of providing insight, created more self-doubt or adversity towards the technology. Participants seemed to rely on the algorithmic stress detections and started questioning the capability of their own judgment when assessing their own mental health.

Acknowledgements. This work was supported in part by VLAIO, Stad GENT, imec through the Nervocity project. Mehdi Montakhabi is funded by the Flemish Government through the FWO-SBO project SNIPPET-S007619. Cora van Leeuwen is funded by SBO-grant S005221N, funded by The Research Foundation – Flanders. The authors would like to thank Tim Coggins and Shirley Elprama for proofreading.

Appendix 1

See Fig. 2.

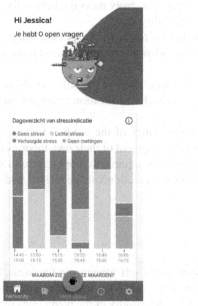

Fig. 2. User interface visualisations: visual on the left show stress prediction during the day, visual on the right shows aggregated stress during the week.

Appendix 2

Technical specifications wearable Chill+

	Parameter	Details	Units	
Physiological signals	GSR	Dynamic range	1–20	μS
		Dynamic range	0.01–2	μS
		Sampling frequency	Configurable (16–256)	Hz
		Resolution	16	bits
	PPG	Dynamic range	50	μA
		Resolution	22	bits
		Sampling frequency	Configurable (64–256)	Hz
	Skin temperature	Dynamic range	10–45	°C
		Sampling frequency	1	Hz
		Resolution	12	bits
Contextual signals	Accelerometer	Dynamic range	±2	g
		Sampling frequency	32	Hz
		Resolution	16	bits
	Gyroscope	Dynamic range	±250	(°/sec)
		Sampling frequency	32	Hz
		Resolution	16	bits

	Details	Units	
System parameters	Operating voltage	3–4.2	V
	Charging time	90	Minutes
	Autonomy (Storage)	24	Hours
	Operating mode	Storage and streaming	–

References

1. Marin, M.-F., et al.: Chronic stress, cognitive functioning and mental health. Neurobiol. Learn. Mem. **96**(4), 583–595 (2011). https://doi.org/10.1016/j.nlm.2011.02.016
2. Richardson, S., Shaffer, J.A., Falzon, L., Krupka, D., Davidson, K.W., Edmondson, D.: Meta-analysis of perceived stress and its association with incident coronary heart disease. Am. J. Cardiol. **110**(12), 1711–1716 (2012). https://doi.org/10.1016/j.amjcard.2012.08.004

3. Brosschot, J.F.: Markers of chronic stress: prolonged physiological activation and (un)conscious perseverative cognition. Neurosci. Biobehav. Rev. **35**(1), 46–50 (2010). https://doi.org/10.1016/j.neubiorev.2010.01.004

4. Murnane, E.L., et al.: Self-monitoring practices, attitudes, and needs of individuals with bipolar disorder: implications for the design of technologies to manage mental health. J. Am. Med. Inform. Assoc. **23**(3), 477–484 (2016). https://doi.org/10.1093/jamia/ocv165

5. Crossley, G.H., Boyle, A., Vitense, H., Chang, Y., Mead, R.H.: The CONNECT (clinical evaluation of remote notification to reduce time to clinical decision) trial. J. Am. Coll. Cardiol. **57**(10), 1181–1189 (2011). https://doi.org/10.1016/j.jacc.2010.12.012

6. Firth, J., Torous, J., Yung, A.R.: Ecological momentary assessment and beyond: The rising interest in e-mental health research. J. Psychiatr. Res. **80**, 3–4 (2016). https://doi.org/10.1016/j.jpsychires.2016.05.002

7. Reisinger, M., Röderer, K.: 'I'm fine, thank you – Contextualizing Wellbeing and Mental Health for Persuasive Technologies, p. 6

8. Müller, J., Fàbregues, S., Guenther, E.A., Romano, M.J.: Using sensors in organizational research—clarifying rationales and validation challenges for mixed methods. Front. Psychol. **10**, 1188 (2019). https://doi.org/10.3389/fpsyg.2019.01188

9. Smets, E., De Raedt, W., Van Hoof, C.: Into the wild: the challenges of physiological stress detection in laboratory and ambulatory settings. IEEE J. Biomed. Health Inform. **23**(2), 463–473 (2019). https://doi.org/10.1109/JBHI.2018.2883751

10. Smets, E.: Towards large-scale physiological stress detection in an ambulant environment, p. 198

11. Eikey, E.V., et al.: Beyond self-reflection: introducing the concept of rumination in personal informatics. Pers. Ubiquit. Comput. **25**(3), 601–616 (2021). https://doi.org/10.1007/s00779-021-01573-w

12. Karter, A.J., et al.: Longitudinal study of new and prevalent use of self-monitoring of blood glucose. Diabetes Care **29**(8), 1757–1763 (2006). https://doi.org/10.2337/dc06-2073

13. Compernolle, S., et al.: Effectiveness of interventions using self-monitoring to reduce sedentary behavior in adults: a systematic review and meta-analysis. Int. J. Behav. Nutr. Phys. Act. **16**(1), 63 (2019). https://doi.org/10.1186/s12966-019-0824-3

14. Baumer, E.P.S.: Reflective informatics: conceptual dimensions for designing technologies of reflection. In: Proceedings of the 33rd Annual ACM Conference on Human Factors in Computing Systems, Seoul Republic of Korea, April 2015, pp. 585–594 (2015). https://doi.org/10.1145/2702123.2702234

15. Wolf, G.I., De Groot, M.: A conceptual framework for personal science. Front. Comput. Sci. **2**, 21 (2020). https://doi.org/10.3389/fcomp.2020.00021

16. Li, I., Dey, A., Forlizzi, J.: A stage-based model of personal informatics systems, p. 10 (2010)

17. Epstein, D.A., Ping, A., Fogarty, J., Munson, S.A.: A lived informatics model of personal informatics. In: Proceedings of the 2015 ACM International Joint Conference on Pervasive and Ubiquitous Computing - UbiComp 2015, Osaka, Japan, pp. 731–742 (2015). https://doi.org/10.1145/2750858.2804250

18. Tadas, S., Coyle, D.: Barriers to and facilitators of technology in cardiac rehabilitation and self-management: systematic qualitative grounded theory review. J. Med. Internet Res. **22**(11), e18025 (2020). https://doi.org/10.2196/18025

19. Feng, S., Mäntymäki, M., Dhir, A., Salmela, H.: How self-tracking and the quantified self promote health and well-being: systematic review. J. Med. Internet Res. **23**(9), e25171 (2021). https://doi.org/10.2196/25171

20. Sharma, S., Singh, G., Sharma, M.: A comprehensive review and analysis of supervised-learning and soft computing techniques for stress diagnosis in humans. Comput. Biol. Med. **134**, 104450 (2021). https://doi.org/10.1016/j.compbiomed.2021.104450

21. Manrai, A.K., et al.: Genetic misdiagnoses and the potential for health disparities. N. Engl. J. Med. **375**(7), 655–665 (2016). https://doi.org/10.1056/NEJMsa1507092
22. Cabitza, F., Rasoini, R., Gensini, G.F.: Unintended consequences of machine learning in medicine. JAMA **318**(6), 517 (2017). https://doi.org/10.1001/jama.2017.7797
23. Lupton, D.: Health promotion in the digital era: a critical commentary. Health Promot. Int. **30**(1), 174–183 (2015). https://doi.org/10.1093/heapro/dau091
24. Morley, J., Floridi, L., Kinsey, L., Elhalal, A.: From what to how: an initial review of publicly available ai ethics tools, methods and research to translate principles into practices. Sci. Eng. Ethics **26**(4), 2141–2168 (2019). https://doi.org/10.1007/s11948-019-00165-5
25. Braun, V., Clarke, V.: Using thematic analysis in psychology. Qual. Res. Psychol. **3**(2), 77–101 (2006). https://doi.org/10.1191/1478088706qp063oa
26. Vandendriessche, K., Steenberghs, E., Matheve, A., Georges, A., De Marez, L.: imec. digimeter 2020: Digitale Trends in Vlaanderen (2021). https://biblio.ugent.be/publication/8717212/file/8717464
27. Cohen, S., Kamarck, T., Mermelstein, R.: A global measure of perceived stress. J. Health Soc. Behav. **24**(4), 385 (1983). https://doi.org/10.2307/2136404
28. Roth, G., Assor, A., Niemiec, C.P., Ryan, R.M., Deci, E.L.: The emotional and academic consequences of parental conditional regard: comparing conditional positive regard, conditional negative regard, and autonomy support as parenting practices. Dev. Psychol. **45**(4), 1119–1142 (2009). https://doi.org/10.1037/a0015272
29. Suh, H., Shahriaree, N., Hekler, E.B., Kientz, J.A.: Developing and validating the user burden scale: a tool for assessing user burden in computing systems. In: Proceedings of the 2016 CHI Conference on Human Factors in Computing Systems - CHI 2016, Santa Clara, California, USA, pp. 3988–3999 (2016). https://doi.org/10.1145/2858036.2858448
30. Donnelly, T.T., Long, B.C.: Stress discourse and western biomedical ideology: rewriting stress. Issues Ment. Health Nurs. **24**(4), 397–408 (2003). https://doi.org/10.1080/01612840305316
31. Lupton, D.: The digitally engaged patient: self-monitoring and self-care in the digital health era. Soc. Theory Health **11**(3), 256–270 (2013). https://doi.org/10.1057/sth.2013.10
32. Alexander, V., Blinder, C., Zak, P.J.: Why trust an algorithm? Performance, cognition, and neurophysiology. Comput. Hum. Behav. **89**, 279–288 (2018). https://doi.org/10.1016/j.chb.2018.07.026
33. Bray, E.P., Holder, R., Mant, J., McManus, R.J.: Does self-monitoring reduce blood pressure? Meta-analysis with meta-regression of randomized controlled trials. Ann. Med. **42**(5), 371–386 (2010). https://doi.org/10.3109/07853890.2010.489567
34. Fletcher, B.R., Hartmann-Boyce, J., Hinton, L., McManus, R.J.: The effect of self-monitoring of blood pressure on medication adherence and lifestyle factors: a systematic review and meta-analysis. Am. J. Hypertens. **28**(10), 1209–1221 (2015). https://doi.org/10.1093/ajh/hpv008
35. Kanejima, Y., Kitamura, M., Izawa, K.P.: Self-monitoring to increase physical activity in patients with cardiovascular disease: a systematic review and meta-analysis. Aging Clin. Exp. Res. **31**(2), 163–173 (2018). https://doi.org/10.1007/s40520-018-0960-7

The User-Centred Design in the Development of a Platform for Teletherapy for People with Aphasia

Bianca Spelter[1]([⊠]), Sabine Corsten[2], Lara Diehlmann[2], Almut Plath[2], and Juliane Leinweber[1]

[1] Faculty of Engineering and Health, University of Applied Sciences and Arts Hildesheim/Holzminden/Göttingen, Health Campus Göttingen, Göttingen, Germany
{bianca.spelter,juliane.leinweber}@hawk.de
[2] Faculty of Healthcare and Nursing, Catholic University of Applied Sciences Mainz, Mainz, Germany
{sabine.corsten,lara.diehlmann,almut.plath}@kh-mz.de

Abstract. Aphasia is an acquired neurogenic language disorder. Teletherapy can improve the access and frequency of care, and is comparable to face-to-face therapy. However, the use of technology can be difficult for people with aphasia (PWA). The project TELL aims to develop and evaluate a platform for teletherapy especially for PWA including a videoconferencing system and therapy-management tools. The primary aim was to specify the known requirements for the platform in user-centred design (UCD) workshops. The secondary aim was to gain first information whether UCD workshops can be conducted via videoconferencing systems with PWA and speech and language therapists (SLTs). On the basis of a catalogue of requirements of the first project phase, initial drafts (wireframes) of the platform were developed. In the UCD workshops the participants were asked to perform tasks within the platform giving verbal feedback. Qualitative analysis and ad-hoc observational checklists were used for evaluation. The analysis of the checklists showed which functions were accessible und intuitive for the users (e.g. set reminders, start therapy session). The qualitative content analysis revealed which elements were experienced positively (e.g., design) or negatively (e.g. font size, location of buttons) as well as further needs expressed by the participants. Results are integrated into constant iterations of the platform development. The user workshops were crucial to specify and revise initial drafts of the platform. UCD allows to constantly focus on the accessibility and user goals of PWA as well as SLTs within the development process. The digital workshops were feasible with both groups.

Keywords: User-centred design · Teletherapy · Aphasia

1 Background

Aphasia is an acquired neurogenic language disorder resulting from an injury to the brain. It involves varying degrees of impairment in spoken language expression and

© The Author(s), under exclusive license to Springer Nature Switzerland AG 2022
M. Antona and C. Stephanidis (Eds.): HCII 2022, LNCS 13308, pp. 342–359, 2022.
https://doi.org/10.1007/978-3-031-05028-2_23

comprehension as well as reading and writing. Depending on an individual's unique set of symptoms, aphasia may result in the loss of the ability to use communication as a tool for life participation [1]. It can lead to several limitations in the daily living of people with aphasia (PWA) such as social isolation [2]. Speech and language therapy aims to reduce the symptoms of aphasia and/or their negative effects on quality of life [3].

For PWA, teletherapy and videoconferencing was temporarily the only way to maintain care in speech and language therapy during the COVID-19 pandemic. Furthermore, teletherapy can improve the access and frequency of care [4]. Although evidence is still scant, the benefit of face-to-face therapy and teletherapy for PWA seems to be comparable [5–7] with initial trends toward better language outcomes in teletherapy via videoconference than usual care [8]. However, the use of technology is linguistically and cognitively demanding and can therefore be challenging for PWA [9]. Current platforms for videoconferences are not completely usable for the therapy with PWA [e.g. 10].

The project TELL[1] aims to develop and evaluate a teletherapy platform especially for PWA with a videoconferencing system and therapy-management tools. Overcoming some of the limitations of standard videoconferencing systems requires a platform which is customized to the needs of PWA [11] and offers features specific to intervention requirements. Therefore, the project TELL focuses on the needs of PWA as well as speech and language therapists (SLTs) working with PWA.

There are different methods for designing web applications. While other approaches focus on other aspects like the user's goal or the activity, user-centred design (UCD) concentrates on the user [12]. The UCD approach [13] aims to specify the known requirements by continuously conducting user workshops during the development of the platform. As a multidisciplinary process, the UCD approach actively involves end users in a development process and is therefore a collaboration between designer and user [12]. This leads to better understanding of users' needs and goals, and enables knowledge about needs-based requirements [14]. As PWA have special needs in regard to the use of technology [9], this focus is crucial for therapy success.

In phase one of the project, which has already been completed, user requirements were analysed. The results of this phase are now briefly summarized to provide a basis for our further research work. A literature review was conducted on the requirements of PWA as well as SLTs for teletherapy and digital therapy-management with PWA.

The literature describes some technical conditions that have a negative influence on the success of teletherapy with PWA. For example, technical issues such as unreliable video and audio transmission or loss of internet connectivity [15, 16], difficulties in using technology such as pictorial icons without supporting text prompts to access key functions, complex multi-step actions [17], or distractions from crowded screens [18] are named as an obstruction to successful implementation of teletherapy via videoconferencing.

The use of an alternative and more reliable videoconferencing platform or server independent of a large network may resolve technical issues [10]. User manuals [19], step-by-step instructions [20] and a remote control [21] proved to be useful in solving technical barriers.

---

[1] The current work is supported by a grant of the German Federal Ministry of Education and Research [BMBF, 01IS19039].

For the therapy itself, offering multimodal ways of communication enables PWA to express themselves effectively [22]. A number of authors point out that one major advantage of technology is the use of personal material like photographs as a means of communication facilitator [16, 20, 23–26]. To open up other ways of communication and increase interactivity, chats, drawing tools, dynamic whiteboard displays, screen share features, pointers [16] and mind-maps [27] can be included. Neate et al. [28] emphasize the importance of the capacity to read-aloud text.

In the literature, useful requirements regarding digital therapy-management tools specific for speech and language therapy could not be identified. Moreover, none of the studies collected requirements directly expressed by the users, i.e. PWA as well as SLTs.

Project phase one also contained two digital focus groups, one with four PWA and the other with five SLTs, to specify and extend the known requirements. Some findings of the focus groups were consistent with the literature, e.g. incorporating personalised materials and low-stimulus design when possible. Overall, it was possible to expand the requirements for the platform. To name some examples, PWA added a request for icons as used in messenger services to support non-verbal communication within the video conference. Further, PWA and SLTs considered explanatory videos to be helpful. In the field of therapy-management, this allowed a novel collection of requirements of PWA and SLTs, such as digital to-do lists, a reminder function for appointments and exercises or digital documentation of therapy sessions.

The basis for the further development is a catalogue of requirements from literature and the results from both digital focus groups. It included the categories "design, technology, preparation, implementation, therapy, therapy-management and diagnostics". The requirements were discussed within the project group with the developers and evaluated in terms of their technical feasibility.

The conceptual development was followed by a piloting phase, in which UCD workshops played a key role. This paper concentrates on this phase. The primary aim was to specify the known requirements for the further development of the platform. Therefore, we wanted to observe whether users (i.e. PWA and SLTs) can intuitively operate within the platform and receive their feedback. Since digital implementation has not yet been studied the secondary aim was to gain first information whether UCD workshops can be conducted via videoconferencing systems with PWA and SLTs.

2 Methods

2.1 Participants

For the UCD workshops, we recruited four PWA and four SLTs. All participants met the inclusion criteria. Two of the PWA and three of the SLTs already took part in the focus groups.

Inclusion criterion for PWA was the presence of aphasia for at least six months with good to moderately impaired speech comprehension according to the SLT researcher's judgment. Exclusion criteria were 1) a diagnosed depression or 2) other psychiatric-neurological disorders. Since recruitment and initial contact also occurred digitally, only the essential characteristics of PWA were collected for accessible participation in digital format. The included PWA (see Table 1), three male and one female, are between 34 and 60 years old. All are experienced with videoconferencing. The PWA have various levels of severity of aphasia according to SLT research judgment, ranging from single word utterances to fluent language. Three PWA have additional apraxia of speech.

Table 1. Characteristics of the included PWA

	Sex	Age (years)	Experience with videoconferencing	Apraxia of speech
PWA1	male	60	Yes	No
PWA2	male	51	Yes	Yes
PWA3	female	34	Yes	Yes
PWA4	male	49	Yes	Yes

Furthermore, four SLTs from cooperating practices for speech and language therapy were recruited. Inclusion criterion for SLTs was the continuous treatment of aphasic patients in the past 12 months. The SLTs, three female and one male, are between 30 and 52 years old. They differ in years of work experience as well as current employment status as well as technology use and commitment (see Table 2). The technology commitment was measured with the *Brief Measure of Technology Commitment* [29] in which a higher score symbolises a higher level of commitment.

While two of the four SLTs have treated PWA almost exclusively for many years, one SLT occasionally has PWA in her practice. One SLT has had a focus on working with people with primary progressive aphasia for several years.

Table 2. Characteristics of the included SLTs

	Sex	Age (years)	Work experience (years)	Current status	Devices within the practice (use)	Technology commitment*
SLT1	female	30	6	Employed	Computer (daily), tablet (never)	TC 45 TC-Acc 12 TC-Comp 19 TC-Cont 14
SLT2	female	52	25	Practice owner	Computer (daily), tablet (daily), smartphone (daily)	TC 49 TC-Acc 13 TC-Comp 17 TC-Cont 19

(*continued*)

Table 2. (*continued*)

	Sex	Age (years)	Work experience (years)	Current status	Devices within the practice (use)	Technology commitment*
SLT3	female	31	7	Employed	Computer (daily)	TC 41 TC-Acc 10 TC-Comp 14 TC-Cont 17
SLT4	female	51	30	Employed + work in aphasia centre	Computer (rarely), tablet (daily)	TC 40 TC-Acc 11 TC-Comp 16 TC-Cont 13

* *Brief measure of technology commitment* [29]: TC = Total score technology commitment (max. 60), TC-Acc = Subscore technology acceptance (max. 20), TC-Comp = Subscore technology competence conviction (max. 20), TC-Cont = Subscore technology control conviction (max. 20)

2.2 Setting

The study was approved by the ethics committee of the German Federal Association for Academic Speech/ Language Therapy and Logopaedics (dbs; 20-10065-KA-ESpK).

The UCD approach is an iterative development process (see Fig. 1). After the analysis of user requirements (catalogue based on literature and focus groups), we conducted UCD workshops for further development. The workshops were facilitated by researchers who are SLTs and familiar with the work with PWA. The feedback and observations from the workshops were compiled and assembled for the software developers by the researching speech and language therapist. This led to a new and more detailed analysis of user needs and thus supports the user-centred development.

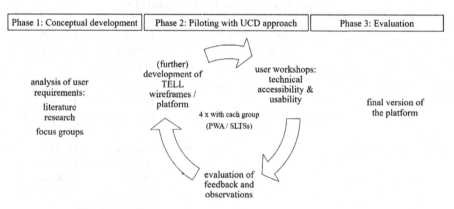

Fig. 1. UCD in the project TELL following Heitplatz et al. [30]

In total, four workshops were planned with each group, PWA as well as SLTs. The aims of the different workshops are summarized in Table 3. In the first workshop, the initial drafts (wireframes) were evaluated to receive feedback for the general design and structure. In the second workshop, the PWA focused on the support within the platform while the SLTs assessed the wireframes regarding the digital documentation system. In the third workshop, the platform will be used to obtain feedback on the therapy-management. In a last workshop, both groups will evaluate the final version of the platform. So far, two workshops with PWA and three workshops with SLTs took place.

Table 3. Overview of the UCD workshops within the project TELL

Workshop	PWA	SLTs
1	First wireframes therapy-management and videoconferencing system	First wireframes therapy-management and videoconferencing system
2	Support within the platform, esp. explanatory videos	Revised wireframes First wireframes on digital documentation system
3	Testing of the therapy-management tools within the platform	Testing of the therapy-management tools within the platform
4	Testing of the final platform including videoconferencing system	Testing of the final platform including videoconferencing system

The workshops were originally intended to take place in face-to-face settings, as this approach would have allowed specific observation of the participants on the laptop and technical assistance on site. Due to the COVID-19 pandemic the workshops had to be conducted digitally. First studies indicate that digital UCD workshops via videoconferencing systems are feasible with people with dementia [31] and people with chronic pain [32]. The concern of lacking active participation within the digital setting, could not be confirmed since the participation in discussions was higher than expected [32]. It seems to be relevant that participants can use their own devices to attend the workshops [31].

The workshops were conducted via the videoconferencing system zoom [33]. In the workshops with the SLTs, all participants attended at the same time. Break-out sessions (one participant and one researcher) were used to perform tasks and evaluate wireframes. For the PWA, a pilot run was conducted to test the digital setting. It revealed that the UCD workshop via videoconferencing is generally feasible with PWA. However, it is important that participants join the meeting with a notebook, not a tablet, in order to be able to engage during the entire workshop. It also became apparent that participants should have experience with videoconferencing systems to avoid the need for analogue third-party assistance. While SLTs completed the tasks in break-out-sessions in one-on-one situations, we wanted to reduce this added technical complexity for PWA. For this reason, it was decided to conduct the user workshops for PWA in individual rather than group sessions. In individual workshops the specific needs of PWA can be addressed and individual assistance can be provided. We prepared to support PWA for example via telephone instructions when technical problems occurred (e.g. difficulties with log-in).

2.3 Material

For visualisation in the UCD workshops, wireframes, the platform and a sample for an explanatory video were used depending on the development stage and content.

In the first two workshops, wireframes (see Fig. 2 for an example) of the platform were used. They were developed based on the catalogue of requirements with the software Justinmind [34]. Wireframes are used to quickly and economically display a prototype of a page in order to repeatedly test and modify the design through feedback [35]. Wireframes can be used to illustrate how the web page will function and be displayed [27, 35]. The wireframes were developed in close collaboration of the interdisciplinary research team consisting of people with expertise in speech-language therapy, health science, platform design and software developers.

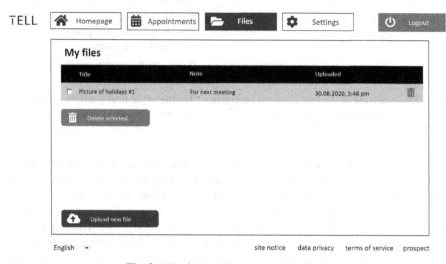

Fig. 2. Wireframe of the screen "My files".

In certain areas, two different versions of the presentation of a web page were created in order to work out preferences in the workshops. For example, there were two visualisations of the videoconferencing system, a highly minimalist version with more "hidden" features and a more detailed version showing all features (see Fig. 3).

Fig. 3. Two versions of the videoconferencing system (PWA view).

Based on the wireframes, the platform will be developed and tested in the two final workshops.

In the first project phase, the need for explanatory videos was expressed. For this, one sample video was provided for the second UCD workshop with PWA. As suggested by the PWA, the aim was to show one function of the platform per video to improve navigation. It seems to be useful to start and end with text and icons for multimodal support [36, 37]. The explanatory video sample started with an introduction screen title "How to complete my tasks?" and the fitting icon which is also used in the platform to mark the tasks. It was followed by a step-by-step screencast of the function itself. The text was highlighted [36, 38] and the cursor was enlarged and hand-shaped [38]. To ensure comprehension of PWA, a script in simple language in the first-person perspective and elements to secure understanding at the end are relevant [38, 39]. The video ended with a final screen indicating "Did you understand everything? You can watch the video again." and corresponding icons. The audiotape was recorded in reduced time with clear intonation [38–40]. To keep the video compact, a maximum duration of three minutes was not exceeded.

2.4   Data Collection

For data collection, digital UCD workshops were conducted and video recorded. Within the workshops, the wireframes and the platform were shown via screen sharing. The participants were asked to perform tasks within the platform giving verbal feedback during and after the task. The tasks were performed with the researcher sharing control over the cursor. After each task, the researchers asked which aspects the participants received as positive or negative as well as for further comments and ideas. Tasks for the SLTs were, for example, to create appointments and patient files, fill out digital session documentation or start a therapy session. They were also asked to give feedback on the patients' view of the front page and the videoconferencing system. Comparable to the workshops with the SLTs, PWA were also asked to perform tasks within the wireframes giving verbal feedback during and after the task. Those tasks included, for example, to start and end a therapy session, to set a reminder or to cancel an appointment via the platform. After each task, the researcher asked for positive and negative feedback and further ideas giving linguistic support. Multimodal communication was facilitated if necessary.

For all workshops, interview guides were written beforehand and followed by the facilitators. The introduction and ending of the interview guides were written in key points to allow natural formulation of facilitators. The tasks were formulated verbatim to ensure comparable workshop conditions between the participants, for example the SLTs were asked the following: „*You had the first group session, in which Mr. Schiller participated. Now, you would like to document the session. Open the documentation for the appointment of 10.01.2022 at 3 pm.*" The participants were asked to give feedback during and directly after each task. The questions for feedback were prepared within the interview guide. However, the facilitators remained open for new aspects of discussion. When problems were observed, the researcher addressed the difficulty on a meta-level and asked for improvements. For the PWA a PowerPoint presentation was used to visualise (in writing and pictures) the important aspects (e.g., aim of the project in general, aim of the UCD -workshop) in order to secure comprehension. At the end of each workshop, we asked for feedback regarding the workshop itself with open questions.

To analyse the performances on the given tasks, ad hoc observational checklists (see Table 4 for an example) were used for evaluation. The videos were evaluated regarding the reactions of the participants. The reactions were categorised as "without any problems", "feasible after try-out/short time", "feasible only with help/after a long time" and "not feasible". Additional observations were noted under "commentary".

Table 4. Observational checklist for the task "start session"

action	Without any problems	Feasible after try-out/short time	Feasible only with help/after a long time	Not feasible	commentary
Person starts session	o	o	o	o	
Person confirms security question	o	o	o	o	

2.5 Data Analysis

In order to evaluate the wireframes and the platform comprehensively, we used quantitative and qualitative methods. For quantitative analysis, the checklists were counted for each task to identify functions, which were not used intuitively by the participants. For semi-structured qualitative analysis, we worked with a predetermined category system with the three categories positive, negative and further ideas/comments. In the following step, we allocated the feedback to each wireframe or screen within the platform to visualise the results. Finally, those visualised results were discussed with the developers regarding technical feasibility and specific realization.

3   Results

The primary aim was to specify the known requirements for the further development of the platform. The results of the observation checklists and the feedback are described in the following. We concentrate on the results that can be generalised for platform designing for teletherapy with PWA.

The secondary aim was to evaluate the feasibility of digital conduct of UCD workshops with PWA and SLTs. We therefore describe our experiences of the workshops at the end of this chapter.

3.1   Observation Checklists

Using the wireframes, user requirements were specified regarding the design and accessibility of the platform. The analysis of the checklists showed which functions were accessible and intuitive for the users. The SLTs were able to successfully execute the tasks with only few exceptions where they tried out different options before solving the task (see Table 5 for an example).

Table 5. Summary of the counted reactions of the four SLTs with the observational checklist SLTs "create new patient file" (workshop 3)

Action	Without any problems	Feasible after try-out/short time	Feasible only with help/after a long time	Not feasible
Person opens tab „patients"	3	1		
Person opens „new patient"	4			
Person sets first and last name, gender, date of birth	3*		1**	
Person sets phone number and email address	4			
Person saves new patient file	4			

* 3 SLTs entered date of birth manually, ** 1 SLT hesitated whether to type phone number throughout

While some PWA solved tasks without difficulty, others struggled with certain tasks. For example, ending therapy sessions or cancelling an appointment via the platform (see Table 6 for an example) were challenging. However, some tasks were completed without any problems by all participants like starting the therapy session or uploading a file. In the commentary, further observations like needed support (e.g., a reminder of the tabs or the location of the searched button) were documented.

Table 6. Summary of the counted reactions of the four PWA with the observational checklist PWA "cancel appointment" (workshop 1)

Action	Without any problems	Feasible after try-out / short time	Feasible only with help / After a long time	Not feasible
Person opens tab *"appointments"*"	3		1*	
Person clicks on *"cancel appointment"*	3		1**	
Person confirms security question	4			

* looked on front page and didn't look for tabs, ** could not distinguish *"cancel appointments"* from *"transfer appointments to my calendar"* and needed linguistic support

3.2 Qualitative Feedback

The participants were asked to give feedback during and after each task. The qualitative analysis showed which elements were experienced as positive or negative as well as further needs and ideas expressed by the participants.

As positive aspects, the PWA as well as the SLTs named the general design, the colours and the clarity especially of the front page. The PWA further emphasised the importance of understanding everything. While three participants described the front page as clearly arranged and understandable, for one participant there was too much information on one page.

The negative feedback mostly concerned texts and wording as well as the design (i.e. font sizes and location of buttons). Different texts and wording were discussed by both, PWA and SLTs, on personal initiative or when asked why a button was not found within a task. For example, the text "Here, you can test the videoconferencing system alone." was considered too long and "Test alone" was proposed. Both groups considered the smallest font size within the platform to be too small. Buttons on the left bottom of the platform caused frequent difficulties. For example, the button "Upload files" was described to be more intuitive directly under the page headline "my files" (see Fig. 2). In addition, drop-down menus were experienced as difficult and PWA wished for all options to be visible.

Moreover, the participants expressed further needs and ideas regarding the platform. For example, PWA asked for always-visible support buttons on every page of the platform. One participant would find a feature to read-aloud text useful to support his reading, especially when the differences of functions are close (e.g., delete file vs. upload file).

The SLTs considered a reminder on when a new prescription is needed useful. They also expressed the wish to scan new prescriptions to automatically enter the information into the platform.

For the two different versions of the screen during the teletherapy via videoconferencing, consisting of a videoconferencing system and multimodal assistance (minimalist versus detailed version), SLTs and PWA decided differently. Two out of four SLTs found the more detailed design for SLTs better, as all functions are visible immediately and there is no need to search for further functions and options. The other two SLTs preferred the minimalist design due to the screen clarity. The verbal exchange with the patients was rated as most important by these SLTs and would be the key aspects in this design, which puts its focus on the large representation of the persons in the video conferencing system. Three of the four PWA preferred the more extended version. The multimodal support of the platform, such as the chat, are fully visible in the extensive version and can thus be used more intuitively. One PWA preferred the minimalist version because the design was clearer with a focus on the large display of the videos. In contrast, three out of four SLTs preferred the minimalist design for PWA because it appeared cleaner with less text and yet all the advanced features, such as chat, could be operated through picture-based displays.

The explanatory video was found to be generally helpful. One PWA noted he would not need explanatory videos for the platform, since he had no problems using all functions. Only few changes, like wording choices, were suggested.

3.3 Feasibility of Digital UCD Workshops

All participants could attend the workshops. There were no problems with internet connectivity or login into the videoconferencing systems. We did not have to provide any technical support. One PWA with limited productive language skills had support of a relative for linguistic assistance. There were difficulties in the observation of some kinds of technology use of people in our digital workshops. While the SLTs (and one PWA) could explain and verbally express all of their feedback, some PWA had difficulties. The digital setting reduces some non-verbal communication options. For example, in a videoconference, one cannot see when a person is pointing to something on the screen and referring to this part in the feedback. In UCD workshops with persons with communication difficulties, we often rely on observations which are compromised via videoconference. However, we could also observe positive effects of the videoconferencing setting. Because the PWA were situated in their home environment, they could use the setting to overcome word finding difficulties. One PWA answered a question whether he would use a drawing tool on the platform by getting his computer pencil and showing it to the camera. In contrast, for SLTs the digital setting was feasible and none of the described challenges occurred.

We further recognised, that it is crucial to adjust the procedure to the PWA´s needs. When preparing the workshops we made sure to phrase our interview guidelines in simple language.

The participants themselves received the digital user workshops positively. The PWA gave the feedback that the instructions were understandable, they had enough time and were happy to try out a lot. Three PWA said that they are looking forward to further workshops. The SLTs praised the good organization and structure of the workshop. They wished for more time to try-out the platform.

4   Discussion

The workshops according to the UCD approach fulfilled the aim to specify the known requirements in the development of the platform TELL. The UCD allows a constant focus on the accessibility and requirements of PWA and SLTs within the development process of technical solutions.

4.1   Implications for the Development Process of the Platform TELL

The first UCD workshops were necessary to proceed with further development of the platform. For example, through discussions by the PWA and SLTs on arrangements on the screen and wordings on the wireframes, the requirement of a "distraction-free screen" [18] could be specified for the platform.

For the videoconferencing system, we had contrary requirements. On the one hand, a distraction-free screen is important to support the concentration on the therapy itself [18]. On the other hand, a reduction of complex multi-step actions [17] and a variety of functions to facilitate multimodal communication, such as icons, chats, whiteboard and personal photos [16, 20, 23–26] are needed. However, a distraction-free screen with many multimodal support options at the same time is difficult to realise. This contradiction is also reflected in the participants' different views on the two opposing versions of the videoconferencing system (see Fig. 3). The majority of SLTs preferred the minimalist design for PWA while the PWA themselves preferred the more detailed version. This might indicate different prioritisation of SLTs and PWA. However, the interpretation can only be made with caution due to the small number of participants.

The results of the observation checklists and the qualitative analysis of user feedback are integrated into constant iterations of the platform development as well as the explanatory videos. In response to user feedback, for example, long and misleading texts were shortened and rewritten, font sizes adjusted and the positions of control buttons changed. The UCD workshops in TELL were crucial to specify and revise initial drafts and to develop the platform exactly according to the end users' preferences.

It must be taken into consideration that there will always be requirements that are technically unworkable. As seen with the screen during the videoconferencing, it is difficult to implement a distraction-free design and include numerous functions at the same time.

There were also requirements in the UCD workshops that were valuable for platform development, but not feasible within this project. For example, a videoconferencing meeting room that can be used privately without the SLTs was requested. The SLTs expressed the wish for simplification of billing, for example the note of the co-payment obligation and automatic invoicing. Since those requirements exceed the project aim, they cannot be taken into account but used for further development projects.

4.2 Digital Setting in UCD Workshops

For conducting the workshops with PWA, the digital setting was challenging. Due to the digital format, PWA already had to bring technical skills such as the use of a video-conferencing system. Since the group of PWA is very vulnerable, it is necessary to plan the workshops with wireframes or versions of the technical solution that are aligned with their technical competencies. Dixon et al. [31] described difficulties in observing some types of technology use of people with dementia in digital workshops. In our workshops with PWA, we faced similar challenges. Since the observation during the digital workshop is limited, verbal feedback gains importance. One PWA with deficits in speech production could only participate with a relative as support. However, the presence of other persons may influence the results of the research. For instance, the supporting relative sometimes helped the participants even though this might not have been necessary.

Despite the challenges, our digital workshops with PWA were feasible with some advantages compared to analogue workshops. Especially people with good technical competences and experiences in videoconferencing can successfully participate, even with severe deficits in language production. Similar to Dixon et al. [31], the included PWA were able to take advantage of their home environment and use personal items for linguistic support. Furthermore, comparable to teletherapy, we could reduce travel costs and time [4]. In order to include a broader patient group (i.e. persons with little technical experiences as well as persons with a variety of aphasia severity), additional support and/or analogue workshops should be offered. If analogue workshops include people with low technical skills, digital applications can also be developed accessible for this target group. During a pandemic, digital workshops contribute to social distancing and thereby less risk of contact spread, particularly relevant when working with users in elevated risk demographics [32].

In contrast, for SLTs the digital setting was feasible, and no challenges occurred. Therefore, the advantages of digital in comparison to analogue workshops predominate. As pointed out by Smaradottir et al. [32], in terms of iterative development and evaluation, the remote approach might facilitate increased user-involvement in the collection of user requirements and later on in assessment of user interface design, interactions and usability.

4.3 Methodological Reflection

There are advantages and disadvantages for different starting points of user involvement within the development process. Within the project TELL, the user involvement was started five months after the beginning of the project. While the importance of user involvement from the beginning is often underlined [41], the start after a few months gave the opportunity to conduct literature research first and formulate evidence-based questions for the interview guides. With every UCD workshop, there is a possibility of new requirements to arise. This has to be considered in the project planning and the time schedule might have to be adjusted. To avoid unnecessary changes for the scope of the project and frustration for the developer team and the others involved, it is crucial to clarify the maximum size of the project [41]. A detailed description of the project aim and scope was necessary to determine which requirements could be implemented within the project TELL.

The conduction of digital UCD workshops needs to be well prepared and adapted individually to the participants. The visualisations through wireframes, the platform or the explanatory videos are crucial for specific feedback, because they enable discussion on what specific requirements mean to PWA and SLTs.

Both methods for data analysis, the observation checklists and the qualitative analysis of user feedback, proved to be relevant. The checklists assisted to systematically evaluate the tasks comparable for each participant. They revealed which functions were used intuitively. If, for example, a participant took a long time to find the appropriate button for a task, it became apparent that intuitive operation was missing. Qualitative feedback was often consistent with the observations. For example, the task "creating a new patient file" was conducted without any problems by all SLTs in the first workshop. As qualitative feedback, they indicated a fast and uncomplicated completion of the task. As shown in Table 6, one PWA had difficulties clicking on "cancel appointment", because he could not distinguish "cancel appointments" from "transfer appointments to my calendar". He expressed the need for a function to read-aloud text which was already named by Neate et al. [28] as an important feature for PWA. It also occurred that a lot of qualitative feedback was provided on tasks, even if they were intuitively performed without any difficulties. For instance, all SLTs could find and fill in the case history in the patient file. Still, there were many comments and ideas for adaptations for this area of the platform.

The workshops were conducted with only four participants in each group. All participant had sufficient technical competences. A larger and more diverse sample size in UCD workshops could help to get a richer picture of preferred designs and accessibility. In addition, more information on the PWA included would have been useful for a more detailed analysis.

5 Conclusion

The UCD is a need-based approach and might increase technology use and access to teletherapy. Through this approach, it became apparent which functions of the platform can be used intuitively. Feedback on functions and suggestions for improvement on design and usability were gathered. According to the UCD approach, the results are integrated into constant iterations of platform development. In the last workshops still to come, the final platform will be tested.

The UCD workshops via videoconferencing were feasible with both, PWA and SLTs. In order to include PWA with different degrees of severity of aphasia as well as technical skills, additional support and / or analogue workshops should be provided. The digital setting has had some advantages over the analogue up to this stage of the project and could even further facilitate increased user-involvement.

References

1. Threats, T., Worrall, L.: The ICF is all about the person, and more: a response to Duchan, Simmons-Mackie, Boles, and McLeod. Adv. Speech Lang. Pathol. (2004). https://doi.org/10.1080/14417040410001669435

2. Nätterlund, B.S.: A new life with aphasia: everyday activities and social support. Scandinavian J. Occupat. Therapy (2010). https://doi.org/10.3109/11038120902814416

3. Brady, M.C., Kelly, H., Godwin, J., Enderby, P., Campbell, P.: Speech and language therapy for aphasia following stroke. Cochrane Database Systemat. Rev. (2016). https://doi.org/10.1002/14651858.CD000425.pub4

4. Keck, C.S., Doarn, C.R.: Telehealth technology applications in speech-language pathology. Telemed. J. e-health Official J. Am. Telemed. Associat. (2014). https://doi.org/10.1089/tmj.2013.0295

5. Cacciante, L., et al.: Telerehabilitation for people with aphasia: a systematic review and meta-analysis. J. Commun. Disord. (2021). https://doi.org/10.1016/j.jcomdis.2021.106111

6. Dial, H.R., Hinshelwood, H.A., Grasso, S.M., Hubbard, H.I., Gorno-Tempini, M.-L., Henry, M.L.: Investigating the utility of teletherapy in individuals with primary progressive aphasia. Clin. Interv. Aging (2019). https://doi.org/10.2147/CIA.S178878

7. Woolf, C., et al.: A comparison of remote therapy, face to face therapy and an attention control intervention for people with aphasia: a quasi-randomised controlled feasibility study. Clin. Rehabil. (2016). https://doi.org/10.1177/0269215515582074

8. Øra, H.P., et al.: The effect of augmented speech-language therapy delivered by telerehabilitation on poststroke aphasia-a pilot randomized controlled trial. Clin. Rehabil. (2020). https://doi.org/10.1177/0269215519896616

9. Menger, F., Morris, J., Salis, C.: The impact of aphasia on Internet and technology use. Disabil. Rehabil. (2020). https://doi.org/10.1080/09638288.2019.1580320

10. Pitt, R., Theodoros, D., Hill, A.J., Russell, T.: The impact of the telerehabilitation group aphasia intervention and networking programme on communication, participation, and quality of life in people with aphasia. Int. J. Speech Lang. Pathol. (2019). https://doi.org/10.1080/17549507.2018.1488990

11. Theodoros, D.: Speech-language pathology and telerehabilitation. In: Kumar, S., Cohn, E.R. (eds.) Telerehabilitation. Health Informatics, pp. 311–323. Springer London (2013). https://doi.org/10.1007/978-1-4471-4198-3_21

12. Williams, A.: User-centered design, activity-centered design, and goal-directed design. In: Mehlenbacher, B., Protopsaltis, A., Williams, A., Slattery, S. (eds.) Proceedings of the 27th ACM international conference on Design of communication - SIGDOC 2009. The 27th ACM international conference, Bloomington, Indiana, USA, 10/5/2009 - 10/7/2009, p. 1. ACM Press, New York, USA (2009). https://doi.org/10.1145/1621995.1621997

13. Norman, D.A., Draper, S.W.: User centered system design: new perspectives on human-computer interaction (1986)

14. Mao, J.-Y., Vredenburg, K., Smith, P.W., Carey, T.: The state of user-centered design practice. Commun. ACM (2005). https://doi.org/10.1145/1047671.1047677

15. Marshall, J., et al.: A randomised trial of social support group intervention for people with aphasia: a novel application of virtual reality. PLoS ONE (2020). https://doi.org/10.1371/journal.pone.0239715

16. Pitt, R., Theodoros, D., Hill, A.J., Russell, T.: The development and feasibility of an online aphasia group intervention and networking program - TeleGAIN. Int. J. Speech Lang. Pathol. (2017). https://doi.org/10.1080/17549507.2017.1369567

17. Roper, A., Davey, I., Wilson, S., Neate, T., Marshall, J., Grellmann, B.: Usability Testing - An Aphasia Perspective (2018). https://doi.org/10.1145/3234695.3241481

18. McNaney, R., et al.: Giving a voice through design. In: Huybrechts, L., et al.: (eds.) Proceedings of the 15th Participatory Design Conference: Short Papers, Situated Actions, Workshops and Tutorial - Volume 2. PDC 2018: Participatory Design Conference 2018, Hasselt and Genk Belgium, 20 08 2018 24 08 2018, pp. 1–3. ACM, New York, NY, USA (2018). https://doi.org/10.1145/3210604.3210648

19. Hill, A.J., Breslin, H.M.: Refining an asynchronous telerehabilitation platform for speech-language pathology: engaging end-users in the process. Front. Hum. Neurosci. (2016). https://doi.org/10.3389/fnhum.2016.00640
20. Hoover, E.L., Carney, A.: Integrating the iPad into an intensive, comprehensive aphasia program. Semin. Speech Lang. (2014). https://doi.org/10.1055/s-0033-1362990
21. Øra, H.P., Kirmess, M., Brady, M.C., Winsnes, I.E., Hansen, S.M., Becker, F.: Telerehabilitation for aphasia - protocol of a pragmatic, exploratory, pilot randomized controlled trial. Trials (2018). https://doi.org/10.1186/s13063-018-2588-5
22. Neate, T., Roper, A., Wilson, S., Marshall, J., Cruice, M.: CreaTable content and tangible interaction in Aphasia. In: Bernhaupt, R., et al. (eds.) Proceedings of the 2020 CHI Conference on Human Factors in Computing Systems. CHI 2020: CHI Conference on Human Factors in Computing Systems, Honolulu HI USA, 25.04.2020–30.04.2020, pp. 1–14. ACM, New York, NY, USA (2020). https://doi.org/10.1145/3313831.3376490
23. Brown, J., Thiessen, A.: Using images with individuals with aphasia: current research and clinical trends. Am. J. Speech Lang. Pathol. (2018). https://doi.org/10.1044/2017_AJSLP-16-0190
24. Cruice, M., Woolf, C., Caute, A., Monnelly, K., Wilson, S., Marshall, J.: Preliminary outcomes from a pilot study of personalised online supported conversation for participation intervention for people with Aphasia. Aphasiology (2020). https://doi.org/10.1080/02687038.2020.1795076
25. Palmer, R., et al.: Self-managed, computerised speech and language therapy for patients with chronic aphasia post-stroke compared with usual care or attention control (Big CACTUS): a multicentre, single-blinded, randomised controlled trial. Lancet Neurol. (2019). https://doi.org/10.1016/S1474-4422(19)30192-9
26. Palmer, R., et al.: Computerised speech and language therapy or attention control added to usual care for people with long-term post-stroke aphasia: the Big CACTUS three-arm RCT. Health technology assessment (Winchester, England) (2020). https://doi.org/10.3310/hta24190
27. Marshall, J., et al.: Technology-enhanced writing therapy for people with aphasia: results of a quasi-randomized waitlist controlled study. Int. J. Lang. Commun. Disord. (2019). https://doi.org/10.1111/1460-6984.12391
28. Neate, T., Roper, A., Wilson, S., Marshall, J.: Empowering expression for users with aphasia through constrained creativity. In: Brewster, S., Fitzpatrick, G., Cox, A., Kostakos, V. (eds.) Proceedings of the 2019 CHI Conference on Human Factors in Computing Systems. CHI 2019: CHI Conference on Human Factors in Computing Systems, Glasgow Scotland UK, 04.05.2019–09.05.2019, pp. 1–12. ACM, New York, NY, USA (2019). https://doi.org/10.1145/3290605.3300615
29. Neyer, F.J., Felber, J., Gebhardt, C.: Entwicklung und Validierung einer Kurzskala zur Erfassung von Technikbereitschaft. Diagnostica (2012). https://doi.org/10.1026/0012-1924/a000067
30. Heitplatz, V.N., Leinweber, J., Frieg, H., Bilda, K., Ritterfeld, U.: Konzepte zur Nutzer*inneneinbindung am Beispiel der Entwicklung einer digitalen Anwendung zum Training der Sprechverständlichkeit (ISi-Speech). Nutzerorientierte Gesundheitstechnologie, pp. 183–194 (2019)
31. Dixon, E., Shetty, A., Pimento, S., Lazar, A.: Lessons learned from remote user-centered design with people with dementia. In: Brankaert, R., Raber, C., Houben, M., Malcolm, P., Hannan, J. (eds.) D-Lab 2021. DFI, vol. 2, pp. 73–82. Springer, Cham (2021). https://doi.org/10.1007/978-3-030-70293-9_6
32. Smaradottir, B.F., Bellika, J.G., Fredeng, A., Fagerlund, A.J.: User-centred design with a remote approach: experiences from the chronic pain project. Stud. Health Technol. Inf. (2020). https://doi.org/10.3233/SHTI200722

33. Zoom Communications Inc.: Zoom, San José (2021)
34. Justinmind Inc.: Justinmind, San Francisco (2021)
35. Qu, Z.: Remote Delivery: A Guide to Software Delivery Through Collaboration Between Distributed Teams. CRC Press, Boca Raton (2021)
36. Cherney, L.R., Braun, E.J., Lee, J.B., Kocherginsky, M., van Vuuren, S.: Optimising recovery in aphasia: Learning following exposure to a single dose of computer-based script training. Int. J. Speech Lang. Pathol. (2019). https://doi.org/10.1080/17549507.2019.1661518
37. Palmer, R., Enderby, P., Paterson, G.: Using computers to enable self-management of aphasia therapy exercises for word finding: the patient and carer perspective. Int. J. Lang. Commun. Disord. (2013). https://doi.org/10.1111/1460-6984.12024
38. Oud, J.: Guidelines for effective online instruction using multimedia screencasts. Ref. Serv. Rev. (2009). https://doi.org/10.1108/00907320910957206
39. Goldsworthy, M.A., Fateen, W., Thygesen, H., Aldersley, M.A., Rowe, I.A., Jones, R.L.: Patient understanding of liver cirrhosis and improvement using multimedia education. Front. Gastroenterol. (2017). https://doi.org/10.1136/flgastro-2016-100761
40. Cistola, G., Farrús, M., van der Meulen, I.: Aphasia and acquired reading impairments: what are the high-tech alternatives to compensate for reading deficits? Int. J. Lang. Commun. Disord. (2021). https://doi.org/10.1111/1460-6984.12569
41. Chammas, A., Quaresma, M., Mont'Alvão, C.: A closer look on the user centred design. Proc. Manuf. (2015). https://doi.org/10.1016/j.promfg.2015.07.656

Dance Through Visual Media: The Influence of COVID-19 on Dance Artists

Ryosuke Suzuki[✉] and Yoichi Ochiai

University of Tsukuba, Tsukuba, Japan
`ryosuke.suzuki@digitalnature.slis.tsukuba.ac.jp`

Abstract. Among the arts, dance is regarded as a "dynamic spatiotemporal art using the body as a medium," and it is considered better to appreciate it live [10]. By appreciating dance work live, the theme, movement, and impressions of the work are communicated [12]. However, because of the spread of COVID-19, the first emergency state was declared in Japan in March 2020. Under these circumstances, theaters were closed because of the risk of infection, and all dance performances were cancelled. Live dance appreciation is no longer possible, and dance performances using visual media have soared. Therefore, to clarify how Japanese dance artists have shifted to video distribution in response to the spread of COVID-19 and how this shift has been perceived, we first conducted semi-structured interviews with dance artists who have engaged in video distribution of dance owing to the spread of COVID-19. The interview revealed the merits and demerits of video-delivering dance, problems that emerged, points particular to video-delivering dance, and new physical sensations obtained by video-delivering dance. Based on these results, we suggest room for improvement and then discuss how to provide better computer support.

Keywords: Contemporary dance · Visual media · COVID-19

1 Introduction

Among the arts, dance is regarded as a "dynamic spatiotemporal art using the body as a medium," considered better appreciated live [10]. By appreciating dance work live, the theme, movement, and impressions of the work are communicated [12]. With the development of visual media, the recording of dance videos has become popular. Since the 1960s,s, it is not only a tool for recording and preservation but also a "new art form" called "videodance" has emerged that pursues dance effects that cannot be achieved on stage by adding video technology [22]. Therefore, it can be observed that opportunities to appreciate dance art through videos are increasing. However, "artistic expression of the body," which can be felt in a live performance, is lost through video. Harada et al. (2007) found that the theme, movement, and impressions of work were more clearly conveyed in live appreciation than in video appreciation [12]. In other words, "how to communicate abstract thoughts expressed by the body through videos" is a difficult problem.

© The Author(s), under exclusive license to Springer Nature Switzerland AG 2022
M. Antona and C. Stephanidis (Eds.): HCII 2022, LNCS 13308, pp. 360–378, 2022.
https://doi.org/10.1007/978-3-031-05028-2_24

The reason such a problem remains today is that appreciation through videos results in the materialization of the human body. This is a phenomenon that occurs when the aura is lost through the intervention of new technologies and the artistry that the body represents is lost. Benjamin states, "A work of art exists only once, in the place where it exists, but this property, the property of being here and now, is lacking in reproduction [27]. Because of materialization of the human body, audiences and dancers have been reluctant to intervene in new technologies.

However, because of the spread of COVID-19, the first emergency state was declared in Japan in March 2020. Under these circumstances, theaters were closed owing to the risk of infection, and all dance performances were canceled. Live dance appreciation is no longer possible, and dance performances using visual media have soared. For example, it was possible to appreciate dancing safely at home in the form of a live or on-demand distribution.

Thus, as in other fields, such as sales activities [14,32] and school education [9,20], there is a move toward computer-mediated communication and the introduction of alternative forms of events. It is anticipated that examining the impact of visual media on dance artists here will provide novel insights for the HCI community. This is because dance has a unique characteristic, which differs from other situations that have been examined in previous studies, in that the "artistry of the body" that is felt during live appreciation is important. Recognizing the abstract nature of body movements and mediating between the various actors involved in a singular creative process presents a key challenge for HCI researchers.

Against this background, in a society living with infectious diseases, people must be able to enjoy performing arts without the necessity to gather at a theater, and for the production side to be able to work with a few people at low cost. Therefore, we considered it necessary to develop a technology to deliver dances with artistry through visual media.

Therefore, to clarify how Japanese dance artists have shifted to video distribution in response to the spread of COVID-19 and how they perceive this shift, we first conducted semi-structured interviews with dance artists who have engaged in video distribution of dance owing to the spread of COVID-19. The interview revealed the merits and demerits of video-delivering dance, problems that arose in this context, points particular to video-delivering dance, and new physical sensations obtained. Based on these results, we suggest room for further improvement and discuss ways to provide better computer support.

2 Related Work

In this section, we explain how art, including dance, has been researched in HCI. Next, we review related studies that examined appreciation experience, especially through visual media, and explain the background of this work. This also shows how dance activities have been carried out in the COVID-19 epidemic.

2.1   Dance Researches in HCI

In recent years, progress in digitization and the development of the Internet have enabled the integration of different media fields. Media research, which has traditionally been conducted separately in various research fields, is now being conducted as integrated interdisciplinary research under media informatics. Particularly, the close relationship between art and technology has received considerable attention. Research has discussed the history of interactive art and how art and HCI can contribute to each other with contemporary examples of art in immersive environments, robotic art, and machine intelligence in art [17]. Discussions include the direction of HCI research in the arts, particularly in dance. Here, we propose a multimodal approach to understand the dancer's bodily senses, and to recognize and develop physical creativity and expression [19,34]. In addition, because of the interaction between dance and various elements at work, specific research has been conducted in a variety of directions. For example, studies have attempted to extend physical expressions using technology as a means of expression [3,8,15,28,31]. Moreover, since the production of dance involves not only dancers but also multiple teams involving costumes and lighting, research has been conducted to develop systems and tools to coordinate communication among them [5,6,26]. Interactions with audiences are essential elements. Several examinations have been conducted on how the audience enjoys live viewing [11,13,16,30]. Others have contributed to the growing literature on audience research on technological performance by analyzing the impact of interactive videos in contemporary dance from the audience perspective [7].

2.2   Changes in the Experience of Appreciating Dance Through Visual Media

With the development of video technology, recording and preservation of dance videos have become popular. And since the 1960s, it has established a different realm from dance and video as a "new art form" called "videodance" that pursues dance effects that cannot be achieved on stage by adding video technology as well as a tool for recording and preservation. Matsuoka (2012) analyzed the videodance work "Roseland" (1990) by Wim Vandekeybus (1962-) using three analytical perspectives from "Theory of the Film" by Vera Burrage [22].

The ability to appreciate dance art through video has led to research that compares live performance with video appreciation and clarifies how each audience perceives the characteristics and impressions of the work. Harada et al. (2007) conducted live and video viewing of solo works created by a student and professional, respectively, to examine how the audience viewed and approached the works [12]. For both works, it was clear that the theme, movement, and impression of the work were communicated more clearly through live performance than through video appreciation. It was also identified that differences in expressive techniques between professionals and students could be distinguished in live viewing but this was difficult to achieve with video viewing. Therefore, how to communicate abstract thoughts expressed by the body, in other words, "embodiment in dance art," through video is a pertinent problem.

It has been consistently difficult to communicate through visual media, however, in recent years, with the development of video technology, a solution can be found. One option is the improvement of resolution. According to Sakamoto et al. (2015), when viewing 65-inch TV 4 K video, there were significant differences and trends between the 2 K and the 4 K video in many psychological indicators, including "sense of presence" in natural landscape content, and significant differences and trends were identified in psychological indicators in material and material-feeling content in A3-sized 4 K tablets [25]. In addition, research on camera-work analysis for video appreciation is underway. Lauser (2020) examines how pre-programming the camerawork of performance using a tool called CuePilot can affect the viewing experience of live music broadcasts [21]. Moreover, as drones become increasingly popular, shooting techniques are changing. To date, the mainstream method of filming from locations beyond the reach of human hands has been the use of cranes and other large types of equipment, resulting in significant costs incurred. However, the cost of a drone is only approximately 100,000 yen, no license is required for operation, and its compact size makes it possible to shoot from any viewpoint. These drone characteristics are considered important in a society that is in harmony with COVID-19. However, it is difficult for beginners to operate drones and there are qualifications for drone operation. Therefore, to enable drone usage, research is being conducted on automatic flight videography [2, 4, 18, 18]. These studies may be based on visual theories for filming movies.

2.3 Investigation of Dance Activities Under the Spread of COVID-19

Dance arts dealing with the body has evolved in various forms. Owing to the spread of COVID-19, the first emergency state was declared in Japan on March 2020. Under these circumstances, theaters were closed owing to the risk of infection, and all dance performances were cancelled. Live dance appreciation is no longer possible, and dance performances using visual media have soared. We are being torn away from our everyday body, and a new way of life is being established. As a result, video culture has become a part of our daily lives, an expansion of a culture has emerged in which video is broadcast through a multitude of content where viewers make their own choices. Under such circumstances, this investigation was conducted from the perspective of the activities of Japanese artists working in Japan, particularly the impact on the health and performance of dancers in a broad sense [24]. Mochizuki (2021) investigated the current state of dance creation activities of artists in the context of the spread of COVID-19 and identified that the everyday use of the visual body may lead to the body in videos approaching us with a greater degree of reality, and the perception of "my body" may fade [23]. In a society where the visual body has become an everyday reality because of the popularity of COVID-19, it is necessary to investigate the audience's perspective on the experience of appreciation through visual media.

3   Method

Semi-structured interviews were conducted to clarify how Japanese dance artists shifted to video distribution in response to the spread of COVID-19 and how they perceived this shift. As the transition to video dance with COVID-19 remains in its infancy and has not yet been published in the literature, we used semi-structured interviews to elicit deeper perspectives, because information on the topic is nascent, it was not possible to design a questionnaire without further insight that would lead to meaningful results. Semi-structured interviews were therefore conducted with nine dance artists (seven males and two females) who distributed dance videos during the declaration of a new coronavirus emergency. The age of the interviewees ranged from 31 to 50 years (mean 39.33 ± 5.64), ranging from mid-career to experienced. As all interviewees were Japanese speakers, a video call was conducted in Japanese and then translated into English. Each interview required less than an hour, and the questions mainly comprised of the following three topics: "Advantages and disadvantages of video-distributing dance," "Filming methods, problems, and particular points when video-distributing dance," and "Changes in embodiment due to video-distributing dance. Based on previous studies investigating the use of computer-mediated communication [29,33] and the current status of dance activities in COVID-19 [23], we analyzed the transcriptions of the interviews using open coding [1]. The analysis was performed using MAXQDA software. Then, through iterative refinement processes, we obtained several themes for each topic, which are discussed later in Sect. 4.

The purpose of the study explained to each interviewee in writing, alongside the research methodology, the right to freely participate and withdraw, the protection of personal information, the guarantee of anonymity, and assurance that the data would not be used for any purpose other than specified. Participants were requested to sign a consent form. This study was also approved by the Ethics Committee of the University of Tsukuba (Notification No. 21–48).

4   Results

As a result of conducting and analyzing the above semi-structured interviews, we identified the advantages and disadvantages of the video distribution of dance. Many other comments and insights were obtained, categorized into problems that arose and points particular to video distribution and new physical sensations obtained through video distribution.

4.1   Findings: Advantages of Video Distribution of Dance

4.1.1   Ease of Access
Eight out of the nine respondents mentioned ease of access to work. The following comments were made as typical examples.

P3: *This means that people who are far away, such as people from overseas, will be able to appreciate the works. In addition, people who have difficulty moving, such as small children and the elderly, will view the works safely.*

P4: *One of the first things we want to do is to make it possible for people who have difficulty going to the theater to enjoy dance under the situation where COVID-19 is spreading. In addition, it will be possible for distant audiences, such as those who live in the countryside but want to go to Tokyo to see the show and enjoy the show through video distribution, so I think it will be possible to secure a wide range of audiences.*

This is often discussed as an advantage of computer-mediated communication citeeaseofaccess1. One advantage of the Corona disaster was that it could be appreciated safely at home, even by the elderly and small children. Others commented that it could be observed by people who do not usually visit theaters and accessed from distant places such as overseas and rural areas, thus providing an opportunity for many people to view it:

P2: *Maybe the video is more likely to come back if it's associated with a famous place. Something that can reach one million or two million people will occur.*

4.1.2 Ease of Emphasis

The following comments were made about the possibility that the artist's intentions can be more easily communicated in the video compared to a live performance on stage as the direction in which to focus is already cut out and every detail can be shown:

P2: *In a normal physical performance, the angle of view is up to the audience, and we are seen through their frame, so there is a possibility that something we do not want to emphasize or show will be communicated, but with video, that possibility is reduced. However, with videos, this possibility is reduced. I think the merits of this are the same as those of films.*

P3: *In the performing arts, sometimes when you do not have a specific place or focus to look at. In the case of live performances, each viewer focuses on various places, and there are cases where the focus is clear and cases where it is not clear. In the latter case, the viewer is free to make choices or is confused. In video distribution, the focus is set in a certain manner by the frame. It is also possible to capture the facial expressions of the dancers, which are difficult to see in detail on the stage or to capture the very fine details, which depend on what the filmmaker wants to capture in the frame. In other words, I think it is possible to communicate things that are not usually communicated on stage.*

Some participants also added subtitles to emphasize when they used dialogue in their work:

P5: *I sometimes use lines and words in my works. Such things are overlooked in actual theatrical productions. I think that adding subtitles to a work can be advantageous in that it makes the intention and theme of the work clearer than on stage.*

There were comments that stage performances have a wider range of possibilities in terms of the contingency of the audience taking things in a manner that the artist did not intend.

P5: *In my case, I create various movements on stage simultaneously in a group dance work, and I think there is a lot to be said for being able to choose the point of view from which the audience chooses to be cut. I think that video may be stronger in clarifying the theme of the work and what you want to show, but when you are performing on stage, there is a wide range of possibilities for accidental things like the way you perceive something that you did not intend, or the way you feel in that scene.*

4.1.3 Expanding Artistic Expression

The following comments were made regarding expanding artistic expression through the use of camera angles to determine viewpoints, the addition of subtitles, and the use of cut editing to combine the unique effects of video:

P4: *I think it is possible to make use of the difference between the potential of works seen in theaters and the potential of works seen in video works. As artistic expression, I think it can expand possibilities.*

P9: *With video, we can create effects that can't be seen on stage, such as angles, backgrounds, getting closer, and other effects that are only possible with video.*

In particular, one participant described how the change in camera angle created a new sense of movement that could not be generated by the human body alone, as follows:

P3: *The camerawork movement can do what the human movement cannot do. I think that's a very wonderful thing because it will go beyond the raw human movement, or it will be something different. [...] I believe that dance is something that is created between relationships, and I think that the dance that occurs between the movement of the human body and the movement of the camera is a new sense of movement, a sense of movement that cannot be created by the human body alone.*

4.1.4 Changes in the Concept of Dance

Some participants mentioned that the advantage was that it changed the way they used to think about dance:

P7: *I think there was an advantage in expanding the concept of dance that we had always had, and in rethinking and questioning it. In other words, the attractive elements of dance itself have kind of disappeared, and on the other hand, there are parts that have come out more strongly. I think it was advantageous in the sense that it expanded the concept of the dance work.*

P8: *When it comes to video, we have to communicate the appeal of our own dance without the heat of live performance, so in that sense, it's not nice to say, but it's good for those who are good, and it's not good for those who have been fooling around. If dance is a form of physical expression, I feel that the people who really expressed themselves with their bodies and the people who put themselves in the word "dance" and thought they were dancing with a sense of security will be sorted out.*

As the concept of dance has changed, society has accepted the idea of consuming dance works in the form of images, and the advantage of creating works from a perspective different from the existing concept of dance is that they can be presented as dance works.

P7: *Until now, video works have been seen as something secondary, or as a kind of advertisement for seeing something real. However, as society began to accept the idea of viewing dance works on video, it became clear that dance works would not be able to circulate unless they were also viewed on video. As society began to accept the idea of consuming dance works in video form, I thought it was advantageous to be able to distribute them as dance media and information. [...] There is an advantage in the sense that you can create work from a different point of view and present it as dance work, beyond the existing concept of dance for the time being.*

In addition to the above advantages, they have the ability to generate revenue and reproduce the same image repeatedly.

4.2 Findings: Disadvantages of Video Distribution of Dance

Despite these advantages, the participants cited several disadvantages of the video distribution of dance. Mainly because of the lack of live performance, that is, not being there instead of in the theater, these points are categorized into four topics.

4.2.1 No Real Feeling

The following comments indicate that watching dance work on a video is less enjoyable than watching it in a theater:

P2: *I don't really feel it, so it's hard to concentrate no matter how much I'm doing on live streaming. When I watch live streaming as an audience, I don't find it very interesting either.*

P6: *I feel that when I watch a video distribution, I tend to receive it as information. [...] With video streaming, I feel like I'm seeing the whole thing, so I feel like I'm taking on too much of a meta-view.*

4.2.2 Lack of Feeling at the Site

This is similar to Sect. 4.2.1, however, the following comments demonstrate that video distribution cannot deliver the onsite feeling that only live performance can deliver, considering it no match for a live stage to expose the fact that we are alive:

P5: *This may sound abstract, but I think the difference between this and seeing a live performance is the subtleties of sweat and breath, and the sensations at the site that cannot be captured by sight alone. I feel that it is difficult to deliver these sensations, which is disadvantageous. [...] I feel that the disadvantage is that it is harder to reach the sensations at the site of actually appreciating dance in the same space, or in other words, experiencing it in a two-dimensional form.*

P9: *Performing on stage means exposing the rawness of our bodies, our smells, our sweat, and so on. I think there are some aspects of live performance that cannot be compared to video in exposing what it means to be alive.*

4.2.3 No Shared Experience

The following disadvantage was cited as a lack of shared experience because of the audience's inability to be in the same place.

P3: *It is said that the data of mirror neurons is clearly different between the state of seeing a video and that of seeing a live performance. I think that the sense of unity, sympathy, resonance, and so on, which are the primary pleasures of dance, will be diminished.*

P5: *It's not just about the expression on stage, but also about sharing time and space with the audience next to you and in front of you. I can't really put it into words, but I feel like it turns on something or makes me more sensitive to the audience. This shared experience may be difficult to achieve with video distribution.*

There was also a comment that sharing the same space with others creates a sense of tension:

P1: *Video distribution has a different texture, a different atmosphere of being in the space. In a theater, we sit next to other people, so there is a sense of tension because the atmosphere we share is with other people.*

4.2.4 Difficulty in Dancing Because of the Absence of an Audience

The comments on shared experiences were made from the perspective of the audience. From the dancers' perspective, the following comments were made about the difficulty of dancing without an audience:

P2: *If the audience's clear reaction cannot be seen, the improvisation that should exist no matter how fixed the dance is, is lost.*
P7: *When I'm a dancer, I feel that it's easier to perform with an audience.*

There were also comments unique to online delivery, such as connection problems and inability to immediately ask for feedback after watching work. Other comments concerned that as video works become more widespread, the value of videos that simply record what happens on stage will diminish. Other comments involved the anxiety of not having audiences come to the theater anymore and losing confidence in one's original dance, such as the feeling that one's axis as a dancer might be shaken.

4.3 Findings: Problems Encountered When Distributing Video

4.3.1 Communications Among Production Staff

Many participants mentioned that the ideas of the production staff (dance artists, lighting, stage director, etc.) who usually work on stage did not match the image of the videographer and that it took a long time to communicate with them. The following are some typical responses.

P3: *Shooting video means filming people, so rather than filming movement, there are shots of people's facial expressions or the way they stand, which are important from a cinematographer's point of view. That part and the part that captures the importance of movement and the appeal of dance from the choreographer's point of view sometimes merge and sometimes conflict. We had a lot of discussions about this, and I took my side and the cinematographer's side to find the best answer. I think that was the biggest problem.*
P8: *Especially the stage lighting staff. The same goes for the stage manager. It was a very difficult task to carry the experience that each of them had cultivated over a long period of time to some kind of new frontier beyond compromise.*

In particular, it was mentioned in Sect. 4.1.1, that the viewpoint can be defined by the camera in video distribution, and some participants mentioned that this may cause the angle imagined by the artist and videographer to differ. As the following comment shows, many participants left all the shooting and editing to the videographer:

P1: *I think the camera angle is the problem. But it's a matter of taste because the videographer can choose the point of view. Normally, if it's a dance, we can' t guide the point of view. Even if the image is different, it's okay.*

4.3.2   Technical Problems

The following comments were made about difficulty in preparing the performance of technical aspects, such as equipment and Internet speed, which are important for video distribution, and that they are still currently lacking:

P7: *There were some technical problems and hurdles, but for what I'm trying to do now, the infrastructure of the world, such as the speed of the Internet and the speed of computers, still hasn't caught up yet. That's a little bit of a problem, but I'm hoping it will develop in the future.*

P9: *I realized that it's not easy to do, and that it takes a lot of skill to make sure that the video is delivered without delay. If it's a YouTube video, you have to make a link to the video and make sure it gets to everyone. Also, if you don't have the proper wiring and internet connection, it may stop working.*

4.3.3   Uncomfortable Feeling of Dancing Against the Camera

Some participants were uncomfortable with the idea of dancing for the camera instead of the audience.

P2: *In the case of video distribution, we were dancing to this camera at this time because the camera was here, so it felt strange.*

This is considered equivalent to the difficulty in dancing owing to the absence of an audience, as described in Sect. 4.2.3. On the other hand, as mentioned in Sect. 4.5.2, we would like to note that some participants said that they felt nervous when dancing for the camera, as they did during the live performance.

In addition, there were many comments concerning problems relating to shooting, such as difficulty shooting group dances, lack of time to make shooting plans, and asking to shoot when dance artists dance themselves. Some participants also mentioned issues such as the consideration of music copyright during distribution.

4.4   Findings: What Dance Artists Focused on in Their Video Distribution

Some comments were particular to the angles required to show parts of the performance that those who came to see the performance would not otherwise be able to observe or to communicate the dancing bodies:

P8: *I think it's important to put the camera in the line of sight of the people who came to see the performance but couldn't look into it. [...] Nowadays, even if the screen is large, people watch it on their computers, or if it's not so good, almost 70% of the audience is watching it on their smartphones. When that happens, if you want to communicate the structure of the stage but the camera is pulled back, the dance doesn't come across. In that sense, I wanted to communicate the body of the dance, so I thought about leaning in a little more.*

In addition to these angles, some participants were particular about editing and music to create unique video effects. In addition, some participants stated that the camera is often moving constantly in recent videos and that it is easy to get bored with a fixed camera, additional switching was therefore used:

P5: *The dancers are at a fixed point, and the camera is moving all the time, isn't it? I think our modern eyes are unconsciously used to that, so if the camera is fixed, we would get bored.*

Apart from the advantages of video, as described above, some participants were particular about following the movement of the dance in a comfortable state in the video as well:

P3: *In the creative process, there is a certain order in which movements occur, and a certain order of priority, but videographers shoot from a completely different perspective. In some cases, that's good. Movement is a connection, and it doesn't leave traces like a painting. I think it is necessary to follow it in a comfortable way, as it continues and disappears.*

Some participants believed that there are qualities of movement for video works, and that it is important to extract them:

P3: *There is a possibility that a movement that is communicated in a live performance, for example, a movement with high tension that vibrates and trembles minutely, may appear to be just standing in a video. If you are going to make a video work, it would be more interesting to extract the quality of movement for video, or the vocabulary of movement that incorporates this quality.*

In addition, some participants tried to create the lost sense of live performance mentioned in Sect.4.2. Using video streaming in addition, as follows:

P5: *There were about 8 performers in the zoom, so I wanted to make it look like an apartment complex. I wanted to make it look like if what happened upstairs had an effect on what happened downstairs in real time. Like if someone thumped on the wall, it would affect other people's choreography. If I were, to sum up, what I was obsessed with, it would probably be the sense of live performance. I put a lot of importance on the fact that it's happening somewhere right now.*

4.5   Findings: New Physical Sensations Gained from Video Distribution

4.5.1   Specific Physical Sensations

Among the new physical sensations discovered through video distribution, a few were particularly concrete and scattered. Several participants were able to obtain a delicate physical sensation, such that even the body not shown in the video remained as a sensation:

> **P8:** *I feel like I have to take more responsibility for my body parts, and I need to do that a lot. Also, even when only my right hand is on the screen, the feeling of my left foot is reflected in the video. I've come to imagine my body more sensitively than when I dance on stage. It's actually necessary on stage too. I feel that dancing on video helps me to brush up my senses and feelings.*

A similar feeling was expressed by some participants, who stated that they focused on slowing down and stopping. The reasons were that the resolution of the video was not in time for the movement and that being filmed gives us the calmness of knowing that we are going to see it, as follows:

> **P1:** *It is better to dance according to the number of pixels in the camera. There is a big difference between raw texture and video texture, so if you know how much clarity, how fast the arms move, and how much they stop, you will be able to specialize in the video.*

> **P3:** *I think maybe there is a sense that the slow movement is less scary. There's a big difference between the gaze you get from the audience on stage and the gaze you get from the camera. When the audience looks at us, there is a fear that they might not see us, that they might not look at us. On the other hand, with a camera, you are supposed to shoot, so you already know that you will be seen. I think it gives us a sense of calmness to think about how many variations of movement we can make within that fixed framework.*

> **P5:** *In my own feeling, I was really interested in moving fast. But now, I understand that it's not possible to do it in time with video. For example, the resolution or panning the camera if it involves movement. In this way, I think the point of view and the time axis have changed a little. As a physical sensation in dancing. When I check the filmed videos, I feel that I can understand what I am doing, such as having intonation, slowing down, and concentrating on each and every move.*

There were also comments about coating the body with power such that it could be delivered clearly in the video, and clearly outlining the body without relying on atmosphere was asserted:

P4: *I think a good dancer is one who can change the way he moves his body, coating it with power and the way he relaxes as much as possible. But in the case of video, I think it's a bit coating. In other words, you can see more of the visuals than the atmosphere. In order to make it look clearer, I coat the video a little more.*

P9: *As is often the case with contemporary dance, it creates a vague atmosphere or mood. Instead of that kind of presentation, I try to make it clear what I want to deliver to the camera lens. Also, I was told that I should dance with a clear outline of my body and not rely on the atmosphere, because I wouldn't be able to convey the lingering atmosphere. I thought that was a good idea, so I challenged myself with a slightly different physical sensation from the live stage.*

In addition, some participants valued the feeling, stating that they could see it in the video as follows:

P8: *When we dance with only our senses, our ideals go further and further away from our bodies. When I touch my own hands, there is a big difference between the videos of people who have this feeling and people who just grab their hands based on words, and there is a sense of skin, so I've become more conscious of that when I dance.*

Others commented that they now look at their bodies more objectively than when normally dancing on stage and that they now place greater value on violence, hypnotism, dynamism, and lines of sight.

4.5.2   Conscious Physical Sensation

Some, participants discovered new physical sensations at a conscious level. Other participants stated that they showed what moved from the heart, rather than the superficial interest of the dance:

P9: *In the end, it's not enough to be clever. I used to like the superficial fun of dance. However, if I don't know where the heart is that I want to dance, rather than the choreography, I will end up showing a skeleton or just an empty form of dance.*

Some participants also asserted that by focusing on the camera lens, they felt like they were dancing in a duo with the cameraman, and that feeling that they were on stage made them feel nervous.

P9: *I had a great feeling that I was dancing in a kind of duo relationship with the cameraman. [...] It was a one-shot recording, so when it came time to shoot, I was really nervous and felt like I was on stage. [...] It was during the shooting that I was able to believe that there were people watching me on the other side of the camera. That feeling was really strange. Up until now, even though I couldn't see the audience on stage* *because of the lighting, I could feel their presence, and I danced while talking and interacting with them. I couldn't actually communicate with the audience, but I could believe that they were there and that was a new feeling for me.*

In addition, based on the above experience, this participant made a conscious discovery to push herself to become more stoic.

P9: *I want to strengthen my hips and be able to move my lower body properly, so I have no excuses and want to push myself even more stoically. So, I realized that if I don't have a really strong appeal as a dancer and as a piece of art, I won't be able to make it.*

Some participants wanted to go beyond the neat angle of view and pursue a sense of dynamism and movement that exceeded the sensation of seeing.

P5: *I discovered that there is a part of me that wants to go out of my comfort zone. I don't find it very appealing to keep the image within the angle of view. I think I'm trying my best to look for a sense of movement that goes beyond the sensation of looking at the image from a fixed point or for interesting movements.*

5   Discussion

The semi-structured interviews revealed the advantages and disadvantages Japanese dance artists felt in distributing videos, and what challenges, particular points, and new physical sensations were discovered. Now that COVID-19 has increased current video distribution, the concept of original dance has changed. While there are advantages as described in Sect. 4.1, the absence of an audience continues to remove the unique feeling of a live performance that is missing, and the problems described in Sect. 4.3 suggest that there is room for improvement. Based on these results and those obtained from Sects. 4.4 and 4.5, we discuss ways to provide better computer support. The implications of the findings for other HCI studies outside the context of videos are also discussed.

5.1   Dance Specializing in Visual Media

As mentioned in Sect. 4.5, the fact that new physical sensations are obtained by distributing videos suggests that dances may be specialized for visual media. Delicate movements, slow movements, and stops look better on videos than live movements. In particular, the effect of the difference in frame rates on dance seems significant. If the frame rate is low, and stops, slow movements may look better; conversely, if the frame rate is high, dances that move smoothly may look better.

It also suggests a new sense of motion and relationship between the dancer and the camera. Dance that occurs between the motion of the human and that of the camera will become a new sense of motion that cannot be generated solely by human motion. Some participants also felt they were dancing with the cameraman as a duo. From these points, it can be observed that effective camera work exists which is different from that of theatrical performances such as movies, dramas, and music concerts [21], and that it must be investigated from a different perspective than the context of other fields.

5.2 Implications for HCI Research Other Than Visual Media

Furthermore, some technologies may be useful for video-based dance art. For example, VR can be used to virtually enrich the content of scenes. Therefore, it is possible that the enriched or dynamic VR scenes assist in performing video-based artistic dance for artists, conducting quality video dance for videography practitioners, or improving the quality perceived by possible audiences. For example, VR may be able to compensate for the lack of shared experiences, as suggested by its disadvantages.

Some participants found it difficult to dance owing to the absence of an audience, however, some stated that by focusing on the camera, the same tension as on a regular stage could be felt. This suggests that it is possible to create a sense of tension that can be observed by the audience. For example, the eyes of the audience watching video streaming could be reflected on the monitor of the theater auditorium to create a sense of tension of being watched.

In addition, the difficulty of communication among the production staff was frequently cited as a problem. Several studies [5,6,26] assist communication among production staff, however, no studies are published on communication with video staff, and this challenge has emerged because of the increase in video distribution in this particular context, caused by COVID-19. This may be because the cameraman does not understand the concepts that were important in dance, the dance artist cannot convey the image well. Therefore, it is necessary to develop a support system to bridge this gap. For example, a tool that can easily create a dance storyboard would be useful for both parties to coordinate images during shooting.

6 Conclusion

In this study, we investigated how Japanese dance artists shifted to video distribution in response to the spread of COVID-19 and how they perceived this shift. Semi-structured interviews were conducted with nine dance artists to clarify the advantages and disadvantages of video-distributing dance, problems that arose when video-distributing dance, particular points and new physical sensations obtained using video-distributing dance. These results will provide relevant knowledge not only for researchers but also for active dance artists in a society living with COVID-19. Based on these results, we identified aspects of specialized dance for visual media and of the need to investigate this from a different context than other fields, such as theater and music. Room for improvement in the interaction with the audience and the communication between the production staff was also discusses alongside ways to provide better computational support using VR, support systems, and visual media.

However, some limitations should also be discussed. Semi-structured interviews were chosen to elicit in-depth perspectives, however, the interviewee sample was small. As mentioned in Sect. 3, designing a questionnaire based on the above results and collecting a more widespread number of responses from not only dance artists but also viewers would provide additional accurate feedback and a greater degree of generalization for the findings. Nevertheless, we believe that the results, which began as an attempt to adapt to the changes brought about by COVID-19 via computers, provide a basis for improved understanding in this context and are instructive for HCI researchers attempting to design novel interaction techniques.

Acknowledgement. We thank all dance artists who contributed to this study. We would also like to express our gratitude to Associate Professor Motoko Hirayama of Tsukuba University for connecting us with dance artists. We would like to thank Editage (www.editage.com) for English language editing.

References

1. Anselm, S., Juliet, C.: Basics of Qualitative Research: Grounded Theory Procedures and Techniques. Sage Publications, Newbury Park (1990)
2. Ashtari, A., Stevšić, S., Nägeli, T., Bazin, J.C., Hilliges, O.: Capturing subjective first-person view shots with drones for automated cinematography. ACM Trans. Graph. **39**(5) (2020). https://doi.org/10.1145/3378673
3. Bermudez, B., Ziegler, C.: Pre-choreographic movement kit. In: Proceedings of the 2014 International Workshop on Movement and Computing, MOCO 2014, pp. 7–12. Association for Computing Machinery, New York (2014). https://doi.org/10.1145/2617995.2617997
4. Caraballo, L.E., Montes-Romero, Á., Díaz-Báñez, J.M., Capitán, J., Torres-González, A., Ollero, A.: Autonomous planning for multiple aerial cinematographers (2020)
5. Carroll, E.A., Lottridge, D., Latulipe, C., Singh, V., Word, M.: Bodies in critique: a technological intervention in the dance production process. In: Proceedings of the ACM 2012 Conference on Computer Supported Cooperative Work, CSCW 2012, pp. 705–714. Association for Computing Machinery, New York (2012). https://doi.org/10.1145/2145204.2145311
6. Ciolfi Felice, M., Fdili Alaoui, S., Mackay, W.E.: Knotation: exploring and documenting choreographic processes, pp. 1–12. Association for Computing Machinery, New York (2018). https://doi.org/10.1145/3173574.3174022
7. Correia, N.N., Masu, R., Pham, A.H.D., Feitsch, J.: Connected layers: evaluating visualizations of embodiment in contemporary dance performances. Association for Computing Machinery, New York (2021). https://doi.org/10.1145/3430524.3440621

8. Fujimoto, M., Naotaka, F., Terada, T., Tsukamoto, M.: Lighting choreographer: an led control system for dance performances. In: Proceedings of the 13th International Conference on Ubiquitous Computing, UbiComp 2011, pp. 613–614. Association for Computing Machinery, New York (2011). https://doi.org/10.1145/2030112.2030240

9. Goldschmidt, K.: The covid-19 pandemic: technology use to support the wellbeing of children. J. pediatr. Nurs. **53**, 88–90 (2020). https://doi.org/10.1016/j.pedn.2020.04.013

10. Group, D.E.S. (ed.): Dance Studies Lecture: Dance and Dance Education. Taishukan Shoten, Tokyo (1991)

11. Harada, J.: A case study on viewpoints of dance appreciation. Memoirs Osaka Jogakuin (1), 1–12 (2004). https://ci.nii.ac.jp/naid/110001159939/

12. Harada, J., Sakata, M., Tokuka, M.: Communication structure in dance appreciation: comparison of live and video. Dance Stud. **2007**(30), 53–53 (2007). https://doi.org/10.11235/buyougaku1978.2007.53

13. Harada, J., Sakata, M., Tokuka, M., Uchida, O.: Study on the appreciation of dance works. Dance Stud. **2006**(29), 32–32 (2006). https://doi.org/10.11235/buyougaku1978.2006.32

14. Hartmann, N.N., Lussier, B.: Managing the sales force through the unexpected exogenous covid-19 crisis. Ind. Market. Manag. **88**, 101–111 (2020). https://doi.org/10.1016/j.indmarman.2020.05.005. https://www.sciencedirect.com/science/article/pii/S0019850120302972

15. Hsueh, S., Alaoui, S.F., Mackay, W.E.: Understanding Kinaesthetic creativity in dance, pp. 1–12. Association for Computing Machinery, New York (2019). https://doi.org/10.1145/3290605.3300741

16. Ito, M., Shirai, A.: A study regarding appreciation of dance performance: how the p.e. students assimilate a dance performance by people with intellectual disabilities and their families. Res. J. JAPEW **31**, 19–33 (2015). https://doi.org/10.11206/japew.31.19. https://ci.nii.ac.jp/naid/130005130555/

17. Jeon, M., Fiebrink, R., Edmonds, E.A., Herath, D.: From rituals to magic: interactive art and HCI of the past, present, and future. Int. J. Hum. Comput. Stud. **131**, 108–119 (2019). https://doi.org/10.1016/j.ijhcs.2019.06.005, https://www.sciencedirect.com/science/article/pii/S1071581919300758. 50 years of the International Journal of Human-Computer Studies. Reflections on the past, present and future of human-centred technologies

18. Joubert, N., et al.: Towards a drone cinematographer: guiding quadrotor cameras using visual composition principles (2016)

19. Jürgens, S., Correia, N.N., Masu, R.: The body beyond movement: (missed) opportunities to engage with contemporary dance in HCI. Association for Computing Machinery, New York (2021). https://doi.org/10.1145/3430524.3440624

20. Kerres, M.: Against all odds: education in Germany coping with covid-19. Postdigital Sci. Educ. **2**(3), 690–694 (2020). https://doi.org/10.1007/s42438-020-00130-7

21. Laufer, G., Åblad, A.: Spirit in the screen: the effect of CuePilot on the viewer's experience in live broadcasted music competitions (2020)

22. Matsuoka, A.: An approach to video dance from film theory. J. Grad. Sch. Hum. Sci. **14**, 137–145 (2012)

23. Mochizuki, T.: The current situation of dance creation activities under the situation of coronavirus infection spread. Bull. Teikyo Univ. Sci. **17**, 121–128 (2021). https://ci.nii.ac.jp/naid/40022564617/

24. NPO Total Health Care for Artists Japan: Effects of Corona on Dancers' Physical Condition and Performance: A Questionnaire Survey Report. NPO Total Health Care for Artists Japan (2021)
25. Sakamoto, K., Tanaka, Y., Yamashita, K., Okada, A.: Effects of different display resolutions on physiological and psychological evaluation: comparison by viewing mode. Tech. Rep. Inst. Image Inf. Telev. Eng. **39**, 23–26 (2015). https://doi.org/10.11485/itetr.39.43.0_23. https://ci.nii.ac.jp/naid/110010016002/
26. Singh, V., Latulipe, C., Carroll, E., Lottridge, D.: The choreographer's notebook: a video annotation system for dancers and choreographers. In: Proceedings of the 8th ACM Conference on Creativity and Cognition, C&C 2011, pp. 197–206. Association for Computing Machinery, New York (2011). https://doi.org/10.1145/2069618.2069653
27. Taki, K., Benjamin, W.: The Work of Art in the Age of Mechanical Reproduction. Intensive Reading. Iwanami Shoten (2000). https://books.google.co.jp/books?id=kGWwPAAACAAJ
28. Tsuchida, S., Takemori, T., Terada, T., Tsukamoto, M.: Mimebot: spherical robot visually imitating a rolling sphere. Int. J. Pervasive Comput. Commun. **13**(1), 92–111 (2017). https://doi.org/10.1108/IJPCC-01-2017-0006
29. Tu, P.Y., Yuan, C.W.T., Wang, H.C.: Do you think what I think: perceptions of delayed instant messages in computer-mediated communication of romantic relations, pp. 1–11. Association for Computing Machinery, New York (2018). https://doi.org/10.1145/3173574.3173675
30. Uchiyama, M., Terayama, Y.: On the determinants of perspective in dance appreciation. Dance Stud. **2013**(36), 93 (2013). https://doi.org/10.11235/buyougaku.2013.36_93
31. Van Nort, D.: [radical] signals from life: from muscle sensing to embodied machine listening/learning within a large-scale performance piece. In: Proceedings of the 2nd International Workshop on Movement and Computing, MOCO 2015, pp. 124–127. Association for Computing Machinery, New York (2015). https://doi.org/10.1145/2790994.2791015
32. Wang, Y., Hong, A., Li, X., Gao, J.: Marketing innovations during a global crisis: a study of china firms' response to covid-19. J. Bus. Res. **116**, 214–220 (2020). https://doi.org/10.1016/j.jbusres.2020.05.029. https://www.sciencedirect.com/science/article/pii/S014829632030326X
33. Wen, J., Kow, Y.M., Chen, Y.: Online games and family ties: influences of social networking game on family relationship. In: Campos, P., Graham, N., Jorge, J., Nunes, N., Palanque, P., Winckler, M. (eds.) INTERACT 2011. LNCS, vol. 6948, pp. 250–264. Springer, Heidelberg (2011). https://doi.org/10.1007/978-3-642-23765-2_18
34. Zhou, Q., Chua, C.C., Knibbe, J., Goncalves, J., Velloso, E.: Dance and choreography in HCI: a two-decade retrospective. In: Proceedings of the 2021 CHI Conference on Human Factors in Computing Systems, CHI 2021. Association for Computing Machinery, New York (2021). https://doi.org/10.1145/3411764.3445804

Apps and Digital Resources in Speech and Language Therapy - Which Factors Influence Therapists' Acceptance?

Benedikt Szabó, Susanne Dirks[(⊠)], and Anna-Lena Scherger

Department of Rehabilitation Sciences, Research Unit of Rehabilitation Technology,
TU Dortmund University, Emil-Figge-Str. 50, 44227 Dortmund, Germany
{benedikt.szabo,susanne.dirks}@tu-dortmund.de

Abstract. The aging of society, an increasing shortage of skilled professionals, and the digitization of the healthcare sector will continue to intensify in the future. To meet these challenges, new developments in the field of health technologies, such as digital therapy or teletherapy, are gaining importance.

The aim of the present study was to investigate speech and language pathologists' (SLPs) acceptance of apps and digital resources for interventions. Guided expert interviews with practicing SLPs ($N = 5$) were conducted focusing self-assessment of technical competence, technology use and reasons for non-use, experience of using apps, conditions of use, assessment of effort, barriers, and potentials.

Results show that although all interviewees rated both the potential of apps and digital resources for the quality of their work and their own technical competencies as high, only two out of five regularly used digital resources in their daily work. Feedback from the clients on the use of apps in therapy is predominantly positive. In contrast, the effort required to obtain the apps, to learn how to use them, and for the initial preparation are high. The equipment of the therapy rooms with devices and WLAN access and the support provided by co-workers and supervisors are also rated as inadequate. Regarding their attitudes toward technology, the therapists' self-image and rather conservative mindsets toward digital technologies are described as hindering.

The study revealed that the structural environment and various personality traits of the therapists have great relevance for the use digital resources in speech and language therapy.

Keywords: Technology acceptance · Speech and language pathologists · Apps in intervention

1 Introduction

1.1 General Background

In the context of digitalization, everyday life is changing increasingly. This is also the case in speech and language therapy, along with the increasing number of different tools

© The Author(s), under exclusive license to Springer Nature Switzerland AG 2022
M. Antona and C. Stephanidis (Eds.): HCII 2022, LNCS 13308, pp. 379–391, 2022.
https://doi.org/10.1007/978-3-031-05028-2_25

available to the speech and language pathologists (SLPs). They are faced with the task of constantly adapting to a changing field and finding their own role and identity in the midst of this transformation. Especially, the areas of assessment and intervention can be affected by the advancing digitalization, as speech therapy applications and PC programs are becoming more and more widespread [1]. The Covid-19 pandemic has further stimulated these changes towards more use of technology, urging SLPs to use digital tools like video platforms to enable communication with their patients at all. Teletherapy and digitally-supported face-to-face therapy include the use of therapy apps. These applications, which can be used on mobile devices such as smartphones or tablet PCs, open up new, innovative treatment methods. They can be used as a supplement to original approaches in (tele)-therapy or for autonomous home exercise by patients.

Another relevant aspect for the future of speech and language therapy will be the growing expenditure of the health system. It is foreseeable that the discussion about cost reductions and efficiency increases will become increasingly louder. The speech and language therapy sector will also be confronted with these demands. As a consequence, this will "lead to more competition within health care providers for increasingly scarce resources" [2]. In order to meet these challenges, great hope is placed in new developments in the field of health technologies. In this way, practical, alternative access routes to therapeutic care are to be established and expanded [3] as a beginning of a digital transformation of health care [2] being currently underway.

Although some researchers claim the acquisition of knowledge and skills in relation to digital forms of intervention to be an ethical duty of therapeutic professionals [4], specific evidence for the use of new media and digital components in speech and language therapy, especially for children with developmental language disorders, is still limited [5]. The actual use of digital components in speech and language therapy with children and the motivations for this (non-)use therefore remain under-researched to date.

Therefore, the aim of the present study is to investigate which factors influence the acceptance of therapy apps and the willingness to use them in speech therapy. The objective is to identify facilitating and hindering factors that have an impact on their use. A qualitative approach was chosen to answer these research questions. In five interviews with SLPs, practical experiences, digital competence and openness as well as acceptance attitudes of the experts were explored.

As acceptance attitudes towards technologies and the actual use are of interest for these purposes, the next section sums up models of acceptance and use of technology.

The remainder of this article will focus on the methodology followed by a presentation and a discussion of the results. A conclusion section will wrap up the contribution.

1.2 Technology Acceptance Models

Technical innovations should always be examined in terms of their acceptance by individuals or social groups, as up to 80% of users drop out when using assistive technologies [6]. By assessing the prerequisites, preferences, and abilities of potential users at an early stage, the dropout rates can be minimized.

To capture user-specific usage indicators, technology acceptance models can be used.

The acceptance of a technology is often equated with its actual use. However, the term has deeper dimensions of meaning. Thus, in addition to the practical action component, the behavioral level of the intention to use the new technology is also relevant to the construct of acceptance [7]. To assess the acceptance of a new technology, individual and/or group-related attitudes and user behavior are examined to identify indicators that can be used to predict the subsequent adaptation of a technical innovation as precisely as possible. In this way, technology acceptance research contributes to ensuring the most sustainable application of technological innovations. In the following, the most important technology acceptance theories and models are presented.

TAM

The Technology Acceptance model (TAM), developed by Davis [8] integrates the core idea of the Theory of Reasoned Action [9]. This theory states that an individual's intention can usually be inferred from his or her behavior. The TAM forms the basis for many subsequent models and theories of technology acceptance. Davis identifies *Perceived Usefulness* and *Perceived Ease of Use* as the central determinants for the *Intention to Use* a new technology. This intention in turn usually results in *Usage Behavior*, which he interprets as acceptance. However, the TAM could not adequately explain the complexity of these processes, as revealed in empirical studies. Therefore, as successor models, TAM2 and TAM3 extended the initial model with further acceptance indicators [10, 11].

UTAUT

For the Unified Theory of Acceptance and Use of Technology (UTAUT), Venkatesh et al. [12] combined the results from various existing technology acceptance models. The theory was specifically designed for application within an organizational context.

The main indicators already known from the TAM, *Performance Expectancy* and *Effort Expectancy*, were enhanced by two new indicators, *Social Influence,* and *Supportive Conditions*. Social influence refers to the influence that (professionally) important persons, such as superiors or colleagues, have on the intention to use a new technology. The supporting conditions refer to the technical and infrastructural equipment that can be resorted to when using the new technology. These supporting conditions directly influence the usage behavior, while the other three constructs influence the behavioral intention. Furthermore, Venkatesh et al. [12] identified secondary factors, such as *Gender, Age, Experience*, and *Voluntariness of Use*, which moderate the influence of the main variables on behavioral intention and use behavior.

In a quantitative study, Liu et al. confirmed the suitability of the UTAUT for the acceptance of rehabilitation technologies by therapists [6].

UTAUT2

In the follow-up theory UTAUT2, Venkatesh, Thong & Xu [13] extended the original model by three main indicators. In this way, the theory should achieve better applicability for users of a technology ('consumers') outside the organizational context.

The added indicator *Hedonic Motivation* refers to the enjoyment that the use of a technology generates in the user. Its impact on acceptance and usage behavior has been investigated and confirmed in various studies. According to the theory, this component has an influence on behavioral intention. By adding the dimension *Price Value*, an economic factor has been integrated into the theory. In contrast to the original UTAUT, the costs of a technology represent a relevant factor for the acceptance and use of private users. A positive influence on the intention to use would therefore be given if the advantages of use outweigh the economic costs of acquisition for the user. The newly introduced indicator *Habit* needs to be distinguished from the indicator *Experience*, which already exists in the UTAUT. Venkatesh et al. [13] explain that habit describes the degree to which an action is performed automatically due to previous learning processes. In contrast, experience describes the time span between the first use of a technology and the time of the investigation.

Technology acceptance models, such as TAM and UTAUT, provide comprehensible explanations for the acceptance of new technologies in various fields of application, and have been verified in many scientific and practical studies. However, they are repeatedly criticized for not adequately capturing the complexity of technology acceptance processes and for assuming very different individual intentions and perceptions [14]. One of the central aims of the presented study is the exploration of whether the existing models can explain the attitudes and usage behavior of SLPs towards the use of apps in speech and language therapy.

1.3   State of Research and Research Questions

The available research in the field of technology acceptance and the use of apps in speech and language therapy, is rather limited so far. Moreover, the studies focus on the needs and attitudes of the patients rather than the therapist's perspective. An exception is the acceptance of video therapy by therapists and patients; some studies were conducted on this in the course of the COVID19 pandemic [15, 16].

Jakob and Späth [17] published in 2021 a study in which, among other things, the acceptance of SLPs for the Neolexon articulation app was evaluated. The results showed a high level of overall acceptance, and the SLPs were convinced of the professional benefits of the application. They rated the use of the app as beneficial for the achievement of therapeutic goals. With n = 58, the sample was rather small for a quantitative study and the survey dimensions showed little depth. Nevertheless, the results of the study indicate that the use of apps in speech and language therapy is accepted by SLPs, if it meets their therapeutic quality standards.

Malchus [18] investigated technology acceptance factors for therapists in the context of social robot use in speech therapy. In this work, the following indicators were assessed as particularly relevant: openness to digital technologies, ease of use and affordability. Inhibiting factors were a lack of prior technical knowledge and a high effort to use the technology. In addition, SLPs showed defensive reactions when they perceived the technology as a substitute for themselves. Although the study does not specifically address the use of apps, it does provide valuable information regarding the significant acceptance factors of technological innovations in the field of speech therapy.

These findings are largely consistent with results from various studies in the U.S., where the use of new technologies in therapeutic professions is more widespread and therefore the body of research is more comprehensive. In a UTAUT-based study on the technology acceptance behavior of occupational and physical therapists, Liu et al.

[6] found that the intention to use the technology was significantly influenced by the performance expectancy of the technology and that the actual use of a technology was most strongly promoted by the technical and organizational infrastructure available in the workplace. They found no evidence for the relevance of effort expectancy and social influence on the therapists' behavioral intention. Contrary to this, a study by Albudoor and Peña [19] showed that the intention to use technology in therapy is strongly influenced by the perceived attitude of close people around the therapist. They thus saw social influence as one of the main shaping factors for behavioral intention.

The present study aims to contribute to the identification of acceptance factors in SLPs that promote the motivation to use apps in speech and language therapy. To achieve this, facilitating and hindering factors need to be identified based on the indicators extracted from the known acceptance models and the current state of research. To address these research questions, a qualitative approach was chosen, which is described in more detail in the following section.

2 Methods

2.1 Methodological Procedure

For answering the research question, qualitative data from guided expert interviews with SLPs was collected. This is considered to be an adequate approach to gain knowledge about the experience and actions of the experts. For the purposes of this study, an expert is defined as a person who has specific knowledge about an issue or a certain group. He/she is constructed as an expert from the outside because of his/her function, position or activity. The interviewees for this study are thus given the status of experts in that they, as professionals working in speech and language therapy, have at least theoretically dealt with the use of new technologies for therapy purposes and have individual experiences and attitudes to the topic. Although there is a comprehensive body of research on technology acceptance in general through various quantitative studies, the theoretical basis is not very extensive, especially in the field of speech and language therapy and the use of apps for therapy purposes.

Within qualitative research, guided expert interviews belong to the so-called semi-standardized or semi-open approaches. In addition to the claim of qualitative research to uphold the principles of openness, flexibility, and communication [20, 21], the guideline integrates a minimum of structure. In this way, it serves as a concrete aid in the survey situation and to structure the topic [22]. Likewise, the use of a guideline increases the comparability of the collected data and facilitates the later evaluation.

For the construction of the guideline, the dimensions of the research question and the findings from the technology-acceptance models were used to form nine thematic question blocks. The questions within the blocks were developed with the help of the principles 'collect - check - sort - subsume' according to [22]. In a first step, all possible questions were collected that arose in the process of creating the guideline. In the second step, these questions were checked for their suitability. Irrelevant or unsuitable questions were sorted out and the list of questions was structured. Pure fact queries and those questions that only contributed insufficiently to answering the research question were eliminated. After this revision, only a fraction of the original questions remained, which were then sorted in a further step. The questions were grouped into thematic blocks which were put into a natural conversational order, placing the conversation-opening questions at the top of each of them. In the fourth step, the guideline was put into its final form. In order to motivate free narrations, each topic block was preceded by an impulse. The content-related aspects to be dealt with within the thematic complex were listed in bullet points in a separate column. In case the interviewee did not come up with these contents him/herself, concrete follow-up questions were collected in a further column. Moreover, maintenance questions were prepared to keep the conversation flowing and to avoid long pauses.

The individual thematic complexes were preceded by fact-finding questions about the interviewee, in which age, educational background, work experience and questions about the job were asked. In doing so, relevant information was collected at the beginning of the interview in order to continue with the content-related questions. These addressed the aspects of previous experience with apps in intervention, self-assessment of one's own level of competence in the use of technologies, description of one's own use or reasons for non-use, experience of using apps, feedback on use, conditions of use, assessment of effort, assessment of barriers and potentials of the technology, as well as an open-ended creative question to initiate the end of the interview.

The guide was tested in a pretest interview with a SLP for its practicality. The order of the topic blocks was slightly adapted to the 'natural' course of the interview, and individual question aspects were sorted out or added.

2.2 Participants

The selection of the interview partners was based on two main criteria, an occupation in the field of speech and language therapy in a practice and the motivation to explain one's own attitude to the topic of apps/digital media for intervention purposes. It was not a requirement to use apps in speech and language therapy or to have done so in the past. Rather, it was of interest to understand the subjective attitude backgrounds of the respondents. When compiling the sample, the focus was also placed on gaining interviewees of different genders and with different educational backgrounds[1], as well as covering a broad age range. By recruiting people who have been working in the field for many years and those who are relatively new to the field, the variability within the group of interviewees was to be increased. Thus, the principle of the 'formation of counter horizons' was considered [22]. The selection principles mentioned here are intended to consider the qualitative research claim to narrowly define the group of interviewees while at the same time maximizing the variability of the individual members [22]. For an overview of participants, see Table 1.

To address the research question, interviews were conducted with five experts working in speech and language therapy. Three of these interview partners were acquired through personal contacts. Another interview partner was recruited through the referral of an interviewed person. The fifth interview was initiated by contacting a practice by

---

[1] In Germany, there are several possible ways to become a SLP. One way is through vocational training to become a state-approved speech therapist, another is through academic studies in speech therapy, clinical linguistics, patholinguistics, or speech therapy education.

Table 1. Participant overview.

Participant	1	2	3	4	5
Educational background	Academic	Academic	Academic	Vocational training	Academic
Age	23 years	57 years	45 years	44 years	23
Professional experience	2 years	32 years	16 years	17 years	1,5 years
Gender	Female	Female	Male	Male	Female

email via its website, where the practice presented itself as working explicitly with digital methods. The practice in turn selected the interviewee internally as suitable because of his special experience in the field.

2.3 Interview Procedure

The data collection took place in July 2021. All interviews were conducted at the workplaces of the interviewees in personal meetings. The hygiene rules applicable in the respective practices were adhered to. The interviewees gave their written informed consent before starting the interview which were audio-recorded for further data processing. The average duration of the interviews was 30 min.

One of the interviews can be claimed an outlier. The interviewee herself was the only one among the participants who had no practical experience in the use of therapy apps. The interview conducted with her is the shortest at 15 min, but overall, it provides an interesting contrast to the other interviews.

2.4 Interview Analysis

In a first step, the audio recordings were transcribed verbatim, with slight smoothing of the speech according to the transcription rules of [9]. In a second step, the content-structuring qualitative content analysis according to [9] was chosen for further investigation of the data, representing a 7-phase, linear analysis process.

In a first text work phase with the transcripts, an initial global understanding of interrelationships was gained and a case summary for each interview was written. In a second phase, the main categories were developed deductively: personal information, technical competence, openness, previous experience, app use, barriers, potentials, feedback, user experience, practical conditions, effort and future scenario. Phase 3 involved an initial coding process in which the main categories were applied to the entire data. Therefore, assigned text passages from all five interview transcripts were labelled accordingly with the help of the MAXQDA 11 software (11.1.14) [24]. Phase 4 and 5 consisted of the compilation of all coded text passages and the inductive development of the subcategories. This resulted in between three and six sub-categories per main category. In order to differentiate further, a second coding process was carried out in phase 6, in which the newly formed subcategories were subsequently integrated into the software and applied to the entire data set and the respective text passages collected under each main category. In order to carry out a category-based evaluation, short summaries for the main categories and subcategories that were assessed as particularly relevant were prepared in phase 7 at the end of the analysis process, thus further compressing the data material and focusing it in terms of answering the research question.

The following section presents the most important results of the interviews in relation to the indicators from the technology acceptance models.

3 Results

To relate the outcomes of this research to the known technology acceptance theories, the results are described according to the main factors of the UTAUT model: Performance Expectancy, Effort Expectancy, Social Influence and Supportive Conditions. Work by other researchers has shown that technology acceptance models are very well suited for surveying user acceptance of assistive technologies and therapy software [25].

In addition to the factors covered by existing models, aspects such as Professional Skills and Lack of Openness were identified in this work as important factors and are subsequently elaborated.

3.1 Performance Expectancy

Therapy apps are rated better by the interviewed experts than the frequency of their use would suggest. All experts see a tangible added value, both for their patients and for themselves in terms of work organization. They evaluate their use within the therapy setting or as an accompanying home exercise as positive. All respondents acknowledged the increased motivation of the patients as a major benefit. Since digital devices such as smartphones and tablets are of high relevance in everyday life and most patients are familiar with their use, they are widely accepted by almost all of them. The use of apps also generates organizational advantages for the therapists. As less material needs to be printed, transported, or organized, schedules can be optimized, and the daily work routine can be made more effective.

In relation to UTAUT, these aspects can be summarized under the term *Performance Expectancy*. In line with other studies, this factor seems to be the strongest predictor for a behavioral intention to use a new technology and thus ultimately a predictor for a concrete use of the technology. Therapy apps can improve the 'Job Performance' of the therapist, i.e. they create a benefit for the therapist in his or her work processes. Increased motivation and greater progress of patients are also perceived as quality factors in the work of SLPs. This related to the indicator *Perceived Usefulness*, which is also known from the TAM as a significant factor influencing the intention to use new technologies.

3.2 Effort Expectancy

The interviewed SLPs described the required effort as particularly high, especially at the beginning of the use. The effort includes the costs of acquiring the devices and apps, the effort required to learn how to use them, and the effort required to gather information about which apps can be used for which patient groups and disorders. The perceived effort varies depending on the therapists' level of technical and digital competence. Once a basic familiarity has been established, the effort no longer represents a barrier to future use. In some cases, a lower level of effort is described compared to conventional non-digital therapy methods.

In addition to the technical profile of the SLPs, the crucial factor for the intention to use apps in speech therapy is the effort required to start using them.

3.3 Social Influence

In line with other studies, this study found only few indications of the relevance of social influence on the use of therapy apps. The interview results indicated no interrelation between the use of an app and an affirmative exchange about it between colleagues. However, it can be assumed that younger professionals with less confidence and experience might be more influenced by an encouraging collegial environment. This could at least provide impulses to reflect upon the topic, especially for experts who have not considered using therapy apps yet.

3.4 Supportive Conditions

The supporting conditions from the UTAUT also show their relevance in this research. They comprise the necessary technical resources, such as a working internet connection, the provision of app-enabled end devices and the availability of the required apps. They also include the necessary knowledge to competently use therapy apps. The technical and structural conditions for the use of apps are generally rated as insufficient. SLPs who plan to use an app usually must resort to their private end devices, as the practices do not own app-enabled devices. In addition, the poor capacity of the existing internet connections does not allow a widespread use of apps. At present, the cost factor still seems to be not in proportion to the expected benefit.

3.5 Professional Skills

Regarding the necessary knowledge required to use therapy apps, an ambivalent result emerged. The younger professionals, who were also academically trained, can rely on better technical skills. As so-called 'digital natives', they have a greater familiarity and competence in using applications and end devices, which was enhanced at university with regard to the use of apps for therapeutic purposes. However, these skills had only a small influence on the actual use. Both younger academically trained experts did not use any or only sporadically non-specific apps in therapy. The older interviewees used apps more regularly and extensively, without having any formal qualification. One expert attended a few specific training courses, the other two followed a 'learning by doing' approach. Thus, competences are primarily developed through trying things out and applying them. This requires an explorative attitude, which results from an open mind and curiosity towards the topic.

These results suggest that professional experience and confidence may be a significant factor in the technology acceptance of SLPs that has so far remained undescribed.

3.6 Lack of Openness

The results of this work clearly show that the knowledge about the potential advantages of using apps is not sufficient to use them. The interviewees who have used apps only rarely or not at all so far are absolutely convinced of their positive application possibilities. It seems that in the context of speech and language therapy, other aspects are more relevant for the acceptance and use of apps. From the interview results, another aspect was identified that has not been sufficiently mentioned in the models and theories on which this paper is based. It should be described as a lack of openness due to obstructive ways of thinking. References to this aspect and its relevance were found in different parts of the interviews and across several participants. There are overlaps with the 'habit' indicator from UTAUT2 [13]. There, the term 'habit' refers to a mindset that can be understood as a lack of receptiveness to innovations. In this work, the criterion of lack of openness is defined more broadly. In addition to habit, the lack of openness includes skepticism towards innovation based on specific ways of thinking and the fear of being replaced by 'digital therapists'. This combination creates a basic attitude characterized by caution and rejection of innovation, which can be described as conservative.

The SLPs interviewed repeatedly referred to the importance of the interpersonal level for therapeutic success. They considered this to be endangered by the integration of digital elements into therapy. The possibility to use the apps as a complement to the therapeutic intervention or as a home exercise seemed irrelevant in this context. This shows a lack of understanding that SLPs do make themselves dispensable through the use of digital technology, but rather expand their therapeutic possibilities and the patients' exercise options.

4 Discussion

With $N = 5$, the number of interviews is considered sufficient to gain a first impression of patterns in the attitudes of SLPs. The indicators derived from the known technology acceptance models and theories seem to be not sufficient to explain the intention to use and the usage behavior of SLPs for therapy apps.

In addition to the factors of performance expectancy and effort expectancy, the structural environment of the speech therapy activities and personality traits of the therapists are highly relevant for acceptance of apps in speech therapy. A basic attitude, characterized by curiosity, openness, and therapeutic security, proves to be conducive to the usage behavior of SLPs. Due to the novelty character of therapy apps, which results from the lack of evidence and proven concepts, their use requires courage and openness towards the new. The willingness to use apps is fostered by many years of professional experience and a high degree of perceived freedom in the choice of treatment method, which in turn results from the professional position and work situation. SLPs with extensive professional experience, who work in a leading position or have their own therapeutic practice, use therapy apps more frequently than therapists who are new to the profession or employees with limited decision autonomy.

The perceived high acquisition and start-up costs discourage the adoption of therapy apps. Due to the limited cost coverage by health insurance companies, SLPs must bear the costs for the acquisition and use of the apps on their own. In addition to the costs for the apps themselves, the costs for the appropriate devices and the information technology infrastructure also need to be raised. Furthermore, many therapists have rather limited digital competences and are not confident in using therapy apps.

Due to the overall positive attitude of SLPs towards the use of apps in speech therapy, it can be assumed that a change in the structural framework and a modernization of the professional training of SLPs will lead to an increase in the use of apps in speech and language therapy.

In sum, the present study adds information on influence factors on therapists' acceptance of apps and digital resources going beyond existing models of technology acceptance. By highlighting Professional Skills and Lack of Openness, we were able to identify two important factors that were not covered by the existing models (TAM and UTAUT).

5 Conclusion

The work presented here provides important insights that can be used for further research into the acceptance and use of apps in speech and language therapy.

Like other fields of therapeutic activity, speech and language therapy will face further challenges in the future. These result from changes in social, structural, and political circumstances. To ensure that patients continue to receive high quality care in the future, the discourse on new, digital treatment methods and concepts must be intensified. This requires openness of speech and language therapists to new approaches and the acquisition of new competences. In addition, politicians, professional associations, research and development, doctors and health insurance companies are called upon to provide enabling and supportive conditions for this and to continue to set new impulses.

It can be assumed that speech therapy will become more digitalized in the future. To meet this need, the framework curricula for education and training need to be adapted for a stronger focus on digital competences. In addition, continuing education should be expanded to provide already practicing SLPs with adequate opportunities to enhance their skills.

Research is also required to promote studies on the effectiveness of digital treatment formats. Based on this evidence, therapy concepts can be designed that combine analogue and digital approaches. Furthermore, health insurance companies could be persuaded to open up to digital treatment methods and to provide supportive impulses through the financing of apps or loan devices. The experiences from the COVID-19 pandemic show that a hesitant and passive attitude towards digitalization and its possibilities can only be compensated for with a lot of extra effort and improvisation.

The results of the present study have shown that the attitude of SLPs is a decisive factor for the use of therapy apps. In addition to teaching digital competences, new training and education concepts should also develop the therapists' self-image and attitude. The expansion of competences and an analysis of one's own attitude increases the professional confidence and leads to empowerment. SLPs can thus become competent practitioners who consciously decide to use technology in therapeutic practice and can thus actively shape future developments in therapy and health care.

References

1. Alber, B., Starke, A.: Digitale Kompetenzen von Sprachtherapeut*innen – Therapieren (DioST-T). Forschung Sprache **2**, 3–11 (2021)
2. Bilda, K.: Grundlagen. Potenziale und Barrieren. In: Bilda, K., Mühlhaus, J., Ritterfeld, U. (eds.) Neue Technologien in der Sprachtherapie, pp. 20–34. Thieme, Stuttgart (2017)
3. Beushausen, U.: Teletherapie in der Logopädie im deutschsprachigen Raum: Ein Überblick über aktuelle Studienergebnisse. Forum Logopädie **25**(3), 6–10 (2021)
4. Leinweber, J., Schulz, K.: Digitalisierung in der Aphasietherapie – eine ethische Betrachtung. Aphasie und verwandte Gebiete **46**, 34–41 (2019)
5. Starke, A., Mühlhaus, J., Ritterfeld, U.: Neue Medien in Therapie und Unterricht für Kinder mit dem Förderschwerpunkt Sprache. Praxis Sprache **61**(1), 28–32 (2016)
6. Liu, L., Miguel Cruz, A., Rios Rincon, A., Buttar, V., Ranson, Q., Goertzen, D.X.: What factors determine therapists' acceptance of new technologies for rehabilitation – a study using the Unified Theory of Acceptance and Use of Technology (UTAUT). Disabil. Rehabil. **37**(5), 447–455 (2015)
7. Schäfer, M., Keppler, D.: Modelle der technikorientierten Akzeptanzforschung. http://www.depositonce.tu-berlin.de/handle/11303/4758. Accessed 7 Jan 2022
8. Davis, F.D.: Perceived usefulness, perceived ease of use, and user acceptance of information technology. MIS Q. **13**(3), 319–340 (1989)
9. Hill, R.J., Fishbein, M., Ajzen, I.: Belief, attitude, intention and behavior: an introduction to theory and research. Contemp. Sociol. **6**(2), 244 (1977)
10. Venkatesh, V., Davis, F.D.: A theoretical extension of the technology acceptance model: Four longitudinal field studies. Manage. Sci. **46**, 186–204 (2000)
11. Venkatesh, V., Bala, H.: Technology acceptance model 3 and a research agenda on interventions. Decis. Sci. **39**(2), 273–315 (2008)
12. Venkatesh, V., Morris, M.G., Davis, F.D., Davis, G.B.: User acceptance of information technology. Toward a unified view. MIS Q. **27**(3), 425–478 (2003)
13. Venkatesh, V., Thong, X.: Consumer acceptance and use of information technology: extending the unified theory of acceptance and use of technology. MIS Q. **36**(1), 157 (2012)
14. Shachak, A., Kuziemsky, C., Petersen, C.: Beyond TAM and UTAUT: Future directions for HIT implementation research. J. Biomed. Inform. **100**, 103315 (2019)
15. Lauer, N.: Teletherapie – hat die Logopädie eine digitale Zukunft? Ergebnisse eines qualitativen Forschungsprojekts des Studiengangs Logopädie der OTH Regensburg. Forum Logopädie **34**(5), 12–17 (2020). https://www.hs-bremen.de/internet/studium/stg/atw/ljc lauer_2020_teletherapie.pdf. Accessed 17 May 2021
16. Bilda, K., Dörr, F., Urban, K., Tschuschke, B.: Digitale logopädische Therapie. Ergebnisse einer Befragung zum aktuellen Ist-Stand aus Sicht von LogopädInnen. Logos **28**(3), 176–183 (2020)
17. Jakob, H., Späth, M.: Sprachtherapeutische Apps am Beispiel neolexon: Herausforderungen beim Zugang in die Versorgung und Chancen für Therapeuten und Patienten. Sprache Stimme Gehör **45**(01), 17–21 (2021)
18. Malchus, K.: Evaluation emotionaler und kommunikativer Verhaltensweisen in Mensch-Roboter Interaktionen in therapierelevanten Szenarien. https://pub.uni-bielefeld.de/dow nload/2784346/2784347/diss_malchus.pdf. Accessed 10 June 2021
19. Albudoor, N., Peña, E.D.: Factors influencing US speech and language therapists' use of technology for clinical practice. Int. J. Lang. Commun. Disord. **56**(3), 567–582 (2021)
20. Kruse, J., Schmieder, C., Weber, K.M., Dresing, T., Pehl, T.: Qualitative Interviewforschung. Ein integrativer Ansatz, 2nd edn. Beltz, Weinheim (2015)

21. Helfferich, C.: Die Qualität qualitativer Daten. Verlag für Sozialwissenschaften, Wiesbaden (2009). https://doi.org/10.1007/978-3-531-91858-7
22. Bogner, A., Littig, B., Menz, W.: Interviews mit Experten. Eine praxisorientierte Einführung. Springer, Wiesbaden (2014). https://doi.org/10.1007/978-3-531-19416-5
23. Kuckartz, U.: Einführung in die computergestützte Analyse qualitativer Daten. Springer, Wiesbaden (2010). https://doi.org/10.1007/978-3-531-92126-6
24. MAXQDA. https://www.maxqda.com. Accessed 20 July 2021
25. Dirks, S., Bühler, C.: Assistive technologies for people with cognitive impairments – which factors influence technology acceptance? In: Antona, M., Stephanidis, C. (eds.) UAHCI 2018. LNCS, vol. 10907, pp. 503–516. Springer, Cham (2018). https://doi.org/10.1007/978-3-319-92049-8_36

Exploring Video Game Satisfaction of Gamers with Disabilities

Carmen A. Van Ommen[(⊠)] and Barbara S. Chaparro

Department of Human Factors and Behavioral Neurobiology, Embry-Riddle Aeronautical
University, 1 Aerospace Blvd., Daytona Beach, FL 32114, USA
rescoc@my.erau.edu, Barbara.Chaparro@erau.edu

Abstract. It is estimated that 61 million Americans are living with a disability,
and that 33 million of those play video games. Gamers with disabilities face
many barriers in gaming, such as being unable to hear necessary audio or move
various components on a controller, which may impact their game satisfaction.
Since there has been little research to validate gaming satisfaction measures in
gamers with disabilities, an exploratory study was conducted to assess factors that
contribute to satisfaction among this population. Results indicate that the items of
the validated Game User Experience Satisfaction Scale (GUESS-18) are helpful
in understanding video game satisfaction in this population. Participants were able
to use the GUESS-18 without modifications, but suggested the addition of areas
related to game customization, challenges faced, and learnability.

Keywords: Video games · Accessibility · Accessible games

1 Introduction

It is estimated that 61 million Americans, or 26% of the population, are living with a
disability, according to a 2016 survey conducted by the CDC [1]. This included disabilities related to mobility, cognition, independent living, hearing, vision, self-care or
combinations. Of the 61 million Americans that report having a disability, it is estimated
that 33 million play video games [2]. Gamers with disabilities face many diverse barriers
in gaming. These include being unable to hear necessary audio or perceive important
visuals, unable to understand complex language, or unable to easily move various components on a controller. Additionally, video games may not always work well with
the assistive technology a disabled gamer may use to overcome these barriers, such as
text-to-speech systems, modified controllers, on-screen keyboards, voice commands, or
assistive programs like AutoHotkey [3].

1.1 Game Satisfaction

One of the most important aspects of enjoying and continuing to play a video game is
the satisfaction that one experiences when playing the game. Several scales have been
developed to measure game satisfaction, such as the Game Experience Questionnaire

© The Author(s), under exclusive license to Springer Nature Switzerland AG 2022
M. Antona and C. Stephanidis (Eds.): HCII 2022, LNCS 13308, pp. 392–405, 2022.
https://doi.org/10.1007/978-3-031-05028-2_26

(GEQ) [4], the Player Experience of Needs Satisfaction (PENS) [5], and the Game User Experience Satisfaction Scale (GUESS) [6]. The GUESS is the most recent comprehensive, validated measure of assessing game satisfaction. It includes 55 items representing nine subscales: Usability/Playability, Narratives, Play Engrossment, Enjoyment, Creative Freedom, Audio Aesthetics, Personal Gratification, Social Connectivity, and Visual Aesthetics. A short version of the GUESS was recently validated to allow for quicker evaluation of video games (GUESS-18) [7]. The GUESS was validated with over 1400 gamers, but it is unknown how many represented disabled populations.

Since gamers with disabilities experience barriers that may impact their ability to play video games, it is likely that game satisfaction is impacted when a game is not designed to meet the needs of the player. Little research has been conducted to explore the dimensions that contribute to video game satisfaction for disabled gamer populations.

To explore this area, we examined the accessibility guidelines for video games as set forth by Game Accessibility Guidelines [8] and mapped them to the nine dimensions of the GUESS-55. Several of the guidelines directly mapped to dimensions of the GUESS. For example, one guideline suggests support text as well as voice chat, so that gamers with disabilities who could not easily use one of those methods of chat could have an alternative method of communication with other gamers. This would be related to the GUESS dimension of Social Connectivity, and could potentially be reflected in the scale item "I find the game supports social interaction (e.g., chat) between players."

Other guidelines potentially mapped to a GUESS dimension but not to a specific scale item. For example, the guideline "include an option to adjust the game speed" could relate to the GUESS dimension of Usability/Playability, but there are no specific scale items that reflect whether a video game allowed for settings such as game speed to be adjusted. Table 1 shows a summary of the Game Design Guidelines that mapped to the GUESS dimensions.

Finally, there were some guidelines that did not directly map to any dimensions or scale items of the GUESS. For example, the guideline "allow subtitle/caption presentation to be customized" benefits gamers with hearing impairments. Games that do not provide this accessibility feature may be rated with lower satisfaction, but it is unclear as to how this may be measured by the GUESS.

Table 1. GUESS dimensions and corresponding game design guidelines for accessibility [9]

GUESS dimension	Game design guidelines for accessibility
Audio Aesthetics - The different auditory aspects of the game (e.g., sound effects) and how much they enrich the gaming experience	Subtitles/captions; adjustable background noise/music; visual cues as to who is speaking and cues or captions for significant background noise; short and understandable subtitles/captions; surround sound is used
Creative Freedom - The extent to which the game is able to foster the player's creativity and curiosity and allows the player to freely express his or her individuality while playing the game	Adaptable and easy to use interactive elements; separate volume controls or mutes for effects, speech and background/music
Enjoyment - The amount of pleasure and delight that was perceived by the player as a result of playing the game	Alterable difficulty level; option to disable blood and gore
Narratives - The story aspects of the game (e.g., events and characters) and their abilities to capture the player's interest and shape the player's emotions	Subtitles/captions are or can be turned on before any sound is played; no essential information is conveyed by sounds alone; all sound is able to be replayed; narrative progress summaries
Personal Gratification - The motivational aspects of the game (e.g., challenge) that promote the player's sense of accomplishment and the desire to succeed and continue playing the game	Alterable difficulty level; reminders of current objectives during gameplay
Play Engrossment - The degree to which the game can hold the player's attention and interest	All settings are saved/remembered; surround sound is used
Social Connectivity - The degree to which the game facilitates social connection between players through its tools and features	Text, voice, and symbol-based chat supported; preference settings for playing games with players who will only play with or are willing to play without voice chat; real time transcription and signing
Usability/Playability - The ease in which the game can be played with clear goals/objectives in mind and with minimal cognitive interferences or obstructions from the user interfaces and controls	Flexible mapping/reconfiguration/sensitivity of controls; customization of interface and element sizes; alternative input devices and screen reader support; voiceovers for all text; clear indication of what elements are interactive

(continued)

Table 1. (*continued*)

GUESS dimension	Game design guidelines for accessibility
Visual Aesthetics - The graphics of the game and how attractive they appeared to the player	Customizable font sizes; sufficient contrast between text and user interface background; screen reader compatibility; no essential information is conveyed by color, sounds, or text alone

1.2 Adapting Scales for Special Populations

Another consideration in the measure of game satisfaction with a disabled population is the design of the measurement scale itself. Due to various difficulties that people with disabilities can face, there has been a number of studies that suggest modifications to scales or questionnaires when presented to people with disabilities. In a 2020 literature review, Aguado-Delgado et al. proposed a taxonomy for classifying disabilities when used in the context of video games and categorizes them into sensory, motor, and cognitive disabilities, which was adopted for this study [10]. Scale modifications for people with those disabilities are as follows:

Sensory. Scale modifications for people with sensory disabilities, such as sight or hearing, focus mainly on scale presentation. For participants with hearing impairments, the scale or questionnaire may not need to be modified if presented in a written format. If the scale is generally given verbally, it may be necessary to provide an ASL translator or have a written version of the scale available.

For participants with visual impairments, it is suggested that moderators provide the option to use magnification tools, such as a magnifying glass or magnification software if delivered via computer. Additionally, the scale should provide a braille or large print version [11]. Modifying the format of a scale or questionnaire can also enhance understanding. Modifications can also be made by including thorough information about the topic and length of the questionnaire, as well as instructions for completing and returning the questionnaire. The design of the questions or scale items can be modified to enhance understanding in those who have visual impairments, as they provide cues to differentiate question and response options, as well as what type of response may be asked for. Every question and response option should be distinct, which can be achieved by starting questions with a number followed by a period, and starting the response options with a letter followed by a period. The first response option should start with the letter "a" and subsequent response options should be in alphabetical order. Scale items and response options should be grouped together with a line separating the group before each question, but not before each response option. If the scale or questionnaire uses checkboxes, they should be included directly after each response option, rather than having them on separate lines [12].

Motor. When presenting scales to participants with motor disabilities, the content of the questions or scale items should be evaluated to ensure that they are appropriate for the population [13]. Experts can be consulted in order to evaluate if the question or scale item is appropriate and can assist in modifying the items if needed. If the scale items are evaluating motor movement, experts can provide guidance on the level of support that may need to be given to help a participant understand or complete a task [14]. The format of the scale should be presented in a way that allows assistive technology to be used, such as eye-tracking devices or voice-to-text software.

Cognitive. Participants with cognitive impairments are most likely to have difficulties with the comprehension of the question or scale item. Techniques for improving comprehension include reading the question aloud to the participant, providing the scale in large print, presenting each question one at a time [15, 16], presenting the participant with supplemental questions [17], adding photos or symbols that relate to the meaning of the text or question alongside the written text of the question [11, 18] making the questionnaire shorter [19] and simplifying the wording of each question [15, 20].

Response formats for each question may also need to be changed. Likert scales can be simplified to only include three options [19, 21–23], or the response format can be changed to only include yes/no options [21]. Response options can also be modified to include faces or along with or instead of numbers [11, 24], they can include a histogram with bar sizes representing the magnitude each response option symbolizes [16], or changing the response options from having distinct points to being a continuous line that participants can use to mark their responses [25]. It may also be helpful to include an option for caretakers to report responses on behalf of the participant [21, 24, 26].

Another issue that occurs when presenting scales or questionnaires to participants with cognitive impairments is response acquiescence, or responding in the same way to each question. Strategies that can help reduce the likelihood of response acquiescence include asking participants to respond by pointing to a picture that represents the correct response, varying where the correct response is located on the page [18], including questions that have an opposite response [27], including neutral items in the answer options [11], and randomizing the order of response options [17]. This allows the researcher to ensure that participants are not giving the same response to each question or pointing to the same response option each time.

Additional strategies for presenting scales or questionnaires to participants with cognitive impairments includes breaking up the session into smaller chunks to prevent boredom [11] and including a cessation rule to reduce or limit stress at failure, if a participant does not succeed to complete a task multiple times [28].

1.3 Purpose

Given that different aspects of game design influence gamers with disabilities in unique ways, it is important to use a measurement tool that meets the gamers' needs and includes items that accurately and comprehensively measure satisfaction from their perspective. The purpose of this study was to explore how well the GUESS satisfaction scale measured satisfaction of a small group of gamers with disabilities. Specifically, the short version of the GUESS, GUESS-18 [7], was used to determine if the scale design, scale items, and dimensions are inclusive to this population.

2   Method

2.1   Participants

The study sample consisted of 15 participants (9 female, 5 male, 1 self-described) recruited from within the United States. To qualify for the study, participants had to self-report a disability, have played a video game for at least 10 hours and have played that game in the last 3 months. Participants ranged in age from 21–63. 4 participants reported sensory disabilities, 2 participants reported cognitive disabilities, 5 participants reported physical disabilities, and 4 reported both physical and mental disabilities. Participants were asked about how long they have had their disability to determine their level of familiarity and experience with gaming with that disability. 14 participants had self-identified as having a disability for at least 10 years. Participants were also asked whether their disability affected their ability to play video games. 2 participants reported that their disability did not affect their ability to play video games and 13 participants said it did affect their ability to play video games.

2.2   Materials

The study consisted of two phases: (1) the administration of the GUESS-18 survey and (2) follow-up interview questions to better understand the participants' gaming experience and adaptations.

The GUESS-18 consists of 18 statements that are answered on a 7-point Likert scale that represent 9 dimensions of satisfaction [7].

- Usability/Playability (2 items)

  – I find the controls of the game to be straightforward.
  – I find the game's interface to be easy to navigate.

- Narratives (2 items)

  – I am captivated by the game's story from the beginning.
  – I enjoy the fantasy or story provided by the game.

- Play Engrossment (2 items)

  – I feel detached from the outside world while playing the game.
  – I do not care to check events that are happening in the real world during the game.

- Enjoyment (2 items)

  – I think the game is fun.
  – I feel bored while playing the game.

- Creative Freedom (2 items)

  - I feel the game allows me to be imaginative.
  - I feel creative while playing the game.

- Audio Aesthetics (2 items)

  - I enjoy the sound effects in the game.
  - I feel the game's audio (e.g., sound effects, music) enhances my gaming experience.

- Personal Gratification (2 items)

  - I am very focused on my own performance while playing the game.
  - I want to do as well as possible during the game.

- Social Connectivity (2 items)

  - I find the game supports social interaction (e.g., chat) between players.
  - I like to play this game with other players.

- Visual Aesthetics (2 items)

  - I enjoy the game's graphics.
  - I think the game is visually appealing.

    Follow-up interview questions asked participants about their experiences with gaming:

- Are there any aspects of the GUESS that should be changed?
- Are there aspects of game satisfaction that you think are important that are not highlighted on the GUESS?
- What games do you play most frequently?
- Why do you play these games?
- What do you look for in a game?
- What aspects make a game challenging to play?
- What makes a game playable?
- What makes a game enjoyable?
- Are there any shortcuts you take to evaluating a game?
- Are there any games you want to play but can't? Why?
- Can you give an example of how you adapt games to make them easier or more enjoyable to play?

2.3 Procedures

Prospective participants were asked to fill out a screening survey that asked if they had a disability, if they played video games, and to list the last time they had played a video game. Participants that responded that they had a disability, played video games, and had played a game within the last 3 months were invited to the interview portion of the study. This study obtained IRB approval and consent was obtained from all participants before beginning the interview. Participants met with the researcher synchronously via web conferencing software and were asked to complete the GUESS-18 and think aloud or comment as they made their ratings, while sharing their screen to allow the researcher to ask follow-up questions to their responses. Participants were encouraged to use any assistive technology they would normally use and were asked if they preferred to input their own answers or if they preferred to verbalize their responses to the researcher and have the researcher input their answers. After completing the survey portion of the interview, participants were asked the interview questions as well as whether any items of the GUESS-18 should be modified to better fit their needs or understanding.

3   Results

3.1   GUESS-18

All participants were able to comprehend and answer all of the GUESS-18 items without any issues. The survey also was able to be used with the assistive technology utilized by participants, which included screen readers and on screen keyboards. Those with physical disabilities were sometimes unable to comfortably use a mouse or keyboard, and preferred to verbally respond to the researcher and have the researcher input their responses, but all participants were able to complete the screening survey and did not report having difficulties inputting their answers on their own. The wording of the GUESS-18 was understood by all participants in this study.

Results of the responses to the GUESS-18 showed that some dimensions were impacted by the challenges gamers with disabilities face. For example, participants who were deaf or hard of hearing said that they did not enjoy the sound effects or find the audio to enhance their gaming experience, or they did not find those items applicable to their experience. If the participant was able to experience the audio or sound effects through another method, such as wearing a haptic vest that allowed them to feel vibrations that coincided with the audio in the game, they rated those items more positively (Table 2).

Table 2. Participant comments on selected GUESS-18 items

Selected GUESS-18 items	Selected comments from participants about GUESS-18 items
Usability/Playability	
I find the controls of the game to be straightforward	"Controls aren't as familiar compared to other games. For example, most first-person games use the right trigger to shoot, but if a game uses another button it can be tricky to remember/play, which is the case for Rainbow Six Siege." P7, Neither agree nor disagree, Rainbow Six Siege, Cognitive Disability
I find the game's interface to be easy to navigate	"It takes many clicks to get where you need to, the text is small and cramped, and the contrast makes text hard to read against background." P2, Disagree, Civilization 6, Cognitive Disability
Narratives	
I am captivated by the game's story from the beginning	"I wouldn't say "captivated", [the game] doesn't have a great story but [it] is still fun for other reasons." P10, Somewhat disagree, Borderlands 3, Physical and Cognitive Disability
Play Engrossment	
I feel detached from the outside world while playing the game	"It's fun to pass the time with games, but they do not entice me enough to bring me out of reality." P8, Strongly disagree, iAssociate, Sensory Disability (Visual)
I do not care to check events that are happening in the real world during the game	"In general, I never really get "detached" when playing games." P1, Somewhat disagree, The Sims 4, Sensory Disability (Hearing)
Enjoyment	
I think the game is fun	"I don't like how certain updates have affected the game. I don't like how matchmaking works, makes it unfun to play if you're put with people with less hours than you. I keep playing because it's fun at first, but it does get more punishing as you continue. I have a "love-hate" relationship with the game." P13, Somewhat disagree, Call of Duty: Modern Warfare, Physical and Cognitive Disability
I feel bored while playing the game	"The game is repetitive, but I play it to talk to friends." P7, Neither agree nor disagree, Rainbow Six Siege, Cognitive Disability

(continued)

Table 2. (*continued*)

Selected GUESS-18 items	Selected comments from participants about GUESS-18 items
Creative Freedom	
I feel the game allows me to be imaginative	"It can be somewhat imaginative by how you get to locations, but you must follow by game rules mostly." P7, Somewhat disagree, Rainbow Six Siege, Cognitive Disability
I feel creative while playing the game	"I kind of use it when I'm trying to think of something else but I need to keep the front of my brain occupied." P9, N/A, Instant Farmer, Physical Disability
Audio Aesthetics	
I enjoy the sound effects in the game	"I cannot always hear sound effects, some helpful cues are not heard/noticed." P1, Somewhat disagree, The Sims 4, Sensory Disability (Hearing)
I feel the game's audio (e.g., sound effects, music) enhances my gaming experience	"Some of them are painful to hear because it's too loud, some of them are helpful such as enemy footsteps." P13, Somewhat agree, Call of Duty: Modern Warfare, Physical and Mental Disability
Personal Gratification	
I want to do as well as possible during the game	"The Sims isn't about doing well, it's about doing what you want. There's no right or wrong." P12, Somewhat disagree, The Sims 4, Physical Disability
Visual Aesthetics	
I enjoy the game's graphics	"It's an older game, the graphics are not good." P6, Somewhat disagree, Final Fantasy VII, Physical and Mental Disability

3.2 Interview

After responding to the GUESS-18, participants were asked if they felt like there were areas of game satisfaction that they found important that were not addressed. Several participants responded that they felt there were not adequate questions about game customization, such as customization of controls, settings or the ability to add modifications. Also, some participants suggested that questions about barriers or challenges faced in the game were not addressed, as well as if the game was easy to learn or if the game supported the player by reminding them what their goals were and how to accomplish them. Participants were asked additional questions about their gaming experience, but these were intended to be used to provide the researcher context to their gaming experience and were not analyzed.

4   Discussion

The results of this exploratory study indicate that the items of the GUESS-18 are helpful in understanding video game satisfaction in this population. The scale format did not need to be modified to be used with the gamers with disabilities in this study, however the instructions could allow for the scale items to be read aloud, or for the researcher to input answers on behalf of the participant.

Results also indicated that participants would respond negatively or with N/A to areas of games that they could not experience due to their disability, such as Audio Aesthetics in players who are deaf or hard of hearing. However, if the player could interact with the sound effects in the game through a wearable that allowed them to feel vibrations that coincided with the sound in the video game, they would rate items about the game audio more positively. This suggests that it should not be assumed that there is no way for gamers with disabilities to experience all aspects of the game. Rather, that may be an area in which the game is deficient when played by a gamer with a specific disability, and adaptations should be made so that they can experience that aspect of the game in a different way than traditionally thought.

When recruiting for the study, participants were asked if their disability affected their ability to play video games. While the majority stated that it did, some participants stated that their disability did not affect their ability to play video games. This may be due to those participants selecting games that accommodate for this disability, or it may be due to their disability not being as severe and impacting game performance. This suggests that, while most gamers with disabilities may prefer or even require adaptations made to video games, it is not guaranteed that this is necessary for all gamers with disabilities.

When designing this study, the GUESS-18 was chosen instead of the original GUESS with 55 items, due to it being shorter and more manageable to discuss in a 60-min interview. However, there may have been items on the original GUESS that related to accessibility needs that were not included in the GUESS-18. For example, participants mentioned that they did not feel that the learnability of the game was addressed, or if the game supported them in reminding them of their goals and how to accomplish them. In the GUESS-18, there are only two items that address usability/playability: "I find the controls of the game to be straightforward" and "I find the game's interface to be easy to navigate" [7]. In the original GUESS, however, there are other items that may address learnability and supporting progress towards goals, including "I think it is easy to learn how to play the game", I always know how to achieve my goals/objectives in the game", "I always know my next goal when I finish an event in the game", and "I feel the game provides me the necessary information to accomplish a goal within the game" [6]. Additional items about the ability to customize controls and settings, or items about experiencing barriers and challenges in the game, however, are not included in the original GUESS which may mean that this is an area that needs to be further developed for use when evaluating the accessibility of a video game.

Previous literature suggests that modifying existing solutions for game development could have an impact on increasing accessibility in video games [10]. The GUESS was originally designed as a tool for game developers to assess video game satisfaction and be able to determine specific areas where game satisfaction could be lacking. If the GUESS is able to be used to assess game satisfaction in gamers with disabilities, this could allow game developers to better understand areas of game satisfaction that may be deficient when played by this population. This could provide a tool to increase the level or prevalence of accessible games.

4.1 Limitations and Future Research

One limitation of this study is that it had a small sample size and recruited only a few participants of several disability types. Since disabilities are so varied, this was likely not a representative sample. However, this study was intended to be exploratory in nature to determine whether future research in this area should be conducted and what the nature of that research would be, rather than a comprehensive study that would make recommendations on adaptations in this area.

When the GUESS was validated, it required participants to choose video games that they have played for more than 10 hours and have played in the last 3 months. To use the scale how it was validated, the participants in this study also were asked to follow these requirements. However, if a player is not able to play a game due to the game not meeting their accessibility requirements, it is very likely that their experience with the game would not meet these requirements, and thus not be able to be evaluated with the GUESS. Therefore, participants are more likely to choose games that they enjoy and have met a certain level of their accessibility requirements, so their responses may not be the same as if they were evaluating a game that does not meet their accessibility requirements. Future research should evaluate games that participants have not played as long or report to have difficulties playing.

Future research should psychometrically validate the GUESS-18 or the original GUESS, with a wide range of gamers with disabilities and to explore whether the items are answered with a similar pattern as gamers who do not have disabilities or if more items should be added to be a more inclusive measure.

References

1. Okoro, C.A., Hollis, N.D., Cyrus, A.C., Griffin-Blake, S.: Prevalence of disabilities and health care access by disability status and type among adults – United States, 2016. MMWR Morb. Mortal Wkly Rep. **67**, 882–887 (2018)
2. Barlet, M.C., Spohn, S.D.: A Practical Guide to Game Accessibility. The Ablegamers Foundation, Charles Town (2012)
3. Porter, J.R., Kientz, J.A.: An empirical study of issues and barriers to mainstream video game accessibility. In: Proceedings of the 15th International ACM SIGACCESS Conference on Computers and Accessibility, pp. 1–8 (2013)
4. IJsselsteijn, W., et al.: Measuring the experience of digital game enjoyment. In: Proceedings of Measuring Behavior, vol. 2008, pp. 88–89. Noldus Information Technology, Wageningen, Netherlands (2008)
5. Ryan, R.M., Rigby, C.S., Przybylski, A.: The motivational pull of video games: A self-determination theory approach. Motiv. Emot. **30**(4), 344–360 (2006)

6. Phan, M.H., Keebler, J.R., Chaparro, B.S.: The development and validation of the game user experience satisfaction scale (GUESS). Hum. Factors **58**(8), 1217–1247 (2016)
7. Keebler, J.R., Shelstad, W.J., Smith, D.C., Chaparro, B.S., Phan, M.H.: Validation of the GUESS-18: a short version of the game user experience satisfaction scale (GUESS). J. Usability Stud. **16**(1), 49–62 (2020)
8. A straightforward reference for inclusive game design. http://gameaccessibilityguidelines. com/
9. Van Ommen, C., Chaparro, B.S.: Assessing video game satisfaction of gamers with disabilities. Proc. Hum. Factors Ergonomics Soc. Annu. Meet. **65**(1), 822–826 (2021)
10. Aguado-Delgado, J., Gutierrez-Martinez, J.M., Hilera, J.R., de-Marcos, S., Otón, S.: Accessibility in video games: a systematic review. Univ. Access Inf. Soc. **19**(1), 169–193 (2020)
11. King, N.J., Josephs, A., Gullone, E., Madden, C., Ollendick, T.H.: Assessing the fears of children with disability using the revised fear survey schedule for children: a comparative study. Br. J. Med. Psychol. **67**, 377–386 (1994)
12. Kaczmirek, L., Wolff, K.G.: Survey design for visually impaired and blind people. In: Stephanidis, C. (ed.) UAHCI 2007. LNCS, vol. 4554, pp. 374–381. Springer, Heidelberg (2007). https://doi.org/10.1007/978-3-540-73279-2_41
13. Washburn, R.A., Weimo Zhu, W., McAuley, E., Frogley, M., Figoni, S.F.: The physical activity scale for individuals with physical disabilities: development and evaluation. Arch. Phys. Med. Rehabil. **83**(2), 193–200 (2002)
14. Salavati, M., et al.: Reliability of the modified paediatric evaluation of disability inventory, Dutch version (PEDI-NL) for children with cerebral palsy and cerebral visual impairment. Res. Dev. Disabil. **37**, 189–201 (2015)
15. Dagnan, D., Jahoda, A., McDowell, K., Masson, J., Banks, P., Hare, D.: The psychometric properties of the hospital anxiety and depressions scale adapted for use with people with intellectual disabilities. J. Intellect. Disabil. Res. **52**, 942–949 (2008)
16. Lindsay, W.R., Skene, D.D.: The Beck depression inventory II and the Beck anxiety inventory in people with intellectual disabilities: factor analyses and group data. J. Appl. Res. Intellect. Disabil. **20**, 401–408 (2007)
17. Lindsay, W.R., Michie, A.M.: Adaptation of the Zung self-rating anxiety scale for people with a mental handicap. J. Intellect. Disabil. Res. **32**, 485–490 (1998)
18. Illingworth, K., Moore, K.A., McGillivray, J.: The development of the nutrition and activity knowledge scale for use with people with an intellectual disability. J. Appl. Res. Intellect. Disabil. **16**, 159–166 (2003)
19. Nezu, C.M., Nezu, A.M., Rothenberg, J.L., et al.: Depression in adults with mild mental retardation: are cognitive variables involved? Cogn. Therapy Res. **19**, 227–239 (1995)
20. Ramirez, S.Z., Lukenbill, J.: Psychometric properties of the Zung self-rating anxiety scale for adults with intellectual disabilities (SAS-ID). J. Dev. Phys. Disabil. **20**(6), 573–580 (2008)
21. Cuthill, F., Espie, C., Cooper, S.: Development and psychometric properties of the Glasgow depression scale for people with a learning disability: individual and carer supplement versions. Br. J. Psychiatry **182**(4), 347–353 (2003)
22. Finlay, W.M.L., Lyons, E.: Methodological issues in interviewing and using self-report questionnaires with people with mental retardation. Psychol. Assess. **13**(3), 319–335 (2001)
23. Lindsay, W.R., Michie, A.M., Baty, F.J., Smith, A.H.W., Miller, S.: The consistency of reports about feelings and emotions from people with intellectual disability. J. Intellect. Disabil. Res. **38**, 61–66 (1994)
24. Cummins, R., McCabe, M., Romeo, Y., Reid, S., Waters, L.: An initial evaluation of the comprehensive quality of life scale-intellectual disability. Int. J. Disabil. Dev. Educ. **44**(1), 7–19 (1997)

25. Dagnan, D., Sandhu, S.: Social comparison, self-esteem and depression in people with intellectual disability. J. Intellect. Disabil. Res. **43**, 372–379 (1999)
26. Esbensen, A.J., Rojahn, J., Aman, M.G., et al.: Reliability and validity of an assessment instrument for anxiety, depression, and mood among individuals with mental retardation. J. Autism Dev. Disord. **33**, 617–629 (2003)
27. Stancliffe, R.J., Parmenter, T.: The Choice Questionnaire: a scale to assess choices exercised by adults with intellectual disability. J. Intellect. Dev. Disabil. **24**(2), 107–132 (1999)
28. Masson, J.D., Dagnan, D., Evans, J.: Adaptation and validation of the Tower of London test of planning and problem solving in people with intellectual disabilities. J. Intellect. Disabil. Res. **54**, 457–467 (2010)

Multimodal and Psychophysiological Interaction in Universal Access

Neuro-Voting: An Accuracy Evaluation of a P300-Based Brain-Computer Interface for Casting Votes

Rupal Agarwal$^{(\boxtimes)}$ and Marvin Andujar

University of South Florida, Tampa, FL 33620, USA
{rupalagarwal,andujar1}@usf.edu

Abstract. Reliable and accessible voting systems are essential for democratic societies as they are a vital link between the democratic representation and its citizens. The current voting systems need further accessibility features to aid people with disabilities to vote more independently. This paper describes "Neuro-Voting" a novel P300-based Brain-Computer Interface (BCI) voting application that allows the users to vote for their preferred candidate using their brain activity and without requiring any physical movement. Neuro-Voting uses the P300 wave activity elicited in the users to predict their vote. This paper discusses the design and implementation of the created system including the descriptions of the classification method that was implemented. The application is evaluated through a user study with five participants and the results show that it is highly accurate in predicting the votes of the participants. The application also received positive qualitative feedback from the participants after interacting with the system. The findings from this study demonstrates that it is possible for people to vote with their brains.

Keywords: Neuro-Voting · Brain-computer interfaces · EEG · P300

1 Introduction

Voting is the cornerstone of democracy. It is a crucial process with the help of which a democratic society elects its government. Therefore, a safe, and reliable voting system is essential not just for the democratic nation, but also for the voter's trust and secrecy of the votes. Different forms of voting methods are used throughout the world, the most common of which is the paper ballots. In this method, the ballot paper lists all the candidates, and the voters select their favorite candidate accordingly. Another form of voting that has gained significant popularity over the last two decades is electronic voting. This form of voting method uses machines like computer systems and touch screens for casting votes. The above-mentioned voting methods are widely used in many countries; however, they have several limitations [1]. Both methods require the use of hands to make selections on a ballot paper or a screen, making it difficult for people who have motor disabilities to cast their votes. Another potential drawback of electronic voting is the use of a computer mouse to navigate the voting application [1]. This can likely lead to more

© The Author(s), under exclusive license to Springer Nature Switzerland AG 2022
M. Antona and C. Stephanidis (Eds.): HCII 2022, LNCS 13308, pp. 409–419, 2022.
https://doi.org/10.1007/978-3-031-05028-2_27

errors being made by the older adults because of their possible lack of eye-hand coordination and manual dexterity.

In recent years, the field of brain-computer interface (BCI) has garnered a lot of attention, especially as a novel control mechanism in the field of Human-Centered Computing. BCI technology is developing at an unprecedented speed and has shown its potential in creating innovative applications in several areas such as art, education and gaming [5,13]. In addition, another area where BCI has the potential to serve as a novel control modality is voting. A voting application based on a P300 brain-computer interface creates a direct communication link between the voting system and the voter's brain, thus allowing the latter to vote for their favorite candidate using the P300 component of their electroencephalogram (EEG) brain activity. In the past, the BCI researchers have used the P300-based BCI's to spell words [3] and also paint on a digital canvas [2]. These applications allow the users to select from a N × N matrix by focusing on an option of their choice, without physically performing the selection. Together, these studies demonstrate that P300 based BCI's are fast and straightforward to use, require very little training, and are effective for most users, especially those who have physical disabilities such as Amyotrophic Lateral Sclerosis (ALS).

This research explores the use of 'Neuro-Voting', a novel P300-based BCI that allows the users to vote for their favorite superhero character (supergirl, superman, black widow, or wolverine) using their brain activity. The application in use can be seen in Fig. 1. In addition to testing the accuracy of the application, this study also acquires feedback from the participants to get a qualitative understanding of their experience after interacting with the system.

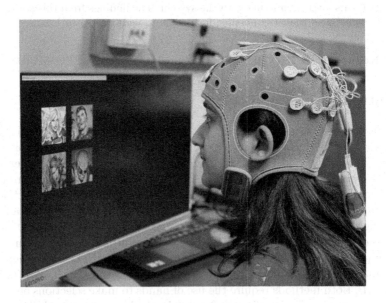

Fig. 1. A user engaged in the Neuro-Voting task.

2   Related Work

Farewell and Donchin [3], developed the first P300-based BCI that allowed the users to spell words using brain activity. Their application used a P300-speller displayed in the form of a 6×6 matrix, containing letters of the alphabet and digits from 0 to 9. Through a user study with able-bodied adults, they achieved an average accuracy of 95% with a bit transfer rate of 12 bits per minute, thus allowing the users to communicate effectively through a computer.

In another research [12], Sellers and Donchin evaluated the effectiveness of using P300-based communication for users with ALS. They tested their system with three able-bodied participants and three participants diagnosed with ALS, who were shown four stimuli ('YES', 'NO', 'PASS', 'END') in a random order. Their results indicated that the event-related potentials elicited by the target stimuli and the event-related potentials elicited by the non-target stimuli are different for both ALS and non-ALS users. Their results also showed that P300-based communication is possible for participants who are suffering from ALS.

In [2], a Brain Painting application was developed to allow users to paint on a digital canvas using EEG brain activity. The application consisted of two components: a P300 matrix containing painting options and a canvas for digital painting. The P300 matrix was based on the P300 speller, proposed by Farewell and Donchin [3], however it was modified to include shapes, colors, directions, etc., instead of the letters and numbers. Their application was used for 3.5 months by a participant, diagnosed with ALS, who showed high satisfaction and low frustration after constant use. Since, their results were based on only one end user, they could not be generalized to the population of potential end-users, however the attainment of high satisfaction after constant home use showed the benefit of using this BCI in day-to-day life. Brain Painting has also been extended to be performed in 3D and virtual environments [8,9]. Such applications have received positive feedback from the users, demonstrating their usefulness in communicating through physiological means such as brain activity.

Another form of P300-based BCI that allowed the users to browse the internet using EEG activity was presented in [10]. Three ALS patients and ten healthy individuals evaluated the application and achieved average accuracies of 73% and 90%, respectively. These results demonstrate the system's potential to help people with paralysis to navigate the internet browser without requiring any assistance.

Previous studies have used the P300-based BCI's for painting [2,8], navigating the internet browser [10] and spelling words [3]. However, none of them have explored their use for voting purposes. An EEG-based BCI voting application will be secure to use, eliminating the problem of fake voter IDs. This is potentially due to the fact that each person exhibits unique patterns of EEG in their brain [11], because of which no two individuals have similar EEG activities. Furthermore, such an application will also allow people with physical disabilities such as those with ALS, to take part in the voting process without requiring any external assistance, thus maintaining the privacy of their votes. For this reason,

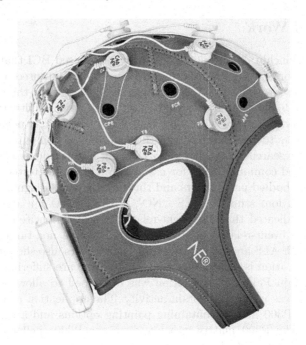

Fig. 2. The Enobio brain computer interface headset.

this study proposes Neuro-Voting, a BCI application that allows the users to cast votes in a hands-free and easy to use voting environment.

3 Methodology

3.1 Participants

A total of five participants were recruited to take part in the Neuro-Voting user study. Two participants were female and three were male with an age range from 18 to 34 years (mean = 24, sd = 5.49). Out of the five participants, four had a master's degree and one had a bachelor's degree. Two participants were familiar with BCI technology and had used a BCI application before, however, none of them had previously interacted with a P300 speller.

3.2 EEG Device

The Enobio headset was used for measuring participant's EEG data. It is a wireless and lightweight device that uses dry electrodes for reading electrical activity from the user's scalp, as shown in Fig. 2. This headset collects high quality data with 19 movable EEG sensors placed at Fp1, Fp2, F3, Fz, F4, Cz, CP5, CP6, P7, P3, Pz, P4, P8, PO7, PO3, PO4, PO8, O1 and O2 locations according to the 10–20 International System, as shown in Fig. 3. The sensors were

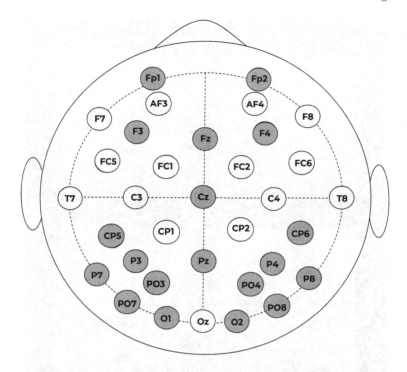

Fig. 3. The 10–20 international system with the used channels highlighted.

placed predominantly in the parietal region where the P300 wave is captured [7]. Some of the sensors were also placed in the frontal lobe region as it carries relevant information for the detection of P300 activity [4].

3.3 Design and Implementation

Neuro-Voting User Interface. The user interface of the P300-based Neuro-Voting application consisted of a 2×2 matrix containing images of four super-hero characters (supergirl, superman, black widow and wolverine), as shown in Fig. 4. These superhero characters represented the potential candidates that participants could vote for. The 2×2 matrix was chosen to shorten the training period and to ensure that there were less candidates to concentrate on. Initially, the images in the matrix were displayed in grey color, however, in the flashing state they transitioned between grey colored images and colored images at regular intervals. The voting interface was developed in C++ programming language using the Win32 Application Programming Interface (Win32 API).

Fig. 4. User interface of the voting application consisting of four superhero images arranged in 2×2 matrix. Supergirl (top left),superman (top right), black widow (bottom left) and wolverine (bottom right).

Data Preprocessing. Data preprocessing was performed by filtering the raw EEG data in the 1–7 Hz frequency band using the fifth-order Butterworth filter. After the filtering process, the P300 and non-P300 feature vectors were derived by extracting 400 ms segments of data following each intensification of the target and non-target stimuli, respectively. The feature vectors were then moving average filtered and decimated by a factor of 12 before being fed into the classifier for training.

Classification. The presence or absence of the P300 evoked potential in the EEG data can be expressed as a binary classification problem. Therefore, during the training process, the P300 feature vectors (target stimuli) were assigned a class label of $+1$ and the non-P300 feature vectors (non-target stimuli) were assigned a class label of -1. The vectors were then trained using the Linear Discriminant Analysis (LDA) classifier. During the voting process, assuming that the P300 event-related potential (ERP) was elicited for one of the two row/column intensifications, the classifier predicted the resultant row and column by taking the maximum of the sum of the weighted feature vectors for the respective rows and columns. The resultant row and column were predicted using Eqs. 1 and 2, respectively,

$$predicted(row) = argmax_{rows}[\Sigma_{i_{row}} w.x_{i_{row}}]$$ (1)

$$predicted(column) = argmax_{columns}[\Sigma_{i_{column}} w.x_{i_{column}}]$$ (2)

where w represents vector of classification weights, $x_{i_{row}}$ represents a row feature vector and $x_{i_{column}}$ represents a column feature vector [6]. The predicted superhero character was then determined by taking the intersection of the predicted row and column in the matrix.

3.4   User Study

Study Design. The user study was conducted to explore and evaluate the accuracy of the application for casting votes and acquire qualitative feedback from the participants to get an understanding of their experience after interacting with the system. First, the participants completed a pre-experiment survey containing demographic questions. Following this, they interacted with the Neuro-Voting application. For the experiment, the participants had to complete six training sessions and five online voting tasks while wearing the EEG device. In the end, to evaluate the experiment after interacting with the system, the participants were asked to take part in an audio interview. In the interview, they were asked a series of questions to get their qualitative feedback regarding their experience with the application.

Experimental Procedure. At the beginning of the study, a member of the research team explained the experiment and acquired informed consent from the participants. Following this, the participants filled out the pre-experiment survey using Qualtrics Survey software. Afterwards, a member of the research team helped the participants in wearing the BCI device on their scalp and using the Neuroelectrics Instrument Controller (NIC2) software, the study personnel ensured that the headset had successful contact with the scalp with proper signal quality. The participants then completed six training sessions while using the Neuro-Voting BCI application. During each session, the EEG data of the participants was recorded while they focused attention on the flashing images of the four superheroes one by one. The four superhero images were arranged in a 2 × 2 matrix (see Fig. 4) and the rows and the columns of the matrix flashed in a random sequence with regular intervals of 100 ms. Each session continued for 20 series of flashes with four flashes in each series and P300 event-related potentials were elicited in the user, during the times when the rows and the columns containing the target superhero character were flashed. Following the sixth training session, a rest period of five minutes was given to the participants. During this time, the acquired EEG data was preprocessed based on the preprocessing steps described in Sect. 3.3. And then trained by the Linear Discriminant

Table 1. Task performance and accuracy scores for each participant.

Participant ID	Task 1	Task 2	Task 3	Task 4	Task 5	Average accuracy
P01	No	No	Yes	No	No	20%
P02	Yes	Yes	Yes	Yes	Yes	100%
P03	Yes	Yes	Yes	Yes	Yes	100%
P04	Yes	Yes	Yes	Yes	Yes	100%
P05	Yes	Yes	Yes	Yes	Yes	100%

Analysis (LDA) classifier. Following the rest period, the participants engaged in the online voting task in which they were instructed to complete the following five tasks:

1. **Task 1** - Vote for supergirl.
2. **Task 2** - Vote for wolverine.
3. **Task 3** - Vote for superman.
4. **Task 4** - Vote for black widow.
5. **Task 5** - Vote for the superhero character of your choice.

During the first four voting tasks, the participants had to vote for supergirl, wolverine, superman and black widow, respectively, by focusing on the corresponding superhero image. In the last voting task, the participants had to vote for the superhero character of their choice. The final part of the study was an audio interview in which the participants were asked to answer a series of questions. These questions were designed to: (1) determine how intuitive and useful they found the application; (2) get feedback regarding their voting experience; and (3) get suggestions for improving the application in the future. The entire experimental procedure took approximately one hour and fifteen minutes.

4   Results

4.1   Accuracy Scores

Table 1 shows the results and the average accuracy scores obtained by the participants for each of the five tasks. As seen in the table, for a task, "Yes" represents that the application was able to correctly predict the vote of the participant and "No" represents that the application was not able to correctly predict the vote. Four participants (P02, P03, P04 and P05) were able to cast their votes in all the five tasks with 100% accuracy, whereas, one participant (P01) could only get one task correct. The average accuracy for this participant was 20%. The poor performance of this participant could potentially be due to fatigue and their inability to focus on the tasks, as they participated in the study during the mid-term exams at their university.

4.2   Participant Qualitative Feedback

At the end of the study, the participants provided their feedback by answering a series of open-ended questions. Four participants found the voting application to be quite intuitive as it correctly predicted the superhero characters they wanted to vote for. All the participants agreed that they liked the idea of voting with their brain. Three of the five participants found the application easy to use. Participant P03 stated that "the application was quite simple to use" and P05 mentioned that "Neuro-Voting was easy to use and understand". One participant (P04) mentioned that the Enobio device was uncomfortable to wear for the duration of use and another participant (P01) was unable to focus on the voting tasks because of fatigue. Participants were also asked if there was anything that could be improved about the application. Some answers included reducing the training times and providing a more comfortable headset. Furthermore, when asked whether they could foresee this kind of voting BCI being implemented in the future, all of them agreed. Participant P01 said, "I think that people would definitely use this system", P04 said, "I think voting in this manner is the safest way to vote" and P02 stated that "Neuro-Voting could increase the current accuracy of voting". Overall, the Neuro-Voting BCI application received positive feedback. The participants suggested to improve the application's long training times and EEG headset's comfortableness.

4.3   Discussion

The results obtained from the user study showed that the application has the potential to accurately predict the votes of the users as out of five participants, four were able to cast their votes with 100% accuracy. This indicates that the proposed application is a reliable voting system as it can guess the votes of the users with high accuracy. As seen in Table 1, one of the five participants (P01) only got 20% accuracy. This potentially happened due to their lack of concentration during the voting task as in the audio interview, this participant mentioned that they were feeling tired and were unable to focus. The application received positive feedback from the participants. They found the proposed voting system interesting and intuitive and indicated that they could foresee this type of voting system to be implemented in the future. Some participants mentioned the application's long training times and EEG devices poor comfortableness as areas of improvement. In the future, these issues would be addressed by exploring new ways to shorten the training procedure and possibly use another BCI headset that is comfortable to wear and can collect high quality EEG data.

5   Conclusion

This paper presented Neuro-Voting, a novel P300-based BCI application that allows users to cast their votes using their brain activity. This application would be beneficial to people who are diagnosed with ALS and have limited physical mobility, allowing them to vote without requiring any assistance. In addition, the use of this application could potentially remove the problem of forged voter IDs, as users have unique patterns of brain activities and it would be difficult for a user to use another user's profile to vote. A user study was conducted to evaluate the efficiency and accuracy of the application. The accuracy results obtained were promising as the application was able to predict the votes of majority of users with 100% accuracy. The feedback from the study was encouraging with some suggestions for improvements such as increasing EEG devices comfortableness and reducing the overall training time. The results indicate that Neuro-Voting has the potential to provide an accurate, safe, hands-free and easy to use voting environment. The application has the ability to scale upwards as in the future iterations, the application would be improved based on the recommendations received in the user study.

References

1. Bederson, B.B., Lee, B., Sherman, R.M., Herrnson, P.S., Niemi, R.G.: Electronic voting system usability issues. In: Proceedings of the SIGCHI Conference on Human Factors in Computing Systems, pp. 145–152 (2003)
2. Botrel, L., Holz, E.M., Kübler, A.: Brain painting V2: evaluation of P300-based brain-computer interface for creative expression by an end-user following the user-centered design. Brain-Comput. Interfaces **2**(2–3), 135–149 (2015)
3. Farwell, L.A., Donchin, E.: Talking off the top of your head: toward a mental prosthesis utilizing event-related brain potentials. Electroencephalogr. Clin. Neurophysiol. **70**(6), 510–523 (1988)
4. Hoffmann, U., Garcia, G., Vesin, J.M., Diserens, K., Ebrahimi, T.: A boosting approach to P300 detection with application to brain-computer interfaces. In: Conference Proceedings. 2nd International IEEE EMBS Conference on Neural Engineering, pp. 97–100. IEEE (2005)
5. Kaplan, A.Y., Shishkin, S.L., Ganin, I.P., Basyul, I.A., Zhigalov, A.Y.: Adapting the P300-based brain-computer interface for gaming: a review. IEEE Trans. Comput. Intell. AI Games **5**(2), 141–149 (2013)
6. Krusienski, D.J., et al.: A comparison of classification techniques for the P300 speller. J. Neural Eng. **3**(4), 299 (2006)
7. Manyakov, N.V., Chumerin, N., Combaz, A., Van Hulle, M.M.: Comparison of classification methods for P300 brain-computer interface on disabled subjects. Comput. Intell. Neurosci. **2011**, 1–12 (2011)
8. McClinton, W., Caprio, D., Laesker, D., Pinto, B., Garcia, S., Andujar, M.: P300-based 3D brain painting in virtual reality. In: Extended Abstracts of the 2019 CHI Conference on Human Factors in Computing Systems, pp. 1–6 (2019)
9. McClinton, W., Garcia, S., Andujar, M.: An immersive brain painting: the effects of brain painting in a virtual reality environment. In: Schmorrow, D.D., Fidopiastis, C.M. (eds.) HCII 2019. LNCS (LNAI), vol. 11580, pp. 436–445. Springer, Cham (2019). https://doi.org/10.1007/978-3-030-22419-6_31
10. Mugler, E.M., Ruf, C.A., Halder, S., Bensch, M., Kubler, A.: Design and implementation of a P300-based brain-computer interface for controlling an internet browser. IEEE Trans. Neural Syst. Rehabil. Eng. **18**(6), 599–609 (2010)

11. Ruiz-Blondet, M.V., Jin, Z., Laszlo, S.: CEREBRE: a novel method for very high accuracy event-related potential biometric identification. IEEE Trans. Inf. Forensics Secur. **11**(7), 1618–1629 (2016)
12. Sellers, E.W., Donchin, E.: A P300-based brain-computer interface: initial tests by ALS patients. Clin. Neurophysiol. **117**(3), 538–548 (2006)
13. Szafir, D., Mutlu, B.: ARTFul: adaptive review technology for flipped learning. In: Proceedings of the SIGCHI Conference on Human Factors in Computing Systems, pp. 1001–1010 (2013)

Analyzing Gaze Data During Rest Time/Driving Simulator Operation Using Machine Learning

Kazuhiro Fujikake[1]([✉]), Yoshiyuki Itadu[2], and Hiroki Takada[2]

[1] Chukyo University, 101-2, Yagotohonmachi, Showa-ku, Nagoya, Aichi 4668666, Japan
fujikake@lets.chukyo-u.ac.jp
[2] University of Fukui, 3-9-1 Bunkyo, Fukui-shi, Fukui, Japan

Abstract. Research on drivers often uses the driving simulator (DS). Visually induced motion sickness (VIMS) has been pointed out as a problem in DS experiments. Although there are many methods to evaluate VIMS, reducing the burden on the experimental collaborators is an issue. As a method of measuring physiological indices that is less burdensome to the participants and has many applications, the use of noncontact eye-tracking system has been mentioned. This study developed a VIMS evaluation index using data collected with a noncontact eye-tracking system for DS experiments. The participants included eight elderly people with visual and balance functions that did not interfere with their daily life. The participants' gaze data were measured at all DS trials and they answered the simulator sickness questionnaire (SSQ) before and after each trial. The participants were divided into two groups on the basis of their SSQ results. One group experienced VIMS during the DS trial (four people; average age, 79.0 years), whereas the other group did not experience it (four people; average age, 72.0 years). The results of the learning model's validation showed a high rate of correct answers. The results suggested that the learning model obtained using machine learning was an effective evaluation index for VIMS during the DS trial.

Keywords: Visually induced motion sickness (VIMS) · Gaze data · Rotational eye movement · Driving simulator (DS) · Elderly people

1 Introduction

Driving simulators (DS) have been widely used in research related to elderly drivers. As advantages of experiments utilizing a DS, no injuries occur from accidents because it is a simulated experience, it is easy to set up and reproduce the traffic scenarios, and the experiment conditions can be adjusted. As one of the disadvantages associated with the use of DS, visually induced motion sickness (VIMS) can occur. Other disadvantages include a deviation from the sense of reality and high costs incurred. In recent years, DS-related hardware has become more powerful and less expensive, and thus the issues of realism and cost are being resolved. However, these are not an effective solution for VIMS. By contrast, because the symptoms of VIMS worsen as the field of view is expanded, it has been pointed out that the risk of VIMS increases as the size of the display screen increases [1].

© The Author(s), under exclusive license to Springer Nature Switzerland AG 2022
M. Antona and C. Stephanidis (Eds.): HCII 2022, LNCS 13308, pp. 420–434, 2022.
https://doi.org/10.1007/978-3-031-05028-2_28

VIMS occurring through the use of DS is considered to be a type of motion sickness [1]. Motion sickness caused by visual information is classified as visual motion sickness. Because VIMS is thought to be caused by a mismatch between visual information and the vestibular system such as the semicircular canals, involvement of the oculomotor control system is expected. The physical symptoms associated with VIMS include sickness, nausea (upset stomach), dizziness, and lightheadedness.

The occurrence of rotational eye movement is known to be a physical symptom of VIMS [1]. Rotational eye movement is the movement of the eye as it rotates around the line of sight. Rotational eye movement is generated by vestibular (in particular, the otolith organs) and visual stimuli. The rotational eye movement generated by vestibular stimulation is called vestibular counter rolling (vestibular torsional counter rolling). When the body (head) is tilted in either direction, the eyeballs rotate in the direction opposite the tilt of the body (head) to maintain the field of vision [2]. Furthermore, rotational eye movement is a reflex caused by linear acceleration from the otolith organs, and rotational eye movement is also thought to occur when the posture fluctuates as a physical symptom of motion sickness [3].

There are many methods for applying an evaluation index of VIMS. A simulator sickness questionnaire (SSQ), which is a subjective evaluation of VIMS, and measurements of the center of gravity sway while standing have been used [4, 5]. In addition, a method for evaluating an impulse to vomit (upset stomach) by measuring an electrogastrogram has also been investigated [6]. Furthermore, an evaluation based on rotational eye movement has also been considered by measuring the area around the eyeball through electromyography [7].

As evaluation indices for VIMS based on data on the center of gravity sway, the total locus length, area of sway, trajectory length per unit area, and sparse density are known [8–11]. The total locus length indicates the total movement distance of the center of gravity, and the numerical value increases when the posture is in fluctuation. The area of sway is the inner area enclosed by the outer contour of the trajectory of the moving center of gravity, which increases when the posture is wobbly. The trajectory length per unit area is the length of the total locus divided by the area of sway, and the value increases when the posture is stable and decreases when wobbling occurs. The sparse density is a quantification index that shows the variation of data on the planar view, and is a numerical value calculated by the number of times the center of gravity passes through each division of the sway diagram separated by squares. The sparse density value will be close to 1 if the posture is stable, which will result in locally dense divisions. If the posture fluctuates, the sparse density value increases. These quantification indices of the center of gravity sway have been shown to be effective in the evaluation of VIMS, which occurs as a result of gazing at moving images displayed on a screen [12, 13]. Furthermore, it has been shown to be effective as an evaluation index for VIMS that occurs when gazing at stereoscopic images [12–14]. As one of the features of these evaluation indices, they are calculated from the center of gravity sway data when gazing at moving and stereoscopic images.

There are several issues that need to be resolved in the evaluation of VIMS. The physiological indices of eye-movement induced sickness from electrogastrograms and electromyography require electrodes and special equipment, and thus their burden on the experiment participants is large, and their use is limited. In addition, in the case of a VIMS evaluation using the DS, an evaluation based on the center of gravity sway is inappropriate because it involves a pedal operation in a sitting position. Furthermore, with regard to the physiological indices of sickness caused by eye movements such as center of gravity sway, gastric electrocardiograms, and electromyograms, no consistent results have been obtained for the complex changes in the progression of sickness [8, 9]. Although an SSQ allows a high degree of freedom in an evaluation, it is neither objective nor accurate. If the symptoms progress to the point where the VIMS can be subjectively perceived, the symptoms of sickness may last for approximately 24 h [15]. It is therefore necessary for DS experiments to detect the signs of VIMS at an early stage before the symptoms become serious.

The use of a non-contact gaze measurement device is a less burdensome method of measuring physiological indices for experiment participants and has many different applications. Because a non-contact gaze measurement device does not require electrodes to be attached, there is little burden on the experiment participants in terms of data acquisition. The corneal reflection method is used as a measurement method for non-contact gaze measurement devices. The corneal reflection method is a method of irradiating a light source onto the cornea to distinguish between the reflection points of light on the cornea and the pupil, and the direction of the eye is calculated based on the reflection points of light and other geometric features [16–18].

The purpose of this study is the development of an index that can evaluate VIMS from gaze data using a non-contact type gaze measurement device. Gaze data were collected at rest before and after the DS was run, as well as during a portion of the DS run itself. We will consider the development of an evaluation index that enables the early detection of VIMS by using the gaze data as the analysis target while driving the DS. The evaluation index will be developed through machine learning on the acquired eye gaze data. The hypothesis of this study is as follows:

The machine learning model obtained through a machine learning analysis can determine the characteristics of the gaze data associated with the VIMS, such as rotational eye movement.

2   Method

2.1   DS Configuration and Driving Content

The DS used in the experiment consisted of five screens (the viewing distance from the experiment participants in the driver's seat to the front screen was approximately 1 m), a steering wheel, gas pedal, brake pedal, and a control PC (Figs. 1 and 2).

The experiment participants experienced driving in the DS a total of six times: once for a 1-min practice run and five times in a 5-min test run. In addition, it is generally believed that VIMS associated with DS driving is induced by the screen display when decelerating by braking and when turning right or left. For this reason, the experiment driving course of the DS was set at two temporary stop intersections and two right/left turn points.

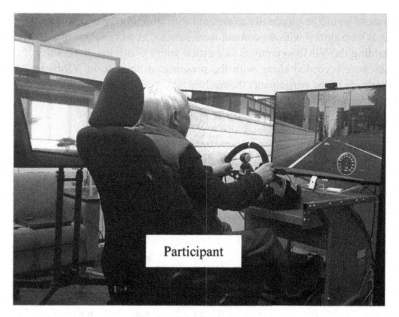

Fig. 1. Experimental setup.

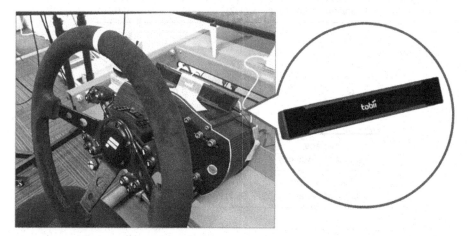

Fig. 2. Measurement device (Tobii Pro X2–30).

2.2 Experiment Participants

Eight elderly individuals recruited through a temporary employment agency and having no visual or equilibrium problems participated in the experiment (Table 1). We explained to the experiment participants that DS driving may cause symptoms similar to motion sickness, and that they should indicate whether they felt sick or unwell, and that if so the experiment would be stopped immediately. Furthermore, we explained that if their symptoms did not ease after a certain break period, the experiment would be stopped and that there would be no penalty associated with stopping the experiment. The elderly individuals who agreed with the content were selected as participants in this experiment.

Regarding the VIMS symptoms associated with DS driving, the results of the SSQ responses were recorded along with the presence or absence of VIMS based on the internal reports of the participants themselves before and after the experiment (Fig. 1).

This experiment was conducted with the approval of the Ethics Review Committee of the University of Fukui (Approval No. H2018003).

Table 1. Participants' score (SSQ).

Participant	VIMS	Age	SSQ (Total score) pre	post
A		76	0.0	0.0
B	Without (N/A)	73	0.0	0.0
C		74	0.0	0.0
D		73	0.0	0.0
Average (standard deviation)		74.0 (1.2)	0.0 (0.0)	0.0 (0.0)
E		81	33.7	59.8
F	With (A)	72	1.9	11.2
G		79	0.0	3.7
H		84	3.7	11.2
Average (standard deviation)		79.0 (4.4)	9.8 (13.8)	21.5 (22.3)
Overall average (standard deviation)		77.9 (4.5)	4.9 (10.9)	10.8 (19.1)

2.3 Measurement of Gaze Data

During the experiment, gaze data were measured at rest before and after, as well as during, the operation of the DS. The experiment participants were instructed to gaze at the optotype displayed at the center of the DS screen when at rest. A machine learning analysis was conducted on 60 s of resting gaze data before and after the DS was run (pre/post), and on 30 s of the latter half of the first and fifth DS runs. The experiment participants were instructed to pay attention to the safety of their surroundings while driving in the DS, as they would during a daily drive.

A Tobii Pro X2–30 (sampling rate of 60 Hz) was used as the gaze measurement device, and Tobii Pro Studio (ver. 3.3.2) was used as the analysis software. The gaze measurement device in question measures eye movements using the corneal reflection method. The gaze measurement device was installed on the steering wheel control unit in front of the experiment participants (Fig. 2). In addition, a scene camera was set up at a height of 1.5 m above the head, approximately 1 m behind the experiment participants. The gaze data were plotted corresponding to a pixel resolution of 640 (width) × 480 (height) of the scene camera (Logitech HD Webcam C270) (one pixel of which is approximately 1 mm in size on the screen to be gazed at). In addition, the gaze data were output for each of the left and right eyes. Therefore, the gaze data acquired by the eye measurement device are the values of the plane coordinates for each eye. In this study, the mean value calculated from the gaze data of each eye was analyzed as the gaze point of the corresponding eye.

3   Gaze Data Analysis Processing

Pre-processing was conducted to analyze the gaze data through machine learning. First, the acquired gaze data were standardized (mean 0, variance 1) and missing values were removed. A dataset was then created by extracting time series data with a series length of 5 s at 0.1-s intervals.

Machine learning was applied by analyzing the created dataset. The learning model was a one-dimensional (1D) convolutional neural network, and features were extracted and classified (binary classification) in the convolutional and pooling layers. In regard to the verification method for the training and test data used in machine learning, the leave-one-out method was applied, for which verification was repeated such that the data from all of the experiment participants became the test cases (Fig. 3, Table 2).

The model was created through machine learning performed for 60 s at rest before and after the DS run, and every 30 s in the latter half of the first and fifth DS runs. Validation of the learning model obtained from the resting gaze data was conducted for 60 s at rest before, 60 s at rest after, and 60 s before and after the DS was run (only for

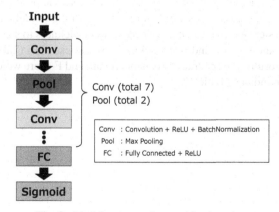

Fig. 3. Model structure for machine learning.

Table 2. Machine learning procedure.

No.	Layer Name	Output Shape	Kernel Size	Filters	Parameters
1.	Input	300×2			0
2.	Conv	300×64	8	64	1,344
3.	Conv	300×32	8	32	16,544
4.	Pooling	150×32			0
5.	Conv	150×32	8	32	8,352
6.	Conv	150×16	8	16	4,176
7.	Conv	150×16	8	16	2,128
8.	Pooling	75×16			0
9.	Conv	75×8	8	8	1,064
10.	Conv	75×8	8	8	552
11.	Flat	600			0
12.	Dropout (0.3)	600			0
13.	Dense	128			76,928
14.	Dense	1			129

the group with VIMS). In addition, the validation of the learning model obtained from the gaze data of the first and fifth DS runs was conducted for a 30-s period for the first DS run, a 30-s period for the fifth DS run, and a 30-s period for the first and fifth DS runs (only for the group with VIMS).

No VIMS was considered negative (negative), whereas the presence of VIMS was considered positive (positive). For validation of the learning model, each dataset was classified from no sickness to no sickness (TN), from no sickness to sickness (FP), from sickness to no sickness (FN), and from sickness to sickness (TP) (Table 3). Based on the classification results, the accuracy, precision, recall, and F-score were calculated and used as evaluation indices (Table 4).

Table 3. Classification of analysis results.

Classification item		Contents
TN	(TrueNegative)	: Classify without VIMS into without VIMS (Correct)
FP	(FalsePositive)	: Classify without VIMS into with VIMS (Not correct)
FN	(FalseNegative)	: Classify with VIMS into without VIMS (Not correct)
TP	(TruePositive)	: Classify with VIMS into with VIMS (Correct)

Table 4. Evaluation index of classification.

Index	Contents	Formula
Accuracy	Percent correct for all predictions	(TP+TN)/ (TP+FP+FN+TN)
Precision	Percentage of correct predictions	TP/ (TP+FP)
Recall	Percentage of correct responses to positive	TP/ (TP+FN)
F-score	Harmonic mean of fit rate and recall rate	(2×Precision×Recall)/ (Precision+Recall)

4 Results

The experiment participants were classified into two groups, "with VIMS (4 subjects)" and "without VIMS (4 subjects)" based on their SSQ results (Table 1). Although having a high SSQ score before the experiment, Participant E stated, "I don't feel sick," and "I'm sweating because I hurried," and thus it was determined that the individual could participate in the experiment and was thus included in the original group.

The resting gaze data before and after the DS run are plotted on a plane (Figs. 4 and 5). In the non-VIMS gaze data for participant C, no significant differences were observed before or after the DS was run (Fig. 4). In the gaze data with VIMS for participant F, the result indicated that the gaze data after driving seemed to be diffused compared to before driving (Fig. 5). In addition, when both were compared to the gaze data before driving, the gaze data of the experiment subjects with VIMS appeared to be more diffuse.

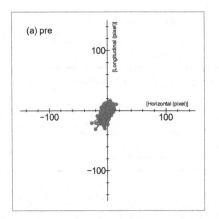

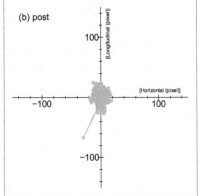

Fig. 4. Example of without VIMS (Gaze data at rest time). Gaze data of participant C before (left) and after (right) the DS run. The vertical axis is the longitudinal movements of the gaze, and the horizontal axis is the right and left movements of the gaze.

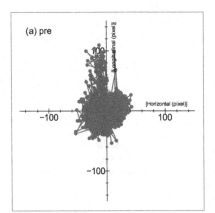

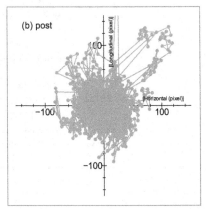

Fig. 5. Example of with VIMS (Gaze data at rest time). Gaze data of participant F before (left) and after (right) the DS run. The vertical axis is the longitudinal movements of the gaze, and the horizontal axis is the right and left movements of the gaze.

4.1   Results of Resting Gaze Data

The evaluation results of the learning model obtained through machine learning while at rest are shown. In the results for the evaluation indices validating the learning model with the gaze data before running the DS, the mean accuracy was 54.43% and the mean precision was 41.80% (Table 5). The results of the evaluation indices after the DS were run showed that the mean accuracy, precision, recall, and F-score exceeded 70% (Table 6). In the number of classified datasets after driving, TNs and TPs occurred more than before driving. For the results for the evaluation indices in which the learning model was validated with the gaze data before and after running only in the group with VIMS, the mean accuracy, precision, recall, and F-score exceeded 70% (Table 7). In the number of datasets classified for only the group with VIMS, TNs occurred more than after driving.

Table 5. Result of before DS trial (Pre).

VIMS Without	With	TN	FP	FN	TP	Accuracy	Precision	Recall	F-score
A	E	0	315	4	256	44.52	44.83	98.46	61.61
B	F	341	1	355	0	48.92	0.00	0.00	–
C	G	186	123	129	203	60.69	62.27	61.14	61.70
D	H	137	198	51	298	63.60	60.08	85.39	70.53
					Average	54.43	41.80	61.25	64.62
					Standard deviation	7.93	25.05	37.81	4.18

Table 6. Result of after DS trial (Post).

VIMS Without	With	TN	FP	FN	TP	Accuracy	Precision	Recall	F-score
A	E	130	120	8	316	77.70	72.48	97.53	83.16
B	F	181	111	21	288	78.04	72.18	93.20	81.36
C	G	191	141	102	220	62.84	60.94	68.32	64.42
D	H	302	2	110	154	80.28	98.72	58.33	73.33
					Average	74.72	76.08	79.35	75.57
					Standard deviation	6.93	13.87	16.48	7.42

A one-tailed Wilcoxon signed rank test was conducted on the results of the evaluation index of the learning model for the gaze data before and after DS driving, with the null hypothesis that there is no difference in the population mean. The results showed that the accuracy of the learning model tended to be significantly higher after DS driving than before ($p < 0.1$). It was also shown that there was a significant tendency for the accuracy of the learning model in the VIMS group to be higher than that before DS driving ($p < 0.1$). Furthermore, the precision of the learning model in the VIMS group tended to be significantly higher than that before DS driving ($p < 0.1$).

Table 7. Result of with VIMS (Pre and Post).

Pre	Post	TN	FP	FN	TP	Accuracy	Precision	Recall	F-score
E	E	308	41	138	186	73.40	81.94	57.41	67.51
F	F	234	98	82	227	71.92	69.85	73.46	71.61
G	G	215	140	19	303	76.51	68.40	94.10	79.22
H	H	129	131	14	250	72.33	65.62	94.70	77.52
					Average	73.54	71.45	79.92	73.96
					Standard deviation	1.80	6.24	15.56	4.67

4.2 Results of Gaze Data While Driving

The evaluation results of the training model obtained through machine learning while driving is shown. The results of the evaluation indices validating the learning model with the gaze data from the first DS run showed that the mean accuracy and precision exceeded 60%, the mean recall was 87.35%, and the mean F-score was 72.97% (Table 8). The results of the evaluation index for the fifth DS run showed that the mean accuracy and precision exceeded 65%, the mean recall was 87.60%, and the mean F-score was 75.57% (Table 9). For the results for the evaluation indices in which the learning model was validated with the gaze data from the first and fifth DS runs for only the group with VIMS, the mean accuracy and precision exceeded 60% (Table 10). In the number of datasets classified for only the group with VIMS, TNs occurred more than in the first and fifth drives.

Table 8. Result of DS trial (1st).

VIMS		TN	FP	FN	TP	Accuracy	Precision	Recall	F-score
Without	With								
A	E	109	98	58	141	61.58	59.00	70.85	64.38
B	F	0	50	0	95	65.52	65.52	100.00	79.17
C	G	0	102	0	209	67.20	67.20	100.00	80.38
D	H	64	108	44	161	59.68	59.85	78.54	67.93
					Average	63.49	62.89	87.35	72.97
					Standard deviation	3.00	3.53	12.94	6.94

A one-tailed Wilcoxon signed rank test with a null hypothesis, assuming that there was no difference in the population mean, was conducted on the results of the evaluation index of the learning model for the DS run and the fifth set of the gaze data. The results showed that the accuracy of the 5th DS run learning model tended to be significantly higher than that of the first DS run ($p < 0.1$).

Table 9. Result of DS trial (5th).

VIMS Without	VIMS With	TN	FP	FN	TP	Accuracy	Precision	Recall	F-score
A	E	95	42	52	142	71.60	77.17	73.20	75.13
B	F	18	27	5	52	68.63	65.82	91.23	76.47
C	G	0	84	0	199	70.32	70.32	100.00	82.57
D	H	85	109	23	141	63.13	56.40	85.98	68.12
					Average	68.42	67.43	87.60	75.57
					Standard deviation	3.23	7.54	9.71	5.14

Table 10. Result of with VIMS (1st and 5th).

1st	5th	TN	FP	FN	TP	Accuracy	Precision	Recall	F-score
E	E	170	29	132	62	59.03	68.13	31.96	43.51
F	F	55	40	5	52	70.39	56.52	91.23	69.80
G	G	151	58	102	97	60.78	62.58	48.74	54.80
H	H	200	5	115	49	67.48	90.74	29.88	44.95
					Average	64.42	69.49	50.45	53.27
					Standard deviation	4.67	12.94	24.65	10.49

4.3 Comparison Between Resting and Driving

The evaluation indices of the learning model were compared between the resting state before the DS run and after the first run, with the indices being higher for the first run. However, when the evaluation indices of the learning model were compared between the resting state after the DS run and the fifth run, those for the resting state after the run were found to be higher. In addition, when the evaluation indices of the resting state before and after driving the DS and of the driving state were compared for only the group with VIMS, those for the resting state before and after driving were found to be higher.

A one-tailed Wilcoxon signed rank test with a null hypothesis, assuming that there was no difference in the population mean, was conducted for the evaluation indices for the state at rest prior to the DS driving and the first run, the state at rest after DS driving and the fifth run, and the state at rest before and after the DS driving only for the group with VIMS. The results showed that the accuracy at rest before and after DS driving in the group with VIMS only was significantly higher than the accuracy rate while driving ($p < 0.05$).

5   Discussions

In this study, we investigated the development of an index used to evaluate the VIMS by measuring the resting gaze before and after DS driving using a non-contact gaze measurement device. The evaluation index was developed through machine learning for the acquired gaze data.

As a result of validating the learning model created by the resting gaze data before and after DS driving, the accuracy was higher after driving than it was before. In addition, the accuracy was higher in the VIMS group than before DS driving. Similarly, we tested a learning model based on gaze data during the DS run and found that the correct answer rate was higher for the fifth run than for the first run. In addition, the accuracy was higher in the VIMS group than in the first DS run. This result can be said to be influenced by the fact that, in the model validation before the DS driving and in the first drive, the number of datasets classified as VIMS-free to VIMS presence (FP) and VIMS presence to VIMS-free (FN) were relatively large. This result suggests that the created learning model may not be able to sufficiently judge the gaze data before the DS run or after the first run, when VIMS is not considered to occur.

In addition, as a result of comparing the learning models created by the gaze data during the resting state and driving state before and after DS driving, the accuracy during the resting state was higher than that during the driving state only in the group with VIMS. As a background factor, it is considered that the data included gaze behavior associated with driving. From this, it may be necessary to increase the number of data such that the characteristics of the VIMS can be extracted even for the gaze data while driving.

For the evaluation index of VIMS using gaze data, studies have shown the effectiveness of the evaluation index calculating the total locus length and sparse density of the gaze data with reference to the evaluation index of the center of gravity sway [19]. However, because this evaluation index targets the eye gaze data at rest, an issue occurs in that it does not target data while gazing at the image, such as with the center of gravity sway data. As a particular factor worth mentioning, the image content that affects the gaze data while gazing was not targeted as an evaluation index of VIMS based on the gaze data. In this study, the gaze behavior aimed at the surrounding area for safety confirmation during DS driving falls under this category. The results of this study do not cover the gaze data while gazing at the video screen. However, because it is also possible to analyze the gaze data while gazing at the video, we plan to work on the analysis of the gaze data while driving the DS in the future.

From the results of this study, the hypothesis that the model obtained through a machine learning analysis can make judgments regarding the characteristics of the gaze data associated with VIMS, such as rotational eye movement, was supported. However, there is a need to further improve the accuracy of gaze data while driving the DS. Therefore, it is necessary to increase the number of data in the future. In addition, it will be necessary to verify the effectiveness of the system in the case of gaze data where the driver is gazing at complex surrounding environments, such as when driving on public roads.

6 Conclusion

In this study, we investigated the development of an index that can evaluate the VIMS by measuring the gaze at rest before and after, as well as during, the driving of the DS using a non-contact gaze measurement device. As a result of creating a judgment model through machine learning for the eye gaze data before and after driving the DS, a highly accurate judgment model for VIMS was shown through verification using the eye gaze data after driving. In addition, the results of the gaze data during DS driving showed a highly accurate judgment model through verification using the gaze data from the fifth driving run.

Therefore, the hypothesis that the model obtained through machine learning analysis can make judgments about the characteristics of the gaze data associated with VIMS, such as rotational eye movement, was supported.

Future tasks include increasing the number of data and validating the system for long-term gaze data when driving on public roads.

Acknowledgment. This work was supported by JSPS KAKENHI Grant Number 20K11905.

References

1. Ohmi, M., Ujike, H.: Eizou Jouhou ni yoru Jiko Teii to Eizou Yoi. Bio Med. Eng. **18**(1), 32–39 (2004). (in Japanese)
2. Howard, I.: Human Visual Orientation. John Wiley & Sons Ltd., New Jersey (1982)
3. Marg, E.: Development of electro-oculography; standing potential of the eye in registration of eye movement. AMA Arch. Ophthalmol. **45**, 69–185 (1951)
4. Golding, J.F.: Phasic skin conductance activity and motion sickness. Aviat. Space Environ. Med. **63**(3), 165–171 (1992)
5. Wan, H., Hu, S., Wang, J.: Correlation of phasic and motion sickness-conductance responses with severity of motion sickness induced by viewing an optokinetic rotating drum. Perceptual Motor Skills **97**(3), 1051–1057 (2003)
6. Kinoshita, F., Fujita, K., Miyanaga, K., Touyama, H., Takada, M., Takada, H.: Analysis of electrogastrograms during exercise loads. J. Sports Med. Doping Stud. **8**(2), 285–294 (2018)
7. Shackel, B.: Eye movement recording by electro-oculography. In: Venables, P.H., Martion, I. (eds.) A Manual of Psychophysiological Methods, pp. 300–334. North-Holland Publishing Co., Amsterdam (1967)
8. Nakagawa, C., Ohsuga, M.: The present situation of the studies in VE-Sickness and its close field. Virt. Soc. Jpn. **3**(2), 31–39 (1998). (in Japanese)
9. Hirayanagi, K.: A present state and perspective of studies on motion sickness. Jpn. J. Ergon. **42**(3), 200–211 (2006). (in Japanese)
10. Fujikake, K., Miyao, M., Honda, R., Omori, M., Matuura, Y., Takada, H.: Evaluation of high quality LCDs displaying moving pictures, on the basis of the results obtained from statokinesigrams. Forma **22**(2), 199–206 (2007)

11. Fujikake, K., Takada, H., Omori, M., Hasegawa, S., Honda, R., Miyao, M.: Evaluation of moving picture image quality on LCDs using Stabilometer. Jpn. J. Ergon. **44**(4), 208–217 (2008). (in Japanese)
12. Kinoshita, F., Takada, H.: Numerical analysis of SDEs as a model for body sway while viewing 3D video clips. Mech. Syst. Control **47**(2), 98–105 (2019)
13. Miyao, M., Takada, M., Takada, H.: Visual Issues on Augmented Reality Using Smart Glasses with 3D Stereoscopic Images. In: Antona, M., Stephanidis, C. (eds.) HCII 2019. LNCS, vol. 11572, pp. 578–589. Springer, Cham (2019). https://doi.org/10.1007/978-3-030-23560-4_42
14. Tanimura, T., Takada, H., Sugiura, A., Kinoshita, F., Takada, M.: Effects of the low-resolution 3D video clip on cerebrum blood flow dynamics. Adv Sci Tech Eng Syst J **4**(2), 380–386 (2019)
15. U.S. Navy: OPNAVINST, 3710.7T (2004)
16. Young, L.R., Sheena, D.: Methods and designs; Survey of eye movement recording methods. Behav. Res. Methods Instrum. **7**, 397–429 (1975)
17. Cornsweet, T.N., Crane, H.D.: Accurate two-dimensional eye tracker using first and fourth Purkinje images. J. Opt. Soc. Am. **63**, 921–928 (1973)
18. Crane, H.D., Steele, C.M.: An accurate three-dimensional eye tracker. Appl. Opt. **17**, 691–705 (1978)
19. Fujikake, K.: Measurements for visual function, including gaze, and electrooculography (EOG). In: Takada, H., Yokoyama, K. (eds.) Bio-information for Hygiene, pp. 45–56. Springer, Berlin (2021)

MTeacher: A Gamified and Physiological-Based Web Application Designed for Machine Learning Education

Bryan Y. Hernández-Cuevas$^{(\boxtimes)}$ and Chris S. Crawford

Department of Computer Science, The University of Alabama, Tuscaloosa,
AL 35401, USA
byhernandez@crimson.ua.edu, crawford@cs.ua.edu

Abstract. Everyday devices are becoming smarter. Machine Learning (ML) is increasingly more utilized in technology to augment the user experience. Furthermore, it is applied to improve the overall performance of systems. People constantly use intelligent agents in different forms through online shopping, social media, and entertainment. However, they do not understand the intrinsic functionality of the technology. Brain-Computer Interfaces (BCI) are more prominent in non-medical fields. Advances in hardware enable better ways to implement and use BCIs in more ubiquitous ways. There are also software advances that allow devices to connect and achieve signal processing in lower-end environments like the web. There is a need for the public to understand the social and ethical implications of Machine Learning. This research project aims to provide novices and non-CS majors with an explainable educational experience. Machine Teacher (MTeacher) is a web-based Machine Learning educational system that aims to implement less typical types of data (e.g. EEG) and gamified elements. Players can explore the concepts of Machine Learning through interactive activities, and our objective is to help increase their engagement, general ML knowledge, and self-efficacy. Initial results of a study reveal that physiological signals are more appealing to the users than traditional types of data, though they would prefer collecting the data themselves. Our future work aims to explore the addition of real-time physiological data acquisition and improve the application of gamification elements to study their effects on the learner's experience.

Keywords: Machine Learning education · Explainable machine learning · Physiological computing

1   Introduction and Background

Today, interactions with e-commerce websites, social media, and entertainment platforms are all mediated by a powerful piece of technology: Machine Learning (ML). People are constantly encountering some type of output from ML. Typical applications include recommending items [10, 18], showing similar products [15],

© The Author(s), under exclusive license to Springer Nature Switzerland AG 2022
M. Antona and C. Stephanidis (Eds.): HCII 2022, LNCS 13308, pp. 435–445, 2022.
https://doi.org/10.1007/978-3-031-05028-2_29

and personalized experiences [8]. Other ML use cases are seen in social media platforms [1] to predict human mental health, and online entertainment [19] to improve user accessibility. This amount of exposure that people have can lead to situations that require them to critically think and make important decisions. Moreover, with the imminent integration of ML into people's everyday lives, everyone might have to make policy decisions on the technology in the future. The main goal is to inform the general public through easily-accessible educational platforms, for them to have the necessary knowledge to make critical decisions on ML personally and for others.

Current literature shows a trend for exploring Machine Learning Education, however, most of the current solutions focus on the assumption that users have previous experience or the required background to understand complex processes. There is a need to create more explainable ML educational applications, leveraging effective teaching methods to engage users onto more difficult topics (e.g. mathematics, algorithms, signal processing). There are underlying challenges in ML education involving visualizations [17], mathematical complexities [12], and interest levels [5]. Current solutions aim at solving some of those with glyph-based visualizations [16]. Furthermore, others explore the use of real-life interactions with a mobile app that classifies sports movements [21]. Nonetheless, there are not many applications focusing on the use of gamification to leverage interactivity, visuals, and possible increase of engagement. Gamified systems have previously been effective at improving levels of interest. Physiological computing is an emerging field integrated into non-medical areas. There are educational applications that use physiological signals, like electroencephalography (EEG), to understand the user's mental states during the experiences [13]. But instead of utilizing these components to understand user states, other literature explores the use of block-based programming techniques to teach the creation of physiological-based systems [2,4].

The objective of this article is to present a system that intersects gamified elements and physiological signals in an ML educational application. The goal is to increase user engagement and interests based on the assumption that novel technologies (e.g. physiological data) can be more personally relevant to the learner. Machine Teacher (MTeacher) is a web-based solution that implements gamification elements and physiological computing to teach the ML pipeline along with important basic concepts. The system design is presented in detail, with its different components and overall findings in terms of limitations.

2   Challenges in ML Education

To understand the components included in MTeacher, this section discusses the different existing challenges in ML education today. The most common learning barrier is the **mathematical complexities** of every process involved in the pipeline [20]. Students are normally not familiar with the components themselves, and asking for an understanding of the back-end mathematical operations can become overwhelming. In [12], participants considered themselves as "not able to do math", which is a negative connotation that can affect their motivation and self-perceived capability of creating ML-based applications. There are attempts to help visualize certain operations in a more explainable manner for those with limited mathematical backgrounds [17], but these are very specific to algorithms.

Another important barrier in ML education is **programming experience**. Students that do not have previous programming expertise can feel unable to achieve more complicated tasks like an ML model. In [9], the authors make use of Snap!, which can help lower any entry barriers associated with programming. If students can feel confident in their ability to program, they might feel more confident to create ML applications. However, it can be useful to use non-programming interfaces that create a sense of control in participants. They can focus on the task at hand, without the hurdle that programming logic can contribute to the learning experience. Other approaches would be to provide guided tutorials and apply methods such as "Use-Modify-Create" [7] to ease participants into the topic [3,20].

Finally, **engagement** of learners is difficult to maintain in these types of educational platforms [5]. One of the main reasons for this barrier is that the topics are complicated, and people do not feel connected. Unless the learner already has the motive to study ML, others do not feel interested due to the lack of accessibility of the field. Because of their limited knowledge about the possibilities of ML, users do not understand the ways in which they can apply the technology. Therefore providing a clear objective, instead of teaching specific concepts, can increase their level of interest. Nonetheless, they can feel more connected to the application if they are able to apply personally-relevant information (e.g. their physiological data). The learners can be given a guide and a goal, which they can follow to create a model that solves the proposed problem.

3   System Design

MTeacher is a web-based application, created using modern programming languages like TypeScript, under the Angular framework. The system can be deployed and hosted statically, which makes it easier to distribute. The basic components of MTeacher are as follows: gamification, physiological computing, and machine learning. The gamification aspects are used to create a sense of completion, progression, and therefore motivate students during the learning experience. Physiological computing is a novel technology, applied in MTeacher to develop an interest in participants to further explore the topic. Moreover, the signals can help students feel that their involvement in the system is meaningful to them due to the nature of physiological data. Machine Learning is the core component in the system, with a focus on visualizations and real-time interactivity to help provide a better understanding of concepts and processes.

The application uses a storytelling approach that provides students with a problem to solve during the experience. They are role-playing as scientists trying to teach their robot how to detect when a person is moving their hand or foot via classification of the physiological signals. Therefore, they have had a clear objective since the beginning: creating a classifier to identify right hand or left foot movement using motor imagery data. Students are introduced to the story through an introductory animated video that explains the situation. Once inside the application, users can select their preferred scientist avatar and begin at Level One. At the start, all players are Level 0 with no XP points earned (see Fig. 1).

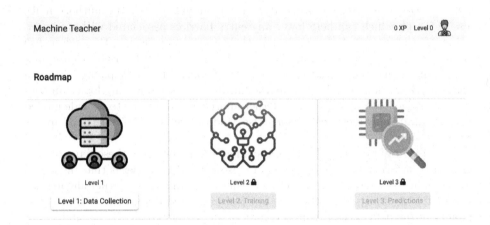

Fig. 1. The main menu of MTeacher. Players have to start at Level One to unlock the other steps in the ML pipeline. They begin with 0 XP points and at Level 0, with their selected avatar on the top right.

3.1 System Components

Machine Learning. The application focuses on making the basic concepts of ML easier to visualize and understand for novice users. Players have a roadmap representing each step in the pipeline: data collection, model training, and model evaluation. The system implements pre-recorded data from the BCI Competition IV [14], which contains motor imagery data. This data is loaded and manipulated according to each of the levels, therefore players are handling the data. Our back-end integrates BCI.js [11], a library developed for web-based signal processing. There are also ML methods to train and predict throughout the entire system.

Physiological Computing. The application leverages the fundamental requirements in EEG signal processing and classification to help learn ML topics. The physiological signals use the band power format, a standard visualization approach for EEG data. This uses different waves and represents them into their corresponding bands (alpha, beta, delta, theta, and gamma) [6]. Signals are explained in a tutorial video for those with no previous knowledge of the topic. It is not expected that users will interpret the data since the goal is for them to leverage the ML approach for this purpose.

Gamification Elements. MTeacher has multiple types of elements used to resemble a gaming application. First, the storyline helps provide context to the situation. Players are told that they are scientists trying to help a robot learn to classify left foot or right-hand movements from humans. This establishes a goal and a clear purpose for the Machine Learning model they are building. The system has levels, which are indicators of progress and structure. This helps provide a sense of advancement while providing a clear path for players to follow. Moreover, there are points and XP, which motivate players to get good results in each of the levels. This can also drive competitive players to replay certain mini-games to improve their scores.

3.2   Level One: Data Collection

Level One is Data Collection, a mini-game that visualizes the process of collecting the signals and shows the users how to split the collected data into training and testing buckets. See Fig. 2 for the level design. Players can put a Brain-Computer Interface (BCI) on the icon and see a graph representing the signals starting streaming into the application. Once they finish with the visualization, they start splitting pieces of EEG data into Training or Testing. Players are told the rule of thumb is 70% training and 30% testing, and the reason behind this process is to have a set of data for testing and avoid incorrect accuracy results.

The mini-game shows ten pieces of data on the screen as graphs. These graphs are processed to use power bands instead of raw signals, this is to make the visuals meaningful and easier to read by humans. The goal is to assign each piece of data to one of the available buckets (training or testing) by clicking on the buttons. There are real-time counters that represent each bucket, and change once the player selects any of the buttons below the graphs. To create a sense of improvement, a timer is running and it is used to calculate the final score based on the speed at which the player finished the section. Every level has written instructions apart from the introductory tutorial, in case they forget certain details or need hints.

3.3   Level Two: Model Training

Level Two allows players to explore the basic concept of training a Machine Learning model. They can visualize different pieces of data and the label that they should have (right hand or left foot movement). See Fig. 3 for a glimpse at the design of this level. The section is based on the classic Memory game,

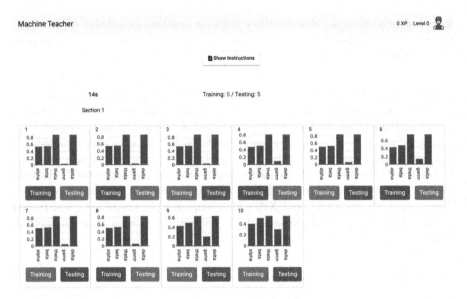

Fig. 2. Level One of MTeacher teaches the fundamentals of data collection and splitting. Players can interact with a time-based mini-game in which they will split training and testing data into their respective buckets.

where players would have to remember the value of each piece of data and then label it manually. The level resembles the process behind training a model, which requires a set of markers to identify which class it represents. After the player labels all of the pieces of data, they can drag and drop them into the corresponding buckets (hand or foot movement). The activity helps understand the back-end process of labeling the data.

After the player finishes all the sections, they can click on the Training button, which tells the robot to work on what was labeled. Then, they are ready to continue to Level Three. The XP for Level Two is calculated based on the player's memory game performance. Incorrect answers deduct points, therefore they are encouraged to get all correct answers. This might motivate those learners that like challenges, and could encourage the repetition of the level to improve their final score. This level combines multiple approaches to engage the learner. Moreover, the section abstracts the step-by-step process of training a model to an explainable mini-game that simulates the same procedures. Students can interact with the data and visualize how training algorithms behave behind the scenes.

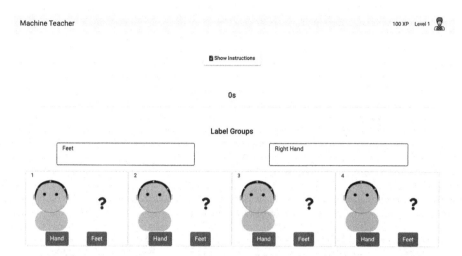

Fig. 3. Level Two focuses on displaying a Memory game that requires the player to remember the label for each piece of data and then assign them to the corresponding bucket. The process is an interactive depiction of what machines achieve while model training is in progress.

3.4   Level Three: Model Evaluation (Predictions)

Level Three is the final step for the player, where they can evaluate the model they worked on during the previous two levels. The user has a Predicter box, representing a place where they can include pieces of data and the robot can provide a prediction (See Fig. 4). The robot is shown on the top left of the screen, along with an accuracy formula and the accuracy percentage based on the current predictions. The goal for the learner is to drag and drop each piece of data and see how the robot responds. Each time they interact with the Predicter box, they will see an update to the accuracy percentage on the top right. Users can associate the formula to the current value based on the pieces of data they add to the box, resulting in an easy way to visualize how the model predicts data points.

Once they finish adding all ten pieces of data, they will be able to continue. A pop quiz asks them to choose the correct formula for accuracy, a situation that might come as a surprise to the learner. However, they could easily associate the formula to their actions in the previous step. This process dictates how many points they receive for Level Three. The level aims to help the learner understand that ML models predict certain outcomes. The player can recognize the objective of creating these models, which is to predict classifications based on statistical analysis. Moreover, the level provides a change of pace for them to independently analyze what is happening. They do not have any pressure to finish the level and it is for them to freely explore the evaluation of the final model.

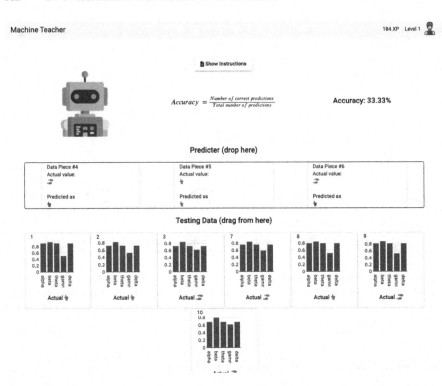

Fig. 4. Level three simulates the process of evaluating the machine Learning model that players created. The robot predicts a piece of data from the testing bucket, and users can see the model performance (accuracy) on the top of the page along with the formula used to calculate that score.

4   Limitations

4.1   Data Collection Visualizations

The data collection level (Level One) was the hardest to design, with multiple variables and steps involved. Due to the limitation of pre-recorded data, the actual collection of physiological signals had to be simulated understandably. Therefore, an interactive avatar was used to model the BCI placement and data streams via graphs. However, a real-time interaction would probably provide a better understanding of the entire data collection process. The players could become a part of the process and their level of interest might increase. The level could be designed for a more friendly interaction to split the data. Instead of having buttons to tag each piece of data, we recognize that having a more visual activity might help. An example could be a quick-paced mini-game that requires players to drag and drop the pieces of data to buckets placed on the sides of the screen. During the initial study results, participants are mentioning their difficulties in understanding what to do at the level and their lack of involvement in the process of data acquisition.

4.2   Limited Gamified Elements

Even though the system already contains multiple gaming elements, there are possibilities to improve based on the integration. In the case of XP, there is no way to use it in the current version. A good use case would be to have an in-game store that users can access and spend their XP to buy components that would help in certain levels. This does not only give XP a purpose, but it would require a redesign of the levels to can allow replayability. Players can buy algorithms to test, data types to use, and more. The concept of repeating the game is directly related to the iterative nature of Machine Learning systems. These models are mathematical representations of the data, which predict different possibilities. Participants can start again to improve their accuracy scores is another goal that provides a basic fundamental of ML applications.

4.3   Real-Time Physiological Data

As mentioned earlier, our system was originally intended to use real-time physiological signals for players to manipulate their data. However, due to limitations regarding in-person studies during the COVID-19 Pandemic, this version of the application implemented pre-recorded physiological data. The current iteration is a good start for physio-based ML educational platforms, though we hypothesize that real-time data could yield better learning outcomes. Participants that can interact with their data might perceive the experience as more meaningful, therefore increasing their interest levels. Moreover, players could take part in the process of collecting the data. This is closely related to their learning gains since with pre-recorded data they are not exposed to the process.

5   Conclusion

This article presents the details of a system design aimed at implementing physiological data and gamified elements to teach Machine Learning concepts. The system involves a storyline that provides context for students, the goal is to create a sense of purpose for the experience. Levels and XP are implemented for motivation and completion. Players can go back and improve their scores on each level. Applying gamification elements contributed to the simplified visualizations of each ML process. Moreover, players could interact with each element on the screen, which allowed them to directly manipulate the data. Based on the initial results of a study, participants overwhelmingly preferred the gamified aspects of MTeacher.

Furthermore, the system included a non-traditional type of data for ML-based applications: physiological signals. In this specific iteration, MTeacher used EEG motor imagery data as the main set used to classify right hand or left foot movements. The goal was for players to feel more connected with the integrated data type, providing a sense of meaningfulness to the learning activity. Initial study results show that physiological data is more appealing to participants, however, they would prefer a real-time version that allowed them to collect the data. Compared to traditional data (images), pre-recorded physiological signals were considered equally as personally relevant.

Our future work aims to expand on MTeacher with more gaming elements that can provide more motivation and replayability. A fundamental concept in ML is iterative development, and it is important to measure how many students consider starting over to improve their results. Moreover, participants could understand which step in the pipeline might be best to tune for better accuracy. These evaluations, along with the integration of real-time physiological data acquisition can help improve self-efficacy. MTeacher allows novice programmers and non-CS majors to explore machine learning concepts through an interactive experience that imparts more personally-relevant data by leveraging novel technologies.

References

1. Chancellor, S., Baumer, E.P., De Choudhury, M.: Who is the "human" in human-centered machine learning: the case of predicting mental health from social media. In: Proceedings of the ACM on Human-Computer Interaction (CSCW), vol. 3, pp. 1–32 (2019)
2. Crawford, C.S., Gilbert, J.E.: Neuroblock: A block-based programming approach to neurofeedback application development. In: 2017 IEEE Symposium on Visual Languages and Human-Centric Computing (VL/HCC), pp. 303–307. IEEE (2017)
3. Gresse, C., Jean, V.W., Pacheco, F.S., Bertonceli, M.F.: Visual tools for teaching machine learning in K-12: a ten-year systematic mapping. No. 0123456789. Springer, US (2021). https://doi.org/10.1007/s10639-021-10570-8. https://doi.org/10.1007/s10639-021-10570-8
4. Hernandez-Cuevas, B., Egbert, W., Denham, A., Mehul, A., Crawford, C.S.: Changing minds: exploring brain-computer interface experiences with high school students. In: Extended Abstracts of the 2020 CHI Conference on Human Factors in Computing Systems, pp. 1–10 (2020)
5. Long, D., Magerko, B.: What is AI Literacy? competencies and design considerations, pp. 1–16. Association for Computing Machinery, New York (2020). https://doi.org/10.1145/3313831.3376727
6. Lotte, F.: A tutorial on eeg signal-processing techniques for mental-state recognition in brain-computer interfaces In: Guide to brain-computer music interfacing. pp. 133–161 (2014)
7. Lytle, N., et al.: Use, modify, create: Comparing computational thinking lesson progressions for stem classes. In: Proceedings of the 2019 ACM Conference on Innovation and Technology in Computer Science Education, pp. 395–401 (2019)
8. Ma, L., Sun, B.: Machine learning and AI in marketing-connecting computing power to human insights. Int. J. Res. Mark. **37**(3), 481–504 (2020)
9. Michaeli, T., et al.: Looking Beyond Supervised Classification and Image Recognition-Unsupervised Learning with Snap! (May 2020)
10. Portugal, I., Alencar, P., Cowan, D.: The use of machine learning algorithms in recommender systems: A systematic review. Expert Syst. Appl. Expert Syst. Appl.= Expert Syst. Appl. **97**, 205–227 (2018)

11. Stegman, P.: Bci.js. Software (February 2020), (Retrieved Feb. 11, 2022). https://bci.js.org/
12. Sulmont, E., Patitsas, E., Cooperstock, J.R.: Can You Teach Me To Machine Learn? In: Proceedings of the 50th ACM Technical Symposium on Computer Science Education - SIGCSE 2019 (2019). https://doi.org/10.1145/3287324.3287392
13. Szafir, D., Mutlu, B.: Pay attention! designing adaptive agents that monitor and improve user engagement. In: Proceedings of the SIGCHI conference on human factors in computing systems, pp. 11–20 (2012)
14. Tangermann, M., et al.: Review of the BCI competition IV. Front. Neurosci. **6**, 55 (2012)
15. Vangipuram, S.k., Appusamy, R.: A survey on similarity measures and machine learning algorithms for classification and prediction. In: International Conference on Data Science, E-learning and Information Systems 2021, pp. 198–204 (2021)
16. Wan, X., Zhou, X., Ye, Z., Mortensen, C.K., Bai, Z.: SmileyCluster: supporting accessible machine learning in K-12 scientific discovery. In: Proceedings of the Interaction Design and Children Conference, IDC, pp. 23–35. (2020). https://doi.org/10.1145/3392063.3394440
17. Wang, Z.J., et al.: CNN 101: interactive visual learning for convolutional neural networks, pp. 1–7 (2020). https://doi.org/10.1145/3334480.3382899
18. Yi, S., Liu, X.: Machine learning based customer sentiment analysis for recommending shoppers, shops based on customers' review. Complex Intell. Syst. **6**(3), 621–634 (2020)
19. Yuksel, B.F., et al.: Human-in-the-loop machine learning to increase video accessibility for visually impaired and blind users In: Proceedings of the 2020 ACM Designing Interactive Systems Conference, pp. 47–60 (2020)
20. Zhou, X., Van Brummelen, J., Lin, P.: Designing AI learning experiences for K-12: emerging works, future opportunities and a design framework (September 2020). http://arxiv.org/abs/2009.10228
21. Zimmermann-Niefield, A., Polson, S., Moreno, C., Shapiro, R.B.: Youth making machine learning models for gesture-controlled interactive media. In: Proceedings of the Interaction Design and Children Conference, IDC, pp. 63–74 (2020). https://doi.org/10.1145/3392063.3394438

Simulation of ECG for Cardiac Diseases Using Generative Adversarial Networks

Kohki Nakane[✉], Tatsuki Kawai, Rintaro Sugie, and Hiroki Takada

University of Fukui, 3-9-1 Bunkyo, Fukui-shi, Fukui, Japan
nkd21007@g.u-fukui.ac.jp, takada@u-fukui.ac.jp

Abstract. Every year, the fundamental technology related to deep learning evolves. Recently, remarkable progress has been made not only in the fields of classification and regression, but also in the field of generation. To date, various models have been proposed for generative models using deep learning, including generative adversarial networks (GAN) and variational auto-encoder (VAE). In this study, we attempted to simulate an electrocardiogram (ECG) using GAN. In addition, ECG may have various states simultaneously, such as AV block and WPW syndrome. Therefore, we propose a method for generating ECGs that considers the fact that multiple states exist simultaneously. The generated ECG validated the basic elements that compose an ECG, such as R and T waves. We demonstrated that AI system can be applied to numerical simulations of bio-signals such as time sequences measured by 3D motion capture, ECGs, and electrogastrograms (EGGs). Furthermore, we conducted experiments to study the effects of stereoscopic video clips on the elderly.

Keywords: Generative Adversarial Networks (GAN) · Electrocardiogram (ECG) · Simulation

1 Introduction

Today, it is not necessary to have technical knowledge for the investment because the automatic algorithms to sell/buy the investment destination have been developed with artificial intelligence (AI). However, because these mechanical trading systems were developed using past time series data from investment outlets or time sequences generated by stochastic processes to verify the systems, they may not be able to sustain future variations. Therefore, we considered applying GAN, which has gained attention in the field of image generation, to a time series of the exchange rate. After learning the properties of variations in the exchange rate whose factors are not elucidated in detail by GAN, the pseudo exchange rates were generated to be used as data for verification of the mechanical trading system.

© The Author(s), under exclusive license to Springer Nature Switzerland AG 2022
M. Antona and C. Stephanidis (Eds.): HCII 2022, LNCS 13308, pp. 446–458, 2022.
https://doi.org/10.1007/978-3-031-05028-2_30

In a previous study, to measure the similarity (stationarity, fractality, and degree of determinism) of variations in the exchange rates to the pseudo-exchange rates generated by GANs, we compared Wiener processes with the GANs [1]. In terms of stationarity, the similarity of sequences in the pseudo exchange rates was higher than those generated by the Wiener processes, and high scores in similarity resulted from both sequences in terms of degree of determinism.

February 2, 2018 marked the day of the largest Dow Jones industrial average decline [2]. The exact reasons for this decline are unknown, but one possibility is the use of artificial intelligence (AI), or automated trading algorithms, to continuously sell shares (mechanical trading) [3]. In recent years, mechanical trading has not been limited to major hedge funds. For example, many financial institutions (such as securities firms) provide mechanical investment services to general consumers. Mechanical investment offers the advantage of relieving the consumer of the burden of deciding what and when to buy. However, there is the risk that mechanical investment may not be able to predict future fluctuations. In general, automated trading algorithms are tested against past fluctuations to evaluate their effectiveness; however, there is a possibility of overfitting if the system solely relies on past fluctuations. Overfitting is a common problem with machine learning. Thus, to address this problem, a test may be performed on a large number of time series generated by using a stochastic process. Many researchers have conducted studies in which stock prices are considered stochastic processes [4, 5]. However, a time series generated by a stochastic process does not reflect actual stock prices and exchange rate fluctuations, making it unreliable. Therefore, in this study, we used stochastic process-generated time series data.

This study also includes the use of neural networks to classify images [6]. In 2014, the concept of GAN was proposed by Goodfellow et al. [7]. Additionally, the amount of research that entails using neural networks to generate images, has been increasing. In this study, G is defined as a network that generates simulative sequences (SSs) or fake data from input noise, and network D distinguishes whether the data generated by the generator G is the desired real data (i.e., true data). The generator G learns as the discriminator D mistakes the SS with the true data, and D is trained to correctly distinguish between the true and SS. Repeated training of networks G and D (Fig. 1) can result in the generation of a large number of SSs if the output of G can generate data that are very similar to the true data. Therefore, we identified that we could improve the reliability of automated trading algorithms by examining various fluctuation patterns using a GAN-generated pseudo time series.

The aim of this study is to design an artificially intelligent GAN by generating one-dimensional time series data that are similar to the true exchange rate data. We compared the pseudo exchange rates, generated by a model based on stationarity [8], fractality, and the degree of determinism [9], to the actual exchange rate and time series data generated by a stochastic process.

In this study, we applied this AI system to numerical simulations of bio-signals such as stabilograms and electrocardiograms (ECGs).

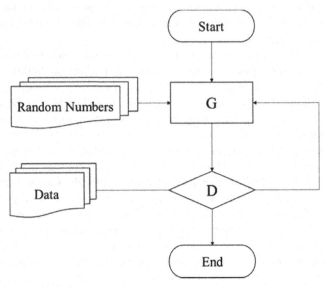

Fig. 1. GAN model.

2 Model Design

GAN learning is considered to be difficult to stabilize. We designed and trained several models to generate pseudo exchange rates, but only a few models exhibited stable learning.

Alec Radford et al. provided some suggestions regarding how to stabilize GAN learning [10]. In this study, we used the hyperbolic tangent function (i.e., tanh) as the activation function in the output layer of the generator. Except for the output layer/fully connected layer, LeakyReLU [11] was used to design the discriminators, each of which acts as an activation function. To design a model, various parameters need to be set. Moreover, because the accuracy of the generated pseudo exchange rate is dependent on the parameters, it is necessary to optimize various parameter settings. Neural network model optimization often entails using the accuracy rate as an objective variable for classification and prediction [12]. However, the purpose of this study was to identify the characteristics of exchange rate fluctuation, and generate a pseudo time series that simulates the fluctuations. Therefore, GAN learning cannot be evaluated based on the degree of similarity between the actual exchange rate and the generated pseudo exchange rate. In addition, it is difficult to describe the characteristics of exchange rates because the factors and systems of exchange rates are not clearly understood. Therefore, an objective variable must be defined. In this study, we discovered two metrics that would facilitate network training. These metrics are as follows: 1) the total output errors for the generator and discriminator training data must be small, and 2) lower output error values for the generator and discriminator training data indicates stable learning. Thus, we developed and optimized the optimization function (1), which takes into account these two metrics:

$$OptimisationFunction(G_{Loss}, D_{Loss}) = ln\frac{G_{Loss} + D_{Loss}}{D_{Loss}/G_{Loss}} \tag{1}$$

where G_{Loss} is the training error for the generator network, and D_{Loss} is the training error for the discriminator network.

In this study, the number of convolutional layers (i.e., four), number of filters per layer (16, 32, 64, 128), and filter sizes (1–10) were set to minimize the value of the optimization function for the generator model (Fig. 2). The value was evaluated after the parameters were optimized. It should be noted that, because of the high computational cost, the discriminator model was not optimized (Fig. 3).

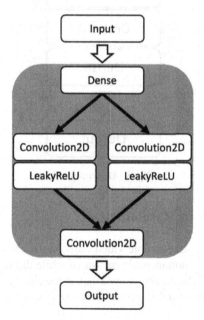

Fig. 2. Generator

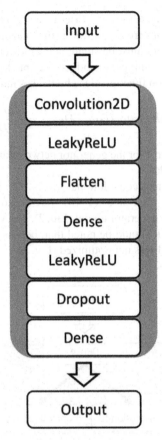

Fig. 3. Discriminator

3 Empirical Study in Stabilometry

We studied the effects of stereoscopic video clips on the elderly. In addition to radial motion, body sway was simultaneously measured while the young and elderly viewed stereoscopic video clips. The results showed that, in the elderly, the equilibrium function is affected by tracking the visual target in stereoscopic video clips.

3.1 Experiment 1

As a basic study, the stabilometry was conducted for 238 elderly people that stood with Romberg posture on a gravicorder GS3000 (Anima Corp. Ltd., Tokyo). Stabilograms were recorded at 20 Hz sampling with their eyes open/closed for 60 s each. This experiment was approved by the Ethics Committee of the Graduate School of Information Science, Nagoya University.

3.2 Experiment 2

In this experiment, 12 healthy volunteers, including 6 young and 6 elderly, aged 22.5 $\pm$ 1.0 yrs. (mean $\pm$ standard deviation) and 75.0 $\pm$ 8.2 yrs., respectively, participated. The experiment was fully explained to the participants, who could view stereoscopically before they signed the written consent. The experiment was also approved by the Ethics Committee of the Department of Human and Artificial Intelligent Systems in the Graduate School of the Engineering University of Fukui (No. H2019003). Stabilometry and radial movements were simultaneously measured and recorded at 100 Hz and 60 Hz sampling rates, respectively.

Stereoscopic images used for this experiment were recreated based on Sky Crystal (Olympus Memory Works Corp, Tokyo) with permission (Fig. 4). The details of the 3D video clips are as follows:

VC1) A normal 3D video clip with full backgrounds (Fig. 4a).
VC2) A 3D video clip with the static regulation of backgrounds (Fig. 4b).

These clips were played in visual pursuit for 60 s or in peripheral vision for 60 s in a dark room on a liquid crystal display (LCD), 55UF8500-JB (LG Electronics, Seoul). In the VC1, the peripheral visual field was forced to be narrowed. An order effect was herein excluded in the procedure of this experiment, which included a test with the participant's eyes closed after each simultaneous measurement.

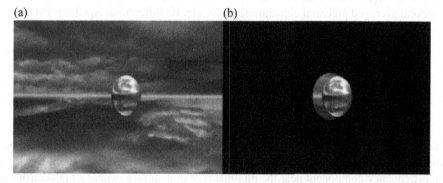

Fig. 4. Visual stimulus; (a) a normal image, (b) an image with static regulation of backgrounds

In this experiment, the stabilometry was conducted using a Wii balance board (Nintendo, Kyoto). Typical examples of stabilograms are shown in Fig. 5a.

Furthermore, we used an eye mark recorder, EMR-9 (Nac Image Technology, Tokyo), to measure the radial movement. The position of the viewpoint for each sampling time is composed of x-y coordinates [pix]. Total locus length, area of radial sway, and total locus length per unit area, as well as the body sway, were evaluated. In addition, we performed statistical tests for each analytical index. The significance level was set at 0.05.

4   Results and Consideration

The elderly volunteered to participate in this study. Their stabilograms were recorded while standing in the Romberg posture (Fig. 5a). In previous studies, the mathematical models of body sway have been described by stochastic processes based on the following properties for each component:

(i)   Markov property.
(ii) non-anomalous diffusion.

In stabilograms, variables x (right designated as positive) and y (anterior designated as positive) are regarded to be independent [13]. A linear stochastic differential equation (Brownian motion process) has been proposed as a mathematical model to describe body sway [14–16]. To describe the individual body sway, we suggest that it is necessary to extend the following nonlinear stochastic differential equations:

$$\frac{\partial x}{dt} = -\frac{\partial}{\partial x}U_x(x) + \mu_x w_x(t), \tag{2}$$

$$\frac{\partial y}{dt} = -\frac{\partial}{\partial y}U_y(y) + \mu_y w_y(t), \tag{3}$$

where $w_x(t)$ and $w_y(t)$ express the white noise [17]. The following formulas describe the relationship between the distribution in each direction, $G_x(x)$ and $G_y(y)$, and the temporal averaged potential constituting the stochastic differential equations (SDEs):

$$U_x(x) = -\frac{\mu_x^2}{2}\ln G_x(x) + const., \tag{4}$$

$$U_y(y) = -\frac{\mu_y^2}{2}\ln G_y(y) + const. \tag{5}$$

The variance of stabilograms depends on the temporal averaged potential function (TAPF), with several minimum values when it follows the Markov process (i) without abnormal dispersion (ii). SDEs can represent movements within local stability with a high-frequency component near the minimal potential surface, where a high density at the measurement point is expected. In the numerical analysis of Eqs. (2) and (3), the SDE was rewritten as a difference equation with the term $w_x(t)$ or $w_y(t)$ substituted by pseudorandom values generated by white Gaussian noise [17] or 1/f noise [18].

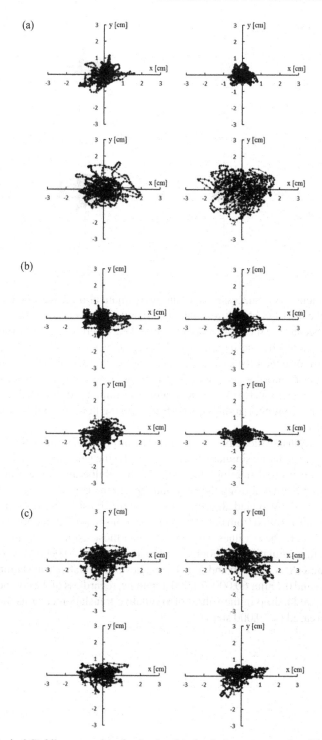

Fig. 5. (a) Typical Stabilograms; data for 1 min, (b) simulation patterns after 10,000 steps, (c) simulation patterns after 20,000 steps, (d) simulation patterns after 30,000 steps.

(d)

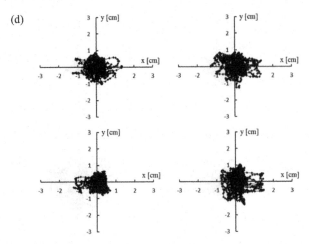

Fig. 5. continued

In experiment 1, we successfully found mathematical models of body sway in the elderly with the use of GANs. It was validated that training was not stable in the created GAN-model because of the small amount of real data. Therefore, first, two-dimensional noise was generated by the independent Wiener processes; 1,000,000 kinds of time sequences were provided for each component by the Wiener processes. Then, by substituting the noise into the generator G, fine-training was conducted for the optimal parameter of the neural network as a generator/discriminator of the GANs (Table 1 and 2). After the fine-training, training was performed using the 256 stabilograms measured in experiment 1–2.

Subsequently, using the stabilograms stated in the previous section, machine learning was conducted to generate simulative stabilograms by the generator G and to distinguish fake data from measured stabilograms. Finally, all stabilograms were evaluated by the translation error estimated using the Wayland algorithm [19].

According to the Wayland algorithm, values of the translation error were distributed around 0.7, which resulted from both components of the measured stabilograms (Fig. 5a). As shown in Fig. 6, these values were greater than those estimated from x-component sequences in the simulative stabilograms after iterations (<20,000 steps) on the deep-learning of the GANs (Fig. 5b and 5c). The values of simulative translation error were distributed around 0.7 after 60,000–70,000 iterations, regardless of the component. However, we observed a drop in the values of simulative translation error as the number of iterations increased (>70,000 steps).

Table 1. Optimal parameter of the neural network as a generator of the GANs

Layers	Layer Name	Units	Kernel Size	Filters	Output Shape	Activation
0	Input	-	-	-	-	-
1	Dense	150	-	-	150	LeakyReLU
2-1	Dense	150	-	-	150	LeakyReLU
3-1	BatchNormalization	-	-	-	150	-
4-1	Convolution	-	1×3	128	1×300	LeakyReLU
5-1	BatchNormalization	-	-	-	1×300	-
6-1	Convolution	-	1×3	128	1×300	LeakyReLU
7-1	BatchNormalization	-	-	-	1×300	-
8-1	Convolution	-	1×3	64	1×600	LeakyReLU
9-1	BatchNormalization	-	-	-	1×600	-
10-1	Convolution	-	1×3	64	1×600	LeakyReLU
11-1	BatchNormalization	-	-	-	1×600	-
12-1	Convolution	-	1×3	32	1×1200	LeakyReLU
13-1	BatchNormalization	-	-	-	1×1200	-
14-1	Convolution	-	1×3	32	1×1200	LeakyReLU
15-1	BatchNormalization	-	-	-	1×1200	-
16-1	Convolution	-	1×1	1	1×1200	Tanh
2-2	Dense	150	-	-	1×150	LeakyReLU
3-2	BatchNormalization	-	-	-	1×150	-
4-2	Convolution	-	1×3	128	1×300	LeakyReLU
5-2	BatchNormalization	-	-	-	1×300	-
6-2	Convolution	-	1×3	128	1×300	LeakyReLU
7-2	BatchNormalization	-	-	-	1×300	-
8-2	Convolution	-	1×3	64	1×600	LeakyReLU
9-2	BatchNormalization	-	-	-	1×600	-
10-2	Convolution	-	1×3	64	1×600	LeakyReLU
11-2	BatchNormalization	-	-	-	1×600	-
12-2	Convolution	-	1×3	32	1×1200	LeakyReLU
13-2	BatchNormalization	-	-	-	1×1200	-
14-2	Convolution	-	1×3	32	1×1200	LeakyReLU
15-2	BatchNormalization	-	-	-	1×1200	-
16-2	Convolution	-	1×1	1	1×1200	Tanh
17	Concatenate	-	-	-	2×1200	-

In experiment 2, we recorded the radial motion of participants while viewing the stereoscopic video clip. The radial motion of the elderly was quantitatively different from that of the young. We applied this AI system to numerical simulations of stabilograms in this study. In the next step, this AI system can be applied to numerical simulations of figure patterns in radial motion to evaluate the anomalous radial motion due to the deterioration of visual function with aging. In addition, the AI system can be applied to numerical simulations of bio-signals such as time sequences measured by 3D motion

Table 2. Optimal parameter of the neural network as a discriminator of the GANs

Layers	Layer Name	Units	Kernel Size	Filters	Output Shape	Activation
0	Input	-	-	-	-	-
1	Convolution	-	1×3	32	2×600	LeakyReLU
2	Convolution	-	1×3	64	2×300	LeakyReLU
3	Convolution	-	1×3	128	2×150	LeakyReLU
4	Convolution	-	1×3	256	2×75	LeakyReLU
5	Convolution	-	1×3	512	2×38	LeakyReLU
6	Convolution	-	1×3	32	1×38	LeakyReLU
7	Flatten	-	-	-	1216	-
8	Dense	32	-	-	32	LeakyReLU
9	Dense	1	-	-	1	Sigmoid

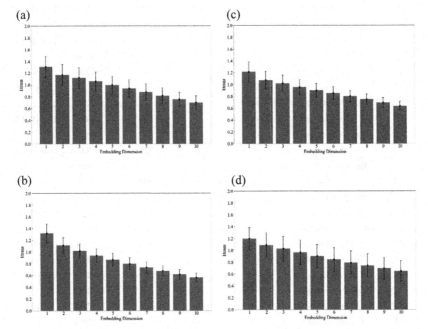

Fig. 6. Translation error estimated from the following x-component in each embedding space; measured stabilograms for 1 min (a), simulation patterns after 20,000 step (b), simulation patterns after 70,000 step (c), simulation patterns after 100,000 steps (d).

capture, ECGs, and electrogastrograms (EGGs). This study shows an example of the application.

5   Application to ECG Simulation

In this study, we applied GAN, which is mainly used for image generation problems, to time series generation to simulate ECGs. Because the ECG shows characteristic waveforms reflecting various cardiac diseases, we developed a model that can control the ECG simulation under the conditions of those diseases. To create this generative model, we trained on "PTB-XL, a large publicly available electrocardiography dataset" by Patrick Wagner et al. [19]. There are a total of 71 ECG statements annotated in this data set. All 71 different ECG statements, which include diagnostic, form, and rhythm statements, conform to the SCP-ECG standard. In addition to these statements, we also added gender as a condition for control. Therefore, a total of 72 conditions were controlled and simulated in this study. It is important to note that the 72 conditions are not necessarily independent. Therefore, in this study, we treated the 72 conditions as vectors and trained the condition vectors to match the cosine similarity between the condition vectors input to the generator and the condition vectors determined by the discriminator.

Figure 7 shows the results of the ECG simulated by the generative model developed in this study. The top row shows the ECGs of a man and the bottom row shows the ECGs of a woman. In order from the left column, normal, sinus arrhythmia, and atrial fibrillation are shown. Compared to a normal ECG, an arrhythmia shows an irregular RRI. In addition, atrial fibrillation shows an increased dispersion between S and P waves. In the future, we would like to evaluate the similarity of the generated ECGs and the similarity in each condition for further improvements.

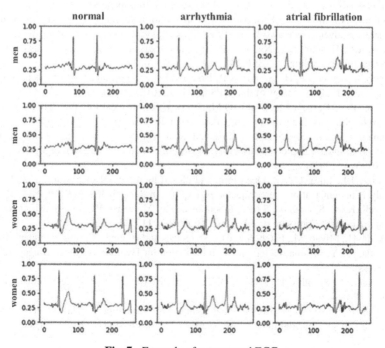

Fig. 7. Example of a generated ECG

Acknowledgments. This work was supported in part by the TAKEUCHI Scholarship Foundation, Japan Society for the Promotion of Science, Grant-in-Aid for Research Activity Start-up Number 15H06711, Grant-in-Aid for Young Scientists (B) Number 16K16105, and Grant-in-Aid for Scientific Research (C) Number 17K00715.

References

1. Wang, L., Wittenstein, J.: Dow Jones industrial average, worst decline in history - drops nearly $1600, Bloomberg (2018). https://www.bloomberg.co.jp/news/articles/2018-02-06/P3PHW0 6TTDS601
2. Ponczek, S., Popina, E., Wang, L.: Dow average, who dropped-machine criminal theory emerging, Bloomberg (2018). https://www.bloomberg.co.jp/news/articles/2018-02-06/P3P JGE6JIJVN01
3. Black, F., Scholes, M.: Pricing of options and corporate liabilities. J. Polit. Econ. **81**(3), 637–654 (1973)
4. Tasaki, T.: Motion equation of for stock prices. Bussei Kenkyu **81**(4), 518–519 (2004). (in Japanese)
5. Wakabayashi, K., Namatame, T.: Examination of applicability of deep learning to consumers' purchasing behavior. J. Jpn. Soc. Data Sci. Soc. **1**(1), 48–57 (2017). (in Japanese)
6. Goodfellow, I.J., et al.: Generative adversarial Nets, pp. 1–9 (2014)
7. Matsuba, I.: Statistics of Long-Term Memory Processes: Self-Similar Time Series Theory and Method, pp. 144–146. Kyoritsu Shuppan, Tokyo (2007). (in Japanese)
8. Aihara, K., Ikeguchi, T., Yamada, T., Komuro, M.: Basics and Applications of Chaos Time Series Analysis, p. 13. Sangyo Tosho, Tokyo (2000). (in Japanese)
9. Radford, A., Metz, L.: Unsupervised representation learning with deep convolutional generative adversarial networks. In: Proceedings of the ICLR, pp. 1–16 (2016)
10. Maas, A.L., Hannun, A.Y., Ng, A.Y.: Rectifier nonlinearities improve neural network acoustic models. In: Proceedings of the ICML, vol. 30, no. 1, p. 3 (2013)
11. Snoek, J., Larochelle, H., Adams, R.P.: Practical Bayesian optimization of machine learning algorithms. In: Proceedings of the NIPS, pp. 1–9 (2012)
12. Goldie, P.A., Bach, T.M., Evans, O.M.: Force platform measures for evaluating postural control: reliability and validity. Arch. Phys. Med. Rehabil. **70**, 510–517 (1986)
13. Emmerrik, R.E.A., Sprague, R.L.V., Newell, K.M.: Assessment of sway dynamics in tardive dyskinesia and developmental disability, sway profile orientation and stereotypy. Mov. Disord. **8**, 305–314 (1993)
14. Collins, J.J., Luca, C.J.D.: Open loop and closed-loop control of posture: a random-walk analysis of center of pressure trajectories. Exp. Brain Res. **95**, 308–318 (1993)
15. Newell, K.M., Slobounov, S.M., Slobounova, E.S., Molenaar, P.C.: Stochastic processes in postural center of pressure profiles. Exp. Brain Res. **113**, 158–164 (1997)
16. Takada, H., Miyao, M., Fateh, S. (eds.): Stereopsis and Hygiene. Springer, Singapore (2019)
17. Takada, H., Yokoyama, K. (eds.): Bio-information for Hygiene. Springer, Singapore (2021, in Press)
18. Wayland, R., Bromley, D., Pickett, D., Passamante, A.: Recognizing determinism in a time series. Phys. Rev. Lett. **70**, 580–582 (1993)
19. Wagner, P., Strodthoff, N., Bousseljot, R., Samek, W., Schaeffter, T.: PTB-XL, a large publicly available electrocardiography dataset (version 1.0.0). PhysioNet (2020). https://doi.org/10.13026/qgmg-0d46

EMS-Supported Throwing: Preliminary Investigation on EMS-Supported Training of Movement Form

Ryogo Niwa[✉], Kazuya Izumi, Shieru Suzuki, and Yoichi Ochiai

Research and Development Center for Digital Nature, University of Tsukuba,
Tsukuba, Japan
`niwa.ryogo@digitalnature.slis.tsukuba.ac.jp`

Abstract. We propose a learning support system with extremely low latency and low cognitive load to correct the user's motion. In previous studies, visual and haptic feedback has been mainly used to support motion learning, but there is a delay between the presentation of the stimulus and the modification of the action. However, this delay is due to reaction time and cognitive load and is difficult to shorten. This study proposed a system for solving this problem by combining Electrical Muscle Stimulation (EMS) and prediction of the user's motion. In order to improve the control ability of the underhand throwing, we used the system to tell the subject the release point during the underhand throwing motion and verified the learning effect. This experiment revealed that EMS tended to be effective in teaching the ball's release point, although it did not improve the control ability of the underhand throwing motion. In addition, although the effectiveness of EMS for motion learning was not yet fully evaluated, this study showed the possibility of applying EMS to support learning of motion.

Keywords: Motor skills · EMS · Electric stimulation · Skill learning

1 Introduction

It is difficult and time-consuming to learn movements in sports and other activities [30]. It is common to receive instruction from an instructor because receiving appropriate feedback is vital to understand and improve these movements [21].

The timing of giving feedback to the user may be during operation (real-time) or after the motion, but it has been suggested that real-time feedback is more effective for beginners [11]. Therefore, many systems have been proposed to provide real-time feedback to novices. Among them, many methods using visual feedback [1,7,12] and haptic feedback [6,16,18,18,20,26] have been suggested to be effective for learning.

© The Author(s), under exclusive license to Springer Nature Switzerland AG 2022
M. Antona and C. Stephanidis (Eds.): HCII 2022, LNCS 13308, pp. 459–476, 2022.
https://doi.org/10.1007/978-3-031-05028-2_31

1.1   Background

It is challenging to apply existing systems that provide real-time feedback using visual, auditory, and tactile stimuli to teach movements in sports. This is because even if feedback is provided at the user motion correction timing, the position where the user starts to correct the motion is slightly displaced for a small amount of time until the user responds to the feedback. Motion in sports is often fast, and this causes much larger displacement. For this reason, it is not easy to use the existing methods for sports motion instruction.

We simplified the delay until the user corrects the motion after receiving a stimulus, as shown in Fig. 1, and discussed two factors: reaction time and cognitive load.

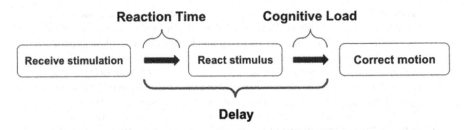

Fig. 1. The process from when the user receives a stimulus to when they correct their motion.

Reaction time is the time from when a stimulation is provided to the user to when an externally observable response to that stimulation is confirmed [29,31] (Reaction Time in Fig. 1). It is known that reaction time is about 200 ms for visual stimuli, 150 ms for auditory stimuli, and 200 ms for tactile stimuli [29,31]. This time is not constant every time, even for the same user but can vary, ranging from several milliseconds to several tens of milliseconds.

In addition to the reaction time, there is a time for the user to interpret the information fed back (Cognitive Load in Fig. 1). On the other hand, when the action to be transmitted by a stimulus is complex, the cognitive load of the user becomes high. Therefore, the existing stimulus methods have a limitation that the actions to be transmitted are limited to simple ones.

Two factors, reaction time and cognitive load, cause a delay between receiving the feedback and correcting the motion (Delay in Fig. 1). For this reason, if we want to provide feedback at the target position and timing, providing the stimulus as early as the delay is necessary. However, since the reaction time and the time for interpreting the stimulus are not constant but vary each time, it is challenging to provide the stimulus earlier than these times.

For these reasons, it is not easy to apply the conventional motion acquisition system with real-time feedback using visual, auditory, and tactile stimuli to motion instruction in sports.

1.2   Research Motivation

EMS (Electrical Muscle Stimulation) can be applied to the teaching of high-speed movements. EMS is an electrical stimulation for semi-forced muscle movement, mainly used in rehabilitation therapy. It has been attracting attention as a method of tactile stimulation in the field of human interface since the late 2000s [15].

EMS forces the user's muscles to move externally. Therefore, when the EMS is used to provide feedback to the user, the process of the user responding to the stimulus, interpreting the stimulus, and converting it into movement, as shown in Fig. 1, does not occur. Therefore, by using EMS, no delay occurs until the user receives the stimulus and starts to correct the motion. Thus, it is possible to communicate the correction to a user moving at high speed with minimal displacement from the feedback position.

In this study, we propose a real-time feedback system for high-speed movements using EMS and motion capture. We propose a real-time feedback system for high-speed movements using EMS and motion capture. Specifically, when a user throws an underhand throw or performs a bare hand swing, EMS stimulates the user's muscles at a pre-designated release point and informs the user of the release point. There have been many attempts to have users perform specific movements using EMS, but few have examined the effects of learning the movements. In this study, we implemented the above-mentioned system and verified its effectiveness in correcting the release point and improving the control ability of the throwing motion by actually using the system. We selected the underhand throwing motion represented by Softball as the motion which proposed system support.

1.3   Contribution

The contributions of this research are as follows:

- Proposal of a real-time feedback motion learning support system for users performing fast motion such as throwing, by combining EMS and motion prediction
- Qualitative and quantitative evaluation and discussion of the applicability of EMS to support learning of motion in sports and other activities.

2   Related Work

In this section, we will discuss the strengths and weaknesses of visual, auditory, and haptic feedback in previous studies and the effectiveness of EMS feedback compared to them in motion learning support.

For learning behaviors, it has been found that a high frequency of feedback can improve the learning effect for beginners [32]. Furthermore, it has also been suggested that real-time feedback is more effective for novices [11]. For this reason, many methods have been proposed to provide users with real-time feedback in various modalities to try to support the learning of movements.

2.1 Visual Feedback

Visual information is helpful for accurately grasping spatial information. For this reason, dancers have long used mirrors to check and train their form, and it has been confirmed that they are helpful for correcting form [4]. Anderson et al. [1] proposed a system that superimposes images of the trainer's skeletal information on a mirror. The learning effect was improved by increasing the amount of information compared to the conventional mirror. Mirrors are the mainstream method of providing real-time feedback to vision, but they have the limitation that they can only be viewed within the neck's range of motion. With the advent of Head Mounted Displays (HMDs), it has become possible to provide instruction with real-time visual feedback not limited to the neck's range of motion. Higuchi et al. [7] proposed a system that allows users to view their appearance from a third party's perspective captured by a drone camera using an HMD. It is said that athletes can imagine their movement from the perspective of an external observer [17], and the system proposed by Higuchi et al. supports the formation of this image and discusses whether it can be used for sports training. Higuchi et al. [7] used this system to support the formation of mental images and discussed the possibility of using it for sports training.

Lin et al. [12] proposed an HMD system that can visualize the trajectory of free throws in real-time for skilled basketball players. In addition, many methods using training in a virtual environment with HMDs have been proposed [3,9]. However, it is still a debate whether training in a virtual environment can improve athletic performance in the real world [19].

2.2 Audio Feedback

Since auditory perception is often not used during the task, its strength is that it can be used with other stimulus modals. For example, Houri et al. [8] attempted to support beginners of calligraphy with audio feedback in order to improve calligraphy strokes. However, the problem is that users need to learn how to map parameters such as the pitch of the sound to physical movements, which places a high cognitive load on them. Houri et al. [8] also pointed out that the problem is that general rules for generating sounds that match physical sensations have not yet been determined. In addition, the method using auditory feedback has only been proposed for applications, and the learning effect has not been sufficiently verified.

2.3 Haptic Feedback

Real-time feedback using haptic stimuli has been proposed more often and reported to be more effective than other stimulus modalities for learning support [6,16,18,26].

Fujii et al. [6] attempted to support the performance of a musical instrument that the user plays for the first time by using a robot arm installed on the desk. This method made it possible to teach temporally continuous movements but had the limitation that the supported movements were limited to those performed at a desk. Finally, Maekawa et al. [16] proposed a system in which a robot arm is carried on the back and showed the possibility of teaching not only desk-based but also temporally continuous movements.

It has been pointed out that these positional control-based methods may be effective for beginners but may not be effective for skilled users. It is thought that this may be because the positional control-based method does not strengthen the motor control loop in the central nervous system between Eigen sensory input and motor output [23]. It has also been pointed out that the equipment is large, expensive, and difficult to disseminate [25].

The vibration feedback method requires smaller equipment and costs less than a robot arm. Many methods have been proposed to support action learning using vibration feedback [2,20,26]. For example, for sports action learning, Ruffaldi et al. [20] tested the effect of vibration feedback on a rowing task. However, few studies have applied vibration feedback to complex motor tasks, so the applicability of vibration feedback to complex motor tasks has not yet been clarified.

As in the case of visual and auditory feedback, if the user cannot receive and correctly interpret the vibration feedback, the system will not be effective as a learning support system. For this reason, McDaniel et al. [18] have investigated the relationship between vibrations, more natural stimuli, and body movements that are easy for users to understand.

2.4 EMS for Human Computer Interaction

EMS is a small, lightweight, and low-cost wearable device compared to large tactile stimulus output devices like robot arms.

Therefore, in the field of the human interface, it is attracting attention as a method of outputting tactile stimuli and is used for tactile feedback [13] in mobile games and tactile presentation in mixed reality [14,15].

In addition, several studies use EMS to make users perform movements. For example, EMS has been used to play the Japanese harp [27] and to play rhythmic instruments such as percussion [5].

The advantage of EMS is that it requires lower cognitive load on the user than visual, auditory, or vibrational stimuli because electrical stimuli semi-forced move the user. Zindulka et al. [28] used EMS to teach bowling throwing form and achieved form modification only ten interventions on the throwing motion. Thus, EMS may be effective in learning physical movements, but the learning effect has rarely been verified [28]. In this study, we investigate the possibility of applying EMS to support physical movement learning.

2.5 Position of This Study

In this study, we investigate the possibility of applying EMS to support physical movement learning. Table 1 shows the position of this study. This study proposes

464   R. Niwa et al.

a motion learning support system that uses EMS to force users to correct their motions, minimizing the reaction time and cognitive load until the users correct their motions.

Table 1. Comparison of feedback modalities for real-time learning support

Feedback modality	Reaction time	Cognitive load	Learning effectiveness
Visual	200 ms	Low	Largely effective
Audio	150 ms	High	Largely unconfirmed
Haptic	200 ms	High	Effective (vibration)
EMS	**Extremely short**	**Extremely low**	**Possibly effective**

As shown in Table 1, many existing methods are effective in learning, but they do not take into account the problem that the user cannot correct the motion in real time due to a short delay. EMS solves these problems and can perform motions with very short delays, but whether it is effective in learning motions has not been fully verified. For this reason, we propose a system using EMS, conduct experiments, and verify the learning effect.

3   System Design

We developed a system to support the learning of high-speed movements using EMS. This study focused on the release point of underhand throwing, represented by Softball. Figure 2 shows an overview and Fig. 3 shows the workflow of this system. This system consists of two modules:

Release Timing Detection Module Tracks the ball and calculates the appropriate release timing for the user. Based on the calculated approximation equation, the module send a signal to EMS Module when the predicted release point is in the pre-defined area.

EMS Module Outputs a pulse to the EMS circuit and sends an electric current to the user's muscles to move them when the microcontroller receives signals from Release Timing Detection Module.

3.1   Release Timing Detection Module

This module tracks the ball and calculates the appropriate release timing for the user. The ball was covered with a retroreflective sticker, and the spatial coordinates of the ball were obtained by motion capture. Based on the obtained coordinates, this module predicts the position of the ball after 80 ms. If the predicted position is in the area of the pre-specified release point, this module sends a signal to the microcontroller of EMS Module.

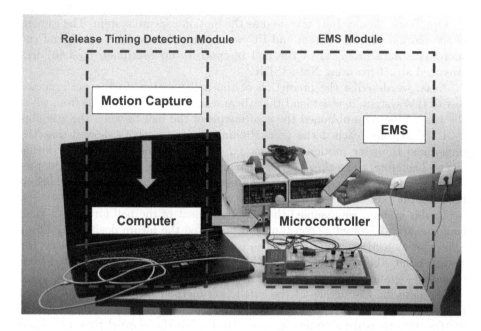

Fig. 2. Proposed system overview

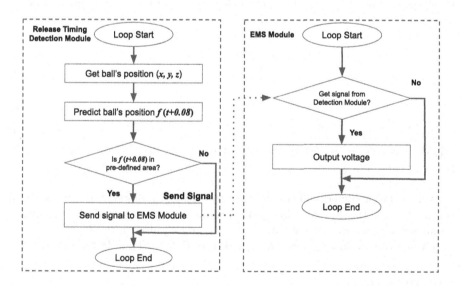

Fig. 3. Flowchart of the proposed system

OptiTrack, Acuity Inc., was used as the motion capture system. The camera of the motion capture system and PC were connected by LAN cable, and the coordinate data (x, y, z) of the ball in space (y-up coordinate system) was streamed at 250 fps using NatnetSDK.[1]

Next, we describe the prediction of the ball position. In the performance test of this system, it was found that there was a delay about 80 ms from when the tracking system obtained the coordinates of the ball to when the stimulus by EMS Module reached the user. Preliminary experiments showed that the underhand throwing motion study moved a maximum of several 10 cm during 80 ms. Therefore, when the electrical stimulus to the user is provided at the pre-specified release point, it is necessary to send a signal to EMS Module before reaching the position.

In this system, we assumed that the movement of the ball for a short time could be approximated as constant and predicted the future position by linear approximation. By sending a signal to EMS Module before the ball reaches the release point, the point where the EMS stimulation reaches is prevented from deviating significantly from the assumption.

We describe the details of the prediction method using linear approximation. Since the proposed system uses motion capture at a measurement speed of 250 fps, the interval per frame is 4 ms, 0.004 s. For the elapsed time t (s) since the start of ball tracking, the relationship between the ball's coordinates and the elapsed time from t to 20 frames before $(t - 0.08$ to $t)$ is obtained by curve fitting using the least-squares method as shown into

$$J = \sum_{i=1}^{20} \{x_i - (at_i + b)\} \tag{1}$$

$$f(t) = at + b \tag{2}$$

From Eq. (1), we calculated a and b such that the value of error J is minimized. This resulted in the approximation equation, Eq. (2), for the relationship between time and x-coordinate, and $f(t + 0.08)$ (m) was calculated to predict the position of the ball about 80 ms later $(t + 0.08$ (s)).

When the predicted ball coordinate was $0.40 \leq f(t + 0.08) \leq 0.45$, the signal was sent to EMS Module using serial communication. EMS Module output a stimulation waveform with a voltage of 3.3 V and a pulse width of 500 μs at 2 Hz only when the module receives the signal from Release Time Detection Module.

3.2   EMS Module

We developed EMS Module for the proposed system because it is necessary to control the stimulus First, it was necessary to apply a large voltage to the human body due to its sizeable electrical resistance. However, if a large voltage is applied to the microcontroller, it will malfunction. To avoid this, we divided the circuit

---

[1] NatnetSDK: https://optitrack.com/software/natnet-sdk.

into two parts: one to control the flow of electricity to the human body, and the other to control the current running to the human body. In addition, the current amount of the current control part and the part where the current flows through the human body are designed to be the same.

Since the human body's electrical resistance varies, the EMS device we developed was designed to deliver a constant current regardless of the human body's electrical resistance.

In this study, it was assumed that it was sufficient to present force in the direction of bending the subject's wrist and that the EMS should be used with a maximum current of about 10 mA, considering the amount of current that would not affect the human body according to Kono et al. [10]

The maximum electrical resistance of the human body was assumed to be about 10 kΩ, which means that an electrical voltage of about 100 V is required.

It is dangerous to directly connect the human body to the stabilized power supply because the stabilized power supply can cause damage to the human body if the stabilized power supply is operated incorrectly during the experiment.

Therefore, in the EMS device that we developed, we used an isolated DCDC converter to achieve electrical isolation from the outside and power supply from the outside. A DCDC converter is a device that converts DC current to DC current and can change the output voltage. In DCDC converters, the input and output currents are electrically isolated to prevent the unintended inflow of electric charge. The upper limits of the output voltage and current are predetermined. We selected the upper limit of the output current of the DCDC converter to be 25 mA for safety, and the upper limit of the current flowing to the human body was designed to be 25 mA.

Kono et al. [10] have shown that this amount of current does not pose any problem to the human body. The stabilizing power supply applied a voltage of 15 V to the boost type DCDC converter, and the output of the boost type DCDC converter was designed to output up to 200 V.

The current control part consists of a microcontroller and a variable resistor (0 to 1 kΩ), and the current flowing through the human body can be obtained from these output voltages and variable resistor values. When the signal is sent from Release Timing Detection Module via serial communication, the microcontroller outputs a pulse wave with an output voltage of 3.3 V. In this way, it is possible to apply EMS stimulation to the human body at computer-controlled timing. M5StickC, from M5Stack Technology Co., Ltd., was used for the current control.

4   Experiment

We recruited nine right-handed participants (3 females and 6 males) between the ages of 22 and 24 (M = 23.0, SD = 0.89). Figure 4 shows an experiment environment. Participants threw a ball downward five times per session toward a target placed on the floor 3 m away. The participants performed this throwing task for a total of 4 sessions. In session 2 and training of the four sessions, electrical stimulation by EMS Module was applied at specific points in the space tracked by motion capture to correct the release point and improve the control ability.

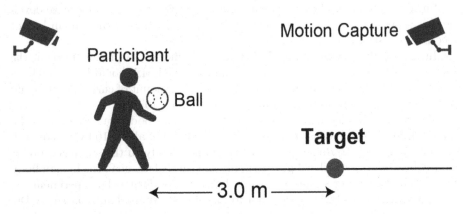

Fig. 4. Experiment environment. A participant throws the ball downward at a target 3.0 m away in a space equipped with motion capture cameras.

For the presentation of the electrical stimulation, participants wore the electrode pad as shown in Fig. 5, so that their wrist was bent inward when they received the electrical stimulation.

Fig. 5. Electrode pad placement (left). A participant wore wristbands over the pad during the experiment to keep placement (right).

In addition, to analyze the position where the ball was released, we used a high-speed camera to capture and measure the throwing motion at 996 fps.

4.1 Procedure

The outline of the experimental procedure is shown in Table 2. The Ethics Review Committee approved this experiment of the University of Tsukuba.

Table 2. Procedure of the experiment

Session	Process
Session 1	Throwing the ball without stimulation
Rehearsal	Rehearsal of throwing the ball with stimulation
Session 2	Throwing the ball with stimulation
Session 3	Throwing the ball without stimulation
Training	Training of swinging with the ball with stimulation
Session 4	Throwing the ball without stimulation

In Session 1, participants threw a ball five times without electrical stimulation to check their proficiency in the downward throwing motion.

Before the Rehearsal session, we adjusted the current amount by EMS Module so that the contraction of the muscles caused by the electrical stimulation did not change the throwing motion, but the user could feel the sensation. After adjustment, one throwing task was performed to ensure that the current amount was acceptable and that the participant did not feel any discomfort. At this time, participants were told to be aware of releasing the ball simultaneously as the electrical stimulation.

In Session 2, participants performed a ball-throwing task five times with electrical stimulation from the wearing electrode pad to confirm the effect of presenting electrical stimulation in real-time during the throwing task.

At this time, participants were told in advance to release the ball when they felt the electrical stimulation.

In Session 3, in order to confirm the learning effect of using EMS in real-time, participants performed the throwing task five times toward a target without the electrode pad of EMS Module. At this time, participants were told to release the ball where the electrical stimulation was presented in Session 2.

In the Training session, participants wore the electrode pad and performed five swinging motions with the ball in their hands. At this time, the electrical stimulation by EMS Module was presented at the same position as in Session 2.

In Session 4, participants removed the electrode pad and performed the ball throwing task again five times to confirm the Training session's effectiveness. At this time, participants were told to release the ball at the position where the stimulation moved their muscles in the Training session.

5   Result

5.1   Qualitative Evaluation by Questionnaires

After the experiment, the following three questions were asked on a 5-point Likert scale:

Q1. Was the proposed system's presentation of the release point easy to understand (1: Difficult, 5: Easy)?
Q2. Was the EMS system helpful in correcting the timing of releasing the ball (1: Not helpful, 5: Helpful)?
Q3. Did you feel that the timing of releasing the ball was corrected by the proposed system (1: Did not feel, 5: Felt)?

Figure 6 shows the results for all questions. The results show that the EMS presentation of release point is easy to understand and that the proposed system was useful in correcting the timing.

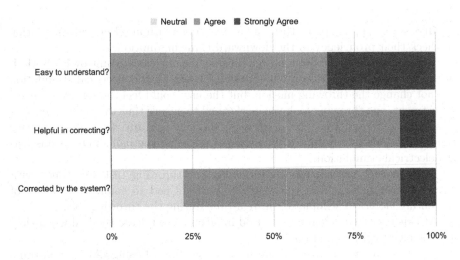

Fig. 6. Qualitative evaluation of the system by questionnaires

5.2 Task Performance Improvement

The results of the task performance of each participant are shown in Fig. 7.

In Session 2, with electrical stimulation during the underhand throwing task, testing by t-test showed a tendency for task performance to decline ($p < 0.05$). In addition, the mean error of the task performance in Session 4 tended to be higher than that in Session 1 slightly ($p < 0.5$). It is considered that the control of throwing tends to become worse by the intervention of the release point by the electric stimulation.

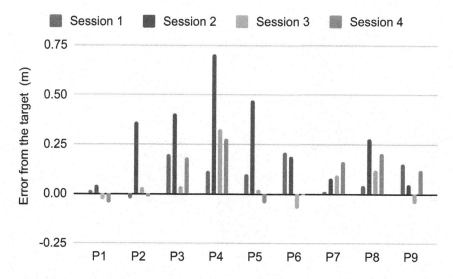

Fig. 7. Distance between the point where the ball falls and the target

5.3 Release Point Improvement

Since it is impossible to accurately measure the ball's release point using motion capture alone, we used a high-speed camera (996 fps) to capture the throwing motion in this experiment. The time from the moment the ball leaves the hand to the moment the ball first touches the floor was measured from the video taken by the high-speed camera and was named as ball's flight time. Next, from the time and spatial coordinate data obtained from the motion capture, the time when the ball first touched the floor was named as drop time. The time and spatial coordinate data were used, and the spatial coordinate at the time before ball's flight time from the time of drop time was used as the release point. We calculated the error between the release point and the median value of 0.425, the range in space where the stimulus was applied ($0.40 \leq x \leq 0.45$), and the actual release point of the participant.

6 Discussion

From the experiment results, the stimulus by the EMS was found to be helpful in correcting the release point, but the points to be improved were also revealed.

6.1 Negative Effects on Learning Effect in Terms of Cognitive Overload

As a result of EMS feedback during the underhand throwing task in Session 2, Figs. 7 and 8 show that the control performance and the release point errors increased. Sho et al. [28] also found that EMS feedback during the task resulted

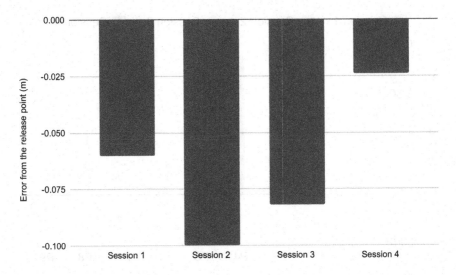

Fig. 8. The difference between the position where the stimulus was presented and the actual release point

in worse task performance, similar to this study. Sho et al. discussed that this is because the user reacts to the stimulus late without considering the reaction time. However, in this study, the delay in response to the stimulation was minimized by predicting the user's motion, suggesting another cause. Some participants said that they became too aware of the release point and did not focus on control in the questionnaire. However, the results show that both the control and the release point did not improve. Therefore, we discuss that participants' attention to both control and release points led to cognitive overload, which worsened both results. During the swing training, participants did not need to focus on control, which means they were in low cognitive load. Therefore, we discussed that participants could only focus on correcting the release points, which led to improvements. Based on these factors, we suggest that it is essential not to place the excessive cognitive load on the user and design the training method so that the subject can concentrate only on what is being taught.

6.2   Feedback on Other Factors Required for the Throwing Motion

The experiments suggest that the proposed system may teach release points; however, it did not improve control ability.

We discuss that this is caused by the proposed system only giving the feedback of the release point. For the user to throw the a toward a target point, it is necessary to consider the swing of the arm and the direction of the wrist besides the release point. It is known that the wrist direction during the throwing motion can be instructed by EMS [28], and the system can be implemented in the proposed system.

In addition, as shown in the results of Session 2, if the cognitive load is high for the user, positive learning effects may not be obtained. Therefore, it is necessary to separate the training to teach the release point and the training to teach the wrist direction.

6.3 Potential Learning Effects of EMS

The results of Session 4 do not confirm a statistically significant difference in the effect of the training phase on task performance. The learning effect of the training phase on the modification of the release point was not statistically significant, but a useful trend was suggested. In the questionnaire results, there are many comments such as *"I forgot the location instructed in the training phase from the third time in Session 4"*. Despite these comments, it is essential to see that Session 4 shows the trend for the most improved release points. This means that there may be no correlation between the subjective report of whether the user remembers and the actual quantitative confirmation of the effect of the instruction. Therefore, we would like to improve the training method and continue to verify the results of this study because it is possible that the users of the EMS-based movement learning method have improved their movements without feeling it themselves.

7 Limitation and Future Work

7.1 Limitations of the Movements that Can Support

As pointed out in the Introduction and Fig. 1, it takes about 150 ms from the stimulus to correct the motion in the conventional method. The proposed system successfully reduces this time and presents the stimulus with a slight deviation from the intended body position. The proposed system uses a linear function curve fitting to predict the body position. However, further consideration will be needed to verify whether the linear approximation model used in the proposed system can provide feedback with sufficient prediction accuracy when feedback is provided for faster motions such as the overhand throwing motion.

7.2 Learning Support with Multimodal Feedback

This experiment confirmed that the proposed system tended to help correct the release point, but we could not confirm a statistically significant difference. In the questionnaire results, it is said that the participants forgot the stimulated point in the middle of the experiment, which suggests that it is difficult for participant to remember the stimulated point by EMS. For this reason, we will explore more memorable and effective learning methods in the future. For example, we can use HMDs to display the points we want the subject to release at all times. Thus, since previous studies have suggested that multimodal feedback could be more effective than a single stimulus modality [22,24], we will investigate this possibility in the future.

8   Conclusion

In this paper, we propose a system that predicts the user's underhand throwing motion and supports learning the release point of the ball in real-time by providing electrical stimulation by an EMS device. The proposed system forcibly corrects the user's motion by EMS. The system is designed to solve the delay of the user's motion correction caused by the cognition of feedback and to correct the user's motion without delay, even for high-speed motion such as throwing. The delay caused by calculation in the system is solved by predicting the ball's position and calculating the timing considering the delay.

An experiment was conducted using the proposed system to test the learning effect. The experiment results show that the control ability of participants does not improve, but the error of the release point shows a tendency to improve. In addition, some participants said that they forgot the release point presented in Session 4 in the questionnaire after the experiment. However, the analysis results show that the release points of participants tended to improve, showing a specific learning effect of the system. Notably, this suggests no relationship between quantitative results and subjective impressions of the EMS-based instructional method.

Furthermore, compared to conventional methods using visual, auditory, or haptic feedback, the proposed method can provide detailed instruction such as arm direction or swinging speed in real-time without requiring a cognitive load on the user. In this paper, We focused on only the release point and provided feedback. In the future, it would be beneficial to correct other factors for throwing motion, such as arm swing and wrist direction.

References

1. Anderson, F., Grossman, T., Matejka, J., Fitzmaurice, G.: YouMove: enhancing movement training with an augmented reality mirror. In: Proceedings of the 26th Annual ACM Symposium on User Interface Software and Technology, UIST 2013, pp. 311–320. Association for Computing Machinery, New York (2013). https://doi.org/10.1145/2501988.2502045
2. Choi, S., Kuchenbecker, K.J.: Vibrotactile display: perception, technology, and applications. Proc. IEEE **101**(9), 2093–2104 (2013). https://doi.org/10.1109/JPROC.2012.2221071
3. Cmentowski, S., Krueger, J.: Exploring the potential of vertical jump training in virtual reality, pp. 179–185. Association for Computing Machinery, New York (2021). https://doi.org/10.1145/3450337.3483503
4. Dearborn, K., Ross, R.: Dance learning and the mirror: comparison study of dance phrase learning with and without mirrors. J. Dance Educ. **6**(4), 109–115 (2006). https://doi.org/10.1080/15290824.2006.10387323
5. Ebisu, A., Hashizume, S., Suzuki, K., Ishii, A., Sakashita, M., Ochiai, Y.: Stimulated percussions: method to control human for learning music by using electrical muscle stimulation. In: Proceedings of the 8th Augmented Human International Conference, AH 2017. Association for Computing Machinery, New York (2017). https://doi.org/10.1145/3041164.3041202

6. Fujii, K., Russo, S.S., Maes, P., Rekimoto, J.: MoveMe: 3D haptic support for a musical instrument. In: Proceedings of the 12th International Conference on Advances in Computer Entertainment Technology, ACE 2015. Association for Computing Machinery, New York (2015). https://doi.org/10.1145/2832932.2832947

7. Higuchi, K., Shimada, T., Rekimoto, J.: Flying sports assistant: external visual imagery representation for sports training. In: Proceedings of the 2nd Augmented Human International Conference, AH 2011. Association for Computing Machinery, New York (2011). https://doi.org/10.1145/1959826.1959833

8. Houri, N., Arita, H., Sakaguchi, Y.: Audiolizing body movement: its concept and application to motor skill learning. In: Proceedings of the 2nd Augmented Human International Conference, AH 2011. Association for Computing Machinery, New York (2011). https://doi.org/10.1145/1959826.1959839

9. Jiang, S., Rekimoto, J.: Mediated-timescale learning: manipulating timescales in virtual reality to improve real-world tennis forehand volley. In: 26th ACM Symposium on Virtual Reality Software and Technology, VRST 2020. Association for Computing Machinery, New York (2020). https://doi.org/10.1145/3385956.3422128

10. Kono, M., Takahashi, T., Nakamura, H., Miyaki, T., Rekimoto, J.: Design guideline for developing safe systems that apply electricity to the human body. ACM Trans. Comput.-Hum. Interact. 25(3), 1–36 (2018). https://doi.org/10.1145/3184743

11. Liebermann, D.G., Katz, L., Hughes, M.D., Bartlett, R.M., McClements, J., Franks, I.M.: Advances in the application of information technology to sport performance. J. Sports Sci. 20, 755–769 (2002). https://doi.org/10.1080/026404102320675611

12. Lin, T., et al.: Towards an understanding of situated AR visualization for basketball free-throw training. Association for Computing Machinery, New York (2021). https://doi.org/10.1145/3411764.3445649

13. Lopes, P., Baudisch, P.: Muscle-propelled force feedback: bringing force feedback to mobile devices. In: Proceedings of the SIGCHI Conference on Human Factors in Computing Systems, CHI 2013, pp. 2577–2580. Association for Computing Machinery, New York (2013). https://doi.org/10.1145/2470654.2481355

14. Lopes, P., You, S., Cheng, L.P., Marwecki, S., Baudisch, P.: Providing haptics to walls & heavy objects in virtual reality by means of electrical muscle stimulation. In: Proceedings of the 2017 CHI Conference on Human Factors in Computing Systems, CHI 2017, pp. 1471–1482. Association for Computing Machinery, New York (2017). https://doi.org/10.1145/3025453.3025600

15. Lopes, P., You, S., Ion, A., Baudisch, P.: Adding force feedback to mixed reality experiences and games using electrical muscle stimulation, pp. 1–13. Association for Computing Machinery, New York (2018). https://doi.org/10.1145/3173574.3174020

16. Maekawa, A., Takahashi, S., Saraiji, M.Y., Wakisaka, S., Iwata, H., Inami, M.: Naviarm: augmenting the learning of motor skills using a backpack-type robotic arm system. In: Proceedings of the 10th Augmented Human International Conference 2019, AH2019. Association for Computing Machinery, New York (2019). https://doi.org/10.1145/3311823.3311849

476 R. Niwa et al.

17. Mahoney, M.J., Avener, M.: Psychology of the elite athlete: an exploratory study. Cogn. Ther. Res. **1**(2), 135–141 (1977). https://doi.org/10.1007/bf01173634
18. McDaniel, T.L., Goldberg, M., Bala, S., Fakhri, B., Panchanathan, S.: Vibrotactile feedback of motor performance errors for enhancing motor learning. In: Proceedings of the 20th ACM International Conference on Multimedia, MM 2012, pp. 419–428. Association for Computing Machinery, New York (2012). https://doi.org/10.1145/2393347.2393408
19. Michalski, S.C., Szpak, A., Loetscher, T.: Using virtual environments to improve real-world motor skills in sports: a systematic review. Front. Psychol. **10**, 2159 (2019). https://doi.org/10.3389/fpsyg.2019.02159
20. Ruffaldi, E., Filippeschi, A., Frisoli, A., Sandoval, O., Avizzano, C.A., Bergamasco, M.: Vibrotactile perception assessment for a rowing training system. In: World Haptics 2009 - Third Joint EuroHaptics Conference and Symposium on Haptic Interfaces for Virtual Environment and Teleoperator Systems, pp. 350–355 (2009). https://doi.org/10.1109/WHC.2009.4810849
21. Schmidt, R.A., Lee, T.D.: Motor Control and Learning: A Behavioral Emphasis, 3rd edn. Human Kinetics, Champaign (1999)
22. Seitz, A.R., Dinse, H.R.: A common framework for perceptual learning. Curr. Opin. Neurobiol. **17**, 148–153 (2007). https://doi.org/10.1016/j.conb.2007.02.004
23. Shadmehr, R., Mussa-Ivaldi, F.A.: Adaptive representation of dynamics during learning of a motor task. J. Neurosci. **14**(5 Pt 2), 3208–3224 (1994)
24. Shams, L., Seitz, A.R.: Benefits of multisensory learning. Trends Cogn. Sci. **12**(11), 411–417 (2008). https://doi.org/10.1016/j.tics.2008.07.006
25. Sigrist, R., Rauter, G., Riener, R., Wolf, P.: Augmented visual, auditory, haptic, and multimodal feedback in motor learning: a review. Psychon. Bull. Rev. **20**(1), 21–53 (2013). https://doi.org/10.3758/s13423-012-0333-8
26. Spelmezan, D., Jacobs, M., Hilgers, A., Borchers, J.: Tactile motion instructions for physical activities. In: Proceedings of the SIGCHI Conference on Human Factors in Computing Systems, CHI 2009, pp. 2243–2252. Association for Computing Machinery, New York (2009). https://doi.org/10.1145/1518701.1519044
27. Tamaki, E., Miyaki, T., Rekimoto, J.: PossessedHand: a hand gesture manipulation system using electrical stimuli. In: Proceedings of the 1st Augmented Human International Conference, AH 2010. Association for Computing Machinery, New York (2010). https://doi.org/10.1145/1785455.1785457
28. Tatsuno, S., Hayakawa, T., Ishikawa, M.: Supportive training system for sports skill acquisition based on electrical stimulation. In: 2017 IEEE World Haptics Conference (WHC), pp. 466–471 (2017). https://doi.org/10.1109/WHC.2017.7989946
29. Welford, A.T., Brebner, J.M.: Reaction Times. Academic Press, London (1980)
30. Williams, A.M., Hodges, N.J.: Skill Acquisition in Sport: Research, Theory and Practice (2004)
31. Woodworth, R.S., Schlosberg, H.: Experimental Psychology. Holt, Oxford (1954)
32. Wulf, G., Shea, C.H., Matschiner, S.: Frequent feedback enhances complex motor skill learning. J. Mot. Behav. **30**(2), 180–192 (1998)

Facial Emotions Classification Supported in an Ensemble Strategy

Rui Novais⬤, Pedro J. S. Cardoso⬤, and João M. F. Rodrigues$^{(\boxtimes)}$ ⬤

LARSyS & ISE, Universidade do Algarve, Faro, Portugal
{a49095,pcardoso,jrodrig}@ualg.pt

Abstract. Humans are prepared to comprehend each other's emotions from subtle body movements or facial expressions, and from those, they change the way they deliver messages when communicating between them. Machines, user interfaces, or robots need to empower this ability, in a way to change the interaction from the traditional "human-computer interaction" to a "human-machine cooperation", where the machine provides the "right" information and functionality, at the "right" time, and in the "right" way. This paper presents a framework for facial expression prediction supported in an ensemble of facial expression methods, being the main contribution the integration of outputs from different methods in a single prediction consistent with the expression presented by the system's user. Results show a classification accuracy above 73% in both FER2013 and RAF-DB datasets.

Keywords: Facial emotions · Ensembles · Computer vision · Machine learning

1 Introduction

Emotion and sentiment analysis methods are the automated processes of analyzing information to determine the emotion (e.g., happiness, sadness, fear, surprise, disgust, anger, and neutral) or sentiment (e.g., positive, negative, and neutral) expressed by the user. The sentiment influences the emotion, and the emotions influence the sentiment. Humans are prepared to comprehend each other's emotions from subtle body movements, facial expressions, the way they speek, or simply by the tone of voice. They use this capacity when communicating between them, changing the way they pass the message based on those responses/emotions/sentiments.

We are living in the so-called Information Society, Society 4.0. However, we are starting to notice that the cross-sectional sharing of knowledge is not enough. So, in Japan appeared a new designation, Society 5.0, which should be one that "through the high degree of merging between cyberspace and physical space, will be able to balance economic advancement with the resolution of social problems by providing goods and services that granularly address manifold latent needs regardless of locale, age, sex, or language." [1]. Simplifying, Society 5.0 is a super-smart, people-centric society.

To achieve this degree of development, one of the keys is to empower machines, user interfaces, or robots with the same communication capabilities that humans have between them. This changes the interaction between machines and humans from the traditional

© The Author(s), under exclusive license to Springer Nature Switzerland AG 2022
M. Antona and C. Stephanidis (Eds.): HCII 2022, LNCS 13308, pp. 477–488, 2022.
https://doi.org/10.1007/978-3-031-05028-2_32

"human-computer interaction" (HCI) to a "human-machine cooperation" (HMC) [2], where the machine provides the "right" information and functionality, at the "right" time, and in the "right" way.

One of the solutions to achieve HMC relies on machine learning algorithms with a performance that depends greatly on the quality of the algorithm (and proper tuning), but also on the data's (high) quality. There are several ways to improve algorithms results, being the more usual way to train them repeatedly with all available data, with different settings, until the best possible result is achieved (fine-tuning the algorithm). Training might be extremely time-consuming, as well as it implies spending a lot of energy during the training phase, also increasing the algorithm's "carbon footprint".

Of course, there are ways in the literature to mitigate this problem, one of those is Active Learning [3]. The idea behind Active Learning is that the algorithms can achieve greater accuracy with fewer labelled training instances if they are allowed to pick the training data from which they learn, achieved by letting the learners to ask queries in the form of unlabeled instances to be labelled by an oracle (e.g., human annotator). This filtered use of data might even have a greater effect on performance and costs since many times labelled data is scarce and extremely expensive to obtain (unlabeled data may be abundant but labels are difficult, time-consuming, or expensive to acquire).

A different solution is applying assembly techniques, using for instance the results from algorithms previously thought and available in the community, e.g., open-source code. This use of hybridization and ensemble techniques allows empowering computation, functionality, robustness, and accuracy aspects of modelling [4], as well as allows to reduce the "carbon footprint" of the algorithm, once we use already trained algorithm(s), and now we are working with those results to develop the ensemble model. In short, the ensemble aggregates by (possibly) training with the results from the adopted methods. For instance, as it will be the case in this paper, the ensemble/aggregator method uses floating-point numbers returned by running established algorithms over an image, each number corresponding to a class of the emotion detection algorithm, instead of using an original color image.

This paper explores the last solution, a framework supported in the use of ensembles/aggregation of algorithms/methods to make the facial emotion classification from video clips or live streaming. The complete method receives information in the form of images (or frames) that will be passed to different types of facial emotion classifiers (available as open-source code), returning the same type or different types of results (corresponding to the emotions classes), which are then combined to return a (single) final result. The main contribution of the paper is the ensemble tool, which shows generically better results than using the methods individually.

In this Section, it was introduced the goals of the paper. Next sections present some related work (Sect. 2) and the proposed ensemble facial expression classification method (Sect. 3), followed by the developed tests and results in Sect. 4. Section 5 draws some conclusions and defines some potential future work.

2 Related Work

Expression recognition to interpersonal relation prediction needs input from different sources, e.g., sound, body, and facial expressions, as well as age or cultural environment. Zhang *et al.* [5] devise an effective multitask network that is capable of learning from rich auxiliary attributes such as gender, age, and head pose, beyond just facial expression data. Noroozi *et al.* [6] presented a survey on emotional body gesture recognition. While works based on facial expressions or speech abound, recognizing affect from body gestures remains a less explored topic. The authors in [6] present a new comprehensive survey hoping to boost research in the field. They first introduce emotional body gestures as a component of what is commonly known as "body language" and comment on general aspects as gender differences and cultural dependence. Then they define a complete framework for automatic emotional body gesture recognition.

Other solutions were also presented as, for example, the fusing of body posture with facial expressions for the recognition of affect in child-robot interaction [7]. The opposite also exists, i.e., the dissociation between facial and body expressions (in emotion recognition), as in a study done with impaired emotion recognition through body expressions and intact performance with facial expressions [8]. Further recent examples exist in the literature, such as, mood estimation based on facial expressions and postures [9] or, e.g., in the following works [10–14].

In the present case, we are focusing on a single aspect which is facial expression. Ekman and Friesen demonstrated that facial expressions of emotion are universal, i.e., the human way of expressing an emotion is supposed to be an evolutionary, biological fact, not depending on the specific culture [15]. Nevertheless, different methods for facial expression classification return different results when presented with the same input (face). The idea of facial expression recognition (FER) using an ensemble of classifiers is not new. For example, Zavaschi *et al.* [16] presented in 2011 a pool of base classifiers created using two feature sets: Gabor filters and Local Binary Patterns (LBP). Then a multi-objective genetic algorithm has used to search for the best ensemble using as objective functions the accuracy and the size of the ensemble. Later (in 2019), Renda *et al.* [17] compared several ensemble deep learning strategies applied to facial expression recognition (for static images only). Ali *et al.* [18] presented an ensemble approach for multicultural facial expressions analysis. Intending to get high expression recognition accuracy, the study presents several computational algorithms to handle those variations. They use facial images from participants in the multicultural dataset that originate from four ethnic regions, including Japan, Taiwan, "Caucasians", and Moroc.

Wang *et al.* [19] presented OAENet (oriented attention ensemble for accurate facial expression recognition). The authors used an oriented attention pseudo-siamese network that takes advantage of global and local facial information. Their network consists of two branches, a maintenance branch that consisted of several convolutional blocks to take advantage of high-level semantic features, and an attention branch that possesses a UNet like architecture to obtain local highlight information. The two branches are fused to output the classification results. As such, a direction-dependent attention mechanism is established to remedy the limitation of insufficient utilization of local information. With the help of the attention mechanism, their network not only grabs a global picture but can also concentrate on important local areas. In [20] the authors present a facial emotion recognition system that addresses automatic face detection and facial expression recognition separately, the latter is performed by a set of only four deep convolutional neural networks concerning an ensembling approach, while a label smoothing technique is applied to deal with the miss-labelled training data.

The LHC is a Local (multi) Head Channel (self-attention) method [21], which is based on two main ideas. First, the authors hypothesize that in computer vision the best way to leverage the self-attention paradigm is a channel-wise application, instead of the more explored spatial attention, and that convolution will not be replaced by attention modules like recurrent networks were in NLP (natural language processing); second, a local approach has the potential to better overcome the limitations of convolution than global attention. With LHC, the authors managed to achieve a new state of the art over the FER2013 dataset [22], with significantly lower complexity and impact on the "host" architecture in terms of computational cost.

Py-Feat [23] is an open-source Python toolbox that provides support for detecting, preprocessing, analyzing, and visualizing facial expression data. Py-Feat allows experts to disseminate and benchmark computer vision models and also for end-users to quickly process, analyze, and visualize face expression data.

For two recent (2021) surveys on various deep learning algorithms for efficient facial expression classification and human face recognition techniques, please refer to the works of Banerjee *et al.* [24] and Revina & Emmanuel [25].

All the above-mentioned methods need a huge amount of data (images) from which they learn from. Differently, we intend that our method learns from the result of previously established models, simplifying the learning phase and reducing the time required to teach the classification model, as well as computing power that is needed for that (decreasing this way the local "carbon footprint" of the framework). The next section explores the proposed framework in more detail.

3   Facial Emotions Prediction Supported in Ensembles

As mentioned before, the framework to develop an emotion classifier should be supported in several sources/attributes, such as facial expression, body expression, speech, text, environment etc. Figure 1 illustrates that principle: the combination of an "undetermined" number of primary classifiers, that is dynamically added/removed/updated to/from the framework, to return a final prediction. The main idea behind the framework presented in Fig. 1 is that the primary methods are off-the-shelf methods, i.e., methods that have their code publicly available and can be easily added into the ensemble/aggregation model, by providing final and raw classification results that will be processed by the ensembled/aggregator for the final classification prediction. We stress that the framework does not intend to improve any of the primary models, but only to work with the results they return. In this context, the emotions classifications models used in this paper, had their code extracted from some repository and no changes of any kind were done in the code, meaning that the individual results presented by the emotion classifier, when applied to the datasets, are the collected and presented results, despite many times those are not coincident with the ones in the original publication.

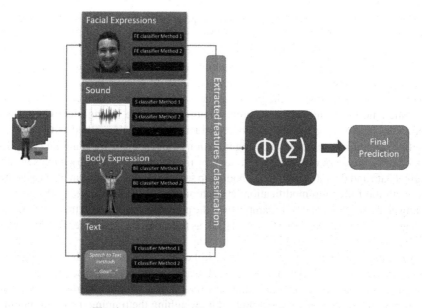

Fig. 1. Emotion classification framework scheme.

3.1 Framework

To facilitate the description, this paper only addresses the use of static images (i.e., it does not consider sequences of images, sounds, text, and body expressions) and considers that primary methods return 7 values corresponding to the different emotions, as we will see next. However, the framework is easily adaptable to different outputs from the primary classifiers, e.g., the number and type of returned features.

Within the expressed restriction, the pipeline of the framework consists in presenting the same image, to (i) n primary emotions classifiers (in the present case $n = 3$). Then, from the input image, each primary classifier returns a value between 0.0 (less likely to be) and 1.0 (more likely to be) for each of the seven classes/emotions (happiness, sadness, fear, surprise, disgust, anger, and neutral). (ii) The returned values are then injected to the ensemble/aggregation model, to produce a single final classification. This means that for each presented image there will be $n \times 7$ inputs to the aggregation model and an expression/emotion as output.

For the initial part (i) of the framework pipeline, the following primary emotion classifiers were used: (i) LHC [21] with its code available at [26]; (ii) Py-Feat [23] with its code available at [27]; and (iii) FERjs which is a free implementation done by Justin Shenk and has its code available at [28]. The reason to choose these three methods to build the baseline was: (a) they present state of the art results, (b) are recent methods, from 2021, (c) have publicly available code (implementation), and (d) represent different architectures. Again, it is important to stress that there is a huge number of different methods that could be used, as mentioned in [24, 25].

For the second part (ii) of the framework pipeline, the models used were: (a) Voting; (b) Random Forest [34]; (c) AdaBoost [35]; and (d) a Multi-layer Perceptron/Neural Network (MLP/NN) [36]. Models (b–d) were tested without ranking the values returned by the initial classifiers, as we will see later. In more detail, the (a) Voting method used the classes predicted by the primary classifiers to make a prediction if there is a majority of opinion between the guesses, that is, if at least two of the predictors guess the same emotion. If all return different emotions, then the Voting method returns no prediction. The Voting method can be considered as a naïve method but serves as a baseline for building more advanced aggregation strategies. The (b) Random Forest [34] is *per se* an aggregator of predictors. It starts by the draw of k bootstrap samples from the original data and then, for each of the bootstrap samples, grow an unpruned classification tree, with the following modification: at each node, rather than choosing the best split among all predictors, randomly sample m of the predictors and choose the best split from among those. The (c) AdaBoost method [35], as the name suggests, uses boosting which involves combining the predictions from many weak learners, being a weak learner a (very) simple model, although it has some skill on the dataset. The AdaBoost algorithm uses short (one-level) decision trees as weak learners that are added sequentially to the ensemble. Each subsequent model attempts to correct the predictions made by the model before it in the sequence. This is achieved by weighing the training dataset to put more focus on training examples on which prior models made prediction errors. Finally, the (d) Multi-layer Perceptron [36] is a feedforward artificial neural network model that maps sets of input data onto a set of outputs. An MLP consists of multiple layers and each layer is fully connected to the following one. There can be one or more non-linear hidden layers between the input and the output layer.

The next section details the tests and achieved results.

4   Tests and Results

For the tests, it was used, as mentioned, two different datasets, namely: (i) FER2013 [22, 32], where the data consists of 48×48-pixel grayscale images of faces. The faces have been automatically registered so that they are centered and occupy about the same amount of space in each image. Each face is annotated to a facial expression, of the seven previously mentioned categories. The training set consists of 28,709 examples and the public testing set consists of 3,589 examples; The second dataset used is (ii) RAF-DB [33], which is a facial expression database with 29,672 facial images, downloaded from the Internet. Images in this database have great variability in subjects' age, gender and ethnicity, head poses, lighting conditions, occlusions (e.g., glasses, facial hair, or self-occlusion), post-processing operations (e.g., various filters and special effects) etc. The images were classified into two different subsets: single-label subset, including the 7 classes of basic emotions (same as FER2013), and two-tab subset, including 12 classes of compound emotions. It also includes 5 accurate landmark locations, 37 automatic landmark locations, bounding boxes, race, age range, and gender attributes annotations per image. As usual, to be able to objectively measure the performance for the followers' entries, the database has been split into a train set and a test set, where the size of the training set is five times larger than the one of the testing set, and expressions in both sets have a near-identical distribution.

It is important to stress that in the case of RAF-DB, before applying the emotion classifier, a face detector was applied. As the goal of the paper is not to select the best detector to apply in this situation, it was applied one of the most well-known face detectors - Haar-Cascate face detector [34].

Regarding both datasets, Table 1 shows the accuracy for each primary emotion classifier and the Voting model, serving as a reference for the latter tested and more advanced aggregation models.

Table 1. Accuracy for the individual emotion classifiers and voting model.

Dataset	LHC	Py-Feat	FERjs	Voting
FER2013	70,59%	**77,98%**	65,67%	**73,37%**
RAF-DB (2)	60,68%	62,04%	62,19%	62,60%

Besides the Voting model, the other aggregators' methods were tuned using a grid search stratified 5-fold cross-validation, i.e., for each set of classifier parameters, the training data was divided into 5 folds with the same classes ratio as the training set and then the algorithms were trained and tested 5 times, where each time a new set (a fold) is used as testing set while remaining sets are used for training. The scoring (the accuracy in this case) for each set of parameters is computed as the mean score over the 5 train-test runs. Next, the full training dataset and best scored set of parameters are used to obtain the final model for each of the methods (i.e., Random Forest, AdaBoost, and MLP/NN). Used the Scikit-learn machine learning library for the Python programming language [35] (version 1.0.1), besides the default values, the parameters used to tune the methods are summarized in Table 3 (Appendix). The remaining section's results were attained in a personal computer running Kubuntu 21.10 over an Intel(R) Core(TM) i7-4770 CPU @ 3.40 GHz with 16 GiB of RAM.

Considering the methods and datasets above introduced, different combinations of those were used, obtaining different aggregation models. So, Table 2 shows the results of the different models applied to the different datasets where the results per row were obtained in the following manners. The FER2013 row shows the results considering that the outputs of the primary methods (LHC, Py-Feat, and FERjs), namely the methods' estimated confidence of being each of the emotions, are injected into the aggregators' methods (Random Forest, AdaBoost, and MLP/NN). In this case, 21 features are injected, since 3 primary methods returning 7 expressions were used, either directly with no transformation or ranked within each method (resulting in the "Without ranking" and "With ranking" table's columns). Furthermore, in the aggregators training phase, the injected values were the results of applying the primary methods to the FER2013 training dataset, and the results shown in the table are the values obtained by applying the final aggregator model (the model with parameters obtained from the grid-search cross-validation phase and trained over the full FER2013 training dataset) to the FER 2013 testing dataset. Row RAF-DB (1) shows the results of applying the above models (the model trained for table's RAF2013 row) directly to the full RAF-DB dataset, which in this case can be considered as a testing dataset since the model never saw that data. Finally, row RAF-DB (2) was built similarly to row RAF2013, with the difference being that the training and testing datasets were RAF-DB training and testing datasets, respectively. The parameters obtained from the grid-search cross-validation are summarized in Table 4 (Appendix).

Table 2. Results of the different models applied to the different datasets.

Dataset	Without ranking			With ranking		
	Random Forest	AdaBoost	MLP/ NN	Random Forest	AdaBoost	MLP/NN
FER2013	71,08%	71,41%	70,95%	70,68%	70,79%	70,84%
RAF-DB (1)	**60,24%**	60,17%	60,01%	59,47%	59,53%	59,75%
RAF-DB (2)	**76,17%**	64,94%	74,14%	38,98%	38,98%	67,07%

Some conclusions can be drawn from Table 1 and Table 2. The first conclusion is that, although in some cases the values are close, the ranking of the values is not justified as it always returned worst accuracy than the corresponding method without ranking, i.e., it seems to be a better solution to inject the values from primary methods directly into the aggregation methods. Considering the results over the FER2013 test dataset, the best aggregation method was the Voting model with an accuracy of 73,37%, which is worse than the accuracy of the Py-Feat model (77,98%). As a curiosity, which is not presented in the tables, is the fact that the accuracy of the models over the FER2013 training dataset was 99.18%, 81.84%, and 74.96%, respectively. This seems to indicate overfitting of the first method since it drops from 99.18% accuracy over the training dataset to 70,59% accuracy in the testing dataset. In the reverse, Py-Feat suffered a very small drop from 81.84% to 77,98% of accuracy. This is relevant since having a 99.18% accuracy, the aggregation methods might have had some somehow misleading predictions from method LHC – this was an expectable risk and provides us with further studies to mitigate this threat. Applying the aggregated model trained for FER2013 to RAF-DB is interesting by the fact that it produces results very similar to the primary methods without the need to train them with that dataset. In more detail, LHC, Py-Feat and FERjs trained with RAF-DB training dataset produced an accuracy of 60,68%, 62,04%, and 62,19%, respectively, which is very similar to the aggregation methods trained with FER2013 accuracies (60,24%, 60,17%, and 60,01%, respectively), but without the need to train a new model. If the aggregation models were trained using the prediction from LHC, Py-Feat and FERjs for the RAF-DB training set, then their prediction improve the base methods in all (the without ranking) cases, i.e., the best accuracy was 62.19% for method FERjs, and the aggregation methods attained an accuracy of 76,17%, 64,94%, and 74,14% (for Random Forest, Ada-Boost, and MLP/NN, respectively).

Between the aggregation methods, AdaBoost was the one performing worst. Random forest and MLP/NN had similar results, being the Random Forest slightly better in the tested cases.

5   Conclusions

This paper presents a simplified version of a facial expression/emotions predictor framework supported in ensembles. The pipeline of the frameworks consists in presenting an image, to several (primary, pre-trained) emotions classifiers. Then, each classifier returns for each image and for each of the seven considered classes/emotions (happiness, sadness, fear, surprise, disgust, anger, and neutral) its confidence values. Those results are then fed to an ensemble/aggregator model returning a single predicted class.

The best results for the aggregators methods in the case of FER2013 dataset were achieved with the Voting model (supported on the majority of the models' predictions), being above two of the primary emotion classifiers but below one of them. This result is achieved probably because the emotion classifiers were taught with FER2013 but have different accuracy behaviors (one of the classifiers is probably overfitted since the accuracy dropped from almost 100% on the training set to nearly 70% on the test set). In the case of RAF-DB, the best result was achieved with the model Random Forest aggregator, and the result is above all the results achieved individually by the primary emotion classifiers.

In future work we intend to explore different datasets, like the ones mentioned in [36, 37] and datasets that have motion (video or streaming). We will also try to improve the final results by increasing the number of emotion classifiers, and studying the influence of their characteristics, like the fact that they are over or underfitted.

Acknowledgements. This work was supported by the Portuguese Foundation for Science and Technology (FCT), project LARSyS - FCT Project UIDB/50009/2020.

Appendix

This appendix presents the parameters (Tables 3 and 4) used for Random Forest, AdaBoost and MLP/Neural Network for the results presented in Sect. 4.

Table 3. Grid search parameters (although the majority of the naming of the parameters is self-explicative, we suggest that the readers refer to the library's documentation [35] for a more detailed explanation).

Random Forest	
Number of trees in the forest (n_estimators)	{25, 50, 100, 500}
Function to measure the quality of a split. (criterion)	{gini, entropy}
Maximum depth of the tree(max_depth)	{None, 2, 5, 10, 20}
Minimum number of samples required to split an internal node (min_samples_split)	{2, 5, 10}
Minimum number of samples required to be at a leaf node (min_samples_leaf)	{1, 2, 5, 10}
Number of features to consider when looking for the best split (max_features)	{1, 2, sqrt, log2}
Number of samples to draw from X to train each base estimator (max_samples)	{None, 0.1}
AdaBoost	
The maximum number of estimators at which boosting is terminated (n_estimators)	{25, 50, 100, 500}
Boosting algorithm (algorithm)	{SAMME, SAMME.R}
MLP/Neural Network	
The i-th element represents the number of neurons in the i-th hidden layer (hidden_layer_sizes)	{(10,), (100,), (10, 10), (100, 100), (10, 10, 10), (100, 100, 100)}
Learning rate schedule for weight updates (activation)	{identity, logistic, tanh, relu}
L2 penalty (regularization term) parameter (alpha)	$\{10^{-3}, 10^{-2}, \ldots, 10^{3}\}$
Learning rate schedule for weight updates (learning_rate)	{constant, invscaling, adaptive}

Table 4. Sets of parameters used to obtain the results for the different models (tuned using grid search stratified cross-validation).

		With ranking		Without ranking	
		FER2013	*RAF-DB*	*FER2013*	*RAF-DB*
Random Forest	n_estimators	100	500	50	100
	criterion	gini	entropy	gini	gini
	max_depth	10	None	None	20
	min_samples_split	10	5	2	10
	min_samples_leaf	10	1	10	1
	max_features	Sqrt	2	2	1
	max_samples	0.1	None	None	None
AdaBoost	n_estimators	500	50	500	500
	algorithm	SAMME.R	SAMME	SAMME.R	SAMME.R

(continued)

Table 4. (*continued*)

		With ranking		Without ranking	
		FER2013	*RAF-DB*	*FER2013*	*RAF-DB*
MLP/NN	hidden_layer_sizes	(100, 100, 100)	(100,)	(10, 10)	(100,)
	activation	identity	relu	tanh	tanh
	alpha	0.01	0.1	0.1	1
	learning_rate	invscaling	constant	constant	constant

References

1. Deguchi, A., et al.: What is Society 5.0. Chapter 1 in Society 5.0 – A People-centric Super-smart Society. Hitachi-UTokyo Laboratory (eds.), pp. 1–23. Springer (2020). https://doi.org/10.1007/978-981-15-2989-4

2. Rothfuß, S., Wörner, M., Inga, J., Hohmann, S.: A study on human-machine cooperation on decision level. In: Proceedings of the IEEE International Conference on Systems, Man, and Cybernetics, pp. 2291–2298. IEEE (2020)

3. Kumar, P., Gupta, A.: Active learning query strategies for classification, regression, and clustering: a survey. J. Comput. Sci. Technol. **35**(4), 913–945 (2020). https://doi.org/10.1007/s11390-020-9487-4

4. Ardabili, S., Mosavi, A., Várkonyi-Kóczy, A.R.: Advances in machine learning modeling reviewing hybrid and ensemble methods. In: Várkonyi-Kóczy, A.R. (ed.) INTER-ACADEMIA 2019. LNNS, vol. 101, pp. 215–227. Springer, Cham (2020). https://doi.org/10.1007/978-3-030-36841-8_21

5. Zhang, F., Zhang, T., Mao, Q., Xu, C.: Joint pose and expression modeling for facial expression recognition. In: Proceedings of the IEEE Conference on Computer Vision and Pattern Recognition, pp. 3359–3368 (2018)

6. Noroozi, F., Kaminska, D., Corneanu, C., Sapinski, T., Escalera, S., Anbarjafari, G.: Survey on emotional body gesture recognition. IEEE Trans. Affect. Comput. **12**(2), 505–523 (2018)

7. Filntisis, P.P., Efthymiou, N., Koutras, P., Potamianos, G., Maragos, P.: Fusing body posture with facial expressions for joint recognition of affect in child–robot interaction. IEEE Robot. Autom. Lett. **4**(4), 4011–4018 (2019)

8. Leiva, S., Margulis, L., Micciulli, A., Ferreres, A.: Dissociation between facial and bodily expressions in emotion recognition: a case study. Clin. Neuropsychol. **33**(1), 166–182 (2019)

9. Canedo, D., Neves, A.J.: Mood estimation based on facial expressions and postures. In: Proceedings of the RECPAD 2020, pp. 49–50 (2020)

10. Bänziger, T., Mortillaro, M., Scherer, K.R.: Introducing the geneva multimodal expression corpus for experimental research on emotion perception. Emotion **12**(5), 1161 (2012)

11. Kleinsmith, A., BianchiBerthouze, N.: Affective body expression perception and recognition: a survey. IEEE Trans. Affect. Comput. **4**(1), 15–33 (2012)

12. Senecal, S., Cuel, L., Aristidou, A., Magnenat-Thalmann, N.: Continuous body emotion recognition system during theater performances. Comput. Animat. Virtual Worlds **27**(3–4), 311–320 (2016)

13. Ahmed, F., Bari, A.H., Gavrilova, M.L.: Emotion recognition from body movement. IEEE Access **8**, 11761–11781 (2019)

14. Liang, G., Wang, S., Wang, C.: Pose-aware adversarial domain adaptation for personalized facial expression recognition. arXiv preprint arXiv:2007.05932 (2020)

15. Ekman, P., Friesen, W.V.: Constants across cultures in the face and emotion. J. Pers. Soc. Psychol. **17**(2), 124 (1971). https://doi.org/10.1037/h0030377

16. Zavaschi, T.H., Koerich, A.L., Oliveira, L.E.S.: Facial expression recognition using ensemble of classifiers. In: Proceedings of the IEEE International Conference on Acoustics, Speech and Signal Processing, pp. 1489–1492 (2011). https://doi.org/10.1109/ICASSP.2011.5946775

17. Renda, A., Barsacchi, M., Bechini, A., Marcelloni, F.: Comparing ensemble strategies for deep learning: an application to facial expression recognition. Expert Syst. Appl. **136**, 1–11 (2019)

18. Ali, G., et al.: Artificial neural network based ensemble approach for multicultural facial expressions analysis. IEEE Access **8**, 134950–134963 (2020)

19. Wang, Z., Zeng, F., Liu, S., Zeng, B.: OAENet: oriented attention ensemble for accurate facial expression recognition. Pattern Recognit. **112**, 107694 (2021)

20. Benamara, N.K., et al.: Real-time facial expression recognition using smoothed deep neural network ensemble. Integr. Comput.-Aid. Eng. (Preprint) **28**, 1–15 (2021)

21. Pecoraro, R., Basile, V., Bono, V., Gallo, S.: Local multi-head channel self-attention for facial expression recognition. arXiv preprint arXiv:2111.07224 (2021)

22. Goodfellow, I., et al.: Challenges in representation learning: a report on three machine learning contests. In: Lee, M., Hirose, A., Hou, Z.-G., Kil, R.M. (eds.) ICONIP 2013. LNCS, vol. 8228, pp. 117–124. Springer, Heidelberg (2013). https://doi.org/10.1007/978-3-642-42051-1_16

23. Cheong, J.H., Xie, T., Byrne, S., Chang, L.J.: Py-Feat: Python facial expression analysis toolbox. arXiv preprint arXiv:2104.03509 (2021)

24. Banerjee, R., De, S., Dey, S.: A survey on various Deep Learning algorithms for an efficient facial expression recognition system. Int. J. Image Graph., 2240005 (2021)

25. Revina, I.M., Emmanuel, W.S.: A survey on human face expression recognition techniques. J. King Saud Univ.-Comput. Inf. Sci. **33**(6), 619–628 (2021)

26. LHC-NET: Local multi-head channel self-attention (code) (2021). https://github.com/bodhis 4ttva/lhc_net. Accessed 28 Dec 2021

27. Py-FEAT: Python facial expression analysis toolbox (code) (2021). https://pythonrepo.com/ repo/cosanlab-py-feat-python-deep-learning. Accessed 28 Dec 2021

28. Shenk, J.: Facial expression recognition (code) (2021). https://github.com/justinshenk/fer. Accessed 28 Dec 2021

29. Breiman, L.: Random forests. Mach. Learn. **45**(1), 5–32 (2001)

30. Hastie, T., Rosset, S., Zhu, J., Zou, H.: Multi-class Adaboost. Statistics and its. Interface **2**(3), 349–360 (2009)

31. Ayyadevara, V.K.: Pro Machine Learning Algorithms. Apress, Berkeley (2018)

32. FER2013: Learn facial expressions from an image (2021). https://www.kaggle.com/msa mbare/fer2013. Accessed 28 Dec 2021

33. RAF-DB: Real-world affective faces database (2021). http://www.whdeng.cn/raf/model1. html. Accessed 28 Dec 2021

34. OpenCV: OpenCV: Cascade classifier – face detection (2021). https://docs.opencv.org/4.5.5/ db/d28/tutorial_cascade_classifier.html. Accessed 28 Dec 2021

35. Pedregosa, F., et al.: Scikit-learn: machine learning in Python. J. Mach. Learn. Res. **12**, 2825–2830 (2011)

36. Li, S., Deng, W.: Reliable crowdsourcing and deep locality-preserving learning for unconstrained facial expression recognition. IEEE Trans. Image Process. **28**(1), 356–370 (2019)

37. Cheong, J.H., Xie, T., Byrne, S., Chang, L.J.: Py-Feat: Python facial expression analysis toolbox. arXiv preprint arXiv:2104.03509 (2021)

Haptic Pattern Designer Toolkit – HaptiDesigner: Software and Hardware for Creation of Actuation Patterns

Nasrine Olson[1(✉)] [iD] and Jonas Jarvoll[2]

[1] Swedish School of Library and Information Science, University of Borås, Allégatan 1, 501 90 Borås, Sweden
Nasrine.Olson@hb.se
[2] AIVA Robotics, Mor Kerstins väg 46, 511 53 Kinna, Sweden

Abstract. In this paper we present a software and hardware toolkit called HaptiDesigner, useful for work with creation of haptic patterns and beyond. The toolkit includes two printed circuit boards each with 32 and 40 channels which can also be connected for an extended number of channels. It also includes a PC-based interface for ease of design and the software needed for encoding and storing the related instructions for activation of actuator motors. HaptiDesigner toolkit has been successfully used for the design of meaning bearing patterns for haptic communication. Some examples are provided.

Keywords: Haptic · Actuation patterns · Designer toolkit

1 Context

1.1 Introduction

Technological innovations for remote communication have been sky-rocketing in recent decades. These days, many new tools and devices incorporate haptic stimuli as well as the typical audio and visual modes of communication. Even so, in the majority of these solutions, haptic stimuli are offered as a complement and to enhance the reception of information by other senses rather than being offered as the primary mode of information delivery. That is, the haptic elements are not extensive enough to enable full haptic communication without reliance on either visual or auditory cues. Therefore, there remains a great need for further development of haptic communication, not only as a supplement to other forms of communication, but also as the main mode of communication. Not only such solutions are needed e.g., for people with deafblindness, the use of haptic communication systems is scalable to many other areas.

Research in the field has steadily gained momentum and many have explored the use of various forms of actuators (in wearables or otherwise), for conveyance of information to the receiver (e.g., [1–3]). Often different patterns of actuation are designed to denote

© The Author(s), under exclusive license to Springer Nature Switzerland AG 2022
M. Antona and C. Stephanidis (Eds.): HCII 2022, LNCS 13308, pp. 489–509, 2022.
https://doi.org/10.1007/978-3-031-05028-2_33

various messages; those involved typically design their own circuit boards and devise individual methods for encoding different sequences of activation. Detailed reports on how this is done, however, remain limited and each project in essence would need to reinvent the wheel. In this paper we propose a useful toolkit comprising scalable printed circuit boards (PCB) and, more importantly, a software interface that can help encoding of the actuation patterns in a user-friendly and yet sophisticated manner.

1.2 Background

In a recent H2020 project called SUITCEYES, one of the objectives was to create haptic communication solutions for people with deafblindness. Accordingly multiple prototypes were developed for this purpose (e.g., [4, 5]). Towards that, the concept of haptograms was presented to denote "a tactile symbol composed over a touchscreen, its dynamic nature referring to the act of writing or drawing" [6, 7]. That is, a haptogram, as developed within SUITCEYES, is a tactile symbol or a meaning-bearing synthetically generated haptic pattern to be communicated as stimuli to the human body. The system of patterns, or the haptogram vocabulary developed within that project were inspired by, and emulated, the Social Haptic Communication system. Social Haptic Communication (SHC) consists of hand gestures made on appropriate body parts of the receiver, such as the back or arms, to convey meaningful messages. The decision to emulate SHC was based on the familiarity of that system for many potential users, eliminating the need to learn a new language or mode of communication (Fig. 1).

 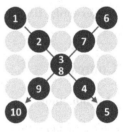

Fig. 1. (**a**) The hand gesture for the word "danger" in SHC. (**b**) The Haptogram for the word "danger".

A major consideration in design of haptograms was perceptibility of haptic messages and the placement of vibrotactile stimulation based on the guidelines resulting from psychophysical experiments (e.g., [8, 9]). Other constraints were also considered including wire-management, flexibility for user preferences, similarity between haptograms, or the number of frames in each haptogram, and more. The patterns that can be created with the help of the HaptiDesigner toolkit, however, are not limited by those constraints or any specific set of rules; HaptiDesigner can be used to create any pattern based on the needs or imagination of the designer. Furthermore, HaptiDesigner is not limited to activation of vibrotactile actuation motors; it can also be used for designing patterns of activation of units such as LED lamps, or other devices. However, while multiple

PCBs can be daisy-chained for an extended number of channels, the number of actuation motors that can be activated remain restricted by the level of power supply, issue of latency, and practical wire management. The presented interface is therefore currently designed to enable activation of a maximum of 96 actuator motors. For an extended number of actuators, further experiments with connecting a larger set of HaptiBoards will be needed. In SHC, variables such as pressure or lightness of touch, or the speed of movement are important in conveying a message depicting nuances in the meaning. Similarly, in actuator based haptic communication elements such as speed and intensify play a role (e.g., see [10]) and need to be adjustable based on user needs and preferences. HaptiDesigner is therefore developed to fully support such design considerations.

1.3   Related Work

We argue that HaptiDesigner has the potential of being a useful tool for many. This claim is based on the steady rise in the number of research in the area as indicated by a simple search on the term "haptic*" in indexed databases. For example, a search for this term on Google Scholar returns over 400,000 hits. The same search in the Web of Science database (WoS) returns a more modest number of just over 23,250 hits and an examination of publication patterns in this set (Fig. 2) indicates that publications on the topic have appeared as far back as 1922, to then continue in modest numbers (<20 per year) until the 1990s. From then on, the number of publications has steadily risen (with temporary dips in 2010–2012) until 2019, with 1714 publications in that year. Slightly lower numbers are, however, reported again for 2020 (which may be due to the pandemic and lack of ability to conduct tests that involve human subjects in close proximity). What the total number of publications will be for the year 2021 will be fully known in the early months of 2022.

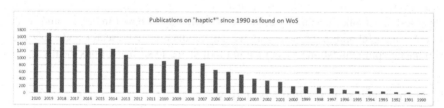

Fig. 2. An overview of publication trends related to the term "haptic*" as found in WoS in December 2021.

This trend indicates a steady interest in haptics-related research, where the value of skin's receptors in capturing information and interaction with the surrounding is acknowledged and touch as a medium for communication is of core interest. Many of these publications explore various modes of stimuli (e.g., mechanical, electrical, thermal) and modalities (e.g., vibration, pressure) to stimulate skin receptors by implementing various actuating devices.

In an overview paper on tactile displays, [11] provides information about skin physiology including receptors and modalities of the skin, as well as related devices that exploit modalities of the skin's sensors. In a related paper, while critiquing traditional tactile displays that use large size actuators [12] present a microelectromechanical system as tactile display that conveys tactile sensations to users.

Various methods of stimulations are also explored, e.g., in soft wearables [13], audio-haptic feedback in mobile phones [14], bracelets and haptic feedback to forearm [15, 16], belts [17, 18] or various types of vests (e.g., [19]). Many of these explore various types of actuators and actuator-based interfaces as tactile displays in a variety of different areas [20]. For example, in an interactive setting [3] presents, among others, both a vibrotactile vest, also vibrotactile patterns as a form of vibrotactile language to convey information to the wearer in a playful way. Even [21] describes two vests as torso-based haptic displays to be used for presentation of navigational cues to a human operator, concluding that these systems produce useable tactile inputs to provide directional information. Further related works by this team of researchers also present development of an actuator [22] and a wirelessly controlled tactile display [23]. A further vest that is intended to be used as a haptic interface for situational awareness is presented in [24]. The intention is to create an intuitive and safer route guidance alternative, improving road safety for motorcyclists. Actuator based haptic stimuli is also used to reduce stress and anxiety [25].

In such studies, not only is there a need for hardware and controller boards, there is also a need for means of encoding the different actuation sequences, hence re-inventing the wheel from scratch in each project. While there are papers that describe the hardware and software components developed by the authors (e.g., [26, 27]) detailed descriptions of systems similar HaptiDesigner are not that common.

In this paper we present the use of haptograms to convey meaningful messages. Even other haptic messaging systems [28, 29] exist, all of which would similarly require tools for designing and testing the encoded symbols. Again, there is a lack of papers that present the systems that are developed for designing haptic symbols and messages, the hardware required, or the codes for activation of actuators. We, therefore, present the HaptiDesigner toolkit (including a couple of PCBs, a PC-based interface, and related codes) as a useful option for those who wish to conduct related research and experiment with haptic communication without having to first create such solutions locally[1].

2 HaptiDesigner Toolkit Overview

The HaptiDesigner Toolkit consists of a database or a Haptogram Library, the HaptiDesigner software, a number of HaptiBoards and a set of vibration motors. These components are presented in the Fig. 3.

---

[1] HaptiDesigner toolkit is currently being revised for improved functionality and user-friendliness. The updated version will become available online in due course. Information about this will be published on the SUITCEYES website when ready: https://suitceyes.eu/.

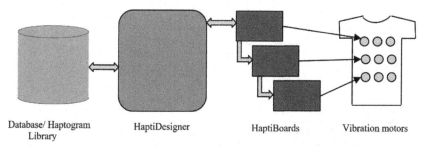

Database/ Haptogram   HaptiDesigner   HaptiBoards   Vibration motors
Library

Fig. 3. An overview of the different components in the HaptiDesigner Toolkit

The HaptiDesigner is a PC application that allows the user to create or modify haptograms and store them in the database (haptogram library). The application is intuitive to use and has several unique features to support designing new, or modifying existing haptograms, e.g., simulation, activation of multiple nodes simultaneously, or recurrent inclusion of the same node on multiple times in the same haptogram.

The database stores information about the haptograms so that they can be reused when needed. The details are saved as an XML file which can be edited by a standard text editor if required. In addition to the features that enable intuitive use of the toolkit, without the need for any coding, there are a number of extra features that can be further customized through modification of the XML codes directly in the application. These features include adding new templates, modifying background colours or nodes (to group them into more intuitive sections) and modifying which nodes are connected to which channels.

The hardware part is a custom-designed board, HaptiBoard, to which e.g., the vibration motors are connected. The board is controlled by the HaptiDesigner application using USB communication. The following sections provide further details; we first describe how the HaptiDesigner works and then describe the hardware and software components in more details.

2.1 HaptiDesigner Interface

The HaptiDesigner interface provides a number of features for creation and management of haptograms and respective libraries. Initially, when the application is invoked for the first time, the haptogram library is empty; as new haptograms are created, these are added to the library. The empty interface, before use, is shown in Fig. 4. The application window is divided in different areas including spaces for (i) the name of the library; (ii) application menu; (iii) action buttons related to the haptogram list; (iv) a list of haptograms stored in the library; and (v) the area that is used for editing individual haptograms. A new library is named *Untitled* until saved, and while editing, if the library contains changes that have not yet been saved, the library name precedes with an asterisk. In subsequent use, the HaptiDesigner always loads the last used haptogram library if found. The actual shape and size of the HaptiDesigner interface is flexible as the borders can be dragged to achieve the desired format.

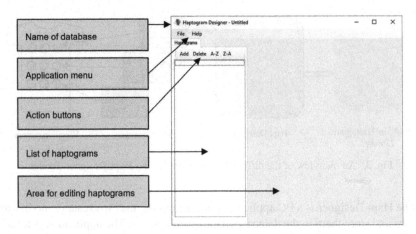

Fig. 4. Sub-areas included in the HaptiDesigner interface

Application Menu – The menu bar is located at the top of the application window and the available options are listed in Table 1. Under the menu option *File*, one can create a new database, open an existing database, save, save as, and exit the toolkit. The menu option *Help* provides further information about the HaptiDesigner toolkit.

Table 1. List of menu options available in the HaptiDesigner interface.

Menu option	Description
File – New database	Creates a new and empty database / haptic library.
File – Open	Opens a previously saved library.
File – Save	Saves the current library. (If the library has not been saved before, the application will ask the user of a filename.)
File – Save as	Allows saving the current library under a different name.
File – Exit	Exits the application. If there are unsaved changes, it will issue a notification asking if the user wishes to save the library before exiting.
Help – Version history	Opens a separate dialog window for version information that also provides a list of updates in each version.
Help - About	Opens a separate dialog window with further information about the application and its background and license.

Action Buttons – The action buttons are used for interaction with the haptogram library. The options here allow the user to create a new haptogram (Add), delete an existing haptogram (Delete), and sort the list of existing haptograms in ascending (A–Z) or descending (Z–A) alphabetical orders.

The *Add* option allows the user to create a new haptogram. By pressing the *Add* button a dialog box (Fig. 5 the upper image) appears that allows the user to define a (unique) name for the new haptogram. The dialog box also provides access to a set of predefined default grid-sizes to choose from. The grid-sizes currently available in the interface are 3 × 3, 4 × 4, 5 × 5, 6 × 6, and 8 × 12 (Fig. 5 lower images), however, additional grid-sizes can be added through modifications in the toolkit's main XML file.

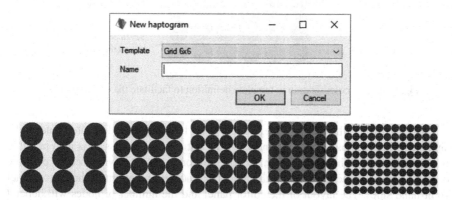

Fig. 5. The function for adding a new haptogram to the library. Top: the dialog window where the user is able to name the haptogram and choose among pre-defined grid-size templates. Bottom: Currently available predefined grid-size options (3 × 3, 4 × 4, 5 × 5, 6 × 6, and 8 × 12).

Each of the nodes in the grid (represented as circles in the editor panel), corresponds with one channel. The idea is not, however, to create a display screen with this number of nodes on one screen, rather, the designer will make the decision about the location of each corresponding actuator. The users may choose to utilize a colourization scheme to facilitate mapping of the nodes to related channels. As an example, in common experiments by us, a set of 5 × 5 actuators was placed on the back, a set of 2 actuators on each shoulder, and 7 actuators were placed around the waste. Therefore, the haptograms that utilised this placement specification were designed by using a 6 × 6 grid template. For this, the 6 × 6 grid template was designed with a grey background marking the 5 × 5 nodes that were to be placed on the back to facilitate recognition in the design process (Fig. 6). Similar colourizations and additional templates can be crated in the XML file to hold useful mapping information and correspondence with related channels.

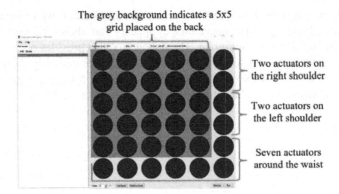

Fig. 6. Use of colourization in template definition to facilitate the design process.

Once a name for a haptogram is registered, it will be listed in the dedicated space (left-hand side). New items are placed on top of the list for easy access. It is also possible to sort the list in alphabetical order. By clicking on a name, it will become possible to design, or subsequently modify, the associated actuation pattern in the editor panel (right-hand side). The layout of the editor panel and the number of nodes will depend on the template chosen when registering the name. Figure 7, illustrates the creation of a haptogram that uses the 5 × 5 grid template.

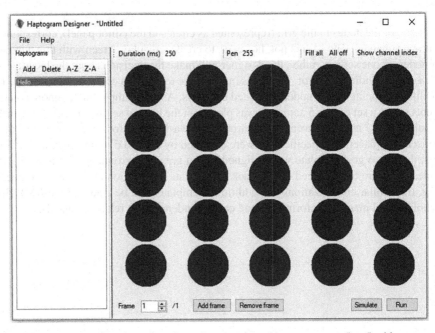

Fig. 7. HaptiDesigner interface when creating a haptogram on a 5 × 5 grid.

Table 2. HaptiDesigner interface's functions and features.

Name	Description
Duration	The duration for each frame is set by this option in terms of milliseconds, e.g., for one second delay, 1000 is entered.
Pen	Actuation intensity for each node is set by the pen option. The intensity can be between 0 (channel off) and 255 (maximum intensity). As well as the ability to set up the desired intensity by the pen option, one can also choose from a set of pre-defined intensity options (Off, Low (100), Middle (128) and Max (255)) by right-clicking on a node.
Fill all	Automatically enters the current pen intensity for all nodes (including those that already have another value)
All off	Automatically sets all nodes to 0 (including those that already have another value)
Show channel index	Shows the relationship between the node and the channel to help the user to keep an overview of the associations between each node and their decided placement. Normally node 0 corresponds to channel 0, node 1 to channel 1 and so on, but this can be overridden in the haptogram library.
Frame	The frame counter lists the current frame number and the total number of frames in the actual haptogram. Users can switch between frames using the up- and down buttons in the textbox or enter the requested frame number directly in the box and press enter.
Add frame	Pressing on this option will add a new empty frame at the current position
Remove frame	The current frame is removed.
Simulate	Opens a separate window that allows the user to simulate the current haptogram on the computer screen in real time. No connected hardware is required to simulate a haptogram. On the simulation screen, a status bar provides information about the cu rrent frame being displayed as well as the duration.
Run	Runs the current haptogram on real hardware and opens up the Run dialog window. A correct serial port is selected. A Scan button is available that helps scan for available ports. There is a Stop button if the user chooses to stop a haptogram from running before conclusion. A log window provides the user the information sent between the application and the hardware. Any errors during the playback will be displayed, as will other potential error messages, e.g., if hardware is not found or the selected serial port is wrong.

A haptogram consists of one or more frames. Each frame refers to activation of one or more nodes, sequentially, simultaneously, or both. In the editor mode, one can easily define the desirable pattern of actuation for each haptogram. Here, one can define (i) the nodes to be activated, (ii) the order of their activation, (iii) the intensity, (iv) the duration of each activation, (v) the duration of pause in between each activation, and (vi) whether the order of activation is sequential or simultaneous or both. One can create new haptograms or frames or choose to modify an existing haptogram by making adjustments directly in some of the frames as desired. By defining and adding each new haptogram, the haptogram vocabulary or entries in the haptogram library grows. The defined haptograms can also be deleted if one so chooses. Towards these, the editor panel provides a number of functions and features as listed and described in Table 2 to support the user in creating haptograms.

2.2 Implementation

Two PCBs have been developed to offer 32 channels (Fig. 8, Left) and 40 channels (Fig. 8, Right) respectively. Each channel can control one actuator motor. To enable activation of an even larger set of actuator motors, it is possible to daisy chain a number of these boards together (Fig. 9), e.g., the 32-channel board × 2, or 3 (etc.) achieving 64, or 96 channels respectively. The number of connected boards is only limited by the power supply and the timing requirements.

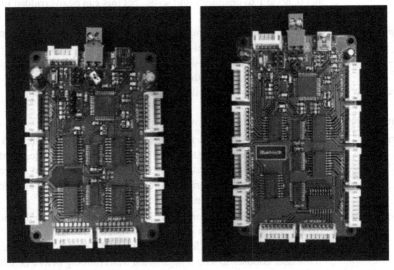

Fig. 8. PCBs created as part of the HaptiDesigner Toolkit. Left: the 32-channel board. Right: the 42-channel board.

In a daisy chained case, it is fully possible to mix 32ch and 40ch boards together.

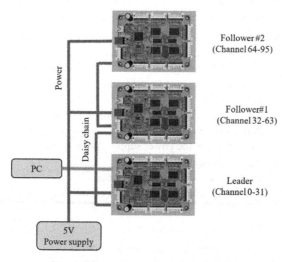

Fig. 9. Daisy chaining multiple boards

On the board there are 5 LEDs (Fig. 10) that indicate different status of the board (Tables 3 and 4):

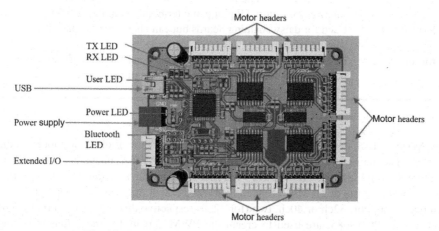

Fig. 10. LED indicators and the connectors on the board.

Table 3. LED indicator functions and descriptions.

LED	Function
TX LED	Blinks when board transmits to the USB port
RX LED	Blinks when the board receives from the USB port.
User LED	Standard Arduino LED is currently not used. Can be controlled from firmware.
Power LED	Turns on when the power supply is connected.
Bluetooth LED	Indicates Bluetooth status blinking→ waiting on connection solid on→ communication link established

Table 4. Connector descriptions.

Connector	Function
USB	Standard mini-USB connector for communicating with host. Max 500 mA (protected by a poly-fuse)
Power supply	Main power supply supports both all-motor-headers and microcontroller. Max +5V and note polarity when inserting cable. Mating connector: TE pluggable terminal block P/N 284506-2
Extend I/O	Used for daisy chaining boards but can also serve as spare I/Os Mating connector: 6 ways JST PH series
Motor headers	Each header supports 4 motors. The exact number of headers depends on the number of support channels of the board. Mating connector: 8 ways JST PH series

System block description - Fig. 11 provides an overview of different blocks in the system. The main controller of the board is a Microchip AVR ATmega32U4. This MCU features 32 KB Flash, 2.5 KB SRAM, 1 KB EEPROM and an integrated USB controller. It is clocked to run at 16 MHz. Since the ATMega32U4 does not have enough PWM outputs to support 32ch or 40ch, two (for 32ch) respective three (40ch) external PWM generators, PCA9685, are used to create the PWM signals for the actuators. Using PWM the intensity of the actuator can be controlled stepless. The PWM frequency is approximately 1500 Hz, limited by the PCA9685 IC. The main controller communicates with the PCA9685 using I2C and the PCA9685s on the board have a unique I2C address. The PWM signals from the PCA9685 IC are connected to an 8-channel DMOS transistor array, TBD62083. The DMOS driver is rated to approximately 400 mA per channel.

The board supports power through the USB connector or an external power supply. The power supply can be selected using a jumper on the board. Note that using a USB connector restricts the maximum output to 500 mA by poly-fuse to protect the feeding device e.g., the computer. It is however recommended to ensure that the current is below 500 mA when supplying the board through the USB connector. There is no voltage regulator onboard and the outputs as well as the electronics are directly fed from the power supply. The power supply must therefore not exceed 5 V.

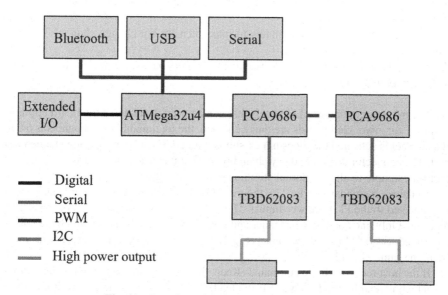

Fig. 11. Overview of different blocks in the system

The board supports several ways of communicating to a host: for USB connector, the board will be registered as a serial port on the host; for serial communication, it is possible to communicate directly with the MCU using a standard serial line communication; for Bluetooth communication, a HC-06 module is used. The Bluetooth is configured to act as a follower node and will be seen as a virtual serial port by the host. The default device name of the Bluetooth module is HC-06.

The protocol used for communication is a pure text format, making it easy to develop unique applications for the board. It is designed to be compact, fast, and yet readable for developers. The standard setup is 9600 baud, 8N1 for all communication variants (USB, Bluetooth, daisy chained bus and direct serial port communication). As a failsafe mechanism, if no communication is detected for 2 s, all the outputs of the board are automatically deactivated. All messages sent from host to device are surrounded by opening and closing square brackets "[]". These are used by the board to detect start of message resp. end of message. The following commands are recognized by the board:

[V] – Returns the firmware version.
[K] – Keep alive (send from host to device to prevent the board to enter failsafe mode)
[L,…] – Motor control message

The L command is used to activate the channels. It takes a list of which channels to activate and the output intensity level. The intensity level can be a number between 0 (channel is turned off) to 255 (channel is fully turned on). The parameters are parsed from left to right. For example:

[L,1:255] => Set channel 1 motor to max intensity
[L,1:255,3:128] => Set channel 1 motor to max intensity, set channel 3 to half intensity
[L,1-5:255,3:128] => Set channel 1 to 5 motor to max intensity, set channel 3 to half intensity
[L,all:255,3:128] => Set all channels to max intensity but change channel 3 to half intensity
[L,all:0,10-12:255, 14-16:255] => Turn off all motors but set channel 10 to 12 and 14 to 16 to max intensity

The maximum number of channels that can be used depends on the board configuration. If e.g., two 32ch boards are daisy chained, the total number of channels is 64ch. If a channel is activated that does not exist it is ignored. Each board has an extended I/O port. The connector is used to daisy chain boards, but it can also be used as a regular I/O port for example to allow external stimulus to trigger patterns.

To daisy chain boards (Fig. 12), the pin LO (Leader Output) from the leader board is connected to the FI (Follower Input). The connection for each follower board is then repeated. Only one board can be leader and it is defined as the board to which the host is connected. Each follower then connects its LO to the next follower FI. All boards must share the same ground.

If the host receives the K-command (Keep alive) it is mirrored to the Leader Output pin which is read by the followers. If the leader receives a L-command (Motor control message) it is transformed to a F command before it is sent on the Leader Output. No other commands are not passed down the daisy chain. The F-command uses the same parameters as L command but with the number of supported channels added as the first parameter. This informs the follower what the virtual number of its first channel is, e.g., [F,32,all:0,2:255] (Table 5).

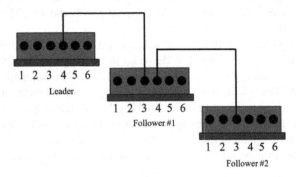

Fig. 12. Daisy chained boards

Table 5. Pin descriptions

Pin	Function
1	GND
2	IO1 (spare digital I/O)
3	FI (Follower Input)
4	LO (Leader output)
5	IO2 (spare digital I/O)
6	IO3 (spare digital I/O)

If a 32ch leader and a 32ch follower is daisy chained the first virtual channel for the follower will be 32. The leader controls channels 0 to 31 and the first virtual channel for the follower is 32. For the host to activate the first channel of the follower board, it will need to send the following command [L,32:255]. The host cannot read how many channels are available and the host can only use the L-command (the F command is completely handled by the board internally).

Fig. 13. Latency related to a message consisting of 14 characters

Regarding potential latency, numerous experiments have been conducted. The process in general is as follows, the leader passes on the message to its followers by manipulating the string received from the source. As the message is passed down in the daisy chain to every follower, a delay is also introduced in each follower. The delay is due to the need to parse the command from the leader or the previous follower, act on it and pass it to the next follower in the chain. The exact delay is heavily depending on the size of the message. In the example below (Fig. 13), with a message consisting of 14 characters, each follower will add a delay of approximately 15 ms. In a daisy chain with one leader and three followers, the final follower would therefor receive the command after 15 ms * 2, i.e. 30 ms. As the message gets more complex, for example 44 characters (Fig. 14), the number of characters that needs to be forward will increase and as such the delay will increase to 48 ms per follower.

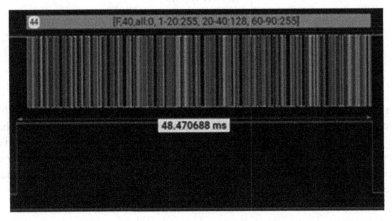

Fig. 14. Latency related to a message consisting of 44 characters

2.3 Firmware

The firmware (or embedded software) is written using the Arduino IDE. Its overall function is to supervise the serial ports for any incoming messages, parse the message and update the PWM output buffer. If the PWM output buffer differs from the previous buffer value, the PWM output buffer is sent to the PCA9685 drivers on the I2C bus. If no communication is detected for 2 s, it will disable all channels by updating the PWM output buffer to zero.

There are two variants of the firmware, one that supports 32 channels and the other 40ch. The number of support channels is defined in the file *pwm_outputbuffer.h* (Table 6).

As the number of hardware serial ports in the ATmega32U4 is limited to two, the daisy chain function uses a software simulated serial port.

Table 6. The firmware files

Filename	Function
suitceyes_40ch.ino	Make initial setup and contain the main loop
pca9586.cpp	Low level driver for the PCA9586 IC
pca9685.h	Header file for PCA9586 IC
pwm_outputbuffer.cpp	Keep the duty value for each channel on the board. Translate channel number to the specific output pin of the PCA9586 IC.
pwm_outputbuffer.h	Header file

3 Schematics and Components

Figures 15 and 16 provide an overview of the main controller and communication, and channel drivers respectively. The schematics show the 40ch variant. In the 32ch board the bottom driver and corresponding components are not mounted.

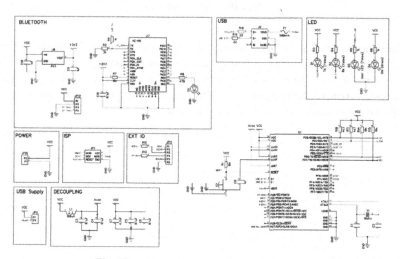

Fig. 15. Main controller and communication

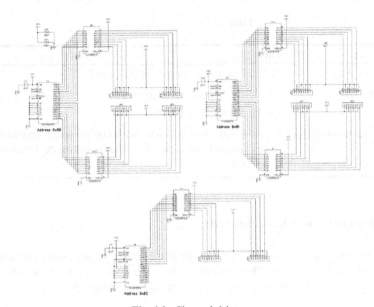

Fig. 16. Channel drivers

The components that are needed for these configurations are listed in the Table 7.

Due to space restriction in this article, GitHub is used to provide access to full details of the toolkit online including the related codes, schematics, and instructions (see: https://github.com/NasrineOlson/HaptiDesignerToolkit). Information on further improvements will also be made available as developments mature.

Table 7. Bill of materials

Ref	Value	Description
C1, C2	16pF	Load capacitors
C3, C4, C5, C6, C7, C11, C12, C19, C48	0.1uF	Decoupling capacitors
C8, C9, C10	1uF	
C46, C47	100uF	
Q1, Q2, Q4, Q33, Q34	ULN2803	Drivers
U1	ATMega32u4	MCU
U2, U3, U4	PCA9685	PWM circuits
U8	MCP1703-33	Voltage regulator for Bluetooth
Y1	16MHz	Crystal for ATMega32u4
U7	HC-06	Bluetooth module
S2	Micro switch	Reset button
L1	100uH	Inductor
R1, R7, R14, R15, R16	10k	
R18, R22	22	USB resistors
R2	2k	
R5, R6, R9	1k	
R10, R11	4k7	
R8	470	
F1	500mA polyfuse	For USB protection
JP1	6-pins 2.54mm	AVR ISP
JP2	2-pins 2.54mm	Jumper for selecting between USB power supply or external power supply
JP3, JP4, JP5, JP6, JP7, JP8, JP9, JP10, JP13, JP14	8-pins 2.0mm	Channel I/O
JP11	6-pins 2.0mm	External I/O
JP15	2-pins jackable plug 3.5mm	Main power supply
D1, D2, D3, D4, D5	LED	For misc. indications on board
J2	USB connector	

4   Known Limitations and Future Plans

The current version of the HaptiDesigner toolkit has a number of limitations. For example, since all commands are passed down in the daisy chain, each follower adds a small delay for processing the message before passing it to the next follower. Therefore, if too many boards are daisy chained, there can be latency issues. Furthermore, the PCB track of the board supports approximately 3 A. If there are certain channels that are always activated at the same time, it would be a good practice to ensure they are distributed across the TBD62083 ICs to avoid potential but unlikely heat related issues. Even so, we hope that this toolkit can be useful as a starting point for those who plan to experiment with haptic patterns. There are already a number of improvements planned including availability of the HaptiDesigner interface online, additional templates, sound-word-haptic conversations and more.

Acknowledgements. This work has been partially funded by the European Union's Horizon 2020 research and innovation programme under grant agreement No 780814 SUITCEYES.

References

1. Dijour, D., Krishnaprasad, A., Shei, I., Wong, E.: Haptic pattern exploration in an arm-mounted solenoid array. In: Stephanidis, C., Antona, M. (eds.) HCII 2020. CCIS, vol. 1224, pp. 213–222. Springer, Cham (2020). https://doi.org/10.1007/978-3-030-50726-8_28
2. Kelling, C., Pitaro, D., Rantala, J.: Good vibes: the impact of haptic patterns on stress levels. In: Proceedings of the 20th International Academic Mindtrek Conference, AcademicMindtrek 2016, pp. 130–136. ACM, New York, USA (2016)
3. Morrison, A., Manresa-Yee, C., Knoche, H., Jensen, W.: Vibrotactile and vibroacoustic communications: pairs in interaction and play—an interactive structure and bodies in an urban environment. Univ. Access Inf. Soc. **17**(3), 585–605 (2017)
4. Gay, J., et al.: Keep your distance: a playful haptic navigation wearable for individuals with deafblindness. In: The 22nd International ACM SIGACCESS Conference on Computers and Accessibility, ASSETS 2020, article 93, pp. 1–4. Association for Computing Machinery, New York, USA (2020)
5. Theil, A., et al.: Tactile board: a multimodal augmentative and alternative communication device for individuals with deafblindness. In: 19th International Conference on Mobile and Ubiquitous Multimedia, MUM 2020, pp. 223–228. Association for Computing Machinery, New York, USA (2020)
6. Darányi, S., et al.: Communicating semantic content to persons with deafblindness by haptograms and smart textiles: theoretical approach and methodology. Int. J. Adv. Intell. Syst. **13**(1 & 2), 103–113 (2020)
7. Darányi, S., Olson, N., Riga, M., Kontopoulos, E., Kompatsiaris, I.: Static and dynamic haptograms to communicate semantic content: towards enabling face-to-face communication for people with deafblindness. In: vor der Brück, T., Kontopoulos, S. (eds.) The 13th International Conference on Advances in Semantic Processing, SEMAPRO 2019, Porto, pp. 16–20. IARIA, Porto, Portugal (2019)
8. Plaisier, M.A., Sap, L.I.N., Kappers, A.M.L.: Perception of vibrotactile distance on the back. Sci. Rep. **10**, 17876 (2020)
9. Kappers, A.M.L., Bay, J., Plaisier, M.A.: Perception of vibratory direction on the back. In: Nisky, I., Hartcher-O'Brien, J., Wiertlewski, M., Smeets, J. (eds.) EuroHaptics 2020. LNCS, vol. 12272, pp. 113–121. Springer, Cham (2020). https://doi.org/10.1007/978-3-030-58147-3_13
10. Ying, Z., Morrell, J.B.: Haptic actuator design parameters that influence affect and attention. In: 2012 IEEE Haptics Symposium (HAPTICS), pp.463–470. IEEE (2012)
11. Chouvardas, V.G., Miliou, A.N., Hatalis, M.K.: Tactile displays: overview and recent advances. Displays **29**(3), 185–194 (2008)
12. Ishizuka, H., Miki, N.: MEMS-based tactile displays. Displays **37**, 25–32 (2015)

13. Koo, I.M., Jung, K., Koo, J.C., Nam, J.-D., Lee, Y.K., Choi, H.R.: Development of soft-actuator-based wearable tactile display. IEEE Trans. Rob. **24**(3), 549–558 (2008)
14. Chang, A., O'Sullivan, C.: Audio-haptic feedback in mobile phones. In: CHI 2005 Extended Abstracts on Human Factors in Computing Systems, CHI EA 2005, Portland, USA, pp. 1264–1267. ACM (2005)
15. Meli, L., Hussain, I., Aurilio, M., Malvezzi, M., O'Malley, M.K., Prattichizzo, D.: The hBracelet: a wearable haptic device for the distributed mechanotactile stimulation of the upper limb. IEEE Robot. Autom. Lett. **33**, 2198–2205 (2018)
16. Stanley, A.A., Kuchenbecker, K.J.: Design of body-grounded tactile actuators for playback of human physical contact. In: 2011 IEEE World Haptics Conference, pp. 563–568 (2011)
17. Golan, Y., Serota, B., Shapiro, A., Shriki, O., & Nisky, I.: A Vibrotactile Vest for Remote Human-Dog Communication. In: 2019 IEEE World Haptics Conference, pp. 556–561 (2019)
18. McDaniel, T., Krishna, S., Villanueva, D., Panchanathan, S.: A haptic belt for vibrotactile communication. In: 2010 IEEE International Symposium on Haptic Audio Visual Environments and Games, Phoenix, USA, pp. 1–2. IEEE (2010)
19. Garcia-Valle, G., Ferre, M., Brenosa, J., Vargas, D.: Evaluation of presence in virtual environments: haptic vest and user's haptic skills. IEEE Access **6**, 7224–7233 (2018)
20. Choi, S., Kuchenbecker, K.J.: Vibrotactile display: perception, technology, and applications. Proc. IEEE **101**(9), 2093–2104 (2013)
21. Jones, L. A., Nakamura, M., Lockyer, B.: Development of a tactile vest. In: 2004 12th International Symposium on Haptic Interfaces for Virtual Environment and Teleoperator Systems, Chicago, USA. IEEE (2004)
22. Nakamura, M., Jones, L.: An actuator for the tactile vest - a torso-based haptic device. In: 2003 Proceedings of the 11th Symposium on Haptic Interfaces for Virtual Environment and Teleoperator Systems, HAPTICS 2003, Los Alamitos, USA, pp. 333–339. IEEE (2003)
23. Jones, L.A., Lockyer, B., Piateski, E.: Tactile display and vibrotactile pattern recognition on the torso. Adv. Robot. **20**(12), 1359–1374 (2006)
24. Prasad, M., Taele, P., Goldberg, D., Hammond, T.: HaptiMoto: turn-by-turn haptic route guidance interface for motorcyclists. In: Proceedings of the SIGCHI Conference on Human Factors in Computing Systems, CHI 2014, pp. 3597–3606. ACM, New York, USA (2014)
25. Kelling, C., Pitaro, D., Rantala, J.: Good vibes: the impact of haptic patterns on stress levels. In: Proceedings of the 20th International Academic Mindtrek Conference, AcademicMindtrek 2016, pp. 130–136. ACM, New York, USA (2016). Paper presented at the Media-Business, Content, Management, and Services
26. Juan, W., Zhenzhong, S., Weixiong, W., Aiguo, S., Constantinescu, D.: Vibro-tactile system for image contour display. In: Jong-Il Park, J., Wan, W., Kajimoto, H., Nii.H. (eds.) IEEE International Symposium on VR Innovation, pp. 145–150. IEEE (2011)
27. Youngjae, K., Heesook, S., Minsoo, H.: A bidirectional haptic communication framework and an authoring tool for an instant messenger. In: 11th International Conference on Advanced Communication Technology, vol. 3, pp. 2050–2053. IEEE (2009)
28. Zhao, S., Israr, A., Lau, F., Abnousi, F.: Coding tactile symbols for phonemic communication. In: Proceedings of the 2018 CHI Conference on Human Factors in Computing Systems, CHI 2018, April 2018, paper no. 392, pp. 1–13. ACM, New York, USA (2018). Paper presented at the Conference on Human Factors in Computing Systems
29. Prasad, M., Russell, M., Hammond, T.A.: Designing vibrotactile codes to communicate verb phrases. ACM Trans. Multimed. Comput. Commun. Appl. **11**(1s), 1–21 (2014)

DRAM Performance Sensor

Jorge Semião[1,2]([✉]) [iD], Luís Santos[1], and Marcelino B. Santos[3] [iD]

[1] University of Algarve, Faro, Portugal
jsemiao@ualg.pt
[2] INESC-ID, Faro, Portugal
[3] IST-UL, INESC-ID, Silicongate, Lisbon, Portugal
marcelino.santos@tecnico.ulisboa.pt

Abstract. Human-machine environments require computers with capacity to store large amounts of data, and it's important that memories do not fail, otherwise it will jeopardize the Human-machine interface. Moreover, as battery operated devices are becoming widely used in everyday Human-Machine environments, it's also imperative to reduce power consumption in these devices. The present work presents a new DRAM performance sensor, to be used in DRAM memories of Human-Machine environments, especially in battery operated devices. Effects such as process variations (P), power-supply voltage variations (V), temperature variations (T) and aging (A) variations (PVTA – Process, Voltage, Temperature and Aging) are key parameters that affect chips performance and reliability. The new performance sensor for DRAM memories has the purpose to signalize when these PVTA variations, or any other parameter, change performance of the memory above a certain threshold limit, jeopardizing memory operation, signal integrity, and the Human-Machine system where it is used. Sensor's sensibility to PVTA variations can be changed in run-time, which allows the sensor to be tuned during circuit's life time. Another important feature is that it can be applied locally, to monitor the online operation of the memory, or globally, by monitoring a dummy memory in pre-defined conditions. These features allow the development of intelligent hardware to be used in Human-Machine systems which allow anticipating system failures and also improve power optimization. Moreover, as far as authors know, this is the first online performance sensor for DRAM memories.

Keywords: DRAM · Sensor · Performance · Aging · PVT variation

1 Introduction

Human-Machine Interaction (HMI) environments use hardware that is shrinking in sizes, and transistors are reaching limits that are near the atom sizes. This small sized hardware imposes the need to reduce power consumption, and as HMI applications increase in complexity, they push the hardware to continue increase circuit complexity and power density, making ways to reliability problems in the hardware. And this gets worse if we consider that semiconductor aging can cause unacceptable degradation in the devices, causing errors during product's lifetime. These issues pave the way for considering today's systems to be manufactured with embedded features, not only to improve error

© The Author(s), under exclusive license to Springer Nature Switzerland AG 2022
M. Antona and C. Stephanidis (Eds.): HCII 2022, LNCS 13308, pp. 510–521, 2022.
https://doi.org/10.1007/978-3-031-05028-2_34

detection, but also to monitor circuit operation and performance, and to predict some errors before they happen.

Systems-on-a-Chip (SoCs) and CMOS circuits' performance is sensitive to parametric variations, such as Process, power-supply Voltage and Temperature (PVT) [2], as well as aging effects (PVT and Aging – PVTA). CMOS circuits' aging degradation is mainly caused by the following effects: Bias Temperature Instability (BTI), Hot-Carrier Injection (HCI), Electromigration (EM) and Time Dependent Dielectric Breakdown (TDDB) [3]. The most relevant aging effect is the BTI, namely the Negative Bias Temperature Instability (NBTI), which affects PMOS MOSFET transistors, and the Positive Bias Temperature Instability (PBTI), which affects NMOS transistors [4]. These effects degrade digital circuits' performance over time, increasing the variability in CMOS circuits. Performance degradation decrease the switching speed, eroding time margins and leading to potential delay faults, and eventually chip failures.

As today's SoC face an increasing need to store more and more information produced in HMI, memories occupy most of the SoC silicon area, being currently about 90% of the SoC density [5]. Therefore, the robustness of memories is considered crucial to guarantee the reliability of HMI.

In the past, significant research has been carried out on PVTA degradations on circuits, and a set of performance sensors for digital logic circuits were proposed, either in the design style of a cell library in custom SoCs or in an FPGA programmable fabric (see, for example, [6, 7, 9]). However, research on performance sensors for semiconductor memories has been much more limited, so far. We recognize that there is a lot of previous research dealing with aging sensors for SRAM cells, and especially focused on the BTI effect. These are attempts to increase reliability in the operation of memories. However, they do not simultaneously consider variations in PVT and aging, and more importantly, very few works are focused on DRAM memories, when compared with SRAM. Therefore, considering PVTA in memory circuits, previous works deal mainly with the detection of aging in SRAMs, but there is a lack on a simple generic sensor to deal with the performance and, simultaneously, PVTA variations in memories.

Moreover, research on performance sensors for digital synchronous logic is much more advanced when compared to its memory counterparts. As an example, the Scout Flip-Flop sensor [6, 10] acts as a performance sensor for tolerance and predictive detection of delay faults in synchronous digital circuits (ASIC). However, sensors for memories (DRAM or SRAM) that can identify abnormal time response, regardless of their origin, are still limited. In fact, as far as the authors know, there are only two previous works on performance sensors [1, 8], which are an initial attempt by the authors to develop a performance sensor for SRAM. Unfortunately, the sensor architecture proposed in [8], is complex and leads to a significant area overhead, and the performance of the sensor is limited in the presence of reduced VDD voltages. Moreover, the sensor proposed in [1], although it solves part of the referred problems, it still has implementation problems that prohibit its use in a real memory circuit. In addition, for DRAM circuits, as far as the authors know, there are no solutions available for performance sensors.

The main purpose of this work is to develop a new online performance sensor for DRAM circuits used in HMI. The performance sensor, compatible with PVTA variations, should allow to detect delay degradations when accessing CMOS DRAM cells, namely in read/write operations. The sensor must be connected to the memory bit line, to monitor transitions that occurred in these signals during these read/write operations. It should monitor any online performance variation with a very low performance overhead and reasonable area overhead.

2   The DRAM Performance Sensor

Process, power-supply voltage, temperature and aging (PVTA) variations are main conditioning factors in the design of technology nowadays [11, 12]. Given the PVTA variation problems in memories, these will naturally be reflected in the processing of data that are in bit lines. Therefore, as we want our sensor to be able to monitor the information from all the processing problems which may exist at the moment, we use the bit lines as the place to monitor memory performance. The problems that most of PVTA variations places in the memory components are, ultimately, reflected in the speed with which transition occur in the bit lines, which means that the slower these transitions are, the greater the probability of an error occurrence, or it means that an error is in the eminence to occur, and our sensor will be able to detect it. Working online, the sensor will monitor bit line transitions and analyze its delays to detect performance degradations in the memory, which reflects a PVTA variation and may cause an error. The purpose is to avoid error occurrence by detecting errors predictively, or predicting the eminence of an error.

2.1   DRAM Cell

DRAM cells have been tested and studied over the years to achieve the best possible implementation. In this work, the DRAM cell used as case-study is presented in Fig. 1, which is the standard DRAM memory cell. This cell is made up with one single NMOS transistor, called an access transistor, and a Cs capacitor that will store the voltage value that should be kept safe, and which needs the periodic refreshment characteristic of DRAM memories. This cell is known as one-transistor cell, in which the transistor gate is connected to the Word line and the drain to the bit line, so that when active it is able to charge the Cs capacitor, which is loaded to VDD if the purpose is to save a 1, or to the VSS if it is to save a 0. In a DRAM, only one bit line is used, unlike in an SRAM, which always use two, one being the complement to the other. Another interesting feature in the DRAM is that the Cs capacitor discharges over time, making it necessary to refresh the memory periodically, so that the stored value is kept. During this update, the value saved is read and rewritten, but with the maximum voltage concerning the bit stored in the Cs capacitor (VDD or VSS). Anyway, regardless of the DRAM cell used, sense amplifier, or memory architecture, the performance sensor that will be presented in the following section is only connected to the bit lines, which means that its operation is independent of the DRAM cell, or even the Sense Amplifier circuitry used.

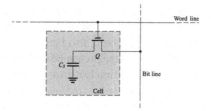

Fig. 1. DRAM memory cell [13].

2.2 Sensor Architecture

The sensor which will be presented in this section has the purpose to alert the user for performance variation problems. It will not alert which problem happened, or which PVTA variation occurred (or any other), but it will give a warning that something is affecting the performance of the memory and, with this, it triggers an alert or some corrective measures (e.g., changing power-supply voltage, refresh rate, etc.).

As depicted in Fig. 2, the DRAM performance sensor is connected to the bit lines of the memory and consists of 4 main blocks: the Transition Detector, the Pulse Detector, the Comparator and the Controller. The following sections will explain in detail how each block works and their architecture.

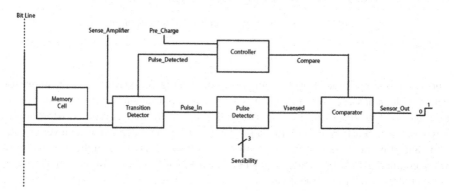

Fig. 2. SRAM performance sensor block diagram.

1) **Transition Detector**

When a memory is being read/write, there are changes in its bit lines signals. The purpose of the Transition Detector is to detect those signal transitions in the bit lines, in order to be able to generate a pulsed signal, with the pulse width being proportional to the delay of the bit line signal transition, which will be used in the reminding parts of the sensor. According to the memory performance status, the transition speed of the bit lines from low-to-high and from high-to-low has a tendency of becoming slower when the memory ages, or generally when a PVTA degradation occurs.

In this work, we consider that in the DRAM reading/writing operations, the bit lines are initialized at VDD/2 value. Nevertheless, with small changes in the transition detector architecture, this could also be used with an SRAM, even for a VDD initialization value. The advantage presented in this work is that, regardless of the implementation type of the Transition Detector chosen, the circuit onwards will always be the same.

Some memory implementations use in the bit lines a pre-charge value different than VDD, i.e., the initialization of the bit lines, prior to a read/write operation, is made with a value that is not VDD. For instance, in a DRAM memory (and in this work), the bit lines' initialization is made to VDD/2, making the transition to VDD or VSS powered by the sense amplifier, to be faster and with smaller amplitude in volts. This is a constraint that may require a specific transition detector implementation, and this is needed for DRAMs, but also for SRAMs, or any other memory initialized at VDD/2.

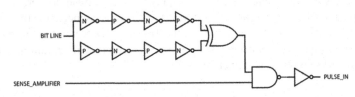

Fig. 3. Transition detector architecture for one bit line.

The structure for the transition detector is presented in Fig. 3. As we can see, the transistor detector block has a set of p-type and n-type inverters, placed alternately along two paths (one for each bit line), and in the upper path the first inverter is type N, while in the lower other path is type P. Note that a p-type inverter is here defined as an inverter with unbalanced n and p transistors, but with the p transistor having a higher conductivity when compared with the n transistor, which means that its output will rise quickly when compared to its fall transition. In the same way, an n-type inverter has a more conductive n transistor, when compared with the p transistor, meaning that when a signal switches in the bit line from 0 to 1 (this will put on the n transistor of the inverter), n-type inverters will process that signal faster than p-type inverters (if a 1 to 0 transition occurs in the bit line, the opposite will occur). Consequently, as the different inverters are placed alternately along the paths, one path is always faster than the other. To create these unbalanced inverters, and comparing their implementation with a balanced inverter (with similar conductive transistors), the highly conductive transistor has a channel that is 5 times bigger than the minimum size used in the balanced inverter (please refer to Table 1, for transistors' size). In turn, these 2 inverter paths are connected to an XOR gate, which works by outputting a logical value "1" when the input signals are different, and the logical value "0" when the input values are equal. Since we have one of the paths faster than the other (one is faster for the low-to-high transition, while the other is faster for the high-to-low transition), this will cause the XOR gate to have a period of time in which both input lines are with a different logic value, causing the output of this XOR gate to be activated during a period of time proportional to the bit line transition delay. This will create a pulse at the output of the XOR gate. At the output, there is an AND gate, connected to an input signal that comes from the Sense_Amplifier, and this is to control the transitions that should be monitored, as the pre-charge of the bit lines could also generate transitions on the bit lines, creating false pulses in the transition detector and jeopardizing sensor operation.

Table 1. Transition detector transistors' size

Inverter	Nmos	Pmos	L	V_{th_n}	V_{t_p}
Type N	5*WNmin	WPmin	65n	0.423 V	−0.365 V
Type P	WNmin	5*WPmin			

2) **Pulse Detector**

The Pulse Detector will receive the information that comes from the Transition Detector (a pulse) and convert it to a DC voltage value (Vsensed, in Fig. 4), proportional to the pulse width. In a simple manner, its operation is based on receiving the pulse from the Transition Detector and charging a capacitor with a voltage level proportional to the pulse width.

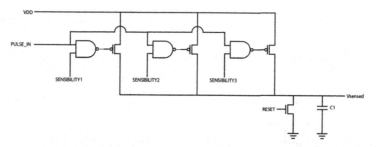

Fig. 4. Pulse detector architecture.

The Pulse Detector presented here (Fig. 4) includes the possibility to change sensor's sensibility during online operation, which allows tuning the sensor according to the specific memory that is being monitored and its operating conditions, or to perform sensor calibration procedures during its life-span. To implement this feature, the Pulse Detector has 3 NAND gates controlling 3 PMOS transistors (with different sizes), which makes it possible to change sensor's sensitivity by changing the current that will charge C1 capacitor. This is carried out through a 3-wire input signal, SENSIBILITY, which allows C1 capacitor to be charged quicker or slower, according with the required sensor's sensitivity, with 7 different sensibility levels (note that if more sensibility levels are required, more bits can be used, controlling additional NAND gates and PMOS transistors). The voltage in capacitor C1 (Vsensed) will represent a sensed voltage obtained from the bit line transition, i.e., a DC voltage proportional to the bit line transition delay. This sensed voltage (Vsensed) stored in C1 should be compared with a reference voltage (Vref) in the Comparator block. The sensed voltage must be calibrated for the "decision" to be made when the sensor should consider a bit line transition as an error or as a success. There is also the possibility of calibrating the Pulse Detector through a change in the capacity of the C1 transistor, since changing its capacity it will also change its charged voltage. Therefore, sensor's sensibility could also be implemented by controlling the connection of several capacitors in parallel, but this approach would require higher silicon area, when compared with the used approach.

3) **Comparator**

It is extremely important to be able to create a reference value that will serve as a basis for comparison with the value stored in the Pulse Detector's C1 capacitor and, thus, be able to know whether the sensor is facing a performance error or not. This reference circuit consists of a small circuit designed in order to, presumably, age more than the memory. This higher aging degradation will assure that the sensibility of the sensor is higher when aging conditions are worse. As it may be seen in Fig. 5, the reference value placed in the output is controlled by the threshold voltage of the NMOS transistor (Vref = VDD-V_{TH}), which is always in a stress-mode condition and charging the C2 capacitor. The Vref output will have VDD-V_{TH}, thus causing our reference value to be slightly below VDD.

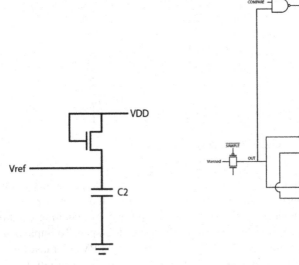

Fig. 5. Reference voltage.   **Fig. 6.** Comparator architecture.

The Signal Comparator presented in Fig. 6 has the purposed to amplify the differences between Vsensed and Vref voltages, triggering the values to the extreme Low/High voltages, VSS/VDD. This means that the signals Vsensed and Vref will be sampled through the transmission gates, activated by the Sample signal, and these sample voltages will be compared and amplified just like a sense amplifier does, when reading a memory cell. This is done by activating the Compare signal, causing the two cross-coupled inverters to be turned on. So, using the cross-coupled inverters to amplify the differences between Vsensed and Vref voltages that were sampled through the transmission gates, the amplifier works as a comparator, by identifying the weakest and the strongest signal and forcing the weakest value to go to VSS and the strongest value to VDD, thus remaining at each other's extreme value and generating a result.

In Fig. 6 it is possible to see the flip-flop and two NAND gates at the output, with the purpose to retain an active OUT signal at the sensor output port (Sensor_Out). This is important so that a predictive error detection occurrence can be interpreted in the following clock cycles, and corrective actions can take place. In this implementation, a predictive error detection will remain active at the output until a new sensor monitoring takes place, by resetting the sensor (and the flip-flop) with the Reset signal.

4) **Controller and Sensor Operation**

For the correct operation of the entire sensor, there was the need to implement a sensor controller, i.e., a Finite State Machine (FSM) which receives some input signals and generates the control signals for the remaining blocks, in order to control all sensor operation. In Fig. 7 it is possible to see the state diagram implemented in the FSM. It consists of 3 main states, Reset, Sample and Compare, as it will be explained ahead.

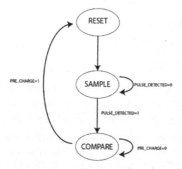

Fig. 7. FSM state diagram for controller block.

The Reset state's purpose is to reset the entire sensor operation to an initial state, ensuring that the values in the capacitors and main nodes are discharged and having the necessary values for the correct operation of the sensor, not misleading the measurements that will be made. This state is executed in a single clock cycle.

The Sample state purpose is to place the FSM waiting for a transition to happen in the bit line. When it occurs, it will generate a pulse, and the FSM will change to the Compare state. To implement this behavior, an auxiliary variable holds the state machine in the Sample state until this pulse is detected (Pulse_detected = 0). When a new pulse is detected, the FSM will move on to the following state (Pulse_detected = 1).

The Compare state is where the comparator is activated, in order to compare the value stored in the C1 capacitor and the reference value, to make the decision whether the measured pulse is an error or a successful reading. This state activates the Compare signal, which enables the comparator to perform the comparison between Vsensed and Vref signals by powering the two cross-coupled inverters. The FSM will remain in this state, until a new Read/Write of the memory occurs. Therefore, prior to a Read/Write operation, there is a pre-charge signal to trigger the initialization of the bit lines, and this pre-charge signal indicates that a new Read/Write operation will take place. So, this signal is also used in the Compare state, to trigger a state change to the Reset state, to prepare the sensor for a new monitoring procedure. While there is no pre-charge signal activation, and consequently no new Read/Write operation, the FSM remains in the Compare state.

3   Layout and Simulation Results

To ascertain sensor design robustness, it is important to test sensor's behavior in a complete memory circuit, in order to apply the correct stimuli to the sensor and to test it in a real situation. Therefore, the sensor was deployed and connected to the bit line of a DRAM cell. The test environment includes the sensor, a DRAM memory cell (one transistor cell) and all of its peripheral circuitry, namely the sense amplifier, the pre-charge and the equalizer circuit. A 65nm CMOS technology, using Berkeley's Predictive Technology Models to simulate the behavior in HSPICE, was used in simulations. Nominal values are: T = 27 °C; VDD = 1.1 V; Aging degradations are induced by increasing |Vth| value on all transistors (p and n).

3.1   Transition Detector Results

To test the transition detector effectiveness, several transition delays were used to simulate different bit line transitions, low-to-high and high-to-low, to demonstrate that the Transition Detector would generate a different pulse width for each transition (i.e., the higher transition times in the bit line produce longer pulses generated by the Transition Detector). In Fig. 8 we can see the transition time varying from 0 to 200 ps, which shows a visible increase in the pulse generated in the Transistor Detector. Similar results are obtained for degradations in any PVTA parameter. Figure 9 shows results for only one transition, but changing temperature (from 27 °C to 100 °C, with an increase step of 20 °C) and power-supply voltage (from 1.1 V down to 0.8 V, with a step of 0.1 V). Similar results can be obtained for aging degradations (increase in transistors' |Vth|), and also if a cumulative effect of simultaneous VTA variations.

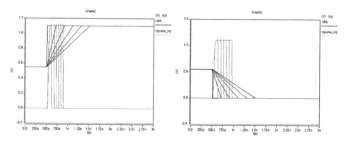

Fig. 8. Transition detector simulation results for several bit line transitions.

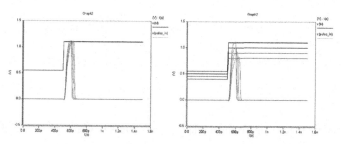

Fig. 9. Transition detector simulation results for temperature (27 °C to 100 °C) and power-supply voltage (1.1 V down to 0.8 V) variations.

3.2 Pulse Detector and Reference Voltage Results

For the pulse detector simulation, several sensibilities were evaluated for the same initial pulse. Also, it is also shown the reference voltage defined in the Comparator block, so that easily we can understand how the sensor works. Figure 10 presents the pulse (pulse_in), the Vref (n2) and the Vsensed (n1), which is the output of the pulse detector. In the graphs in Fig. 10, we can see that the sensibility is increased and, in the final graph, the Vsensed value surpasses the Vref value, which means that, in this case, the sensor would signalize an error.

3.3 Complete Sensor Results

For complete sensor results, a read procedure was performed in the one-cell memory and a high sensibility was used to trigger a predictive error in the memory. Figure 11 resumes all the signals in the simulation. As it can be seen in the 2nd graph of Fig. 11, a bit line transition in the BL signal (the bit line – node bl in simulation – change from VDD/2 to VDD) generates a pulse (pulso_in signal). The pulse generates a Vsensed value higher than the Vref value (respectively n1 and n2 signals in 5th graph), which results on a high sensor output in the last graph of Fig. 11.

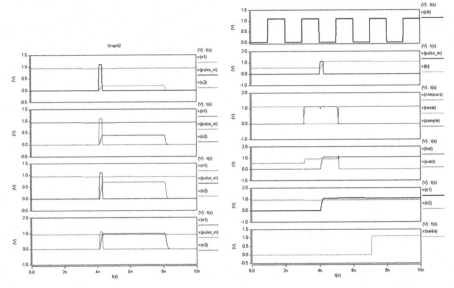

Fig. 10. Pulse detector simulation results.   **Fig. 11.** Complete sensor results.

4 Conclusions

In this work a new performance sensor was presented, to be used in hardware for HMI environments. It is capable of detecting performance variations (or PVTA variations) in CMOS DRAM memories, signalizing when these variations impose unsafe memory operations, i.e., operations in the eminence of an error. The results demonstrate that the performance sensor has the ability to detect PVTA variations or any other that may affect the DRAM performance and those reflected in the bit line transitions' performance, whether if a single parameter change, or in a combination of more than one parameter with a degradation. It is also possible to change sensor's sensibility, which allows calibration during online operation. Moreover, with the increase of signal degradation, the sensor becomes more sensitive. This is an important feature, as the burden is not placed in the sensor design, as it happens in common sensors. Finally, it is important to mention that sensor application in memories can be used as a local sensor, by monitoring few key memory cells, or as a global sensor, using one sensor with a dummy memory cell to mimic the operation of the real memory.

Acknowledgment. This work was partially supported by KTTSeaDrones project, funded by the European Regional Development Fund, FEDER, through the Interreg V-A Spain-Portugal program (POCTEP) 2014–2020 and by INSPECT project 70291, funded by P2020 and national funds through EU funds.

References

1. Semião, J., Santos, H., Cabral, R., Santos, M. B., Teixeira, P.: PVTA-aware performance SRAM sensor for IoT applications. In: Monteiro, J., et al. (eds.) INCREaSE, pp. 337–353. Springer, Cham (2020). https://doi.org/10.1007/978-3-030-30938-1_27
2. Semião, J., et al.: Signal integrity enhancement in digital circuits. In: IEEE Design and Test of Computers, vol. 25, no. 5, pp. 452–461, September–October 2008. http://dx.doi.org/10.1109/MDT.2008.146
3. Wang, W., et al.: The impact of NBTI on the performance of combinational and sequential circuits. In: Proceedings of the ACM/IEEE Design Automation Conference, pp. 364–369, San Diego, CA, USA, 4–8 June 2007. http://dx.doi.org/10.1109/DAC.2007.375188
4. Kim, T., Kong, Z.: Impact analysis of NBTI/PBTI on SRAM VMIN and design techniques for improved SRAM VMIN. J. Semicond. Technol. Sci. 13(2), 87–97 (2013). https://doi.org/10.5573/JSTS.2013.13.2.87
5. Ceratti, A., Copetti, T., Bolzani, L., Vargas, F.: On-chip aging sensor to monitor NBTI effect in nano-scale SRAM. In: Proceedings of the 2012 IEEE 15th International Symposium on Design and Diagnostics of Electronic Circuits and Systems, DDECS 2012, pp. 354–359, Tallinn, Estonia, 18–20 April 2012. http://dx.doi.org/10.1109/DDECS.2012.6219087
6. Semiao, J., et al.: Performance sensor for tolerance and predictive detection of delay-faults. In: Proceedings of the International Symposium on Defect and Fault Tolerance in VLSI and Nanotechnology Systems (DFT) 2014, Amsterdam, The Netherlands, 1–3 October 2014. http://dx.doi.org/10.1109/DFT.2014.6962092
7. Martins, C., et al.: Adaptive error-prediction flip-flop for performance failure prediction with aging sensors. In: IEEE 29th-VLSI Test Symposium (VTS), pp. 203–208, Dana Point, CA, USA, 1–5 May 2011. http://dx.doi.org/10.1109/VTS.2011.5783784
8. Semião, J., et al.: Aging and performance sensor for SRAM. In: Proceedings of the 31th Design of Circuits and Integrated Systems Conference (DCIS 2016), Granada (Spain), 23rd–25th November (2016)
9. Valdés, M., et al.: Design and validation of configurable on-line aging sensors in nanometer-scale FPGAs. IEEE Trans. Nanotechnol. 12(4), 508–517 (2013). Special Issue on "Defect & Fault Tolerance in VLSI and Nanotechnology Systems
10. Semião, J., Cabral, R., Leong, C., Santos, M., Teixeira, I., Teixeira, J.: Dynamic voltage scaling with fault-tolerance for lifetime operation. In: The 4th Workshop on Manufacturable and Dependable Multicore Architectures at Nanoscale (MEDIAN 2015)/DATE'2015 Workshop W06, Grenoble, France, 13 March 2015
11. Farahani, B., Habibi, S., Safari, S.: A cross-layer SER analysis in the presence of PVTA variation. School of Electrical and Computer Engineering, University of Tehran, Tehran, 14395–1515, Iran. http://dx.doi.org/10.1016/j.microrel.2015.04.008
12. Mintarno, E., Chandra, V., Pietromonaco, D., Aitken, R., Dutton, RW.: Workload dependent NBTI and PBTI analysis for a sub-45nm commercial microprocessor. In: International Reliability Physics Symposium, p. 3A-1 (2013)
13. Sedra, A., Smith, K.: Microelectronic Circuits, 7th edn., pp. 1236–1283 Oxford University Press, Inc. New York (2014). cap. 16

Calmbots: Exploring Madagascar Cockroaches as Living Ubiquitous Interfaces

Yuga Tsukuda[1], Daichi Tagami[1], Masaaki Sadasue[1], Shieru Suzuki[1], Jun-Li Lu[1,2(✉)], and Yoichi Ochiai[1,2]

[1] Research and Development Center for Digital Nature, University of Tsukuba, Tsukuba, Japan
jllu@slis.tsukuba.ac.jp
[2] Faculty of Library, Information and Media Science, University of Tsukuba, Tsukuba, Japan

Abstract. We introduce Calmbots, insect-based interfaces comprising multiple functions (transportation, display, drawing, or haptics) for use in human living spaces by taking advantage of insects' capabilities. We utilized Madagascar hissing cockroaches as robots because of advantages such as mobility, strength, hiding, and self-sustaining abilities. Madagascar hissing cockroaches, for instance, can be controlled to move on uneven cable-lines floors and push light-weight objects such as tablespoon. We controlled the cockroaches' movement using electrical stimulation and developed a system for tracking and communicating with their backpacks using augmented reality markers and a radio-based station, the steps of controlling multiple cockroaches for reaching their goals and transporting objects, and customized optional parts. Our method demonstrated effective control over a group of three or five cockroaches, with, at least, 60% success accuracy in dedicated experimental environments involving over forty trials for each test. Calmbots could move on carpeted or cable-lines floor and did not become desensitized to stimulation under a certain break interval.

Keywords: Interfaces of insects · Control of multiple insects

1 Introduction

Humans regard certain insects, animals, and plants as unwanted and attempt to eliminate them from their surroundings. Although some of these creatures share human living spaces, they often evade human notice. In this research, we aim to control insects as interfaces for performing selected tasks in living spaces. The applicability of common robots may be limited under some conditions, such as on vertical, narrow, or uneven floors owing to their limited mobility. Our study is related to the concepts of *ubiquitous computing* and *calm technology* [40]. According to *Mark Weiser*, *"The most profound technologies are those that*

© The Author(s), under exclusive license to Springer Nature Switzerland AG 2022
M. Antona and C. Stephanidis (Eds.): HCII 2022, LNCS 13308, pp. 522–541, 2022.
https://doi.org/10.1007/978-3-031-05028-2_35

disappear. They weave themselves into the fabric of everyday life until they are indistinguishable from it." [40]. This is the idea underlying our innovation.

Based on the capabilities of insects, we explore the possibility of creating ubiquitous interfaces whose applications are not limited to specific spaces, timing, or functions, as in existing many Tangible User Interfaces (TUIs) [29]. In building the interface, we get inspiration from cockroaches, specifically, the Madagascar hissing cockroach. Owing to their simple nervous system, this species of cockroaches can be easily controlled via electrical stimulation. Furthermore, they can move on uneven floors and exhibit remarkable strength; for instance, they can move common lightweight objects such as tablespoons. Their ability to hide indicates their ability to co-exist with humans. Furthermore, they can be designed to be working or non-working and are capable of self-maintenance (can be used for a long duration without actuators).

In this study, we designed *Calmbots*, which are composed of multiple cockroach robots with defined functions in living spaces, including object transportation, display, drawing, haptics, sensing, and sound. We implemented *Calmbots* as follows. First, we performed surgery on Madagascar hissing cockroaches to make them controllable via electrical stimulation. We also attached customized optional parts to these cockroaches depending on the intended purpose and built a system that can track and communicate with these backpacks in real-time applications using augmented reality (AR) markers and a radio-based station. To achieve the necessary functions in living spaces, we proposed the processing steps for controlling multiple cockroaches to reach their goals, transporting objects, and drawing (e.g., letters). In addition, we proposed optional parts with customizable shapes or materials to achieve object transportation and drawing.

We evaluated *Calmbots* based on experiments that included controlling multiple cockroaches to reach defined goals. We also investigated the effect of floor flatness on mobility, workload (continuous controlling success), the effect of stimulating body parts, and control performance across successive experiments with breaks. *Calmbots* exhibited effective goal attainment ability (87.5% and 60% accuracy for 3 and 5 cockroaches, respectively). Furthermore, they moved effectively on carpeted or cable-lined floors. Additionally, we ascertained that the individual cockroaches remained effective within a certain duration. We also observed that the performance of the individuals under electrical stimulation was not affected by previous experiments. With the abilities of maneuverability, mobility on uneven floors, and a certain level of ability to work continuously, *Calmbots* might be capable of executing multiple daily life tasks, including object transportation, by controlling multiple cockroaches. Our contributions are as follows.

- We argue the advantage of building *Calmbots* (insect-based interfaces for living spaces), by leveraging the Madagascar hissing cockroaches' capabilities, such as mobility, strength, hiding, and self-maintenance. *Calmbots* can be used for object transportation, display, drawing, haptics, and even as devices for sensing or sound.
- We implemented *Calmbots* including a system of tracking multiple cockroaches in real-time, controlling the movement directions of cockroaches via

Table 1. A list of related works and *Calmbots*.

	Zoobids [10]	HERMIT [25]	TUI (inFORM) [9]	Swarmrobots [17]	Calmbots by Cockroaches
Applicable range	Flat floors	Uneven floors	Limited range	Flat floors	Ubiquitous
Robot scale	cm	cm	cm	cm	cm
Maintenance (energy)	Electrical	Electrical	Electrical	Electrical	Biological (themselves)
Silent (when using)	x (Motor)	x (Motor)	x (Pin actuators)	x (Motor)	o (Muscle)
Control accuracy	o	o	o	o	Δ (Effective reaching, staying was limited)
Controllable time	o	o	o	o	Δ (Controlled under certain duration)

electrical stimulation, the methods of controlling multiple cockroaches on reaching their goals and transporting objects through cooperation, and the customized optional parts.

- We showed the effectiveness of *Calmbots* in controlling three or more cockroaches toward their goals. Further, we demonstrated their mobility on carpeted or cable-lined floors and the maximum workload under continuous control within a certain duration.

2   Related Work

2.1   Development of Remote Controlling Insects and Creatures

There are various ways to control the movement of creatures [21,38]. Direct electrical stimulation is the most common and feasible approach [32] because it affords greater immediacy compared to other control methods. For example, in a study [12], the attempt was made to control a group of cockroaches by introducing a robot into the group. However, the results obtained were unsatisfactory. Therefore, in this study, we electrically stimulated multiple cockroaches to achieve immediate and accurate control. Control via electrical stimulation entails attempting to control movements by stimulating the nerves, muscles, and sensory organs of creatures. It has been studied for a wide variety of creatures, ranging from vertebrates, such as birds [1], rodents [39], fishes [6] and reptiles [33], to simple neural creatures such as insects [28] and even plants [34]. Substantial research has yielded effective control of the movements of these creatures. Because the fundamental methods for controlling movements have been established, we aimed to utilize the creature-control technique in diverse applications, including in living spaces.

Multiple applications have exploited the advantages of immediate and accurate remote creatures control, considering creatures such as rodents and insects, using various control methods. *Latif et al.* [19] investigated how to maneuver a cockroach on a specified course using radio signals. In another study [32], cockroach control was automated using a tracking camera based on the research data of [19]. Further, various studies have been conducted in the context of search and rescue operations. An application has been developed that enables a cockroach to walk through a maze and remain on a specified course [20]. In another study, [42], a special cockroach attached to an ultrasound sensor was leveraged to effectively explore the surrounding environment. From the perspective of rescue operations using robots, terrain exploration using drones and robots that can be connected with the base control unit have been studied [2].

However, few studies exist on how to control multiple insects such as a group of cockroaches. Therefore, the proposed interface that leverages the advantages of multiple cockroaches (i.e., creature characteristics), such as mobility and hiding and self-maintenance abilities, for multiple and diverse applications in living spaces is novel. *Cyborg botany* [34] is the process of applying plant sensors in living spaces using special lab equipment; however, limited mobility and special equipment might limit the applications of plant sensors. Accordingly, our approach utilizes the advantages of using cockroaches (e.g., mobility) and controlling them using simple and low-cost surgical methods.

2.2   TUIs and Swarm Robots and Their Limitations

Table 1 shows a comparison of TUIs, SwarmRobots and *Calmbots*. Most of the research on TUIs utilize stationary interfaces, which limit the maneuverability of objects, owing to the space restriction [29]. Existing methods involve the use of pin arrays [26], electromagnet arrays [41], ultrasound [27], electrostatic adsorption [3], and vibration [44]. Using small and movable robots, *Zooids* [10] constitute an interface with multiple functions, such as moving objects or providing haptic feedback. However, owing to the limitations of small robots (i.e., attached actuator), *Zooids* cannot easily move on nonflat surfaces (e.g., asphalt ground) and might be limited to flat and simple spaces. *Hermits* [25] contain multiple functions and can move on nonflat surfaces. However, they might be limited in moving on vertical planes or more complex grounds. On the other hand, *LiftTiles* [36] leverage pin-array devices that improved mobility and are usable in multiple living spaces. However, the large size of pins may limit users' interaction with digital information on a tiny scale (in centimeters).

Furthermore, there are problems pertaining to mobility or space in swarm robotics, which may be summarized as follows [30]. In the human-computer interaction community, mouse-based maneuvering [18] is used; the input is achieved through aerial gestures [16], tablet devices [11], and through sketches [13]. Display information is set up as a physical display [22]. *Zooids*, *UbiSwarm* (which exploited haptic capability based on *Zooids*) [17], *RollingPixels* (a display device that moves by rolling) [23], and *ShapeBots* (which are designed to improve mobility through pins that can extend vertically and horizontally) [37], have implemented useful interfaces or functions for multiple situations, especially on flat or two-dimensional space. However, these studies may not be applicable under difficult conditions such as nonflat or asphalt surfaces and walls or ceilings that need to be climbed. In *GridDrones* [4], drones are used as an interface; however, although they are movable in three-dimensional space, they can only be deployed

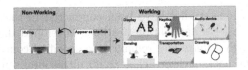

Fig. 1. Calmbots is designed as a ubiquitous interface in living spaces.

in large spaces. *FreeBOT* [24] robots can climb walls, demonstrating increased mobility owing to their use of magnets. However, they may not be applicable to common walls without embedded metal. Another problem in swarm robotics is that actuators must be attached to the robots. However, not only the actuators are noisy, but they also reduce the mobility of the robots. Therefore, we propose the use of the biological muscles of cockroaches as support for actuators. By using biological muscles as actuators, our cockroaches can maintain mobility while working quietly. We selected the Madagascar hissing cockroach, being an excellent climber and having strong legs and high mobility, to create powerful insect robots that can function in multiple daily life situations.

2.3 Ubiquitous Robotics

Ubiquitous robotics entails developing physical mobile platforms for ubiquitous computing such as multi robots, multiagent coordination, and localization. The focus in ubiquitous robotics has been on introducing mechanical robots into living spaces [15]. To this end, various models have been proposed from the engineering perspective, such as experimental multirobots [31], multiagent coordination [14], and network localization [35]. In a study [7], an attempt was made to perform complex tasks in living spaces through the cooperation of multiple robots. However, these studies on ubiquitous robotics might not be applicable to the introduction of nonmechanical robots (e.g., insect robots) into living spaces because they might not support the method for controlling multiple insect robots for functions in living spaces as well as the required system and backpacks.

3 Calmbots Design: Interfaces by Cockroaches

3.1 Exploring Madagascar Hissing Cockroaches as Robots in Living Spaces

In Fig. 1, we present the design of *Calmbots*, an approach to building interfaces using insects as robots, based on the following considerations. The recent developments of ubiquitous computing techniques have focused on methods of introducing robots into living spaces to create smart living spaces [5]. In addition, the literature on TUIs [29] has focused on the methodologies of controlling objects in a wider range. Further, we consider insect-based interfaces and select cockroaches. Among the diverse species of cockroaches, we select an ideal and powerful species, the *Madagascar hissing cockroach*, based on the following considerations.

- Easy maneuverability owing to their simple nervous system. We can easily control an individual Madagascar hissing cockroach through electrical stimulation because of the cockroach's clear response to electrical stimulation of its simple nervous system.
- Mobility. Madagascar hissing cockroaches usually have superior mobility; they can move between walls, uneven surfaces, glass surfaces, and sandboxes, unlike common insects.
- Strength. In living spaces, force is required to implement certain actions such as object transportation. The Madagascar hissing cockroach is strong and large and may be suitable for transporting heavy or large objects. Further, we conducted a simple experiment and observed that the maximum pulling force was 50 g and the maximum pushing force was 30 g. Consequently, the weight or size of the backpack (used for control) may not affect the mobility of the cockroaches.
- Hiding and self-maintenance abilities and noiselessness. Cockroaches can co-exist with humans in living spaces because they can hide; furthermore, they are capable of self-maintenance within a lifespan. Therefore, cockroach robots can be activated or deactivated, depending on the requirements of the human users. Note that the Madagascar cockroaches are noiseless, unlike common robots whose actuators are noisy.

3.2   Functions of Cockroaches in Living Spaces

Object Transportation. We utilize cockroach robots for transporting objects, a function that is often required in daily life. Specifically, for transporting multiple objects of different sizes or weights, we design the necessary optional part (in Subsect. 4.6), which is installed on the front of the cockroach, to which objects are attached. Thus, we could modify the shape of the optional parts, depending on the size of the object to be transported, and modify their shapes for enhanced grip when tightly attaching objects.

Display and Drawing for Symbols. We consider using cockroach robots for movable display or drawing, unlike common display devices. Specifically, we aim to control multiple individuals to display diverse information. For example, if the display information required by a user is the letter "A," we can control a few cockroaches to occupy each of the points comprising "A," in rightmost of Fig. 1. Further, we control multiple cockroaches to convey useful information through drawing symbols, such as marks, at locations that are difficult to access (e.g., the ceiling of the room). Specifically, for this purpose, we attach a customized pen to the front of each cockroach and control multiple cockroaches to move, achieving the desired trail of a pen.

As Devices for Haptics, Sensing, or Sound. We propose the use of cockroaches as movable devices of haptics, sound, or sensing and execute tasks at the desired time because they can reach difficult-to-access spots (e.g., the ceiling).

528   Y. Tsukuda et al.

For example, we can control cockroaches to touch the body of objects, making sounds (additional circuits are installed for triggering sound), or sensing the environment through attached sensors. Notably, we make the haptics function and will design the functions for sound and sensing.

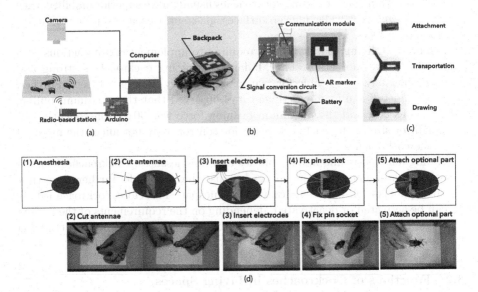

Fig. 2. We implement *Calmbots'* functions based on (a) a system tracking and communicating cockroaches' backpacks by AR marker and radio-based station, (b) the backpack on a cockroach, and (c) the flexible optional parts for functions. Note that (d) we conduct the improved surgery on a cockroach.

4   Implementing Calmbots' Functions

4.1   Surgery on Cockroach

We controlled the movement of the cockroaches via electrical stimulation. We surgically implanted the electrodes on individual cockroaches in Fig. 2(d). We achieved this by placing the cockroach on ice for 30 min. Next, we cut off the tips of both the antennae and cerci of the individual and inserted the five electrodes into the antennae, cerci, and the second prothorax of the individual. Notably, the electrodes were inserted approximately one centimeter into the antennae, stopping short of the brain. Similarly, the electrode of the cerci was inserted approximately five millimeters into the body.

4.2   Controlling the Movement of Cockroach Through Electrical Stimulation

The process of controlling the cockroach is as follows. (a) Forward: electrically stimulate both cerci. (b) Move left: electrically stimulate the right antenna. (c)

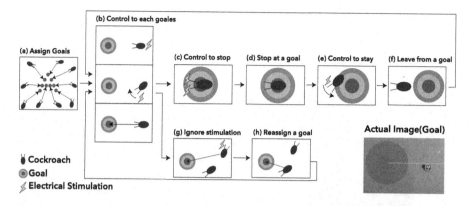

Fig. 3. We control multiple cockroaches simultaneously for reaching their respective goals.

Move right: electrically stimulate the left antenna. (d) Stay: electrically stimulate both antennae. The signal pattern of the electrical stimulation used on the cockroach individual is explained subsequently. When the cockroaches were electrically stimulated, electrolysis occurred between the electrodes. Consequently, impurities adhered to the electrodes, and no electrical stimulation was provided. In the case of the monopolar pulse resulting from the electric current in one direction, impurities adhering to the electrodes accumulated, and electrical stimulation was not provided. Consequently, we could not control the cockroaches. Additionally, in the bipolar pulse, the impurities generated were decomposed by the current of the electricity in the opposite direction, which made it possible to control the cockroaches for longer, compared to when monopolar pulses were used. However, even if impurities are not generated, the cockroaches may become desensitized to the electrical stimuli over time. We hypothesized that this problem could be avoided by providing stimulation at regular intervals. From the above analysis, we decided to provide a one-time electrical stimulus lasting 200 ms at the interval of 300 ms at least based on the literature [43]. Therefore, we electrically stimulated an individual cockroach using a bipolar pulse of 2 V, 50% duty ratio, 50 Hz, based on [8].

4.3 System for Tracking and Communicating with Cockroaches' Backpacks in Real-time

To implement the functions executed by cockroaches, such as object transportation, we proposed a system that can control and track their movement and send them signals for executing tasks. Notably, the proposed system can be implemented in real-time because of the possibility of real-time tracking and communication with the cockroach's backpack.

In Fig. 2, we track the movement of the cockroaches in real-time based on the position of an affixed AR marker using a camera. Notably, based on our

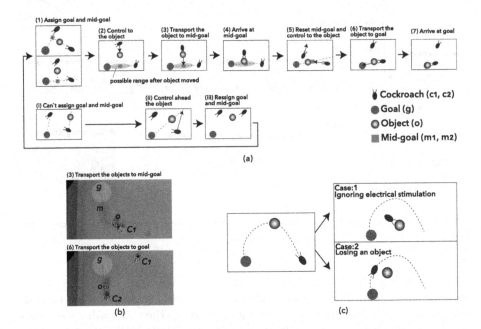

Fig. 4. (a) We control multiple cockroaches in cooperating to move an object to the specified destination. (b) The image of transporting the object to mid-goal and transporting the object to goal. (c) Only a single cockroach can be difficult to transport an object through a curve path since the cockroach can be lost control when making turns.

observations, a common method in the literature [58] might be incapable of identifying individuals in real-time. Second, to send the commands from the user's device, we utilized the communication mechanism using a radio-based station. Specifically, we set a radio-based station that communicated with each cockroach by sending the commands via a radio station to the circuit attached to each cockroach. Notably, we put the required items, including an AR marker and a circuit module, which we refer to as a backpack, on each cockroach.

4.4 Controlling Multiple Cockroaches to Reaching Their Respective Goals

Set Goals with Shortest Paths. In Fig. 3, at this phase, goals are set with shortest paths in Fig. 3(a). Given multiple goals of number n and cockroaches, we assign a goal for each cockroach without overlapping. Therefore, in all possible assignments of pairs of each goal and cockroach, we will take the assignment $\{(g_i, c_i)\}$, where each goal g_i is assigned with cockroach c_i and the total distance $\sum_{i=1}^{n} d_{c_i, g_i}$ is minimal among the total distance of each other assignment. Note that we utilize the AR markers attached to the cockroaches and the goals for computing the locations of cockroaches and goals and the distances among them. The coordinates of the cockroaches is updated every 500 ms based on [43].

Controlling the Cockroaches to Attain Goals. In this phase, cockroaches are controlled for reaching each goals in Fig. 3(b). We control the cockroaches to advance toward the goals based on the angles of the cockroaches toward their goals, their distances, and whether they are moving or not. Note that the angle is computed in a straight trajectory from the controlled cockroach to the goal based on the default horizontal line. When the angle is more than 10° or less than −10°, we make the cockroach move to the right or left, respectively, via electrically stimulating the left or right antenna automatically. Whenever the cockroach stop moving, the cerci are electrically stimulated to make it move forward. If the distance between the goal center and the cockroach is less than 10 cm, the stimulation to the cerci stop. This is to prevent the cockroaches from running out and stepping out of the goal area.

Keeping Cockroach at the Goal Area. In this phase, cockroaches are kept to stay at the goal area in Fig. 3(c)–(f). For scenarios where a cockroach approaches the goal area, we propose control to keep the cockroach there as long as possible. We consider the distances between a cockroach and the goal center for 3 distances, 1 cm, 5 cm, and 10 cm. When the cockroaches are within 1 cm of the goal center, they are stimulated electrically. When they are between 1 to 5 cm away, we stop them electrically by stimulating both antennae continuously. When they are far from the goal center, between 5–10 cm away, we attempt to force them to return to the goal using a turnaround move. To perform the turnaround move, we control the cockroach to move either left or right, depending on which side it is facing.

Reassigning the Goals and Providing Substituted Cockroach Robots. In this phase, cockroaches are reassigned the goals in Fig. 3(g) and (h). When controlling multiple cockroaches, some may become uncontrollable or desensitized to the electrical stimulus over time. Therefore, to increase the number of cockroaches reaching their goals, we propose reassigning goals to those that are not assigned goals. Note that a cockroach will be deemed unresponsive if it does not respond to stimulus for 100 frames (approximately 3.3 s). In the mechanism, a cockroach is deemed unavailable (unassigned goals), if it is unresponsive and far from the available goals. Further, we reassign goals to the available cockroaches at a specific time. Therefore, we may enhance the sustainability of a group of cockroach robots by running our system using available (nonworking) cockroaches and developing a mechanism to switch a robot between working and non-working status.

4.5 Object Transportation Using Multiple Cockroaches

We propose steps for transporting objects effectively using multiple cockroaches in Fig. 4. Note that it might not be efficient to transport an object using only one cockroach, especially when it is necessary to move it through a winding path. For instance, in the scenario depicted in Fig. 4(c), it is easy to lose control over a cockroach when making turns. Therefore, multiple cockroaches are set up to cooperate to move an object. Each of them is positioned such that they move the object in straight lines. Hence, we may increase the accuracy of transporting objects by using multiple rather than single cockroaches and reduce the continuous controlling time on single individuals (when a cockroach completes the subtask of reaching a goal or transporting an object, it can attain nonactive status).

Select Short and Straight Paths. Given an object o, a goal g, and two cockroaches c_1 and c_2, to make both cockroaches move in straight trajectories and shorten the total distance of paths, we propose two possible cases. In case one, cockroach c_1 moves the object to the mid-goal m_1 as a straight path p_{c_1,m_1} and thus cockroach c_2 moves the object to g through m_1 as the path $p_{c_2,g}$. In case two, inversely, cockroach c_2 moves the object to another mid-goal m_2 as a straight path p_{c_2,m_2} and thus cockroach c_1 moves the object to g through m_2 as the path $p_{c_1,g}$. We then set the paths, from either $p_{c_1,m_1} + p_{c_2,g}$ or $p_{c_2,m_2} + p_{c_1,g}$, which has a shorter distance for the two cockroaches.

One Cockroach Moves Object to the Mid-goal and the Other Continues to Move It to Goal Destination. Based on the defined paths, the first cockroach c_a (either be c_1 or c_2) is controlled to move object o to the mid-goal; another cockroach c_b is kept on standby. When object o is moved to the mid-goal, cockroach c_b is controlled toward the location of o and move o to goal g using the reset straight paths. Note that the first cockroach c_a is prevented from disturbing cockroach c_b's task by being controlled to move in other directions. Finally, when cockroach c_b moving o is at goal g (within 5 cm), c_b is controlled to leave g. In some cases of the relative positions among object o, goal g, and cockroaches, setting all the cockroaches to follow straight paths is not feasible (Fig. 4 (8)) and the need arises to move one cockroach to another location, at which the mid-goal can be set on the intersection of the line between a cockroach and object o and the line between another cockroach and goal g.

4.6   Optional Parts

We designed the shape, surface, and materials of the optional parts, which are attached to the external objects and touch the ground.

Object Transportation. We designed the optional parts for the cockroach robots transporting objects while taking cognizance of cockroaches' natural tendency to avoid objects touching their antennae. In Fig. 2(c), we produced an optional part, a Y-shaped horn, for object transportation. The Y-shaped horn could be used to move objects by making the cockroach move forward in front of the objects with the given stimulus to both cerci. The design of the Y-shaped optional part was as follows. First, we had to prevent the cockroach from climbing on the object to be moved by adjusting the position of the installed optional

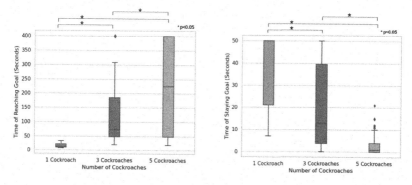

Fig. 5. Controlling performance of multiple cockroaches on reaching goals. (a) The reaching times and (b) the staying times on one cockroach, three cockroaches, and five cockroaches, respectively. Our method controlled one cockroach better than controlling multiple cockroaches at the same time.

part. Therefore, we avoided cockroaches from climbing on the object by setting a slope on the tip of the optional parts so that the optional parts would go underneath the object. The Y-shape horn can prevent the cockroach from losing objects, especially large ones, when it is moving from side to side (moving forward, left, or right). However, a large optional part may impede the mobility of the cockroach. Therefore, to investigate the cockroach's ability to move stably and with mobility, we set the size and weight of the optional part as 3 × 3 cm and 1 g, respectively.

Drawing. In addition, we designed the optional part for drawing (e.g., letters). In the drawing experiment using the controlled cockroach with a pen attached, we observed that the cockroach might find it hard to draw using a ballpoint pen, which may draw small, blurry lines. Therefore, we opted to attach a thick brush pen that could draw thick and legible lines when the cockroach is moving. In addition, we used a brush pen because the timing and pressure of the attached brush touching the ground were suitable.

5   Experimental Results

5.1   Experimental Setting

Because of the influence of environmental factors on the behaviors of cockroaches, we set up a closed room such that the lighting was perpendicular to the ground; daylight penetration was blocked out. Therefore, during the experiments, the outside factors influencing the cockroaches could be reduced; for instance, there was almost no shadow (which cockroaches could perceive as hiding places) and almost no wind (which could stimulate cockroaches).

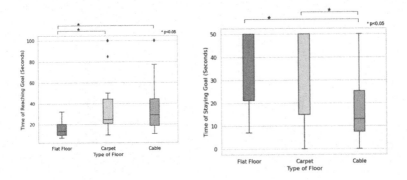

Fig. 6. The mobility performance of cockroach individuals on the affect of floor flatness. (a) The reaching times and (b) the staying times on a flat floor, a floor of carpet, and a floor with cables, respectively.

5.2   Controlling Performance of Multiple Cockroaches on Reaching Goals

We evaluated the success of controlling multiple cockroaches simultaneously to reach the defined goals. In our method, the factors were the criterion of electrical stimulus, tracking or communicating with cockroach backpacks using AR markers and a radio station, and the proposed method with multiple parameters. In each experiment, each cockroach was aligned horizontally and controlled to reach the goal, which was 70-cm away in the same direction. The time taken to reach the goal area and the duration of remaining within it was measured for each cockroach. We experimented on three cockroach teams of varying numbers, one cockroach, three cockroaches (with one for substitution), and five cockroaches (with one for substitution), to observe the effect of the number of cockroaches on the control performance. We included multiple cockroaches in each team to ensure the fairness of the performance evaluation. In the experiment, we used four teams, each with unique individuals. We had 40 trials, 10 for each team.

Results. In Fig. 5(a), the time taken to perform a task by one cockroach (the median time: 13.5 s) was significantly better than that of three or five cockroaches. Additionally, the variances of the reaching times of 3 or 5 cockroaches were high, such that the lower to the upper quartiles were between 50 s to 200 s. Similarly, for the staying times in Fig. 5(b), 1 cockroach could be controlled to stay for approximately 21 s, whereas 3 and 5 cockroaches had less staying time, less than 5 s in many instances. These results implied that the performance of our control method decreased when more cockroaches were being controlled to reach their goals.

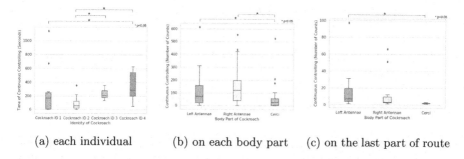

(a) each individual   (b) on each body part   (c) on the last part of route

Fig. 7. The performance of continuous controlling on cockroach individuals.

5.3 Effect of Floor Flatness on Mobility

We evaluated the mobility of cockroaches based on the floor flatness. We performed experiments on uneven floors, such as those with cables, on which typical robots Toio[1] cannot move. We evaluated the effect of the flatness of floors, such as a flat, carpeted floor, and cable-lined floor, on the mobility of a cockroach approaching a destination 70 cm away. We used 4 individual cockroaches for 10 trials each, making a total of 40 trials.

Results. In Fig. 6(a), the arrival time of one cockroach on a flat floor was significantly better than on the carpeted and cable-lined floors. In Fig. 6(b), one cockroach could be controlled to stay on a flat floor or carpet, as opposed to the cable-lined floor. These results might imply the following. First, we showed that, unlike typical robots, cockroaches could be controlled to move on an uneven floor. Note that one cockroach was more controllable on flat floors than on uneven floors, such as carpeted or cable-lined floors. Further, we observed that a cockroach could be controlled to stay longer on an uneven floor such as carpet, even if the control over it had diminished and mobility was impeded. This might be because the movement of cockroaches may be impeded by the materials of uneven floors (carpet). Similarly, on the cable-lined floors, cockroaches might have low mobility because the backpacks on them might get caught, thus affecting the movement of the cockroach; for instance, the center of gravity of the cockroach's body could be shifted backward.

5.4 Analysis of Continuous Control Success on Individual Cockroaches and Stimulated Body Parts

Results for Individual Cockroaches. In Fig. 7(a), among the results for 4 individuals, we observed that the medians of continuous controlling times for 3 individuals (Cockroach ID 1, ID 3, and ID 4) were more than 167.5 s, and the variances of the controlling times of 2 individuals (Cockroach ID 1 and ID 4) were

---

[1] https://www.sony.com/en/SonyInfo/design/stories/toio/.

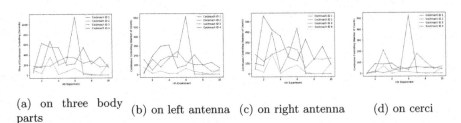

(a) on three body parts   (b) on left antenna   (c) on right antenna   (d) on cerci

Fig. 8. The controlling performance on cockroach individuals across consecutive experiments, where the time interval between experiments was twenty minutes. The controlling performance on cockroach individuals across consecutive experiments, where the time interval between experiments was twenty minutes.

large. We can infer that individual cockroaches can be continuously controlled over a period of time. However, this may result in instability.

Results for Body Parts and Last Part of Route. In Fig. 7(b), among the results for three body parts, we observed that the times for the left and right antennae were close, and their values might be bigger than those for the cerci. Note that the route was a figure eight. We observed that on this route, with more turns than straight lines, controlling cockroaches required more stimulations to the left or right antennae, which corresponded to the left or right directions, compared to the cerci for straight direction. Additionally, a similar number of stimulations was required for both antennae, indicating that the route had equal left and right turns. The results might be considered as proof that our control methods for directions were effective and consistent with the expected movement of cockroaches. Finally, we observed the performance on the last part of a route where the cockroach's response to stimulation might have deteriorated. In Fig. 7(c), the left or right antenna required greater stimulations than the cerci. This might imply that, when the response to the stimuli had deteriorated, it was more useful to stimulate the antennae (for left or right directions) instead of the cerci (for straight direction).

The Controlling Performance Between Experiments with Time Break. In Fig. 8, we observed that the controlling performance on the four individuals was dynamic for the results of stimulation on all body parts (Fig. 8(a)), left antenna (Fig. 8(b)), right antenna (Fig. 8(c)), or cerci (Fig. 8(d)). We aimed to observe if individual cockroaches became desensitized to electrical stimuli over a long period, resulting in reduced control accuracy. However, in Fig. 8, the results for the individuals were dynamic (not gradually reduced) on either all or individual body parts. We can infer that, with sufficient time-break, the electrical stimulation on individual cockroaches will remain effective across series of experiments. This bodes well for long-term usage of *Calmbots* in daily life, which contains periods of working and non-working.

6 Discussion

6.1 Analysis of Experimental Results

The Controllability of Madagascar Cockroaches Was Considered. The experimental results proved that the proposed method was effective for controlling multiple cockroaches to reach defined goals (the reaching accuracy was quality). However, the following issues were observed. When multiple cockroaches were controlled for moving objects to defined points, some of them collided (e.g., climbing on top of another), and as a result, their backpacks could get tangled up, which could make the AR markers temporarily untraceable. In controlling multiple cockroaches toward their goals, individuals that have already attained their goals within the reach of others could become less controllable. Additionally, the reaching time of an individual could not be estimated accurately. Therefore, in achieving multiple goals using the cockroaches, the entire performance may be improved by providing more substitute cockroaches for the tasks, that is, deploying as many cockroaches as possible for a task (goal).

Appropriate Tasks Conducted by Cockroach Robots. We observed that controlling cockroaches such that they remained in specific areas was difficult. Therefore, *Calmbots* might not be effective for tasks that require responsiveness or cost-intensive tasks. This implies that tasks that do not require responsiveness, can be executed off-line, or at a delayed time can be performed using cockroach robots. *Calmbots* may be suitable for moving nonprecious objects or executing the carriage of objects at a later specified time or when the users are not present. In addition, we observed that the controlling accuracy for the cockroaches could decrease over time and the cockroaches could be affected by internal or external factors. Therefore, we can design a system that can sort the cockroaches according to usability and control time and, based on this, assigned tasks at suitable timing.

Effect of Backpack on Cockroaches. We discussed the effect of backpacks on the mobility of cockroaches. Note that a cockroach's mobility and balance are related. We observed that when the backpacks were off-balance, sometimes the cockroaches were unable to crawl on vertical surfaces and took longer crawling over obstacles (e.g., cables). Additionally, when multiple cockroaches were close to each other, their accessories (e.g., antennae) could get tangled, which reduced their mobility. Therefore, to reduce the effect of the backpacks, we propose putting the backpacks close to the center of gravity of the cockroach's body and reducing the backpack weight by using lightweight materials.

Feasibility of *Calmbots* as Interfaces. We discussed the performance and feasibility of *Calmbots* as interfaces in living spaces. Madagascar hissing cockroaches are silent and self-sustaining; furthermore, they have high mobility. There are some concerns about the control accuracy for multiple cockroaches. In use as a display, we may need greater control accuracy because the display

Fig. 9. (a) *Object transportation*: A cockroach was controlled to transport a large box. (b) Three cockroaches are interactive on the person's arm

requires multiple cockroaches to occupy specific locations (long staying time may be needed). In addition, when using them as pixels, the proper directions they face are required since the shape of each cockroach is oval. For transportation or haptics in living spaces, *Calmbots* may be feasible because they have demonstrable reaching ability and considerable staying time. However, for haptics proper tactile should be presented by devising optional parts in terms of *calm computing*. Furthermore, although cockroaches can be used to draw large characters, drawing small characters is a challenge owing to the size of a cockroach and requisite control accuracy. Within a certain workload of continuous controlling time, the system may perform short-period tasks in living spaces. From the current experimental performance, tasks requiring high responsiveness and precise control may not be suitable for *Calmbots*. Therefore, the tasks requiring a long duration or that can be repeatedly executed may be appropriate for *Calmbots* (Fig. 9).

6.2   Realizing Flexible Insects'Interfaces for Living Spaces

Interfaces of Hybrid Cockroaches and Robots. We observed limitations in the functionality of the cockroaches, such as the control performance decreasing as the number of cockroaches increased. To deploy *Calmbots* in living spaces, we hold that novel interfaces integrating cockroaches and common robots may have the complementary advantages of cockroaches and robots. In terms of mobility, common robots can move easily under ideal conditions, such as flat or dry floors; cockroaches, on the other hand, are movable under diverse conditions, such as narrow paths or vertical floors. Additionally, the entire control performance can be improved by using cockroaches, owing to their ability to execute diverse tasks in living spaces, such as tasks needing quiet or minimal noise.

Flexible Optional Parts. The optional parts can be customized for realizing multiple operations such as object transportation and drawing. In object transportation, to move a large object, we may choose to use optional parts with suitable shapes or a high shape-tack to attach the large object. Similarly, for drawing using a specified pen or representing specified expressions, we may use an optional part that can attach the pen and set it in the right position for the expression. In addition, users can customize the design of the optional parts. Note that optional parts can be flexibly customized using digital fabrication, such as 3D printing or computer-aided design.

Factors Affecting Insect Robots Used in Living Spaces. We examined other factors such as biological behaviors or environmental effect. For example, cockroaches may have specific behaviors pertaining to food intake or excretion, which can necessitate the presence of additional things, such as food, around the circuits or backpacks, thus possibly triggering a short- circuit. Additionally, co-existing creatures (e.g., cat) might induce unusual behaviors in the cockroach robots. For such contexts, we may propose ideas that are unrelated to the (*Calmbots*) system, such as limiting the movable area of the cockroach robots. We can consider another control method that is not based on electric stimulation such as utilizing special materials or spices. For instance, we could use Vaseline petroleum jelly to reduce the movement of the cockroaches. Note that there are other problems pertaining to users or appropriate usage situations.

Acknowledgement. This work was supported by Pixie Dust Technologies, Inc. in Japan.

References

1. Cai, L., Dai, Z., Wang, W., Wang, H., Tang, Y.: Modulating motor behaviors by electrical stimulation of specific nuclei in pigeons. J. Bionic Eng. **12**(4), 555–564 (2015)
2. Dirafzoon, A., Bozkurt, A., Lobaton, E.: A framework for mapping with biobotic insect networks: from local to global maps. Robot. Auton. Syst. **88**, 79–96 (2017)
3. Amano, K., Yamamoto, A.: Tangible interactions on a flat panel display using actuated paper sheets. Association for Computing Machinery, New York (2012)
4. Braley, S., Rubens, C., Merritt, T.R., Vertegaal, R.: GridDrones: a self-levitating physical voxel lattice for 3d surface deformations. Association for Computing Machinery, New York (2018)
5. Chaimowicz, L., et al.: Deploying air-ground multi-robot teams in urban environments. In: Parker, L.E., Schneider, F.E., Schultz, A.C. (eds.) Multi-Robot Systems. From Swarms to Intelligent Automata, vol. III, pp. 223–234. Springer, Dordrecht (2005). https://doi.org/10.1007/1-4020-3389-3_18
6. Choo, H.Y., Li, Y., Cao, F., Sato, H.: Electrical stimulation of coleopteran muscle for initiating flight. PLoS ONE **11**(4), 1–9 (2016)
7. Ducatelle, F., Di Caro, G.A., Pinciroli, C., Gambardella, L.M.: Self-organized cooperation between robotic swarms. Swarm Intell. **5**(2), 73 (2011)
8. Erickson, J.C., Herrera, M., Bustamante, M., Shingiro, A., Bowen, T.: Effective stimulus parameters for directed locomotion in Madagascar hissing cockroach biobot. PLoS ONE **10**, e0134348 (2015)
9. Follmer, S., Leithinger, D., Olwal, A., Hogge, A., Ishii, H.: Inform: dynamic physical affordances and constraints through shape and object actuation. Association for Computing Machinery, New York (2013)

10. Goc, M.L., Kim, L.H., Parsaei, A., Fekete, J., Dragicevic, P., Follmer, S.: Zooids: building blocks for swarm user interfaces. In: Rekimoto, J., Igarashi, T., Wobbrock, J.O., Avrahami, D. (eds.) Proceedings of the 29th Annual Symposium on User Interface Software and Technology, UIST 2016, Tokyo, Japan, 16–19 October 2016, pp. 97–109. ACM (2016)

11. Grieder, R., Alonso-mora, J., Bloechlinger, C., Siegwart, R., Beardsley, P.: Multi-robot control and interaction with a hand-held tablet

12. Halloy, J., et al.: Social integration of robots into groups of cockroaches to control self-organized choices. Science **318**(5853), 1155–1158 (2007)

13. Hauri, S., Alonso-Mora, J., Breitenmoser, A., Siegwart, R., Beardsley, P.: Multi-robot formation control via a real-time drawing interface. In: Yoshida, K., Tadokoro, S. (eds.) Field and Service Robotics. STAR, vol. 92, pp. 175–189. Springer, Heidelberg (2014). https://doi.org/10.1007/978-3-642-40686-7_12

14. How, J.P., Behihke, B., Frank, A., Dale, D., Vian, J.: Real-time indoor autonomous vehicle test environment. IEEE Control Syst. Mag. **28**(2), 51–64 (2008)

15. Kim, J., Lee, K., Kim, Y., Kuppuswamy, N.S., Jo, J.: Ubiquitous robot: a new paradigm for integrated services. In: Proceedings 2007 IEEE International Conference on Robotics and Automation, pp. 2853–2858 (2007)

16. Kim, L.H., Drew, D.S., Domova, V., Follmer, S.: User-defined swarm robot control. Association for Computing Machinery, New York (2020)

17. Kim, L.H., Follmer, S.: UbiSwarm: ubiquitous robotic interfaces and investigation of abstract motion as a display, vol. 1, no. 3 (2017)

18. Kolling, A., Nunnally, S., Lewis, M.: Towards human control of robot swarms. Association for Computing Machinery, New York (2012)

19. Latif, T., Bozkurt, A.: Line following terrestrial insect biobots. In: 2012 Annual International Conference of the IEEE Engineering in Medicine and Biology Society, pp. 972–975 (2012)

20. Latif, T., Whitmire, E., Novak, T., Bozkurt, A.: Towards fenceless boundaries for solar powered insect biobots. In: 2014 36th Annual International Conference of the IEEE Engineering in Medicine and Biology Society, pp. 1670–1673 (2014)

21. Le, D.L., et al.: Neurotransmitter-loaded nanocapsule triggers on-demand muscle relaxation in living organism. ACS Appl. Mater. Interf. **10**(44), 37812–37819 (2018)

22. Le Goc, M., Perin, C., Follmer, S., Fekete, J., Dragicevic, P.: Dynamic composite data physicalization using wheeled micro-robots. IEEE Trans. Visual Comput. Graphics **25**(1), 737–747 (2019)

23. Lee, Y., Kim, M., Kim, H.: Rolling pixels: robotic Steinmetz solids for creating physical animations. Association for Computing Machinery, New York (2020)

24. Liang, G., Luo, H., Li, M., Qian, H., Lam, T.L.: FreeBOT: a freeform modular self-reconfigurable robot with arbitrary connection point - design and implementation, October 2020

25. Nakagaki, K., Leong, J., Tappa, J.L., Wilbert, J.A., Ishii, H.: HERMITS: dynamically reconfiguring the interactivity of self-propelled TUIs with mechanical shell add-ons. Association for Computing Machinery, New York (2020)

26. Nakagaki, K., Liu, Y.R., Nelson-Arzuaga, C., Ishii, H.: TRANS-DOCK: expanding the interactivity of pin-based shape displays by docking mechanical transducers. Association for Computing Machinery, New York (2020)

27. Ochiai, Y., Hoshi, T., Rekimoto, J.: Pixie dust: graphics generated by levitated and animated objects in computational acoustic-potential field. ACM Trans. Graph. **33**(4), 1–13 (2014)

28. Panzenhagen, S.J.: Characterization of the 2-phase turning response of Madagascar hissing cockroach biobots to antennal stimulation. Ph.D. thesis (2019)

29. Poupyrev, I., Nashida, T., Okabe, M.: Actuation and tangible user interfaces: the Vaucanson duck, robots, and shape displays. Association for Computing Machinery, New York (2007)
30. Rezeck, P.A.F., Azpurua, H., Chaimowicz, L.: HeRo: an open platform for robotics research and education. In: 2017 Latin American Robotics Symposium (LARS) and 2017 Brazilian Symposium on Robotics (SBR), pp. 1–6 (2017)
31. Riggs, T.A., Inanc, T., Zhang, W.: An autonomous mobile robotics testbed: construction, validation, and experiments. IEEE Trans. Control Syst. Technol. **18**(3), 757–766 (2010)
32. Romano, D., Donati, E., Benelli, G., Stefanini, C.: A review on animal-robot interaction: from bio-hybrid organisms to mixed societies. Biol. Cybern. **113**(3), 201–225 (2019)
33. Sanchez, C.J., Chiu, C.W., Zhou, Y., González, J.M., Vinson, S.B., Liang, H.: Locomotion control of hybrid cockroach robots. J. R. Soc. Interface **12**(105), 20141363 (2015)
34. Sareen, H., Zheng, J., Maes, P.: Cyborg botany: augmented plants as sensors, displays and actuators. Association for Computing Machinery, New York (2019)
35. Stubbs, A., Vladimerou, V., Fulford, A.T., King, D., Strick, J., Dullerud, G.E.: Multivehicle systems control over networks: a hovercraft testbed for networked and decentralized control. IEEE Control Syst. Mag. **26**(3), 56–69 (2006)
36. Suzuki, R., Nakayama, R., Liu, D., Kakehi, Y., Gross, M.D., Leithinger, D.: LiftTiles: modular and reconfigurable room-scale shape displays through retractable inflatable actuators. Association for Computing Machinery, New York, (2019)
37. Suzuki, R., et al.: Shapebots: shape-changing swarm robots. Association for Computing Machinery, New York (2019)
38. Visvanathan, K., Gianchandani, Y.B.: Locomotion response of airborne, ambulatory and aquatic insects to thermal stimulation using piezoceramic microheaters. J. Micromech. Microeng. **21**(12), 125002 (2011)
39. Wang, Y., Lu, M., Wu, Z., Zheng, X., Pan, G.: Visual cue-guided rat cyborg. In: Guger, C., Allison, B., Lebedev, M. (eds.) Brain-Computer Interface Research. SECE, pp. 65–78. Springer, Cham (2017). https://doi.org/10.1007/978-3-319-64373-1_7
40. Weiser, M.: The computer for the 21st century. SIGMOBILE Mob. Comput. Commun. Rev. **3**(3), 3–11 (1999)
41. Weiss, M., Schwarz, F., Jakubowski, S., Borchers, J.: Madgets: actuating widgets on interactive tabletops. Association for Computing Machinery, New York (2010)
42. Whitmire, E., Latif, T., Bozkurt, A.: Acoustic sensors for biobotic search and rescue. In: SENSORS, 2014 IEEE, pp. 2195–2198 (2014)
43. Whitmire, E., Latif, T., Bozkurt, A.:
44. Yamanaka, S., Miyashita, H.: Vibkinesis: notification by direct tap and "dying message" using vibronic movement controllable smartphones. Association for Computing Machinery, New York (2014)

Indoor Auto-Navigate System for Electric Wheelchairs in a Nursing Home

Zhexin Zhang[1]([✉]) [iD], Jun-Li Lu[1], and Yoichi Ochiai[1,2]

[1] Research and Development Center for Digital Nature, University of Tsukuba,
Tsukuba, Japan
jacobzhang@digitalnature.slis.tsukuba.ac.jp
[2] Faculty of Library, Information and Media Science, University of Tsukuba,
Tsukuba, Japan

Abstract. We are currently living in an age of COVID, where we wish to reduce physical contact as much as possible. It is even more important for patients who live in nursing homes and need wheelchairs. It is noticeable that people who live in nursing homes usually have an elder average age, and are more likely to have some underlying disease. Therefore they need extra care to resist COVID. As we all know, the most common and effective countermeasure against COVID is to avoid close contact. However, for most people who lives in a nursing home, there are plenty of daily activities that are mandatory for them. They have to spend considerable time moving on a wheel chair with a assistant pushing the wheelchair. Which made the assistant and the user a close contact to each other. We plan to design a auto-navigation computer system for electric wheelchairs. So it can be possible for electric wheelchair users to go to various places in nursing home without a assistant aside, reducing the risk of infection, as well as the human resource needed.

Keywords: Computer vision · Deep learning · Medical assistant technology

1 Introduction

We are currently living in an age of COVID, where we wish to reduce physical contact as much as possible. It is even more important for patients who live in nursing homes and need wheelchairs.

Usually patients who live in nursing homes have an elder average age, and are more likely to have some underlying disease. Therefore they need extra care to resist COVID. As we all know, the most common and effective countermeasure against COVID is to avoid close contact. However, for most people who lives in a nursing home, there are plenty of daily activities that are mandatory for them, such as daily health check and rehabilitation training. These activities are under the guidance of doctors, and may change according to the situation. They have to spend considerable time moving on a wheelchair with a assistant pushing the

© The Author(s), under exclusive license to Springer Nature Switzerland AG 2022
M. Antona and C. Stephanidis (Eds.): HCII 2022, LNCS 13308, pp. 542–552, 2022.
https://doi.org/10.1007/978-3-031-05028-2_36

wheelchair. Which made the assistant and the user a close contact to each other. We plan to design a auto-navigation computer system for electric wheelchairs. So it is possible for electric wheelchair users to be guided to various places in nursing home without a assistant aside.

2 Related Works

2.1 Indoor Navigation Using YOLOv5

You Only Look Once, or YOLO [9], is a popular deep learning architecture of object recognition based on transformers [1]. YOLO has had several iterations and a lot of development since recent years. The pre-trained YOLOv5 models has proved their efficiency on object recognition. A typical object recognition task is license plate detection. This includes two sub-tasks: detect the presence of one or several license plates in the picture frame, and detect the exact number on each license plate.

Shortly after the release of YOLOv4 Glenn Jocher introduced YOLOv5 using the Pytorch framework, which we are planning to use. Wang et al. proposed a neural network method [11] to do the traffic sign detection. In our experiment, we implemented the YOLOv5s [4] model for better performance.

2.2 Stereo Vision

Stereo vision is a well-developed computer vision technology. However, stereo vision still has some severe flaws that make it unable to be broadly used on motion systems.

The first is shaking issue. A stereo system always assumes the two stereo cameras maintain a fixed relative position. However, in most moving systems, there is usually some shaking. Shaking can be caused by inertia as the whole system accelerates or decelerates. Stereo system stop working properly as long as cameras leaves the initial position.

The second is object detecting issue. Stereo vision systems calculates distance by disparity method. In a stereo vision system, the same object projects at two different position on left and right camera planes. By calculating the difference we can find out how far the object is from the camera plane. However, it is not always clear to clarify which point in left and right frame are corresponding to the same certain point in real world. Humans have the ability to recognize objects in their integrity. But computer have problems to do so, hence there are usually a lot of "holes" in a parity map. This is because stereo vision system has difficulty in recognizing these parts as individual objects. A usual case is the system recognizes the shadow of an object as another object, therefore has a wrong estimation of distance. This situation can be even worse when encountering humans. Stereo vision systems detect objects by its edge. However, humans wearing different kinds of clothes can have some blurred edge. And so is also true for objects with shadow.

Despite these problems, stereo vision is still one of the most cost-less and decent method for 3D object recognition. In recent years, AI assisted stereo vision [2] has became a popular solution in many commercial circumstances.

3   Problems

3.1   Flaws of Stereo Vision

Though being a old and mature computer vision method, stereo vision has some unique flaws. One of the most significant flaw is that depth maps generated by stereo vision systems often come with some miscalculation. Especially when estimating depths of far away objects that are not bright.

3.2   Transplanting

Nursing home can refer to a various type of long-term care facilities, including old people's homes, assisted living facilities, etc. The definition and function may vary from facility to facility. But we want to make a system that is transplantable for most kinds of nursing homes.

3.3   The Mandatoriness of an Assistant Aside

Mandatory daily activities can vary as the situation of patient differ. However, Such as rehabilitation training, regular medical examinations, or going out for a stroll to get fresh air. They have to spend considerable time moving on a wheel chair with a assistant pushing the wheelchair. Which made the assistant and the user a close contact to each other. A close contact, by the definition [6] of CDC of United States, means someone who was less than 6 ft away from an infected person for a cumulative total of 15 min or more over a 24-h period.

The reasons that the assistant is needed includes several factors: Firstly, though the wheelchair can be pushed by the passenger, it takes a lot of power to manually pushing a wheelchair for a patient who lives in nursing home. Secondly, navigation is usually needed for patients because the destination may vary.

3.4   Lack of Computer Vision Dataset

Nursing homes can be quite different from one to another. Hence it is very hard to build up a indoor computer vision dataset that can include and efficiently represent all kinds of Nursing homes. Which brings difficulty to develop and evaluate a computer vision method to analyze the indoor environment.

4   Methodologies

The auto-navigation system includes two subsystems: Indoor marker navigation system, and computer-vision autopilot system. The auto-navigation system then communicate to the motion system of electric wheelchair in order to perform a slow and stable automatic movement.

4.1 Motion System

For a patient that needs to live in a nursing home, we must consider their safety first as they might have some underlying disease. The electric wheelchair will move and turn in a very slow speed under the guidance of IMNS. Also, there will be a hint on a mini screen installed on the handle of wheelchair as a guidance of turning left, right, or go straight. So that user can turn the wheelchair manually if they hope to do so. The main control authority is always given to the user, which means any inputs will interrupt control of IMNS and give the full control of electric wheelchairs back to the user until the IMNS is manually started again.

There is no software speed limit in manual mode, allowing the user to move the electric wheelchair at a higher speed in their need.

We plan to use a stick controller, which is the way most electric wheelchair in the market now use. However, we plan to preform some turning on the controller considering the features of the motion system. The speed of the wheelchair is very limited since it is used only under indoor circumstances. So we do not need to allow the controller to have a wide range of input values. Which allows us to adjust the controller's dead-band to meet our need.

Under ideal situation, the user is told to grab the stick constantly, and if there's any unexpected big movement, such as a big shake, jitters, or sudden brake. The stick will be pushed or pulled out of the dead-band and the control authority would be given back to the user instantly.

4.2 Indoor Marker Navigation System

The target of indoor marker navigation system, or IMNS, is to recognize the indoor location. Considering the complex indoor surroundings which may block radio signals, it is not possible to locate a indoor position with a normal radio-navigation system, such as GPS, in an indoor environment. A more decent way of doing this is to hang visible marks in some fixed position, as hints to both humans and computer vision systems. The marks can be painted on the wall or simply glued there. They shall be put in a high position onto the wall, so they can avoid being damaged and also be visible with people walking around in the facility. Also, it's very easy to deploy as well as to replace since they are just visual marks. We plan to imply YOLOv5 as the method to recognize these marks. Karkar et al. has designed a indoor navigation system [7] with YOLOv5 for blind people, which worked pretty well with a handhold camera as input. This suggests that YOLOv5 has some robustness against vertical and horizontal shaking.

4.3 Computer Vision Autopilot System

The target of computer vision autopilot system, or CVAS system, is to constantly monitor the surroundings and perform some motion control. While the main control authority is always given to the user, we want to allow the CVAS to be able to stop the wheelchair if there's something or someone in the way. Simpson et al. has developed a method [8] using an array of 12 ultrasonic sensor to allow wheelchair to detect surroundings and autopilot. However, ultrasonic goes in a narrow beam, thus can only detect things in a narrow area. We want a wider vision and we want it to be robust against the vertical shaking. Also, humans with clothes on them can absorb ultrasonic and blind the sensors. So we plan to have a stereo vision system which allows the computer to accurately measure the distance from anything ahead of the wheelchair. We are not using a Neural Network method to measure the distance as we want it to be more accurate. However, we are also using the YOLOv5 Neural Network to detect humans and other things in the way, like long bench in the hallway for instance. So the wheelchair can behave differently when it found a human in front of it or a thing. For example, we can let the wheelchair stop when it is one meter away of any human or 50 cm away from a thing. The specific distance can be varied to adapt the environment in different nursing homes.

4.4   YOLO Assisted Stereo Vision

The method we plan to implement includes mainly three points. Firstly, evaluating the distance between camera and the human detected by YOLO with stereo vision system. Secondly, detecting and analyzing the surroundings by stereo vision system. Lastly, detecting the mark to realize the location inside the facility.

4.5   Camera System Equipped on Wheelchair

Usually a wheelchair's handle is about 90–110 cm in height. The camera system should not be too low, otherwise the camera view may be blocked by the head of user. The camera system should not be too high, otherwise the fixture may be unstable, and weaving back and forth during moving.

Also, the system must be able to detect marking text of normal size. Apparently these markings should be high enough to have a clear vision. A normal standard of ceilings height in Japan is 240 cm. We assumed a marking of 40 cm height with a text of about 35 cm at height of 190 cm. In experiment, we set our camera system on a fixture of 150 cm height.

4.6   Marking in Nursing Facility

As mentioned above, maybe it is a better way if we choose to standardize the markings itself, rather than try to train a model to adapt all kinds of situations in facilities. We choose to make the markings with the font that are widely used among North America. Since there has been a lot of Neural Network methods to recognize numbers on licensing plates. And a lot of them has been adopted, verified and used by police departments. Also, licensing plates datasets usually contains quite a lot of different negatively effected samples, such as dirty, blurred, or low brightness. Thus neural networks trained on these datasets have some robustness against the obstructions of recognition.

4.7 Parity Characters

Parity Character is a method to validate the sequence of characters in case there are some character missing. Hereby we only propose an example of parity algorithm.

Example 1. Example, a nursing home mark every spot with 4 characters, 2 are numbers and 2 are alphabets. Each of them guaranteed to be different. Let us consider a spot marked "AC13". First of all we can have them interlaced. So if there is only one character not being detected, we can have clue that it is a alphabet or a number. Next step is we append 2 characters after them. One is number and the other is alphabet, which are called parity alphabet and parity number. If we use x_1, x_2, x_p to represent the first, second, and the parity number. They meet the following conditions:

$$x_1 + x_2 \equiv x_p (mod\ 11) \tag{1}$$

Given $0 \leq x_1, x_2, x_p \leq 9$, we will be able to calculate any one of them given the other two. A likewise method can be implemented for alphabets if we map them into their orders in the English alphabet.

There can be a lot of parity methods, nursing homes can have their own parity methods given their own ways of encoding spots with characters.

5 Experiments

5.1 Stereo Camera System Experiment

We built a customize stereo vision system with two 4K cameras. However, the frame rate drops when recording under high resolution. Also, it can be hard for Neural Network models to analyze a high-resolution frame. So we decided to record with the resolution of 1080 by 1920. The frame rate is 20 in experiments.

5.2 Mark Detection

We plan to put markers on every significant point where the wheelchair needs navigation. These points includes turnings, doors and crossroads. Here we assume these doors are opened and electronic wheelchair is able go over the level difference over the door and pass through.

A marker should be visible from all angles that a wheelchair can approach. We plan to design a marker that consists of 4 different marking codes, so that a wheelchair can trace its exact position. For some indoor landmarks like a door, the markers can be put directly onto the wall above the door. We implied a pre-trained model [3] of YOLOv5 model used to recognize License Plates of cars. We printed these in the font of "PLAT NOMOR" on A4 papers. And we paste them above a door.

However, usual use case of License Plates recognition is to detect them from a horizontal picture. So we decided to cut our vertical picture into small pieces. Every piece is distanced half of the height of a piece. So that code in any position can be detected in at least one piece (Figs. 1, 2, 3 and 4).

Fig. 1. A sample of left view, right view, and depth map of the stereo vision system we build. The miscalculation on the shoe shelf in the middle left of the view can be observed.

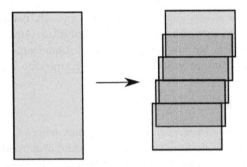

Fig. 2. Cropping method of vertical frame

Fig. 3. Full picture from one of the camera, which we used for detection

Fig. 4. The part of the image where the letters and numbers are recognized and labeled by YOLO models

5.3 Human Detection

We deployed a pre-trained model YOLOv5s [4] published by Glenn Jocher. It is based on YOLOv4 [5] and perform better on a lot of kinds of recognition tasks (Fig. 5).

Fig. 5. A sample of left view, right view, and depth map of the stereo vision system we build. The miscalculation on the shoe shelf in the middle left of the view can be observed.

5.4 Next Stage Experiments

So far, outdoor computer vision methods are still under development and sometimes unstable. There exists a lot of factors that can interfere the camera itself, such as dust or rain. Also, outdoor ground is not always as flat as indoors, therefore may have more jitters and shaking. On a motion platform the miscalculation can be worse in outdoor use cases.

We plan to test the stereo systems on a slow moving motion system in nursing facilities. We also plan to do some fine-turning to the camera mounting platform to make it more stable while moving, as well as to do some re-train for our YOLO models to increase the recognition accuracy if needed.

6   Other Computer Vision Methods

Some other computer vision methods can also be mounted onto the multi-camera system. Putting bar code or QR code on the mark is a decent and broadly used way for labeling in computer vision technology. Also, bar code or QR code is both capable of carrying much more information.

However, bar code and QR code may lose accuracy when seen in a slightly slanting angles, especially from a far distance. Also, since we are putting marks in places where everybody in the hallway can see, we wish to make these markers readable for human. But bar code and QR code can be added aside of the text part as a method.

7   Future Work

7.1   Building Datasets

As mentioned above, a fine-turning can always be done if nursing homes managed to build up their own indoor dataset and re-train the yolov5 model with it. However, it is a huge amount of work to took pictures from all angles inside the facility and to label them. Also, a model trained under a dataset of a certain facility may have trouble migrating to another.

7.2   Increasing Robustness

In our experiment, we have noticed some factors that influence the recognition. For instance, if the light got too bright or too dark, computer vision system can have trouble detecting the characters. However, the brightness can often vary as the weather changes and the level of sunlight shifts. Increasing the performance under these circumstances is a major concern for the future developing.

8   Conclusions

With this system, it is possible for patients to move around the facility alone, doing daily stuff without assistance, reducing the risk under the COVID. Also, even when the COVID pandemic comes to an end. This can also be a solid method for a nursing home to reduce manpower needs and maintain a more clean environment, as a lot of nursing homes serves for medical services as well.

Acknowledgement. This work was supported by Japan Science and Technology Agency. JST CREST: JPMJCR19F2, Research Representative: Prof. Yoichi Ochiai, University of Tsukuba, Japan.

References

1. Vaswani, A., et al.: Attention is all you need. In: Advances in Neural Information Processing Systems, vol. 30 (2017)
2. Luo, W., Schwing, A.G., Urtasun, R.: Efficient deep learning for stereo matching. In: Proceedings of the IEEE Conference on Computer Vision and Pattern Recognition (2016)
3. https://github.com/bharatsubedi/ALPR-Yolov5
4. https://github.com/ultralytics/yolov5

5. Bochkovskiy, A., Wang, C.-Y., Liao, H.-Y.M.: Yolov4: optimal speed and accuracy of object detection. arXiv preprint arXiv:2004.10934 (2020)
6. https://www.cdc.gov/coronavirus/2019-ncov/php/contact-tracing/contact-tracing-plan/appendix.html
7. Karkar, A.G., Al-Maadeed, S., Kunhoth, J., Bouridane, A.: CamNav: a computer-vision indoor navigation system. J. Supercomput. **77**(7), 7737–7756 (2021). https://doi.org/10.1007/s11227-020-03568-5
8. Simpson, R., Levine, S., Bell, D., Jaros, L., Koren, Y., Borenstein, J.: NavChair: An Assistive Wheelchair Navigation System with Automatic Adaptation, pp. 235–255 (1998). https://doi.org/10.1007/BFb0055982
9. Redmon, J., et al.: You only look once: unified, real-time object detection. In: Proceedings of the IEEE Conference on Computer Vision and Pattern Recognition (2016)
10. Redmon, J., Farhadi, A.: Yolov3: an incremental improvement. arXiv preprint arXiv:1804.02767 (2018)
11. Wang, J., et al.: Improved YOLOv5 network for real-time multi-scale traffic sign detection. arXiv preprint arXiv:2112.08782 (2021)

Correction to: Blood Pressure Concerns: Findings from a Usability Study of Culturally Infused mHealth Design

Helina Oladapo and Joyram Chakraborty

Correction to:
Chapter "Blood Pressure Concerns: Findings from a Usability Study of Culturally Infused mHealth Design"
in: M. Antona and C. Stephanidis (Eds.): *Universal Access in Human-Computer Interaction. Novel Design Approaches and Technologies*, **LNCS 13308,**
https://doi.org/10.1007/978-3-031-05028-2_20

In an older version of this paper, there were several errors, which now have been corrected. On page 300, the explanation at the end of the page erroneously referred to "Fig. 2". This was corrected to "Fig. 1". On page 303, a sentence was expanded and corrected from "Participants usage of the Apple Health App were 12%, Samsung Health App for BP, and 72% were not utilizing the health app for BP" to "Participants usage of the Apple Health App for BP were 12%, Samsung Health App for BP were 16%, and 72% were not utilizing the health app for BP". This has been corrected.

The updated version of this chapter can be found at
https://doi.org/10.1007/978-3-031-05028-2_20

© The Author(s), under exclusive license to Springer Nature Switzerland AG 2022
M. Antona and C. Stephanidis (Eds.): HCII 2022, LNCS 13308, p. C1, 2022.
https://doi.org/10.1007/978-3-031-05028-2_37

Author Index

Reprinted in the United States
by Baker & Taylor Publisher Services

Printed in the United States
by Baker & Taylor Publisher Services